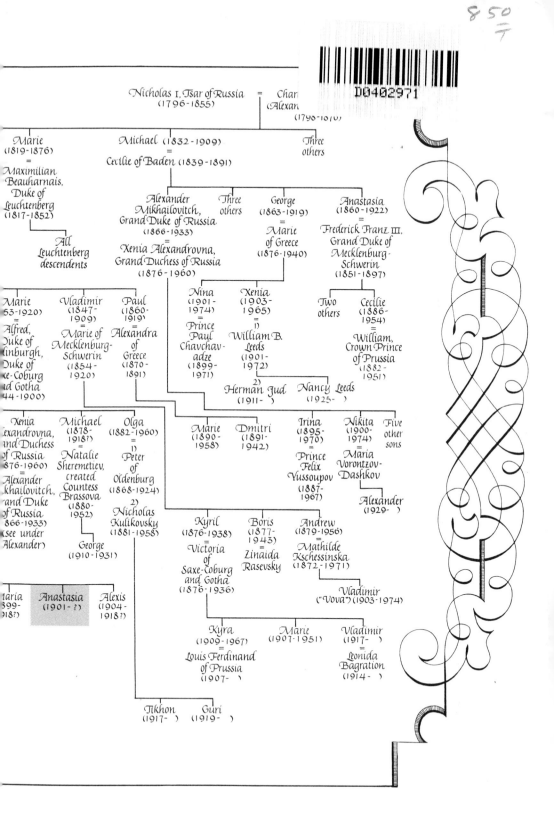

Anastasia

Anastasia

THE RIDDLE OF ANNA ANDERSON

Peter Kurth

LITTLE, BROWN AND COMPANY

Boston   Toronto

Acknowledgment of permission to reprint previously copyrighted
material appears on pages 435–436.

Library of Congress Cataloging in Publication Data

Kurth, Peter.
   Anastasia: the riddle of Anna Anderson.

   Bibliography: p.
   1. Anastasia Nikolaievna, Grand Duchess of Russia,
1901–1918.   2. Anderson, Anna.   3. Soviet Union—
Princes and princesses—Biography.   I. Title.
DK254.A7K8   1983   947.08′092′4 [B]   83-9397
ISBN 0-316-50716-4

VB

Designed by Patricia Girvin Dunbar

Published simultaneously in Canada
by Little, Brown & Company (Canada) Limited

PRINTED IN THE UNITED STATES OF AMERICA

For A.

                                You gods look down,
And from your sacred vials pour your graces
Upon my daughter's head! Tell me (mine own)
Where hast thou been preserved? where lived? how found
Thy father's court? For thou shalt hear that I,
Knowing by Paulina that the oracle
Gave hope thou wast in being, have preserved
Myself to see the issue.

                                — *The Winter's Tale*

PREFACE

I was thirteen when I first saw *Anastasia,* the Ingrid Bergman film based on the life of Anna Anderson, the woman who claimed to be the only surviving daughter of the Tsar of Russia. Time and research have blurred my memory of the initial experience, but I do recall my mother remarking offhandedly, "You know that's a true story, don't you? Sort of . . ." At the time, I didn't know anything at all about the life and mysterious death of the last Romanovs, nor, when I began to read about it, did the question of Anna Anderson's true identity interest me nearly so much as the larger drama of Nicholas and Alexandra, the Rasputin scandal, and the bloody progress of the Bolshevik Revolution. In the first place, I knew that Mrs. Anderson was not the only claimant to the name and title of the Tsar's daughter, that there had been other "Anastasias," would-be Tsarevitches and any number of pseudo–grand duchesses ever since the brutal murder of the Tsar and his family at Ekaterinburg in 1918. I assumed that Mrs. Anderson was only the most notorious of many unfortunate madwomen, but I was mistaken, and I well remember the moment I first suspected it.

On February 17, 1970, the Supreme Court of West Germany handed down a ruling on Mrs. Anderson's claim — a ruling that appeared to confirm history's verdict that she was a fraud, but that impressed me more meaningfully because it existed at all. Why had any ruling been necessary? What had persuaded the judges of West Germany's highest court to hear the plea of a woman who (so her opponents affirmed) "bore not the slightest resemblance to Grand Duchess Anastasia," "did not speak a word of Russian," and knew nothing about life at the Tsar's palace that was not common knowledge? [1] If I was to believe the peremptory disclaimers of Mrs. Anderson's identity issued by those people who had stood nearest to Anastasia — uncles and aunts, tutors, servants, and ladies-in-waiting — how could I believe that anyone, much less the Supreme Court justices, had ever taken her case seriously? Something rang very false in the matter of "Anastasia," and, with a passion that still amazes me today, I set out to discover what it was.

My first attempt to unravel the mystery was exciting, tireless, and, with hindsight, comically sincere. Armed with three outdated books about the "Anastasia" affair, a handful of American newspaper articles, and a lucky interview with a Romanov princess, I created, by stages, a two-hundred-page "book," which, in my innocence, I imagined to be definitive. I made no secret of my newfound conviction — my loud hope, I should say — that I had stumbled onto one of the greatest cover-ups in history and that Mrs. Anderson truly was the Tsar's lost daughter. I saw her then as the very spirit of tragedy, a gentle, unassuming soul, caught in a web of international intrigue and denied her rights by a pack of unscrupulous and mercenary relations. My diatribes on this subject were perfectly in keeping with the near-hysteria that, I knew, Mrs. Anderson's claim had provoked among the surviving members of the House of Romanov and the exiled Russian nobility. Already I had heard about brothers, sisters, and cousins turned against one another on account of her case, about sordid battles for money and jewels, "endless discussions of rights and family misunderstandings." [2] All the same, I was not prepared for my first trip to Europe, where I traveled shortly, in order to clarify a few details and first confronted the veritable mountain of testimony assembled during Mrs. Anderson's thirty-seven-year suit for legal recognition. There were more than forty bound volumes of evidence, amounting to well over eight thousand densely written German pages. At that point, I did not know German. I went home that summer with my enthusiasm intact but my prospects for a quick publication seriously diminished.

Not until ten years later, and after three more lengthy trips to Europe, did I complete the research for this book. I had already finished another draft of the manuscript when, in 1978, I came across thirteen cartons of unsorted "Anastasia" papers at the Houghton Library at Harvard University. By that time I knew enough about Mrs. Anderson's case to know that this scholar's dream, although it needed to be probed, would contain no revelation: the frustration I had for so long experienced in my search for "the Truth" about Anastasia was something shared by everyone whose life had touched hers. It made sense when I finally realized that I had been trying to prove an intangible; when I learned that selfhood is not found on scraps of paper and that true identity rests on more than a set of missing fingerprints.

I had learned much more than that during my quest, however. My initial assumptions about the source of Mrs. Anderson's woes, while logical enough and reassuringly simple, had been naive and insulting. Caught in a web she was indeed, but it was a network of human failing, I am convinced, more than of malevolent design. I had to learn and remember that she was never alone in her struggle for identity. Everyone around her — the exiled grand dukes and grand duchesses, the foreign cousins, former imperial army officers, and canny chambermaids — had all, with her, lost their place and their reason for being. *Anastasia* is a story about refugees. It is about people unanchored, blinded by a past they needed to believe was perfect, holding very deep grudges, and immobilized by uncertainty. It is a story of "anguished indecision"[3] and colossal misunderstanding. Finally, above all, it is the story of a family in crisis, a once-mighty dynasty confronted with a problem its laws and tradition could not comprehend, a family decimated in the Russian Revolution, scattered in exile, and asked to accept as authentic a broken, unstable, and recriminatory woman whom few could bring themselves to acknowledge as sane, let alone as the sole heir of the Tsar. The answer to the riddle of Anastasia does not lie in Russia, but in the heart of the Romanov family, where pride and appearances overruled compassion and condemned a human being to life in a bitter universe of imputation and doubt.

There is a story told about Grand Duke Boris of Russia, a first cousin of the Tsar and renowned libertine, who sat in a drawing room in Paris at the end of the 1920s and heard one Russian cousin dismiss Anna Anderson as a demented Polish factory worker with delusions of grandeur. Another replied that she was a Latvian gun moll with ties to the Soviets, while a third insisted she was an agent of the Pope. Not one of these people had so much as laid eyes on her, and Boris, so the story goes, merely sighed, stubbed out his cigarette — a brand, incidentally, he had seen fit to endorse in exile — rolled his eyes, and exclaimed, "Oh, give the girl a chance!" [4]

Grand Duke Boris knew what the world did not. "Whether the cause of the controversy be a conspiracy on the part of one or the other faction," wrote a friend of Mrs. Anderson, "an unfortunate sequence of accident and coincidence, or merely blind prejudice and ignorance . . . , one fact stands out beyond all the others: the curse of the Romanovs appears to be that they are unable to speak an open word with one another. The argument and counter-argument should never have been forced into a court of law, but discussed without rancor, peacefully and amicably, and settled in the private councils of the family." [5]

The background to Mrs. Anderson's story, when compared with the never-ending argument for and against her identity and the sheer volume of evidence collected over the past sixty years, is disarmingly simple.

In March 1917, after the abdication of Tsar Nicholas II, the seven members of the Russian imperial family — consisting of the Tsar, the Empress Alexandra Feodorovna, their son, the hemophiliac Tsarevitch Alexis, and their four daughters, the Grand Duchesses Olga, Tatiana, Maria, and Anastasia — were arrested by Kerensky's Provisional Government and interned at the Alexander Palace in Tsarskoe Selo, not far from St. Petersburg. The palace had been home to the family ever since the revolutionary disturbances of 1905, and, for the first months of their incarceration, the Romanovs were allowed to continue their lives very much as they were used to doing, in a ceaseless, thoroughly Edwardian round of lessons, promenades, prayers, and five o'clock tea. Even during his lifetime the Tsar was known as an exemplary family man whose happiest hours were spent with his wife and children, reading aloud, gardening, pasting innumerable family snapshots into photograph albums, and quietly discussing the great and small events of the day. Since the outbreak of World War I in 1914, however, these cozy gatherings had been infrequent. The Tsar had often been away at the front, while the Empress, in poor health, obsessed with the strict principles of Russian autocracy and divine right, and fatally devoted to Grigory Rasputin (the Siberian muzhik who, she believed, had saved her son from the worst attacks of his hemophilia), had taken over the affairs of state and almost single-handedly led the country to ruin. Alone together now, the family did not much miss the late impositions of royal life, and they had more to fear from boredom than from the mob that gathered daily at the palace gates to jeer at them.

For weeks, then, while the Revolution spread, the imperial family kept busy with domestic concerns. Each day the four Grand Duchesses pursued their studies and practiced such genteel refinements as befitted European princesses of their rank. They were tutored in history, mathematics, and the natural sciences. They knew how to sew and embroider, to ride, draw, dance, sing, play the piano, and converse politely (if most imperfectly) in Russian, English, French, and German. By the spring of 1917 the girls were almost grown. The eldest, Olga Nicolaievna, was twenty-one, while Anastasia, the fourth and youngest, celebrated her sixteenth birthday on June 18. She was a short, stout, roguish child, nicknamed "Schwibsik" (Imp) by her family and remembered chiefly as a comedienne. One of her mother's friends recalled that she "might have been composed of quicksilver. . . . She was always in mischief, a regular tomboy," a girl with a lively flair for mimicry and a dry, sometimes wicked sense of humor.[6] It was often said in the Romanov family that had Anastasia not been born a Russian grand duchess, she would have made an excellent actress, and, in later years, her antics were credited with lifting her family's spirits during the darkest days of captivity.

The first blow had come in August, when the Kerensky regime — fearing reprisals and hoping to circumvent the persistent demands of the revolutionaries that the Tsar and the Empress be made to stand trial for their crimes against the Russian people — transferred the imperial family some two thousand miles east of Tsarskoe Selo to Tobolsk, in Siberia. There the family, with a devoted handful of tutors, courtiers, and servants, occupied the spacious townhouse of the district's former governor and, for eight more months, endured a still tolerable but deadly dull routine. It was not until Lenin's coup d'état in November, in fact, that the imperial family truly learned what it meant to live as prisoners of the Revolution. The soldiers dispatched to Tobolsk by Alexander Kerensky had been orderly and respectful, on the whole, even sympathetic to the Romanovs' plight, but the new Bolshevik detachments were not. Far from it: they wanted to see "Citizen Romanov" and his family suffer, and they were not to be disappointed. The Tsar was poked and pushed while he tried to work in the garden. The Empress, usually alone in her room, still heard the soldiers' talk about "the German bitch" and saw the crude pornographic sketches they had drawn of herself and Rasputin. And the young Grand Duchesses, the pretty girls who, in the years before the war, had so enjoyed flirting with the officers of their father's retinue, now began to learn how ugly, how very ugly, relations between the sexes can be.

No one knows if the Tsar's daughters were sexually abused in prison. Stories later spread in monarchist circles of their being tied naked to chairs and gang-raped by crazed Bolsheviks. Although the rumor may have been exaggerated, the threat of sexual assault was never far away. When, in April 1918, the Tsar, the Empress, and their third daughter, Grand Duchess Maria, were suddenly taken by the Bolsheviks from Tobolsk to a more secure prison in the Ural mining capital of Ekaterinburg, they left Olga, Tatiana, and Anastasia alone in the governor's mansion with the ailing Tsarevitch Alexis. Afterward, the girls were forbidden to lock their bedroom door at night. Alexis and his tutors, we may be sure, provided scant protection against the swaggering lewdness of Red Army soldiers nursing a grudge. Grand Duchess Olga spoke for all of her sisters when she declared, in one smuggled, understated line to a friend: "Darling, you must know how dreadful it all is." [7]

Olga wrote those words barely three weeks before she descended into what has been called "the hell of Ekaterinburg." [8] When the Grand Duchesses and their brother finally arrived at the Ekaterinburg station on May 23 (the Tsarevitch having recovered sufficiently to travel), they were quickly separated from the remainder of their retinue and taken alone to the Ipatiev house — "the House of Special Purpose," as the Bolsheviks called it — where their parents, their sister Maria, their personal physician, Dr. Eugene Sergeyevitch Botkin, and several other servants awaited them. It was pouring that day, and Ekaterinburg's citizens caught a last glimpse of the Tsar's daughters as, carrying their own luggage, they struggled through the city's muddy streets on the way to their final prison. Those of their suite who were fortunate enough not to be removed to jail and execution stayed on in the city for several weeks hoping to be of some service, but they never saw their masters again. No one did.

Very little is known about the imperial family's two-month captivity in the Ipatiev house. The windows had been whitewashed, and two tall palisades were later erected to shield Bolshevik Russia's supreme prisoners from public view. It is known that the family was confined to two bedrooms, one for the four Grand Duchesses, where they slept on only mattresses, and another for Nicholas, Alexandra, and Alexis. It is known that the family was given a few minutes each day to walk in the enclosed courtyard, that they dined on black bread and soup with their jailors, and that Anastasia, when she "asked for a new pair of shoes out of the loft . . . , was told that those she had would last for the rest of her life."[9] It is known that the Grand Duchesses' trunks were rifled and their possessions stolen, that they were always followed to the single lavatory and forbidden to close the door while they relieved themselves (a pathetic note was later found on the wall: "Please be so kind as to leave the seat as clean as you found it"),[10] and that the girls were reading Tolstoy and Turgenev in the face of these violations. In the first days of July, when the anti-Bolshevik "White" armies began to threaten Ekaterinburg from the east, the Russian interior guard at the Ipatiev house was replaced with foreigners, usually described as "Letts." Finally, on July 14, mass was sung for the last time. The officiating priest later testified that the imperial family, in a moving departure from the order of service, fell in unison on their knees during the prayer for the souls of the dead. Afterward, one of the Grand Duchesses just had time to whisper "Thank you" before the door was closed in her face.

"Something has happened to them in there," the Romanovs' last confessor reflected.[11] He didn't know what it was, and neither does anyone else. Rudolf Lacher, an Austrian orderly attached to Yakov Yurovsky, the last commandant of the Ipatiev house, saw the imperial family the night they vanished from the face of the earth. As they filed down the stairs, Lacher remembered, the girls were sobbing. Half an hour later, shots rang out.

"They all knew they were going to die," the Tsar's sister Olga observed bitterly in exile. "I am sure of that."[12] Apparently she was right. Found among Anastasia's effects after the Bolshevik evacuation of Ekaterinburg was a short theme she had begun for her English tutor. It was Browning's tale of "Evelyn," a pretty nobody whose family name, sadly, was "Hope." Locked away, cut off from the world at sixteen, the Grand Duchess left an eerie précis of the poem. The English is hers:

A young girl who was called Evelyn had just died. She was lying in the cofen, very pretty. All her things [were] on the same place nothing was changed and even the flower which she gatherd, stood in the glace, but was beginning to faid. Whe[n] she died she was only sixteen years old. Ther was a man who loved her without having seen her but new her very well. And she herd of him also. He never could tell her that he loved her, and now she was dead. But still he thought that when he and she will live [their] next life whenever it will be that . . .[13]

That . . . what? "Goodby," Anastasia had written a friend in the winter of 1917. "Don't forget me."[14]

She is alleged to have perished in the cellar of the Ipatiev house during the night of July 16/17, 1918, at the height of the Red Terror. A White Army investigation team later concluded that the entire imperial family and their four remaining servants (Dr. Botkin, a serving girl, a cook, and a valet) had been shot, stabbed, and bludgeoned to death by their Bolshevik captors, the order ostensibly having come from Lenin to prevent the family's liberation by the Whites. According to the official monarchist report, first published in Paris in 1924, the corpses were taken into the forest, hacked to pieces, soaked in gasoline and sulfuric acid, and burned. Then the ashes were pitched down an abandoned mineshaft. Inspector Nicholas Sokolov, the White Army's examining magistrate, maintained categorically that no member of the Russian imperial family could possibly have emerged alive from the Ekaterinburg bloodbath.

Anastasia was specifically cited in the Sokolov report as having survived the first volley of gunfire and having then been put to death with bayonets and blows from a rifle butt. Wrote an aide to Inspector Sokolov: "When the smoke of the firing had cleared a little and the murderers began to inspect the bodies, they found that Grand Duchess Anastasia was alive and unhurt. She had fallen in a dead faint when the firing began and so escaped the bullets. When the assassins moved her body, the Grand Duchess regained consciousness, saw herself surrounded by pools of blood and the bodies of her family, and screamed. She was killed."[15] Louis Mountbatten, a nephew of Empress Alexandra, was still more explicit. "My cousin Anastasia," he declared, "was bayoneted eighteen times as she lay there screaming."[16] And from the biographer of the Tsar's sister we hear: "Eighteen bayonet marks embedded in the flooring of the cellar marked the spot where the horrified young girl writhed her last."[17]

"Writhed her last." Here the story of Grand Duchess Anastasia concludes in the eyes of accepted history. She is gone, as one ardent monarchist expressed it, "fragile and lovely as an opening flower, serene in the divine innocence of childhood and radiant with the bright charm of girlhood and health."[18] The image of the cellar at Ekaterinburg hung like a pall now over the royal houses of Europe, as, one by one, the thrones of Austria-Hungary, Prussia, Saxony, Hesse, and a dozen others ceased to exist, and Anastasia's foreign relations were left to ponder the meaning and the lesson of her demise. "We were told it had taken place," said her cousin, Lord Mountbatten, in a franker moment; "at least we were expecting it to take place, we had no reason to doubt it; and there may not have been any proof, but they in those days were not requiring proof. What else could we believe but the worst, as history appears to have shown was right? What was the alternative?" [19]

Burlington, Vermont
April 1983

CONTENTS

xvii

PART THREE:

Mrs. Anderson

PART FOUR:

Anastasia

PRINCIPAL CHARACTERS

Anastasia Tschaikovsky, also known as *Anna Anderson,* claimant to the identity of Grand Duchess Anastasia

Nicholas II, Tsar of Russia
Alexandra Feodorovna, his wife, Empress of Russia, formerly Princess Alix of Hesse and the Rhine
Alexis Nicolaievitch, their son, the Tsarevitch
Olga Nicolaievna
Tatiana Nicolaievna
Maria Nicolaievna ⎱ their daughters, Grand Duchesses of Russia
Anastasia Nicolaievna

Alexander Mikhailovitch, Grand Duke of Russia, second cousin and brother-in-law of Nicholas II
Alexander Nikititch ([Prince Alexander] Romanov), grandson of Alexander Mikhailovitch and the Tsar's sister Xenia
Andrew Vladimirovitch, Grand Duke of Russia, first cousin of Nicholas II and uncle (in Russian style) of Grand Duchess Anastasia
Barbara, Duchess of Mecklenburg, granddaughter and adopted heir of Princess Irene of Prussia; defendant during the Hamburg trials
Botkin, Eugene Sergeyevitch, physician-in-ordinary to the Russian imperial family; murdered in 1918
Botkin, Gleb Evgenievitch, youngest son of Dr. Botkin

Botkin, Serge Dmitrievitch, first cousin of Dr. Botkin, president of the Office of Russian Refugees in Germany

Botkin, Tatiana Evgenievna (Mme. Melnik), daughter of Dr. Botkin

Buxhoeveden, Baroness Sophie Karlovna, maid of honor to Empress Alexandra

Cecilie, Princess of Prussia and German Crown Princess, married to Crown Prince Frederick William, daughter of Grand Duke Frederick Franz III of Mecklenburg-Schwerin and his wife, Grand Duchess Anastasia Mikhailovna of Russia

Dassel, Felix, Captain of the 9th Kazan Dragoons of Grand Duchess Maria Nicolaievna; during World War I a patient in the military hospital at Tsarskoe Selo under the patronage of the Grand Duchesses Maria and Anastasia

Ernest Louis, Grand Duke of Hesse-Darmstadt, brother of Empress Alexandra

Fallows, Edward H., Anastasia's attorney from 1928 to 1940

Frederick Ernest, Prince of Saxe-Altenburg, brother-in-law of Prince Sigismund of Prussia, uncle of Barbara of Mecklenburg; after 1949 Anastasia's legal proxy

Gilliard, Alexandra ("Shura"), formerly Tegleva, nursemaid of Grand Duchess Anastasia

Gilliard, Pierre, French tutor to the children of Nicholas II

Irene, Princess of Prussia, sister of Empress Alexandra

Jennings, Annie Burr, of New York City and Fairfield, Connecticut, Anastasia's hostess from 1929 to 1931

Kyril Vladimirovitch, Grand Duke of Russia, first cousin of Nicholas II and brother of Andrew, pretender (1924) to the Russian throne

Kleist, Baron Arthur von, a former Tsarist police official, Anastasia's first sponsor in Berlin

Lavington, Faith, governess to the children and grandchildren of Duke George of Leuchtenberg

Leuchtenberg, Duke George Romanovsky de Beauharnais, great-grandson of Tsar Nicholas I, Anastasia's host at Castle Seeon in 1927

Leuchtenberg, Duchess Olga, his wife, born Princess Repnin

Leverkuehn, Paul, Anastasia's attorney (with Kurt Vermehren) from 1938 to 1960

Lilburn, Ian R., a British friend of Prince Frederick and, at Hamburg, Anastasia's "historical advisor"

Manahan, Dr. John Eacott, Anastasia's husband after 1968

Maria Feodorovna, mother of Nicholas II, Dowager Empress of Russia, formerly Princess Dagmar of Denmark

Olga Alexandrovna, sister of the Tsar, Grand Duchess of Russia, married to Colonel Nicholas Kulikovsky

Osten-Sacken Tettenborn, Baron Vassili ("Willy") Lvovitch von der, secretary to Serge Botkin

Peuthert, Clara, German dressmaker and one-time inmate of the Dalldorf Asylum

Rathlef-Keilmann, Harriet von, a sculptress and writer, befriended Anastasia in 1925

Schanzkowska, Franziska, a Polish working girl, born in 1896, missing since 1920

Schwabe, Nicholas von, Captain of the Dowager Empress's cuirassiers regiment, in exile manager of the monarchist newspaper *The Double Eagle*

Sigismund, Prince of Prussia, son of Irene of Prussia, first cousin of Grand Duchess Anastasia

Stackelberg, Curt von, Anastasia's attorney before the West German Supreme Court

Vermehren, Kurt, Anastasia's attorney (with Paul Leverkuehn) from 1938 to 1962

Volkov, Alexis Andreievitch, groom of the chamber to Empress Alexandra

Waldemar, Prince of Denmark, brother of the Dowager Empress

Wingender, Doris, later Frau Rittmann, daughter of Franziska Schanzkowska's landlady

Wollmann, Carl-August, Anastasia's attorney after 1962

Xenia Alexandrovna, sister of Nicholas II, Grand Duchess of Russia

Xenia Georgievna, Princess of Russia (Mrs. Leeds), second cousin of Grand Duchess Anastasia

Zahle, Herluf, Danish Minister Plenipotentiary to Berlin

PART ONE

Fräulein Unbekannt

1

DALLDORF

*L*ater on the unknown woman always insisted that it was the asylum that "broke" her — not the loss of her family and her country, not even the savage attack on her own life, but the two years she spent at Dalldorf in the company of a dozen spitting, jabbering, incontinent lunatics. Before that, she said, she had been "a different person."[1] She had known what she was about. On her arrival in Berlin, hoping to locate her mother's sister, she had walked straight to the gates of the Netherlands Palace,[2] only to realize at the last moment that there might not be anyone there who would know her and that she couldn't simply knock at the front door and announce herself. She tried to explain afterward that she had never before in her life been anywhere unescorted. "Can you understand what it is," she asked, "suddenly to know that everything is lost and that you are left entirely alone? Can you understand then that I did what I did?" She broke off: "I didn't know what I was doing. . . ."[3]

She never knew how she got to the Bendler Bridge or exactly what she thought would happen when she fell the short distance into the river below. The plunge itself she could not recall. She only remembered staring at the water and reflecting that water had always fascinated her, that she had always wanted to know "what lived beneath."[4] From that moment it was out of her hands. She awoke sputtering, drenched, shaking with the cold, and aware of a

3

great commotion around her. There were policemen everywhere, a crowd had gathered, and people were shouting. Suddenly she realized that they were shouting at her, and right then, lying on the embankment of the Landwehr Canal, she made a decision: she would not answer. It was nine o'clock on the evening of Tuesday, February 17, 1920.[5]

She had been wrapped in a blanket and brought to a police post, where they gave her something strong and warm to drink. Then the questions began: who are you? What were you doing? Did you slip? Were you pushed? Did you jump? Why did you do it? Who are you? Where are your papers?

The unknown woman sat shivering in the corner, silent, pale as a sheet and looking as though she might faint. It was plain to see that she was terrified. Only when the police started shouting again and warned her that she might be liable to criminal prosecution did she show any sign that she had been listening. "I have asked for nothing," she said.[6]

She said it in German, her words precise but muffled, in "a completely foreign accent."[7]

She was taken that night to an open ward of the Elisabeth Hospital, in the Lützowstrasse, where she stayed with more than twenty other women at the expense of the city of Berlin.[8] The nurses took off her clothes, rubbed her dry, wrapped her in a white gown, and drew up an inventory of her things: black skirt, black stockings, linen blouse, underwear, boots that laced to the knee, and a heavy, shapeless shawl. But no purse and no papers, no identification of any kind. The nurses looked for initials, laundry marks, labels, anything that could help the police, but the unknown woman's clothes might have been made at home, for all the information they gave.[9] There was nothing to be done. For now they let her sleep.

The next morning the doctors and the police found her stronger, more alert, obviously still afraid of them, but somehow defiant. No, she declared, she would not tell them who she was, or who her family was, where she had come from, or what she did for a living. They would all do well to leave her in peace. This was not a request but a demand, and when the questions kept on coming, one after the other, "in every language," she simply turned her head to the wall, pulled the blanket across her face, and said nothing.[10] Nothing.

The scene was played out every day for the next six weeks. No amount of badgering could move the unknown woman from her course. And she was badgered all the time. She was told that suicide was a crime, that she couldn't expect to get away with it in Berlin, that she had better tell the doctors *now* who she was, that she shouldn't be so stubborn and childish, that her family must miss her very much. Nothing helped. Finally the doctors began to load the questions and shortly got her to "admit" that she had been "a working woman." [11]

Where had she worked, then?

No answer.

At what kind of job?

Silence.

The doctors sent her to the Dalldorf Asylum at the end of March because they had no idea what else to do with her. The diagnosis was "melancholia" — as the doctors clarified it, "mental illness of a depressive character." [12] They offered no opinion about her sanity. She simply arrived at Dalldorf, in the countryside near Berlin, as *"Fräulein Unbekannt"* ("Miss Unknown") and took a bed in House 4, Ward B, a low, flat block reserved for "quiet patients." [13] There were fourteen other women in the room. [14] None but she, strictly speaking, was quiet.

An examination conducted at the asylum on March 30, 1920, recorded her weight at one hundred and ten pounds, her height at just under five feet two. The report continued:

Very reserved. Refuses to give her name, family, age or occupation. Sits in a stubborn posture. Will make no statement, says she has her reasons for this and that if she had wanted to speak she would have done so already. . . . The doctor may believe what he likes; she will tell him nothing. To the question whether she hears voices or hallucinates she is said to have replied, "You are not very well informed, Doctor." She admits to having tried to kill herself but declines to give any reason or explanation. [15]

The doctors at Dalldorf had been warned about Fräulein Unbekannt. Already she had greeted them with the same mixture of terror and contempt that had distinguished her behavior at the Elisabeth Hospital. The very sight of a white coat sent her scrambling under the bedclothes, and when they did persuade her to uncover her face the doctors noticed that she always turned her eyes away from theirs. Particularly remarkable was her resistance to her first physical examination. [16] She seemed to be in agony while they looked at her body, and the doctors quickly saw why: it was covered with scars ("many lacerations," the report said).[17] They saw something else: she was no longer a virgin. This seemed important in a girl of "about twenty,"[18] so the doctors went on a new tack. How would it be if they sent for her "fiancé"?

The response was violent: "*Nichts von alledem!* [None of that!]"

Well, then, what was the matter? How could they help her if she wouldn't tell them anything?

"I will say no more!"

But the next day she broke down and admitted that she was frightened for her life: "Indicates that she does not want to give her name because she fears persecution. Gives impression of fearful reticence. More fear here than reticence."

So it went on, day after day, incessantly and without result. Once in a while the doctors imagined that they were getting somewhere. Fräulein Unbekannt had claimed to be a working woman. Was that true?

Silence. A nod.

And her family — were they working people, too? Wouldn't she tell them something about her family?

All right: her parents were dead. Her mother had died "only recently." She had no brothers or sisters. She had no relations at all.

No one?

No one.

Was she sure?

Silence.[19]

After another two months of this cat-and-mouse the doctors at Dalldorf summoned the Berlin police and told them that they had failed.[20] They asked that a serious effort be made to find out who this woman was and added that they, the doctors, were not equipped to make it. Thus at the beginning of June Fräulein Unbekannt was removed from her bed and taken down the hall to be fingerprinted and photographed. She struggled with all her might when she saw the cameras pointed at her, "screwed up her eyes," and had to be held in position. Finally the flashes exploded, she was shot front and profile and sent back to her room in a sweat.

Her pictures and prints were sent out to Stuttgart, Brunswick, Hamburg, Munich, Dresden — to all the corners of the Weimar Republic.[21] Meanwhile the police looked into some clues nearer to home. The records of all of Berlin's hospitals and madhouses were dutifully checked for missing and discharged patients who fitted Fräulein Unbekannt's description, while mothers who had lost their daughters in the city, and husbands their wives, were sometimes brought out to Dalldorf to look at her. She had already been seen by the brother of a certain Maria Andrecewsky[22] (who shook his head and went home depressed) when she was asked point-blank if she were another Maria, surnamed Wachowiak, who had disappeared recently from the city of Posen, to the east. She laughed. "What kind of game are you playing with me, Doctor? Best of luck to you."[23]

Nobody blamed the Berlin police when they gave up on this case. They had exhausted their resources and had never really expected their efforts in other parts of Germany to succeed. They didn't believe the unknown woman was German, to start with. A doctor at the Elisabeth Hospital had suggested that she might come from Bavaria, but no one at headquarters agreed. There was a note in the bulletin of the Dalldorf Asylum: "It is known that she conversed in Russian with the sisters nursing her."[24]

When the police had gone and the questions stopped, the reaction set in. The head nurse at Dalldorf remembered that Fräulein Unbekannt, during the first days of her hospitalization, had been chronically, dangerously depressed. Days passed when she could not be persuaded to turn her head from the wall. She wouldn't speak and wouldn't eat. She couldn't sleep. When she did she had nightmares. She kept her blanket pulled up over her eyes and arranged the pillows in such a way that they formed a sort of barricade; the nurses had to bend down in order to talk with her. *Leidend* was the word they all used to describe her — *suffering*. She was "very suffering," "a suffering type."[25] In theory, every patient at Dalldorf was supposed to work at something to keep herself busy — washing and mending, tidying the wards and the grounds — but Fräulein Unbekannt rarely did, and no one at the asylum thought to press her. It would have meant violating what one of the nurses called her "fear of being touched."[26] The nurses were hard put to explain it properly, but they had never tried to force Fräulein Unbekannt to do something she didn't want to do. She existed apart from the other patients. She was so *different* from the other patients, and she took no part in their dull, regimented activities. Each morning, with some difficulty, her neighbors were lined up at one end of the room and marched outdoors for their daily constitutional. Fräulein Unbekannt never went with them. Only when the doctors insisted that she walk in the garden for the sake of her health did she agree to do so, and then only in the way she pleased. She would wait for the madwomen to come back before stepping outside "alone, in the company of a nurse."

There is a photograph taken of her in the walled garden at Dalldorf during the second year of her hospitalization, when her spirits had rallied a little and she had made friends with the nurses. She is turned away slightly from the camera, one hand held up against her lumpy hospital gown, her face a study in resignation. It is a well-shaped face, a face that might have been pretty were it not so obviously tired. The line of the profile is gentle and expressive, but the cheeks are puffy and the hair is pulled tightly back, revealing an exceptionally high brow. The nurses heard that Fräulein Unbekannt had plucked her hair away at the forehead. They also heard that when seven or eight of her teeth were extracted by the asylum dentist — Fräulein Unbekannt suffered from constant toothache — she hadn't minded at all. One of the nurses claimed that a perfectly healthy front tooth had been removed at Fräulein Unbekannt's own request, in an attempt to alter her appearance. It was her obsession: never to be found out, to pass her days in total anonymity, to vanish, even. But in the end she wasn't up to the task. She supposed it would be all right for her to leave the asylum one day, she told the nurses mysteriously, but not now — not until "times had changed." [27] And why not? Because she would be killed. Often she said that she was afraid of "the newspapers," "the press." [28] And again, something the nurses at Dalldorf never forgot: "She was afraid of being recognized and transported to Soviet Russia." [29]

She told the nurses a lot of things as the weeks and months went by, after she had convinced herself that they weren't going to betray her trust. She began to ask them for magazines and books — anything they had, it didn't matter — and spent time on her own reading in the small library at Dalldorf. In this way the nurses got to know her for an intelligent person, "an amiable, courteous person, grateful for small things." [30] She was "cultivated," they declared, well educated and well bred, "gracious," meticulous in her habits, clean, "charming." "Her distinguished manners contrasted agreeably with the lack of discipline of the other patients," one of the staff remembered.[31] "She struck us by her good behavior." [32] And further: "From her bearing and her cultured manner of speaking one had to conclude that she came from good circles. . . . In her whole manner she gave the impression of an aristocratic lady. She was now and again even somewhat overbearing. . . ." [33] The nurses rejected out of hand any suggestion that their patient might be insane, even if the doctors had scribbled "psychopathic symptoms" on her chart and called her "abnormal, without doubt."[34] The doctors didn't know anything about it, the nurses thought, because they refused to take Fräulein Unbekannt at her word. There was nothing mad about this girl who told them of her passion for animals and flowers; who talked about some long-ago travels in "Scandinavia";[35] and who, with increasing frequency, joined them at the night desk if she couldn't sleep. When the dreary, unvarying evening meal had ended, the lights had been turned out in the ward, and the other patients had quieted down, Fräulein Unbekannt would rise from her bed and slip noiselessly across the room. "Oh, you have such pretty dresses," she might say to the nurse on duty.[36] Then she would sit down and they would talk — about the weather, about politics, about the doctors, the greasy food, the books she had read and the people whose photographs she ran across in the newspapers. Sometimes they even talked about Fräulein Unbekannt's past. The nurses could always see it coming. An expression of mingled eagerness and despair would pass across her face, and her striking sea-blue eyes grew dark before she spoke: "Tonight I saw my mother in my dream."[37]

The nurses at Dalldorf definitely inclined to the last diagnosis, offered at the end of Fräulein Unbekannt's second year: *Einfache Seelenstörung* ("simple psychic disturbance").[38] One matter-of-fact nurse thought that Fräulein Unbekannt had a tendency "to build castles in the air: she imagined that after her release she would buy an estate and ride horses. She loved this sport."

Her remarks could be far more arresting: "She was well informed about the German Kaiser, and once she spoke of the Crown Prince in such a way that one would think she knew him personally."[39]

Did she? The nurses at Dalldorf began to wonder if their patient's castles were, after all, in the air. Their suspicions only increased when she claimed to be "a working woman" — she with her "very refined, soft hands," her "distinguished manners," and her air of authority.[40] The nurses learned to respect her wishes, and they were not surprised when the Russian monarchists came to take her away. In a moment of confidence she had told them that would happen. "If people knew who I am," she had said, "I would not be here."[41]

Nobody can know what it was that finally made Fräulein Unbekannt give in; why, after nearly two years at Dalldorf, she suddenly proclaimed that she was the youngest daughter of Tsar Nicholas

II.[42] In the wake of her notoriety, people rarely hesitated to make their own claims on her behalf. No one could even sort out the exact sequence of events at Dalldorf, but all accounts do agree on one thing: the scandal that followed the revelation of Fräulein Unbekannt's identity was not of her making. She was no publicity seeker, and her illusions, if they were illusions, were not the kind to win her quick release from the asylum. She must have known that.

Many people later believed that the nurses could have nipped the affair in the bud if only they had gone to the doctors or the police and told them what they knew. The nurses didn't see it that way. How long had it taken them to win the unknown woman's confidence? They weren't about to risk losing it now, just when she had begun to open up to them. As it was, they tried to reason with her and put her fears to rest. They told her that she was safe in Berlin, that all over Germany "princes move about freely and nothing happens to them," but they never convinced Fräulein Unbekannt of that. "There are many Russian spies here," she replied. "One is best sheltered in the asylum. If a revolution came in Russia, then it would be different."[43]

The nurses at Dalldorf had never doubted that Fräulein Unbekannt was Russian. It wasn't just her "Eastern" accent[44] or the fact that she spoke foreign languages in her sleep. "She spoke Russian like a native," said Erna Bucholz, a former German teacher who had lived in Russia, "not like a foreigner who has learned Russian."[45] Nurse Bucholz had been the first to take care of Fräulein Unbekannt at Dalldorf, and later she recalled an event that had taken place already in the summer of 1920:

During the nightshift I had special opportunity to converse with her, as generally she could not sleep. . . . I told her one evening that I came from Russia, talked about the cathedral in Moscow [St. Basil's] and spoke about Russian matters in general. She nodded and said she knew all this. . . . I asked her if she could speak Russian. She answered, "Yes," whereupon we began to converse in Russian. She did not speak it faultily. Rather, she used whole, complete, connected sentences without any impediments. . . . I absolutely got the impression that the patient was completely conversant in the Russian language, Russian affairs and especially Russian military matters.[46]

All the members of the Dalldorf nursing staff could confirm that when Fräulein Unbekannt spoke about Russia she spoke confidently and precisely.[47] "She showed in her conversation such a thorough knowledge of the geography," said one, "and so sure a grasp of the politics, that I could tell she was a lady of the highest Russian society."[48] And she bore such a striking resemblance to the Russian imperial family. So, at least, the nurses thought when they compared her features to photographs of the imperial family printed in a cheap illustrated magazine.[49] There were many of these publications lying about the asylum in the library and on the tables, some of them dating from as far back as 1914 and others, more recent, recounting the sensational news of the murder of the Tsar and his family at Ekaterinburg. One photograph of the Tsar's four daughters had immediately caught the nurses' attention. They had looked at it very carefully, they had discussed it together, and finally they had decided to force the issue: they brought the magazine to Fräulein Unbekannt.

Nurse Bertha Walz maintained that when she saw the photographs in front of her Fräulein Unbekannt "showed quite an altered behavior."[50] She became "utterly sad, quite pale and said, 'I know all these.' "[51] Summoning her courage, Nurse Walz pointed to one of the Grand Duchesses "and asserted that this one daughter of the Tsar was supposed to have been rescued. Fräulein Unbekannt corrected [her] and said no, not the one [Nurse Walz] had pointed out, but another of the Tsar's daughters had remained alive."

Which one? Nurse Walz wanted to know, but Fräulein Unbekannt had said enough: "The following day she was completely prostrate and depressed."[52]

Nurse Walz believed that this was the first time Fräulein Unbekannt had seen the photographs of the imperial family, but according to another report it was not. Thea Malinovsky, a night nurse who had only recently taken up her post, remembered the evening Fräulein Unbekannt had approached her at the desk. The incident took her completely by surprise:

After she had been sitting with me for about half an hour she said that she wanted to show me something. She went to her bed and pulled a *Berliner Illustrierte* out from under her mattress. On the cover was a photograph of the Russian imperial family. She put the magazine down in front of me and asked if I was not struck by something in the picture. I looked closely at the photograph but didn't know what she was driving at. However, as I looked longer it occurred to me that Fräulein Unbekannt bore a distinct resemblance to the youngest of the Tsar's daughters. But I pretended that I couldn't see anything in particular, whereupon she pointed to the young girl and asked if I still didn't notice anything. I said no. She asked, "Then you don't see any resemblance between the two of us?" Now I had to admit that I did indeed see a resemblance. Suddenly she got very upset. I asked her if it was she. She turned away, not wanting to let out any more. I told her that she shouldn't have come this far unless she was prepared to tell me the rest.[53]

It was then, in the autumn of 1921, that Fräulein Unbekannt declared outright that she was Her Imperial Highness the Grand Duchess Anastasia Nicolaievna. In the conversation that followed, as Nurse Malinovsky remembered it, she was "very upset indeed." She spoke of her sisters and the jewels they had sewn into their clothes in Siberia, of the last night in Ekaterinburg, when "a lady-in-waiting ran about with a cushion in her hands, hiding her face behind it and screaming," and of "the leader of the murderers of the Tsar, [who] went straight up to her father with his pistol . . . , mocking him with it and shooting at him."[54]

In a newspaper article published in 1927, Thea Malinovsky wrote further: "She asked me with some emotion to run away with her to Africa. . . . When I objected and said that there was currently fighting down there, she answered that we could join the French Foreign Legion as nurses, since we would be safer there than with the Jews here. . . . She was thoroughly convinced that the Jewish doctors at the asylum were in league with the Russian Bolsheviks and that they would one day betray her."[55] The special significance of these remarks was not lost on Nurse Malinovsky. At this time the Jews, as Europe's eternal scapegoats, were blamed not only openly for the catastrophe of the Bolshevik Revolution in Russia but directly for the slaughter of the imperial family at Ekaterinburg. The murder of the Romanovs, in fact, would be exploited to maximum effect as the Nazis began their rise to power in Germany. As "Grand Duchess Anastasia," therefore, Fräulein Unbekannt did not need to explain or justify her anti-Semitic feeling.[56]

Thea Malinovsky went home and told her fiancé, a doctor, about her conversation with Fräulein Unbekannt. She met with a blank stare: what did she expect to hear in a lunatic asylum?[57] Matters might have ended there had it not been for the admission to Dalldorf of Clara Peuthert, "a big, lean, bony proletarian,"[58] fifty-one years of age, who had lived in Russia before World War I as a dressmaker or a laundress — there seemed to be some confusion about her true profession. Clara herself later claimed that she had been employed in Moscow as a governess, but other reports make it plain that she had also served the Germans as a kind of penny agent, an intermittently reliable source of high-class gossip. In any case, she drank too much, talked too much, and had an annoying habit of slapping people when they said something she didn't like. "Do you think I'm crazy?" Clara asked everybody. "I'm not crazy."[59] After Fräulein Unbekannt had made her famous, Clara was seen to display "with great pride" a medical certificate attesting to the fact that "she was not mad, only pathological."[60]

Clara Peuthert had been committed to Dalldorf at the end of 1921, after she had accused her hitherto patient neighbors of stealing her money. She was bored at the asylum, restless and angry, and it didn't take her long to attach herself to the peculiar girl who lay at the other end of the ward. Clara had been fascinated by Fräulein Unbekannt from the moment of her admission. This was "somebody grand," she remembered. "Everybody in the room had already seen that."[61] But there was more. A Russian monarchist report dated the following June affirms that Clara "had met the unknown woman for the first time at Dalldorf, and the girl's face seemed familiar to her. She [Clara] had wanted to talk but the first attempt failed, because the unknown woman refused to answer. After some time she again addressed her and said: 'Your face is familiar to me, you do not come from ordinary circles.' The unknown woman looked at her, very startled, and put a finger to her lips to indicate that she should be silent. Very soon after that she approached her and made friends with her."

It isn't clear just why Fräulein Unbekannt decided that she could trust Clara Peuthert. Her loneliness may have outweighed her alarm. "We became more intimate when we discovered that we were the only normal beings among the insane people," Clara recalled. "We talked together and even joked."[62] Fräulein Unbekannt may have discovered that she truly liked Clara, with her beery good humor and those motherly attentions Clara knew how to extend on her good days. And it may be that Clara Peuthert, in her excitement, put a good many words in Fräulein Unbekannt's mouth. Clara, too, had seen the photographs of the Russian imperial family in the newspapers. One edition of the popular *Berliner Illustrierte Zeitung*, in particular, carried a cover story: "The Truth about the Murder of the Tsar." There, beneath a portrait of the Grand Duchesses Tatiana, Maria, and Anastasia, Clara Peuthert confronted the rumor that had swept Siberia in 1918 and which now, in Europe, stubbornly refused to die: "Is One of the Tsar's Daughters Alive?"[63]

It wasn't long before Clara jumped to conclusions. As one account has it, she ran to Fräulein Unbekannt's bed, thrust the magazine in her face, and cried at the top of her lungs: "I know you! You are Grand Duchess Tatiana!"[64]

"Tatiana," in this version, neither confirmed nor denied the charge, but began to cry and covered her face with the blanket.

There was no going back after this; the whole ward had heard it. In the end, however, Fräulein Unbekannt found a reason to believe that Clara Peuthert might be a blessing in disguise. Word had spread that the inmates of Ward B were about to be transferred to another public hospital, farther out in the Brandenburg countryside. Suddenly Dalldorf no longer seemed safe. Aware that her garrulous neighbor was due for release — "and visibly suffering because she was obliged to turn to [her]" — Fräulein Unbekannt took the matter in hand. Her "grandmother was living in Denmark," she told Clara. Then there was "an aunt" in Germany. Clara got the name, pronounced in the French mode: "Irene." Write to her, Fräulein Unbekannt said; she would know what to do.[65] But she begged Clara to be careful. It was not alone the people on the outside one had to fear, but others closer by. Again the specter of "the Jewish doctors" was raised. The thought of what they might do to her in a more distant place, said Fräulein Unbekannt, filled her with dread.

Well, said Clara Peuthert, thrilled by these confidences, she would be careful. And she would be back. There were a few more whispered conversations, a closer look at the pictures in the *Berliner Illustrierte,* a dozen more pleas for discretion, and then Clara was let go. She left the Dalldorf Asylum on the twentieth of January, 1922, and the "Anastasia" affair began.

Anastasia, not Tatiana. People later wondered why the nurses at Dalldorf hadn't done something to clear up the muddle that arose when Clara Peuthert returned to Berlin. The answer was too simple for most to believe: Fräulein Unbekannt had asked them not to talk about her, and, as nurses, they took their promises seriously. No one could blame them for a moment's indecision, either. What Fräulein Unbekannt had to say was fantastic. It was profoundly disturbing. Six weeks later, after Clara Peuthert had sounded the alarm, Fräulein Unbekannt summoned the nurses to her bedside. The nurses had never seen her in such agitation. This was "a case of espionage," she cried. What did the doctors know? It would be all over the newspapers, she was sure of it. The *newspapers!* Fräulein Unbekannt pronounced the word in sheer anguish. Then, as one of the nurses recalled, "She asked me very excitedly whether she really bore such a great resemblance to one of the Tsar's daughters as depicted in the illustrated magazine, and then added, 'Because then the photograph could be my ruin.' I confirmed the resemblance but said that Fräulein Unbekannt looked older than the lady in the picture, whereupon she said yes, that was because of the missing teeth. . . . Then she asked me, 'How old do you think I am?' and when I answered, probably in her late twenties, Fräulein Unbekannt began to laugh and said, 'No, not so old.' "

The nurse seized the moment of distraction. Taking up the copy of the *Berliner Illustrierte,* she pointed to the girl Fräulein Unbekannt resembled so much and asked, "Well, what is the lady's name?"

Fräulein Unbekannt answered without a moment's hesitation, "Anastasia."

In the winter of 1922 there were nearly five hundred thousand Russian refugees in Germany. More than a hundred thousand of them had settled in Berlin, making it the largest Russian colony outside Paris. There were Russian shops all over the city. There were Russian restaurants, Russian churches, Russian theatres, clubs, newspapers, charities, and movie houses. And there were more political associations than anyone could count — monarchist, fascist, socialist, even communist. Under the umbrella of the Office of Russian Refugees in Germany — the only émigré organization empowered by the Weimar government to represent these stateless people — factions of every conceivable political persuasion held their rallies and planned for the future. At that time most of the exiles honestly believed that the Soviet regime could not last, and they all wanted to be prepared for the fall when it came. Nobody wanted to be better prepared than the group that had understood the Russian Revolution the least: the monarchists.[66]

Numerically, the monarchists did not constitute a majority in Russian émigré politics. They did not even constitute a single party. In their own minds, however, and in the minds of the people whose cities they lived in, the monarchists were the soul of the emigration, the keepers of the Orthodox flame, symbols, literally, of all that had been Holy Russia. In May of 1921 a monarchist congress had been called in the Bavarian town of Bad Reichenhall to address the question of a successor to the throne of Nicholas II. That it was called at all signified de facto admission that Nicholas, along with his son and his brother, Grand Duke Michael, was dead, and not a single member of the Romanov family turned up at Bad Reichenhall to endorse that tacit resolution. This was a great blow to the congress, inasmuch as the monarchist ranks were already decisively split over the matter of the succession. In the extraordinary circumstances of the Revolution and the emigration, the problem of designating the next Tsar of Russia went beyond purely dynastic considerations. In France, the imposing Grand Duke Nicholas Nicolaievitch enjoyed the wholehearted devotion of the remnants of the imperial armies, whose commander-in-chief he had once been; while in Germany, at Coburg, the Tsar's first cousin, Grand Duke Kyril, was on the verge of demanding his rights as the next in line to the throne. It was a matter of choosing between popularity and international prominence, as claimed by the supporters of Nicholas, and strict legitimacy, as claimed by Kyril and the radical right.

Flummoxed, the delegates to the Congress of Bad Reichenhall managed to decide only two issues. First, a "Supreme Monarchist Council" would be established and would have its seat in Berlin under the leadership of Nicholas Evgenievitch Markov, a powerful, shrewd former member of the Russian Imperial Duma who was known in émigré circles exclusively as "Markov II." Next, it was agreed that the future Tsar must be chosen from among the Romanov family — that is, that a new dynasty must not be created — and it was fervently hoped that the surviving members of the family, not the monarchists, would do the choosing. Having declared these things, the delegates retired to their corners in Paris and Berlin to bicker, plot against each other, draw up charters and manifestos, and await the designation of the Romanov heir.

Nearly a year later, on Sunday, March 6, 1922, Captain Nicholas Adolfovitch von Schwabe, a young Russian exile of striking good looks and impeccable military bearing, sat in the inner courtyard of the Russian embassy church on Unter den Linden selling monarchist propaganda to the faithful. Before the Revolution, Schwabe had been a staff captain of the personal guard detachment of the Dowager Empress Maria Feodorovna. Now, in Berlin, he had become the manager of *Dvouglavy Orel* (*The Double Eagle*), the proto-fascist, rabidly anti-Semitic, right-wing organ of the Supreme Monarchist Council. Captain von Schwabe was in the habit of coming to the church each afternoon to spread the council's word and peddle a variety of its publications: hastily written histories of the recent Civil War, renewed calls to arms, religious tracts, and commemorative photographs of the Russian imperial family. Today a tall, nervous woman, "very poorly dressed," had approached his table and begun thumbing through his wares. It was some time before she asked, in German, "What are you doing with these pictures?"

Schwabe was taken aback. It was unusual to meet a German at the church, and stranger still to meet one so obviously interested in Russian printed matter. He told the woman that he worked for a monarchist publishing firm. "She looked at the pictures of the imperial family," Schwabe remembered, "and then turned to me with the question 'Can I trust you?' "

It was Clara Peuthert. "She wanted to tell me something, obviously," Schwabe continued, but the test had just begun. Clara had to know if Captain von Schwabe was "devoted to the throne," whether or not the pictures he was selling of the Tsar's daughters were good likenesses, what he thought about Jews. Baffled, Schwabe replied that he was selling anti-Semitic propaganda and that "conclusions might therefore be drawn about [his] attitude." To prove his point, Schwabe reached inside his collar and drew out the small metal swastika he wore around his neck.

By now the service in the church had ended and the courtyard was flooded with people. Clara Peuthert's story had to wait. When at last she told it, her narrative continually interrupted by Schwabe's customers, the captain was amazed: "In a lunatic asylum, near Berlin, there is a person interned who very much resembles Grand Duchess Tatiana. I myself am even convinced that she is [the Grand Duchess]. I believe this on account of her social manners, the noble cast of her features, and her well-shaped hands." And now, looking at the photographs of the Tsar's daughters, Clara believed it more than ever. "Yes," she exclaimed, "that is she. What a likeness!" Of course Captain von Schwabe, having been attached to the Dowager Empress, might be in a better position to judge. Wouldn't he go out to Dalldorf and see for himself?

Schwabe undoubtedly wanted to hear more, but the usher was making ready to close the gates. Yes, he told Clara, packing up his things, he would go out. He would go on the next visiting day, and he would not breathe a word to the doctors. He understood "what they were" and that they might try to lock him up if they found out his business. And of course he understood that the Grand Duchess was "very shy and afraid of everybody." Schwabe and Clara exchanged addresses, and then Clara walked away. She had not gone far before she turned around. "You will do something about it?"

Yes, said Schwabe again, he would be sure to do something about it.[67]

Afterward, Captain von Schwabe described this conversation as "peculiar." He was not thinking only of the news about the "Grand Duchess." Clara Peuthert herself made him wonder. Everything about her was strange: her looks, "her great nervousness," her baggy dress and floppy hat, her very involvement in what was, after all, fundamentally a Russian affair. Schwabe had to suspect a provocation, if only because there had been so many cases like this one already. "Grand Duchesses" had been sighted all over the world in the four years since the disappearance of the imperial family from Ekaterinburg.[68] Only the previous autumn a Mlle. Berditch had surfaced in Paris claiming to be Grand Duchess Anastasia. She had been laughed out of town, but the confusion was no less for that. Now there was another claimant, and Schwabe was not entirely certain what to do about her.

After talking it over that night with his wife, Alice, Captain von Schwabe decided that he would mention the matter of "Tatiana" to no one until he had been able to see her in person. But on Monday morning, bearing in mind what Clara Peuthert had told him about the doctors at Dalldorf, "and in view of the absolute mystery of the affair," Schwabe concluded that it would be best to have a witness. He therefore telephoned a friend, Franz Jaenicke, asking him to come along on the trip to Dalldorf. By profession Jaenicke was a flight engineer and the business manager of the German-Russian Club, another monarchist society with anti-Semitism as its creed. Schwabe wanted Jaenicke with him for two reasons: first, because he was a German and thus could more easily "divert the doctors" if necessary, and second, because he had a license to carry a gun. Having heard Schwabe's tale, Jaenicke agreed to meet him at his apartment at two o'clock on Wednesday afternoon.

Schwabe had barely finished talking with Jaenicke when there was a knock at his door. He opened it and there stood Clara Peuthert ("in the same old dress"). She waited a moment and then asked, "Are you really going to go?"

Swiftly Schwabe brought Clara inside and sat her down. All the questions he had wanted to ask the day before now came tumbling out. How had Clara met Fräulein Unbekannt? What made her think the unknown woman was a Grand Duchess? Had Clara ever seen the Grand Duchesses? Had Fräulein Unbekannt asked her to seek help among the Russian monarchists? Had Clara told anyone else about this affair?

Oh yes, Clara replied, she had indeed told someone else about this affair. She had written *two* letters to the Grand Duchess's aunt, Irene of Prussia, and to Irene's husband, Prince Henry. She still had the postal receipts, but they had not answered. Then, because the Grand Duchess had said that her grandmother was in Denmark, Clara had gone to the Danish embassy and to "several private people," but nobody had taken her seriously. And yes, she had seen the Grand Duchesses from a distance three times in Moscow. As for the Grand Duchess asking for help, Captain von Schwabe had to understand how it was: the only thing the Grand Duchess seemed to fear more than Jews was Russians. She was "in constant anxiety for her life." Still, said Clara, she was "very nice," although "very reserved." She was "fond of teasing when she was in a good humor," but "could be very unapproachable, even haughty." She was "very religious and educated"; liked "to receive Russian, English and French books," but spoke "only German"; was "energetic, very firm, never complained about anything [and] never thanked anybody." Altogether a very grand duchess.

Unconvinced, but more intrigued than ever, Schwabe sent Clara home and waited impatiently for Wednesday afternoon. At two o'clock sharp Franz Jaenicke arrived, armed and ready, and the two men set off for Dalldorf. Schwabe carried with him a Russian Bible, a box of chocolates, a copy of the monarchist newspaper *The Double Eagle,* and a photograph of Nicholas II's mother, the Dowager Empress. "It is necessary to state that we were both perfectly calm," he wrote later, "did not expect to find a Grand Duchess there and only went at all in order to clear up the matter finally."

To Captain von Schwabe's surprise, nobody at the Dalldorf Asylum tried to prevent him from seeing Fräulein Unbekannt. Nobody even asked him any questions. When one of the nurses ushered Schwabe and Jaenicke into Ward B she gently pulled the blankets away from her patient's face and said, "Fräulein Unbekannt, somebody has come to call on you."

The unknown woman stared at her visitors for a moment and then spoke: "I do not wish to see anybody." She covered her face again.

There was a long, tense silence. Then, Schwabe reported, Fräulein Unbekannt "pushed the blanket away and asked me what I wanted. I answered that I wanted to learn how she had come here and whether I could be of any assistance to her."

Fräulein Unbekannt would not let down her guard. "Who sent you?" she demanded.

Schwabe had no intention of discussing Clara Peuthert in front of the nurse — he had no intention of discussing anything in front of the nurse — and he answered that he could not tell her "at [that] moment."

Fräulein Unbekannt appeared to understand: "She looked at me very intently for a long time, then covered herself again."

Schwabe turned to the nurse. Would it be all right if he gave the patient some chocolates?

Why not? the nurse replied, but Fräulein Unbekannt had overheard them: "I do not take anything from anybody."

She was speaking in German. "Don't you speak Russian?" Schwabe asked her.

The answer came back, swift and unequivocal: "*Nein!*"

Schwabe had no idea what to do next. He couldn't very well ask Fräulein Unbekannt directly, "Are you Grand Duchess Tatiana?" but neither could he go home without finding out more. It was Franz Jaenicke who came to his rescue. "Why don't you show her the photograph?" Jaenicke suggested.

Now Schwabe brought out the portrait of the Dowager Empress. Once again the nurse bent down and removed the blankets. "The gentlemen want to show you a photo," she said.

Jaenicke observed that when she saw the picture of the Tsar's mother Fräulein Unbekannt "blushed furiously." "She took it from my hand," Schwabe remembered, "sat up in bed, and looked at it for a long time. Then she turned away from us, handed the picture back, and said in a rather sharp way, 'I do not know that lady.' "

Two more minutes went by in awkward silence before Fräulein Unbekannt broke the spell. This time she uncovered her face without assistance and said to the nurse, "I should like to speak with the gentleman in private." Without a word the nurse went with Jaenicke and stood by the door. Then Fräulein Unbekannt, gazing straight into Schwabe's eyes, asked him again, "*Who sent you?*"

There was nothing to worry about, Schwabe replied quickly; it was only Clara Peuthert.

Fräulein Unbekannt let this news sink in. "Forgive me," she said at length, "but I am very much upset." After a few minutes she regained her composure and came to the point. Could the gentleman do anything to secure her release? She was going to be moved that very week to an asylum in Brandenburg, and the thought made her sick with anxiety. Schwabe answered that he would do everything in his power to help: "[I] assured her that she could be absolutely at peace and that she could trust me. . . . Thus I tried to pacify her. For her part, the unknown woman asked me to be as careful as possible."

Fräulein Unbekannt had said all she had to say. Once more Schwabe offered her the box of chocolates, which she now accepted, along with his copy of *The Double Eagle*.

"You do *read* Russian?" Schwabe asked. It was more of a statement than a question, and it was confirmed "with a scarcely noticeable nod."

"Thank you," said Fräulein Unbekannt, and Captain von Schwabe took his leave. When he had reached the doorway he and Jaenicke turned back and bowed. Fräulein Unbekannt answered them with a smile and a quick nod, a gesture of dismissal that impressed them more profoundly than anything she had said.

Out in the hallway the nurse was waiting. Well? Had they recognized anybody?

Schwabe pretended not to understand. No, he replied. But Fräulein Unbekannt was interesting, very interesting.[69]

That night — a sleepless one for her — Fräulein Unbekannt told the nurses, "The gentleman has a photograph of my grandmother."[70]

On the trip back to Berlin Captain von Schwabe and Franz Jaenicke did not speak a word. "The interview with the unknown woman . . . had made such a deep impression on both of us," Schwabe wrote. "[We] were convinced that the patient truly was the Grand Duchess." There was no time to lose. That very evening Schwabe obtained an audience with the monarchist leader, Markov II. "After he had heard me," said Schwabe, "he, too, felt that the unknown woman might be a Grand Duchess." But Schwabe was not prepared to take responsibility for the establishment of her identity. There had to be someone in Berlin, he thought, who had known the Tsar's daughters well "and who could really recognize her." Markov agreed. In the meantime it was essential that nothing happen to Fräulein Unbekannt. He would take care of it. "After this," Schwabe remembered, "Markov took all the initiative and I was only acting on his advice."

It was a late night at the Supreme Monarchist Council. By morning it seemed that the whole émigré colony had heard the news: "A Grand Duchess at Dalldorf!" The Russians were kept busy all day. First, a number of former officers with pistols were dispatched to stake out the Dalldorf Asylum and make sure that no one tried to remove Fräulein Unbekannt. Another group went down to police headquarters to learn what they could there. And finally, while Captain von Schwabe spoke with the doctors at the Elisabeth Hospital about Fräulein Unbekannt's first days in Berlin, a third detachment was sent out to locate Baroness Buxhoeveden.

Sophie Karlovna Buxhoeveden, maid of honor to Empress Alexandra, had been a member of the imperial suite for five years and, as such, had known her mistress's four daughters exceptionally well. She had followed the imperial family into exile in Siberia in 1917 but had been denied permission to live with them in the governor's mansion at Tobolsk. The Baroness had not been able to see any of the family again until May of the following year, when the Tsarevitch Alexis and his sisters were removed to Ekaterinburg and she was allowed to travel with them in their train. At Ekaterinburg the Bolsheviks had given her her freedom and told her to move on. Now, the émigrés discovered, the Baroness was living at Hemmelmark as the guest of Irene of Prussia. Somebody would have to fetch her.

In the meantime the Supreme Monarchist Council had tracked down Zinaida Sergeievna Tolstoy, a woman who had lived at Tsarskoe Selo before the Revolution and who had often come to the Alexander Palace as a friend of the Empress. If Fräulein Unbekannt were genuine, the émigrés thought, she would surely remember "Zina." Mme. Tolstoy and her daughter, consequently, along with Captain von Schwabe and another monarchist officer, Captain Stefan Andreievsky, arrived at Dalldorf later in the morning. There they were met by the medical superintendent of the Elisabeth Hospital, Dr. Winicke, who had treated Fräulein Unbekannt in 1920. Schwabe had persuaded Winicke to act as an intermediary with the doctors at Dalldorf, but, again, nobody at the asylum put up any resistance to the émigrés' demands. The director of Dalldorf himself, after conferring with Winicke, merely asked one of the nurses to bring Fräulein Unbekannt down to the reception room.

"About a quarter of an hour elapsed," Schwabe remembered.

"Our tension mounted constantly." Finally the nurse returned and announced that Fräulein Unbekannt would not come. In that case, said the director, the émigrés would have to go to her.

They found her as usual, turned to the wall, her head covered with the blanket. Schwabe went up first. "You don't have to be afraid," he said softly. "Your friends are here."

There was no answer. At Schwabe's signal Zinaida Tolstoy and her daughter stepped forward and whispered, "Tanechka?" — a pet name of Grand Duchess Tatiana. Slowly Fräulein Unbekannt turned to them, still holding the coverlet over her mouth and nose. Encouraged, the Tolstoy ladies brought out photographs of the imperial family at Tobolsk, a holy ikon, and signed portraits of Empress Alexandra and her daughters.

"The unknown woman looked at them and began to cry," Captain von Schwabe reported. "Several times [the Tolstoys] stooped over her and asked her at least to say a word to them." She would not. It was the same when Captain Andreievsky, "very much excited," ran up to the bed and shouted, "Your Highness! Your Highness!" Schwabe was aghast. Every patient in the room had stopped what she was doing to stare at the scene. "They can hear you!" Schwabe protested, but Andreievsky paid him no attention. "Your Highness!" he cried again.

"Since the unknown woman could not be moved to show herself," Schwabe went on, "the ladies and Captain Andreievsky decided to uncover her face by force. I objected. The unknown woman resisted frantically." Quickly Dr. Winicke stepped in, sat down beside the bed, and calmed the patient. It was all right, he said; it was all right, nothing was going to happen to her. "Cautiously he uncovered her face. The unknown woman did not resist. . . . There were red spots on her face; she had tears in her eyes. Twice she opened them a little. Everyone looked at her very intently and came to the conclusion that she was indeed Grand Duchess Tatiana. . . . The only thing that puzzled [them] all was the unknown woman's smallness."

Now, all of this was going on as if there were some great secret to be hidden. Each time one of the émigrés stepped up to Fräulein Unbekannt's bed another stepped back "to divert the nurses' attention." The nurses had had enough. What was the matter with these people? they asked Dr. Winicke. Had they so little sensitivity that they couldn't see how terrified the woman was? She was being tortured, and it had to stop.

At the bed, Fräulein Unbekannt was still crying. Zinaida Tolstoy's daughter had sat down now and was stroking her hair. Fräulein Unbekannt took her hand and squeezed it. "The ladies and especially Captain Andreievsky wanted to uncover the unknown woman's face again," said Schwabe, "but I and Dr. Winicke insisted that she be left alone." At the headquarters of the Supreme Monarchist Council later that day, Zinaida Tolstoy told Markov II what she had seen and declared that there were no two ways about it: somebody would have to bring Baroness Buxhoeveden to Berlin.

Captain Andreievsky was put on the next train for Hemmelmark.

Schwabe, in the meantime, was still upset by the day's experiences. It had never been his intention to torment the unknown woman. Markov asked him now if there weren't someone Fräulein Unbekannt trusted, someone who might help her to relax and persuade her to cooperate. Suddenly Schwabe remembered Clara Peuthert. Clara had been visiting Fräulein Unbekannt all this while, bringing her newspapers, food and other sundries, chatting with her about life on the outside and generally doing what she could to be cheerful. Surely Clara, if anyone, could help. Schwabe asked her over that night and told her what was on his mind. There was going to be another visit to Dalldorf, he said, an important visit, and the council would be much obliged if Clara would go to Fräulein Unbekannt and prepare her for it.

Late in the evening of March 11 Baroness Buxhoeveden arrived in Berlin; Captain Andreievsky's mission to Hemmelmark had succeeded. Now Markov II set the plan: Clara Peuthert would go to Dalldorf the next morning at 9:30 and inform Fräulein Unbekannt that people were coming to see her and that she had to behave. At ten Baroness Buxhoeveden would arrive with Captain von Schwabe and Zinaida Tolstoy. In this way the meeting would be amicable, civilized, and presumably decisive. But when he arrived at Andreievsky's flat early on Saturday, Schwabe found that Baroness Buxhoeveden had other ideas. She wanted no part of Clara Peuthert, Schwabe discovered, and no part of Schwabe, either. The Baroness had decided to go to Dalldorf by herself and was already on her way. Schwabe couldn't believe it. "For reasons unknown," he wrote later, "Andreievsky *tried visibly to prevent me* from going [*Schwabe's emphasis*]. Thinking my presence important, I went anyway. . . ."

At Dalldorf Schwabe found Baroness Buxhoeveden and Zinaida Tolstoy pacing in the reception room. The Baroness was demanding loudly that Fräulein Unbekannt be brought down to meet *her*. When this failed to take place — and Schwabe could have told her that it would fail — the Baroness ordered Schwabe to stay where he was and to "detain" Clara Peuthert if she happened to show up. Then she and Mme. Tolstoy entered Ward B together.[71]

No one ever found out what went on in the ward during the several minutes of Baroness Buxhoeveden's first visit to Fräulein Unbekannt. All Schwabe knew was that the Baroness emerged from the room blushing, her face turning first red, then white, then red again.[72] The Baroness was obviously "excited," Schwabe wrote. "She said, however, that this was no Grand Duchess." Zinaida Tolstoy was pleading with her now to go back for another look, at least to take more time before making such an important decision, and finally, with plain reluctance, the Baroness agreed. This time Schwabe did not stay behind.

Clara Peuthert had arrived by now and had somehow slipped into the ward unnoticed. Fräulein Unbekannt was sitting up in bed talking with her excitedly. But the moment she laid eyes on Baroness Buxhoeveden, she darted back under the bedclothes and steadfastly refused to budge. The Baroness cried out to her in Russian, in English, and in French; called her "darling"; tried to show her an ikon and a ring that had belonged to "Mamma" — "but no persuasion could move her to appear again."[73] Angry now, the Baroness stood up, ripped off the covers, and dragged Fräulein Unbekannt violently to her feet. Looking her up and down she pronounced the verdict: "She's too short for Tatiana."[74]

Horrified, Fräulein Unbekannt leaped back in bed. The Baroness left the room. Outside, said Schwabe, she "confirmed again that it was not the Grand Duchess, but she added that there was some resemblance."

That, then, was that. To Captain von Schwabe's dismay the peremptory result of this rude confrontation was accepted as negative proof by the Supreme Monarchist Council. "Suddenly they all lost interest," Schwabe complained. Nobody wanted to hear another word about Fräulein Unbekannt, said Schwabe, and nobody wanted to see her again. Schwabe was given to understand that there might be "political repercussions" if he persisted in his efforts to identify Fräulein Unbekannt. "When I pointed out that she was nevertheless an unhappy Russian woman who ought to be helped," Schwabe remembered, "nobody was ready to do so. Even the Russian Charity Committee did not react."[75]

What seemed to Captain von Schwabe like heartlessness was, in reality, cowardice. He would soon learn that Baroness Buxhoeveden's influence had spread to loftier circles, far beyond the émigré colony in Berlin.

Clara Peuthert was beside herself. The outcome of the meeting with Baroness Buxhoeveden, Captain von Schwabe wrote, had "thrown her into great despair. But she did not give up hope." She would go to the Swedish Red Cross! she cried. She would write again to the Grand Duchess's family. She would show "the Buxhoeveden woman" a thing or two.

Schwabe was only half listening to Clara's tirade. He, too, had been badly upset by the recent fiasco at Dalldorf. Schwabe did not dare anymore to bother Fräulein Unbekannt with questions or surprises when he came to see her. But he did keep coming to see her. One day he presented her with a Russian Bible, on the flyleaf of which he had written "the password of the imperial family," given to him by Markov, a promise to save her, a request that she trust him, and an explanation of who he was.[76]

Fräulein Unbekannt had ripped the page out of the book and carefully torn it to bits, but she brought herself to honor the captain's request. She decided to trust him. In this way Schwabe — and Clara Peuthert, too — finally realized the mistake they had made. "I did not say I was Tatiana," Fräulein Unbekannt remarked, simply and accurately.[77] When, soon afterward, one of Schwabe's friends gave her a slip of paper on which were inscribed the names of the four daughters of Nicholas II, he asked Fräulein Unbekannt to strike out the names that did *not* belong to her. She did so willingly, leaving one name free.[78] Thus, with a quick stroke of the pen, the unknown woman captured an identity and sealed her fate as "Anastasia." Anastasia she would now be called, and to that name she answered for the rest of her life.

It was Captain von Schwabe's greatest desire now to find shelter for his mysterious protégée. Anastasia had to be gotten away from Dalldorf, Schwabe felt, not merely for her own peace of mind but in order that the investigation of her identity might proceed under less compromising circumstances. In the end, the publicity Anastasia had feared so much worked to her advantage. Baroness Buxhoeveden's denial of her identity may have satisfied the Supreme Monarchist Council, but it had done nothing to quiet discussion of her case in the Russian colony at large. "Even the more remote circles of the émigrés were talking about it," Schwabe observed. Among the most "remote" were Baron Arthur Gustavovitch von Kleist and his wife, Maria, a baroness in her own right who had once enjoyed a certain far-flung connection with the Russian court. Neither of the Kleists had ever seen the children of Tsar Nicholas, but they hoped all the same to play a role in Anastasia's identification, and, toward the end of March, they came to Captain von Schwabe asking if they could meet her. Finding the couple "very friendly" and seemingly reliable (and knowing that they had a large apartment and rather more money than most of their exiled compatriots), Schwabe quickly arranged for it.[79] By the end of the month the Baron and his family, citing "humanitarian reasons," had obtained a waiver of the usual visiting regulations at Dalldorf and were allowed to see Anastasia — "the unknown Russian woman" — at any time they pleased.[80]

Now began the difficult task of persuading Anastasia to leave the asylum for a new home. "She took up the matter only very gradually," Maria von Kleist remembered.[81] Frequent presents of flowers and candy helped break down her reserve, but the intervention of the Russian émigrés had already won Anastasia a reprieve from the dreaded asylum in Brandenburg, and she was beginning to think again that Dalldorf might not be such a bad place. Still the Kleists were coming to see her three or four times a week. When for any reason the Baron and Baroness could not make it to Dalldorf they sent their daughters, and when their daughters could not go they sent their maid, all in the attempt to convince Anastasia that she would be in good hands if she chose to accept their offer. Anastasia continued to hesitate. She would have to think it over, she said, and think it over she did for the next two months. She discussed the matter repeatedly with the nurses, with Clara Peuthert, with Captain von Schwabe, until, one morning at the end of May, she suddenly announced that she was ready to go.

Baron von Kleist had experienced no difficulty obtaining Anastasia's release from the Dalldorf Asylum. The police, in whose hands the decision finally rested, only wanted assurance that her maintenance would be provided, and they greeted the latest sensational development in her affairs with what looked like complete indifference. "Various attempts are being made in Russian circles to establish the unknown woman's identity," the police wrote laconically, "since there is some question of her being Grand Duchess Anastasia."[82] Only the doctors at the asylum (whom the émigrés had continued to regard with pathological suspicion) worried about the effect her discharge might have on Anastasia's health. Her weight had been dropping steadily for several months now, and she already showed the first signs of tuberculosis, an illness that would plague her for years. When the Kleists came to fetch her on a sunny May morning, the director of Dalldorf stopped them in the hall and asked them to tell him why they wanted to take the girl away.

"Because she is from our country" was Baron von Kleist's frosty reply. Then, because the director seemed unimpressed, the Baron continued: the very fact that Anastasia *might* be a daughter of the Tsar of Russia was sufficient reason to remove her from this place.

That said, the Baron and his wife swept into Ward B to collect their charge. They found her standing by the bed, dressed for the first time in more than two years in a set of proper clothes and looking, according to Baroness von Kleist, "quite radiant."[83] She would not leave the ward, however, until a thick black veil had been tied across her face.[84]

If she had known what kind of life awaited her in the outside world she might never have consented to leave the asylum at all. As it was, she bade farewell to the nurses on a cautious, cryptic note. "Soon, probably, we won't be seeing each other anymore," she said, "and I will be all right, but the mad rush is beginning again."[85]

2

"THE STORY"

*B*aron Arthur von Kleist lived with his wife and two daughters in a roomy fourth-floor apartment at Nettelbeckstrasse 9 in Berlin. The unknown woman from the Dalldorf Asylum joined them there on May 30, 1922, and managed within a few days to turn their domestic life on its head. If the Baron had ever hoped to shelter Anastasia quietly and with a minimum of fuss, he was quickly disappointed. Her presence transformed the Kleist home into a kind of mini-court in exile, "the point of rendezvous for White Russians of *le Tout-Pétrograd*," as one clever reporter called it, where Russian monarchists, the faithful and the doubtful alike, came to stare at the latest Romanov claimant and while away the hours.[1] Baroness von Kleist herself was amazed at the number of people who were suddenly coming to call. Before this, she and her husband had enjoyed no particular prominence. Now, however, with Anastasia under their roof, the Kleists had become the most popular couple in monarchist society. It was not unusual to meet twenty people in their drawing room on any given afternoon, and if the Baron, at least, began to enjoy himself, it was only understandable. Having served as a Tsarist district police officer in Russian Poland, he had now emerged the confidant of royalty, an important man, and by all accounts he encouraged the horde of monarchist hangers-on as testimony to his new prestige.

There were those among the monarchists who strongly suspected

29

that the self-aggrandizement of Arthur von Kleist, and not the identification of Anastasia, had become the primary goal at the Nettelbeckstrasse. Others were less kind and charged that the Baron was
out to make money on the tragedy of the Russian imperial family.
An inspector at police headquarters remarked of Baron von Kleist:
"It should be noted that he went to great trouble to solve the mystery and made no secret of his original conviction that the alleged
Grand Duchess was genuine. It is true that he may have had ulterior
motives, as was hinted in émigré circles. If the old conditions should
ever be restored in Russia, he hoped for great advancement from
having looked after the young woman."[2]

The attacks on Baron von Kleist may be left with that, because
when he and his wife first took her in they were convinced — ar-
dently convinced — that Anastasia was no one other than the Tsar's
youngest daughter. Captain von Schwabe, too, did not waver in his
support of her claim. When Schwabe's wife gave birth to a child
later in the year, the little girl was named for Anastasia, who stood
as godmother at the christening. "Many of the Russian émigrés were
invited," Schwabe's friend Franz Jaenicke remembered. "Many of
them had formerly been attached to the Tsar's court. *All* of them
were convinced that [Anastasia] truly was the daughter of the
Tsar."[3]

This unqualified confidence in Anastasia's authenticity was not
shaken by the fact that she would not speak Russian. The émigrés
accepted her explanation that she no longer wanted to speak the
language because, as Baron von Kleist quoted her, "the Russians
brought so much misery on [her] and [her] family."[4] To others Anastasia confided that the very sound of the Russian language distressed her so profoundly that she could barely control herself. She
told one Russian visitor that "a people who could do what the Russians have done deserve no better fate than to be enslaved."[5] Her
hosts were sorry to hear it, but they experienced no difficulty in
communication: they spoke to Anastasia in Russian, and she answered them in German — "a foreign German," said Maria von
Kleist. "The accent sounded Russian to us, or perhaps Polish, but
more Russian."[6] Zinaida Tolstoy, her curiosity undiminished despite Baroness Buxhoeveden's negative verdict, remembered that she
"always" spoke Russian with Anastasia and that Anastasia understood her perfectly.[7] Often Baron von Kleist read aloud to Anastasia from Russian newspapers and books; the remarks she made and
the questions she posed left him in no doubt of her nationality. One

evening Anastasia even rose from her chair and joined the monarchists in singing "God Save the Tsar." She was nothing if not contradictory.[8]

Indeed, Anastasia seemed truly anxious at first to meet the Kleist
family halfway. She did her best to be friendly, and while she could
not bring herself to converse freely with the swarms of monarchist
Russians who came to see her, she did not as yet openly object to
their presence. The Kleists had been considerate enough to give her
a room of her own and seemed to understand her when she told
them that she required a bath first thing every morning.[9] They had
bought her some simple, pretty dresses and let her borrow anything
else she needed from the Baron's two daughters.[10] In her becoming
new outfits Anastasia accompanied the Baroness on drives in the
countryside and on tours of the museums and palaces at Charlot-
tenburg and Potsdam.[11] The only thing she lacked was an "official"
name. Nobody yet dared call her Anastasia in public, and so, after
flirting with various Russian diminutives, Baron von Kleist settled
on the ambiguous and faintly vulgar "Fräulein Anny."[12]

Everything suggests that "Fräulein Anny Unbekannt" continued
to prize her anonymity above all else. She knew very well who,
precisely, the émigrés thought she was, but the understanding did
nothing to change her tactics. She lived in a state of perpetual anxiety, and she saw the Kremlin's emissaries everywhere. Out for a
stroll one day Anastasia noticed "an old Jew" crossing the street.
Grabbing her companion by the arm, she spun him around and
exclaimed, "*Schon wieder ein Bolschewist!* [Still another Bolshevik!]"[13] "Fräulein Anny was forever afraid that she would be kidnapped by the Bolsheviks," Baron von Kleist's daughter Gerda explained. But this sweeping paranoia extended beyond "Jews" and
"Bolsheviks" to embrace the whole of humankind — and most especially anyone who tried to probe Anastasia for proofs of her identity. "She ruined every chance she had to be recognized," Gerda von
Kleist remarked in bewilderment. "Whenever her identity was supposed to be tested, she showed a peculiar nervousness and would
begin to cry, or would run away."[14] There was nothing the Kleists
or anyone could do but wait for her to cooperate.

That Anastasia had passed through some awful trauma no one
doubted. She seemed sometimes to be overcome by despondency,
and on these occasions the Kleists were careful not to leave her
alone: they were afraid of what she might do to herself. "I was
often awakened in the night by the sound of crying," said Baroness

von Kleist, who took turns with her daughters sleeping in Anastasia's room.[15] She would find Anastasia sitting up in bed, bent over the photographs of the imperial family that her Russian guests had given her. The weeping was a frightful thing to witness. But terror and despair were not the only qualities Anastasia knew how to project. Rarely had the Kleists met anybody with such a wildly unpredictable nature. If Anastasia was polite one minute, she was aloof the next. If she was cheerful, talkative, and even "very gay," she could also be stubborn, opinionated, and downright rude. Later remarks of Gerda von Kleist make it plain that Anastasia's presence in the home was frequently less than pleasant. *Tyrannical* was another word used to describe her.[16]

Her moods doubtless fluctuated in accordance with her precarious health. Anastasia was truly ill. The Kleists' family physician, Dr. T. A. Schiler, saw her periodically during this summer of 1922. "Patient is friendly," Schiler noted after his first visit to Anastasia, "answers questions shortly with a 'yes' or 'no,' does not enter into any explanations." Schiler diagnosed acute anemia and remarked that Anastasia was "very pale, pulse weak." He guessed her to be about twenty-five (the Tsar's daughter at this time would have been just twenty-one).

Three days later Anastasia's condition had got worse: "Patient is very reserved. Gives practically no answer to questions; very pale; supports her head with her hand; smiles a little when a joke has been made." Dr. Schiler also discovered that even mild pressure to Anastasia's skull gave her great pain: "She hesitates to answer questions about injuries to her head; formerly a severe injury of the head has taken place." On June 10 Anastasia was spitting blood, and Schiler reported, "She gives no information, not even her age." On June 14 she was "completely aloof" and refused to eat. Then, nearly a month later, she was "more friendly and confiding toward the family — to others still aloof in the same way."[17]

On June 29 Anastasia was well enough to make an appearance at a small "evening party," but on the thirty-first she fell suddenly to the floor, choking: "She feels very dazed and makes hazy statements. . . . In her sleep she speaks Russian with good pronunciation; mostly unessential things. She calls out distinctly, 'Veronica!' "[18]

Anastasia's collapse now kept her confined to bed. On August 3 she was "totally aloof, very restless. Feels utterly ill." She was treated with digitalis and given morphine, while Zinaida Tolstoy moved into the sickroom to nurse her. And it was then, when Anastasia was "very dazed" and under the influence of narcotics, that the first details of "The Story" emerged.[19]

"What I have gone through! I have gone through everything, dirt and all, everything."

This is how Anastasia later spoke of the eighteen months that had passed between the disappearance of the Russian imperial family at Ekaterinburg and her own attempt at suicide in Berlin. The same stark words run through all her narratives like a refrain: *everything, everything, horrible, dreadful, haste, hurry, dirt, blood.* A woman who knew her later in the 1920s once watched in fascination as Anastasia, her hand pressed across her eyes, sought to recall the events of the summer of 1918, specifically, as Anastasia put it, "the last night, when we had to dress so quickly." Anastasia was confused, there was no doubt about it. She pulled back her hair and asked her companion, "Can you find a scar behind my ear?"[20]

There was, indeed, a deep scar behind Anastasia's right ear. Her friend ventured that it must have been the result of an accident.

"Yes, you are right," said Anastasia bitterly, "it was an accident . . . a very bad accident." She paused. "I don't know how to say exactly. . . . But I fainted, everything was blue, and I saw stars dancing, and there was a great roar."

"Was it a cut?" asked Anastasia's friend, still looking at the scar.

"No," said Anastasia uncertainly, "it should be round, for it was no cut."

"What was it then?"

Anastasia was silent for a moment. "Why were my dresses all bloody?" she asked finally. "Everything was full of blood. . . . Yes, it was then . . . when the end came."

For Anastasia, "the end" meant the night of July 16, 1918, the last time the Russian imperial family was ever reliably reported to be alive. Anastasia herself never mentioned the exact date, but she did know the month and the year and muttered, "Month of July is the worst for me." Beyond that, in detail, she was reluctant to go, and she reacted angrily whenever people came forward with what purported to be accurate descriptions of her experiences. There were "so many untrue statements," she complained, so many "wild imaginations and selfish motives," that it was impossible any longer to sort fact from fiction.[21] When a police inspector once remarked that she had been wearing soldier's boots on the last night in Ekaterinburg, she cried out in sheer exasperation, "What is that man thinking of! It's crazy. . . . We weren't supposed to be going any-where, just into another room; we didn't need to put on boots."[22] It was a minor point, but to Anastasia's mind typical.

Zinaida Tolstoy, nursing Anastasia in the summer of 1922, was the first to hear "The Story," or parts of it. She reported the details as she received them to Baron von Kleist, who in turn drew up a number of protocols and invented for Anastasia a flowing, first-person narrative that bore no resemblance to her actual speech but did introduce, in a guarded way, "a soldier who had rescued [her]" from the general slaughter at Ekaterinburg. This soldier, des-tined to cast a long shadow across Anastasia's life, gave his name as Alexander Tschaikovsky. With Tschaikovsky and his family — "his mother, Maria, his sister, Veronica, and his brother, Serge" — Anastasia traveled out of Russia in a farm cart to Bucharest. There she remained until the beginning of 1920. During the Rumanian sojourn — to be precise, on "December 5, 1918" — she gave birth to Tschaikovsky's child, a boy, whom she called Alexis after her brother. Shortly after that she was married to Tschaikovsky in a Catholic church in Bucharest. No rings were exchanged and no pa-pers were signed. In Bucharest the family had taken up residence with a "gardener," described as a relative of Alexander Tschaikov-sky's mother. Tschaikovsky was shot and killed on the streets of Bucharest at the end of 1919. His young widow, leaving her son behind, then came "alone" to Berlin to seek out her mother's rela-tions. She was "at liberty for less than a week" before she fell — or had she been pushed? — into the Landwehr Canal.[23]

Such was the fantastic gist of "The Story" as Baron von Kleist told it. Anastasia's indignation knew no limit when she heard about the Baron's "lies." Alexis! she exclaimed. She had never called her child Alexis: "The boy is called like the father, Alexander."[24] And where had Baron von Kleist come up with the date of the child's birth? Anastasia had no idea when the boy was born. He would be "almost three" now, in 1922, that was all she knew.[25] What did it matter? She would never be able to recognize the child in any case.

Anastasia had never wanted to talk about the child, and still less about her relations with Alexander Tschaikovsky. This, apparently, is what she had meant when she said that she had passed through "dirt and all." "She told me that she had been raped," said Gerda von Kleist bluntly.[26] There had already been whispers of "innocent flirtations" behind the palisades at the Ipatiev house in Ekaterinburg, and now the Russian monarchists began to pay closer attention to them.[27] Anastasia herself approached the subject with utmost delicacy. Only in the company of other women was she able to overcome her humiliation and explain that "a peasant is not the same as us,"[28] that Alexander Tschaikovsky had been possessed of "a good heart" but, like so many of his class, he was "hot." Anastasia knew what people would think, she said, and she was right: the notion arose in monarchist circles that she had bartered her way out of Ekaterinburg with sexual favors. In 1925, after "The Story" had been made public, a friend asked Anastasia how she, a Russian Grand Duchess, could possibly have brought herself to live with such "simple people" as the Tschaikovskys, and Anastasia became angry. "Look here," she said, "if simple people are kind to me, I do not remember at all that they are simple."[29]

And had the Tschaikovskys been kind to her?

"I would not be here now if they were not kind to me," Anastasia answered coldly.[30]

"She did not seem to want to go on with this topic," wrote Anastasia's friend. No, she did not want to go on with any part of this topic — not the Tschaikovskys, the boy, Bucharest, the flight from Russia, or, before that, the "last night" and the imprisonment in the Ipatiev house. When she talked about it again in 1929[31] Anastasia could not recall how long her family had been held in Ekaterinburg — "a very short time" — but she well remembered their helplessness and the "constant dread" they all had felt. During the conversation, when she was asked why the imperial family had made no attempt to escape, she was incredulous. "How could we get out?" she asked. "How could we arrange it?" People didn't understand, Anastasia protested: "We couldn't talk much. We were not alone. They were always right in the room." The soldiers were everywhere, those "terrible, terrible" Russian soldiers: "They came into the room during the night. . . . The Russian soldiers are something dreadful. . . . You cannot imagine what they are like. . . . If any of them showed the least sign of kindness they were put away. . . . Many things the soldiers took. Nobody took care of the place and they just took everything they could. . . . Of course they were always drinking and using terrible language. . . . They were horrible. They behaved terribly to my father. . . . It makes me ill even today to think about it. They used vile language, they called him terrible names." People didn't understand, Anastasia said again. No one could understand what she had been through, what they had all been through. "They do not feel ashamed when I tell them of how my mother and sisters suffered," she declared hotly, and everyone knew whom she meant by "they" — the Russians, all of them. Now she had said enough. She would not speak of it anymore.

It was thus, over a period of seven years, that Anastasia told "The Story" — in fragments, spurts, bursts of rage and moments of deepest bitterness. Baron von Kleist never heard the half of it. While he wrote dully of Anastasia's escape across Russia in a peasant cart, Anastasia herself still shuddered at the memory:

Do you know what a Russian farm wagon is? No, you do not know. You only know when you lie in one with a smashed head and body. . . . How long was it? My God. A long time. Many weeks. Tschaikovsky was really crazy to rescue me. What I went through. I was as though fallen from the sky. Suddenly among strangers. They took my clothes off right away. I lay in the clothes of the old woman's daughter. But my clothes were hidden in the wagon. And also many bottles with water. For days we went through stretches where there were no people. Also woods. The water was for my head. But sometimes there was no water.[32]

Here Anastasia broke off her narrative and "cried for a long time."

Of course the question on everyone's lips was this: who on earth was Alexander Tschaikovsky, and how had he managed to rescue the daughter of the Tsar?[33] On this point Anastasia could not enlighten anybody. She only knew what Tschaikovsky had told her: "It was a dreadful mixup, then he saw that I was still alive. He did not want to bury a live body and he escaped with me under greatest dangers. It was very dangerous."[34]

So Tschaikovsky had been one of the Bolshevik guards at Ekaterinburg?

Evidently he had, said Anastasia, again turning the conversation away from Tschaikovsky, away from Ekaterinburg and the Ipatiev house. "This part is too horrible," she declared. "I must not think about it."[35] Many who trusted in Anastasia's identity chose, out of sheer tact, not to press the point. Others, and not without reason, began to suspect that she was hiding something. She did once admit that she had "a heavy burden on her conscience,"[36] and, indicating a photograph of Grand Duchess Tatiana, said, "She is dead because of me."[37] Zinaida Tolstoy remembered Anastasia telling her that "the Tsar was killed first" and something more: the body of Grand Duchess Tatiana had fallen on top of her own, no doubt protecting her from the assassins. Then she felt "a terrible blow on her head" and lost consciousness.[38]

Nobody ever heard Anastasia use the word *murder* when she spoke of the "dreadful mixup" of July 1918. It was "the tragedy," "what happened," "the end." "We always expected it," Anastasia confided. "We did not know what would happen. There was always that dread. We never could tell." When, seven years after her release from the Dalldorf Asylum, Anastasia suddenly found herself talking about "what happened," she could only give expression to her enduring bewilderment:

Everything was so sudden. It all happened at once. It came so quick nobody could think. . . . It was late in the evening. We were all in bed. They just came and told us to get ready. We had to dress and follow them. We knew nothing — were just ordered to come along. . . . I do not know what they told my father. We were just ordered to go — to follow the soldiers. Nobody could believe what was going to happen, and to this moment I do not know. There is just one horrible picture in my mind. I do not want to talk about it. I must not think about it.

On this occasion Anastasia's companion had the courage to ask her, "Were you all together?" She answered, "Yes." And then again: "I do not know what happened. . . . There was nobody there to do anything to help us."

About the Rumanian sojourn, the birth of her child, and her marriage to Alexander Tschaikovsky, Anastasia proved less mysterious, if equally vague. She did not know how long the journey out of Russia had taken them — "weeks and weeks" — and she remembered little about it beyond the shaking of the cart and the incessant pain in her head. The wounds she had received — on the skull, at the jaw, behind the ear, in the arm, the chest, and the foot — she said had healed "very quickly" through the application of simple compresses and cold water. She was "always ill," however, and frequently unconscious. She did not recollect the moment the party crossed the Rumanian frontier or even know how to describe the house they had occupied in Bucharest. "I was in one room and never came out," she explained. "I was ill all the time."[39] Would she recognize the house or the street again if she saw them? people asked, and Anastasia answered no, she would not: "I was only brought out of the house twice. . . . I saw nothing in Bucharest."

How about the "gardener," then, the relative of the Tschaikovskys who had sheltered them? Would she know him?

"I cannot say," said Anastasia. "He was Russian. . . . He was not young and he was not old." The information was useless enough.[40]

When Anastasia spoke of being "brought out of the house twice" she was referring first of all to her marriage to Alexander Tschaikovsky and, second, to the latter's funeral later the same year. She clearly remembered seeing Tschaikovsky's body, although, as she explained again, "I never went into the street; once for the wedding I was put into a car, I did not look out. I was frightened. The church, yes, it was large."

And what did Anastasia remember about the marriage ceremony? Nothing: "I did not know the Catholic rites."[41] She had been married in a black dress and veil[42] under the name — she insisted — of "Anastasia Romanov," but she did not know if the civil regulations had been met. When it was later suggested to her that her marriage might not have been a marriage at all, but rather a simple mass designed to appease her in the face of her son's illegitimacy, Anastasia preferred not to consider the possibility. Some reports claimed that she had married Tschaikovsky "out of gratitude,"[43] but Anastasia denied it: she had done it only for the child, and she had allowed the boy to be baptized a Roman Catholic. She did not go to the christening, however, and she had *never* permitted anyone to give him the name of Romanov.[44] At all events, she had handed the baby over to Tschaikovsky's mother and sister at the moment of its birth: "My only desire was that it would be taken away instantly."[45]

During the year in Bucharest, Anastasia continued, the Tschaikovsky family had subsisted on the proceeds of the jewelry which she, like her sisters, had sewn into her clothes while imprisoned at Tobolsk. There were diamonds and other precious stones, together with a long pearl necklace which she wore in a band around her waist and which was one of the last items to be sold.[46] Later it was assumed that Alexander Tschaikovsky had been murdered in Bucharest by vengeful Bolsheviks who knew about his rescue of the Tsar's daughter, but Anastasia was not so sure. "Maybe he wanted to sell the jewels," she suggested. "They may have robbed him. Rumanians are quick with the knife." She sighed: "It was hard." But there had been no reason for her to remain in Bucharest any longer. The Tschaikovskys had not wanted her to leave Rumania in the middle of winter, but Anastasia was adamant. She had only one thought now — to reach her mother's family in Germany: "Yes, my mother loved them. . . . It was always in my mind to go to my mother's relatives. . . . It seemed so natural to me that they would recognize me; I did not think of any difficulties."[47] She had left behind her not only her child, but also "the clothes she had worn on the night of the murder and the underclothes bearing her initials." Even Baroness Buxhoeveden, Anastasia declared, "would recognize these clothes if they were laid before her."[48].

Anastasia could never talk about the trek from Bucharest to Berlin without breaking down. These were brutal, frightful days. Contrary to the initial belief, Anastasia had not traveled to Berlin "alone," but rather in the company of her late husband's brother, Serge Tschaikovsky. "In Rumania we traveled on the train," she remembered, "but many places we were afraid they would ask for the passport. Sometimes I traveled on the train and sometimes I walked."[49] It was the walking that had nearly felled Anastasia, the endless trudging through the snow and the long hours of waiting "in the bedrooms of small hotels"[50] while her companion sought the means to cross the borders secretly: "We could only go a short distance at a time." Only when they had crossed the frontier into Germany did Anastasia feel safe. "Then it was all right," she said. "I went by train to Berlin." At first Anastasia had found it "very hard to remember" her German — "It was hard to make them understand me" — but the language had begun to come back to her by the time she reached the capital. She and Serge had checked into two rooms "in a hotel," the name of which she did not know. "Everything was so new to me," she said.[51]

Anastasia's plan to find the members of her mother's family might have succeeded but for one thing: Serge Tschaikovsky disappeared — or at least Anastasia imagined that he had disappeared when she went down the hall to his room and found him gone.[52] Anastasia could not bring herself to think what this disappearance, following so quickly on the death of her husband, might mean. Panic-stricken, she ran outside, bent on reaching the Netherlands Palace, where, she hoped, her mother's sister might be staying. There followed the realization that none of the Prussian royal family might be in residence; the terrible confusion; the hours of wandering through the streets of Berlin; and, finally, the desperate leap into the Landwehr Canal. This act Anastasia later categorized as her "greatest folly,"[53] but from that moment, in any case, her history was known.

It isn't difficult to imagine the reaction of the Russian monarchist community when news of "The Story" leaked out. Those inclined already to doubt Anastasia's identity naturally believed the fabulous tale of her escape from death even less. Neither could Baron von Kleist soften for the émigrés the hard blow of learning that Anastasia had given birth out of wedlock to her rescuer's child. It did no good for Anastasia to protest (as she later did) that Alexander Tschaikovsky, while simple and rough-hewn, was actually a scion of the old Polish nobility.[54] Nobody in monarchist circles wanted to believe that the daughter of the Tsar of All the Russias was the mother of the bastard son of a Polish-Bolshevik soldier. It was still worse to think that the last descendant of the last Tsar had been "left behind" in Rumania. How many three-year-old orphaned boys might there be in Bucharest? Russian monarchists who knew their history must have trembled when they realized that Anastasia, whoever she was, would probably not be the last claimant to the heritage of the Romanovs.

Ill and habitually morose, Anastasia could not be bothered with the émigrés' problems. In fact she was beginning to lose her temper. She was not a "thing," she declared,[55] and the monarchists had better realize it. Even during her serious illness Baron von Kleist did not consider her state of mind as he herded his friends into the sickroom for what might be a last look. Anastasia began to talk about going back to Dalldorf.

In her distress, she turned to Clara Peuthert for comfort. A peculiar alliance, not appreciated by outsiders, had been forged between these two ex-inmates. But the Kleists abhorred Clara and did everything in their power to minimize her influence. Clara, in turn, deeply resented what she saw as the Baron's theft of her laurels. "He got involved in this affair for self-interested reasons," Clara grumbled, "and now he wants to be her only counselor."[56] It was true: Captain von Schwabe — who, after all, had done more to advance Anastasia's claim than anyone — noted regretfully that since Anastasia had taken up residence with Baron von Kleist, he saw her "seldom."[57] It had become clear to everyone that the Baron meant to keep "the Grand Duchess" to himself.

The result was a backstairs tug-of-war that would have done justice to any royal court in Europe. People began to loiter about the Kleists' apartment in ever greater number, hoping to curry Anastasia's favor and obtain for themselves — what? Anastasia had nothing to offer them but her attention. Evidently that was enough.

Whenever Baron von Kleist brought guests to see her, Anastasia was encouraged not to meet them — by Clara Peuthert, or, increasingly, by Captain von Schwabe's wife, Alice, who threw herself into the intrigue at the Nettelbeckstrasse with relish and proved to be a meddler of the first water. Meanwhile the tension grew daily more intolerable. On August 11 Baroness von Kleist, who so far had tried to rise above the unpleasantness in her house, expressly forbade any further visits from Clara Peuthert.[58] That evening Alice von Schwabe came to call and closeted herself with Anastasia for several hours. Anastasia later emerged from her room in tears, but when Baron von Kleist asked her what the matter was, she replied that she could not discuss it with him: she would have to speak with Mme. von Schwabe first. "There is no doubt," the Baron wrote, "that Mme. Schwabe worked a most disadvantageous effect on the invalid's psychic condition."[59]

In the end, fed up, Anastasia tricked them all. Dr. Schiler observed that she had rebounded from her serious collapse with uncommon vitality. "The status quo ante has been reached," Schiler noted happily. "Patient is up, is extraordinarily cheerful."

When Dr. Schiler returned for his next visit he found that his services were no longer required. "Patient has escaped," he remarked, very puzzled, and indeed Anastasia had vanished.[60]

The mystery enveloping the fate of the Russian imperial family remains as impenetrable today as it was sixty years ago, when Anastasia ran away from Baron von Kleist rather than reveal her secrets. It still surprises people to learn that the popular story of the murder of the Romanovs — that is, the story of their mass execution in the cellar of the Ipatiev house — is, in reality, only a theory of history. Scholars have pointed out for years that the case for the murder of the imperial family rests entirely on circumstantial evidence; that no bodies were ever recovered, nor even were any undisputed witnesses to the crime found. One man alone, a captured Bolshevik formerly in service at Ekaterinburg, signed a statement affirming that he had seen the corpses of the imperial family lying in thick pools of blood on the floor of the Ipatiev house cellar. That document had been drafted by officers of the anti-Bolshevik "White Army" in Siberia, and it was signed under torture.[61] A few days later the star witness died in prison of "typhus" ("I hit him once too often," a White officer later sheepishly confessed in exile). "Don't you agree," said a French military attaché in Ekaterinburg, "it is disconcerting that this damned typhus should have come along and just happened to deprive historians, now and in the future, of the only witness to a momentous event which up till now has been insoluble?" [62]

Disconcerting it is, especially in view of the strange history of the forensic evidence on which the tale of the Romanov murder is based. A box containing what were presumed to be the imperial family's mortal remains — these consisted of smashed jewelry, burned clothing, and a grisly handful of charred "mammal bones" — was passed from hand to hand and from palace to palace for more than a decade when it finally reached Europe; none of the relatives of the imperial family would agree to arrange for its disposal, and it has since vanished completely.[63] Then there were three identical sets of sworn testimony, each of them authenticated and signed by Inspector Nicholas Sokolov, the magistrate appointed in 1919, during the White occupation of Ekaterinburg, to determine the fate of the imperial family. Two copies, including Sokolov's own, have disappeared, while the third found its way eventually to the Houghton Library at Harvard University. There it sat virtually unnoticed for years. When, in 1976, the complete findings of the Sokolov investigation were finally made public, they revealed less about the true circumstances of the murder of the imperial family than they did about the investigation itself: it was no "investigation" at all, but a judicial charade, strategic propaganda expressly designed to cap a mystery that, politically, was getting out of hand.

This is no reckless accusation, nor even a novel one. His superior in the White Army actually described Inspector Sokolov's Siberian mission as a "political command" and advised that "complete revelations concerning the assassination and its circumstances are thus undesirable." [64] There was no room for doubt or speculation at such a critical moment: this was civil war. "It was clearly in the interest of the Whites to accept the fact that all of the family had died," write Anthony Summers and Tom Mangold in The File on the Tsar. "As propaganda, this served the double purpose of exposing the Bolsheviks as vicious murderers of helpless women and children and at the same time elevating the Romanovs to the status of martyrs." [65] As propaganda, the murder of the imperial family served far more than that. It allowed anyone with a political or racist chip on his shoulder to impose his case on a truly horrified public. Thus Inspector Sokolov could point to Lenin as the man responsible for the Ekaterinburg slaughter, while his monarchist colleagues automatically blamed "the Jews" and their imaginary overlords, "the Elders of Zion." [66] Still others, notably Grand Duchess Anastasia's French tutor, Pierre Gilliard, saw an opportunity to vilify the Germans; in 1921 Gilliard declared that the imperial family had been murdered by something he called *austro-allemands*. [67] In other words, as Summers and Mangold rightly conclude, the lack of evidence in this case was a great nuisance: "What was needed was an official enquiry which began with a definite premise — that all the Romanovs died at Ekaterinburg — and which could be firmly dominated from [White Army headquarters at] Omsk." [68]

No one need doubt that Inspector Sokolov's investigation into the murder of the imperial family was in fact "dominated from Omsk." The White Military Command ordered Sokolov on the case, and the White Military Command ordered him off it four months later. Neither is there any doubt that Sokolov wanted to prove what the White Army wanted to hear. Before he left Omsk for Ekaterinburg, in February 1919, Sokolov had already told a worried Pierre Gilliard that "the children suffered the same fate as their parents." He added, "I don't have a shadow of doubt about it." [69] As a result, Sokolov never addressed himself "officially" to the rumor of Grand Duchess Anastasia's escape — a rumor that, as reported by an adjutant to the White military governor of Ekaterinburg, "never ceased to circulate in the town." [70]

The rumor had spread like wildfire, as rumors will. It was carried out of Siberia to Europe by soldiers, diplomats, former prisoners-of-war, nuns, countesses, and peasants seeking to escape the carnage inflicted on them one minute by the Reds and the next by the Whites. The records of the Sokolov investigation, in fact, contain the sworn statements of no fewer than a dozen witnesses who declared, on the one hand, that the Empress of Russia and all of her daughters were still alive in the city of Perm, about two hundred miles west of Ekaterinburg, more than two months after their supposed deaths, and, on the other, that one of the Grand Duchesses, most often designated as Anastasia, had escaped her prison in Perm only to be recaptured by Bolshevik platoons in the woods around the city. The reports on "Anastasia" were especially enlightening — not as proof that the Tsar's daughter had survived, but rather as an indication of the confusion and the manifest alarm of the Bolshevik hierarchy in Siberia. The Bolsheviks at Perm — the new seat of the Ural Regional Soviet, the body that, ostensibly, had murdered the Tsar's daughter at Ekaterinburg — had guarded the mysterious girl with great care and had even called in a doctor to treat her wounds (she had been severely beaten and, probably, raped). The doctor, Paul Utkin, was told that she was "the daughter of the ruler, Anastasia." He had no reason to doubt it. One of the witnesses in the Sokolov file was the sister of the secretary of the Regional Soviet.[71] Was she lying when she said that she had inside knowledge of the survival of the Empress and her daughters? Had the Bolsheviks perhaps planted her as a false witness? It's possible, but her testimony, taken by itself, is as valuable as any other in this lamentable dossier, and, unlike others, it does not stand alone. Princess Helena Petrovna of Russia, a Serbian princess who had married into the Romanov family, was also held prisoner at Perm during the autumn of 1918. One day, Helena remembered, a young girl calling herself "Anastasia Romanov" was brought to her cell. The Bolsheviks wanted to know if she was, as they suspected, the daughter of Nicholas II. Helena said no, and the girl was taken away.[72]

Now, the name Romanov, like the name Anastasia, is one of the most common in Russia. There must have been hundreds of "Anastasia Romanovs" in the vicinity of Perm alone. Why had the Bolsheviks needed to consult Helena Petrovna to find out that this particular "Anastasia Romanov" was *not* the daughter of the Tsar?

The Bolsheviks appear to have been perfectly frank at the beginning about Grand Duchess Anastasia's escape. Thus there is the testimony of Dr. Günther Bock, a retired career diplomat, who had to await security clearance from the West German government before giving his evidence. As German consul at Leningrad in 1927, at a time when Anastasia's case was the talk of Europe, Dr. Bock had consulted S. L. Weinstein, the chief of Moscow's Foreign Commissariat for Leningrad. Weinstein told Bock directly that one of the Romanov women had escaped execution at Ekaterinburg. "Anastasia?" asked Bock, but Weinstein felt he had already said enough and merely shrugged his shoulders: "One of the women."

"I had expected him to deny it," said Dr. Bock, "and I was amazed at the friendly, natural way in which he confirmed my question." Only later, when Anastasia's case had begun to attract too much attention, did Moscow fall back on the tactic it always employs in the face of scrutiny: total silence.[73]

Over and again the Siberian witnesses tell a common story — of house-to-house searches, spontaneous interrogation, and open threats of retribution if any of the citizenry was found harboring "female members of the Romanov family."[74] The roster of witnesses who actually saw posted placards announcing the flight of the Grand Duchesses — at Ekaterinburg and Perm, in Moscow, Orel, Chelyabinsk, and at Soviet missions abroad — is not a small one.[75] Some said it was one of the girls, others that it was two or more, but most of the witnesses spoke with the reticence a legal oath can inspire and could not identify the Grand Duchess or Duchesses by name. A White officer in the Civil War was told to prepare a special train to be held in reserve in the event the Tsar's daughters were found alive.[76] Another, a commanding general in south Russia, led the interrogation of two captured Bolsheviks who had formerly served in Ekaterinburg. Both declared, "in separate interrogations," that "one of the Grand Duchesses got away."[77]

"You've got to remember one very important thing," said Julius Holmberg, a Finn who had been educated in Ekaterinburg and who still saw many of his Siberian friends during the 1920s, "that is, that the [Sokolov] commission was *ordered* to abandon its researches at a time when the White Army was still at the height of its power in Siberia." This is true, and Holmberg thought he knew why: his friends from Ekaterinburg, "to a man," had all heard about the escape of "at least one" of the Grand Duchesses. "Perhaps for their sake it seemed wiser to leave it," Holmberg suggested, remembering what he had been told about the fury of the Bolsheviks when they discovered that their plan to annihilate the entire imperial family had not succeeded.[78] In the absence of proof the matter may be left with a single document. Count Carl Bonde, sent by the Swedish Foreign Ministry to inspect prisoner-of-war camps in Siberia during the Civil War, declared:

In my capacity as the chief of the Swedish Red Cross mission in Siberia in 1918, I traveled in a private railway car. At some place, the name of which escapes my memory, the train was stopped and searched for the Grand Duchess Anastasia, daughter of Tsar Nicholas II. The Grand Duchess, however, was not aboard the train. Nobody knew where she had gone.[79]

She had gone, said Anastasia, to Rumania. It can't be proven sixty years later, after another world war, the Communist takeover, and a violent earthquake that in 1977 leveled most of Old Bucharest. Suffice it to say that investigations conducted on Anastasia's behalf in Rumania have uncovered no trace of the Tschaikovsky family, no trace of her marriage, no record of her son's birth, of her husband's death, or of her subsequent departure for Berlin.

"There is not one tittle of genuine evidence in the story," a Russian Grand Duchess remarked,[80] but she was wrong, and her mistake lies in her notion of what is "genuine" and what is not — in this case, a European princess who had ostensibly turned up in Bucharest and did not at once present herself to the King and Queen of Rumania for identification. Anastasia always reacted bitterly to this constantly repeated criticism of her behavior. Many believed her when she told them that the fact of her motherhood had filled her with a shame so deep she would never have dreamed of approaching the Rumanian court — was Anastasia supposed to introduce the King and Queen to her rapist? — but this royal squabble is a red herring, serving little more than to block that "tittle of genuine evidence."[81]

In the autumn and winter of 1918 Rumania, like every nation in Eastern Europe, remained in a state of utter chaos. Refugees flowed through the country by the tens of thousands, a migration that only intensified as the Whites and the Reds battled it out in Russia. But until November 1918 the Germans were masters in Rumania, just as they controlled south Russia, parts of the Ukraine, and the Crimea. The Germans did not evacuate Bucharest until November 11, the day of the Armistice; it was a further two weeks before the Rumanian government, with the King and Queen, returned from exile in Jassy, and many more after that before a semblance of order was restored. "Everything was upset," Anastasia remembered.[82] It is not awarding her tale any credence to say that there could have been no better time for a refugee — any refugee — to enter the country unnoticed and to remain there without detection. Not until 1920 — that is, after Anastasia had left the country — did Rumania inaugurate a comprehensive identity and domicile registration system similar to the one that had already existed in Germany for years.[83] Said a Rumanian judge in this regard: "Many refugees did not report to the authorities. They had children, died, and disappeared without trace. Why? Because they themselves wanted to hide from officialdom for subjective personal reasons: smuggling, jewelry deals, agents of foreign powers, revenge, murders: *règlements de comptes*."[84]

Only three people ever stepped forward who were willing to swear personal knowledge of the escape of the Tsar's daughter from south Russia — how she got that far, no one could say — and into Rumania, passing through the Nikolaev-Odessa region and continuing on by way of Jassy. One was an Armenian peasant who saw her at a monastery near Jassy, rendered her some small assistance, and received five thousand lei for his trouble.[85] Another was a man who claimed to have known the shady, "good-hearted" fellow whom Anastasia identified as Alexander Tschaikovsky.[86] And the third was a German officer who controlled access to a pontoon bridge at Nikolaev and who was approached by an acquaintance in the White Army — a certain "Kolya" — about granting passage to the wounded Grand Duchess Anastasia and her peasant companions. He referred the matter to his commanding officer and later received a brief note of thanks for his help.[87]

These testimonies, obviously, were not likely to sway anybody who already doubted Anastasia's identity. But there is other evidence to carry the tale forward, evidence that relates specifically to German involvement in the escape of the Grand Duchess.[88] Heinrich Dietz, a former officer of the German military administration in Bucharest, remembered that the presence of the Tsar's daughter in that city after World War I had been something of an open secret. It was "quite generally known," said Dietz, that the Grand Duchess had lived in Bucharest "under the protection of the Germans."[89] Then in 1927 General Max Hoffmann, the former chief-of-staff of the German armies on the Eastern Front and the man who had presided at the German–Russian peace negotiations at Brest–Litovsk, was asked his opinion of Anastasia's claim. At that time General Hoffmann expressed his firm conviction that Anastasia was, in truth, the Tsar's youngest daughter.[90] "I heard him say it over and over," General Hoffmann's daughter recalled: " 'It is she, it is she; I know it.' "[91] When asked if he had ever met the lady, General Hoffmann replied, "I don't need to see her. I know."[92]

Here then, with a cryptic remark, the trail vanishes. No further evidence has come to light to prove the story of Anastasia's rescue. But what would constitute proof? Even if it could somehow be demonstrated that the Tsar's daughter had escaped Russia and fled to Rumania, how, with no papers and no fingerprints, could it then be demonstrated that she and Anastasia were one? That was the dilemma Anastasia now faced, and the problem her monarchist sponsors were determined to solve.

Of course, Baron von Kleist had to find her first.

3

TO AND FRO WITH THE ÉMIGRÉS

*A*nastasia's sudden disappearance from the Nettelbeckstrasse had thrown the Kleist family into disarray. "Where is Anny?" Maria von Kleist asked her daughters when she returned home on the afternoon of August 12, 1922.

"We thought she was with you," the Kleist girls replied. When it dawned on her that Anastasia had run away, the Baroness was more angry than apprehensive. Undoubtedly the girl had gone to Clara Peuthert, the Baroness said when she called her husband's office to complain: something would have to be done to curtail that woman's influence. The Baron encouraged his wife to calm down. Hadn't the police made them responsible for Anastasia's welfare? He would let them know about it. In the meantime the Baroness was not to worry.[1]

By nightfall they were all worried. One of the Kleist girls had thought to surprise Anastasia by calling on Clara Peuthert unannounced, but when she reached Clara's dingy two-room apartment on the Schumannstrasse, Anastasia wasn't there. Clara, moreover, claimed to know nothing about Anastasia's disappearance. When the police arrived later they had no greater success. Why couldn't they leave a decent woman (meaning herself) alone? Clara cried; it was getting so a law-abiding citizen was not safe in her own house. Anyway, she had told them that she had no information about the Grand Duchess's whereabouts. "Certain contradictions suggest that she is not speaking the truth," the police reported,[2] but there was, indeed, no sign of Anastasia at Clara's.

It was neither the police nor the Kleists who at length tracked down the fugitive "Grand Duchess." After a two-day search Franz Jaenicke, Captain von Schwabe's friend, spotted Anastasia standing alone on a footbridge near the Berlin zoo. Jaenicke had remembered Anastasia's fondness for animals and had spent the whole of the previous night hunting for her in the Tiergarten, the largest and loveliest of Berlin's parks. When he finally caught up with her at the bridge, Jaenicke began shouting. What did Anastasia think she was doing? Did she have any idea how much trouble she had caused?

Jaenicke never had time to get his breath. Trouble! Anastasia exclaimed. What did Herr Jaenicke know about trouble? "She told me that she was being very badly treated at the Kleists'," Jaenicke reported, "that they never left her in peace, she was always supposed to be talking about her past." Every day the Baron surprised her with some new face and demanded that she tell him who it was. They wouldn't even let her sleep in her own room at night! It was dreadful: "Baron von Kleist and both his daughters just treated her very badly."[3]

Since Anastasia had made it plain that she would rather spend the night at the zoo than go back to the Kleists', Jaenicke brought her to his own apartment and waited while she settled herself. He, too, had completely lost his patience with Baron von Kleist. That evening, in the company of Alice Schwabe's father, Jaenicke went to inform the Baron that Anastasia would not again, under any circumstances, agree to live under his roof. But the Baron was in just as foul a mood as everyone else. Fine, he replied. Jaenicke and the Schwabes could take the girl themselves. They would have to take responsibility for her upkeep, too, however, and there was the small matter of money: everybody knew that the Schwabes didn't have any.

Never mind that, Alice Schwabe's father chimed in, *he* had now obtained all the money Anastasia would need "from Russian quarters." "Just you keep out of it," he snapped as Baron von Kleist showed him the door.[4]

The Baroness was not so easy to get rid of. She was worried, and she wanted to do what she could to help. On August 17 she arrived at Jaenicke's apartment and found Anastasia sitting quietly in the parlor. Anastasia turned her head away and refused to answer the Baroness's greeting.

"Won't you talk to me?" the Baroness asked. "Why won't you talk to me?"

Anastasia's body seemed to fall in on itself. She was crying. "*Mamschen* [Little Mother]," she said at last, "I am so dirty, I cannot look you in the eyes." She repeated this several times: "I am so dirty."

"What are we going to do?" asked the Baroness.[5]

Jaenicke had had an idea. As a member of the fledgling (and, at the time, seemingly inconsequential) Nazi Party, Jaenicke was already well known at police headquarters. There he had made the acquaintance of a like-minded detective-inspector, Franz Grünberg, who had listened to his stories about Anastasia with pure fascination. Who better to take care of her for a few weeks, Jaenicke suggested, than Grünberg, an amateur historian, nearing retirement, who, as a seasoned investigator, could simultaneously help resolve her case?

Nobody had yet thought to ask Anastasia if she was willing to live with a Berlin police inspector, but the obstacle seemed minor under the circumstances, and on August 21, after she had met Inspector Grünberg in person, Anastasia moved out to the inspector's country estate at Funkenmühle, near Zossen.[6]

She was soon glad she had. Funkenmühle provided a welcome refuge from the hectic, increasingly demeaning life of the Russian monarchist colony. Anastasia spent hours walking in the forest and along the lake, gathering flowers and hunting for wild mushrooms (a pastime, as Inspector Grünberg discovered, that amounted to a science: without a second glance Anastasia could tell which mushrooms to pick and which to leave alone). She began to busy herself with drawing, played happily with the Inspector's young nephews and nieces, and, unless she was feeling unwell, always joined the Grünberg family at the dining table. In this relaxed atmosphere the inspector had occasion to observe her at his leisure. "She claims with the greatest certainty to be Anastasia, the youngest daughter of the Tsar," Grünberg reported, "and has given descriptions of the imperial family's stay at Tobolsk and Ekaterinburg which presuppose exact knowledge."[7] So impressed was Grünberg with Anastasia's conviction, and so troubled by her want of lasting security, that he now undertook her rehabilitation as a personal responsibility. Through the mediation of the chief of police in Breslau, the inspector approached Irene of Prussia, Empress Alexandra's sister, with the suggestion that she come to Funkenmühle for a meeting with Anastasia. The proposal was just bold enough to succeed.

Clara Peuthert had already alerted Princess Irene to Anastasia's predicament in a flurry of enigmatic letters that must have been coolly received at Irene's estate at Hemmelmark. Irene remembered her sister's youngest daughter as a healthy, sprightly, mischievous girl of twelve and cannot have been eager to believe that a well-loved niece had recently emerged from an asylum for the insane: the vision of the cellar at Ekaterinburg was horrible enough to contemplate. Then, too, Anastasia's case was so confusing. Baroness Buxhoeveden had been staying with Irene at the time of her own visit to Anastasia at Dalldorf, when Anastasia was taken to be Grand Duchess Tatiana; the Baroness's negative impressions, assuredly, had not been ignored at Hemmelmark. Taking one thing with another, Irene must still have hoped for the best, for she arrived at Funkenmühle one afternoon in the company of a lady-in-waiting, conscious of her responsibility and determined to do her duty.[8]

Anastasia had been told nothing about the impending meeting. She met Princess Irene and her companion in the dining room, where the two ladies were introduced to her under false names.

"At supper," Inspector Grünberg recalled, "Her Royal Highness was placed opposite Anastasia in order that she might study her closely. The Princess did not think that she recognized her; she was obliged to admit, however, that she had last seen the imperial family ten years before."[9]

Writing, like Grünberg, three years after the event, Princess Irene was emphatic: "I saw immediately that she could not be one of my nieces. Even though I had not seen them for nine years, the fundamental facial characteristics could not have altered to that degree, in particular the position of the eyes, the ears, etc. . . . At first sight one could perhaps detect a resemblance to Grand Duchess Tatiana."

While Irene sat staring at her Anastasia suddenly rose from the table and ran without a word to her room. Although the Princess "had already decided that this was not [her] niece . . . , at Inspector Grünberg's request" she "went into [Anastasia's] room and approached the bed." There followed a fruitless interrogation. Anastasia, her head in her hands, turned away from the Princess and refused to reply to her. "She did not even answer when I asked her to say a word or give me a sign that she had recognized me," Irene wrote. "It was the same when I asked her — not to leave anything out — 'Don't you know me, I am your Aunt Irene.' " After a while the Princess gave up, collected her things, and left.[10]

Franz Jaenicke arrived at Funkenmühle soon afterward to find the Grünberg household in an uproar. The inspector was cursing Anastasia with a vividness that shocked even a fellow Berliner. Upstairs, Anastasia had bolted the door, and Jaenicke was obliged to knock, scold, plead, and threaten for more than twenty minutes before he finally gained admittance to her room. There he found a "very upset" young lady.[11]

For many years Anastasia was to hear that she had been "thoughtless" and "rude" to Irene of Prussia. But she had her own ideas on the subject, which she expressed in her staccato German not long after their meeting:

I was *not* rude. Really not. It was like this, I was ill [a swelling on Anastasia's breast had begun to fester], had to get up, the room was dark, then a lady came, I knew the voice and was listening, but didn't know, because the name was different. Then at table, the face was familiar, but I didn't know, wasn't sure, then I recognized Aunt Irene. I was feverish and excited, went into my room. Aunt Irene came after me, spoke and asked so many questions. I stood at the window, and because I had to cry I turned my back to her; I did not want to turn around, but not because I was rude. I was crying.[12]

Bewildered and *humiliated* were other words Anastasia used to describe her feelings when she realized that "Aunt Irene" had come to visit her under an assumed identity, "as a stranger."[13] It had been in order to see Princess Irene that Anastasia had initially undertaken the long, hard journey from Bucharest to Berlin in 1920. Later, through Clara Peuthert, she had even sent an appeal to the Princess from Dalldorf. Now Irene had suddenly appeared out of the blue, unannounced and lacking even the courtesy to introduce herself: "I was *not* rude."

Irene of Prussia did not stay for explanations. Glumly Inspector Grünberg reported that Irene had been "deeply offended" by Anastasia's behavior — "and with good reason. Since that time she wants to hear nothing more about the matter."[14]

Thus ended the first, brief meeting between Anastasia and a close relative of the Tsar's daughter — a meeting that had waited long enough in the first place. "We had lived earlier in such intimacy," Irene declared, "that it would have sufficed had she given me the

least sign, or had made an unconscious movement to awaken in me
a feeling of kinship and to convince me." [15] There was nothing more
to be said. "I could not have made a mistake," Irene protested when,
years later, she heard her words challenged; "I could not have made
a mistake!" [16] Suddenly the Princess burst into tears. Pacing the floor,
wringing her hands, she exclaimed in real anguish, "She *is* similar,
she *is* similar, but what does that mean if it is not she?" [17]

Really, what does that mean? It was fervently hoped now that
Princess Irene might relent and give Anastasia a second chance. Anastasia herself longed for a reconciliation. But Prince Oscar of Prussia, the Kaiser's son, when asked to influence Irene to that end,
merely replied that another meeting was "out of the question." The
whole affair had upset Irene "so terribly," Oscar reported, that her
husband, Prince Henry, had forbidden Anastasia as a topic of conversation in the house. [18]

Period.

The disastrous meeting with Irene of Prussia marked the beginning of what one of Anastasia's friends called *die Schattenzeit* ("the
time of shadows"): two and a half years of reckless gossip and rumor, missing evidence, and endless, bitter recrimination. The battle
for her favor and her person had recommenced the moment Inspector Grünberg, understandably disappointed, sent Anastasia back to
Berlin to live with Franz Jaenicke and his wife. The Jaenickes did
what they could to make Anastasia's life easier, but before too long
the strain of her notoriety, not to mention the demands of her character, had worn them out. In October 1922 Jaenicke was called to
Munich on Nazi Party business, and his wife, terrified, made it plain
that she could not manage Anastasia by herself. [19] Anastasia understood. She was already packed and ready to go back to Dalldorf
when Baroness von Kleist, hearing the news, rushed to the Jaenickes' apartment and declared that she would stand no more nonsense: Anastasia might live as she wished but she would live with
the Kleists. [20]

Anastasia was too tired to argue, but the Baroness's triumph was
short-lived. Anastasia had not been back at the Kleists' for more
than three weeks before doctors confirmed that a severe inflammation on her chest was, in reality, incipient tuberculosis of the breast-
bone. Shortly afterward, under the name "Anna Tschaikovsky, *née*
Romanovsky," she entered the Westend Hospital at Charlotten-
burg, her bills paid by a sympathetic friend of Baron von Kleist. For

three months Anastasia stayed at Westend, only to be readmitted barely a week after her initial discharge.

Much of the following year, 1923, Anastasia remained hospitalized. "She went back to Kleist for a while," the police noted, "but probably spent longest with the Peuthert woman, . . . who, according to Inspector Grünberg's statement, exerted a strong influence over her." The relationship between Anastasia and Clara Peuthert had never been more devoted — Clara was hostess, domestic, cook, lady-in-waiting, maiden aunt, mouthpiece, and court jester, all in one — but other friends of Anastasia's always stood waiting in the wings. The Jaenickes had Anastasia again for a short time. So did the Schwabes, and Inspector Grünberg was kind enough to offer her shelter at the home of his niece, Eva Wahl.[21] Frau Wahl's young son, Konrad, retained dim memories of "the silent foreign lady"[22] who sat in her chair for hours on end and who, when she conversed at all, "spoke more English than German."[23] "She had decided long before this to pretend that she had forgotten her Russian," said a woman who met her at Inspector Grünberg's country estate, "out of fear of being recognized as Grand Duchess Anastasia and killed by the Bolsheviks. Our host caught her out in his own way, however. He used a Russian swearword in her presence, at which she, as he had expected, 'jerked up,' turned red, and exclaimed in reproach: 'Aber Herr Doktor!' " Indeed, Anastasia "brought a touch of etiquette to any situation," never leaving the house without gloves, for instance, and deferring to her elders "with the politeness and accommodation of a well-brought-up young girl of the highest circles. . . . [I recall that] she never spoke to anybody without the proper salutation and she never forgot a title. . . ."[24]

In and out of hospitals, an object of ceaseless curiosity, Anastasia led a vagabond's life in these days. "She seems to have drifted about from family to family in the strangest way," said a woman who met her several years later.[25] Anastasia was inclined to be more bitter about it: "I was passed from one to the other. People hated each other if someone else had me."[26] But Anastasia played the leading role in this topsy-turvy drama. She quickly became famous for spurning her protectors without apparent provocation, and she did not hesitate to impose herself on anyone when the mood struck. Her allegiances shifted as often as her address. Inspector Grünberg reported that every time she returned to Baron von Kleist she sooner or later ran away again: "She did this four times with the Kleists, and each time they fetched her back." By way of explanation, Anastasia told Grünberg that she was "afraid of her incognito being betrayed by the importunities of the Russian émigrés."[27]

The Russian monarchists showed no consideration whatsoever for her feelings, Anastasia complained. How else could they sit in their cozy drawing rooms and tell such wicked lies about her mother and Rasputin?[28] "He was a saint!" Anastasia declared whenever anyone criticized "the Holy Father" in her presence.[29] "Rasputin was really a loyal friend. He told my mother that people were conspiring against us, and protected us in every way. I believe he was the only real friend we had. . . ."[30] Now the émigrés were saying "the dirtiest things." Kleist was the worst. "Among other things," exclaimed Anastasia, "Kleist told me that for the last years before the Revolution Russia had been ruled by a hysterical woman." A hysterical woman — his Empress!

But Kleist was a buffoon all around. "Kleist never hid from me the fact that he wanted to make money on me," Anastasia continued.[31] He had asked her to sign a paper pledging him fifty thousand Danish kroner, to be paid when she had been acknowledged by her grandmother in Denmark: "He said openly that he expected to get much money from the Dowager Empress." Anastasia, of course, would have none of it. Once the Baron had entered her room with "indecent proposals." She would not elaborate. It was "too dreadful."[32] And then, as if the monarchists weren't bad enough, "the newspaper people" were after her. Franz Jaenicke confirmed later that he had lost a great deal of money by refusing the offers that regularly came his way to write about Anastasia.[33] Others were less scrupulous, however, and the doubtful, blood-and-thunder stories in the newspapers were enough to drive Anastasia to despair. Here were the most intimate and tragic details of her life, "terribly garbled," for all to read.[34] Here was her claim to identity put forward as "a political event of grand import, an affair whose stakes might one day be the throne of the Romanovs."[35] Only Anastasia appeared to understand the impression these stories would create in the ranks of European royalty, where publicity — any kind of publicity — had forever been deemed intolerable.

Opinions were formed on hearsay; minds were made up on rumor. There is a sad image of Anastasia from these days, exchanging her hospital bed at Westend for a grimy sofa at Clara Peuthert's, wandering alone through Berlin's magnificent parks, staring at chocolates and candies in shop windows, and sitting in all-night cafeterias while she wondered where to go next. Once she told Clara, when asked what she had been up to, that she had "just run around the whole night," not caring or not daring to seek a bed among the émigrés.[36] This was the girl Russia's exiled monarchists were asked to believe was the daughter of their Emperor. Many of Anastasia's remarks had already upset them profoundly. She was tired of hearing about her marriage to Alexander Tschaikovsky, for one thing, and reminded her hosts that the Tsar's sister, Grand Duchess Olga Alexandrovna, had divorced her husband shortly before the Revolution and married a mere colonel of her mother's bodyguard regiment. If it was good enough for a daughter of Alexander III, said Anastasia, it was good enough for a daughter of Nicholas II.[37] The émigrés were unanimous in their judgment that this girl was proud, and fearless at heart. In 1923 the rumor reached the monarchist colony that a leading member of Ekaterinburg's Ural Regional Soviet — some said it was the Ipatiev house regicide himself, Commandant Yurovsky — had arrived in Berlin and was staying at the Soviet mission. Anastasia had heard that rumor, too. She walked unescorted through the Brandenburg Gate, somehow talked her way past the caretakers at the embassy and waited for the Soviet envoy in an anteroom.[38] It was never clear exactly what she meant to do there, but it was whispered that she carried a vial of acid in her hand and that the "murderer" was lucky not to appear.

While Anastasia roamed the streets and fed the animals at the zoo, the Russian monarchists accused each other of destroying her chances for recognition. Baron von Kleist, more unpopular than ever, placed the blame squarely on "the extreme caution and reserve" of Markov II's Supreme Monarchist Council.[39] Kleist heard that the council had raised money to provide for Anastasia's basic needs — people were forever claiming to have raised money for Anastasia — but that its leaders were reluctant to take a stand on the matter of her identity without the blessing of the Russian Orthodox Church. The Church, naturally, was reluctant to take a stand on the matter in the absence of any experience of Anastasia herself. And everyone was reluctant to take a stand on the matter so long as the surviving members of the House of Romanov continued to behave as though Anastasia did not exist. But nothing, not even the sincere guarantees of the monarchists, seemed able to shake the Romanovs out of their apathy. For example, Zinaida Tolstoy, Empress Alexandra's friend from Tsarskoe Selo, had found a special reason to believe in Anastasia. One quiet evening she and the Kleists had been sitting with

Anastasia in the Baron's parlor, chatting about nothing in particular and taking turns at the piano.

"Do you play?" asked Mme. Tolstoy.

Anastasia replied that she had had piano lessons as a child but that her arm had been injured and that she could no longer distinguish the notes. "And we danced," she continued; "we so loved to dance."

At the piano Mme. Tolstoy was lightly fingering the keys. Suddenly she broke into a waltz, a tune which her brother had composed and which she had often played for the Tsar's daughters at Tsarskoe Selo while they danced together.

"The result," Baroness von Kleist remembered, "was shattering." Anastasia turned beet red, burst into tears, and threw herself down on the sofa. Mme. Tolstoy, in turn, fell on her knees, "kissed [Anastasia's] hands and asked if she had recognized the waltz. This was confirmed in tears." So shaken was Mme. Tolstoy by the reaction that she immediately telegraphed the Tsar's two sisters, then living with the Dowager Empress outside Copenhagen, and implored them to do something for Anastasia at once.[40] Whatever reply she received must have been peremptory, because from that moment Zinaida Tolstoy suddenly stopped coming to call. Baron von Kleist told Anastasia that Mme. Tolstoy had left the apartment one day with a nasty remark: "A Grand Duchess cannot have a child by a private soldier."[41]

It was some time before Zinaida Tolstoy recovered her balance and dared to challenge the testimony of Sophie Buxhoeveden — for Baroness Buxhoeveden had undertaken a wholehearted campaign against Anastasia in Denmark. "It made no impression on us," said the Tsar's sister Olga when she was later asked to account for the Romanovs' apparent indifference to Anastasia's plight, "because [we knew that] all of our loved ones had been murdered together in Ekaterinburg. We had heard from officers and other trusted persons . . . that all had been killed. . . . Then the faithful Baroness S. Buxhoeveden wrote (and later told us personally) that she had been asked to visit this person, who had hidden her face and refused to speak with the Baroness. So she pulled down the bedclothes and exclaimed, 'Ah, this is absolutely not Tatiana! This person is short, and Tatiana was taller than I am. . . .' She left quite convinced that it wasn't Tatiana."[42]

Tatiana it surely was not, but had "the faithful Baroness S. Buxhoeveden" neglected to mention the alternative possibility? Anastasia had been conducting a campaign of her own, declaring to all who would listen that the Baroness's refusal to acknowledge her had been motivated by a guilty conscience. "At Ekaterinburg," Inspector Grünberg explained, "a rescue of the imperial family was planned, which, however, as Anastasia claims, was betrayed to the Bolsheviks by the lady-in-waiting Baroness Buxhoeveden, in an attempt to save her own life." [43] Said Anastasia: "That there had been a betrayal was clear to us. We spoke about it often in prison. And then. . ." [44]

Anastasia herself had cut off that sentence. Where had "Isa" been when they all needed her? she asked, calling the Baroness by the nickname the imperial family had always used. Why had the Bolsheviks given her her freedom when so many others had gone to the grave? Anastasia continued: "I must always think how Papa and Mamma sat there in Ekaterinburg and said that they could not understand why Isa had changed so during the last time in Tobolsk. We knew that we were supposed to be freed, and when nothing came, no rescue came, Papa and Mamma said that they must connect Isa's changed behavior with the unsuccessful rescue. They believed that Isa had betrayed the rescue plans. And that I cannot forget." [45]

"Isa," needless to say, was furious when she heard that she had become the villainess in Anastasia's piece. But Baroness Buxhoeveden was not the only one to be accused of "treason." A Russian nobleman who met Anastasia in Berlin recalled:

One evening she was particularly talkative, and spoke in an uncommonly lively way, zealously, in fact, about the causes of the Revolution. She blamed Russian society in no uncertain terms. People had thought only of themselves and not of the country; officers had attached more importance to their drinking than to their duties; members of the family had broken their oaths and involved themselves with intrigue; they had not stood behind the Tsar, who, she added (calling him "Papa"), had been too congenial. . . . The invalid always comes back to one point: she cannot understand why no one managed to rescue the family and simply let them be destroyed. On the whole she can't understand why now, as she says, everyone and everything has conspired against her and deliberately complicated what is really a very simple matter. . . . With immense conviction, clearly motivated by a desire for revenge, . . . she said she knew who ought to be punished, with whose skulls "the streets should be paved." [46]

What was anybody going to do with this resentful ghost? Anastasia's determination not to conceal her rather Byzantine opinions may well account for the reaction of another monarchist exile who met her around this time. Captain Nicholas Pavlovitch Sablin, a former officer of the Tsar's yacht, *Standart,* had been only one among many in the Tsar's retinue to desert his master at the outbreak of the Revolution. It was a fact Sablin never lived down, and something a daughter of Nicholas II might not have forgotten. Small wonder, then, that Sablin's confrontation with Anastasia in a Berlin restaurant was negative. Accompanied by Admiral Papa-Federov, another officer of the *Standart,* Sablin had had dinner with Baron von Kleist "and several ladies, among them a person who was supposed to be Grand Duchess Anastasia Nicolaievna, saved by some miracle when the imperial family was killed." Sablin recalled, "I had been asked to talk during dinner with Admiral Papa-Federov about the *Standart,* about Livadia, about the fjords [of Finland, where the imperial family cruised every summer], about the family — all in order to see how the said person would react."

Captain Sablin's report goes on to say, unbelievably, that he could not decide for himself which of the ladies was supposed to be the Tsar's daughter and that he had to ask after dinner: "One of the young women next to Baroness von Kleist was pointed out. . . . I found no resemblance between the said person and the Grand Duchess." Later Baron von Kleist made bold to ask if Sablin had recognized Anastasia: "I was indignant to think that I should recognize the Grand Duchess in this person, and I replied, 'You may cut off my head, but I do not find the slightest resemblance between her and the Grand Duchess.' "

What was "the said person" doing all this time? According to Sablin, "she didn't pay the least attention to the world. . . . When we left the restaurant Admiral Papa-Federov told me that he shared my opinion entirely." [47]

Did he, indeed? To Baroness von Kleist Admiral Papa-Federov had declared: "If she would only speak Russian and awaken some memory of the past, I would acknowledge her on the spot, because the resemblance is great." [48] Then there was Marianne Nilov, the widow of the commander of the *Standart,* who met Anastasia in Berlin and was jolted into recognition by the deep blue of her eyes. "She told us she thought she was looking at the Tsar's eyes," said Mme. Nilov's niece, "and then she heard a little laugh which she recognized at once. Anastasia had a very distinctive laugh." [49]

What is going on here? One witness is struck by Anastasia's resemblance to the Tsar's daughter while another denies it completely. One is ready to acknowledge her if she will only reminisce with him while another watches her fall to pieces at the sound of an old waltz. One is suspicious because she does not speak Russian, while the next — her friend Franz Jaenicke — is ready to swear that besides German and Russian "she spoke English and French."

"The émigrés would have been *happy* if they had been able to recognize her," sighed Gerda von Kleist. But Anastasia "didn't pay the least attention in the world."[50] Contradiction follows contradiction. The pattern was only beginning.

Shunted from one place to another, her health growing steadily worse, Anastasia entered the Westend Hospital again in the autumn of 1924. One morning she left her room without a discharge and without the knowledge of her doctors. Not long after, the Kleists tracked her down at Clara Peuthert's and decided that the moment had come to assert their rights. This time they lodged a formal complaint with the police, which detailed the trouble Anastasia had given them ever since her release from Dalldorf and which requested that she be forced to return to the Nettelbeckstrasse. The police had long ceased to care where Anastasia was staying, however, and they replied that she might as well be allowed to live where she pleased.[51] Triumphant, Clara Peuthert now took over as Anastasia's quasiofficial spokesman in the émigré colony, quickly renewing her attack on the recalcitrant Irene of Prussia, who she refused to believe had actually abandoned Anastasia forever. "Nearly every day," Clara wrote Irene, "Anastasia comes into my little kitchen and asks me to write a letter to the best and dearest Aunt Irene. Up till now I have refused point-blank, because I have a high opinion of myself and I don't want people to think me stupid, or a liar, or worse — crazy." With good sense, but little tact, Clara now begged Irene to bring Anastasia to Hemmelmark — "and then if it should turn out that she is an impostor, or a fraud, or crazy, there will still be time to put her in an asylum."[52]

Toward the end of 1924 an official at Hemmelmark wrote Baron von Kleist on behalf of Irene's husband, Prince Henry of Prussia: "His Royal Highness . . . has requested me to inform you that he as well as his wife, after the latter's visit to your protégée, have come to the unshakable conviction that she is *not* a daughter of the Tsar, specifically not Grand Duchess Anastasia. Prince Henry considers the matter as it concerns himself and his wife as cleared up and finally settled and insists that you refrain from the further sending of letters or requests to himself or to the Princess. It would be appreciated if you would influence your protégée and Fräulein Peuthert accordingly." [53]

That did it. This was the message Baron von Kleist had been waiting for. A follow-up note requested that all material relating to Princess Irene's involvement with Anastasia — "several letters" were mentioned — be returned forthwith to Hemmelmark, a request with which Baron von Kleist all too readily complied. [54] Now, with Kleist's withdrawal from the case, it became nearly impossible to find anyone in Russian monarchist circles who had ever taken Anastasia seriously. The general opinion among the émigrés was that Baron von Kleist was a fool and a dupe. No one doubted that Anastasia —and Clara Peuthert along with her — would be back at Dalldorf before the year was out.

The break with Clara was, probably, the hardest of all for Anastasia. Clara's "high opinion" of herself had been seriously compromised. What had become of all her friends in the émigré colony? Clara wondered. She had enjoyed their friendship, enjoyed their attention, enjoyed the respect they had shown her as "Aunt Peuthert." And now? It had to be Anastasia's fault. What had the Grand Duchess ever brought anybody but ridicule and grief?

Clara began to beat her. Anastasia never mentioned a word about it, but the evidence is plain. "I have also reduced the Grand Duchess to a jelly sometimes," Clara snarled when the subject came up. [55] But Anastasia, when she later spoke of her "quarrel" with Clara, only said that an article attacking her claims had appeared in a Berlin scandal sheet at the end of 1924. Clara had wanted her to reply to the charges of fraud, but Anastasia had had enough. She refused.

Clara threw her out. "She shoved me onto the landing," Anastasia exclaimed in total disbelief. "It was the middle of the night." Two and a half years after her release from the Dalldorf Asylum, Anastasia now found herself utterly abandoned by the Russian émigrés.

A poor working family named Bachmann had heard Anastasia sobbing on the staircase. She said of these people later: "They shared their last bit of bread with me and cared for me as best they could. If ever I have any money my greatest desire is to help these people who sheltered me only through generosity, without asking me who

I was or if they would be paid for doing it." [56] To help with her upkeep Anastasia embroidered a handkerchief, which she later sold to the Baltic Red Cross for about thirty marks. This she imagined was an enormous amount of money, and an idea began to form in her head: if she could only get well, she could work. She could earn her own living. The notion began to obsess her.

At the Bachmanns', "on a hunch," [57] Inspector Grünberg caught up with Anastasia in January 1925; in fact the Berlin Welfare Office had begun to express some concern about her situation.[58] Again Anastasia went to live with the inspector, and again the inspector did what he could to improve the quality of her life. "I tried in vain to interest the Russian émigrés in the unhappy girl," Grünberg wrote later in the year. "The émigrés displayed an incredible indifference and were, moreover, quite unreliable." [59] The extent of that unreliability had been made plain to the Inspector in March, when a bizarre incident completed the rupture between Anastasia and her erstwhile "saviors" in the monarchist colony. The story has been badly muddled in the telling, but it runs something like this.[60]

A young man had turned up at Clara Peuthert's apartment one morning, apparently having been sent there by the staff at the Dalldorf Asylum. At Clara's the stranger saw a photograph of Anastasia and said, "I know that lady." Then he broke into tears. On the back of the picture he scribbled the words, in pencil: "Anastasia Nicolaievna . . . Alexandereva . . . Ivan . . . Alexev . . . Shorov . . . *geb.* [born] Pittersburg."

Clara Peuthert took her stranger to see Captain von Schwabe, her personal favorite among the émigrés. There the man informed Schwabe that he had brought Anastasia from Rumania to Berlin, that he had known Anastasia and her "so-called husband" in Bucharest, that the two had never been legally married, that Anastasia had indeed had a child, and that the boy could now be found at an orphanage in Galatz (now Galati). This information was given reluctantly, in a weird mixture of German, French, and "peasant Russian." No names were named. Clara's caller explained that he had already spent "six months in jail on account of this business in Rumania." Finally, however, when he learned that Anastasia was staying with the Grünberg family in the country, the young man produced a photograph of himself and a letter, which he instructed Captain von Schwabe to give Anastasia when she returned to town.

Clara Peuthert swiftly concluded that the enigmatic stranger must

have been Anastasia's elusive "brother-in-law," Serge Tschaikovsky. Anastasia was not going to meet him, in any case, because by
the time she heard about him the fellow had vanished, never to be
seen again. Clara insisted that she had tried to tell Inspector Grünberg about the young man's search for Anastasia but that Grünberg
had thrown her out when she came to his office ("They all think
I'm crazy"). On Anastasia's return to Berlin, nevertheless, the inspector asked Captain von Schwabe for the letter and the photograph the stranger had left behind. Schwabe replied that he had
"mislaid" them.

Mislaid them! Anastasia was frantic. All of her pent-up hostility
and frustration now burst forth in a torrent of verbal abuse. The
Schwabes and their monarchist cohorts, Anastasia had no doubt,
had done away with this important witness and destroyed his evidence. Her remarks, in fact, made in desperation and the warped
perspective of illness, were sufficient to drive the Schwabes directly
into the ranks of her most bitter opponents. Within a few months
Anastasia would learn to her regret that the Russian monarchists in
Berlin were no longer "indifferent" to her fate.

Anastasia's last days with Inspector Grünberg passed quietly, on
the whole. She divided her time between the estate at Funkenmühle
and the inspector's elegant town house on the Wilhelmstrasse, stopping again with Grünberg's niece for several weeks. Her health continued to get worse: a tubercular lesion had now developed on her
left arm. Soon a friend of Grünberg's, Dr. Josef Kapp, was called
in to see her. "[She] was very reluctant and timid," Dr. Kapp told
the *New York Times* three years later, "and only after I had won
her confidence was she willing to converse with Mrs. Kapp . . .
and myself. . . . I noticed, if memory serves me right, two distinct
deepenings in the parietal bones of [the] cranium, one right on top
and affecting both parietals, another on the left side, corresponding
to that part of the brain right next to the fissure of Sylvius, where
understanding of words is located. That might throw some light on
the fact that at that time the woman was not able to speak Russian.
The deepenings in the skull were distinctly artefacts and might have
been caused by some accident or an act of violence."[61]

For Anastasia the days went by in a fog. Later she had only a
dim impression of the comings and goings at Grünberg's house,
barely recollecting even the important visit she received that spring

from the former German Crown Princess, Cecilie of Prussia. Grünberg, of course, had arranged the meeting. Anastasia remembered how "beautifully dressed" the Crown Princess had been and how ashamed she had felt of her own threadbare outfit.[62] "She was going to a concert," said Anastasia, "but she promised to come back. Then she did not come."[63] The Crown Princess, for her part, recalled that she had been "struck at first glance by the young person's resemblance to the Tsar's mother and to the Tsar himself, but I could see nothing of the Tsarina in her. . . . There proved no opportunity of establishing her identity, [however], because it was virtually impossible to communicate with the young person. She remained completely silent, either from obstinacy or because she was totally bewildered, I could not decide which."[64]

And so another meeting ended badly. "How was she supposed to recognize me in a few minutes?" Anastasia wondered in her bitterness. "I have grown so old, the missing teeth in front make me so strange."[65] If only the Crown Princess had taken the time to come back. "She looks like Xenia [meaning the Tsar's sister]," Cecilie confided to her brother, and added: "I almost believe that it must be she."[66] But Cecilie had informed Inspector Grünberg that "in the opinion of . . . the Grand Duke of Hesse, brother of the murdered Tsarina, it must be regarded as absolutely impossible that a member of the Russian imperial family should still be alive."[67] Why was that? Cecilie didn't know. But since the Grand Duke and his sister, Irene of Prussia, refused to have anything to do with Anastasia, the Crown Princess said, "I felt it was not my business to follow up the question of her identity."[68]

"I have reached a dead end," Inspector Grünberg confessed after this second wasted confrontation.[69] Grünberg was not a patient man. Immediately he set out to find a new protector for the tubercular, malnourished Anastasia, who had now developed a bad case of pleurisy to add to her other maladies. Pressure from his superiors undoubtedly contributed to Grünberg's decision to give up the case — the police had a reputation to maintain — and evidently the inspector took out most of his frustration on Anastasia herself, blaming her failure to be recognized on her own mulishness. "The young lady has rewarded all my efforts with very bad behavior in my house," Grünberg wrote. "If she has not got the identity she claims, it is nothing but her own fault."[70] The most Grünberg would do was provide her with a character reference: "Anastasia is no impostor, nor, in my opinion, is she a mentally ill person who imagines herself to be the daughter of the Tsar. Having lived with her for months, I have come to the firm conviction that she is a lady from the highest circles of Russian society and that she is most probably of princely birth. Every one of her words and movements reveals so lofty a dignity and so absolutist a bearing that it cannot be asserted she has acquired these characteristics in later life." [71]

Inspector Grünberg had set July 3, 1925, as the date for Anastasia's departure (the Grünbergs were going on vacation) and he seemed not to care very much whether she had found anyplace else to live or not. Fortunately, help came in the nick of time. Through an elderly, warmhearted German masseuse who had befriended Anastasia some months before, her case came to the attention of Dr. Karl Sonnenschein, a prominent philanthropist who took a special interest in the problems of Berlin's Russian refugees. It was Dr. Sonnenschein who now sought the means to rescue Anastasia. [72] On June 19, having secured her a bed at St. Mary's Hospital, a Catholic institution in the run-down east end of Berlin, Sonnenschein telephoned a co-worker, a Russian émigré with the un-Russian name of Harriet von Rathlef-Keilmann. Harriet von Rathlef was a divorced thirty-seven-year-old mother of four who had fled the Baltic provinces during the Revolution and now earned her living in Berlin as a sculptor and writer for children. She never forgot her introduction to the case of Anastasia — "an invalid Russian lady who had been resident for the last six months with a police inspector but who could remain there no longer. Dr. Sonnenschein thought I might be able to spare the time and asked me, as I spoke Russian, to deal with the case. 'Have you heard anything about a daughter of the Tsar of Russia still being alive?' he asked." [73]

Frau von Rathlef had not. She arrived at the Wilhelmstrasse that same afternoon, and presently, after Inspector Grünberg had slipped from sight, the door to the drawing room opened. [74]

"I was disappointed and astonished," said Frau von Rathlef. "The Grand Duchess could not have been more than twenty-five years old. . . . But she looked far older than that. She might have been thirty-five. She wore a dark, ugly skirt, a dark sweater." Frau von Rathlef took it all in: "the thin, tiny figure," "the suffering, haggard face," and in the movements, the stance, the politely expectant look, "an astonishing resemblance to the Tsar's mother and to the Empress Alexandra Feodorovna."

Anastasia stepped forward and held out her hand. Frau von Rathlef went on: "Her courtesy was, as it seemed to me, heartily conventional, and her good breeding showed in everything. Later I learned that when she is excited she always becomes frantically pleasant like this. I told her that Dr. Sonnenschein had arranged for her arm to be treated, and then Inspector Grünberg had written him the rest. She thanked me kindly. We agreed that I would bring her to the hospital the next day. When noting down the telephone number, I found that I didn't have a pencil. . . . I asked her in Russian something like 'U vass karandash yest? [Have you got a pencil?]?' She answered softly, 'There ought to be one here.' "

She had spoken in German. Harriet von Rathlef's questioning look moved her to continue: "If you knew how terrible that is. The worst of all, that I don't find the Russian anymore. All forgotten." Anastasia's chin fell on her chest and she began to cry.

Frau von Rathlef took her hands: "Don't worry about it; first you must get well, then your memory will come back."

"Do you think I can get well?" Anastasia asked. "Oh, I want to so much!"

"If you want to with all your strength and trust the doctor and the people around you — certainly!"

Anastasia managed a smile. Then her face fell again. "She wanted to say something," said Frau von Rathlef, "but couldn't." Finally it tumbled out: "I am so afraid, so afraid, again strange new people. You will go soon, when I tell you something else, I cannot decide, I have a child, it is Catholic."

Harriet von Rathlef waited a moment. "Have you become Catholic, too?" she asked.

"No," said Anastasia, "only through the wedding, and they told me that I should become so, too, because of the child. But the step is so hard. Do you understand me, why? And in the Catholic hospital they will try to persuade me. And I cannot. I must still wrestle."

Nobody was going to try to persuade Anastasia to do anything, Harriet von Rathlef replied. She promised it: nobody. Anyway, she continued, "the Roman Church is nearly the same as the Greek [Orthodox]. If a Lutheran converts, it is a much harder decision."

"My mother was a Lutheran before," said Anastasia, "later . . ." She fell silent.

"But your mother was a faithful Orthodox, isn't that so?"

"Oh, yes, she was."

The tears had come back. Frau von Rathlef thought it best to go. As they walked toward the door Anastasia suddenly lost her color, reeled, and sank into a chair: "Forgive me, madam, I cannot stand."

"I said good-bye," said Harriet von Rathlef. Anastasia made no answer, but remained in her chair, silent, staring.

PART TWO

Frau Tschaikovsky

4

THE SHADOWS OF THE PAST

*O*n the morning of June 20, 1925, Harriet von Rathlef found Anastasia waiting for her in the foyer of Inspector Grünberg's town house. The inspector had not come downstairs to say good-bye. As she walked along the Wilhelmstrasse Anastasia turned back three or four times to stare at the house, as though she had forgotten something. At last the building passed from sight, and Anastasia saw that her new companion had picked up her bag.

"No, no!" Anastasia cried. She would carry the bag herself; Frau von Rathlef was not to trouble with it.

"Madam, I am a sculptress," said Harriet von Rathlef, "so I ought to have strength enough for this."

Anastasia looked blank: "She did not seem to know what the word *sculptress* meant."

"Well," Frau von Rathlef continued, "I make figures out of wood."

"Oh, how nice. I, too, used to paint before." Anastasia was smiling now and her voice had become merry. "And it even came out well. My eldest sister was even very gifted. She painted much more beautifully."

"What did you paint, then? Landscapes, flowers? From nature?"

"Yes, we had good lessons."

"What was your teacher's name?"

The question killed the conversation. Anastasia's hand flew up to her eyes, and her voice seemed to drop an octave: "That I can no longer say."

Harriet von Rathlef cursed herself silently and lunged for her cigarette case, nearly dropping it on the ground. "Oh, for heaven's sake," she muttered, "I am losing my beloved cigarettes."

Anastasia laughed. "I, too, like to smoke," she said, "but not now; it is not good for me."

It was as though nothing had happened. "You were allowed to smoke?" Frau von Rathlef asked. "You were still a child not so long ago."

"We were not allowed, but secretly, especially Tatiana. She was already very cunning." Anastasia laughed again.

Harriet von Rathlef had just been given her first lesson in dealing with Anastasia. The trick could be summed up in two words: *Don't push.*

It had begun to take shape already on the train, as the two women made their way to St. Mary's Hospital — the consideration, the confidence, the extraordinary rapport that came to define Anastasia's friendship with Harriet von Rathlef.[1] They were an unlikely duo: a girl who claimed to be the daughter of the last of the Tsars and an obscure Baltic sculptor whom an acquaintance once tried to characterize as "a thoroughly middle-class provincial lady . . . with a sponge-like face."[2] Frau von Rathlef had once been Harriet Keilmann, a doctor's daughter, a Jew who had been converted to the Catholic Church. Thus she had found a way to live unmolested, while still independent, on the periphery of Russian Orthodox society. Despite her own prejudices, Anastasia never mentioned Harriet von Rathlef's Jewish descent. Frau von Rathlef, for her part, worried in her dealings with Anastasia only that she might commit some terrible sin of omission. "I just cannot understand how a simple peasant can have fitted into your life," she said to Anastasia one day in reference to Alexander Tschaikovsky.

Anastasia smiled "as though [Frau von Rathlef] had said something really stupid." Frau von Rathlef went on: "A peasant is rough and without manners. I think I myself might have made mistakes around you."

"How so? What do you mean?"

"Well, if I were with you or your family, I might make the mistake of entering a room before you did, because for me it is quite natural to go first when *I* am the guest."

"Madam," said Anastasia, "I do not understand that at all. How can anyone think like that? It is really indifferent. With Papa and Mamma it is something else. But with us children it was all the same; we were just like others, just children."

In the months ahead Harriet von Rathlef was to learn that with "us children" it was by no means "all the same," but for the moment she appreciated Anastasia's efforts to put her at her ease. Although Anastasia never lost a measure of formality and distance — nor ever broke the social barriers by calling Frau von Rathlef by her first name — she sensed from the beginning Frau von Rathlef's need for warmth and human contact. On her very first night at St. Mary's, when she found herself once again surrounded by a number of noisy, dying women from the Berlin slums, she let Frau von Rathlef tuck her into bed and kiss her goodnight. Of course Anastasia needed warmth and contact, too. "Want to get well quickly," she said in her imperfect German. "Everything so strange here." But even during the worst crises of her illness Anastasia tried to let Frau von Rathlef know how grateful she felt. "I have known many Baltic people," she said on their first afternoon together. "Many were at home. Therefore I am glad that you are with me, because you are Baltic. . . . The Germans are so different . . . somehow different, how shall I say?"

"Yes," Frau von Rathlef answered, "it is said that the Russian has a *shirokaya natura*. Is that the expression you're looking for?"

"Yes, that is what I wanted to say, he is generous, never petty" — the Russian word *shirok* means literally vast, broad. "Are many good ones among the Germans, but different."

They had sat drinking coffee while they waited for Dr. Ludwig Berg, the chaplain at St. Mary's. "I have such longing for home," Anastasia had said.

"None of us are allowed there now," Harriet von Rathlef replied bluntly. "What is your 'home'? Do you mean Petersburg?"

"Gatchina and Tsarskoe Selo," Anastasia answered without a thought. "That is always the nicest time; that is home."

"She took my hands," said Frau von Rathlef; "I felt how they were shaking. She was like a little girl who had lost her parents and whom I had gathered up and had to protect. I who myself am at the mercy of the wind and weather!"

"Thursday I got so old," Anastasia continued. "Thursday [June 18, 1925] I was twenty-four years old." And she looked old, too, Frau von Rathlef thought. She looked a wreck — that is, until something took her fancy and she forgot herself.

"What is that funny thing up there?" Anastasia asked, pointing to a shelf in Dr. Berg's office.

Frau von Rathlef brought it down. It was a hand-made Russian doll: "She laughed brightly and merrily like a child. Suddenly she was very young." But the moment passed as swiftly as it had arisen. The hand, once again, reached up and covered the eyes while Anastasia looked for words: "How was that? Yes, we had *kokoshniki* [Russian headdresses] and red costumes, I and Maria danced, we did many performances for us children, Maria and I, we always danced together." Frau von Rathlef learned that these uncomplicated pleasures — dancing and dolls, music, painting, and drama — always had the power to break Anastasia's gloomy reverie. And perhaps that was the key to their friendship. Anastasia was "happy" one morning when Frau von Rathlef came to St. Mary's dressed in a brightly colored Russian peasant smock.

"Oh yes," said Frau von Rathlef, laughing, "I look just like a Russian muzhik!"

"Not at all," said Anastasia; "you look like a woman, like an artist!"

Anastasia was right: Harriet von Rathlef was an artist to the roots of her soul. She revealed it not just in her sculpture and the fairy tales she published for Russian refugee children; her engagement and her sensitivity found expression in everything she undertook. If a project could not withstand one hundred and fifty per cent of her attention, it received none. She was passionate, fiercely loyal, bossy, impetuous. She was naive and sentimental. Nothing was more beautiful to Harriet von Rathlef than the gifts of nature, nothing more important than the fulfillment of a single individual, nothing more abhorrent than human suffering and injustice. Her friends understood her when she later told them that she did not believe in chance, that her whole life had seemed to lead up to her meeting with Anastasia. They understood her when she said that she had had to write about it.

Harriet von Rathlef's enormous, disorderly chronicle of life with Anastasia, "The Unknown Woman of Berlin," was published in 1928 under the title *Anastasia: A Woman's Fate as a Mirror of the World Catastrophe*. It had not been Frau von Rathlef's intention at the beginning to write for publication. That came later, when Anastasia's case had thrown the royal houses of Europe into a panic, and when Frau von Rathlef herself had been accused of masterminding a plot to defraud the Romanov family. She hoped her work might help to convince people that there had never been a plot to mastermind, that her only goal had been "to find a suitable, humane, decent person, who with patience and goodwill might help the little one to her right." Of course Frau von Rathlef was not unaware of the particular historical significance of this case. Nothing was too trivial for her pen in that regard, no chance remark or narcotic ramble that might finally throw light on Anastasia's true identity. But again her notes were meant to illustrate not just who Anastasia was, but what she was. Only thus could outsiders begin to appreciate the girl's spontaneity, her faith in herself, and her utter lack of guile:

"Where are you from, madam [this from Anastasia on the first day of their acquaintance]?"

"I am from Riga." The expression on her face changed quickly, the thoughts beneath it seemed to be flying.

"Oh, I know Riga. A memorial was dedicated there. We traveled on the ship. Everything in the town was decorated."

"What kind of ship was that?"

"That was our *Standart*. Were there not platforms somewhere?"

"Yes, at the memorial there were platforms."

"*You* were there?"

"I saw you; you were a little girl with your hair down."

"All four of us always had our hair down."

"But your brother, why wasn't he with you in the town?"

"He was not allowed; he was not well."

"I saw him playing on the *Standart*. He was running around in white sailor pants."

"He always wore white sailor suits. If I ever have my boy with me, then he will also wear such long pants; they are the nicest for boys. He [her brother] was such a dear one. He liked so much to roller-skate. He was so clever; later he was often so ill, when these sudden attacks came, then we always thought, now the end is coming. It was dreadful."

"As the youngest [daughter], were you the favorite?"

"No, my mother never had favorites. She liked very much to be with Maria, otherwise, all the same. I had good parents," she said passionately. "Papa was so good." Then passionately: "If Papa had not been so good, then everything would not have happened so. But we all spoiled our little one; quite naturally he was favored over the girls. But we were all satisfied with that, we all together loved him so much. He was so clever, so often he had to stop his lessons, because he was suffering, but there were never gaps, he caught up with everything quickly — *oh he was our dear one*." [*Frau von Rathlef's emphasis.*]

It was pointless, in the end, for anyone to argue about the sub-
stance of Anastasia's memory. Reams of paper were wasted in a
quarrel over detail. No one who saw Anastasia lying in bed with
her eyes squeezed shut, her jaw clenched, her hands running constantly through her thick dark-blond hair as she sought to recall a
name, or a place, or a detail from the past, could possibly have
doubted her sincerity. The sheer exertion required for Anastasia to
remember anything — and names above all — usually left her
drenched with sweat. Harriet von Rathlef told Anastasia one day
that in a bookshop she had seen a photograph of the imperial family: "It was from the time of the imprisonment; you were all sitting
out on a roof."

Anastasia looked as though someone had just slapped her across
the face. "*Wie ist das möglich?*" she cried several times. "How is
that possible? Where did the picture come from? The sisters have
photographed."

"She was trembling," said Frau von Rathlef. "I tried to calm her
down. . . . 'I'll bring you the picture sometime, shall I?' She looked
at me, said nothing." Frau von Rathlef tried again: "In one picture
you had a little dog?"

"No, I had no dog, but Tatiana saved hers."

"What was he called, do you remember?"

Anastasia was dragging her hand across her forehead, as though
she were trying to hold her head in place: "No, I cannot find the
name, cannot."

"Was he called Jackie?"

"No, it was different."

"Try to think; if it is correct, I will tell you."

Frau von Rathlef had the impression that Anastasia's thoughts
were literally whipping her across the brow: "I have seldom been
able to observe so clearly the changing expressions of a face. . . .
She shuts her eyes, the lids are fluttering nervously, the face is working. . . . The whole face is in tension." Then the name flew out:
"Jemmy!"

"Yes, it was called Jemmy."

"You are so good to me," said Anastasia, "so I can think better,
and suddenly a lot comes back that was not clear. Yes, the little
Jemmy, Tatiana's dog." But now her first thought returned: "How
is that possible? Where were the pictures found? Only the sisters
had them."

Frau von Rathlef thought it right to tell Anastasia something she evidently did not know: "Anastasia, the investigation commission [at Ekaterinburg] found everything, even your mother's diary."

The look of horror on Anastasia's face prompted Frau von Rathlef to move on quickly: "I can get it for you, someday, when you are better."

"No, please, not yet, not yet!"

"I arrived home very depressed," Frau von Rathlef remembered. In future, she decided, it would be best not to mention these things. But sometimes Anastasia brought up the subject of Siberia herself. She was speaking once of the imperial family's imprisonment:

"And then, it did not happen suddenly," she says, smiling bitterly, "in Tsarskoe already it began to be bad, then it got worse and worse, the air was too good for us. Everything was already gone there" — she points to her shoulders — "they tore it all off, it was terrible for Papa." Her eyes are filled with tears. [Anastasia was referring to the Tsar's epaulettes.]

"Were you brought straight from Tsarskoe to Ekaterinburg?"

"No, at first we were someplace else, but what was it called . . ." She strokes her forehead, wants to say a name, then she stops.

"Everything has gotten lost, I do not find the word, I knew it once," she says in despair.

"Leave it, Anastasia; it isn't important."

"Tobolsk!" she says suddenly, sitting up straight and looking at me like a child who wants to be praised.

"Like a child" — the words recur again and again in Harriet von Rathlef's notes. A friend of Frau von Rathlef's who met Anastasia at St. Mary's remembered the first time she saw her out of bed: "I was astonished to see how tiny she was."[3] It was something people tended not to notice when they looked at Anastasia reclining among her pillows, with the blanket drawn up to her chin and one hand held up to cover the gaps in her teeth. "Papa was also so small," Anastasia said,[4] and gave "Papa" the credit for whatever presence she was able to muster when she rose to her feet. Frau von Rathlef had never seen such exquisite posture. "I am the true daughter of a soldier," Anastasia remarked with pride, "and always will be. My Papa was the best and the bravest soldier."[5] "*Malenkaya,*" he had called her, and in Harriet von Rathlef's notes and correspondence Anastasia again became *die Kleine,* "the little one."

"Mamma called me something else again," Anastasia went on, "also so funny. As a child I was really fat. That is why she called me so."

"What was the name?"

"I do not know. . . . The meaning of the name was that I was fat."

Certainly Anastasia was no longer fat. At five feet two she now weighed under ninety pounds. Somehow she still managed to take possession of a room when she entered it. Hers was an intensely physical presence. First of all there were the nervous tricks — the hands forever stroking at the forehead, running through the hair, or twisting a handkerchief into knots. Then Anastasia had a certain deliberateness of speech and of motion that reminded one of her friends of nothing so much as "a young deer ready to butt." [6] People always noticed the way she sat: "She appears always to have one foot behind the other, preferably the left behind the right, and sits most appropriately well forward in her chair." [7] Anastasia could turn the act of listening into a physical activity. She would sit with a look of sheer concentration on her face, her expression almost comically solemn, and then when it was her turn to speak her voice emerged like a sudden clap. Her sentences were crisp, brief, often curt. She attacked her words, pounded at them, and rolled over the rules of grammar with perfect unconcern. One minute her voice was high-pitched, even shrill, and then it would suddenly drop to become a soft, throaty rumble. Her movements matched her vocal range. Anastasia did not walk across a room; she practically flew. She would look swiftly about her from side to side, then her chin would snap down to her chest and she would be off, taking "little, short, rapid steps, with her body . . . plunging forward, altogether characteristic." [8] Through it all she retained an indelible refinement and an economy of gesture that few who met her failed to appreciate. Repeatedly there are references to "a certain haughty grace," "a perfect neck," and "those infinitely aristocratic hands, with the long, expressive fingers." A woman who met her at a tea party recalled: "But the most overwhelming feature about her are her eyes. Of a greyish-blue, changing color, they shine like stars. Looking into them one seems to see unfathomable depths, [as] in very deep mountain lakes. I have never seen such eyes before." [9] The witness did not exaggerate. There were people who said they had seen such eyes only once before.

Harriet von Rathlef had been struck from the beginning by Anastasia's pervasive simplicity, her sense of dignity, and her tendency toward self-criticism. Anastasia's taste in fashion, for example, was impeccable. Not for her — at least not yet — the gaudy outfits adopted by many another improbable princess in Berlin. Even when she had the opportunity to choose her own clothes without regard to cost, she chose the most elegantly simple garments, in solid colors and with the straightest cut. This was the kind of thing, she said, by which "her mother had set the greatest store." Not that Anastasia was without extravagance. Take bracelets: "Since I was a child I have always worn bracelets. I do not feel natural without them; I cannot express how I feel — rings and necklaces and other jewelry I should not miss, but without bracelets I cannot exist." [10] Then there was Anastasia's passion for brightness and light: "I am so, how shall I say it right, so dependent on humors, if I put on white, then I am instantly in a good mood. Black dresses, which I wear now, I do not like, but white is so good. . . . Before, I always wore white. . . . And when I come into large, bright rooms I feel that I can breathe properly; that is how it was at home."

In all of these matters Harriet von Rathlef recognized *die Kleine*. She saw that little girl in everything. There was the compassionate little girl, "who wants to own every dog she sees" and had to be forcibly prevented from handing out her pocket money to beggars on the street. There was the gluttonous little girl, who was incapable of hoarding sweets and in fact "usually ate more of the dessert than she did of the main dish." [11] Then the mischievous little girl, the prankster, the pest, who kicked the evening newspaper into Frau von Rathlef's face and tried to tickle her when Frau von Rathlef combed her hair. There was the prim little girl, who professed to be shocked when she found out that Frau von Rathlef was reading a *French novel* ("You should be ashamed of yourself, one does not read such books"); [12] the outdoorsy little girl, the sportswoman, who longed to have a garden, who played tennis like a gifted amateur when she was well, snowshoed with pleasure, and "judged keenly and cleverly the good or bad seat of a rider" [13] (Anastasia could not begin to describe the would-be equestrians she had watched in the park: "*Oy oy oy!* You should have seen how they sat!"); the pious little girl, who wanted to go to church and become "a real person" again; and the frightened little girl, who "trembled at being left alone" [14] and wondered if Frau von Rathlef might not be able to move into the hospital with her. Always there was the fun-loving little girl, the comedian, the girl with the indestructible sense of humor, who thought she had never heard anything so funny as when one of the nuns at St. Mary's asked her if Frau von Rathlef was her mother; and who laughed till she cried when Frau von Rathlef said, "Do you know, I've seen several pictures of the Prince of Wales lately, but always when he's falling off his horse."

The trouble was that Anastasia was not a little girl anymore, and that humor could take her only so far. "I am old, madam," she said one day, "quite old inside."

Harriet von Rathlef had been hoping these moods might pass with time and good care. "Oh, child," she answered, "that will change when you are well."

"No, madam, it will always be like that. . . ." Anastasia paused. "I want to show you something that I carry in my little bag," she said, "something beautiful, Mamma's mascot." She reached inside and pulled out a swastika, the hooked cross already recognized in Germany as the symbol of the Nazis.

Frau von Rathlef recoiled in outrage: "How can you have anything to do with that! These witch-hunts are disgusting!"

"But no, madam, that is here in Germany. But in reality it is an ancient Indian symbol — a symbol of luck. Mamma had it with her everywhere, and right to the end she had it. . . . Mamma believed in this symbol."

"Mamma," as Harriet von Rathlef discovered, occupied a special place in Anastasia's universe. "They tried to bring slander against her," Anastasia said, shaking her head fiercely, "but it is not the truth. . . . They slandered my mother in the same way they now slander me. Now they want to wash their hands. It is a cheap way to do so." [15] Anastasia saw it as a precious duty to uphold the Empress's reputation. She revered Alexandra. She worshipped her. Frau von Rathlef had given her a photograph of the Empress with the young Tsarevitch Alexis, and Anastasia was pleased with the choice. "She laughed so seldom," Anastasia said, "here she is laughing. How beautiful she is, my Mamma. Here my brother was already ill. Really, she was always sad. Madam, the circumstances were so hard. . . . I think Mamma was probably always so quiet and prayed so much, because she always felt that something terrible is coming. Mamma felt everything so easily. Is it not dreadful, that it came just as Mamma felt? Earlier Mamma was a happy woman . . . *Prinzessin Sonnenschein* ['Princess Sunshine']." Anastasia, too, had a marked talent for "feeling everything." There ran through her being a streak of gloomy mysticism, which the peculiar circumstances of her life only helped to encourage. She knew what the name Anastasia meant: "the Resurrection" — "She who will rise again." It did not escape her notice either that she had double life-lines in both of her hands. "Mamma should not have hung that picture in her room," said Anastasia. "It was a bad omen. . . . But I think she had a presentiment of everything, and therefore it hung there."

"What picture?"

"It was the Queen of France [Marie Antoinette], who perished so, same as later Mamma and we all with her."

It was a great burden to Anastasia not to be able to share Empress Alexandra's undying faith in God and the power of prayer. It was a sin, she knew, not to go to church. She had tried it once with the Kleists: "But the air . . . the singing . . . and then I could not stand." She had fainted, creating in the monarchist community a scandal whose ramifications were past computing. "I am at variance with God," Anastasia told Harriet von Rathlef, very seriously. "If I were not so skeptical and divided from God, I could go to Holy Communion, but because I am not one with God, I cannot do so."[16] Anastasia was furious with God, when it came to that, a notion that terrified her: "And why must I torture myself so? Often I do not believe in God anymore. For how can one explain that? Why does He send such pain? And even if things change, I will never be happy. When I laugh sometimes — but then instantly it comes all over me again. This morning, early, I did not want to live anymore. I thought, I want to sleep, to sleep, so then it is over." But Anastasia was superstitious. She kept ikons about her, and she panicked one day when she realized that she could not recall what had become of the little crucifix she had worn as a girl. "Oh, of course," she said with relief, "my child has it. It was gold, and in the middle a colored picture." She had placed it herself around the boy's neck in Bucharest. It had been her sole gesture of motherly concern.

For now the past was Anastasia's god. It was "something sacred" to her, said Harriet von Rathlef. If Anastasia could not live with her memories she could not live without them, either. She needed the bulging packet of photographs she carried with her everywhere. Pictures of the imperial family were the only gifts — "charity," she called it — she would accept without protest: "That is the best that I can get." And Frau von Rathlef's notebooks filled to bursting when the photographs were spread out on Anastasia's bed.

"How awful I look!" Anastasia exclaimed while gazing at a formal portrait of the imperial family.

"I don't think so," Frau von Rathlef chirped.

"Yes, yes, I was terrible then; I only had such a face when I was naughty. — That was in Odessa. . . . No, maybe I am wrong, maybe it was not Odessa, it was —"

"Where, then?"

"I do not know, please forgive me, I am not bright today." But she went on: "We were so bad, did not want to sit still. I and my brother. I still remember, Papa was so angry. Look, you can see here, he was really angry." She stared at the picture for some minutes more. Then: "Tatya was taller than Olga. Olga was always the most quiet. She bore everything with Mamma; she was like Mamma. It is not good when a person feels everything so deeply; better quite frivolous, that is better for the world."

She could look at the photographs for hours, and not just those that depicted her immediate family. Anastasia clipped other pictures out of the newspapers and added them to her file. There was her father's sister, her beloved "Aunt Olga," who had called her "Schwibsik"; "Aunt Mavra," who had been born a princess of Saxe-Altenburg and "had so many sons"; "Uncle Ernie," the Grand Duke of Hesse, with his wife, "Auntie Onor," and their two boys; and Grand Duke Kyril Vladimirovitch, whom she would not call "uncle," who had sworn allegiance to the new Provisional Government in 1917 and who last year, in 1924, had proclaimed himself Emperor and Autocrat of All the Russias: "He in Papa's place! He was the first to desert Papa with his army. A relative!" Anastasia looked at Kyril's photograph with an expression of sheer disgust. "He looks just as nasty as he always did," she told Frau von Rathlef, and shuddered. Then she said it again: "Nasty. Get rid of that picture." [17] But this was a subject that stirred Anastasia's deepest passions — Kyril and "that Coburg," his wife, Grand Duchess Victoria, who had divorced the Empress's own brother and married Kyril against the Tsar's orders. "If he and his wife come into my parents' place," said Anastasia, "then there is no God!" Well, nothing could surprise her anymore: "Madam, there were so many false people with us at court . . . how they all talked and slandered us. But we knew the proprieties. . . . Do you know, I was so bad, I used to wash my hands after these people had kissed them. . . . But it was good for them with us, and they all deserted us! . . . Yes! . . . When I think how the people used to cheer . . . how delighted everybody was when we appeared . . . In all of Mighty Russia there was nobody to protect one family! That I will never be able to understand." [18]

Where were they? Harriet von Rathlef wondered. Where were the only people who could take Anastasia in charge now and do something to settle this case? Sometimes she and Anastasia talked about it. "It would never have occurred to me before that I would have to go through such things in Berlin," Anastasia said. "That my relatives would begrudge me a little piece of bread . . . It would have been better if Tschaikovsky had left me lying there." But Anastasia did have suggestions. "Fetch Gilliard here . . . ," she said. "Is he still alive? . . . If I could write and he was still alive, all would be well. He would help me to find my right. He was with us many years, he knew me well." She continued to Frau von Rathlef:

"The doctor would also know me."
  "What doctor?"
  "Who was with us."
  "What was his name?"
  She doesn't know. Then: "I believe . . . B— Botkin."
  "Do you think he is no longer alive?"
  "I believe to have read something, that he is dead." She looks at me questioningly, holds my hands firmly. "What do you know? Do you know it for sure?"
  "It has been published that they found something to prove it."
  From all of this I see that she does not know that people have written about the murder of the imperial family. She pulls out the little photograph of the Dowager Empress and says quietly: "But she lives, I am sure of that."
  "The Dowager Empress may thank her stars that she was allowed to leave."
  "Who knows if she is happy?" she says bitterly. "I am alive, madam, and I am unhappy; can you explain it to me, why I had to stay alive? The others were allowed to die. But I, what am I now?"

What was she now, indeed? "I will never, *never* see that again!" Anastasia cried when she ran across a photograph of the Tsar's estate at Livadia, in the Crimea. "What has become of all that, what have they done with it?" Frau von Rathlef had to pacify her: "It is all standing just as it was, do believe me."

"In these moments," wrote Harriet von Rathlef, "when she was tired of living, when bodily pain and the shadows of the past overwhelmed her, her temper burst forth in all its passion. We could not leave her alone. We feared, the doctors as well as I, that she might harm herself. How often she complained to us: 'I am still insane, because I cannot understand how I could have gotten into this condition. That I have not the right to be what I am and must always live among strangers.' . . . She was not posing when she said it would be better if she could die, because she did not know how she was going to live." [19] And her patience with the controversy over her identity, above all, was wearing very thin. She did not have the strength for it. "If you do not succeed in helping me to my right," she warned Frau von Rathlef, "then I will not live anymore." She would get a job, earn some money, go to Greece, enter an Orthodox convent, and die there.[20] She was serious: "If you tell me that another refusal has come, then I do not want to live anymore. *This is the last time.* . . . I remain inside who I am, Papa and Mamma's child, even if I am only called Frau Tschaikovsky."

This was not the little girl talking. This was not "Fräulein Anny." "In this poor, tormented creature," wrote Harriet von Rathlef, "there is a deep-rooted consciousness of her eminence and her dignity, which may be anything else but is not ridiculous."[21] Anastasia's pain came out in a pathetic, ironic cry: "I have never said that I am Grand Duchess Anastasia Nicolaievna!" She meant that she had never insisted on the title, never demanded the name, never asked anybody for anything. Baron von Kleist had "jeered at her" and finally gotten angry because she refused to wear linen monogrammed with the imperial crown and the name Anastasia. But she had known that these trappings were "ridiculous" under the circumstances. Now Frau von Rathlef, if she wished, might affix the initials "A.T." to her handkerchiefs — "or better still, just 'A.' But no crown."[22] She had lost those rights in Bucharest: "And if my relations had taken me in, they need not have let me live as a Romanov. I will always remain Frau Tschaikovsky."

So proclaimed "Frau Tschaikovsky."

In the summer of 1925, by the time she entered St. Mary's Hospital, Anastasia was critically ill.[23] The tubercular infection in her left arm had been complicated now by staphylococcus and had formed an ugly, excruciatingly painful open wound at the elbow. "The patient is very anemic,"[24] wrote Serge Mikhailovitch Rudnev, the celebrated high-living Russian surgeon who treated Anastasia during her illness and ultimately saved her life, "and so emaciated that she is little more than a skeleton." Following a detailed report of her physical condition Rudnev remarked, "On the right foot I noted a severe deformity, apparently congenital in nature, in that the big toe bends right in over the middle, forming a bunion."

The malformation of Anastasia's foot — it could actually be seen in both feet — has a clinical name: *hallux valgus*. Although the condition is not unusual, in this case the malady was so pronounced that it could only have been present from birth; Professor Rudnev believed that Anastasia's family could not fail to remember such a striking deformity. Harriet von Rathlef had prepared a list of other identifying marks: "a small white scar on the shoulder blade from a cauterized mole"; another scar at the root of the middle finger of the left hand, which Anastasia said had been caught in a carriage door when she was very young; and a third, "indistinct" scar on the forehead. There were, in addition, the scars that would have been left by the attempt on Anastasia's life: the cut behind the right ear, which Frau von Rathlef, guessing, took to be "a graze from a bullet"; another that pierced the right foot from top to bottom; the infections in her chest and her left elbow, which, her doctors believed, might originally have been stab wounds; and then the head injuries, whose precise nature and even existence were to be disputed for decades.[25] "I still recall that there were cracks in the bone of the upper jaw,"[26] the doctor who had taken X rays of Anastasia's head recalled after the pictures themselves had disappeared,[27] "which pointed to an injury. On the skull there were signs of a probable fracture."

"One cannot say to what degree the memory disturbance is a result of the apparent injuries," wrote Dr. Lothar Nobel, a director of Berlin's exclusive Mommsen Clinic, to which Anastasia was transferred in July 1925, "since the severity of those injuries cannot now be determined."[28] Anastasia's impaired powers of recollection, amounting in effect to a kind of amnesia, puzzled all of her doctors. "The reproduction of her past life is spotty," Dr. Nobel went on, "like islands in a sea. . . . The form of amnesia is extraordinary, and comes under no known category, since it applies equally to the whole of the past, except for the most recent times, where the memory is normal."

Professor Karl Bonhoeffer, the eminent Berlin psychoanalyst and father of the famous Pastor Dietrich Bonhoeffer, was also called in to examine Anastasia over a brief period during her hospitalization. Bonhoeffer noticed no outward sign of violence to her head, but insisted, "This does not in itself speak against the existence of a severe organic disturbance of the memory, since such disturbances are often the result of brain concussion without there being severe damage to the skull." The aftereffects of trauma, in any case, take many forms, and Dr. Bonhoeffer understood that Anastasia had not adequately come to terms with the horrors of her past. What, exactly, those horrors had been Bonhoeffer did not find out: "Concerning the last experiences of the Tsar's family she says that her father was shot first. She remembers a number of men coming and a shining starry sky. What happened next she does not know." Like Dr. Nobel, Bonhoeffer was especially interested to observe that the gaps in Anastasia's memory extended to all the stages of her past life, not only to her childhood or the moment of trauma. He could only conclude that this curious "amnesia" was the result of "a more or less deliberate engagement of the will. . . . It is probably a case of loss of memory by auto-suggestion, arising from a desire to suppress what she has experienced. . . . The possibility must at least be conceded that this [auto-suggestive] influence might have developed in the daughter of the Tsar." [29]

The peculiar blocks affecting Anastasia's memory undoubtedly also accounted for the bewildering problem of her knowledge of languages, a problem Harriet von Rathlef correctly declared to be "the cause of most of the doubt and disbelief in her identity." [30] Although there were people who said that they had heard her speak in Russian, in English, and even in French, by 1925 Anastasia was speaking German exclusively. Her Russian detractors, Germanophobes all, later employed this fact against her to great effect, with the claim that the Tsar's daughter, as a girl, "knew no German at all" and that Anastasia, since she spoke it fluently, could not be she.[31] In reality, however, all four of the Grand Duchesses had studied German seriously right up through their imprisonment at Tobolsk in 1918. It was a language they had little occasion to use and which they never mastered, but, after five years in Germany, neither had Anastasia. Dr. Ludwig Berg, the chaplain at St. Mary's, recalled that Anastasia "spoke German, but slowly, and she often had to search for her expressions. Her sentences were not always of German construction." [32] Indeed they were not. Anastasia once pointed to a small child and called him "*Dieses süsse kleine Sache*" — a literal and, for Germans, impossible rendition of the English "this sweet little thing." [33] Everything was a "*Sache*" for Anastasia — an "object." There were only "good things" and "bad things" in life. People, too, she saw in black and white. They were either *sympathisch* ("agreeable") or *unsympathisch* — the reverse. Anastasia's disregard for the rules of German grammar was nearly total, and she settled for the neutral *das* when she was unsure of anything. *Das* meant "that," "it," "he," and "she." "She always chops off every *h* in German," added a woman who met her when Anastasia had been living in Germany for seven years, "and it is *Aus* [*Haus*] and *Eute* [*Heute*] and so on — her German is extraordinary, and she can only understand quite simple German, she could not follow a German newspaper for example — her poor brain has been so knocked about and yet German is really the only thing she can speak." [34]

This was the problem too often overlooked when Anastasia's use of languages was examined only as it related to her claim to identity: she could not communicate properly in *any* language. So badly had her mental skills deteriorated that in 1926, when Dr. Bonhoeffer examined her, she could neither count past ten nor tell the time. Bonhoeffer wrote:

In longer conversations congestion of the face sets in and her features become taut. In conversation and social interaction, however, she always maintains a kindly, obligingly attentive manner. Her choice of words is often unusually clever, [but] she will never paraphrase anything. In speaking she will indicate that she cannot think of a word she wants to use. . . . Her pronunciation is foreign, with a Russian accent, which, however, has a particular nuance to it. Of a South German touch, which is mentioned in the Dalldorf history of the illness, there is currently no trace. . . .

The tests of her ability to read prove that she can read single Latin letters correctly (she cannot read German [Fraktur]), although only with difficulty and often only under pressure. Putting letters together into words, she says, gives her great trouble; she can spell the name "Anastasia" aloud slowly, but refuses with other words, saying that she is tired and debilitated by the pain in her arm. . . . She is ashamed that she cannot do it. . . . She cannot connect words to sentences when reading. It is the same with writing. She writes laboriously the name "Anastasia" in Latin characters, otherwise nothing spontaneously. She writes slowly, in the manner of a seven- or eight-year-old child. [35]

When Professor Rudnev operated on Anastasia's infected arm he affirmed that she had "raved in English" under the anesthetic. "Before the operation," he went on, "I spoke Russian with her, and she answered all my questions, although in German." [36] This was a phenomenon observed so often and by so many people that Harriet von Rathlef never even bothered to try to prove it. It was absurd to say that Anastasia did not "know" the Russian language. She did not *speak* the Russian language, and there was a world of difference. "Perhaps the avoidance of the Russian language is connected with the dangers of its use in the flight from Siberia and her fear then of being recognized," said Dr. Nobel; "for this obsessive fear is constantly reflected in everything she says and the way she behaves. That is my explanation for her uncooperativeness. . . ." [37] Anastasia herself carried that explanation a step farther. She had said it and said it: she did not *want* to speak Russian. "If you could have heard the sort of Russian we heard at the end in Siberia," she remarked, "you would never want to hear it spoken in your presence again." [38] And if the Russian monarchists could not accept that, it was not her affair. "She has made up her mind about this," said Dr. Nobel, "and will stick to it." [39]

"I will tell you something, madam," said Anastasia to Harriet von Rathlef, "but you must not scold me. I like English better than Russian. I also believe that it will come back more easily." [40] And Anastasia, despite her protestations, did hope that both languages would come back. This, she said repeatedly, was "the most terrible thing of all, that I do not find the words anymore." She frequently dreamed in English and Russian, she said, but with morning the languages were gone: "Sometimes I again understand everything, but if you knew what a terrible torture it is . . . these years in the asylum, all has simply vanished." Once Anastasia tried to explain that she *thought* in English — "I believe" — but that her "tongue simply will not form the right words." Even in German, she said, she would often mean to say one thing and then hear herself saying something else entirely. It was dreadful. "She *has* forgotten a lot," Harriet von Rathlef wrote, "but she inhibits herself by some sort of feeling that she 'cannot.' As soon as she conquers this feeling, often for only minutes at a time, she knows it all again; suddenly she can speak . . . Russian sentences which she has not heard from me." [41]

Such were the blocks, said Harriet von Rathlef, other people had to understand if they hoped to understand Anastasia, and which the doctors who examined her during her ten-month hospitalization had no difficulty reconciling with her claim to identity. The Russian doctor, Rudnev, for one, had no doubt about her identity at all, and in fact became one of her most ardent champions and a lifelong friend ("my good Russian professor," Anastasia called him, "who saved me from death").[42] Only Dr. Bonhoeffer, the psychoanalyst, wondered if, instead, his patient, unwilling to confront some awful fact of her own life, had blocked out her true identity and replaced it with details from the experience of Grand Duchess Anastasia. He did not think it conceivable, however, as was shortly to be charged, that she could have found these details in books or the narratives of others. If she had assumed the Grand Duchess's identity as her own, Bonhoeffer believed, then she must have grown up in the Grand Duchess's immediate environment, as the daughter of an officer, say, or some dignitary of the Russian court. In any case, after so short a period of observation (three weeks), and in view of her unflagging resistance to questions, Dr. Bonhoeffer could not determine with anything like certainty whether Anastasia's memories were her own or not:

The positive establishment of Frau Tschaikovsky's identity is not in itself a matter for psychopathology, but rather — if you want to put it this way — for criminology. . . .
Although her bearing, her manner of speech, and a certain friendly grace in mimicry and in the way she expresses herself all clearly indicate that the patient has come from cultured circles, it is still difficult to receive a complete picture of her personality. . . . In regard to the question of identity concerned here, certain important psychopathological points have been established. The patient is not suffering from a mental illness in the true sense; on the other hand, she does exhibit signs of a psychopathic constitution, evidenced by her emotional excitability, her tendency toward changes of mood, especially toward depression, and by the peculiar disturbance of the memory. . . .
It has been asked if there can be any question of hypnotic influence on the patient by some third party.
That is to be denied, as is the other supposition that this is a deliberate fraud.[43]

Dr. Nobel, who had observed Anastasia for eight months, disagreed on some points with Dr. Bonhoeffer. He wrote:

In conclusion, I would like to state that in my opinion no mental illness of any kind exists; I, at least, have noticed no trace of derangement in the patient during the long period of observation, and also no trace of auto-suggestion or suggestion by others. Although her memory has certainly suffered, perhaps owing to the evident head injury, and although she is subject to moods of depression, these in my opinion have nothing pathological about them.

Now a few remarks concerning the patient's identification. Naturally there can be no question of proof on my part. Yet it seems to me impossible that her memories rest on suggestion, or that her knowledge of many small details is due to anything but her own personal experience. Furthermore, it is psychologically scarcely conceivable that anyone who, for some reason or other, is playing the part of another person should behave as the patient does now and show such little initiative toward the realization of her plans.[44]

It was left to Harriet von Rathlef to take the initiative, for the moment. After only a week in Anastasia's company Frau von Rathlef felt confident enough to appeal directly for help to Grand Duke Ernest Louis of Hesse-Darmstadt, the only brother of Empress Alexandra. Certainly she assumed that the Grand Duke must take Anastasia's case seriously when he read her letter, which briefly outlined Anastasia's history and drew his attention to such physical peculiarities — scars and bodily marks — as an uncle might remember in a niece. Finally, Frau von Rathlef enclosed a set of X rays showing Anastasia's head injuries and then sat back to await the Grand Duke's reply.

When it came, it took her by surprise. "I certainly received an answer to my letter," Frau von Rathlef sniffed, "but not a very encouraging one. It was impossible to think that one of the Tsar's daughters might still be alive. That was the answer."[45] Later, when she knew the case better, Frau von Rathlef had to admit that she had hoped for too much from this first appeal, especially in view of the unsuccessful meeting between Anastasia and the Grand Duke's other sister, Irene of Prussia. Still Frau von Rathlef could not believe that the Grand Duke would disown a woman who might be his sister's only surviving child without at least examining the evidence to back her claim. So she tried again. This time she took copies of all her notes, attached a number of photographs to them, and sent the whole package off to Darmstadt in the hands of a trusted friend, Amy Smith.

Amy Smith was the intrepid granddaughter of a mayor of the free city-state of Hamburg. A report of her adventures in the former grand duchy of Hesse was presently added to Harriet von Rathlef's files. "When I decided, in the summer of 1925, to go to Darmstadt," Fräulein Smith recalled, "my only motive was to comply with the repeated request of a fellow creature who was pitifully helpless, absolutely neglected, and seriously ill." [46] Anastasia herself had urged Fräulein Smith to make the trip: "She was heartily in favor of it. She had it all worked out: when I could leave, when I would be back, and she was even convinced that her uncle, the Grand Duke, might come back with me and take her away. Then — or so she thought — all would be well." [47]

Amy Smith arrived at Darmstadt with a letter of introduction from the Unruh family (the German writer Fritz von Unruh was a close friend of the Grand Duke of Hesse and had been his sons' tutor). But the Grand Duke had left the palace in Darmstadt for Schloss Wolfsgarten, his hunting estate, and Fräulein Smith was obliged to deliver her report to Count Kuno Hardenberg, the Grand Marshal of the Hessian court. There followed two solid days of argument and equivocation — quarreling over Anastasia's memories,[48] for the most part, as reported in Harriet von Rathlef's notes — with Amy Smith defending Anastasia and Count Hardenberg taking the role of devil's advocate. "Evidently this kind of thing had been brought to the Grand Duke before," Fräulein Smith explained, "and each time it had turned out to be a hoax." In the end, the mission to Darmstadt failed miserably. Before leaving the palace Fräulein Smith asked the Count, "If Frau Tschaikovsky is not Grand Duchess Anastasia, and if she is not an impostor or mentally ill, what possibility remains?" [49]

"Oh," Count Hardenberg replied, "there still remains the possibility that some powerful unknown hypnotist is behind all this."

"Whom did Darmstadt take this marvelous hypnotist to be?" Amy Smith grumbled as she rode back to Berlin in defeat. "Frau von Rathlef?" At St. Mary's, in the meantime, Anastasia's health had gotten worse. Fräulein Smith did not know how to break the news to her. "Unfortunately," she said, "your uncle was not able to come back with me right away, as we had hoped when I left here. But everything is going to be all right. You must just be patient a little longer."

Anastasia would not be consoled. Crying, she turned her head to the wall and murmured, "Oh, they will all come when I am dead."

Amy Smith never hid her low opinion of the Grand Duke of Hesse: "I felt I was up against someone quite lacking in the humanity and sense of responsibility which should have made him anxious to clear up this strange and tragic case completely. . . . My repeated requests that the Grand Duke come to Berlin incognito in order to settle the affair ran up against unshakable opposition. It would be impossible for the Grand Duke to come to Berlin for this purpose. It might get into the newspapers." But Amy Smith knew an excuse when she heard one. She knew the real reason for the Grand Duke's intransigence. "It was something Frau Tschaikovsky had said about the Grand Duke," she admitted carefully. ". . . I understood at once that I had unwittingly hit on a sore point."[50]

Some days before Amy Smith had left for Darmstadt, Harriet von Rathlef had thought to ask Anastasia if she knew the Grand Duke of Hesse personally. "Oh yes," Anastasia had replied, "he was called Ernest, Mamma's brother."

"And when did you see him last? You must have been very young."

No: "*Im Kriege bei uns zu Hause* [In the war, with us at home]".

Frau von Rathlef had stared at Anastasia in disbelief. During World War I the Grand Duke of Hesse had been fighting with the Germans against Imperial Russia. It was inconceivable that he had been received at the Russian court in the midst of hostilities or that Anastasia could have seen him there. "You're confusing things," said Frau von Rathlef, who normally did not contradict; "perhaps you mean before the outbreak of the war?"

"No, no, he was with us quite secretly. He wanted to persuade us that either we should leave the country or make peace quickly. My uncle can confirm it, that I speak the truth."

"I was amazed," said Frau von Rathlef. "It wasn't possible, a prince of the enemy powers . . . in Russia, with the imperial family. How could that have been?"

"No, you must be mistaken," Frau von Rathlef insisted, until Anastasia lost her temper: "He even told Mamma, 'That is no longer Princess Sunshine!' "

"I was amazed," said Harriet von Rathlef again. But the thought had already come to her: "If it were true, if it were so, and nobody else knew about it" — so she had asked Anastasia one more time: "You are certain? You are certain?"

"Certain, yes," said Anastasia. "Quite, quite certain."[51]

5

THE FAMILY REACTS

*I*n 1929, long after the scandal of her claim had broken in the world press, Anastasia was asked to account for the undying hostility toward her at the court of her "Uncle Ernie," the Grand Duke of Hesse. She explained as best she could:

It started from the moment I told . . . about the time [the Grand Duke] came to Russia. Then started their campaign against me. . . .

I didn't know what was going on. . . . I was at that time near death and didn't know what was going on. . . .

It was during the war — in 1916. He came to arrange with my mother and father a treaty. He came under an assumed name, but all of us children knew him because we had seen him before. If it had been known, they would have put him out of Germany, and he was terribly afraid . . .[1]

But what was this about "a treaty"? How could Anastasia know that the Grand Duke had come to Russia in order "to persuade us that either we should leave the country or make peace quickly"? She went on:

I heard my mother talk about it. We were great friends together and we all knew what was going on at home. . . . I was then about fifteen years old. Of course I would understand. We were so much together in everything. . . .

93

I dislike very much to mention anything about my relatives and what
they did during the war, but when I thoughtlessly mentioned the fact
about my uncle coming to see my mother in 1916, I did not realize that
he had gone without the proper authority. It was indeed thoughtless
of me to mention it . . . for it evidently brought about much serious
complications for my uncle.[2]

"A sore point," Amy Smith had called it. She well remembered
the sequence of events at Darmstadt: how she had met Count Hardenberg, the Grand Duke's aide; how Hardenberg had been doubtful but not antagonistic; how he had looked through Harriet von
Rathlef's notes with interest and sympathy. At their first meeting,
in fact, the Count had appeared to be "deeply shaken" by all Frau
von Rathlef had to report, but when Amy Smith met him again the
next day, after Hardenberg had consulted with the Grand Duke,
"he was completely changed. . . . He was almost rude to me, and
he greeted me at once with the statement that [Anastasia] was an
impostor. I explained that I had already gone into that with him
and could assure him that [Anastasia], whoever she was, was not
that." Then Hardenberg exploded: "What does this shameless creature think she's doing claiming that the Grand Duke was in Russia
during the war?" Amy Smith couldn't tell him, but the fury in his
voice made her nervous: "The Count was pacing around the room,
and I got the impression that he felt it was a catastrophe, which I
didn't understand at all. So, in order to calm him down, I said,
simply, 'Well, then, he wasn't there. We didn't believe it, either.' "[3]
That was not good enough for Count Hardenberg. Fräulein Smith
should know that there were laws against fraud in Germany. And
libel. And blackmail. Anastasia was an impostor, Hardenberg declared again, or a lunatic, or both, but she would be well advised
not to mention this matter in the press. "If Count Hardenberg had
simply dismissed [Anastasia's] assertion as nonsense," said Amy
Smith, "a bagatelle, that would have been the end of it so far as I
was concerned. Only his extraordinary agitation made me realize
that we had hit on something important."
It was never any secret that the Grand Duke of Hesse, with two
sisters in the Russian imperial family — one of them, the Empress,
plainly headed on a collision course — had been deeply committed
to bringing about a separate peace between Russia and Germany in
World War I. Nor is there any doubt that the German government
had endorsed the Grand Duke's efforts and empowered him to act

in its behalf until the middle of 1916, at least. The key to the dispute lies not so much in Anastasia's allegation that the Grand Duke had finally come to Russia in person to talk peace with the Tsar and the Empress, but rather that he had done it "without . . . proper authority."[4] In 1925, when Anastasia first mentioned the matter, the Grand Duke of Hesse, by then deposed for seven years, still entertained real hopes of regaining his throne. He could never expect to do so without the support of an increasingly "republican," increasingly recriminatory German population and without a sweeping disclaimer of past errors and associations — royal associations, *family* associations. The Kaiser's daughter, Victoria Louisa, explained the situation this way in her memoirs:

I personally know of no one who has any evidence of the Grand Duke's trip to St. Petersburg [Tsarskoe Selo], neither did I hear anything from my father about it. But I do know that the proposal to send a prince over there was discussed, and also with the military commanders, but Ludendorff was strictly against it. So if such a step had been taken, it was taken without the knowledge of the High Command. That would explain why my father had wanted the strictest secrecy, and it would also explain the Grand Duke's absolute silence, too, particularly as regards his own family. They certainly never got the slightest indication from him.[5]

In the years ahead Anastasia had the satisfaction of hearing her story confirmed by a variety of people who were in a position to know something about it. The wall of secrecy began to crack when, twenty-five years later, the German Crown Princess stepped forward to affirm not only that the Grand Duke of Hesse had undertaken the peace mission to Russia, but that "our circles knew about it even at the time." The Crown Princess's own source had been her father-in-law, the Kaiser. "So in my opinion," she went on, "by making such a statement (which I only heard about much later) Frau A. T. was giving strong evidence that at least she had intimate knowledge of high politics and the most secret dealings of the imperial family."[6] Then Fritz von Unruh declared that he himself had helped the Grand Duke draw up the plans for the journey to Tsarskoe Selo and that those plans, *in defiance of the wishes of the Kaiser,* had indeed been put into effect.[7] There were dozens of other witnesses. One lady of St. Petersburg society remarked innocently, "What *I* don't understand is why everyone keeps talking about the Grand Duke's 'secret' trip. We all knew about it."[8]

"There are no indications," the Darmstadt public archives loyally maintain in the face of all evidence to the contrary, "that the former Grand Duke Ernest Louis of Hesse could have gone to Russia, specifically Tsarskoe Selo, in 1916."[9] The point is well taken, but it does not answer the question: did he go or did he not? Perhaps if the Grand Duke had ever met Anastasia they might have resolved the issue between them. But when it was suggested to her later that she go herself to see the Grand Duke at Darmstadt, Anastasia only answered, "No, I want it to be here, in front of you, when he tells me to my face that he did not come to see us during the war!"[10] And by the time Amy Smith returned to Berlin and St. Mary's Hospital, a campaign had already been set in motion at Darmstadt to prove Anastasia an impostor — in effect, to neutralize her.

"Difficulties exist in order to be overcome," Harriet von Rathlef wrote nervously. "I did not, of course, tell the invalid that the attempt to interest her uncle on her behalf had failed. . . . Although I really had no idea where to turn next, I continued working, gathered together my material, and hoped that somehow and from somewhere help would come.

"It did. And from a direction I had never expected."[11] Frau von Rathlef was sitting outdoors with Anastasia at St. Mary's one sunny afternoon early in July when Dr. Ludwig Berg came out to the garden to tell her that visitors were waiting in his office.

"Visitors?" asked Frau von Rathlef. "What visitors?"

"You will see," said Dr. Berg.[12]

It had required a German, the daughter of the hated Kaiser Wilhelm, to impress on the Russian imperial family the seriousness of the "Anastasia" affair. The whispers and rumors had moved through the ranks of Europe's royalty until, through Crown Princess Cecilie, the reality of Anastasia was brought home to the Kaiser's only daughter, Victoria Louisa, Duchess of Brunswick.[13] Although the Duchess, like Cecilie, had no desire to meddle in the private concerns of the House of Romanov, she did think it right to discuss the matter with her own mother-in-law, the Duchess of Cumberland.[14] In this roundabout way Anastasia found an ally who could really do her some good, for by birth the Duchess of Cumberland was Thyra of Denmark, a sister of Maria Feodorovna, the Dowager Empress of Russia. Thyra agreed now that something had to be done about Anastasia, and she brought a gentle pressure to bear at the Dowager Empress's court-in-exile near Copenhagen. How would it look, Thyra hinted, if the imperial family did not do everything in its power to solve this mystery? It would be simple, surely, "just to clear up the case once and for all." [15]

Thyra was right: it should have been simple. That it proved otherwise was no fault of hers. The Dowager Empress, rather, had the last word in Copenhagen and seemed disinclined to cooperate.

During the Revolution and the Civil War in Russia the Tsar's mother had adamantly refused to leave the country. [16] It shamed her deeply to depend for protection on the German forces of occupation in the Crimea, where she had moved from Kiev, but she preferred that humiliation to the notion of flight. In 1919, finally, alarmed by reports of violence at Ekaterinburg, King George V of England had sent a fleet of warships to Yalta to rescue his "Aunt Minnie." Even then, with the Bolsheviks at the gate, the Dowager Empress would not go until everyone who wanted to leave with her had gotten safely on board. Some six thousand aristocrats, with valets, maids, and chefs in tow, thus sailed into permanent exile at British expense. It was the last time anyone heard "God Save the Tsar" played for a living empress. [17]

For some time after her escape Maria Feodorovna stayed on in England with Queen Alexandra, her eldest and favorite sister. Although one of Maria's daughters, Grand Duchess Xenia, lived out the rest of her life as the guest of the British royal family, the Dowager Empress at length returned to her native Denmark, where, with her younger daughter and inseparable companion, Grand Duchess Olga, she settled down at Villa Hvidøre, a small estate she owned jointly with her sister. At Hvidøre "the Old Ikon" (as Maria Feodorovna was known among waggish Russians) continued to enjoy every deference to which an empress is entitled. She kept her servants and her attendant ladies. Russian émigrés of all classes flocked to Villa Hvidøre to bask in the presence of their "Empress Mother," to dine free of charge at her table, and to lay their complaints with her secretary, while the dutiful Grand Duchess Olga, married to a commoner and with two small children of her own, took over the management of her mother's chaotic social life. In exile, Maria Feodorovna's influence had diminished only in scope. Her patronage, or even her tacit blessing, could make or break an émigré enterprise, for she was the senior-ranking member of the Romanov family, the arbiter of all family disputes, and the spiritual head of the monarchist movement.

It was consequently of no small importance that Maria Feodorovna, to the end of her life, refused to credit the story of the murder of the Tsar and his family at Ekaterinburg. She believed that Nicholas, Alexandra, and all their children were still alive in Russia, and Inspector Sokolov's report of their murder did nothing to change her mind. An ill-informed public swiftly concluded that the Empress had lost her reason, but the verdict was cruel and far too hasty. Something more than an old woman's hope lay behind Maria Feodorovna's attitude. "It may have been pride," an insightful American journalist wrote after her death. "It may have been affection. It may have been superstition. But it was also statecraft. Until the titular head of the House of Romanov admitted that the throne was vacant, all claimants to the throne were in the position of pretenders." [18] Here, of course, the stubbornness of the Dowager Empress had its most profound effect. She had been no less outraged than Anastasia was to learn that Grand Duke Kyril had proclaimed himself Emperor-in-exile. "My heart was painfully depressed," the Empress wrote sourly to Grand Duke Nicholas Nicolaievitch, who himself had been put forward as a claimant to the throne. ". . . If it should please the Almighty to take unto Himself my beloved sons and grandson, I believe . . . that the future Emperor will be designated by our fundamental laws in unison with the Orthodox Church and altogether with the Russian people." [19]

There were many too many of these would-be tsars in Maria Feodorovna's tired opinion. Kyril and Nicholas Nicolaievitch were only at the forefront of the struggle. Kyril now had a son whom he had designated "Tsarevitch." Handsome, enigmatic Grand Duke Dmitri Pavlovitch, a grandson of Alexander II and one of the murderers of Rasputin, had also been suggested as a possibility, while others in the Romanov circle toyed with the idea of staking claims. [20] Now, at her elegant, wind-swept villa on the Baltic, the old Dowager Empress kept quiet. "She felt it beneath her dignity to take sides," her son-in-law Grand Duke Alexander Mikhailovitch explained, "to issue manifestos, to participate in sham battles." [21] And she did not need to say anything to make it plain that the subject of Ekaterinburg was not welcome in her house.

This was the problem, precisely, that prevented the members of her family and her entourage from breathing a word about Anastasia to the Dowager Empress until it was too late to turn back. Thanks to Thyra of Cumberland, however, concern for the mysterious claimant in Berlin had finally been raised where it counted the most. Prince Waldemar of Denmark, the Dowager Empress's brother, wrote immediately to the Danish ambassador to Germany, Herluf Zahle, asking him to proceed "privately" — that is, secretly — with a preliminary inquiry.[22] Waldemar's letter was hand-carried to Berlin by Alexis Andreievitch Volkov, who was further charged to meet Anastasia and report back to the family in Denmark.

Alexis Volkov had been Empress Alexandra's personal servant, what was known as a groom of the chamber. It was Volkov who, in the last years before the Revolution, had pushed the ailing Empress in her wheelchair. Imprisoned at Ekaterinburg with others of the Tsar's retinue, Volkov was later removed to Perm and escaped death only by virtue of his quick wits. One evening in September 1918 the prisoners were led out into the forest. Sensing that the end had come, Volkov broke away from his guards and dashed into the night. Eventually he made his way to White Army headquarters at Omsk and from there to Europe, where his unswerving loyalty to the imperial family had earned him a reputation practically unequaled among monarchists in exile.[23]

These, then, were the two "visitors" — Alexis Volkov and Ambassador Zahle — who were waiting in Dr. Berg's study at St. Mary's on the afternoon of July 3, 1925.[24] Harriet von Rathlef stood by in anticipation while Volkov, peering through the window, watched Anastasia rise from her chair, bid good day to one of the nuns, and walk along the garden to her room. His first impressions were strictly positive: seeing her from a distance, and in motion, Volkov could affirm that "the invalid did indeed resemble Grand Duchess Anastasia." When he met her face-to-face the following afternoon, however, that impression was completely dispelled. "Volkov was disappointed," Frau von Rathlef wrote, ". . . because the Grand Duchess had had a rounder face and a rosier complexion. The features he now saw did not remind him of the Grand Duchess."[25] To make matters worse, Anastasia had greeted the old man with deep suspicion and no remark, failing to show any sign that she might have recognized him. Volkov had to be content to watch her in silence while she conversed with the Danish ambassador in German, a language he did not understand.

Harriet von Rathlef saw how the meeting affected Anastasia: "She gazed long at Volkov with a pained and worried expression. That her memory was torturing her was apparent to us all. Finally she lay back on the sofa cushions, exhausted, and said, *'Ich kann mich nicht zurecht finden* [I cannot make the connection].' " When Ambassador Zahle remarked later that Volkov had come to see her from Denmark, Anastasia shook her head: "But he belonged to our court."[26] Puzzled, she told Volkov that she hoped he could return the next day. As he left, "she extended her hand in a friendly way and said she was glad he would come back another time."

That night Anastasia told Harriet von Rathlef that Volkov's face was familiar to her: "The face reminded her dimly, as though through a fog, of a face from her former surroundings, and she added, 'I believe he was specially attached to my Papa. But things must be going badly for the poor man, because he is not well dressed.'" Here Anastasia stopped. It was as though she had suddenly realized the importance of the occasion. "You must be very careful when you tell my Grandmamma about me," she said. "It could be her death."

Early the next morning Volkov and Ambassador Zahle were back at St. Mary's. While Zahle talked with Anastasia, Volkov continued to express his doubts rather loudly in Russian. But when Frau von Rathlef tried to reason with him Anastasia swiftly cut her short: "*Ich will das nicht mehr!* [I want no more of that]" "She had understood more of our conversation than I had thought," said Frau von Rathlef, and then went on:

Volkov was aware of his responsibility in this matter and told me again and again that he could not say Frau Tschaikovsky was *not* the Grand Duchess, but neither could he say definitely that she was. Finally he asked me to translate a few questions. He mentioned a name (I have forgotten it) and asked Frau Tschaikovsky if she knew this person. She answered immediately, "Yes." When asked who it was [she said]: "He was a special servant for us children." Then Volkov asked if she remembered a sailor who had been with her brother. She said right away: "Yes, he was so tall and was called . . . Nagorny." I asked her to repeat the name again loudly. Volkov was completely astonished and said that was correct. With that, the relations between Volkov and Frau Tschaikovsky became entirely different. The leavetaking was warmer.

When Alexis Volkov arrived at St. Mary's for his third and final visit on July 6, Anastasia's fever had risen and she was too weak to leave her bed. He sat down at her side and within a few minutes, with Harriet von Rathlef as interpreter, asked, "Who was Tatischev?"[27]

"In Siberia — he was Papa's adjutant."

"That's correct," said Volkov. He gave Anastasia a portrait of the Dowager Empress, which she stared at without apparent emotion.

"Is she well?" Anastasia finally asked, and then said, in afterthought, "I am surprised that Grandmamma is not dressed all in black. She always used to wear only black." [28]

For several minutes more Anastasia lay quietly in bed while Volkov and Frau von Rathlef talked together in Russian: "Suddenly she interrupted us: 'There was another sailor with my brother.' Volkov nodded. 'He was called — the name is so hard to pronounce . . . Derevenko.' Volkov said: 'Yes.' Then she went on and asked, 'Did he not also have sons, who played with my brother?' Volkov: 'Yes.' Later she said: 'But there was somebody else there, called that . . . a doctor who always relieved Dr. Botkin.' Volkov: 'Yes.' "

By now an unmistakable empathy had arisen between Anastasia and her guest. When Volkov asked her if she remembered "Olga Alexandrovna," Anastasia laughed happily and replied, "Yes, my aunt. Mamma loved her too, she was very friendly." But when the conversation turned on the imperial family's Siberian imprisonment her smile faded. Volkov wanted to know where the Grand Duchesses had hidden their jewels at Tobolsk.

A pause. Then: "They were sewn in the clothes . . . spread around . . . in the seams."

"Do you remember the St. Ivan convent?"

"That was in Siberia . . . did not nuns come from there to sing with us? . . . Mamma and we four sang with the nuns."

"Volkov was shaken," said Frau von Rathlef.

"He has asked me enough questions," Anastasia declared suddenly. "Now I will ask something." Did Volkov remember the room at Peterhof "where Mamma used to scratch her initials on the windowpane, and the year, whenever we were there?"

Volkov did: "[He] was deeply upset. He was crying and he kissed her hand several times. . . ."

"Don't cry," said Anastasia, "*das kann ich so . . .*" Her voice trailed off. "Everything will be all right," Volkov told her as he left the room.

Was this a recognition? Out in the hallway with Harriet von Rathlef, Volkov took several minutes to compose himself: "Tears were still streaming down his face." But he left Berlin that day without leaving a statement. Nobody asked him for one, since his job was only to meet Anastasia and report back to Copenhagen. That much he did, and if the subsequent dramatic excitement at the

Dowager Empress's villa is any guarantee, there can be no doubt about Volkov's feelings. But to Frau von Rathlef he remarked in distress: "Think of the position I am in! If I now say that it is she, and others later claim the reverse, where would I be then?"

"I can well understand his position," Frau von Rathlef commented dryly, "but a determined word would have been more useful to the invalid than all the hesitant, timid confirmations that later fell to our lot.

"We had to be patient."

While Alexis Volkov sat at St. Mary's looking for traces of the girl he had known in Russia, Zahle, the Danish ambassador, had already been called to Copenhagen for a meeting with Prince Waldemar. The one conversation satisfied the Prince that he had been right to take Anastasia's case seriously. Waldemar now instructed Zahle to conduct a thorough investigation of her identity and further declared that he, Waldemar, was ready to take responsibility for her mounting hospital bills. With the unqualified backing of the Danish royal family, therefore, Zahle returned to Berlin and the most extraordinary adventure of his career.

The intervention of Ambassador Zahle lent Anastasia's case a measure of legitimacy and authority it could ill afford to lose. Well known and well liked in diplomatic circles, Zahle was a former president of the Assembly of the League of Nations. He could not have known in 1925 how gravely his involvement with Anastasia would threaten his reputation, but, in the end, he was not a man to back down from what he regarded as a trust. Anastasia had said of him after their first meeting, "The Danish gentleman will be my friend for life; I feel it." [29] She was right. But Zahle was more than a friend. He was a champion, whose tacit faith in her identity and whose steadfastness under pressure ultimately rescued Anastasia from a royal maelstrom she could not escape on her own. The ambassador never knew what it was that had first persuaded him of Anastasia's authenticity — whether her "inborn distinction," which expressed itself immediately in a certain detached politeness and a simple gesture to be seated; or her sincerity, manifested by her panicked reaction to a letter on black-edged stationery ("Who has died in Copenhagen? I am so afraid. How is my Grandmamma?"). Zahle had endeared himself from the start by treating Anastasia with all the courtesy due to the rank she claimed: he always made an appointment to see her, and he always called ahead to make sure the appointment stood. A special, playful friendship quickly developed. Zahle — so imposing, so polite, so *distingué* — was "the Tall Man." Anastasia, of course, was "the Little One."

As his investigation progressed and his visits to the hospital became an almost daily ritual, Ambassador Zahle was drawn nearer to one certain conclusion: Anastasia, whatever her true identity, was not fooling with him. Who might she be? Zahle wondered. What family and what background had produced a woman who did not know, incredibly, that if she bought a chocolate bar with a ten-mark note she would undoubtedly get money back from her bill? Anastasia was deeply embarrassed to realize that she had been leaving change behind her in shops all over Berlin.[30] She was a woman who could discuss intelligently music and painting,[31] but did not know that she needed reservations for trains and hotels. She was heard to speak frankly, even gleefully, about the amorous scandals and lesser-known peccadillos of the Romanovs, but cast aside Lytton Strachey's *Queen Victoria* as "impertinent" and declared of Leo Tolstoy, when his name came up, that "she did not want to hear anything about Tolstoy; she could not stand him, as he was one of the many causes of the Russian Revolution." Very definitely, too, with an assurance the more striking because it was taken for granted, Anastasia corrected her entourage on the finer points of royal etiquette. Having seen a newsreel film of Queen Alexandra of England out for a drive with a lady-in-waiting, Harriet von Rathlef remarked that the attendant's face was "horribly devoid of expression."

"That is how she has to sit," said Anastasia, surprised. "Do you think that she ought to be greeting people, too? I imagine you would be ready to join right in. They could not let you sit there. . . . You had better stay at home."

"She laughed heartily at this," Frau von Rathlef recalled. Another incident proved the point:

After she had gotten a little better we went out to a Russian restaurant, because she very much wanted to have some Russian cabbage soup. There were only a few people in the restaurant, and the waiters were standing around. Suddenly it struck me that as we moved through the restaurant she was bowing left and right to the waiters. It was rather embarrassing, and I told her that she shouldn't do it. Very startled, she said: "Please forgive me, I was not thinking, only I was brought up always to acknowledge people. They told me again and again that I must never forget it. . . . Thank you very much for telling me."

Here was the woman Ambassador Zahle met, then, bowing to the waiters in Berlin restaurants but "beside herself with anxiety" because the staff at St. Mary's had discovered who she claimed to be. ("Why don't you say it?" one of them asked her while filling out forms. "I have to write it down." Anastasia fled the room.) She was utterly incapable of concealing her reactions. In January 1926 she was introduced to a Baltic-Russian émigré with the tremendous name of Vassili Lvovitch von der Osten-Sacken Tettenborn ("Willy"). Baron Osten-Sacken was private secretary to Serge Botkin, a cousin of the imperial family's private physician and currently president of the Office of Russian Refugees in Germany. During their conversation Baron Osten-Sacken asked Anastasia for permission to smoke a cigarette. She nodded politely and watched as the Baron removed from his pocket a small cigarette holder fashioned in the shape of a tobacco pipe. Suddenly Anastasia, as Harriet von Rathlef observed, was "seized by agitation," and when the Baron had gone she said, "For God's sake, tell me, where did the Baron get the pipe?"

"The holder was given to me in 1917 by a friend who had bought it at Alexander's in Petersburg," Baron Osten-Sacken told Frau von Rathlef next day. "It was the model from which Alexander made a similar one for the Tsar."

"Thank God," said Anastasia when she heard this explanation. "I was so upset, I could not sleep the whole night, because I was afraid it was Papa's pipe. . . . If you knew how startled I was when I saw that pipe . . ."

Toward the middle of July, shortly after Alexis Volkov had been to see her, Anastasia's health took an alarming turn for the worse. Her tubercular arm "swelled to a shapeless mass," Harriet von Rathlef reported, "and it was fearful to see the patient's agony." The doctors at St. Mary's, in the meantime, were still arguing about the preferred course of treatment. Frau von Rathlef only hoped that they would do something for Anastasia quickly: "She lay in bed crying softly and incessantly. . . . After ten days the doctors finally decided to operate. . . . Her arm was pierced right through to enable the pus to escape."

Now Frau von Rathlef dropped her other concerns and moved into St. Mary's to be with Anastasia day and night. The operation, unfortunately, had done nothing to improve the state of Anastasia's arm; if anything, the infection grew worse and the hideous wound grew deeper. Morphine, while it gave her some relief from the pain, naturally only increased Anastasia's mental confusion. For the next six weeks she lay in a state of recurring delirium. Nights were the worst. Frau von Rathlef had never heard such crying: "She said . . . that she had flown a long way and come by her people, who were sitting apart from one another by the wayside." All were dressed entirely in white except "Grandmamma," who wore black. She had called their names and stretched out her arms, but her family was out of reach, from her and from each other. Then she had been perched on a rooftop, facing downward and clutching at her brother's belt as he slid over the edge. "Go into the garden," Anastasia cried to Frau von Rathlef, "and see if the Catherine Vase is still standing there. I am so afraid that the soldiers might already have destroyed it." [32]

"This thought seemed to torment her a great deal," said Frau von Rathlef; "she asked me again and again if I had gone to look, and said in her fever that she would have to go herself. She also called for a Lisa and a Shura to help her get dressed. . . . She had to go away so as not to be shot."

A girl named Lisa had served at the Russian court as a maid for the four daughters of Nicholas II.[33] And "Shura," as Harriet von Rathlef learned soon enough, was the former Alexandra Tegleva, the woman who had been Grand Duchess Anastasia's nursemaid from babyhood. After leaving Russia in 1919, Shura had married Pierre Gilliard, the Grand Duchesses' French tutor; the couple now made their home in Lausanne, Switzerland, where Gilliard taught at the university. Whatever the Gilliards may have heard about Anastasia's case before this, they now found out that the matter was urgent. Shura received an impassioned note from the Tsar's sister Grand Duchess Olga:

Please go at once to Berlin with M. Gilliard to see the poor lady. Suppose she really *were* the little one. Heaven alone knows if she is or not. It would be such a disgrace if she were living all alone in her misery and if all that is true. . . . I implore you again to go as quickly as possible; you can tell us what there is in this story better than anyone else in the world. . . . May God grant you his aid. I embrace you with all my heart.

P.S.: If it really is she, please send me a wire and I will come to Berlin to meet you.[34]

Shura Gilliard lost no time. She and her husband arrived at the Anhalt Station on July 27, 1925, and went directly with Ambassador Zahle to St. Mary's. Zahle, who had just returned from Copenhagen, asked the Gilliards to wait a moment in the hall while he entered the sickroom alone. In her fever, Anastasia was hallucinating. She had been hoping to see "the Tall Man," she said, but now his head was brushing against the ceiling and his face was crossed with colored stripes — "red, blue, and green."[35] The Ambassador turned from the bed and told Harriet von Rathlef that "a lady and a gentleman" were waiting outside. He asked her to escort them in, but, said Frau von Rathlef, "I was not to ask their names . . . only later did I find out who they both were."

The Gilliards sat by Anastasia's bedside for about an hour. Frau von Rathlef reported that they "seemed moved by the invalid's condition" and watched her mostly in silence. When Gilliard had gone into the hall for a moment Shura asked Frau von Rathlef to show her Anastasia's feet. Gently Frau von Rathlef removed the blankets.[36]

"*The feet look like the Grand Duchess's,*" Shura exclaimed, "*— with her it was the same as here, the right foot was worse than the left*" [Frau von Rathlef's emphasis].[37]

Now the Gilliards asked for an opportunity to see Anastasia alone, but they spent no more than a few minutes in her room. "There is no sense in torturing the sick woman with questions in her present state," said Pierre Gilliard. "We will both come back as soon as her condition improves." Anastasia, in the meantime, had grown cross and resentful. Why had the gentleman asked her if she still ate as much chocolate as she used to? "Did he want to make fun of me . . . ?" Afterward, wrote Frau von Rathlef, "the fever seized her again with all its might. She kept fantasizing about her Aunt Olga Alexandrovna, who [she thought] was standing outside the door laughing at her because she had come so low in the world. I had to open the door wide in order to calm her."

That evening Harriet von Rathlef was called to a conference at the Danish embassy. There it was decided that Anastasia should be moved without delay to another hospital, where she might receive better treatment. "Herr Gilliard claimed that this was essential, in fact," said Frau von Rathlef, "because the most important thing at the moment was to keep her alive."[38] On the very next morning, accordingly, Anastasia was taken across town to a private room in the Mommsen Clinic, where Professor Serge Rudnev was on hand to treat her infected arm. The Gilliards went home to Lausanne.

At the Mommsen Clinic, Professor Rudnev opted for radical surgery, "to save her life and, possibly, her arm, because the question of an amputation was not remote." The muscles around the elbow and part of the bone were taken out, and twice more in the month of August the arm was lanced to drain the pus. At the elbow Rudnev inserted a silver joint, which paralyzed the arm at an eighty-degree angle and left what remained of the bone permanently exposed. For a full month and a half, while the infection cleared, Anastasia's life hung in the balance. Said Rudnev: "She could not get along with injections of morphine." Finally, at the end of September, Anastasia's fever dropped to one hundred degrees, where it hovered for many weeks. Her skin, never healthy looking, had turned an awful grayish white. Her lips were swollen from malnutrition and her bones stood out like knobs. "There was not an ounce of fat on her body," Rudnev reported, noting that her weight had declined to less than seventy-five pounds.[39]

As her arm slowly healed and the delirium lifted, Anastasia began to take an interest in her new surroundings. A white Angora kitten, christened Kiki and promptly adopted as a true friend in a world of disappointment, was "a happy thought" of Frau von Rathlef, who gladly took second place to the cat. During the last days of summer Anastasia spent hours at her window, gazing down at the children playing in the open courtyard below. "Listen!" she said one day. "Somebody is calling Shura. I have been racking my brain for that name for so long. . . . It was Shura who was always with us. . . . But what has happened to her? I do not know if she is even alive."[40]

Harriet von Rathlef had not told Anastasia that Shura had already been to see her with Pierre Gilliard. It was Ambassador Zahle who set her mind at rest.

"Where does she live?" asked Anastasia eagerly. "Can she come to me?"[41]

Zahle replied that Shura now lived in Switzerland and could not make the trip alone.

"Well," said Anastasia, who knew nothing about Shura's marriage, "can Gilliard not fetch her, if he is not too far away from her?"

Yes, said Zahle, Shura and Gilliard were both going to come.

Autumn arrived and Anastasia grew impatient. *When* was Shura going to come? Why hadn't she come already? Finally, on "a lovely, sunny day in October," Harriet von Rathlef returned to Anastasia's room from an errand and found Pierre Gilliard — "the little dark gentleman" she had met in July — sitting in a chair by the bed. "It struck me at once that [Anastasia] was inspecting his face with extraordinarily close attention," Frau von Rathlef observed. "She was breathing with difficulty on account of the excitement. But she pulled herself together and gave him her hand with her usual courtesy."

"Do you know who I am?" asked Pierre Gilliard.

"I know the face," said Anastasia, "but there is something strange about it, so I cannot say who it is. I must think first." Plainly uncomfortable, Gilliard inquired after Anastasia's health, made a few remarks about the beautiful Indian summer, and quickly left the room. Then, and only then, Anastasia turned to Ambassador Zahle and said, "It can only be my brother's tutor, Mister Gilliard. But I did not dare say so, because he seemed so strange to me."

The following morning it had come to her. When Gilliard sat down again at her bed Anastasia passed over the formalities and abruptly demanded, "What have you done with your beard? You had something on your chin before."

Gilliard replied that he had shaved his beard while in hiding from the Bolsheviks and had never grown it back.

There was nothing more to be said. Anastasia "seemed exhausted," Harriet von Rathlef explained, "and lay listlessly among the pillows. No real conversation could get underway." But Gilliard wanted more. "Please chat with me a little," he suddenly demanded. "Tell me everything you know about your past."

There was a moment of shocked silence before anger overruled Anastasia's surprise. "I do not know how to chat," she replied coldly. "I know of nothing I could chat with you about." Smiling, Gilliard wondered aloud at Anastasia's poor memory. Her eyes blazed: "Do you think that if someone had tried to kill you, as they did me, you would know much from before?"

Pierre Gilliard did not answer the question. The atmosphere in the sickroom was too ugly for words. For a moment Anastasia stared at Gilliard in total amazement. Then she asked if he knew when Shura was coming. Gilliard replied that he did not, rose, and left.

"On the afternoon of the same day," Frau von Rathlef recalled, "there was a knock at the door. A lady in a violet cloak came in, followed by the Danish ambassador. She went directly to the patient's bed and, smiling, offered her hand. We saw how the thin, pale face changed and flushed a glowing red. Her eyes, which were always tired and glazed, sparkled. She looked happy."

The lady was Nicholas II's sister, Grand Duchess Olga. The reports she had received from Ambassador Zahle, from old Volkov, and, plainly, from the Gilliards, had moved Olga to honor her promise: "If it really is she, please send me a wire and I will come to Berlin to meet you." The Grand Duchess sat down now at Anastasia's side.

"How is Grandmamma?" Anastasia asked at once. "How is her heart?"

Grandmamma was well, Olga replied — she used the word *babushka* [42] — and the two women began to talk, one in Russian, the other in German. "The conversation turned on nothing earthshaking," said Harriet von Rathlef. "The cat Kiki was admired, they talked about her illness." When Olga had left the room for a few minutes Ambassador Zahle asked, "Well, who is the lady?"

"Papa's sister, my Aunt Olga."

"Why didn't you address the Grand Duchess right away by name?"

"Why should I have done that? I was so happy I could say nothing."

Grand Duchess Olga stayed with Anastasia for the rest of the afternoon. As she left for supper Anastasia bent over her hand and kissed it, a gesture of humility no one who knew her had ever expected to witness. That night she was too excited for sleep. "I wanted to ask you," she said to Frau von Rathlef, "will everything be all right now? Do I never again need to be afraid of being put into the street? . . . Can I go now to Grandmamma? There are good doctors there, too, who could treat my arm. . . . You must get a basket for Kiki so I can take him with me."

"Don't think," said Frau von Rathlef. "Just go to sleep." She put out the lights.

Anastasia's voice came from across the room: "You must let your hair grow. Grandmamma will be annoyed that your hair is bobbed." She slept.

Olga was back at the clinic the next morning before nine o'clock. Anastasia welcomed her "with a radiant little face" and presently asked after her children. Olga began to talk about her two young sons, Tikhon and Guri, about "their first reading lessons, their characters, their games . . ." She brought out photographs.[43] And what about Anastasia's own child? Olga asked.

Anastasia blushed to the roots of her hair and made no answer. Olga changed the subject.

The morning passed swiftly by, the sickroom "filled with an atmosphere of happiness and hope." Again the conversation revolved around trivialities. "The invalid asked questions incessantly," Frau von Rathlef remembered, "could not be told enough, and laughed merrily with the Grand Duchess." Finally, following a luncheon at the Danish embassy, Olga returned to the clinic with Shura Gilliard.

"Shura herself was excited," wrote Frau von Rathlef. "She approached the bed and asked, smiling, in Russian, 'How are you?' "

Anastasia stared as though she could not believe her eyes. She extended her hand and answered in German that she felt better.

"Now," said Olga, "who is that, won't you introduce me?"

"Shura," Anastasia replied. ("We all heard it.")

Olga clapped her hands in delight: "*Verno! Verno!* But now we must speak Russian, because Shura understands no German."

Anastasia paid no attention. She motioned for Shura to sit: "She would not take her eyes off her. Then she grasped her bottle of eau de cologne and poured some of it into Shura's hand. She asked her to moisten her forehead."

Shura's mouth dropped open, and then "she laughed with tears in her eyes." Later that day she explained: "That was just like Grand Duchess Anastasia Nicolaievna, who was mad about perfume. In earlier days she used to cover her Shura with it so that she might be 'as fragrant as a bouquet of flowers.' "[44]

Soon Grand Duchess Olga called Harriet von Rathlef out onto the balcony. She pointed into the sickroom and said, "Our little one and Shura seem very happy to have found one another again."

Frau von Rathlef waited. Olga continued: "If I had any money, I would do everything for the little one, but I haven't any and must earn my own pocket money by painting."

What was the Grand Duchess trying to say? Finally it came out: "I am so happy that I came, and I did it even though Mamma did not want me to. She was so angry with me when I came. And then my sister [Grand Duchess Xenia] wired me from England saying that under no circumstances should I come to see the little one."[45]

This curious conversation went no farther. Frau von Rathlef returned with Olga to the sickroom to find Anastasia in a state of indignation: Shura had already been in Berlin for three days! Why had she not come before this? "She could not understand it," said Frau von Rathlef, "and she looked at us, all three, questioning."

"Do you know that I am married?" asked Shura in Russian.[46]

"Married?"

"Yes. Guess who to."

"I cannot imagine."

"I have married M. Gilliard."

"Oh, *pfui!*" Anastasia cried, rolling her eyes, and the room exploded in laughter. "It's just that I was surprised," Anastasia explained in embarrassment. "I would never have thought that Shura would get married, particularly not to Mister Gilliard." She thought a moment, shook her head and said again, "I cannot grasp it."

Later in the day Gilliard himself arrived at the clinic with Grand Duchess Olga's husband, Colonel Nicholas Kulikovsky. "The whole room was full of people," wrote Frau von Rathlef, "and a mood of happy excitement ruled, as never before in this room of suffering. . . . That day I had the impression that all doubt had vanished. . . . The invalid's joy was so obvious." Frau von Rathlef went into the hall to find Professor Rudnev. "I have the impression that this affair is drawing happily to a close," she said. Rudnev could only shake his head and repeat, "My God, my God." When Gilliard joined them in the hallway Frau von Rathlef saw that the sarcastic, openly skeptical mood he had earlier brought to bear in the sickroom had vanished completely. She was aware of what she was doing when she now quoted Gilliard verbatim: "*Mon Dieu, que c'est horrible! Qu'est devenue de la grande-duchesse Anastasie? C'est une ruine, une véritable ruine! Je veux faire tout, pour aider à la grande-duchesse* [My God, how awful! What has become of Grand Duchess Anastasia? She's a wreck, a complete wreck! I want to do everything I can to help the Grand Duchess]!" Then Gilliard, in Frau von Rathlef's presence, turned to Professor Rudnev and asked, "What is Her Imperial Highness's condition? Can she get well?"

"I thought it right to ask which Imperial Highness he meant," Rudnev said later.[47]

"Why, the patient whose room I have just been in."

"Ah," said Rudnev, "then you mean Frau Tschaikovsky." No, he could not guarantee that she would get well.

On the following day, October 30, 1925, the Gilliards and Grand Duchess Olga paid their last visits to Anastasia. "Although she did take part in the conversation," wrote Harriet von Rathlef, "she spoke very little, because she was suffering from a severe headache." Gilliard continued to ask her to talk about her past, and especially about her experiences in Siberia, but whenever he did so the conversation ground to an awkward halt: "She answered that she knew nothing. She did not know where she should begin, and on the whole did not know what she could tell him." Colonel Kulikovsky, in the meantime, remained at a distance in the corner with a grim look on his face. "He just sat there," Frau von Rathlef recalled, "wouldn't say a friendly word to the invalid, and you could plainly see what a bad mood he was in."[48] When she thought about it later, Frau von Rathlef would remember that everyone had seemed out of sorts that last morning — everyone but Anastasia: "She was happy, exceedingly happy."

The time came for Olga to leave, and Anastasia burst into tears. "Don't cry," Olga told her, kissing her on both cheeks. "I will write, and Frau von Rathlef will also write me often. You must get well, that is the main thing." The Grand Duchess's parting words to Ambassador Zahle were to become famous: "My reason cannot grasp it, but my heart tells me that the little one is Anastasia. And because I have been raised in a faith which teaches me to follow my heart before my reason, I must believe that she is."[49]

The Gilliards' departure was harder, more emotional, and oddly disquieting. Shura had begun to sob even before she left the sickroom. She wept all the way out the front door of the Mommsen Clinic and cried to Harriet von Rathlef, "I loved her so much, I loved her so much! Why do I love this patient just as much? Can you tell me that? If you knew how agonized I am now!"

Frau von Rathlef did not fail to observe Pierre Gilliard's uneasiness as he hastened his wife from the clinic. He paused only a moment to speak with Ambassador Zahle. "We are going away," he said, "without being able to say that she is *not* Grand Duchess Anastasia Nicolaievna."

For two months there were friendly letters in the mail. "How are things in Berlin?" Pierre Gilliard wrote Harriet von Rathlef on November 19, 1925. "Is she well behaved? Is she eating more to get back her strength, or does that horrible Kiki devour everything?" Then on December 30: "How is the invalid? Has she recovered enough of her strength to get out of bed? Do you find that her memory is stronger? And that her responses are clearer and more precise? My wife was very moved when she got the card you sent.

. . . It is true that the signature reminds one a lot of Grand Duchess Anastasia's signature when she was 13–14 years old. It would
be very important to know if the invalid has seen the Grand Duchess's signature on cards or in books." [50] Finally, there were five notes
from Grand Duchess Olga to Anastasia herself:

[Undated]

    I am sending you all my love, am thinking of you all the
time. It is so sad to go away knowing that you are ill and suffering and lonely. Don't be afraid. You are not alone now and
we shall not abandon you. Kind regards to Mrs. Ratcliffe [Frau
von Rathlef]. Eat a lot and drink cream.

October 31, 1925

    My thoughts are with you — I am remembering the times we
were together, when you stuffed me full of chocolates, tea and
cocoa. How is your health? You must be a good girl — must
eat a lot and do as Mrs. Ratcliffe says. Kind regards to Professor Rudnev. My children were glad to see us back — I hear that
the youngest was crying every evening because he had to go to
bed without his Papa and Mamma. He kept on hugging and
kissing me today. I hope you will soon be quite well. Am waiting for your letter.

Olga

November 4, 1925

    I am sending to my little patient my own silk shawl which is
very warm. I hope that you will wrap this shawl around your
shoulders and your arms and that it will keep you warm during
the cold of the winter. I bought this shawl in Japan before the
war. Have you received the postcard? I am waiting for your
news. Thinking of you all the time. Am sending my kindest
regards to the three inhabitants of No. 18. How is the white
"Kiki"? Kindest regards to Professor Rudnev.

Love from Olga

November 21, 1925

    It is a long time since we heard from Mrs. Ratcliffe. I heard
from Mr. Zahle that the poor arm is getting better. Thanks for
your greetings. My boys have lessons every morning, but before
their lessons we go for a walk, run about in the wood and look

for frozen pools, etc. Now it is warm again. I was very busy
with a Russian bazaar which was very successful. Yesterday
evening I went to a concert in the Danish church which was
arranged for the benefit of our church. I had only one letter
from Mme. Gilliard since their arrival. They are probably busy
with their own affairs. Kindest regards to both of you as well
as to "Kiki."

December 25, 1925

Very many thanks for the book. Am longing to see you. It
was so kind of you to think of my boys — they enjoyed the
story very much indeed. I was so glad to hear that your health
permits you to go to church. I had already packed one of my
"sweaters" for you which I wore myself and like very much,
but cannot make use of it now, as I am in mourning for my
aunt. So I hope you will not mind wearing it — please do —
you have to pull the thing over your head and then slip in your
arms. We shall still keep our Russian Christmas. In the meantime everyone is celebrating the Danish Christmas. Best wishes.
Kindest regards to Mrs. Ratcliffe. How is "Kiki"?

Olga [51]

Anastasia always treasured these few vague and affectionate notes
from her "Aunt Olga," just as she wore for years one of the presents Olga had sent her — "a beautiful rose-colored pure silk shawl,
six feet long and four wide." It has been pointed out that royalty,
at that time, was not in the habit of giving away its personal property to strangers. But there were no more letters after Christmas. In
January 1926 an article appeared in the *National Tidende* (Copenhagen):

We are able to state, with support from the most authoritative source,
that there are no common identifying marks between Grand Duchess Anastasia, daughter of Tsar Nicholas II, and the lady in Berlin known
under the name of Tschaikovsky, who claims to be the Grand Duchess.
All the rumors currently circulating in the German press are entirely
without foundation. . . .
  By way of a categorical denial, in order to settle the matter once and
for all, we can disclose that Grand Duchess Olga went to Berlin to
see Frau Tschaikovsky, but neither she, nor anyone else who knew Tsar
Nicholas's youngest daughter, was able to find the slightest resemblance
between Grand Duchess Anastasia and the person who calls herself
Frau Tschaikovsky. . . .

Frau Tschaikovsky leaves the impression of a poor highly strung invalid who believes in her story and is confirmed in the belief by the people around her. We hope that she can be freed from this *idée fixe* in the Berlin clinic where she is now being treated.[52]

At that Berlin clinic, with Anastasia, Harriet von Rathlef was left to ponder this unequivocal about-face. Lamely, she hinted at "dynastic considerations"[53] and other "perplexities and complications"[54] which she did not specify and could not fully comprehend. But Frau von Rathlef knew where the denial of Anastasia's identity had originated. She knew that Pierre Gilliard, weeks before he had even met Anastasia, had been in correspondence with the court at Darmstadt; that he had traveled to Darmstadt for conferences with the Grand Duke of Hesse immediately after his last visit to the Mommsen Clinic;[55] that the Grand Duke had also summoned Baroness Buxhoeveden to the court; and that the Grand Duke's right-hand man, Count Hardenberg, had been in touch with Anastasia's one-time "saviors" in the Berlin monarchist colony.[56] Frau von Rathlef knew that while he was still in Berlin Gilliard had embarked on his own quest for information among the émigrés, knew whom he had seen and what Captain von Schwabe, Baron von Kleist, and the rest were now saying about Anastasia. And she knew about the tension-ridden dinner at the Danish embassy before Grand Duchess Olga's departure, when Alice Schwabe had been called in person to tell Olga that Anastasia was "a Polish vagabond [*eine hergelaufene Polin*]" who had studied books and magazine articles about the Russian imperial family in order to better her performance as the daughter of the Tsar.[57]

"I believe this story is now cleared up," Gilliard had announced to Ambassador Zahle after Alice's recital.

"M. Gilliard," Zahle replied, barely able to disguise his contempt, "you have been much too active."

"I have the right to be active!" said Pierre Gilliard.[58]

Under the circumstances, Gilliard had the right to do anything he pleased. "It was I who persuaded Grand Duchess Olga to issue the denial which appeared in the Danish press . . . ," he admitted some months later, and indeed, Gilliard clung steadfastly to his new position as Witness Number One against Anastasia. He wrote articles against her. He solicited testimony against her. He even gave public lectures against her, and, in 1929, he condemned her finally as "a vulgar adventuress" and "a first-rate actress" in a full-length book,

The False Anastasia. By that time, of course, there was no going back. Gilliard's case rested on four points:

(1) that "the invalid of Berlin [did] not bear the slightest resemblance to Anastasia Nicolaievna — apart from the color of the eyes — neither in the features nor in the facial expressions";

(2) that she had failed to recognize various objects Gilliard had shown her — ikons and photographs from Tsarskoe Selo — and was, furthermore, "absolutely incapable of responding to [his] questions" when Gilliard submitted her to "a thorough interrogation" about the private life of the imperial family;

(3) that she had, however, "been put in touch with everything dealing with the imperial family: memoirs (Mme. Viroubova's book, [Gilliard's own] work, etc.), photographs, enquiries, documents of all sorts";

(4) that she could not speak Russian, English, or French and used only German, a language the Tsar's daughter did not know.

Such were Gilliard's allegations — unproven and, of course, unprovable.[59] That was the problem with a case like this: everyone viewed it from his own perspective. Just after he had taken up his investigation of Anastasia's identity, Ambassador Zahle had been approached by Princess Märtha of Sweden, a good friend who would one day become Crown Princess of Norway. Märtha wondered if Zahle might be able to arrange for her a meeting with the woman who claimed to be the daughter of the Tsar. Zahle explained that "Frau Tschaikovsky" rarely received visitors (and never if she suspected that they had come to test her). "I'll tell you what," he suggested. "She's in the habit of stepping out on the balcony to wave good-bye to me when I leave. Why don't you come along in the car?"

It took place exactly as the ambassador had said it would. His audience over, Zahle turned to wave from the courtyard. He had barely raised his arm before he heard a gasp from behind him: "But that isn't Tatiana; it's Anastasia!"

Zahle looked around: "Whatever made you think it was supposed to be Tatiana? It *is* supposed to be Anastasia."

"Well it *is* Anastasia," said Princess Märtha.

This episode — well known to the royal families of Europe — had taken place before Anastasia had passed through the worst of her illness in the summer of 1925: that is, before she was visited by the Gilliards and Grand Duchess Olga.[60] "You have no idea how wretched that woman looked!" Olga confided to her biographer many years later.[61] Small wonder: Anastasia weighed less than eighty pounds; she had no front teeth; she had just begun to recover from an illness that had nearly killed her, and she was still sedated with morphine. Olga and the Gilliards never even had the chance to see her out of bed, to judge her walk, her comportment, or even her height. "Anastasia, to her despair, is now very fat, as Maria was," Empress Alexandra had written from Tobolsk in the winter of 1917, "round and fat to the waist, with short legs. I do hope she will grow."[62] That was when Pierre Gilliard had last seen the Grand Duchess. Olga hadn't seen her since 1916, when they met for only one hour at Kiev.[63]

"Everything in the Gilliards' conduct showed that they plainly admitted the possibility of the invalid being Grand Duchess Anastasia Nicolaievna," an enraged Harriet von Rathlef wrote when she heard about Gilliard's change of attitude, "and when they left they did not dare affirm that she *was not* the Grand Duchess."[64] Frau von Rathlef was prepared to stand by this claim as tenaciously as Gilliard did by his. In the end, the quarrel degenerated into name-calling. There was the matter of the St. Nicholas ikon, for example, which Gilliard had shown to Anastasia at the Mommsen Clinic.[65] "The Empress had given it as a gift to my wife," Gilliard wrote, "in commemoration of an accident which had occurred aboard the *Standart* in the fjords of Finland on 29 August 1907. The Empress also gave each of her daughters an exact replica, which they always carried with them. . . . [We] drew Frau Tschaikovsky's attention to the date on the image; we asked her if she had ever seen it and if she knew what it was. We couldn't get anything from her."

"Of course that is an excuse," Frau von Rathlef replied, "and a poor excuse at that: this exact portrait of St. Nicholas had been hanging the whole time at the head of the invalid's bed. Nobody could expect that she would say anything in particular upon seeing the ikon that was so familiar to her."

No, said Pierre Gilliard: "Frau von Rathlef was playing with words. It was not the same image we had shown to Frau Tschaikovsky, but another image of St. Nicholas given to her by a Russian émigré. . . . If Frau Tschaikovsky were truly Anastasia, she would have let out a cry of surprise at the sight of this image which should have recalled so many memories."

"Would have," "should have" — so much fuss over an ikon! This tedious nitpicking did nothing whatever to resolve Anastasia's case, because her reactions could be interpreted either way at will. If she did not recognize a particular ikon, or a photograph, or a medallion commemorating the tercentenary of the Romanov dynasty and actually bearing the dates "1613–1913," neither did she pretend otherwise. She made no false statement to Pierre Gilliard. She did not answer him at all, a fact Gilliard grudgingly admitted later on: "She didn't speak. I asked her questions, of course, about the family. I asked her if she knew the ikons. She didn't answer. She was very apathetic at the time." [66] Nor was Gilliard's claim that Anastasia had drawn her information about life at the Russian court from books and magazine articles in any way enlightening: anything that could be traced to a source, Anastasia could have found there. Anything that could not, could be denied.

While Gilliard fought his duel of words with Harriet von Rathlef, another battle — far more important and really at the root of Anastasia's troubles — raged in the background. Ambassador Zahle, too, had come under Gilliard's fire. Gilliard depicted Zahle as a man "tricked by appearances," "finally compromised," and determined not to look like a fool. "Before our first visit to Berlin," wrote Gilliard, "[Zahle] had already stirred up the entire Danish court. . . . He threw himself body and soul into this adventure; he moved heaven and earth and found himself caught in an impasse. . . . The events of the last months have convinced me that M. Zahle has decided to prove that he is not mistaken. . . . In order to rescue M. Zahle, the invalid of Berlin must be Grand Duchess Anastasia." [67]

"Don't take Gilliard seriously," Zahle advised when he heard these charges. In later years Zahle characterized Gilliard as "a little man," and "the lickspittle of the Grand Duke of Hesse." [68] For the rest of his life he remained confident that Anastasia, one day or another, would win her recognition as the daughter of Nicholas II — so confident, in fact, that in 1935, on his retirement, Zahle brought his files on the case directly to King Christian X of Denmark. "I thought that, having been charged by Prince Waldemar to proceed with the inquest, I ought to give Your Majesty all the dossiers concerning the matter," Zahle wrote the King. [69] When Christian died twelve years later, the material became part of the Danish royal family's private archives, and there it still sits, untouched and unread by outsiders. All requests for the dossier's release have met with curt refusal. "It is a family matter," Queen Margrethe II has declared. [70] So it was, and an *embarrassing* family matter. One of the few of Zahle's memoranda to escape confiscation affirms that when Grand Duchess Olga came out of Anastasia's room on the first day of her visit to Berlin she had been "extremely excited." She declared on the spot: "I cannot say that it is she, but neither can I say that it is not she." [71] To the Danish foreign ministry Zahle wrote: "In October 1925 Grand Duchess Olga visited Frau v. T., and later on she declared that Frau v. T. was not identical with Grand Duchess Anastasia. But she by no means expressed this view to me immediately after her visit to the lady concerned, and after she had gone back to Denmark she never let an opinion on the matter come my way." [72]

That was not strictly true: Zahle had received one — but only one — communication from Olga. It was a letter written on the very day of her return to Denmark, when she had left Anastasia and begun to submit to a different kind of pressure.

Hvidøre
October 31, 1925

Dear Mr. Zahle,

I and my husband want to express to you and your wife our very warmest thanks for your hospitality.

I have had very long conversations with my mother and U[ncle] Waldemar all about our poor little friend. I can't tell you how fond I got of her — whoever she is. My feeling is that she is *not* the one she believes — but one can't *say she* is *not* as a fact — as there are still many strange and inexplicable facts not cleared up [*Olga's emphasis*]. How is she after our departure? I have sent her a postcard and shall write from time to time so that she may feel we are near her. Once more let me thank you both.

With best wishes to you, your wife, Britta and her governess, I remain yours most gratefully and affectionately,

Olga [73]

It is an open secret in the Romanov family that Grand Duchess Olga hesitated for months before finally committing herself to the denial of Anastasia's identity. Princess Xenia of Russia (a daughter of Grand Duke George Mikhailovitch and not to be confused with the Tsar's sister Xenia) remembered Olga's "anguished indecision" over the matter, [74] and Grand Duke Andrew Vladimirovitch, who would shortly embark on his own investigation of Anastasia's claim, wrote that as late as 1927 Olga still had not satisfied herself that Anastasia was a fraud. "I have been able to determine that Grand Duchess Olga Alexandrovna takes great interest in this affair," Andrew disclosed, "and that, despite the fact that she has been influenced to deal with the matter as though it were a complete fabrication, she still worries over it a good deal. Without doubt, Gilliard's theory has been imposed upon her, and this goes against the grain. . . . Although the Grand Duchess has given in to this influence and sends out letters to affirm that she does not believe in the sick woman, this does not correspond at all to her true feelings and she is suffering severely in spirit as a result." [75]

Ultimately Grand Duchess Olga blamed Ambassador Zahle for her very involvement in Anastasia's life. "All of it was *Zahle's* foolish behavior and his *lies* which brought this whole 'story' up," Olga wrote in self-defense.[76] In a letter to Colonel Anatoly Mordvinov, a former aide-de-camp to the Tsar and a great friend of her own, Olga revealed how deeply this case had upset her:

We tried very hard to get her to say something *new* — but she was just happy and spoke about trivialities. But whenever we would ask her something about the past, she fell silent and covered her eyes with her hand. There is *no resemblance,* and she is undoubtedly *not* A. — but there are many remarkable things here, and she herself is firmly convinced that she is. . . .

It was very difficult. I went away deeply saddened . . . one could say full of tenderness. . . . She cried and said that everybody was going to abandon her again. Curiously, she seems to understand Russian, but answers only in German — not a single Russian word. . . . The peculiarity of the feet is the same as with Anastasia, but it isn't rare and many people have it. . . .

She cried and said that everybody was deserting her. . . .

Well, enough about it. It's a sad story and I'm madly sorry for the misguided girl. . . . It's all obscure and confused. Mamma isn't interested and was against my trip, but I had to go in order to satisfy the relatives.[77]

That was the problem, of course — not Ambassador Zahle, not even "Mrs. Ratcliffe," but "Mamma," the Dowager Empress, who "isn't interested," who was "against my trip." Right to the end of her life Olga wanted it understood that she had gone to Berlin to meet Anastasia "very much against my mother's will and feelings." [78] And Major-General Alexander Spiridovitch, the former chief of the Tsar's secret police, saw a letter Olga had sent to her mother's secretary in Denmark immediately after her first visit to Anastasia: "Poor Mamma, how am I supposed to tell her? It will kill her." [79]

"Poor Mamma"? Poor Olga, who ran her errands, received her guests, arranged her appointments, and bore her never-ending criticism, lived entirely under her mother's thumb, and had done so all of her life. Olga was the Plain Jane of the Romanov family ("She looked like her own cook"),[80] an almost classic Ugly Duckling princess who had finally found happiness in the sincere love of a commoner. After fifteen years of marriage to Duke Peter of Oldenburg, a favorite of her mother's with whom Olga had nothing in common and who made her utterly miserable, Olga had persuaded her brother, the Tsar, to grant her an annulment and had married Colonel Nicholas Kulikovsky, an officer of the Dowager Empress's cuirassiers regiment with whom she had been in love for years. It was the only stab at independence in a long life of subservience and self-effacement, and it was, in the words of one relative, "awfully *mal vu.*"[81] "Within the structure of the imperial family," Princess Xenia of Russia explained, "there existed and still do exist very strict rules in regard to seniority, that is, the accommodation of the elder generation on the part of the younger."[82] Olga paid a heavy price for her happiness: in exile the Dowager Empress never let Olga forget that her second marriage was a disgrace. Colonel Kulikovsky, in fact, was rarely allowed in the Dowager Empress's presence. "My husband was wonderful," Olga said after her mother's death. "He never complained either to me or to anyone else."[83] But Kulikovsky was no innocent bystander in the matter of Anastasia. Perhaps for the first and only time he and his domineering mother-in-law shared the same goal: to take Olga's mind off this nonsense in Berlin. Kulikovsky could see that it was tearing Olga to pieces, that she was, in Pierre Gilliard's words, "*haunted* by the fear of committing an irreparable error."[84] Kulikovsky was the one who had accompanied Gilliard on his rounds in the Berlin monarchist colony. It was he who had insisted that Alice Schwabe be brought to see Olga at the Danish embassy, and he whose "bad mood" had struck Harriet von Rathlef at the Mommsen Clinic. "While we were in Berlin those 4 days," Olga wrote Irene of Prussia, "Mr. G. and my husband ran about seeing all the Russians with whom [Anastasia] had lived the years before and formed [*sic*] out many facts of great importance. . . . As you see, *one can trace many things to their source — if one cares to do so.* [*Olga's emphasis*]."[85]

In November 1925, just when the burden of Anastasia's future had fallen into Olga's hands, at the very moment, in fact, that a decision was expected, something happened to decide the matter for her: in England Queen Alexandra, the Dowager Empress's sister, died at the age of eighty. "The two sisters were like twins in everything except their age," wrote Olga's biographer, Ian Vorres. "The Queen's death dealt an irreparable blow to the old Empress. At first, it left her stunned. When she recovered from the first shock, she had the air of someone who had lost her way in the wilderness. Almost overnight, Maria gave in to the demands of her years. She became feeble. She lost all zest for life. She ceased going out, and Hvidøre held her a virtual prisoner for the remaining three years of her life." [86]

Would Anastasia have been likely to cheer the Dowager Empress and rally her flagging spirits? "How could we have had the heart to ask her here," Olga wondered in a letter to her friend Colonel Mordvinov, "only to send her away again? Where to? To whom?" [87] Returned from Berlin in the autumn of 1925, Olga faced a problem beyond her capacity to solve. There was no precedent in the House of Romanov to help her out of this extraordinary dilemma, and finally, as one of the Romanovs expressed it, "One was sacrificed to save the other." [88] Three years later Grand Duke Andrew had occasion to speak with Ambassador Zahle's wife, Lillan:

The most important matter which I would like to record is the attitude in Copenhagen toward the affair and the reason for the "cooling off." As [Mme. Zahle] explained it to me, her husband delivered two reports to the Empress. Despite the advice not to mention the tragedy of Ekaterinburg, he was unable to avoid this subject, because it was the invalid herself who had related in detail the stages of this drama. The conclusion to be drawn: the others had perished.

The Empress listened in silence to Zahle, did not comment on the matter, but declared dogmatically that the invalid could not be her granddaughter and dismissed him coldly. The second report produced the same result as the first, with the sole difference that the entire suite was annoyed with him because he had dared to shake the Empress's belief in the survival of the whole family. [89]

"Incredible," wrote Harriet von Rathlef, "that the existence of a human being can be decided only in accordance with *rank*." [90] But there it was. Frau von Rathlef wanted to spit when she saw the witnesses falling into line. Even Alexis Volkov, the old servant who had wept on leaving Anastasia's bedside the previous July, now gave an interview to the Russian monarchist newspapers denouncing her as an impostor. [91] Before Volkov's death in 1929 Professor Serge

Ostrogorsky, one of nearly forty physicians who had served at the Russian court, asked Volkov to tell him the truth. "On the one hand he denied her identity," Ostrogorsky reported; "on the other he told me that his interview with the invalid had moved him deeply, that he had been crying and had kissed her hand, which certainly he would never have done if someone other than Grand Duchess Anastasia had been standing before him." [92] Pressed to account for this contradiction, Volkov started crying again and told Ostrogorsky, "It is true, I believe that she is the Grand Duchess, but how can the Grand Duchess speak no Russian?"

So they were back to that. It was hopeless. "From the point of view of ordinary human feeling," a weary Harriet von Rathlef wrote, "I can offer no explanation for the unexpected failure of our hopes at that time." [93] Meantime a war had been declared. The ranks were split and they would never close again. Pierre Gilliard, who shortly began to introduce himself as "the Representative of the Grand Duke of Hesse," denounced Frau von Rathlef as "a fanatic, if not an hysteric, who is herself under the influence of an *idée fixe*." [94] Frau von Rathlef, a match for any glorified French tutor, saw Gilliard as nothing more than a rat, and said so: "M. Gilliard's role is blatant." [95] Alexis Volkov was crying and Grand Duchess Olga was frantic. Her cousin, Grand Duke Andrew, reported that Olga was "so distressed over this whole Anastasia matter that she has told him [Andrew] that she never wants to hear another word about it." [96] Caught in the middle, Ambassador Zahle was stuck with an investigation no one wanted him to bring to a conclusion.

Anastasia kept to her room. She was not told of these developments for many months, and thus did not know where "the Opposition" had crystallized: in Darmstadt, where the Grand Duke of Hesse had instructed his underlings to rid him of a potentially explosive embarrassment; in Copenhagen, where an old woman had gone deaf; and in Lausanne, where a witness had got lost in the scramble for cover. It was Shura. When a letter came for Frau von Rathlef from the Gilliards, Anastasia cried out: "Hurrah! Hurrah! I want to squeeze my Shura to death with joy! It is my Shura! I want to answer them right away, I must practice my writing." [97] And when Frau von Rathlef read the letter aloud to her in the original French, Anastasia understood it. Gilliard had asked for a sample of her handwriting. "Why does he think such bad things?" Anastasia asked. Lillan Zahle saved a letter Shura had sent her on December 14, 1925:

How is the invalid? My long silence might make you think that I have lost interest in her. That is definitely not the case. I think about her very often, and her tragic situation. For you and M. Zahle it must be a constant worry. Have they made a decision about her in Copenhagen? What are they going to do? Has anything new happened?

Tell her, I pray you, that not a day passes but I think of her and send her my most affectionate greetings.[98]

At the Mommsen Clinic Harriet von Rathlef thought back to the moment of Shura's first meeting with Anastasia, when they had barely managed to speak a word to each other; when Anastasia had grabbed her bottle of cologne and poured it into Shura's hand and Shura had "laughed with tears in her eyes." After Grand Duke Andrew had examined Anastasia's case from beginning to end he felt obliged to defend his cousin, Grand Duchess Olga, by saying that he did not think she had ever been "entirely convinced" of Anastasia's authenticity, but that Shura was: "She certainly did recognize Anastasia during the visits to the hospital, and [Andrew] cannot understand why she should not admit it now."[99]

Shura could not admit it now because she was Mme. Pierre Gilliard. When Gilliard launched his attack Shura stepped back into the shadows and let him do the talking, but that was as far as her submission went. She did not join Gilliard in his fight. "You can tell us what there is in this story better than anyone else in the world," Grand Duchess Olga had written. She wrote those words to Shura, not to Shura's husband.

"Do you know," said Anastasia to Harriet von Rathlef, "if they had asked Shura to let herself be shot, so that we might live, she would have done it. She was that loyal."[100] And she was. "I loved her so much," Shura had cried as she stumbled out of the Mommsen Clinic. "If you knew how agonized I am now!"

6

TANYA

*T*hings moved very quickly in the first months of 1926, after word had spread through the Russian monarchist colony that Grand Duchess Olga, the sister of the Tsar, had refused to acknowledge "the Unknown Woman of Berlin." When the time came for Harriet von Rathlef to answer the slander hurled against Anastasia now, she had no idea where to start. Should she begin with Constantine Savitch, the former president of the Court of Assizes in St. Petersburg? Why not: Savitch had told Frau von Rathlef of his "absolute faith" in Anastasia's identity and had suggested that he, as a legal expert, was well qualified to evaluate her material. Encouraged by Anastasia's surgeon, Professor Rudnev — whose great popularity and lighthearted style of life had led him into many a scrape before this — Frau von Rathlef gave Savitch a portion of her notes on the promise that they be returned within three days. "Only five weeks later did I get my notes back again," Frau von Rathlef lamented. "Every line which indicated that the invalid was no one else than Grand Duchess Anastasia had been crossed out." [1]

Within a few weeks Constantine Savitch had started giving lectures at Russian monarchist clubs in Berlin and Paris. As an expert on "the Spurious Anastasia" he enjoyed packed houses wherever he went and did not hesitate to affirm that he and he alone knew Anastasia's true identity. [2] Savitch (said Savitch) had had occasion to

125

examine the records of the Berlin police — nobody else, including
Ambassador Zahle, had been granted that privilege — and he began
to drop broad hints about a gangster from Riga who bore the sur-
name "Tschaikovsky-Arbatschevsky" and whose common-law wife
had disappeared some time previously.[3] Didn't Harriet von Rathlef
hail from Riga? Savitch asked. Couldn't that explain how she and
Anastasia had come into cahoots? What matter if the police in Riga
(on February 3, 1926) denied any connection between Anastasia
and their gangster's vanished mistress? Naturally there would be a
cover-up. Anastasia had "powerful backers." Her "schemes" were
well mapped out. But the Russian monarchists were not to be fooled
by Frau von Rathlef's sob stories. Anastasia was a fraud and an
adventuress, no more, no less.

Now, there were a number of variations on Anastasia's origins
and the precise nature of her schemes. In a manner of speaking, the
whole monarchist colony had hit the lecture circuit. Captain von
Schwabe went public with the "Polish vagabond" version, while
Markov II, the leader of the Supreme Monarchist Council, railed
from the podium about the "Bolshevik-Masonic-Jewish conspiracy"
to establish Anastasia on the Russian throne, murder her later, and
found a new dynasty through her bastard son — "the People's Tsar,"
"the Bolshevik Emperor." Unless, as Constantine Savitch stoutly
maintained, Anastasia had never had a son: pointing out with utmost seriousness that Anastasia had been admitted to the Dalldorf
Asylum as "Fräulein," not "Frau," "Unbekannt," Savitch concluded that the story of the child had been invented by Anastasia's
"backers" only in order to ensure that there would still be a claimant in the event of her demise (it was generally conceded among the
monarchists that she was seriously ill). And no one was able to
forget about the Pope: could it not be assumed that Anastasia was
an agent of the Papal curia and her claim a base attempt to polarize
the Orthodox Church in exile?

While dodging these fanciful tales, Harriet von Rathlef took note
of certain ill-disguised connections and vested interests. Markov II,
she observed, had shifted the Supreme Monarchist Council's allegiance from Grand Duke Kyril to the more popular Grand Duke
Nicholas in the ongoing race for the tsardom. Captain von Schwabe,
meanwhile, like so many of the monarchists, was playing both sides,
declaring himself a supporter of Nicholas but pledging five thousand marks a month toward the establishment of a monarchist army

that *Kyril* one day hoped to lead in holy war against the Bolsheviks. ("I told Schwabe very clearly what I thought about [Kyril]," Anastasia said, "and that I will never forget that he was the first to betray my father.")[4] Now Constantine Savitch had taken to calling himself "the Representative of the Head of the House of Romanov," which in monarchist circles could mean only one person: Kyril himself.

Probably the most pernicious story to make the rounds of the émigré colony at this time concerned Anastasia and her religion.[5] It continued to haunt her conscience (and to scandalize the émigrés) that she never went to church. Once, Harriet von Rathlef told her that it would be just as easy to bring an Orthodox priest to the Mommsen Clinic, but Anastasia vetoed the idea on the grounds that she owed the Church a greater display of humility. Finally, on the nineteenth of December, 1925, the Orthodox name day of Tsar Nicholas II, she had left her bed for the first time in months and had gone with Frau von Rathlef and several friends to the Russian church in the Nachodstrasse. She might as well have stayed at home. Markov II had attended the same service, and in his next lecture he stunned his audience by announcing that Anastasia had crossed herself like a Roman Catholic! (Roman Catholics make the sign of the cross from left to right; in the Orthodox Church it is done from right to left.) Nobody listened to Harriet von Rathlef when she protested that Anastasia had asked for six candles to be placed before the ikon of the Savior in memory of her family; that throughout the hour-long service she had crossed herself "*each time*" in the correct fashion; that she had asked Frau von Rathlef to give ten pfennigs apiece to the seven beggars who stood huddled outside the church; and that one of her new friends, the Russian émigré writer Leo Urvantzov, had said to her in Russian as they left, "It's very close in here."

"Yes," Anastasia had answered, also in Russian, "it is very close and hot."

"I have come to know the Grand Duchess very well," said Gertrude Spindler, a friend of Frau von Rathlef's who had also attended the church service that December, "and can testify that she has not departed a hair's breadth from her Orthodox creed, and that she knows that creed better than most people do."[6] But no one in monarchist circles wanted to hear it. The "tubercular Polish girl" had given herself away once and for all.

The furor over Anastasia did finally die down in Berlin. Markov II dropped the case when it became apparent that Anastasia was in no danger of winning it and devoted what remained of his life to a demented litany of the villainy of the Jews in world history.[7] Captain von Schwabe, whom Anastasia had once liked so much, died unnoticed several years later, while his accommodating wife, Alice, having enjoyed her moment on the stage, disappeared with her small daughter, Anastasia's godchild, leaving behind her nothing but a record of loose talk.[8] But Constantine Savitch — who also disappeared at the end of the twenties — was not content to let the matter rest.[9] In 1929 he, "the Representative of the Head of the House of Romanov," teamed up with Pierre Gilliard, "the Representative of the Grand Duke of Hesse," as coauthor of *The False Anastasia,* the vicious, vituperative book that was meant to put an end to Anastasia's "career" and simultaneously to annihilate Harriet von Rathlef, the woman Gilliard now described as Anastasia's "impresario."

What a lot of work must have gone into *The False Anastasia!* What misplaced concern over "a poor, highly strung invalid" with an *idée fixe.* But Gilliard and Savitch had only been carrying out the wishes of their masters, two of the most unlikely collaborators in the annals of royalty. Ernest Louis of Hesse and Kyril of Russia had both been married to the same woman — Grand Duchess Victoria Feodorovna, who had left the one to marry the other — and were, understandably, not on speaking terms. Anastasia, who succeeded in uniting them against all odds, eventually declared both of these princes to be "creatures."[10] About "Uncle Ernie" she was merely bitter, but Kyril continued to stir the fires of her contempt. "Grand Duke Kyril made himself Tsar," she complained to all and sundry. "When I told it to my father's sister while in Berlin, she just said it was nothing that concerned her. Can you believe it — his own sister!"[11] But here Anastasia allowed herself the luxury of humor: "They say that according to the old laws Kyril is the legitimate pretender. . . . But if they want to obey the old laws they should first try Kyril for high treason in time of war. . . . So if Kyril wants the old laws back he ought to begin by hanging himself."[12]

Anastasia had neither the energy nor the interest now to worry much about "the old laws." Baron "Willy" Osten-Sacken, the secretary at the Berlin Russian Refugee Office, saw her frequently during her last days at the Mommsen Clinic. He reported in February 1926:

She always says that she wants nothing more from life, only to get her health back and to earn her bread quietly. People should leave her in peace. She does not want and is not striving for recognition. Nobody could give her back her peace of mind, in any event; the mental anguish is so unbearable. Her family, by the way, she not only loves boundlessly but literally deifies, and nothing and no one could ever replace it. She wants under no circumstances to return to Russia, and then she doesn't understand either why it is necessary to establish her identity, which even her near relations are contesting. It is often very difficult to convince her not to throw in the sponge. The affair *must* be brought to a conclusion, not just in her interest, but in the interest of history.[13]

Baron Osten-Sacken and his superior, Serge Botkin, had entered Anastasia's life at a critical moment. As president of the Berlin Russian Refugee Office Botkin was the official spokesman for the émigré colony and the man responsible for the legal protection of every Russian exile in Germany.[14] It was Botkin's organization, by sanction of the Weimar government, which granted the refugees their priceless identity cards and enabled them, usually with great difficulty, to enter and leave the country. Beyond that, although technically unaffiliated with any political party, the Refugee Office functioned as a kind of nursery for the monarchists. Botkin was the firm but fair-minded nanny, who gave his attention to everyone's problems while striving all the while to contain those problems within the monarchist community itself. A cousin of Nicholas II's private physician, Dr. Eugene Botkin, Serge had enjoyed a distinguished career before the Revolution in the Imperial Russian diplomatic corps. "He belonged to that school of diplomats who never 'commit' themselves," his nephew Gleb Botkin remembered. "The words *yes* and *no* did not exist in his vocabulary. All he would say on any subject was 'maybe.' "[15]

Neither Serge Botkin nor his deputy, Baron Osten-Sacken, ever went so far as to proclaim openly his faith in Anastasia's identity. Harriet von Rathlef, throwing up her hands, attributed this reluctance to the fact that Botkin and Osten-Sacken were Russian and therefore could not make up their minds about anything, but the reality was rather more complicated. "Practically no one among the Russian refugees believes in her," wrote a man who spoke with Botkin about Anastasia, "but, as he says, it is because they do not know her." Explaining that his "official diplomatic influence might be unfavorably affected if it were known among the Russians that he favored her," Botkin fell back on a masterpiece of diplomatic ingenuity to justify his work on Anastasia's behalf. It was "equally inadmissible," he maintained, "that a stranger should pretend to be the Grand Duchess as it is that the Grand Duchess should find herself in this horrifying position, as a sort of outlaw." [16] And "outlaw" Anastasia had become. It did not require the intervention of Serge Botkin to demonstrate that the stirred-up Russian colony posed a real threat to Anastasia's safety. The flowers that arrived in great bunches at the Mommsen Clinic each day were carefully examined before being brought to her room, while anonymous gifts of food and candy were simply thrown away. "Believe me," Pierre Gilliard had written Harriet von Rathlef before he broke with her completely, "I am more afraid of certain Russian circles than you are." [17]

In March 1926, when her doctors declared that she was well enough to travel, Ambassador Zahle made reservations for Anastasia and Frau von Rathlef at the Hotel Tivoli in Lugano, the popular resort in the south of Switzerland, famous for its glorious sunshine, its panoramic mountain views, and its healthful air. There, Zahle hoped, Anastasia would be able to convalesce in peace. Through the agency of Serge Botkin and the unexpected intervention of the German foreign ministry — which cited "special reasons" — the Berlin Aliens Office now granted a temporary certificate of identity to "Anastasia Tschaikovsky." [18] A senior counselor at the Prussian Home Office remarked that "on the basis of police enquiries so far, the unknown woman is in all probability the same as the Tsar's daughter Anastasia," and with Grand Duchess Anastasia's personal particulars on her visa, she was allowed to enter Switzerland.

As the moment of her departure drew near, Anastasia grew steadily more anxious. She had no way of knowing if she would ever again see Berlin, a city she had come to love, and she spent many of her last days there walking in the woods and parks with Frau von Rathlef. At night she sometimes went out to Russian restaurants, where she would sit in the farthest booth from the door, the curtains drawn to shield her face from the gaze of her fellow diners. Here she would listen in silence, "with burning cheeks and brilliant eyes," to the Russian gypsy music that filled the room.[19] But if anyone made the mistake of drawing attention to her notoriety, she gave them cause to regret it. One morning "a prattling hairdresser" told Anastasia that she had read about her case in the newspapers. Frau von Rathlef wanted to strangle the woman: "The result was a frightful day! The invalid was furious with everyone around her, because they had done such a thing behind her back. . . . In order to calm her down, I read her a part of the article in the *Nachtausgabe*. The last sentence was something like this: 'In everything that she does she is quite a lady, a real princess.' " [20]

This remark struck Anastasia as so inherently ridiculous that she burst out laughing. When Baron Osten-Sacken told her that she ought to be pleased to receive such a fine compliment in the press, she laughed again and said, "Dear Baron, you must take that back; really, I am not always what I should be."

Anastasia's convalescence at Lugano began auspiciously. At the Hotel Tivoli Harriet von Rathlef held her to a strict regimen of balanced meals, long walks and boat rides, and sundry therapeutic occupations: sewing, painting, reading, and the like. "She's now reading English quite nicely," Frau von Rathlef reported to Berlin, "and practices an English dictation every day. . . . Moreover, I am speaking *only* Russian with her. I saw that lecturing and admonishing did no good, so I just went ahead with it. If I push her far enough she answers me in Russian, 'Ya ne mogu' ('I cannot'), or 'Ya ne hotschu' ('I won't'). . . . But the most amazing thing happened one day at table, when I had misunderstood something she had said. Laughing charmingly, she said, '*Dura!*' ('Ass!') . . . and I give you my word, she did not hear that one from me." [21]

Alas, Anastasia's good humor was short-lived. "Only during the first weeks of our sojourn at Lugano, while the novelty still charmed her, did she feel well and happy and content," Frau von Rathlef wrote. Anastasia complained that the mountains around the resort "hemmed her in." They depressed her, she said. [22] Of course, the real reason for her malaise was that she had not received any letters from the Romanovs in Copenhagen. "She forbade me to write to Gilliard," Frau von Rathlef recalled, "because she was so embittered that he no longer wrote to her, and above all she could not understand it of Shura." [23] Now Anastasia began to brood. She sat for hours doing nothing, saying nothing, and staring at her companion with a look that made Harriet von Rathlef nervous. "In June," Frau von Rathlef wrote Serge Botkin pointedly, "it will be a year that I have devoted my whole energy, time, and patience to this poor lady, a task which really her relatives ought to be doing — for it is just when they are in doubt of how to react that they ought to care for her and get to know her so as to reach a conclusion." [24] The idea was a good one, but help did not come. In Berlin, while the monarchists' attacks on Anastasia grew ever more violent, Ambassador Zahle realized that he could not count much longer on financial assistance from Prince Waldemar, the Dowager Empress's brother, and that Anastasia could not long remain at the Hotel Tivoli without it.[25] "Have just received a shattering letter from Osten-Sacken," Frau von Rathlef wrote. "He writes that everything is hopeless, there is no money, and the enemies triumph. . . . My God, what is to happen? Really, people are mad to take such a sin upon themselves."[26]

Ultimately Anastasia denied her friends the opportunity to reach anything but an emergency decision about her future. Not long before, Baron Osten-Sacken had praised her tact and her great desire "to avoid things that are hurtful and unpleasant."[27] But Osten-Sacken had never crossed her. He did not realize how swiftly and wholeheartedly Anastasia could turn against anyone who, in her mind, had let her down. For that matter, until June 1926, Harriet von Rathlef hadn't realized it either. Now, however, casting around for someone to blame for her troubles, Anastasia chose the only person in view. "Everything," she declared, "simply everything" she had suffered during the past year — up to and including bone tuberculosis — had been the fault of "the Rathlef woman." Anastasia had wanted to "get rid" of Frau von Rathlef for months, she said, but her "wishes had not been respected." When Frau von Rathlef asked her to explain herself, Anastasia answered without a blush that "she would do and say all this and more" to drive Frau von Rathlef from her life.[28]

"She's either crazy or truly wicked," Frau von Rathlef exclaimed after a solid week of rudeness and tomfoolery from her "poor lady." "I can't tell you all she's doing to make my life miserable." First, Anastasia had endeavored to win the staff at the Hotel Tivoli to her side, telling the maids that Frau von Rathlef had "refused to change her bandages and clean the wound on her elbow," and then asking that Frau von Rathlef be moved down the hall, because she could scarcely be expected to share a room with "her service." Frau von Rathlef was flabbergasted: "The other day she threw her stockings in my face and said, 'You are supposed to darn them! What have I got a serving girl for!? You Lett! . . . She told me that she had gotten to know the Letts well in Ekaterinburg and that they were all criminals (I, too, no doubt!). Her parents couldn't even leave a pair of scissors lying around without their stealing it. It might be funny to hear. . . . I'd be laughing too if I didn't have to put up with her rudeness every day. My patience is running out."[29]

Before long Harriet von Rathlef's patience did run out. "It can't go on any longer," she wrote Baron Osten-Sacken on June 9. Frau von Rathlef didn't care how she got home — "third class, fourth class" — so long as the Baron or the Danish ambassador sent her the money for the train ticket, and "*so schnell es geht* [as quickly as possible]."[30] When Osten-Sacken arrived at Lugano more than a week later he found Frau von Rathlef in despair and Anastasia in a state of indignation and nervous distress that surpassed anything he had seen in her before. "I hesitate to judge," Osten-Sacken concluded, "but I would think the two ladies have simply gotten on each other's nerves."[31] On June 19, worn out, Harriet von Rathlef returned to Berlin. Anastasia was not prepared to yield an inch and refused even to say good-bye to the woman who had helped her so much. "She categorically denies any improper behavior on her part," said Osten-Sacken, "but of course that isn't true. She has behaved outrageously."

Baron Osten-Sacken now had the strenuous task of persuading Anastasia to enter another hospital (she could hardly stay on at the Hotel Tivoli by herself). In Berlin, Ambassador Zahle and Serge Botkin had decided to send her to Dr. H. Saathof's Stillachhaus Sanatorium at Oberstdorf, in the Bavarian Alps. "Please go there at once," Zahle cabled Osten-Sacken on June 21. "Saathof is informed and money sent."[32]

"After your telegram came," Osten-Sacken wrote Zahle later, ". . . I had a very hard time of it. I had to deal with outbursts of rage against Frau von Rathlef, mistrust of us all, and a lot of tears." For hours Osten-Sacken tried to make Anastasia see reason, telling her how lovely Oberstdorf was and how well she would be cared for at the new sanatorium, but Anastasia said no, it was "an asylum": they were going to put her away in another asylum! Finally, after arguing with her "logically, step by step," Osten-Sacken was able to break the barrier, and, he said, "she admitted that she believed me, that I was right after all. She only asked me to tell her truthfully where I was taking her. After I had told her what Oberstdorf was and that there could be no questions about its being an asylum she said that she was ready to go. From that moment the spell was broken."

The battle was not quite won. Halfway to Oberstdorf, while they waited for a train connection, Anastasia suddenly declared that the doctors at the new sanatorium were not to be told anything about her true identity or her past: they were to treat her infected arm only and not pry into her personal life. When Osten-Sacken replied that this was an absurd request, that any doctor needed background knowledge of a patient's case, Anastasia answered, "Then you may take me to Berlin at once." She had no use for the Bavarian Alps, she said; she didn't like mountains in the first place.

The moment had come, Baron Osten-Sacken figured, to give Anastasia a taste of her own medicine. She could go back to Berlin anytime she pleased, he replied. She would go alone, however, because *he* was traveling on to Oberstdorf.

Without a word Anastasia followed the Baron onto the next train. "She was silent," Osten-Sacken reported, "and stared angrily out the window. I was silent, too, and resolved not to be the first one to speak. . . . After an hour or so she asked me something about the mountains. I answered her very curtly and she clearly noticed my displeasure." When they arrived at Oberstdorf in the pouring rain later that day, Anastasia was all smiles. "It's very pretty," she had to admit, "and much nicer than Lugano." The only thing that seemed to bother her now — to terrify her, in fact — was the knowledge that she would be left alone "with strangers and in the mountains." "People will come to visit me?" she asked.

Osten-Sacken replied that he hoped they would, "but in order not to disappoint her I made no commitments." As the Baron left, Anastasia pleaded with him to give her his telephone number in Berlin. It was a privilege, she promised, she would not abuse.[33]

The Stillachhaus Sanatorium at Oberstdorf was the sixth hospital Anastasia had entered since her suicide attempt in 1920. Set high in the Bavarian Alps, not far from the border with Austria, Oberstdorf in June is a lush, green paradise of hills and rolling meadows, dotted with farms and the chalets of the rich and commanding a spectacular view of the peaks and valleys of the Allgäu. Here Anastasia would remain through the autumn and winter into 1927, while the quarrel over her identity went on without her in distant cities.

"At her reception," wrote Dr. Theodor Eitel, who was assigned Anastasia's case at Oberstdorf, "and during the first days, the patient gave essentially the same impression as depicted in the reports of [Dr.] Bonhoeffer and Dr. Nobel."[34] No different was the final verdict, delivered after Anastasia had been treated at the sanatorium for eight months. "It is, in my opinion, quite unthinkable that Frau Tschaikovsky is an impostor," wrote Dr. Saathof, the director of Stillachhaus. "Even at crucial moments she has almost always behaved in the exact opposite way from what you might expect of an impostor, and not, certainly, out of calculation." The mystery of Anastasia's true identity interested Saathof very little, but he went on:

According to the impression that her character and her remarks made upon me, I regard it as utterly impossible that this woman has emerged from some lower circle of society. Her whole nature was so distinctive and, in spite of the narrow range of her intellect — which may be explained without further discussion by the enormous gaps in her memory — so thoroughly refined that one must, without knowing anything at all about her origins, recognize her as the offspring of an old, highly cultured and, in my opinion, extremely decadent family. . . .

As for Frau Tschaikovsky's actual extraction, I have stayed away from every "pro" and "con" in forming my judgment, especially since it seems to me nearly impossible that anyone, all things considered, will ever succeed in clarifying the matter. But since you do ask me directly, I can only submit my opinion as a sober and impartial observer, and I maintain that it is absolutely out of the question that this woman is deliberately playing the part of another, and [furthermore] that her behavior, when observed in its entirety, does not in any respect gainsay that she is the person she says she is.[35]

At Oberstdorf, Anastasia was looked after chiefly by "Sister Else," a nurse who later married Dr. Eitel, and by Agnes Wasserschleben, the matron, a solicitous and kindly woman who almost overnight replaced Harriet von Rathlef as a reservoir of comfort and good cheer. For the moment Anastasia had no complaints about her "service," although Dr. Saathof, much amused, recalled that the members of his staff had more than once been taken to task for what appeared to be lèse-majesté. Once Dr. Eitel, when a letter had come for Anastasia from Ambassador Zahle, allowed several hours to elapse before he brought it up to her room. "*What* was Dr. Eitel thinking of?" Anastasia demanded to know when she discovered that her letter had been left lying around the main office all morning.[36] "I don't know if you have ever heard anything about the proverbial 'ingratitude of the House of Habsburg,' " Dr. Saathof wrote, "but her behavior has reminded me frequently and in a striking way of a similar mental attitude, . . . which it might be appropriate to describe as an analogous 'ingratitude of the House of Romanov.' "[37]

Toward the end of 1926 Anastasia traveled to Munich with Agnes

Wasserschleben to see a dentist and finally have her front teeth replaced. The next few days were a revelation for her nurse, who hitherto had been "skeptical" about Anastasia's identity. During a tour of the Residenz, the winter palace of the kings of Bavaria, Anastasia suddenly stopped in front of a large green vase, saying, "*Das ick wusste, ist russisch Sack!*" (More or less: "That I knew was a Russian thing!"). As it turned out, the vase had been a gift from the Tsar. There was scarcely a room or an object in the palace that did not excite some comment from Anastasia, just as later that day she nearly caused a scene at a movie theatre by chattering loudly through a film called *The Tsar's Courier*. "She became very vivacious during these conversations," her nurse reported, "and could give most telling descriptions of people and their conditions, though it was always in such faulty German that much of what she found difficult to express in words could be understood only through her animated mimicry." It was odd, to say the least, to converse with someone who was so obviously well informed and yet who had such a hard time with words. Anastasia told her nurse, when the latter had read aloud to her from *Faust,* that she deeply regretted "the savage interruption of her education." "She spoke with deepest respect of 'Alter Fritz' [Frederick the Great]," Nurse Wasserschleben went on, "and rejoiced every time she saw his portrait in Munich: 'If my father had been more like this man with his fist, Russia would not be what it is today.' "

Talk of Russia, as indeed about almost anything in the past, continued to plunge Anastasia into the depths of melancholy. She said again and again that she would never understand why she alone had been left to survive "after *such* experiences . . . particularly since at home she had been surrounded only by the best and most select people and at the age of 15 had never even read about such things in books."[38] The failure of her relations to come to her aid, the staff at Oberstdorf found out, "pained her in her deepest soul."[39] In addition — "slowly" — Anastasia began to feel guilty about the abandonment of her child in Rumania and asked that something be done to find the boy. "She keeps on returning to this with much intensity," Baron Osten-Sacken reported, "which, frankly, set me thinking, and in spite of all doubts has to be taken as an argument in her favor."[40] When her nurse once asked her what she really wanted out of life, Anastasia replied that she would like to see her grandmother again — just once, even from a distance — and then retire to oblivion. She only wanted "*ein klein Wohnung mit ein russisch Samowar* [a little home with a Russian samovar]."[41] To Sister Else she expressed herself more gloomily: she just wanted to die. "Not to be shot again," she said, "or to commit suicide. No — just not to wake up one morning."[42] But while she professed to long for death Anastasia betrayed a deep-rooted horror of the process of dying. Dr. Eitel recalled one bizarre incident:

One evening at dinner the patient was sitting across from a man who swallowed a fishbone. He turned blue, started gasping, and nearly fell from his chair. At that moment the patient suddenly jumped up, ran out of the dining hall and into her room. She shut herself in and that night would not admit me or the nurse.

Next morning I succeeded in gaining admittance. . . . I told her that she needn't worry about the man; after an operation he was doing fine. She answered me immediately that it wasn't the man she had been thinking of, but rather herself. Observing the scene had awakened in her mind all the horrible events of the past, and an obsessive fear had gripped her. I have rarely seen anyone in such fear for her life as in this case. . . . When I saw her that morning she was still wearing her clothes from the night before. The bed had not been slept in.[43]

"I must not let my mind dwell on these things," said Anastasia, "or I shall become ill." Try as they might, the staff at Oberstdorf could not find a crack in her character. "It must be assumed," said Dr. Eitel at the end of his report, ". . . that the patient has actually experienced the things she describes. . . . Our observations . . . allow us to conclude that Frau Tschaikovsky is Her Highness the Grand Duchess Anastasia Nicolaievna."[44] As an unabashed champion of Anastasia's cause, Dr. Eitel left himself open to the same charges of bias and "wishful thinking" that were currently being leveled against Professor Serge Rudnev in Berlin. All the same, Eitel later regretted that his words had not been stronger in Anastasia's support.

Tatiana Botkin-Melnik was the only daughter of Dr. Eugene Sergeyevitch Botkin, Nicholas II's private physician.[45] In 1917 Tatiana and her younger brother, Gleb, had followed their father into exile at Tobolsk, where they lived with other members of the Tsar's retinue in a large house across the street from the imperial family's prison. After being separated from her father in the spring of 1918, Tatiana had married Constantine Melnik, a young officer of the Ukrainian Rifles whom she knew from Tsarskoe Selo, and had fled

Russia by way of Vladivostok, finally settling in France, at Rives, a town near Grenoble.

"My brother Gleb and I were not intimate friends of the imperial children," Tatiana Botkin recalled, "but we certainly knew them for many years. We first met them in 1911 in the Crimea. At that time my father had fallen ill on the imperial yacht, *Standart,* and we visited him on board every day for two weeks or more, playing each afternoon with the Emperor's children, and especially with Grand Duchess Anastasia." [46] It was during these days on the *Standart* that Tatiana, then thirteen and already growing into the elegant Russian beauty she became, first discovered the joys and the perils of friendship with the Tsar's youngest daughter. "Anastasia was a terrible tease," Tatiana remembered. She would sit demurely on the sofa, "seemingly up to nothing and with the most angelic look on her face," and then trip anybody who tried to walk by. At sundown, when the cannon were fired aboard the yacht, the young Grand Duchess dashed into a corner of the stateroom, plugged her ears with her fingers, stuck out her tongue, and made as if to die of fright. Grand Duchess Maria, rarely more than a few steps away, always endeavored to apologize for these scenes, but her sister paid no attention. "Anastasia Nicolaievna," Dr. Botkin exclaimed to her one day, "you are made of gold!"

"Not at all," the tiny Grand Duchess replied; "I am made of leather." [47]

"Only in the Crimea would we play with the Tsar's children," Tatiana Botkin continued, "although we always saw them in church or passing by our house." [48] During the war, Tatiana had chatted with the Grand Duchesses frequently at the magnificent Catherine Palace at Tsarskoe Selo, where she was a nurse and where the Tsar's daughters frequently came to visit the wounded or work for the Red Cross. "They had both inherited those extraordinary, luminous blue eyes of their father's," Tatiana remembered, "only their expressions were different. Maria's was soft, gentle, while in Anastasia's eyes you could see a healthy dose of mischief." [49] They were lovely girls, said Tatiana Botkin, innocent and delighted with the world as it was, and when she spoke with Grand Duchess Anastasia in February 1917 Tatiana never suspected it would be for the last time.

At Tobolsk, during the Siberian exile, it had been Empress Alexandra's express wish that Dr. Botkin's children take their French lessons with her own daughters, who were in danger of perishing with boredom in the governor's mansion. "I hope Tanya will come to see us often," the Empress had said to Dr. Botkin after Tatiana's arrival. Tatiana went on: "Gilliard was already developing schemes of literary lectures and contests when the Soldier's Committee [in charge of guarding the imperial family] declared that they would allow no such thing, and that if we needed lessons Gilliard could come to us." And so "Tanya" had not been able to speak with the Tsar's daughters during their captivity. Her window looked directly down on the courtyard where the Grand Duchesses took their walks, however, and from that spot she continued to watch and wave at them every day. "Their Highnesses undoubtedly had a very dull time of it," Tatiana wrote. "Often they could be seen sitting on the windowsills of the reception room for an hour or two at a time, looking out at the deserted streets of Tobolsk." [50] Then came the night when the Tsar, the Empress, Dr. Botkin, and Grand Duchess Maria were taken away to Ekaterinburg; the removal of the Tsarevitch and his three other sisters several weeks later; the long months of silence; and, finally, the ghastly conclusions of the Sokolov investigation — conclusions Tatiana Botkin, to the end of her life, defended and held to be true on every count but one. It was her consolation to know that her father's last gesture had been an attempt to shield the Tsar from the Bolshevik gunfire.

It was not Tatiana's uncle, Serge Botkin, who in 1926 encouraged her to travel to Oberstdorf for a meeting with Anastasia. While recuperating from a kidney operation that August, Tatiana had met up with Zinaida Tolstoy, who, she discovered, was suffering from severe guilt feelings. [51] Although always inclined to equivocate on the subject, Mme. Tolstoy still knew that the Russian monarchists had been gravely misinformed about virtually everything concerning Anastasia; if Tatiana would only consent to see her, said Mme. Tolstoy, perhaps the affair could, after all, be brought to a close.

"I saw it as my duty either way," Dr. Botkin's daughter reflected, "to recognize the Grand Duchess or to expose the fraud." [52] So she wrote her "Uncle Seryosha" in Berlin and asked him how she ought to go about it. At the Refugee Office Serge Botkin sent Baron Osten-Sacken to Munich, where he met Tatiana in the company of her aunt, Maria Debagory. The trio arrived at Oberstdorf on August 27. "Mme. Melnik's trip was carried out in absolute secrecy," Osten-Sacken reported to Ambassador Zahle. "No one at Oberstdorf knew who the two ladies were. This was especially ensured so that there would not be the slightest suspicion that the invalid knew who was coming to see her." [53] The unexpected arrival of

Baron Osten-Sacken and "two strange ladies," however, meant only one thing to Anastasia: bad news. "Who are they?" she asked sharply. "What are their names?"

Osten-Sacken replied that he was sure Anastasia could answer that question for herself: "I said only that the father of the younger of the two ladies had been close to the imperial family."

"So were many," Anastasia snapped. "And if I do not want to see them? Tell me their names."

Osten-Sacken stood firm. Both of the ladies were "very nice," he assured Anastasia, and she would not regret making their acquaintance.

"All the same," said Anastasia, "I do not want to." Then she sighed in exasperation: "Well, I will do what I can, but not until tomorrow."[54]

That evening at dinner Tatiana Botkin caught her first glimpse of Anastasia: "It was difficult for me to see her, because her face was hidden by the other diners. When dinner was over she walked into the small salon, her head down, sat in an armchair next to the manageress, said a few words to her, got up again, extended her hand, and left. It was at that moment that I was struck by her resemblance to the Tsar's two eldest daughters. . . . The way she turned her head, the movement of her body when she got up to leave, the gesture she used when she offered her hand, her bearing, her walk, were the same as the Grand Duchesses'."

Tatiana had not recognized Anastasia as the daughter of the Tsar. "I had known Anastasia when she was an adolescent," she explained, "lively, rough, mischievous, a real tomboy. . . . I found myself now before a wraithlike young woman, sickly, very sad, much more mature and much more feminine."

After lunch on the following day Anastasia asked Baron Osten-Sacken to get the visitors ready: they were all going for a walk. Everyone rushed into place. As they climbed the hill that led away from the sanatorium Anastasia and Tatiana lagged behind the others. "Because the 'pseudo-Grand Duchess' did not speak Russian," Tatiana wrote, "I began to speak to her in my own defective German. I told her amusing stories of the kind that used to make her laugh so much before." Anastasia kept her handkerchief pressed to her mouth and, for the moment, said nothing. Tatiana went on: "When Anastasia Nicolaievna laughed, she would never turn her head to look at you. She would glance at you from the corner of her eye with a roguish look on her face."[55] Now, suddenly, one of

Tatiana's stories hit home: "It was exactly the same, the same as before. . . . I thought I was going to suffocate." [56]

That evening Baron Osten-Sacken spoke with Tatiana Botkin in her room. "Tell me," he began, "in your opinion, who is the female patient now living in Room 22 at the sanatorium?"

"It is Grand Duchess Anastasia Nicolaievna."

"Why do you claim that . . . ?"

"I am quite convinced and do not doubt it."

"I am asking for a precise answer."

"It is Grand Duchess Anastasia Nicolaievna. I have recognized her. It is the same person I knew before. Only the lower part of the face, the mouth, has changed. Otherwise nothing."

"Then you have actually recognized the Tsar's daughter Anastasia in the invalid who calls herself Frau Tschaikovsky?"

"Yes, I recognize her. I am not relying on arguments."

The next morning Baron Osten-Sacken found Anastasia rather less sure of herself. "She hadn't slept the whole night," the Baron wrote. "She had tried so hard to remember the name of the younger of the two ladies. She remembered her without being able to find the name, and she asked me if perhaps Herr Botkin — 'Mister Botkin,' she said — had sent the lady."

No, Osten-Sacken replied, Botkin lived in Berlin and the young lady had come from France.

"Yes," Anastasia countered, "but Mister Botkin was in Paris."

No, Osten-Sacken said again, they had not seen each other there.

"But the young lady's father was with my Papa." Anastasia covered her eyes with her hand. "You know," she said at last, "I did not mention the name Botkin to no purpose. You can tell me now who she is."

Osten-Sacken confessed that the lady was Tatiana Botkin, and Anastasia nodded. "Yes, that is what I thought." [57]

Three years later Tatiana herself described the meeting at Oberstdorf:

When I first saw her face close up, and especially her eyes, so blue and so full of light, I immediately recognized Grand Duchess Anastasia Nicolaievna. And when we were strolling along together, on this first walk at Oberstdorf, which lasted barely ten minutes, I noticed more and more the resemblance to what she had been before all the tragedies and all the experiences.

The height, the form, the color of the hair are exactly hers. In her face I discovered signs from before; the mouth has changed and coarsened noticeably, and because of the face's leanness the nose appears to be larger than it was. But the eyes, the eyebrows, and the ears are fully the same. Her unforgettable eyes and the look in them have remained exactly the same as in the days of her youth.

Three hours later we went to tea in her room. She came out onto the balcony in great agitation, couldn't speak a word, but urged us to sit down and then began to pour tea, although her hands were shaking violently. The conversation turned on some local festival or other, and she brought out several picture postcards of the region. Then I said: "I also have photographs," and laid a big gray album in her lap, on the cover of which was a small photograph of the military hospital of the Grand Duchesses Maria and Anastasia. She noticed this photograph at once and opened the album, but when she saw her own picture and those of the Grand Duchesses she immediately slammed the cover shut, saying, "This I must see alone." With that she went into her room. Baron Osten-Sacken advised me to go after her: the invalid sat on the chaise longue; the album lay before her; she was carefully contemplating a picture of Grand Duchess Tatiana and saying, "*Ihr Gesicht, ihr Gesicht* [Her face, her face]!" You could see that she was extremely moved; her eyes were brimming with tears. . . . In bad German she asked, pointing at the album: "You knew her before?"

"Yes," I said.

"And me too?"

"Yes."

"When did you last see me?"

"In 1918." She shook her head as though she could not remember. "You don't know me?" I asked.

"No, not sleep and just think, not sleep and just think. . . ." I took this to mean that she thought so much she couldn't sleep. I told her that I had recognized her; that I had not come to ask her questions but only to be with her; and that I had photographs of her family.

"Where?"

"Here in my room." She asked to be allowed to look at the pictures. Anyone who had seen her bent over those photographs, trembling and crying, "My mother! My mother!" would not have been able to doubt any longer. . . .

"Where are the bodies?" she asked me several times. "Do you have nothing left from there?"

"Nothing but you, my *Malenkaya.*"

"*Malenkaya,*" she repeated in Russian. "My father called me that."

After dinner I went up to her room. She was lying on the unlit balcony; but when I arrived she turned on the lights and came in. Through her tears, her eyes were shining with joy. Coming up to me, she laid her head trustingly on my shoulder and stayed like that for a long time.

Then she sat down, but still said nothing and gazed off somewhere in the distance, as though she could see something beyond the walls of the room. I felt she was capable of sitting like that the whole night, and decided to put her to bed.

"I will undress you as my father undressed you when you were ill."

"Yes," she answered, "measles," and I understood that she had become fully aware of who I was. Because on one occasion when the imperial children had measles, and only once then, it happened that my father tended the Grand Duchesses alone and performed nurses' duties for them. This fact has never been published anywhere, and apart from my father I alone knew anything about it.[58]

The news of Tatiana Botkin's recognition of Anastasia spread like lightning to Berlin. "You can imagine, I think, how very impressed we were by the fact that Mme. Melnik has recognized the Grand Duchess," Lillan Zahle wrote. "For more than a year we've been fighting for her, even against her own family!"[59] At the Russian Refugee Office the usually unflappable Serge Botkin confessed in great excitement: "Now that Mme. [Melnik] has formally declared to have recognized [Grand Duchess Anastasia] in the invalid, I do not see how the family and Mr. G[illiard] can continue to deny that there is any resemblance, and I am convinced that the whole affair is going to have to take a different course now."[60] At Oberstdorf, meanwhile, during the fortnight of Tatiana's stay, Anastasia remained in a kind of heaven. "She was radiant," Baron Osten-Sacken reported. "She started beaming whenever she saw Mme. Melnik approaching from the distance, wanted to have her continually at her side, never wanted to part with her, and was *tender* in a way I have never seen her be before. She even brought herself to tell me that she was so happy I had brought 'Tanya' with me, I had been right, the ladies were very nice, and she was so happy."[61] Tatiana went on:

I spoke of my eldest brother [Dmitri Botkin], and I told her that he had fallen in the war with the Germans. "Yes," she said, "I know, my father told us." I knew from my father that the Tsar had informed his children of my brother's heroic death. . . .

Generally, conversation with her is difficult. She is interested only in political questions, in memories of the imperial family and in life at the remaining courts. Apart from that, she loves to hear droll stories, which you must deliver with as much humor as possible. The moment you mention something serious, which does not fit into the three categories mentioned above, she stops listening and stares worriedly ahead. She can discuss political and family questions totally reasonably, and at the same time tell me of her charming, if not very practical, idea to send me a Christmas tree nailed into a crate at Christmastime.

She plays patience, and although she says she played it a good deal in the last days in Siberia, she can't manage to distinguish the eights from the tens.

The defect obviously lies in her memory and in eye trouble. She says that after her illness she had forgotten how to tell the time, so that she had to relearn it laboriously. She still has to practice doing it every day. She adds that without constant practice she forgets nearly everything. Each time she has to force herself to get dressed, to wash, to sew, so that she won't forget how.[62]

Tatiana Botkin's sojourn at Oberstdorf was, to Anastasia's way of thinking, all too brief. "Do not leave me alone again!" she pleaded with Baron Osten-Sacken when the time came for "Tanya" to go home.[63] But Anastasia need not have worried about being abandoned. "I am ready to write to anyone I have to," Tatiana declared, "to entreat, to swear, and to demand."[64] Two letters had already gone out from Oberstdorf — one to Grand Duchess Olga and the other to Pierre Gilliard, who waited more than six weeks before answering. He had nothing to tell Tatiana that he had not said before: "Neither Grand Duchess Olga, my wife, nor I could find the slightest resemblance between the invalid and Anastasia Nicolaievna."[65] Tatiana had had no greater success with Olga herself:

> Dear Tatiana Evgenievna,
>
> I have received your letter and hasten to reply. We took the matter very seriously, as is shown by the visits to the patient paid by old Volkov, twice by Mr. Gilliard and his wife . . . , as well as by my husband and myself.
>
> However hard we tried to recognize this patient as my niece Tatiana or Anastasia, we all came away quite convinced of the reverse.
>
> With every good wish,
>
> Olga[66]

Tatiana did not need to read between the lines of this letter, which she described as "imprudently put together,"[67] to realize that a decision about Anastasia's future could not be left to rest with Grand Duchess Olga. Returned to France, she arranged a meeting with Grand Duke Nicholas Nicolaievitch, the great hope of the more liberal Russian monarchists, and asked for his help. The Grand Duke, as Tatiana remembered, was "frightfully kind, attentive, and obviously upset," but to Tatiana's frustration and bewilderment he refused to intervene. "The Dowager Empress believes that she is going to see her son and his family alive again," said Nicholas Nicolaievitch. "A shock like this could kill her." With that thought the Grand Duke escorted Tatiana into a small salon and introduced her to his wife, the senior Grand Duchess Anastasia Nicolaievna, who had been godmother to the Tsar's daughter and who wept on hearing what Tatiana had to report.[68]

Indeed, Tatiana Botkin recalled, the Russian émigrés "all were profoundly moved by my tale," until — "as soon as I was gone" — they did their level best to forget about it, "as if to divest themselves of all responsibility."[69] Serge Botkin had advised Tatiana to go to Paris and to wait there until the leaders of the monarchist community came to her of their own volition. Tatiana complied, but she was bound to tell her uncle afterward: "Nobody tried to arrange a meeting with me; on the contrary, they all tried to avoid it. They were all so wrapped up in their petty affairs and so determined not to be bothered; the subject was most unwelcome." Disgusted, Tatiana finally went home to Rives. "No one," she remembered, "not even those people who were most convinced, dared to rise up against the Romanovs."[70] Now the assassination of her own character began. In the autumn of 1926 Dr. Botkin's daughter, until recently one of the leading lights of the Russian emigration — a woman Inspector Nicholas Sokolov himself had cited as especially reliable — suddenly found herself an outcast in the monarchist community.[71] Said Tatiana: "The Russian émigré monarchist party let me know that if I did not cease working for Anastasia I would be expelled from its ranks."[72] It was bad enough that Tatiana had acknowledged "that woman," but must she keep on *talking* about it? Her own uncle, Peter Botkin, who had once been Russian ambassador to Lisbon and who now enjoyed the favor and patronage of Grand Duke Kyril, declared that Tatiana had "made a fool of herself" and "done a great deal of harm" to the monarchist cause.[73] Tatiana never ceased to hear about "the powerful, secret organization" that was plotting to put Anastasia on the Russian throne and, through her son, seal the Bolsheviks' hold on Russia. Now Tatiana had the pleasure of hearing her uncle Peter declare, "Even if she *is* Anastasia, this affair must be defeated in the interest of the Russian monarchy."[74]

Such were the noble concerns of the Russian monarchists. When Tatiana tried to talk about Anastasia's case with General Krasnov, the hero of the Russian Civil War and author of the marvelous adventure *From Double Eagle to Red Flag,* she was presented with a less neurotic but equally heartless excuse. "I reject her for purely selfish reasons," General Krasnov declared. "It is too difficult for me to admit my Emperor's daughter could be in her condition."[75] And that, in Tatiana Botkin's opinion, said it all.

One member of the Romanov family was courageous enough to rock the boat. At Villa Alam, his home near Cap d'Ail in the French Maritime Alps, Grand Duke Andrew Vladimirovitch, a brother of Grand Duke Kyril, found himself thinking about Anastasia's affairs and wondering what he could do to protect his family from further embarrassment. "Incredulous inquiries have reached me, too," Andrew wrote, "about how the imperial family can behave so indifferently in this matter! It has even been suggested to me that if such a case had arisen in an ordinary family everything would have been turned upside down just to find out what was going on, but in this case everyone simply shows fierce disapproval."[76] One afternoon, suddenly, Andrew called on Tatiana Botkin while she was in Nice and asked her to go over her story again from the beginning. "I have not seen my niece since her visit to the invalid," Serge Botkin wrote Andrew later, "so I only know of her impressions from her letter; despite her relatively tender years she is a very mature and positive person, boundlessly devoted to the imperial family. I certainly cannot doubt her assertions, as they agree with all the available information."[77]

Grand Duke Andrew was a first cousin of the Tsar, a tall, handsome, and, in his day, fun-loving graduate of the Military Law Academy in St. Petersburg. Having escaped Russia under especially haphazard circumstances — the Grand Duke owed his life to a Bolshevik commissar who chose to remember a former kindness — Andrew, in 1921, had married the brilliant Mathilde Kschessinska, the *prima ballerina assoluta* of the Imperial Ballet. (Kschessinska had been the mistress of Nicholas II before his marriage to Alix of Hesse.)[78] As an active aide-de-camp to the Tsar during the war, moreover, Andrew had been brought in close touch with Nicholas and Alexandra's children and had seen them at a later date than many others in the family.[79] But as yet the Grand Duke had no wish to arrange a meeting with Anastasia. Andrew felt that he could be of more service to his family and to history if, as a trained jurist, he undertook an objective, neutral examination of her claim. He wrote Serge Botkin:

Rumors reaching me indicated that Grand Duchess Olga Alexandrovna and the Empress Maria Feodorovna maintained a negative attitude toward the matter and that any attempt to clarify the situation would meet with disapproval in that quarter. Under these circumstances, I considered it essential to write a sincere letter to Grand Duchess Olga Alexandrovna, and to tell her my opinion on the subject by drawing attention to the defects of the inquiry and to the undeniable need for documentation in order to clarify the problem in one way or the other. . . . Furthermore, I would ask the permission of the Empress . . . to take the investigation into my own hands and carry it through to its conclusion, and if the question were to be resolved the last responsibility would rest with the Empress to instruct us all whether or not to recognize the invalid as Grand Duchess Anastasia Nicolaievna. I repeat that I believe nobody has the right until that moment to take sides dogmatically.[80]

Grand Duchess Olga's reply to her cousin Andrew pleased him "very much." "All of us who were in Berlin in those days," Olga wrote, "could find no resemblance to Anastasia apart from the similarity of the feet." Before granting Andrew the permission to investigate the affair, however, Olga added frankly: "You think I may be wrong. Such mistakes can of course happen. One way or the other it is ghastly."[81]

One way or the other it was. "It is not necessary for me to emphasize that this affair is very complex and delicate," Andrew wrote, "hence the entire investigation must be conducted in an strictly discreet way."[82] Andrew's investigation was going to last him well into the 1930s, but it should come as no surprise to learn that his archives on the case, like Ambassador Zahle's, have been suppressed: the results of Andrew's investigation are now in the hands of his nephew, "Grand Duke" Vladimir Kyrilovitch, the current pretender to the Russian throne. All that remains is Andrew's tantalizing correspondence with Serge Botkin and his niece Tatiana, and, here and there, a cautious disclosure.[83] "I must confess that this affair fascinates me more and more," said Andrew, "in that it inspires such violent passions on the part of the opposition. My own personal opinion is that they are afraid I might uncover what they are intentionally suppressing and develop frenzied activity to frustrate the inquiry at the outset. Perhaps this thought will lead you to the clue which I do not think it advisable to express in writing."[84] Before his death in 1956 Andrew actually declared that his dossier on the "Anastasia" affair should not be opened to the public until the Kremlin, the estate of Kaiser Wilhelm, and the German War Office released their papers.[85] "There is no doubt," Andrew wrote, "that there exists a vital basic relationship between the tragic events of March 1917 and the present circumstances. . . . I am absolutely convinced that this investigation will lead us steadily back to Ekaterinburg, Tobolsk, the events of 1917 and even further."[86] Andrew was not deterred by a letter from Empress Alexandra's brother in Darmstadt, the Grand Duke of Hesse, warning him that the investigation could be "dangerous."[87] Anastasia's friends soon thanked heaven for his determination, because at the beginning of 1927 Darmstadt attacked in earnest and they had a crisis on their hands. "Evidently a scandal will be unavoidable," Andrew wrote Tatiana Botkin. "Certain people have mingled their bad intentions in the case. . . . Let them suffer the consequences."[88]

7

"WHAT HAVE I DONE?"

*T*he tide began to turn when Harriet von Rathlef decided to publish her notes. It was plain to Frau von Rathlef that nothing had been gained by silence, and a book about Anastasia's case had two things to recommend it: by drawing attention to Anastasia's plight, first of all, it could force a resolution of the controversy and, second, it could raise money for her support. Frau von Rathlef was pleased with her idea, and she meant to go ahead with it.

Her plan provoked a loud squawk from Anastasia's other friends in Berlin. "As you well know," Baron Osten-Sacken wrote Frau von Rathlef at Serge Botkin's request, "I consider the appearance of your book to be extremely detrimental to the invalid's case."[1] Any publicity on the matter, Osten-Sacken feared, would lead inevitably to a scandal and, very likely, "nip in the bud any further communication with those people who are now hesitating." Why was Frau von Rathlef not satisfied to leave the investigation in the hands of Grand Duke Andrew? Osten-Sacken wondered: "You will admit that now that the affair has reached this stage and been taken up by a member of the Imperial House we must all put ourselves solely at his disposal. . . . We must not work independently."

Frau von Rathlef reacted angrily to this admonishment. "The Imperial House," in her opinion, had had its chance to help Anastasia and had lost it. Something about Osten-Sacken's attitude irritated

Frau von Rathlef in the extreme: "For four years the Russian émigrés — and you in particular — knew about the little one's existence. Nevertheless, in those four years the affair did not move forward. When I first took the little one in, not a single one of the émigrés was there to help. . . . From the very beginning I have had to carry the responsibility alone, and I will continue to act with full responsibility." [2]

Not even a letter from Ambassador Zahle could change Frau von Rathlef's mind about publication. "Naturally," Zahle wrote, "I can't have anything to do with a book like this." He asked Frau von Rathlef to consider Anastasia's own reaction to it: "Sooner or later she is going to find out that this book has been written about her. . . . You have also got to assume that Gilliard, at the same moment, will try to publish a rebuttal. A press campaign or something like it between you and M. Gilliard must naturally be avoided if possible." [3] But Frau von Rathlef — more offended, perhaps, than she liked to admit — was determined to see the project through. In November 1926 she sold her manuscript to the Scherl-Verlag, an organ of the powerful right-wing Hugenberg Press. [4] Frau von Rathlef had been especially careful not to deal with any left-leaning or even centrist publishing firms, knowing the kind of ammunition that would have given the Russian monarchists, and she hoped that the editors at Scherl would treat Anastasia's story with the restraint and the dignity it deserved. To Frau von Rathlef's horror, however, serialized publication of her book was now scheduled for February 1927 in the *Berliner Nachtausgabe,* a mass-circulation evening tabloid with a reputation for political provocation and rabble-rousing. [5] She could not have chosen a more unsuitable forum.

"The consequences of your decision," Ambassador Zahle wrote Frau von Rathlef, "will not be without significance to the future course of this whole story." [6] Zahle, of all Anastasia's friends, had the most to lose from publicity. Although he always insisted that he had conducted his investigation of her identity "as a private citizen," Zahle was, all the same, a public figure, the representative in Germany of a European power, and his involvement with Anastasia amounted in effect to protection. Initially Zahle had interpreted Grand Duchess Olga's permission for Grand Duke Andrew to investigate Anastasia's case as a sign of renewed benevolence, but he was much mistaken: in Denmark Olga's uncle, Prince Waldemar, had nothing but bad news to report. "Unhappily," Andrew wrote in this regard, "there is a veritable *hatred* of the invalid in Copenhagen" — that is, among the Russian entourage of the Dowager Empress — "and they simply will not budge."[7] Although the Danish royal family, by contrast, "adheres to Zahle heart and soul,"[8] Zahle still had plenty to worry about. Somebody had to keep paying Anastasia's hospital bills, to begin with, and Prince Waldemar, who had so far obliged, was himself under pressure from the family. "It is clear to me," wrote Serge Botkin, "that in Copenhagen people are moving heaven and earth to persuade Zahle to give up this case without actually commanding him to do so. I have reason to believe this is largely Gilliard's work."[9]

At Oberstdorf, while Zahle fretted, Dr. Eitel and Dr. Saathof were dealing with a variety of problems.[10] They were concerned about the prospect of a "pilgrimage" to the sanatorium, first of all, if the controversy over their famous patient did not cease. Already the waiting list for admission to Stillachhaus had lengthened; tourists were stopping by the sanatorium as they passed through the Bavarian Alps; there had been threats on Anastasia's life; and now the local police had begun nosing about the grounds. Dr. Eitel reported later that around this time he had received thinly veiled warnings from the court of the Grand Duke of Hesse, telling him that there were ways to cause a decline in his business if he did not expel Anastasia from the sanatorium.[11] All the while provocative rumors were flying around Bavaria: the Tsar's sister, Grand Duchess Xenia, was on her way to see Anastasia; Xenia's daughter was coming; "Aunt Irene" would be back — there was no end to the talk. Anastasia had no way of knowing that these stories were pure fantasy, but while she declared herself ready to see her relations, and even said that she looked forward to doing so, her doctors very much doubted her ability to withstand their company. Eitel and Saathof both insisted that Anastasia needed "at least one year" of rest, and that *anything* likely to upset her — "such as questioning, unwelcome visits and so on" — was to be strictly avoided. At the very least, there could be no question of surprise meetings and "interrogations." As Baron Osten-Sacken put it, "I really think the invalid herself ought to have a word to say about whom she is willing to see and whom she is not."[12]

When "Aunt Irene" and the others did not come, when, in fact, nobody from the family came, Anastasia's suspiciousness rose once again to the fore. Inexplicably, she chose Osten-Sacken this time as the source of her woes and cast him out with Harriet von Rathlef, declaring that she never wanted to see him again. Osten-Sacken was amused, but he was the only one who was. "I would like to be able to send 'the little one' some good news to cheer her up," Lillan Zahle wrote Oberstdorf at New Year's, 1927, "but what? We don't dare give her too much hope, we've been disappointed so often." [13] When her husband had finally succumbed to the pressure in Denmark and removed himself from the "Anastasia" controversy, Mme. Zahle explained that his reasons for doing so were these: first, in order to force "the Russians" to do something practical toward Anastasia's rehabilitation; and second, because *the family* does not want him to involve himself with her anymore." [14] According to Harriet von Rathlef, moreover, Zahle had been given "a wigging" by his government in Copenhagen and had been advised to drop Anastasia and drop her *now*. [15] Zahle broke the news just after the New Year: he would not be able to support Anastasia, financially or in any other way, after February 1, 1927. Someone else would have to take charge, said Zahle, and why not Grand Duke Andrew? Andrew enjoyed the family's "permission," after all.

Zahle's unsettling ultimatum left Andrew in a quandary. He had no funds of his own to provide for Anastasia, and his attempt to raise money among the Russian exiles had netted something less than five hundred marks (Anastasia's monthly bills were twice that). "In this whole situation," Andrew wrote, "I can clearly see the method of those who have set themselves the task of wrecking the situation. By preventing me from collecting funds they have put Zahle in an impossible position and at the same time by their counteractivities in Copenhagen they have made Zahle withdraw. It is obvious that in this way they wanted to force the invalid out into the street, and expected her to succumb before long so that she would take with her to the grave that secret which is embarrassing and even dangerous for them." [16]

"They," "them" — who? "The number of people who have been drawn into this work is very large," Andrew wrote cautiously, in the belief that his correspondence with Serge Botkin was intercepted, "and among them such strict discipline is apparent as was never present in purely Russian circles." [17] At Oberstdorf the police had arrived again one morning asking to see Anastasia's identity certificate and threatening to take action against her if it were found to be "out of order." Soon Baron Ludwig Knorring, a friend of Pierre Gilliard from Geneva, had hoodwinked the Bavarian authorities into believing that Anastasia had been exposed as an impostor — as someone, that is, who had given out "false particulars about her person." Now Knorring and Gilliard watched in satisfaction as the police issued an order for Anastasia's expulsion: she was given forty-eight hours to leave Bavaria. Only Zahle's emergency appeal to the Bavarian minister in Berlin prevented the order from being carried out.

"What is supposed to happen after February 1?" Zahle wondered, worried now about the ultimatum he had delivered.[18] He might well have had to reconsider his plans to bow out of the case if someone else had not stepped forward at just the right moment to help. That person was George Nicolaievitch Romanovsky de Beauharnais, Duke of Leuchtenberg, a member of the Russian imperial house and a great-grandson of Tsar Nicholas I.[19] Having heard enough about Anastasia's case in Munich, where he was heavily engaged in monarchist politics, Duke George had been influenced in her favor by General Max Hoffmann, an architect of the Brest-Litovsk Treaty, who was, in Serge Botkin's words, "convinced of the identity of the invalid and [continued] to take a benevolent interest in the case."[20] Now Duke George let Grand Duke Andrew know that Anastasia, if need be, would be welcome as a guest at the Leuchtenberg castle at Seeon, in upper Bavaria. Andrew appreciated the offer. "You know that Markov II has moved in with his spies in the vicinity of the sanatorium . . . ," he wrote Serge Botkin angrily, "and that they have even bribed the hospital employees. Where this will all end it is difficult to say, but I have written to G. N. of Leuchtenberg about it, because I must assume that the invalid is in great danger. . . . I am constantly afraid of intrigues from the other side, and they may at any moment deal disaster to the affair, because, I repeat, this case is dangerous for them."[21]

Spies, disaster, danger, bribery — Andrew had good reason to fear the machinations of the group he called "the opposition." In January Ambassador Zahle was approached by representatives of the Grand Duke of Hesse, who told him that the Grand Duke had decided to undertake his own investigation of Anastasia's claim and felt that efforts to elucidate the mystery really ought to be centered in one place: namely, with him. "I could wish nothing better than to see these endeavors concentrated in Darmstadt," Zahle replied carefully, and declared that he was at the Grand Duke's disposal.[22]

The Grand Duke of Hesse's "investigation" had actually been in progress for some time.[23] Pierre Gilliard, although he later denied any overt involvement in the matter, had been darting back and forth from his teaching duties in Lausanne to the palace at Darmstadt, collecting and delivering affidavits from anyone and everyone who was willing to denounce Anastasia. When Serge Botkin soon heard that the Darmstadt investigation had "resulted in the negative" he could hardly believe it: "By whom and in what way this investigation has been conducted I simply cannot fathom. Zahle has been in possession of absolutely everything relating to this affair for a year and a half, and I know . . . that the Grand Duke of Hesse has never turned to him." [24]

Botkin was mistaken: early in 1927 Zahle, over Harriet von Rathlef's protests, had sent the Grand Duke of Hesse samples of Anastasia's handwriting and plaster casts, which Frau von Rathlef had had the foresight to obtain, of her ears and her misshapen feet.[25] Soon word came from Darmstadt that Madeleine Zanotti, one of Empress Alexandra's former maids, now in the employ of the Grand Duke of Hesse, had looked at the casts and could declare positively that Anastasia's feet "bore no resemblance" to the feet of the Tsar's daughter. Likewise the ears.[26] "Ears never change," someone at Darmstadt pointed out.[27] There was as yet no word on the handwriting. Now the Grand Duke of Hesse wrote Grand Duke Andrew to inform him that the case had been settled at last: Anastasia was *not* the Tsar's daughter. Andrew wrote back asking how the Grand Duke knew that. The Grand Duke did not reply. "I am afraid the latter feels offended," said Andrew, "because I told him that his experiment with the measurements was very interesting and that he had presumably preserved plaster casts of Grand Duchess Anastasia's ears." [28]

On January 14 Pierre Gilliard arrived unannounced at the Danish embassy in Berlin in the company of Count Hardenberg, the Grand Duke of Hesse's aide. He was, as Zahle reported later, "extremely nervous," and the visit lasted barely fifteen minutes.[29] "Only the story of the casts of the feet was mentioned," Zahle continued. "I asked M. Gilliard in the Count's presence if he did not remember his wife telling me and my wife quite distinctly that Frau Tschaikovsky's naked feet, which Mme. Gilliard had inspected at my initiative, were very similar to the feet of A. N. Gilliard had to admit this, and so, in my opinion, the story of the plaster casts falls to the ground."

The first of February was fast approaching. At Oberstdorf Dr. Eitel prepared Anastasia gently for a change of surroundings, while Grand Duke Andrew and Serge Botkin made a last-ditch effort among the Russian émigrés to raise money for her support. Then on January 30 Ambassador Zahle traveled to Darmstadt, where, for two days, he remained to talk about the case with the Grand Duke of Hesse.[30] A statement issued from the palace after Zahle's departure opened with a strange commendation: the Grand Duke wished to thank the Danish ambassador for "maintaining the status quo." This odd remark excited a great deal of comment among Anastasia's friends, who reasonably felt that the most urgent task at hand was to establish her identity. The Darmstadt communiqué went on:

Finally His Royal Highness the Grand Duke expressed his heartiest thanks to His Excellency the Danish Ambassador for having handled the affair of Frau T. so carefully on the instructions of Prince Waldemar; and said that in view of the lively exchange of ideas they had had during His Excellency's stay at Darmstadt he could only regret that they had not met sooner. In any case he would follow further developments in the matter with great interest, even though there was no longer any question of its being his niece.[31]

Just how "lively" was Zahle's exchange with the Grand Duke of Hesse? Perhaps his experiences at Darmstadt had something to do with Zahle's sudden willingness to pay Anastasia's hospital bills for another month. "Since I am the only person Frau Tschaikovsky appears to trust at the moment," he wrote Grand Duke Andrew, "I am ready to use this confidence to influence her as common sense dictates."[32] Anastasia had already been informed that Zahle would soon be obliged to cease his work in her behalf (she thought his decision had something to do with conflicting diplomatic duties) and now, as the moment came, she panicked.[33] A report from Dr. Eitel on February 5 galvanized Zahle into further action. "Invalid's mental state alarming," he cabled Serge Botkin, then in Paris. "Seems to me absolutely necessary that Andrew take steps personally. By authorization given to him by family my task has ended automatically. I have asked George [of Leuchtenberg] if now ready to receive her."[34]

"I hope you will understand my position," Zahle wrote in a covering letter. "I have really been left hanging in the air. . . . It is impossible for me or my wife to go to see [Anastasia], because if we had to tell her that the family in the north is no longer behind me, a breakdown and complete depression would naturally result. I must write you quite frankly, of course, and not hide the facts. I really don't know what will happen if Grand Duke Andrew or the Duke of Leuchtenberg does not effectively take charge."[35]

Botkin relayed this letter to Andrew, who made one last, concerted effort to keep Zahle involved in "this melancholy affair." [36]
It was useless. "I have done my utmost [so] that my royal family
may be blameless in the eyes of history," Zahle declared before his
death. "If the Russian imperial family wishes one of its members to
die in the gutter, there is nothing I can do." [37]

The first of Harriet von Rathlef's articles appeared on the front
page of the *Berliner Nachtausgabe* on February 14, 1927, under
the bold headline "The Battle over the Tsar's Daughter — Recognition and Rejection!" [38] To advertise the series, photographs of Anastasia had been posted on walls and kiosks all over Berlin. "I have
not written a novel," Frau von Rathlef explained in a strangely gentle
introduction, "and above all not a sensational work. . . . I hesitated for a long time before I decided to publish the collected notes
and additional documentation which fill this book, because I knew
it would not be the wish of the person for whom I am working."
However, "the untrue reports and distorted representations" of Anastasia's life and hopes — what the Russian monarchists called her
"schemes" — had finally induced Frau von Rathlef to speak out.
"Witnesses," she cried, "come forward!"

This was the signal for an all-out melee that would preoccupy the
German press for more than two years.[39] When the battle had
calmed down and the lawsuits were settled, Harriet von Rathlef had
the grim satisfaction of knowing that publicity got results. In Berlin
now you could buy a pack of cigarettes and a box of candy styled
"*à la Anastasia,*" while from the nightclubs and cabarets there
emerged a simple refrain:

> Nobody knows who you are, little girl,
> But your smile and your glance enchant me![40]

"The 'Anastasia' publications became the theme of all Berlin," wrote
the editor-in-chief of the *Nachtausgabe*. "And it was no different in
the rest of the land. In Breslau and in Stuttgart, in Düsseldorf and
in Bremen — everywhere people were asking, 'Is Anastasia alive?' "[41]
The German press was fairly split down the middle trying to answer
the question, too — hunting for witnesses, soliciting expert opinion,
consulting with historians and psychiatrists, and, finally, each side
accusing the other of "Bolshevik sympathies" and a variety of jour-
nalistic dirty tricks. The Right charged the Left with a conspiracy

to keep Anastasia from telling what she knew. The Left countered that the Right had employed the tawdry concerns of a deposed and discredited royal family in order to smear all progressive social movements in Germany. On it went until Anastasia herself had vanished from the page, to be remembered only as a catalyst for political debate. "Who she is," read an article in the prestigious *Königsberger Allgemeine,* "what secret forces are driving her, what she or the people behind her have in mind — one can for the moment only fantasize, nothing more."[42]

"As far as the publications in the Scherl Press and Frau von Rathlef's book are concerned," Ambassador Zahle wrote Tatiana Botkin, "it seems to me that it would be best to say just as little about them as possible to the invalid."[43] The fact that the *Nachtausgabe*'s mail was running overwhelmingly in Anastasia's favor was no consolation. Her opponents in Darmstadt had not been idle since Zahle's visit to court. Just as expected, Pierre Gilliard responded to Frau von Rathlef's articles by granting to the *Journal de Genève* an interview in which, for the first time, he publicly denounced Anastasia as a fraud.[44] In a letter to Baron Arthur von Kleist, Gilliard added that he intended to "refute [Frau von Rathlef's] book in a single blow" and asked the Baron "to note carefully all of Frau von Rathlef's lies so that later you can point them out to me."[45] While waiting, Gilliard arranged for the publication of the results of a scientific investigation conducted by Professor Marc Bischoff, an expert in criminal anthropology and, not coincidentally, a colleague of his own at the University of Lausanne. Bischoff had attempted to resolve the dispute once and for all through a comparison of photographs, employing for the purpose three pictures of Anastasia and three of the Tsar's daughter. "The contour of the face is not the same in both cases," Bischoff maintained. "The maximum width is found at the forehead (parietal plane) in the Grand Duchess, while the maximum width is found at the ear level (zygomatic plane) in Frau Tschaikovsky." Anastasia's forehead was higher; her mouth was wider; her eyebrows were "flat and low" instead of "high and curved"; her eyelids sloped up instead of down; her nose was "almost horizontal at the end" — in brief, she failed on every count: "It is impossible that Frau Tschaikovsky could be Grand Duchess Anastasia."[46]

Harriet von Rathlef, buoyed, no doubt, by success, wasted no time attacking the Bischoff report. To deny as "impossible" an identity based on a comparison of six photographs was too absurd for words, particularly since the photographs had not been authenticated or selected according to any scientific guidelines. Even the Grand Duke of Hesse wasn't satisfied, apparently, because his aide, Count Hardenberg, now enlisted the help of the Darmstadt police in the fight against Anastasia, telling them how *very* thankful the Grand Duke would be for a photographic study of her ears in comparison with pictures of the Tsar's daughter.[47] When at length the new study was completed and Anastasia had yet again failed to pass muster, the Darmstadt police had the great honor to hear their work praised "in the name of His Royal Highness" as "so superior, scientific and easy to survey that it has excited general admiration at the palace."[48] The Grand Duchess of Hesse wrote her son in pure triumph, "Now we're only waiting for the handwriting analysis." They got one, sure enough, but it can't have been what they were looking for. In 1927 Dr. Lucy Weizsäcker worked at the Cornelius Graphological Institute at Prien. She recalled:

I was sent, without any explanation, a handwriting specimen to analyze. At first sight I thought it might belong to a serving girl, but on looking more closely I discovered thin, delicate and sensitive curves among the other clumsy traits. I concluded that the handwriting did not belong to a poorly educated person at all, but rather to a cultivated individual who had suffered a shock.

Thereupon I received yet another copy of the same specimen; this time it was explained to me that the writing belonged to the woman whose identity with the Tsar's daughter Anastasia was at that time being contested, and along with it were attached older specimens dating from before the murder of the Tsar. I was supposed to compare the recent ones with the older samples. This request had come to the Cornelius Institute from the court of the grand duchy of Hesse. . . . The fact remains that I concluded in a positive sense [that the specimens came from the same hand].

I heard nothing more about it after that. The court of Hesse must have kept this undesirable result secret and destroyed the report.[49]

Dr. Weizsäcker's report, if not destroyed, was never again mentioned in the correspondence of the House of Hesse. Constantine Savitch, who had lectured against Anastasia with such authority the year before, soon explained why this kind of evidence had not and indeed could not put the matter to rest. "There remain a large enough number of people," said Savitch, "who, due to their own particular turn of mind, cannot consider the enigma to be definitively resolved until they are told the unknown woman's true identity." [50]

That was it, of course. Never mind the handwriting.

Castle Seeon sits at the edge of a secluded lake in the farmlands of upper Bavaria, about an hour's drive from Munich. Attached to a tenth-century Benedictine monastery, the castle had belonged to the family of the Dukes of Leuchtenberg since the 1840s. After the Russian Revolution Duke George Nicolaievitch and his wife, Duchess Olga, had converted the main wing into a guest house, where officers of the Tsar's armies, elderly ladies from St. Petersburg, and others of the Russian nobility were wont to stay when they found themselves in the neighborhood. The moors around the lake, the lilacs, and the silver birches all combined with the fake Greek statuary in the garden and "a queer assortment of furniture" to make Seeon look like a cross between "an old Russian mansion and a second-rate German hotel." [51] It was here, in a spacious room on the second floor, that Anastasia would spend the next eleven months of her life.

It had not been easy to persuade Anastasia to move to Seeon. "The Leuchtenbergs!" she exclaimed when she heard about the plan. "What are the Leuchtenbergs?" [52] She asked the question with a haughtiness that did not become her. Anastasia had never met Duke George or his wife — at least not that she remembered — and she had no wish to do so now. No, she said, and no again: she would not go to the Leuchtenbergs. On February 16, 1927, Ambassador Zahle and his wife sent her what amounted to orders. "You have said many times that although you are skeptical of most people you have always retained confidence in us," the Zahles wrote. "You have had good reason to do so, and we have never betrayed your trust. If we both tell you now that in our opinion the best thing you could do at the moment is move to Castle Seeon, then you must believe it is true." [53]

In a cable to Dr. Eitel, Zahle was more emphatic: Anastasia had to leave Oberstdorf *without delay*. It was essential. "This is a sign of some new aggressiveness against the invalid," Grand Duke Andrew feared. [54] Anastasia, too, seemed to sense that something critical was in the air. She was willing to compromise: she would go to Seeon after all, but only if Tanya Botkin would go with her. In France, Tatiana was prepared to drop everything in order to help, but as a refugee she could not expect to obtain a German visa without weeks of delay. Plainly impatient, Zahle used his influence to cut through the red tape and made a point of reassuring Tatiana that all her expenses would be covered while she stayed with Anastasia at Seeon. In the meantime, would she find out what, if anything, Anastasia needed before traveling? [55]

Anastasia, it turned out, needed "playing cards, morning dresses, a rain umbrella, and a parasol." [56] After the ladies had finally reached Seeon Zahle advised Tatiana:

I would like to make it clear to you how colossally important it is, more important at the moment than anything else, for the invalid to have faith in the Leuchtenberg family. We have succeeded in having the invalid taken into a friendly Russian household, and I expect the very best results, if only a trusting relationship can be established between the invalid and the members of the family. It is absolutely essential that you, Mme. Melnik, make the invalid understand that it is in her best interest to become as close to the family as possible. Tell her from me, in whom I hope she still has confidence, that I implore her to conquer her reticence and her fear and meet these good people halfway. . . . Do not hesitate to use your authority. [57]

After two weeks at Seeon it was still slow going. Tatiana informed her uncle Serge that "the invalid is not yet able to accustom herself to her new surroundings. She is alarmed when somebody knocks, is afraid of meeting people and has not become familiar with anyone other than the Duke. . . . Meals are brought to her in her room. . . . Compared with her condition at Oberstdorf, that is to say at the beginning of September, she has lost ground psychologically." [58] It was more than the jolt of sudden change that now kept Anastasia lying with headaches on her sofa; her reaction to the publication of Harriet von Rathlef's articles had been even more violent than her friends had feared. "The Rathlef woman" had certainly known how to take her revenge, said Anastasia: "My tragedy is her only means of livelihood." [59] Zahle, in the meantime, sent to Grand Duke Andrew four thousand marks Frau von Rathlef had earned from the *Nachtausgabe* series with the advice that Anastasia not be told where it had come from: "I think she would rather starve to death than live off this money." [60]

Bit by bit, during the month of March, Anastasia warmed up to Seeon. The gentle landscape reminded her of "home," and she liked to walk along the edge of the lake and gather bullrushes. "We used to make baskets from these," she said, but she had forgotten how to do it now.[61] Tatiana Botkin observed to her surprise that Anastasia seemed to have entirely lost her sense of space and distance. She could never remember how to get to her room, for example: "She would suddenly stop in front of the door and ask me if it led to the right staircase. Even though she had used the same staircase every day for a month she always thought she was using the wrong entrance." Now, at least, "Tanya" was there to help. "I have a proper lady-in-waiting," Anastasia teased.[62] She told Tatiana that she intended to stay at Seeon only through Easter: "She refuses any longer to live at the expense of others."[63] Then she would go to a convent, or a free clinic, whichever seemed easier. Of course by that time an invitation might have come from Grandmamma in Copenhagen.

Tatiana decided that the moment had come to "use her authority" and tell Anastasia the truth: that her "Grandmamma" wanted nothing to do with her. "It was excruciating," she remembered. "It was atrocious." But it wasn't fair to Anastasia to let her keep dreaming. An invitation from Copenhagen was not going to arrive, Tatiana explained: "Your Aunt Olga does not believe that you are her niece. She says that she took an interest in you only out of pity."

There was no collapse, as people had feared, no breakdown, only a kind of concentrated disbelief: "What? What are you saying?"

"The Grand Duchess wrote me that you are not her niece and that another meeting with you would be superfluous."

The words had begun to sink in. Tatiana was struck most of all by Anastasia's widened eyes and the panic that sounded in her voice as she cried, "But I am I! I am I! They cannot take that away from me! I will prove it to them! I want to see my grandmother, I will prove it, I will prove it."

"How? You haven't any documents; you haven't any papers. *You cannot prove it.*"

It appeared to be the first time Anastasia had seen the problem in that terrifyingly simple light. "*Why?*" she asked Tatiana. She said it over and over: "Why do they reject me? What have I done?"

There weren't any answers. "In order to soothe her," Tatiana recalled, ". . . I told her that she had been too honest, that she had frightened her relatives by confessing that she had had a child. 'Imagine,' I said to her, 'if there were a restoration in Russia, and if they were to change the laws in your favor. . . . Would they want your rescuer's son to succeed you?' "[64]

This was the right question to pull Anastasia out of herself. Shocked though she may have been by the choice of words, Tatiana had to be grateful to see that Anastasia's stunned dejection had turned to blazing anger: "What madness! I have not seen my child since he was three months old. I would not know *how* to recognize him. Do you think I would allow any little bastard to proclaim himself the grandson of the Tsar and Emperor of Russia?"[65] Another meeting with Grand Duchess Olga would be "superfluous" indeed, said Anastasia: "It is I now who will not receive her!"

She never had the chance to prove her seriousness.

At the end of March Tatiana Botkin returned to her family in France, and Agnes Wasserschleben, having given up her post at Oberstdorf, came to Castle Seeon to take her place as Anastasia's "lady-in-waiting." There she was party to the establishment of that "trusting relationship" between Anastasia and the Leuchtenberg family on which Ambassador Zahle had put so much stress. Duke George's brother, Nicholas, had already remarked on the powerful resemblance Anastasia bore in manner and appearance to the Dowager Empress,[66] while she, seeing Nicholas in the hallway, said that it gave her "a stab in the heart . . . because I must have seen him before, at home."[67] In fact Nicholas Leuchtenberg had been an aide-de-camp to the Tsar. "You can understand how important that is for me," Grand Duke Andrew wrote.[68] Looking at photographs, Andrew had noted Anastasia's resemblance to the children of the Tsar's sister Grand Duchess Xenia — "the so-called Alexander III type" — and he was elated to hear that the resemblance went farther than that.[69]

Andrew's ongoing investigation was something Anastasia preferred not to think about. "Ah, he," she sighed when Duke George mentioned Andrew in conversation; "why he?" She could not see beyond the fact that Andrew was a brother of Grand Duke Kyril, the pretender, and she knew, too, that there had been no love lost between Andrew's mother and Empress Alexandra. "When I tried to calm her by saying that not just Grand Duke Andrew but other members of the Imperial House had taken an interest in her fate," Duke George wrote, "she said with pained indignation, 'Oh, mainly that family — all of them!' and almost began to cry." The Duke continued in his notes:

Yesterday our invalid wanted to attend the [Orthodox] service in our chapel. She remained standing until the end of vespers, although we

suggested to her many times that she should sit. . . . Later she told me
that it was difficult to follow the service, because in all these years
she had only been to church once. . . . She had quite lost the habit of
going. When I told her in church that she shouldn't overexert herself, and
that it would be better if she sat down, she answered firmly, "No, I do
not want to! At home it was just so . . ." Helping, I said, "So
rigorous?" — "Yes, yes," she said, "exactly." — "Now," I said, "I know
that, but all the same you must not tire yourself. . . ." Then she said
after a while, "Yes, it is really hard for me, but just because of that I do
not want to sit down, it is proper . . ." Evidently this is a kind of
penance she has imposed on herself. In the first days she was always *'im
Konflikt mit dem lieben Gott* [in conflict with God],' now her heart
seems to have softened, and her eyes are shining with an inner light. I am
not imagining this by any means; everyone in the house has been struck
by it.[70]

From her first days at Castle Seeon the tests of Anastasia's identity continued. Maria Hessé, the widow of the former commandant
of the garrison at Tsarskoe Selo,[71] met her several times in the garden, and so did her daughter, Darya,[72] who saw Anastasia and "declared that she was an impostor, out and out."[73] Darya wondered
aloud if Anastasia's plunge into the Landwehr Canal in 1920 had
caused her to forget her Russian. Anastasia replied that Darya was
"impertinent"[74] and made another enemy. But now the inhabitants
of Castle Seeon forgot about the controversy momentarily and made
ready to celebrate Easter, the most important festival in the Orthodox calendar. Seeon was packed, and not because there was anything unusual about the Leuchtenbergs' chapel. Some of the guests
were sympathetic to Anastasia's cause, some were hostile, and some
were only curious, but differences were put aside during Holy Week
and Anastasia delivered a flawless performance, joining in the midnight procession out of the chapel and into the castle, then back
through the chapel again, carrying her lantern and singing with the
rest: "Christ is risen!" "The invalid moved about so naturally and
so happily among the other guests," Nurse Wasserschleben reported. "She practically forgot they were there, in her joy." After
the service she joined the Leuchtenbergs for Easter dinner, sitting
down with the Duke's children, "drinking vodka, sampling the marvelous food, and drawing my attention continually to each one of
the Easter delicacies. She was just overjoyed when the young ones
began to sing."[75] As she climbed the main staircase at three o'clock
that morning Anastasia paused, took the Duchess of Leuchtenberg

by the hands, and said, "*Bolshoe spasibo, vsye bylo otchen horosho* [Thank you very much, it was all very good]." [76] She seemed unaware that she had spoken in Russian, as she always seemed unaware of it now. It had begun to happen frequently — in the garden with her nurse, while boating on the lake, once at her window during a thunderstorm. But the last attack was already on its way.

"I ought to tell you right now," wrote Serge Botkin to Grand Duke Andrew, "what a curious impression a long conversation I had with Zahle a few days ago made on me. Up till now, and even when he was so obviously trying to disengage himself from the case, Zahle never expressed any doubt about the possibility of the identity. On the contrary, his conviction was evident, if not directly through words, then in his tone of voice. This time, however, a note of doubt sounded. . . . I felt he knew something, but he would not tell me what." [77]

Zahle did know something. Get her away from Oberstdorf, he had urged everyone; get her to Seeon under the Leuchtenbergs' protection as quickly as possible: "I really don't know what will happen if Grand Duke Andrew or the Duke of Leuchtenberg does not effectively take charge."

It wasn't long before the paperboys were shouting the news: "Impostor Unmasked! Anastasia Case Solved!" [78] "Gilliard has already informed me in gloating terms that this 'sordid affair' is now at an end," wrote Grand Duke Andrew, "but how strange: it is from Darmstadt that he writes to me — in fact from the palace. All this is most remarkable." [79]

In the last days of March 1927 Duke George of Leuchtenberg had traveled to Paris on business. He was staying at his apartment on the rue de Grenelle when, on April 1, he read about the "unmasking of the false daughter of the Tsar" in the *Berliner Nachtausgabe*, the very newspaper that had recently published Harriet von Rathlef's articles in Anastasia's defense: [80]

The investigation of the *Berliner Nachtausgabe* into the question "Is Frau Tschaikovsky Grand Duchess Anastasia, youngest daughter of the Russian Tsar?" has had sensational results. Our research staff has answered the question "Anastasia or not Anastasia?" finally and forever.

The woman rescued from the Landwehr Canal on 17 February 1920, who calls herself Anastasia Tschaikovsky . . . is, in reality, Franziska Schanzkowska, unmarried, born on 16 December 1896 at Borowihlas.

With this discovery one of the greatest cases of our time has been brought to a close. We will communicate the details to our readers in due time.[81]

In Berlin, at the Russian Refugee Office, Serge Botkin was sending off letters in haste and confusion. "How far the sensational news in this paper conforms to the truth it is as yet difficult to know, of course," he wrote Grand Duke Andrew while forwarding a copy of the article in the *Nachtausgabe*. "But from what I have been able to ascertain so far, it seems distinctly probable." Botkin had already called on Herluf Zahle at the Danish embassy and had found him uncustomarily nervous and withdrawn. It had been plain to see that Zahle believed the report in the *Nachtausgabe* and that he wanted Botkin to leave. One possibility did not escape Botkin's attention, however: "Perhaps the newspaper . . . has simply fallen victim to a cleverly constructed provocation."[82] What did the Grand Duke think?

Andrew was thinking exactly what Botkin was thinking: "We have often mutually observed with what fanatacism certain people have campaigned against the invalid. . . . The conclusion is involuntarily reached that it was in somebody's interest to frustrate the whole affair and simply to persuade any suitable family to recognize their daughter in the invalid." But the report in the *Nachtausgabe* could not be dismissed so easily. An editor of the Scherl Press, Andrew found out, had followed the Duke of Leuchtenberg to Paris and reminded him that Berlin had a new chief of police, a man who could not have wished for a more sensational case to prove his mettle. Now, said the editor, the police had threatened to conduct "a spontaneous interrogation" of Anastasia and were ready to arrest her for fraud if necessary. Only with great difficulty had they been persuaded to wait until the Duke of Leuchtenberg returned to Bavaria.[83] Of course the Duke, anticipating "an awkward moment," had gone home at once, "completely convinced of the identity of Frau Tschaikovsky and Franziska Schanzkowska."[84] Said Andrew: "He wrote me from Paris that the documents shown to him seemed to leave no doubt."[85]

This was serious business. At Castle Seeon the Duke of Leuchtenberg found a Bavarian constable guarding the front door and Anastasia shut up in her room, totally oblivious to the commotion around her.[86] The constable, Duke George discovered, had been his wife's idea. The police in Berlin might threaten all they liked, said the Duchess, but if they or anyone else were thinking about taking Anastasia away they had better think again. Who cared what had been printed in that rag of a newspaper? Her husband was too gullible, the Duchess thought. In France, Grand Duke Andrew was grateful for the Duchess's self-possession. "We shall see what the newspaper publishes," he wrote, "and what the Duke, who will be going through very difficult times these days, will be able to discover. It is said that Mme. Zahle is in total despair." [87]

After the *Berliner Nachtausgabe* had completed its second "Anastasia" serial, Andrew, while still worried about Anastasia's safety, had no more illusions about the "unmasking of the false daughter of the Tsar." "You should not need to waste your time proving the falsity of this story," he declared, [88] echoing the opinion of most of Anastasia's friends. Someone once ventured that the "unmasking" had all the qualities and characters of a Nazi romance: an unknown woman with a shady past, a young reporter with a cause, a bank detective, a host of bumbling foreigners, and, as the heroine, a blond from the working classes whose native decency and courage were a credit to her nation and her *race*. [89] The blond was Rosa Doris Wingender, of the dank gray slums of north Berlin, a girl whose involvement with Anastasia secured her a tiny niche in history and whose prodigious memory was a source of wonderment to all who knew her. Doris had turned up at the offices of the *Nachtausgabe* during the run of Harriet von Rathlef's articles to say that she had some information. From the published photographs of Anastasia, she said, she had recognized her mother's former lodger, Franziska Schanzkowska, who had disappeared from the Wingender home in the first months of 1920. During the summer of 1922, Doris went on, Franziska had suddenly reappeared at the flat in a very distressed state. She explained that she had been living with Russian monarchists in Berlin "who apparently mistook her for someone else." So afraid was Franziska of the monarchists, said Doris, that when she left again after a three-day rest she asked Doris to exchange clothes with her. [90]

Doris complied. She gave Franziska "a dark blue suit . . . trimmed with black lace and red braid, with buffalo-horn buttons and a black-and-white striped lining; a white lace-trimmed blouse, with a round neckline; gray gauze stockings; black laced boots; and a small cornflower-blue hat decorated with six yellow flowers." Franziska, in turn, left behind a mauve dress, a camel's-hair coat, and underwear embroidered with the initials *AR*. The Wingenders had never seen her again. Now Doris wanted to help. Maybe the monarchists were holding Franziska against her will, said Doris.[91]

The editors of the *Nachtausgabe,* naturally, were excited to hear Doris Wingender's tale. They knew from Harriet von Rathlef's articles that Anastasia, in August 1922, had run away from the home of Baron von Kleist and that she had been missing for three days. Accordingly, the *Nachtausgabe* called in "an international bank detective," one Martin Knopf, to see if the identity between Anastasia and Franziska could be formally established. Happily, Doris Wingender had managed to save the clothing Franziska Schanzkowska had left in her possession during her sudden reappearance, five years before. Immediately, Detective Knopf called on Baron von Kleist to see if they were the same clothes Anastasia had been wearing when she disappeared from the Baron's apartment. They were. "That's it!" the Baron cried when he saw the camel's-hair coat. "I bought it for the unknown woman myself at Israel's." Soon the Baroness came in for a look. "That's the underwear," she said. "That is definitely the monogram I embroidered myself. And that's also the coat. True, it must have been worn somewhat, and washed."

"With the declarations of Baron and Baroness von Kleist," wrote Fritz Lucke, the young author of the "unmasking" series, "the chain of evidence was as good as linked." Only one matter remained: what had Anastasia been wearing when she finally returned from her three-day fugue in the summer of 1922? Were they the clothes Doris Wingender had given to Franziska Schanzkowska? Detective Knopf held his breath while the Baroness searched her memory: "The Tschaikovsky woman wore a simple dark blue suit with a black-and-white striped lining and a colored hat decorated in front with some kind of flower."

Done. "Unmasked!" Fritz Lucke cried. "A brutal word. The mask this woman has worn for seven long years is now ripped pitilessly from her face. . . . The 'Riddle of Anastasia' could not withstand impartial German criticism."

This, then, was the evidence at the core of the "unmasking." There was more, to be sure — much more. The ins and outs of Anastasia's life are easy to follow in comparison with the odyssey of poor Franziska Schanzkowska, the "stocky," "big-boned," "filthy and grubby" Polish factory worker and former farm girl, with her "work-worn" hands and the "black stumps" that passed for her teeth,[92] who had been declared insane in 1916 after being wounded in the head during a grenade explosion.[93] Practically nothing is known for sure about Franziska anymore. Her hair has been described as "chest-nut," blond, "reddish," and black. Her family — it was not a close one — could not recall the color of her eyes. There is only one pho-tograph of Franziska in existence, and the copies have been re-touched more than once in order to heighten her resemblance to Anastasia. It is affirmed that Franziska took a size 39 shoe (in Con-tinental measurement), as opposed to Anastasia's 36.[94] And so on: what Harriet von Rathlef called the "Schanzkowska Legend" was nothing but a breathtaking jumble of uncorroborated detail — and a supremely effective diversionary tactic.

In May of 1927 Mrs. Agatha Grabisch, a representative of the Hearst Syndicate, was sent by Frau von Rathlef to the Scherl Press to spy on Fritz Lucke, the chronicler of the "unmasking" operation. Under the pretext of negotiating American rights to the story Mrs. Grabisch was able to find out a good deal.[95]

"We do not care about making it hard for this girl," Lucke told Mrs. Grabisch; "with us it is a matter of politics. The Grand Duke of Hesse and [Grand Duke] Kyril and the *Nachtausgabe* are inter-ested all together. And it is a matter of one political group against another. Grand Duke Nicholas, Grand Duke Andrew, and the Duke of Leuchtenberg are in combination to advance the girl's claims, and this is opposed to Kyril's claim to the tsardom." Of course everyone knew that Anastasia — that is, Franziska Schanz-kowska — was a Communist agent. Naturally the *Nachtausgabe,* as an organ of the extreme Right, wanted to do what it could to shat-ter the opposition.

So, said Mrs. Grabisch, it was politics as usual.

"Yes, and there is a third group who think that the Tsar and his family were never killed at all. The Dowager Empress in Copen-hagen is one of these." Her own brother, Prince Waldemar, said Lucke, had run into trouble with the Empress because of his sup-port for Anastasia: "When Zahle was told to drop her, Prince Wal-demar did so reluctantly. . . . Zahle, who had delivered, felt he had been fooled."

It must have been quite a shock, said Mrs. Grabisch, for Zahle to read about the "unmasking."

"It was. Zahle and Waldemar really believed in her for a long time, but the others convinced them that she was an impostor."

And what about the Grand Duke of Hesse? Mrs. Grabisch asked. Could Lucke obtain some kind of statement from the Grand Duke?

Certainly Lucke could: "When I spoke with the Grand Duke last

Tsar Nicholas II in 1908, on board the
imperial yacht, *Standart*
(*Ian Lilburn Collection*)

Empress Alexandra Feodorovna
(*Ian Lilburn Collection*)

The children of Nicholas II around 1910. Left to right: Grand Duchess Tatiana,
Grand Duchess Anastasia, the Tsarevitch Alexis, Grand Duchess Maria, Grand
Duchess Olga   (*Ian Lilburn Collection*)

Grand Duchess Anastasia in
1916 in the park at Tsarskoe
Selo, shortly before the
Revolution
(*Ian Lilburn Collection*)

Grand Duchess Anastasia,
ca. 1915
(*Mrs. John J. Weber Collection*)

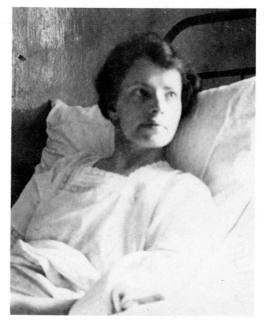

"Uncle Ernie," Grand Duke Ernest Louis of Hesse, brother of Empress Alexandra   (*Houghton Library, Harvard University*)

The Dowager Empress Maria Feodorovna and members of her family in exile at Villa Hvidøre, ca. 1925. Left to right: Grand Duchess Olga Alexandrovna, the Empress, Thyra, Duchess of Cumberland, Colonel Nicholas Kulikovsky (*Ian Lilburn Collection*)

Pierre Gilliard, ca. 1911, with Grand Duchess Olga Nicolaievna in the schoolroom at Tsarskoe Selo *(Beinecke Rare Book and Manuscript Collection, Yale University)*

Herluf Zahle, Danish Minister Plenipotentiary to Berlin *(Ian Lilburn Collection)*

Grand Duke Andrew Vladimirovitch of Russia, who undertook an investigation of the "Anastasia" affair in 1926 on behalf of the imperial family *(Ian Lilburn Collection)*

Anastasia (left) at Oberstdorf with Tatiana Botkin, August 1926 (*Ian Lilburn Collection*)

Castle Seeon. Anastasia secured permission from the Duke of Leuchtenberg to be buried here. She wanted her ashes scattered "beneath a pine tree." (*From a postcard*)

Anastasia (center) debarking from the S.S. *Berengaria* in New York City, February 1928. With her are, from left, Agnes Gallagher, Charles Foley, and Gleb Botkin. (*United Press International Photo*)

An aerial view of "Kenwood," the Leeds estate in Oyster Bay, on Long Island Sound. Anastasia's room was at the far right of the main house (front), directly opposite the tennis court. (*Mrs. Edward J. Wynkoop Collection*)

Princess Xenia of Russia (Mrs. Leeds), Anastasia's hostess at Oyster Bay (*Mrs. Edward J. Wynkoop Collection*)

Anastasia on the private dock of "Kenwood," Oyster Bay, summer 1928 (*Mrs. Edward J. Wynkoop Collection*)

Anastasia in 1930. She wore white whenever possible and spent thousands of dollars on clothes during her sojourn in New York.
(*Mrs. John J. Weber Collection*)

Self-portrait of Anastasia, taken in the mirror at Garden City, September 1928   (*Ian Lilburn Collection*)

Anastasia in 1937, picture taken at Hannover by Gertrude Madsack and presented to Edward Fallows with best wishes from his client   (*Houghton Library, Harvard University*)

Anastasia in 1949, on the day she moved into the barracks at Unterlengenhardt. With her are Prince Frederick of Saxe–Altenburg and Adele von Heydebrandt, who became her companion. (*Ian Lilburn Collection*)

Anastasia in the garden at Unterlengenhardt. "I am the true daughter of a soldier," she declared, and her posture did nothing to contradict it. (*Ian Lilburn Collection*)

The barracks at Unterlengenhardt, where Anastasia was "stormed by curiosity seekers" (*Ian Lilburn Collection*)

Anastasia's key supporters during her suit for recognition. Clockwise from top left: Prince Frederick of Saxe–Altenburg, Carl–August Wollmann with Princess Marianne of Hesse-Philippsthal, Dominique Auclères, Ian Lilburn, and Curt von Stackelberg (*Ian Lilburn Collection*)

Dr. and Mrs. John E. Manahan, photographed at Fairview Farm in Scottsville, Virginia, 1969 *(Transgas)*

Anastasia, 1967 *(Ian Lilburn Collection)*

he told me: 'The outcome of this case has rolled a great stone off my heart.' " But Count Hardenberg was the man to deal with, said Lucke — Hardenberg and Pierre Gilliard.

At a second conversation a few days later Mrs. Grabisch and Fritz Lucke talked about rights and permissions. Mrs. Grabisch wanted to know if the Hearst Syndicate would have any difficulty reprinting the photographs and other original material published in the *Nachtausgabe,* and Lucke said no, he didn't think so. The Scherl Press had purchased everything the *Nachtausgabe* printed: "He said that Scherl had paid Gilliard . . . $100 for a single picture of importance." Then there was the one and only photograph of Franziska Schanzkowska, taken, Lucke said, when Franziska was sixteen. "It had been heavily retouched," said Mrs. Grabisch. "The Chinese white on the light parts was thick; the mouth had been retouched thickly almost to the point of encrustation, so that the mouth appeared heavy and wide." But the *Nachtausgabe* had more material than this, Lucke said — much more than he had been allowed to publish.

Allowed?

Yes, said Lucke, Anastasia's backers were powerful indeed. The police had been ready to arrest her for fraud, in fact, until "higher authorities" ordered them not to.

And who were these "higher authorities"? Mrs. Grabisch wondered.

Well, Lucke answered evasively, "higher authorities."

The threat of police intervention turned out to be one of the *Nachtausgabe*'s many hoaxes. "The Anastasia Affair," Fritz Lucke admitted later on, "was taboo for the police." [96] And so it appears to have been until the scandal of the "unmasking" more or less demanded a response. When Harriet von Rathlef sent Fritz Schuricht, a private detective, down to police headquarters in the spring of 1927, Schuricht found that the police did indeed regard Anastasia's case as closed, but not because they knew any more about it than he did. [97] On the contrary, their colleagues in *Darmstadt* had written to inform them that the "unmasking" was a fact. As matters stood, however, no one was willing to take the responsibility. "We did not establish the identity," the police in Darmstadt were quick to explain. "We did not take part in the work of the identification. As we have been informed today by the manager [Count Hardenberg] of the estate of the former Grand Duke of Hesse, the name of Schanzkowska was ascertained by a detective for the *Berliner Nach-*

tausgabe." [98] And it was detective Martin Knopf, in truth, ostensibly working for the *Nachtausgabe* and no one else, who informed the Berlin police on April 8, 1927, that Anastasia's identity with Franziska had been established beyond all doubt and that "concerned princely houses are interested in exposing her *officially.*" [99] Said Grand Duke Andrew: "It is now known that the detective was hired by Darmstadt and not by the *Nachtausgabe.* The newspaper simply printed the material he gathered." [100]

One other detail Fritz Lucke had been careful not to reveal during the "unmasking" series. When Doris Wingender, the *Nachtausgabe's* star witness, arrived at his office, her first words were: "Look, I've got some information about your Anastasia. How much is it worth to you?"

"We didn't have much time," Lucke remembered. "We were under pressure. . . . What could we do? We didn't want to look foolish. It's understandable to a journalist." And so, "Berliner to Berliner," the Scherl Press had agreed to give Doris an "honorarium" of fifteen hundred marks, to be paid if and when the *Nachtausgabe* satisfied itself of the truth of her story and to be contingent on her meeting with Anastasia at Seeon. [101]

Put more plainly, Doris Wingender was not to get her fifteen hundred marks until she had recognized Franziska Schanzkowska in the flesh. Fritz Lucke and detective Knopf escorted Doris to the pointless, utterly farcical confrontation that took place at Castle Seeon on April 5:

Just to the right of the grand main staircase lies the room where
Franziska Schanzkowska lives. Only rarely has anyone seen her scurrying along the lengthy, lonely corridor in the former Benedictine monastery. She shuns people, she always smells danger.

A sultry roll of thunder hangs over these broad rooms this Tuesday morning; a steady trickle of rain outside completes the dark picture. The closeness and the tension seem to have carried over to the inhabitants. Restlessly the Duke paces up and down; again and again the Duchess tries to put off the moment of the confrontation with the witness — finally the Duke goes in and informs Franziska Schanzkowska that a lady she knows well wants to see her. . . .

The witness, Fräulein Doris Wingender, enters the room. Franziska Schanzkowska lies on the divan, her face half-covered with a blanket. The witness has barely said "Good day" before Franziska Schanzkowska jerks up and cries in a heavily accented voice: *"Das soll 'rausgehen!* [That must go away!]" And again, her eyes glaring, "That must go away!"

The sudden agitation, the wild rage that sounds in her voice, the horror in her eyes leave no doubt: *she has recognized the witness Wingender!*

Fräulein Wingender stands as if turned to stone. *She has immediately recognized the lady on the divan as Franziska Schanzkowska.* That is the same face she saw day after day for years. That is the same voice, that is the same nervous trick with the handkerchief, *that is the same Franziska Schanzkowska!* [102]

"I can swear it! I can swear it!" Doris Wingender cried as the Duchess of Leuchtenberg drove her back to Munich. Leaving Seeon, they passed over a rickety old bridge that spanned the lake. It was called the Liar's Bridge in Seeon, said the Duchess to Doris. Legend had it that the bridge would collapse if liars crossed: "You'd better take care. You don't know what might happen to you." [103]

Harriet von Rathlef was not finished with Fräulein Doris. Posing as a journalist, Frau von Rathlef's attorney, Dr. Wilhelm Völler, made a date with Doris to talk about her future. Fresh from her triumph at Castle Seeon, Doris was in an expansive mood. Yes, indeed, she told Völler over dinner at the Hotel Regina Palast in Berlin, while Frau von Rathlef took frantic notes a few tables away, it had all turned out exceptionally well. Every newspaper in Berlin wanted to make a deal with her now. Unfortunately, said Doris, she had an exclusive contract with the *Nachtausgabe*.

Surely the contract could be broken, Völler replied, pouring a little more wine. After all, fifteen hundred marks was only a year's wages by Doris's standards, and the Schanzkowska story was worth so much more!

"It isn't so bad," said Doris. Still, it was a shame about the contract.

When Doris had left the table for a few minutes to powder her nose, Dr. Völler fumbled through the contents of her bag. He found the copy of the *Nachtausgabe* contract and pocketed it. Upon her return he asked Doris about the small notebook she was carrying. He had noticed that she never let it out of her hands and that she referred to it continually when talking about Franziska Schanzkowska.

Oh, Doris replied, the notebook was just her little aide-mémoire. She had written down everything she remembered about Franziska, she explained, before calling on the editors of the *Nachtausgabe*. She hadn't wanted to leave anything out. And, if truth be known, there had been liberties taken with her memory. Those three days in August 1922, for example, when Franziska had suddenly turned up at the Wingenders' apartment — they hadn't been in August at all. No, Doris was sure of it: she had just bought her spring outfit at the time, and she would hardly have bought her spring outfit in August. It must have been May or June. But, then, detective Knopf had said that it had to be August, so they had compromised: they had said summer. It was close enough. But it was too bad about that contract.[104]

The *Nachtausgabe* was beginning to look ridiculous. The Duke of Leuchtenberg reported:

The confrontation with Doris Wingender took place at Castle Seeon on April fifth with my permission and in my presence as the only witness. It lasted only a few minutes in all, because from the very first there was not the least sign of an earlier connection between the Wingender woman and the invalid. . . Because the strange person seemed sinister to her, and also disagreeable, [Anastasia] said, *"Bitte, das soll hinausgehen!* [Please, that must go out!]" And when this did not at once take place she repeated those words, whereupon the Wingender woman left the room immediately and in her typical fashion. It was not much different with the visit of [detective] Knopf, whose obviously quite incomprehensible words of greeting from the Schanzkowski family the invalid greeted with silent amazement. . . . I had a hard time trying to give the affair even a semblance of plausibility to her. . . . I must say that this confrontation, which was supposed to be the pièce de résistance of the *Nachtausgabe*'s seemingly overwhelming case, rather gave me the impression that there was something fundamentally wrong going on here.[105]

It soon became clear enough to the Duke what was "fundamentally wrong" about the Schanzkowska affair. Later in the year the Berlin daily *Tägliche Rundschau* printed a letter from the Duke's attorney, in which it was affirmed that Fritz Lucke, during his sojourn at Castle Seeon, had remarked to the Duchess of Leuchtenberg that "the Scherl Press had received from the Grand Duke of Hesse for its researches into the affair of 'Anastasia' the sum of 20,000 marks (or 25,000 marks — the Duchess is not sure any longer which of the two sums was named . . .)."[106] With accusations like these, it is no wonder the "unmasking" led to libel suits. Although Fritz Lucke vehemently denied the report, the Duchess was not the only one at Seeon to hear about the twenty thousand marks. "It appears that Lucke at that time also spoke to my eldest

son about the business of the Grand Duke of Hesse and the money,"
Duke George wrote,[107] while Agnes Wasserschleben, Anastasia's
nurse from Oberstdorf, had been present in the room during the
conversation. If the story wasn't true, the Duke wondered, "why
did he tell us about it? It's a mystery to me. Stupidity, perhaps?" It
was a great relief to the Duke, in any case, when the Bavarian police
renewed Anastasia's identity certificate under the name of Tschaikovsky. For the rest of the year they let her keep it, refusing to give
in to repeated requests from Darmstadt that she be expelled or arrested for fraud.[108]

The police had undoubtedly been influenced in their decision by
the surprising results of another confrontation. In May Harriet von
Rathlef had seized control of the "Schanzkowska Legend" by arranging a meeting between Anastasia and a member of Franziska
Schanzkowska's family. It was something the *Nachtausgabe* had
conspicuously not tried to do. At Ammendorf Frau von Rathlef and
her attorney, Dr. Völler, had tracked down Felix Schanzkowski, a
miner, Franziska's younger brother.[109] Although plainly uninterested and resentful of the attention, Felix had at length been persuaded to meet Anastasia on the understanding that he would not
be liable for her financial support if she turned out to be his sister.
In a dig at Doris Wingender, Frau von Rathlef emphasized that Felix had received no payment for his trouble beyond wage compensation and the cost of a round-trip ticket to Seeon.

The earlier confrontation with Doris had been Anastasia's first
experience of the Schanzkowska scandal. "Oh, how clever of him,"
she remarked of detective Martin Knopf when the reality of the
"unmasking" finally sank in.[110] Her contempt had quickly turned
to fury, however — not against the detective, either, but against the
Duke of Leuchtenberg. He had lied to her! He had told her that
Doris Wingender was an acquaintance! It was dreadful. She could
never trust the Duke again. Now, before the confrontation with
Felix Schanzkowski, Duke George did not dare make any excuses.
When Anastasia left Castle Seeon on the afternoon of May 9, 1927,
she knew exactly whom she was going to see and exactly why.

The meeting took place at an inn in Wasserburg, some few miles
northwest of Seeon. Felix Schanzkowski was sitting in the beer garden with Dr. Völler, while Harriet von Rathlef wisely kept out of
sight. As she walked toward his table, Anastasia asked the Duke,
"Which one of the gentlemen is it?"

Felix stared at her.

"Who is the lady?" asked Dr. Völler.

"That is my sister Franziska," said Felix.

All eyes turned to Anastasia. "Well," stammered the Duke, thoroughly amazed, "go and talk with your brother."[111]

Anastasia obeyed.

Dr. Völler had already prepared an affidavit: "From her face (front and profile), her hair, her teeth, her figure, her walk, her feet and her hands, I have recognized my sister, Franziska Schanzkowska, beyond any doubt."[112] That evening Frau von Rathlef, crushed, handed the document to Felix for his signature. Her relief was intense when she suddenly heard Felix declare: "No, I won't do it. She isn't my sister."[113]

It was the most stunning about-face to date. "She isn't your sister!" Frau von Rathlef exclaimed.

No, said Felix again, adding that he would not sign a false declaration that might land him in jail.[114]

Now what? Dr. Völler drew up another affidavit, and this time Felix did not hesitate to sign it:

There does exist a strong resemblance between her and my sister. The resemblance is strong when you look from the front, but not when you look from the side. . . . Frau Tschaikovsky's speech . . . as well as her general manner of expression is totally different from that of my sister, Franziska. . . . At today's consultation, I spoke repeatedly with Frau Tschaikovsky. There can be no doubt that she did not have the slightest idea who I was. You could clearly see that she did not know me. I went toward her and she gave me her hand and talked to me with perfect unconcern. She showed no sign either of astonishment or of the slightest fear. She behaved rather as one behaves toward a third party to whom one is just being introduced.

Harriet von Rathlef went over her checklist. There were scars and birthmarks: "My sister Franziska had no scars and birthmarks." Teeth: "My sister Franziska had a full set of teeth." Languages: "My sister Franziska spoke a little Polish and good German." Feet: "My sister Franziska had no deformities of the feet."[115] Here Felix Schanzkowski took off his shoes and, "with a sort of vanity," declared that Franziska had had "pretty" feet, "just like mine."[116] Before he went back to the mines at Ammendorf Felix asked Dr. Völler to try to find him a new job.

At Seeon the Duke of Leuchtenberg had been following these developments with mixed amusement and outrage. He reserved his harshest critcism for the man who, whatever his active role in the caper, carried the responsibility for the "unmasking" — "Uncle Ernie," the Grand Duke of Hesse. General Max Hoffmann, Anastasia's dogged champion in Bavaria, was content to dismiss the Grand Duke as "an idiot," but Duke George was loyal to his class and hoped for more. "If I were *completely* convinced," he wrote, "that the Grand Duke knows that the whole Schanzkowska affair is a sham, I would not have the least sympathy for him — not in any way, neither as a prince nor as a man." [117] But did the Grand Duke know that? Duke George wondered. What if he himself had been duped by his overeager minions?

In Berlin, Harriet von Rathlef had no patience for the Duke's bigheartedness. She had witnessed firsthand the consequences of "Uncle Ernie's" work. Ambassador Zahle had almost been lost. In the first days of the "unmasking" scandal Zahle had shut himself in his embassy, refusing any comment, refusing Frau von Rathlef's calls, refusing the Duke of Leuchtenberg's appeals that he send a reassuring word to "the little one" at Seeon.[118] "She asks me every day whether 'No mail has come?' " the Duke wrote, "and then when I add the question, 'From Zahle? No,' then she says, 'Yes,' and is very miserable." [119]

It was weeks before Harriet von Rathlef was able to barge through Zahle's office door, sit him down, and give him a good talking-to. Certainly she understood that he had been compromised, she said. Certainly she knew that he had been publicly embarrassed, that his government was furious and had warned him once and for all to stay away from Anastasia. But what was more important to Zahle — the opinion of a misinformed public or Anastasia's trust? Or could it be the heavyhandedness of a certain ex-Grand Duke that now had the Danish ambassador quaking in his boots?

"The little one is not going to lose him," Frau von Rathlef was able to report after this conversation — "he must just find his way." It would not be easy for Zahle to reenter the fold. Now, however, after looking through Frau von Rathlef's bulging file on the Schanzkowska affair, Zahle was "speechless." He would have his wife send Anastasia a note right away, he said. He would do it himself, except that his government would never allow it.[120]

The damage was already done. The "defection" of Ambassador Zahle had hit Anastasia harder than any other consequence of the "unmasking." It was about the only aspect of the affair that excited any comment from her at all, in fact. After their meeting in Wasserburg she declared that she felt "very sorry" for Felix Schanzkowksi, "the poor man who cannot find his sister,"[121] but her sympathy went no farther than that. The confidence she had developed in the Leuchtenberg family had been smashed. She had been tricked, paraded about like a freak, forced to sit still while she was stared at by peasants, detectives, and Berlin shopgirls. She had never been so humiliated. And when delayed greetings finally came to her from the Zahles, Anastasia feigned indifference. "She was, naturally, delighted," said the Duke, "but do you think she admits it? Not at all. 'Too late,' she says, 'earlier that would have made me *so* happy, but now . . . too late.' That's how she is: never forgets a disappointment, an injustice, or what she imagines to be one."[122]

It was true. Anastasia was keeping score. Why not? She already lived with the daughter of the Tsar in a world of pure allegation, and now Franziska Schanzkowska had joined them there. As Serge Botkin, who did not believe the Schanzkowska story, wrote Grand Duke Andrew, who didn't either, "The solution to the problem of who the invalid may in fact be has been utterly bedeviled."[123]

8

AT CASTLE SEEON

I can't tell you if she is the daughter of the Tsar or not," the Duke of Leuchtenberg confided in the autumn of 1927. "But so long as I have the feeling that a person who belongs to my tight circle of society needs my help, I have a duty to give it. And not once, not even in her feverish fantasies, has the invalid committed a faux pas to violate our unwritten laws."[1]

Anastasia needed the Duke's help more than ever in the wake of the Schanzkowska affair. Her powerlessness in the face of attack was not the invention of her partisans. What could she do? Technically, she didn't exist. Her identity as "Anastasia Tschaikovsky" was little more than a bureaucratic convenience, to be reviewed periodically and subject to revocation without notice. If, therefore, someone were able to convince the authorities that Anastasia was a fraud, or a lunatic, the consequences could be dire indeed. Only the shelter of Castle Seeon and the high protection of the Duke of Leuchtenberg now stood between her and calamity.

Through her muddled comprehension of the struggle over her identity Anastasia came to realize what a fix she was in, and her resentment knew no bounds as the fact of her total dependency on the Leuchtenberg family grew daily more obvious to her. She took a hard line. Any plans she may once have had to win the family's favor she now cast aside. Henceforth she was going to listen to her own counsel or none at all. Duke George learned to cope good-naturedly with both her icy reserve and her frequent "nerve storms,"[2] but his wife, Duchess Olga, was harder to please. Born Princess Olga Repnin, the Duchess of Leuchtenberg was a chubby-faced, full-blooded aristocrat, who in exile had proclaimed herself an anarchist and took no nonsense from the "princess" upstairs.[3] Residents of the ducal guest house told stories of hair-raising clashes between Anastasia and her hostess. They quarreled over the linen; they quarreled over the tea service; they quarreled over the food; they even quarreled over the flower arrangements. It was Anastasia's opinion that the Duchess "behaved terribly in everything. . . . The Duke . . . informed me on the side that the Duchess was not normal and I should not be surprised if she suddenly stood on her head in the salon."[4]

"Who does she think she is?" Duchess Olga roared, although she knew the answer perfectly well. Anastasia had reminded her more than once: "I am the daughter of your Emperor."[5]

She stood stock still as she delivered her reproaches, her anger rising up from her throat in waves and covering her face with red blotches. The blotches tended to quiet the anarchist Duchess sooner than any haughty reminder of her guest's exalted rank. Olga of Leuchtenberg had known Empress Alexandra and remembered, as many did, that Alexandra's face always spotted red and white when she became angry or upset. Here at Seeon was a woman who claimed to be Alexandra's daughter and who had evidently inherited one of her mother's less attractive traits.[6]

After an altercation with Anastasia the Duchess would stamp down the stairs carrying on about ingrates. Her husband reminded her that Anastasia had had a hard time of it, that she was "nervous" and needed to be handled with kid gloves, but the Duchess wasn't interested: "She is not nervous, she is crazy, that's what she is. You know what she answered me when I told her that I picked her up on the street out of pure charity? She said: 'I did not ask you to take me, I will gladly go away.' The fool, where is she going to go? I asked her that, and she said: 'It makes no difference to me, where I go.' In her own room, meanwhile, Anastasia would have summoned one of her lady companions to say that her patience with the Duchess had finally run out. "*How* can she be so rude," Anastasia wailed; "she is a lady, after all!" No, no, it was too late, she would not stay at Seeon another moment, she would go back to Berlin at once, she would go back to Dalldorf: "There I shall at last be in peace!"[7]

Did she mean it? Probably not, although she was already famous for moving out without a word and would remain so. In the meantime the Duke usually managed to arrange some kind of truce. Anastasia liked the Duke. She pretended otherwise when it suited her, but with his great height, his commanding air, and his beautifully groomed military moustache Duke George was just the kind of striking man she enjoyed seeing around her. He had served in the Emperor's horse guard, she would never forget that. The Duke, of course, never knew when he knocked at Anastasia's door whether he would be received with a scowl or a dazzling smile, but he was more likely than anyone else in the castle to gain entry to her room, and in fact was the only person at Seeon who could ever persuade her to cooperate if something needed doing in the matter of "her affair." [8]

Oh, but Anastasia was tired of all that! How long could this "mess" continue? [9] "She has taken it into her head that within two months at the most 'that must be settled,' " Duke George wrote in June 1927. "She won't last much longer, she is quite broken, etc. It is very difficult to fight against this mental attitude; in the course of the work I am always having to report nasty things to her . . . , because she has got to know, of course, what is going on." [10]

What was going on, really, had not changed much since the "unmasking." It had only intensified. In Paris the Russian monarchists kept up the smear campaign against Anastasia while Pierre Gilliard prepared his answer to Harriet von Rathlef's book; in Berlin, Frau von Rathlef was looking for another newspaper to publish *her* answer to the "Schanzkowska Legend"; while at Seeon Russian visitors were loitering behind statues in the garden and poking their heads around corners in the hope of catching a glimpse of "Her." Anastasia never knew how far the quarrel had spread or how heated it had become. She did not see Gilliard's article, "The Story of a Fraud," in the French journal *L'Illustration*, in which he called her "a cunning psychopath" and "a little peasant." [11] It was a good thing. She was quite furious enough with the treachery of "the Rathlef woman," who had already "done bad things in the newspapers" [12] and was, Anastasia felt, personally responsible for "all the shouting." [13] Frau von Rathlef was beginning to get tired of Anastasia's bullheadedness. "Perhaps you will be able to convince the wicked little girl *how* devoted I am to her and how hard I am fighting for her rights," Frau von Rathlef wrote the Duke. [14] But Anastasia would not yield. "She cannot get over the fact that you have brought her intimate, confidential information to the knowledge of all the world," the Duke replied. "This seems to hurt her more than the Schanzkowska affair, the importance of which, it seems to me, she is not fully aware of." The most Duke George could report after months of trying to "break her resistance" was that Anastasia no longer started yelling when Frau von Rathlef's name was mentioned — "she only asks ironically 'if something will soon be published in the newspapers, perhaps?' . . . Childish, yes, but for the moment, anyway, not to be overruled. . . . The day will come, do rely on me. Only patience, and courage. . ."[15]

Everyone was going to need patience and courage in the days ahead. "Why, this is getting terrible," the Duchess of Leuchtenberg exclaimed. "My own children are now quarreling with one another."[16] So they were. Duchess Natalie, the eldest, had quickly convinced herself of Anastasia's authenticity and leaped to her defense at any provocation. Duke Dmitri, however, and his wife, Duchess Catherine, remained skeptical, even hostile, and eventually disowned Anastasia altogether.[17] Anastasia didn't care. She barely saw the Leuchtenberg children anyway. She spent most of her time at Seeon lying on her divan in a state of nervous exhaustion or sitting at the rose-covered window that overlooked the lake. Since the Duke would not allow her to go outdoors alone — he and the Duchess were worried about assassination attempts — Anastasia was sometimes seen walking along the stone corridor, back and forth, until a stranger's face sent her dashing for the safety of her room. Besides the Duke, the only people who saw her with any kind of frequency were the four women who alternated as her "ladies-in-waiting" and who, one by one, were sent packing when she got tired of them.

The first to go was Anastasia's nurse from Oberstdorf, Agnes Wasserschleben. She had had the bad luck to be in attendance during the disquieting days of the Schanzkowska scandal and was swiftly held responsible for the disturbance. Professional to the end, Nurse Wasserschleben smiled and remarked, "This had to happen, for no one who is with her for any length of time escapes it."[18] Meantime Maria Baumgarten — "Miss B" — an elderly Russian lady who kept a room at Seeon, eagerly stepped in to fill the gap. She was seconded by Vera von Klemenz, a piano teacher who had sometimes played for Empress Alexandra and vaguely remembered Grand Duchess Anastasia from Tsarskoe Selo. Finally there was Faith Lavington, the solid, attentive, forty-year-old Englishwoman who served as governess to the children and grandchildren of the Duke of Leuchtenberg. Miss Lavington's diary[19] provides a new and very vibrant picture of life with Anastasia — "the *Unbekannte*," "the Sick Lady," "the *Kranke Dame*":

We have had a regular field day today with the Sick Lady — for she has been wild *all day* and finished up in a screaming gale of passion. The first drama, was when the Old Duchess found out that the Sick Lady was using towels — probably hand towels — as compresses, and as she has a history of tuberculosis you can imagine that this simply cannot go on, so that not so many towels were sent up to her — which was her first grief. Secondly the cover of her "*plumeau*" was too short, and when I approached the Duchess about it, I nearly had my head bitten off for my trouble — second grief, and thirdly, 3 dresses arrived from Munich, having been altered, and the Sick Lady has cast them entirely forth from her room, refusing even to look at them, third grief, so you see that Grand Duchesses are not easy to deal with.

It took Anastasia a number of weeks before she was sufficiently comfortable with Faith Lavington to welcome her into her circle (it took her *months* before she could remember Miss Lavington's name and ceased to call her "*Das*"). Miss Lavington was frankly amazed at Anastasia's imperviousness to the everyday concerns of other people. Proud of her work, proud of her Britishness, the English governess regarded Anastasia with a deeply sympathetic but always skeptical eye and was not afraid to laugh at each new "drama" in the Leuchtenberg household — as when Anastasia had agreed to go shopping in Munich with the Duchess and was then left to wait in the hall while the Duchess got ready: "This upset the *Kranke Dame* very much, and she became very angry, even outraged, and declared in front of the Russian governess, who repeated this to me, that 'She could not understand how the Duchess could keep her waiting, the hour for starting had been named and *why* was the Duchess not there.' " But all was not pomp and hauteur about "the Sick Lady." There was the time Miss Lavington entered her room and found Anastasia trying desperately to pin up her long, thick hair, which she had just washed and which was "*à la* Beulah tumbling down her back. Suddenly it became quite undone, and she left it so, saying laughingly, '*Mein Frisure ist ganz kaputt!*' " There were the lengthy, madcap, "*very fast*" drives in the country that Anastasia enjoyed so much — "no speed is too much for her" — but which usually left her companions fearing for their lives.[20] And there was the unfailing dignity with which Anastasia greeted any upset, great or small. "I saw Miss Baumgarten flurrying about with a distressed face and a jug of hot water," Miss Lavington reported one day, "and heard that the poor creature had fallen in her bath." In fact Anastasia had slipped and landed directly on her left arm, where the tubercular wound was still open and the bone exposed. "I was much struck by the air of authority with which she gave directions what to do," said Miss Lavington, "and for nothing in the world would she allow me to use my little basin which I had brought in with hot water, and she besought me to [wash my hands] before I washed in it again. She was trembling all over and I held her head, whilst Miss B flew for a glass of wine for her, for she was near to fainting."

As the weeks passed and Faith Lavington saw more and more of Anastasia she found herself drawn inextricably toward the mystery of her true identity. "There is the most extraordinary something about her which one cannot explain," Miss Lavington wrote, "a sort of weird charm. . . . I feel certain it is she, it cannot be otherwise." And yet — how to explain the negative reactions of so many people who had known the Tsar's daughter in her youth; people like Darya Hessé, who had been a special friend of Grand Duchess Anastasia's sister Olga, and who declared to Miss Lavington, "Miss Faith, I *lived* with the Grand Duchesses, I knew them as real friends all of my life until I married, and that woman is *not* Anastasia Nicolaievna, not in looks, manner, or speech!" Miss Lavington had no way of knowing that Darya Hessé, in the heat of her conviction, had drastically padded her tale.[21] "One cannot utterly disbelieve evidence of that kind," Miss Lavington sighed, and wondered, too, how a Russian grand duchess — how a lady of any description — could be so ungrateful as Anastasia was when she felt like it: "This last week she has absolutely refused to see the Duke, her dresses lie outside the door upon the ping-pong table, . . . her new fur coat hangs in the cupboard, quite scorned, although I put it on and showed her how nice it was, but nothing, nothing helps, one might be a small still voice crying in the wilderness — she takes no notice of anybody's advice or recommendations, it is 'unsympathisch' and that is an end of it. . . ."

"Poor, poor thing!" Faith Lavington exclaimed in her diary many times. "She has no one who will own her. . . . She has no place, no home, no past, no future and no hope of anything better. . . ." That state of affairs, Miss Lavington had no doubt, did nothing to diminish Anastasia's towering pride. "You know," Anastasia said one day, "that I am not ashamed of my name Tschaikovsky — no, not at all, it is a very good name and the name of the good man who saved me, it is all the newspapers which have spoilt this name for me, but I myself, I do not want to change it, for my husband saved me at the risk of his own life."

If Faith Lavington approached Anastasia with the practiced distance and trained eye of a governess, the other two, the Misses Baumgarten and von Klemenz, dealt with her only from a position of subservience and awe. "Miss B" was the runner and the flatterer, while Vera von Klemenz found herself caught up daily in Anastasia's mournful retreats into the past. "I love the water so much," said Anastasia as she stood at her window looking down on the lake at Seeon, "because it reminds me of Finland." There were few things, indeed, that did not remind Anastasia of something or someone she had known before, and when Vera von Klemenz began to practice the piano with her in the summer of 1927 her own diary spilled over with anecdote: "She is very musical and has a good sense of rhythm. . . . I have noticed that when she takes pains she generally cannot place her fingers on the keys correctly, but when she plays automatically, without thinking about it much, she does very well, and it is completely clear to me that she has played the piano before." One morning Miss von Klemenz played Anastasia a song from *"Tschizhik"* and then "suggested that she repeat it. She laughed happily and said: 'That I know very well.' At first she found it difficult. I had the impression that she could not see well, and could not distinguish the individual keys. Then suddenly she repeated the song without the music, by ear."

"I have always like it," Anastasia said simply. "At home, I studied music and wrote tunes." So it continued for weeks, with Vera von Klemenz at the piano playing Russian folksongs — *"Po ulitze mostovoi"* and *"Akh, vy Seni moi Seni"* — and Anastasia standing in the center of the room, crying as likely as not and holding her handkerchief to her mouth ("as if to keep her false teeth from falling out," said Miss Lavington). "I know all these songs," Anastasia might say; "I love them." Or: "Please, please, once again: I am at home when I hear these songs." Once Miss von Klemenz ventured that Anastasia had probably heard the songs while living with the Russian monarchists in Berlin, and Anastasia answered in real distress, "No, no, not in Berlin! I heard these songs at home, that is why I like to hear them. I sang them, my sisters and I! We did many things — sang, played and also danced, we danced Russian dances, too." The day came when Miss von Klemenz located a book containing the music for the marches of the Russian regiments of the guard.

"I know that," said Anastasia, "that was at home."

"I said I hoped to find a hussars' march in this book," Vera von Klemenz remembered, "and she answered me quite positively, 'In this book there are marches of all our regiments.' " Anastasia listened to the music in exquisite pain, saying, "It is so beautiful, but it makes me so sad."

In that case, said Miss von Klemenz, she had better stop. But Anastasia wouldn't hear of it. Only when her companion began, very softly, to play "God Save the Tsar" did Anastasia grab her hand away from the keys and exclaim, "You must never play that!" [22]

On June 18, 1927, the Leuchtenberg family gave a party for Anastasia in celebration of her twenty-sixth birthday. It was meant as a gesture of goodwill and it was accepted with grace. "Yesterday, at her birthday, she was happy," Duke George wrote, "because after a certain estrangement 'peace' rules again between her and my wife, because we have celebrated her birthday, so that she, at last, for the first time, has been sitting with us at table in the evening, and was very content." [23] Harriet von Rathlef had not forgotten the occasion either. One of her readers had written to ask if there were anything Anastasia might like as a gift, and Frau von Rathlef replied that he could do no better than to locate a copy of the poetry of Prince Schönaich-Carolath, "and in particular the poem 'Dank [Thanks].' " Anastasia had spoken about it frequently: "Mamma very much likes the poems of a Prince Carolath; she was sent a poem of his called 'Dank' because Mamma had sent him some violets to tell him how much she liked his poems." When the volume reached Seeon Anastasia was delighted. "She reads the poem over and over," Duke George wrote, "and then told [me] that it was Mamma's poem." All manner of gifts and greetings had arrived at Seeon, the Duke informed, "and it is sometimes really touching." [24]

All this while, Harriet von Rathlef had been searching for another forum to air her objections to the "unmasking." Although she wanted to carry the job farther and publish new evidence of Anastasia's identity, Grand Duke Andrew and the Duke of Leuchtenberg thought it would be wise to limit the rebuttal to the one topic; there would be time enough to prove Anastasia's authenticity when the Schanzkowska business had been put to rest. Again it seemed im-

ortant to employ a newspaper of the political Right for the purpose. Duke George was especially hopeful that Frau von Rathlef
would not be obliged to "turn to the press of the Left, but if it
cannot be helped — then in the name of God! The worse for those
who will be hit by it." The Duke was thinking first and foremost of
Pierre Gilliard, whose recent "imbecilities" [25] in *L'Illustration* had
been so patently offensive that even Serge Botkin, in Berlin, had
begun to mutter about "the self-righteous Swiss." [26] "At last he has
revealed himself as a petty man, capable of lying," Grand Duke
Andrew wrote after breaking off his correspondence with Gilliard,
"but incapable of seeing that his own lies give him away." [27] In the
meantime there had been no letup in the long parade of witnesses
at Seeon. The moment somebody stepped forward to confirm Anastasia's identity, somebody else came around to deny it. Colonel
Anatoly Mordvinov, who had already heard a great deal about Anastasia from his patroness, Grand Duchess Olga, arrived at the castle one afternoon and rejected Anastasia out of hand.[28] "I came
here so hoping to find my Grand Duchess," said Mordvinov, who
had been the Tsar's aide-de-camp and who had deserted him at the
outbreak of the Revolution, "and what did I find?" [29] He did not
answer the question. "Mamma was so happy to know that you
were in Seeon," Grand Duchess Olga wrote her dutiful friend, "and
that you have also confirmed my words about the invalid." [30] If
Mordvinov's testimony was not altogether convincing, there was
more on the way. Prince Felix Yussoupov came to Seeon now and
shattered the Leuchtenbergs' illusions on the spot.[31]

Thanks to his role as the murderer of Rasputin, Felix Yussoupov
is today one of the most notorious figures in Russian history. He
belonged to a fabulously wealthy princely clan — richer, it was said,
than the Romanovs themselves — and was married to the Tsar's
niece Irina Alexandrovna. A pact of silence had been solemnized by
the conspirators in the Rasputin murder, a pact Yussoupov, in exile,
broke with a flourish. "At that time he was seriously imagining
himself an historic figure of considerable importance," wrote Grand
Duchess Maria Pavlovna, whose brother, Dmitri, was the only one
involved in Rasputin's murder to keep his vow of secrecy, "and all
he did was calculated to enhance this position. . . . His desire to
be talked about at all costs made no discrimination as to method
or manner." [32]

Prince Yussoupov happened to find himself in Berlin in May of
1927. While there he met up with Harriet von Rathlef and her part-

ner-in-arms, Professor Serge Rudnev, both of whom, naturally, were anxious to plead Anastasia's cause with a member of the imperial family. Twelve years after he had last seen the Tsar's youngest daughter, as a result, Yussoupov agreed to travel to Seeon with Rudnev for the test. Rudnev, Yussoupov remembered, had gone up to Anastasia's room to inform her of his arrival, then come downstairs again to say that her reaction had been one of unmixed delight: "Felix, Felix! What a joy to see him again! I will get dressed and come down immediately. Is Irina with him?"[33]

"This joy at seeing me again seemed exaggerated," Rasputin's assassin wrote in a letter to Pierre Gilliard,[34] and it had been, either by Rudnev or by Yussoupov himself. When she found out who had come to see her in fact, Anastasia had actually rushed to the Duchess of Leuchtenberg for protection. "Yussoupov is there!" she cried. "Felix . . . Yussoupov!" She was terror-stricken. Finally she did go out to the garden to meet him, but only after much cajoling (and not alone).[35]

The meeting lasted less than fifteen minutes. Yussoupov chatted with Anastasia in the four usual languages; asked her if she would like some new dresses (he had recently gone into the fashion business); promised to get some for her; said good-bye; and went off to denounce her as "nervous, hysterical, vulgar and common."[35] In a letter to Grand Duke Andrew Yussoupov wrote:

I claim categorically that she is not Anastasia Nicolaievna, but rather just an adventuress, a sick hysteric and a frightful playactress [Yussoupov's emphasis].

I simply cannot understand how anyone can be in doubt of this.

If you had seen her, I am *convinced* that you would recoil in horror at the thought that this frightful creature could be a daughter of our Tsar. . .

These false pretenders ought to be gathered up and sent to live together in a house somewhere.[37]

Grand Duke Andrew filed this letter under "Against."

New "scientific" evidence against Anastasia was shortly forthcoming. Feet, ears, face, and handwriting had all been considered. Now teeth had their turn. Anastasia had been to Munich several times to see the Leuchtenbergs' dentist, since her newly acquired dentures gave her a great deal of pain. The doctor had noticed a certain structural peculiarity about her incisors and told Duke George that any dentist who had treated the teeth before could not fail to remember it. Meanwhile, the imperial family's dentist, Dr. Serge Kastritsky, had survived the Revolution and was living in Paris. Grand Duke Andrew and Serge Botkin had both pleaded with him to come to Seeon to examine Anastasia, but Kastritsky refused — adamantly. On his next trip to Paris, therefore, Duke George called on Kastritsky with casts of Anastasia's teeth and demanded an appraisal.[38] Taking one look at the casts, Kastritsky declared, "Impossible! Would I have left the teeth of one of the Grand Duchesses in this condition?" Kastritsky made no mention of the peculiar incisors.[39]

The imperial dentist's verdict spread rapidly in Russian circles and was quickly accepted as the last word on the subject of Anastasia's identity. Few of the monarchists realized that Dr. Kastritsky had not managed to bring his dental charts out of Russia.[40] In correspondence with Grand Duke Andrew, Kastritsky had to concede that without the records and in the absence of an examination of Anastasia his opinion could be taken as only that, an opinion. "He was not sure enough . . . to make an affidavit against her," said Andrew, and indeed he never did.[41]

Anastasia's spirits were lifted somewhat in September when another in the long series of confrontations took place. This next meeting had a special fascination and poignancy about it, because the witness was far removed from the concerns and intrigues of the Russian court and had known the Tsar's daughter only in very topical, very unusual circumstances.[42] Captain Felix Dassel, of the 9th Kazan Dragoons of Grand Duchess Maria Nicolaievna, had been severely wounded in the leg while fighting on the Eastern Front in the autumn of 1916 and was privileged to convalesce in the small military hospital at Tsarskoe Selo set up under the patronage of Grand Duchess Maria and her sister Anastasia. Unlike their mother and their elder sisters, the two youngest Grand Duchesses were not qualified nurses. Their service at the hospital was limited to frequent visitation, but they were thrilled by any opportunity to go out and, according to Dassel, approached their new duties "rather as a game." Dassel remembered Grand Duchess Anastasia as a lively, dumpy, impish teenager, with a laugh "like a squirrel" and an extremely rapid walk: "It was as though she *tripped* along."[43] The hospital at Tsarskoe Selo had had room for only seven or eight patients at a time, Dassel went on, and the Tsar's daughters came to chat, play cards or billiards, and otherwise while away the afternoons. For six months, then, until the Revolution put an end to these quaint missions of mercy, Captain Dassel had seen the Grand Duchesses two or three times a week for several hours at a stretch. In January and February of 1917, although he had recovered sufficiently to return to the front, Dassel had stayed on at Tsarskoe Selo at the Empress's request as an "adjutant" to the girls.

During the Russian Civil War, Captain Dassel had fought with the Whites in the Baltic provinces and had finally emigrated to Berlin, where he worked as a journalist. He had heard about Anastasia's case already in 1923 but had not thought it necessary to meet her, because, as he frankly admitted, "I had no confidence whatever in Baron Arthur von Kleist. . . . I knew that circle of émigrés."[44] Only four years later, when he learned that Anastasia had come under the protection of the Duke of Leuchtenberg, did Dassel begin to think that there might be more to Anastasia's claim than met the eye. Still skeptical, almost as a lark, he set off for Castle Seeon in the comany of Otto Bornemann, a friend and fellow officer of the German youth organization *Jungdeutscherorden*.[45] Before leaving Berlin Dassel had a prudent thought: he wrote a detailed report of his memories of the hospital at Tsarskoe Selo, showed it to no one, sealed it, and later gave it to the Duke of Leuchtenberg for safekeeping.

"She doesn't think too much of me anymore," Duke George laughed during Captain Dassel's first evening at Seeon. Lately Anastasia had given new vent to her outrage against the Russian monarchist community, declaring that she would never receive another Russian émigré while there was breath in her body. It was not a good moment. But on the morning of September 15, 1927, Maria Baumgarten tiptoed into Anastasia's room and made the first attempt: would Anastasia consent to see a gentleman who had once known her well?

"A decided no!" Anastasia wished to be spared; there was no point; everyone was wicked; everything was finished; she wanted nothing; she expected nothing; she was a broken woman!

Out in the garden, through the open window, Felix Dassel listened to Anastasia's tirade. "It was a nervous and somewhat shrill voice," he wrote. "It said nothing to me. It did not awaken the slightest memory."

Now Miss Baumgarten made bold to tell Anastasia that her visitor had once been a patient in her hospital at Tsarskoe Selo. A look of anguish crossed Anastasia's face and she began to weep: "He was there? He was *there?*"

Yes, said Miss Baumgarten, trembling, and he had brought photographs. Would Anastasia like to see them?

"No, I cannot!" It was too dreadful. But finally she took up one of the pictures and looked at it. It depicted the entrance to the Grand Duchesses' hospital, which had been built into a church on the grounds of the Alexander Palace.

"Is that not a church?" asked Miss Baumgarten.

"No," said Anastasia, "that is our hospital." Then she thrust the picture away and almost screamed the words: "Please! Please leave me in peace!"

Miss Baumgarten crept from the room. "Perhaps tomorrow," she told Captain Dassel.

On the morning of the sixteenth the Duke of Leuchtenberg gained entry to Anastasia's chamber and pleaded with her to receive her visitor. She was angry now. All right, she cried, she would receive the gentleman and his companion "ten minutes after tea." She lay on the divan at the appointed hour, covered with a blanket, her handkerchief pressed to her mouth. As Dassel approached he found himself doing something he had not intended. He didn't know why, but he saluted and presented himself in military style: "Captain of the Dragoons of H.I.H. the Grand Duchess Maria."

The problem with this kind of greeting was that Dassel now had to remain at attention until Anastasia responded. And she did, correctly: "She held out her hand to me, quite naturally and according to custom, as I had expected. It was just as natural for me to kiss her hand. Under other circumstances in the better Russian circles it was usual to kiss the hands of married ladies only."[46]

Duke George was standing by to make sure that Dassel's visit remained brief: "We don't want to tire you out; our guests can come back." Meantime Dassel limited the conversation to neutral topics. "The invalid looked almost entirely at Dassel," wrote his companion, Otto Bornemann. "As the visit obviously upset her very much we cut it short. She said practically nothing. She was grateful for the flowers we gave her. She kept her handkerchief constantly in front of her mouth. On being asked if we could come again, she nodded."[47]

Nothing about this brief and uneventful meeting had helped Dassel reach a decision. Anastasia's hands, he told the Duke, and the way she twisted her handkerchief did remind him very much of the Tsar's daughter, but that was all: "The emaciated face was completely unfamiliar to me." That evening, as Dassel and Bornemann sat drinking beer in the small tavern attached to the main building at Seeon, Maria Baumgarten suddenly burst into the room. "Thank God I've found you!" she gasped. "You can't imagine what's just happened. I've never seen anything like it in the invalid before. She'd been in bed for several hours; we all thought she was long asleep. Suddenly she got up, put on her robe and sent for me. I was to come at once! I was alarmed, I thought perhaps she'd taken ill again. Not a bit of it, she was standing in the middle of the room shaking like a leaf with excitement and told me that I should ask 'the young officer' immediately if, when he left the hospital, he received from her and her sister Maria the small gold medallion with the initials M and A."

Miss Baumgarten stopped for a breath: "She wants to know if you still have it."

Dassel was confused: "Medallion? What medallion?" Then suddenly he remembered the little gift the Grand Duchesses had given to all of the officers in the hospital before they returned to the front. No, he replied, he had not received the medallion because he had left Tsarskoe Selo only after the outbreak of the Revolution, when the Grand Duchesses were prisoners.[48]

There was something more, said Miss Baumgarten. She had told Anastasia that Dassel had been "very moved" to see her again — which was only to be expected, "since he saw you every day for months at the hospital."

Anastasia had cut her off: "Every day? No, no, not every day. We did not go every day."

This remark, Dassel observed, was perfectly accurate, and he wondered how Anastasia would have known to contradict Miss Baumgarten. Even in Tatiana Botkin's memoirs, Dassel knew, it was mistakenly written that the Grand Duchesses had visited their hospital *every day* during the war years.[49] Obviously Anastasia had not taken her information from that source.

"I was very troubled," said Dassel.

From the diary of Vera von Klemenz:

Today, at the Duke's pressing request, the invalid decided to receive the two gentlemen in her room. She knew that one of them had lain in the hospital of the Grand Duchesses Maria and Anastasia, and that upset her very much. She kept on repeating, "So sad, so sad . . ."

When the men had left the room after a few minutes, she burst out: "Why did I not die with all my people! Then I would be set free, would not have to suffer so dreadfully as in this moment. You must understand me, he is a person from 'there,' from before, when I was so happy. Now again I feel all I have lost, feel everything dreadful again. . . . *Why do I have so much life?* . . .

"It will pass again, the excitement will pass. I could not speak — I could not see well, because I see almost nothing when I am excited. It all dances before my eyes, I see only spots. Now it is already better; when I came from the asylum it was always so; I could see nothing. Tomorrow when I see him I will be calmer, because it will not be the first time, already the second — I will see him better."

Then she took the flowers the officer had given her and asked if they came from the Duke's garden. I told her the officer had brought them himself. At once she decided:

"These flowers must have the nicest place."

She put them next to the little ikon and the photograph of the Empress. The whole time I was with her she stared constantly at the flowers, and I heard her whisper over and over, "Dreadful, too dreadful!" Then she said to herself softly, over and over, "Someone from there, from there, for the first time from there."

On the morning of September 17 Maria Baumgarten rushed Captain Dassel and Otto Bornemann up to the corridor outside Anastasia's room. "She's going to pass this way!" Miss Baumgarten cried. The two men stationed themselves in front of a massive painting and pretended to admire it. When Anastasia came out they stood at attention and saluted. "Herr Dassel declared at once that the gait was exactly the same as that of Grand Duchess Anastasia as he remembered it," Bornemann wrote. "She walked quickly, with assurance, with little steps. She answered our military salutation with a quick bow."[50]

Anastasia seemed happy to see Dassel again this morning. She asked that he and Bornemann join her in the sitting room, where she and Dassel began to talk about Tsarskoe Selo. Dassel informed her now that he had not received his medallion upon leaving the hospital. What was worse, he said, he had been away on leave at Christmas 1916 and thus had missed the other presents given to the officers — watches, he said, and sabers.

Dassel waited for Anastasia's reply, but she said nothing. Only later did she remark to Vera von Klemenz, "He remembers all the little, stupid things, and it is so far from me. . . . I know we gave presents, but I do not know what anymore, it is so far, I cannot see it. . . . Watches — yes, but I do not think sabers. . . . I don't know. . . . Sabers? Sabers? Perhaps in my mother's hospital? . . . But he says it — then it must be so. I do not know anymore what it was."

In the notes he had written about his stay at Tsarskoe Selo, which were locked away in the Duke of Leuchtenberg's safe, Dassel had observed: "At Christmastime the Grand Duchesses gave the officers cigarette cases and watches." They had *not* given sabers. Dassel had invented the detail only in order to test Anastasia's memory. It was getting better by the minute. Later in the morning Maria Baumgarten went upstairs to tell her that Captain Dassel had claimed that her father, the Tsar, had had a tattoo on his arm.

Nonsense, said Anastasia. Miss Baumgarten was to inform the young officer that Papa did not have a tattoo.

"But I expect you never saw his arms," said Miss Baumgarten.

"How can that be! He often used to row with us on the sea in Finland, and I often saw his arms. . . . No, no, that I know for sure, he had nothing whatever on his arms." Soon Anastasia called Vera von Klemenz to her room. "When I have some money," she announced, "he must have his watch. He worked for us, he was wounded, he must have it." Then she asked when Dassel was leaving Seeon: "If he is leaving soon, he must come [again] right after lunch, if he is leaving later, I would like to rest, and so should he. It is so sad that I have nothing, he will come, and I would like to give him something, a little glass of liqueur, and I cannot."

Miss von Klemenz replied that the Leuchtenbergs could easily provide Anastasia with a bottle of liqueur.

"But that is not mine," said Anastasia; "I want to give from me." After lunch she looked through her things and uncovered a check she had received recently from "one of the public."[51] She asked Miss von Klemenz to buy some liqueur with it. Then, for the first time, she fell into Miss von Klemenz's arms, sobbing and saying, "I am so happy he is here, I am so happy he has come, but it is so frightfully sad!"

The recognition came that afternoon. "Tell us, Captain," said Duke George as he, Dassel, Otto Bornemann, and Anastasia sat sipping their liqueurs, "what did you do in the hospital all day long? You must have been awfully bored."

"Oh, no," Dassel replied, turning to Anastasia, "I wouldn't say that. We read, we played checkers, and upstairs there was even a billiard table."

The interruption was immediate: "No, no, not upstairs! Billiards was downstairs. Don't you remember? Maria played well, I, not well at all."

Dassel did remember — where the billiard table had stood, how inept the Tsar's daughter had been with the cue, and how she had thought nothing of cheating to win. He also remembered that the Tsarevitch Alexis had never once come with his sisters to visit the hospital, but he claimed otherwise to the Duke and was not surprised when Anastasia, "in a sharp tone of voice," broke in: "How you have forgotten! Alyosha was never with us." [52]

One remark and a certain "transformation" settled it for Felix Dassel. He had given Anastasia a photograph of a group of officers at the Tsarskoe Selo hospital, among them a Colonel Sergeyev, who had been known at court as an opponent of Rasputin and had been sent back to the front lines as soon as he was well enough to go.

"Who is that?" asked the Duke of Leuchtenberg.

"The invalid looked at me quickly," Dassel remembered, "and just as I was going to open my mouth she broke out in a little laugh, a little laugh that sounded a bit stifled to me, a bit jerky, but exactly, exactly the same as before." The eyes lit up, the face shone with pleasure, and the words came out in a delighted peal: "The Man with the Pockets!" At that moment Dassel recognized the daughter of the Tsar.

"The Man with the Pockets" — Grand Duchess Anastasia herself had chosen the nickname, Dassel recalled, because Colonel Sergeyev had frequently displayed a shocking lapse of manners and spoken to the Grand Duchess with his hands in his pockets. There was no one alive, Dassel affirmed, who could possibly have told Anastasia anything about it: "But I no longer needed to be convinced."

When Dassel and Bornemann took their leave they told Anastasia that they would be returning to Berlin very early the next morning. She promised to come downstairs to say good-bye.

"Oh, no, Highness," Dassel objected, "it is far too early."

"But I will come downstairs," said Anastasia. To prove it she declined to give Dassel her hand. ("Too stupid!" Dassel wrote afterward. "I should have known better than to contradict her.")

She was there at six o'clock in the morning, as she had promised. She shook hands with Bornemann and with Dassel, and then, just before Dassel climbed into the car, she pressed a small envelope into his palm. Then she hurried back into the castle.

Dassel opened the envelope. Inside were a tiny gold crucifix and a note:

> Blessing instead of the Christmas present not received in the hospital of Their Imperial Highnesses A. and M. Nicolaievna.

> A.

"The *Unbekannte* is appearing in a rather queer light just lately," Faith Lavington confided to her diary shortly after Felix Dassel had been to Seeon, "not that she is any the less 'unbekanntish,' but because she has had a violent access of wounded pride, or whatever queer emotion it might be, and has had a dramatic and complete rupture with Miss Baumgarten."[53]

The story was getting too familiar: Anastasia had thrown over one of her "ladies-in-waiting." Ordinarily she attempted no justification for these sudden breaks, but this time she departed from tradition with a vengeance: "the little Russian lady" had tried to poison her. Yes! She had brought Anastasia her tea three days running, and each time Anastasia had become violently ill. Poor Miss Baumgarten, of course, had no idea what to make of this bizarre accusation. "The official rupture between the *Unbekannte* and Miss B is evidently *for ever,*" Miss Lavington wrote. ". . . This Imperial dropping of favorites is quite striking."

Vera von Klemenz having left Castle Seeon for San Remo at the beginning of October, Faith Lavington now took over Maria Baumgarten's duties full-time. Anastasia gladly welcomed the exchange, partly because a long-standing wish of hers was finally fulfilled: she began to renew her study of English. "I am to have the doubtful pleasure of giving the last of the Tsar's daughters a small English lesson every day at five o'clock," Miss Lavington wrote, "but am determined *not* to be treated in the same way, for I shall drop these rather unwelcome lessons like hotcakes if there is any sign of ill temper, as inwardly I feel quite as good as she — ha ha!" Miss Lavington need not have worried. At the first "lesson" she found Anastasia "much more nervous than I was. . . . In order to get her to talk, I took a nursery rhyme book with me, with very gay colors, and by asking her questions about these pictures, I got her to speak quite a lot and could see quite well that she does know English very well, but the trouble is to get her to speak. . . ." Miss Lavington was fascinated to see that when Anastasia let herself do it she could read, write, and even speak English — "with the purest and best English accent. . . . I was quite amazed at the purity of her speech" — but if she had to stop and think she simply froze and would not continue.

During the weeks that followed Anastasia and Miss Lavington grew ever closer to one another. "People keep saying she is ugly," Miss Lavington wrote, "but personally I do not see it, she has great distinction, and it is difficult for anyone to be a raving beauty when one lives in a dressing-gown all day, but she always looks nice, and has most beautifully kept hands, I always hide my ugly old claws when I go in to see her."

Late in the autumn Miss Lavington was witness to an event which, as described in her diary, was truly extraordinary. Her sister had sent her an article clipped from the *New York Times*, headlined "First Uncensored Photos from Soviet Russia" and depicting various rooms from the Tsar's palaces at Tsarskoe Selo and Livadia — "study, bathroom, bedrooms, drawing rooms," and so on. Miss Lavington was already on her way upstairs to give the pictures to Anastasia when Duke George's younger daughter, Tamara, suggested that they use the photographs as a test of Anastasia's memory. Feeling guilty, but excited at the prospect of uncovering new evidence, Miss Lavington "carefully cut away *every scrap* of printed matter which could show in any way what these illustrations were. . . . The next thing was to arrange matters in such a way that [Anastasia] would not know [they] were testing her memory at all. . . ." Miss Lavington waited until Anastasia had emerged from her room, consequently, and then handed her the pictures, "saying at the same time that [her] sister had sent these to [her] from America and [she] did not know what they were."

Anastasia took up the first photograph "quite indifferently," Miss Lavington went on, until suddenly she turned "very red" and exclaimed, "But this is my Papa's bathroom." Grabbing the whole pile, Anastasia "looked at them as though she could not believe her eyes," and said again, "But these are all our rooms." Then she put the pictures down and walked quickly away, "evidently very upset."

"I was standing by positively trembling," said Miss Lavington, "and Tamara, too, for she was equally sure that the plot had been seen through and that we should all be cast into outer darkness — together with Miss B, who is there already." Finally Miss Lavington gathered her courage and knocked at Anastasia's door, "expecting nothing less than a *pied au dérrière*":

Anastasia Nicolaievna was standing in the middle of the room, very much upset, biting her handkerchief as she always does, and before I could explain why I had come she asked me 3 or 4 times, "How could such photographs be in that newspaper?" by which I understood that she was disgusted at finding her private affairs in a public newspaper. My answer was that unfortunately for money anything could be done nowadays, at which she calmed down a bit and seated herself at her table telling me to sit down. She then took up the pictures and upon [my] very *innocently* enquiring all about them she told me every one *right,* though there was not a scrap of anything to show where they came from. . . . It was just as if she were living there again.

At the end of October Felix Dassel came back to Seeon for a short visit.[54] It was the last thing about her stay with the Leuchtenberg family that pleased Anastasia. The two went for long walks together and took a motor excursion down to Bad Reichenhall, where Anastasia, "all nerves and energy," insisted on buying a camera: "Kodak! Kodak! I take that. Please wrap up." But with Dassel's departure Anastasia fell into a mood so foul as to be truly frightening. An inflammation of her left leg and an eruption of boils on her back did nothing to improve her spirits. "Today was another day straight from Dante's Purgatory," Miss Lavington wrote.[55] ". . . All the accumulated bitterness of all her terrible past experiences poured out like a flood, and nothing seemed too bad or farfetched for her to say. We all passed under it, though being English, I fancy she supports me fairly well, but the Duke, the Duchess, Tamara, all, all had their reputations simply played from them. She positively dissects people, and leaves one without a word to say."

Christmas came and Anastasia made one last appearance at the Leuchtenbergs' table. During Christmas dinner she was the chance recipient of the silver wishbone, an event that gave her "superstitious delight," but she had fallen so far into paranoia that she suspected it had been planted in her food. Then in January 1928 she broke with every last one of her friends. Felix Dassel was the first. Recently he had published a series of articles in the *Tägliche Rundschau* in Berlin and had made the mistake of admitting it in a letter to Catherine Leuchtenberg, the Duke's daughter-in-law, who had already made up her mind that Anastasia was unbalanced and who greeted her verbal abuse now with silent hatred. Finally it was Miss Lavington's turn. When Dr. Lothar Nobel, who had been Anastasia's physician at the Mommsen Clinic, came for a brief visit to Seeon, Anastasia concluded that Miss Lavington had arranged the matter to some nefarious purpose, and that was the end.

"Sie können nicht herein kommen!" Anastasia bellowed when Miss Lavington knocked at her door one morning. *"Ich werde niemand sehen* [You cannot enter! I will see no one]!"

"Oh," said Miss Lavington to herself, "my head has to pay for this, I suppose." When she finally saw Anastasia in the corridor two days later Miss Lavington decided to be bold: "I walked straight up to her and said, 'Why are you cross with me Anastasia Nicolaievna?' not thinking that she was really out to slaughter, for I saw she was very much moved."

Anastasia twisted her handkerchief and replied, "*Wir wollen nicht mehr sprechen* [We will not speak anymore]."

"Anastasia Nicolaievna, you have no right to cause me so much pain; why are you so upset?"

"*Wir wollen nicht mehr sprechen.*"

"It took me just one day to decide that I was going to take the offensive," Miss Lavington continued, "for after all, a Britisher is as good as anyone, and as all the Russians hitherto have crawled around asking her pardon and demanding explanations, I thought to myself that I would go on another tack." Miss Lavington asked one of the maids to return to Anastasia's room all the little gifts Anastasia had given her over the weeks — a silk handkerchief, a photograph of herself, and so on. "Probably for the first time in her life the Sick Lady had this happen to her," Miss Lavington wrote, "and she was very miserable over it. . . . Of course I expected my small presents . . . to come whizzing into my room in return, but the extraordinary thing is that she has never returned one." And when Miss Lavington met Anastasia unexpectedly in the hallway a few days later she had "the agreeable sensation . . . that in some curious way I had the upper hand of her, and I calmly looked, through and through her as if she were glass positively, and passed calmly out in front of her without a word, as if she simply was not. . . . Just for once, she got as good as she gave."

Nobody at Castle Seeon ever forgot Anastasia's behavior during these last days, and her alienation of certain members of the Leuchtenberg family was to cost her dearly. The Duke was tired and ill — he was suffering from the first effects of the brain tumor that was going to kill him — and his family, not surprisingly, blamed Anastasia for making things worse. The Duchess had taken to slamming doors and muttering under her breath, while her children sat in the drawing room in speechless indignation. Only Faith Lavington still kept one ear open for a call from Anastasia. "You will think me awfully sentimental," she wrote, "but I must own that I feel it most terribly, for I gave of my very best. . . . *I* can't work myself up into a tempest — if I could I should feel happier. I feel a miserable, gnawing pity and anxious solicitude still for this poor woman — a sort of feeling as if some living part had been torn right out of me."

9

"SHE WAS HERSELF"

*I*n the spring of 1927 Anastasia had been introduced to a man who would change the whole course of her life. At his home in Hempstead, Long Island, Gleb Evgenievitch Botkin, the youngest son of Dr. Eugene Botkin and brother of Tatiana, had suddenly found himself swamped with press inquiries about the Tsar's daughter, his "childhood playmate,"[1] and about Anastasia, the claimant at Castle Seeon. It had taken some time for the wild and romantic stories about Anastasia to cross the ocean to the United States, but when they did, she captured the headlines. The *New York Times* described her in a front-page article as "this shred of a woman whose deranged brain continually forces her wracked body to shrink from imaginary dangers,"[2] while the *Herald Tribune*, taking note of the veritable war over Anastasia in the German press, raised her up in the public mind as "the reigning enigma of Europe."[3] Anastasia's actual identity was not the main attraction for American readers. "The mystery is too appealing," read an editorial in the *Tribune*, "the hope is too dramatic. . . . The records of every social upheaval are studded with these strange, half-furtive figures, who may have been somebody or who may only have been somebody else. Were they really? Historians and enthusiasts produce their mountains of proof; but one never really knows, and one is never quite sure that one would want to."[4]

Gleb Botkin had nothing to tell the reporters when they engaged him on the telephone. Like so many of his fellow Russian exiles, he had found the news of Anastasia's claim offensive and degrading. Only when he ran across a feature article in the *Times* containing photographs of Anastasia and recounting her meetings with Pierre Gilliard and Grand Duchess Olga at the Mommsen Clinic did Gleb begin to wonder.[5] Immediately he wrote Gilliard asking if there were any truth to the story that he had recognized Anastasia. A cable from Lausanne quickly informed him that the Tschaikovsky affair was "the result of Bolshevik propaganda" and that Anastasia was "an absolute fraud."[6] That took care of Gleb's interest until his sister Tatiana wrote to say that she had seen Anastasia and that Anastasia truly was the Tsar's daughter. Pondering these two unreserved opinions, Gleb next got in touch with his uncle, Serge Botkin, who answered that the case was a confused mess and warned Gleb not to believe anything he read in the newspapers.

In exile, Gleb Botkin earned his living as a novelist and illustrator. At the end of April 1927 he was invited by the North American Newspaper Alliance in New York to travel to Castle Seeon for a meeting with Anastasia. In return for his expenses, of course, a story was expected.[7] Gleb did not have to think twice before accepting. "Arrived in Paris," he wrote later, "I found the whole Russian colony up in arms. Much as I had already heard about the fight which had developed around the question of Frau Tschaikovsky's identity, I was nevertheless surprised to learn what a burning issue it had become. . . . I left for Bavaria my head fairly bursting with the confusing and conflicting information I had obtained."[8]

At Seeon Gleb Botkin was welcomed amiably and told to get ready for a siege. Word of his arrival had preceded him. "Oh, we had an awful time," said Catherine Leuchtenberg, "and she is furious that you came."

"Furious? Why furious?"

"She says that you have come only to write for the newspapers."

Gleb was taken aback. Later he attributed to Anastasia an ability to read people's thoughts, but it is more than likely that publicity was on her mind already: Gleb's arrival at Seeon had coincided with the Schanzkowska storm. For several days, in any case, Anastasia stuck to her decision not to receive "Tanya's" brother. Word emerged that everything was useless; everything was hopeless; it was too dreadful, and so on. One remark only was directed at Gleb: "Ask him if he has brought his funny animals."

"God alone knows what she meant by that," said Natalie Leuchtenberg.[9] Gleb knew, but for the moment he said nothing.

The meeting came on the afternoon of May 9, 1927, as Anastasia
left Castle Seeon for Wasserburg, there to meet Franziska Schanzkowska's brother Felix. As prearranged with the Duke of Leuchtenberg, Gleb stood idly by in the main foyer when Anastasia came
down the stairs. Seeing him, she stopped short, looked around her
quickly, and then, resigned, extended her hand with the words "Oh,
how do you do?"

"The shock was so great," said Gleb, "that I remained standing
unable to utter a word. She [was] changed, of course. She was now
a grown woman. . . . She looked sick, tired, as it seemed to me
frightened." But the recognition was unconditional: "As she went
in her swift manner toward the car she slightly bowed her head
with an absent and benevolent smile, in that inimitable manner of
royalty who know that wherever they go they are greeted from all
directions and automatically return these salutations, bowing and
smiling to everybody and to no one in particular."[10]

A week at Castle Seeon set Gleb Botkin off on a lifelong quest to
win Anastasia's rights. She had never had a champion like this one.
Articulate, sensitive, with pallid skin and soulful green eyes, Gleb
was a talented artist, a wicked satirist, and a born crusader. The
friendship he forged with Anastasia was unlike any other in either's
experience. There were many who thought they had fallen in love
(many, indeed, who said they were lovers). But in fact humor and
playfulness were at the root of the relationship, just as earlier, Gleb
said, *fun* had been the key to his dealings with the Tsar's daughter.
After their first, quick meeting in the hallway at Seeon, when Anastasia had relented completely and received him in her room, Gleb
unpacked his "funny animals." There were exceptionally clever car-
toons he had drawn of various beasts — mostly pigs — dressed in
human clothes and depicting the more pompous functionaries at the
Russian court. Gleb used to amuse the Tsar's children with them.
To drawings made before the Revolution and at Tobolsk he had
now added newer ones, which he brought out without remark for
Anastasia's consideration. She laughed at the new pictures, Gleb
remembered, but seemed bothered by the old ones.

"You have made these drawings long ago," Anastasia said.

"Yes."

"You have made them in Russia."

"Yes."

Who could have told Anastasia, Gleb wondered, which of his pictures had been made in Russia and which had not? Who but the Tsar's daughter would have laughed so hard when she learned that Kaiser Wilhelm had shaved his beard and no longer had a moustache that "stuck up in the air"; or would have declared with such a straight face, when asked if she would like to visit France, "Oh, no, I don't like the French. It always seems to me that none of them had a bath for several years"?

This was Gleb Botkin's Anastasia — "witty," "cheerful," "charming," "delightful." [11] In the many articles and the two books he later published about her — while admitting that she was "exasperating" and "hopelessly stubborn" — Gleb tended to gloss over the less attractive elements of Anastasia's personality and to present them, not as defects of character, but as evidence merely of her autocratic heritage. She was, to Gleb's way of thinking, an almost magically noble tragic princess, and he saw it as his mission to restore her to her rightful position by any means necessary.

"I understand that you are convinced that the invalid is Grand Duchess Anastasia," said a Russian nobleman to Gleb as they drove away from Seeon.

"Exactly."

"May I ask whether your conviction is based on any specific evidence . . . or whether it is simply your feeling?"

"It is simply my knowledge."

"But have you any facts to support your contention? What would you tell, for instance, to people who may not accept your opinion as infallible?"

"I would tell them to go to the devil." [12]

That is just what Gleb Botkin proceeded to do. He was going to shout Anastasia's plight from the treetops. He was going to write, he was going to publicize, he was going to make a noise so loud that the Romanov family would be forced to come to Anastasia's aid or risk public humiliation. [13] Of that plan Anastasia knew absolutely nothing. "Nothing will ever come of it," she had warned Gleb. "Nothing will ever be well again." But Gleb did not agree. He'd had an idea: "I asked Anastasia if she wanted to go to the United States? She replied that she would like to go to America, but that the journey could hardly be arranged. I promised to do everything in my power to bring her to my adopted country, where, I felt, she would be reasonably safe." [14]

It was a promise Gleb Botkin meant to keep. Returned to New

York, Gleb wasted no time bringing Anastasia's case to the attention of the American public and the growing Russian colony in Manhattan. Several of his articles in the *Herald Tribune* quickly caught the attention of Margharita Derfelden, whose late husband had been a member of the personal guard detachment of the Dowager Empress and who herself remained a close friend of the Empress and her two daughters.[15] Mme. Derfelden asked Gleb now if there was anything she could do to help. There was indeed, Gleb replied: she could spread the word. It was thus, in the summer of 1927, that Gleb had a call from Mrs. William B. Leeds, the former Princess Xenia Georgievna of Russia, a daughter of Grand Duke George Mikhailovitch and a second cousin of Grand Duchess Anastasia.[16]

As a child Princess Xenia and her sister, Nina, had often played with the two youngest daughters of the Tsar and with their brother, Alexis. Although Xenia and Nina had left Russia in 1914, passing the war years with their mother in England, they both retained vivid memories of their "frightfully temperamental," "wild and rough" cousin Anastasia,[17] who cheated at games, kicked, scratched, pulled hair, and generally knew how to make herself obnoxious. "Anastasia was madly jealous of me because I was taller than she was," Princess Nina recalled. "As the daughter of the Emperor she thought she ought by rights to tower over everyone."[18] After the Revolution and the execution of their father, both of Grand Duke George's daughters were married, Nina to the Georgian prince Paul Chavchavadze, and Xenia, at eighteen, to Billy Leeds, son and heir of the American tin magnate.[19] It was regarded as one of the great matches of the twenties — Leeds, "the Tin Plate Croesus," and Xenia, "the Daughter of a Thousand Earls" — and the two were among the leaders of Long Island's North Shore society.[20] Now, after consultation with Gleb Botkin, Xenia extended an invitation for Anastasia to live as a guest at Kenwood, her estate at Oyster Bay, the millionaires' haven on Long Island Sound.

Princess Xenia had offered her hospitality to Anastasia for a very simple reason. "I had heard that Botkin was arranging to bring 'the invalid' to the United States through a newspaper organization," she explained. "This bothered me because I had heard so many conflicting stories. It then occurred to me that I should take her myself and avoid all this proposed publicity. For if she were indeed an impostor it would save much unpleasantness for my family, and if she were the real Anastasia it was ghastly to think that nothing was being done for her. . . . This solution would be simple, so it seemed to me."[21]

"There is a universal feeling of compassion here for poor little Princess Xenia," Faith Lavington wrote at Castle Seeon, "who has no idea what she has landed herself in for."[22] Earlier in the year Anastasia had been pleased and touched by Gleb Botkin's proposal to bring her to the United States. It was another matter entirely when concrete plans materialized. "She is totally unstrung at the idea of leaving Europe," Miss Lavington reported.[23] More than ever Anastasia feared that she would never get the chance to see the Dowager Empress: "This seems to bother her more than anything else, and certainly when I happened to see her today she looked like a ghost, so white and wretched." Anastasia's supporters in Europe had also greeted the news of Xenia's invitation with mixed feelings. Grand Duke Andrew, for one, did not want to see Anastasia leave Europe until the question of her identity had been legally clarified.[24] A trip to America smacked of flight from the Schanzkowska scandal, first of all. On the other hand, there was the constant problem of money to be considered, and the Leeds' had no worries in that regard. While regretting the move, Andrew realized that Xenia's offer was probably the only answer. "Why must I go away from Europe," Anastasia cried when the matter was settled, "because my family will not give me just a little to live in some tiny corner, it is because of them that I must go, and I feel I can't go so far away to a strange country, oh why will my family not know me?"[25]

In January 1928 the arrangements for Anastasia's trip had been completed. On Princess Xenia's assurance that she would be responsible for Anastasia's financial maintenance the American consul at Munich granted Anastasia a six-months' visa. Then at the end of the month Xenia sent Agnes Gallagher,[26] her daughter's Scottish nanny, to Seeon to bring Anastasia to New York. Miss Gallagher arrived to find the Leuchtenberg household still in a turmoil. "Anastasia was at war with them all," she remembered. No one at Seeon believed that Anastasia really meant to go ahead with the trip, but to general amazement she told Miss Gallagher that she was ready to leave immediately. Anastasia wanted to know only why Princess Xenia had not come to fetch her in person. Surprised, Miss Gallagher replied that Xenia had been ill and had just left with her husband for a cruise in the West Indies. "Oh," said Anastasia, before asking that her bags be packed at once.

The original idea had been for Anastasia to arrive in New York at the moment of Xenia's return from her ocean cruise, but in January word reached Seeon that she would have to be brought to Berlin for "interrogation" before leaving Germany.[27] The Duke of Leuchtenberg was too tired to fight against the new threat, but Miss Gallagher told him not to worry about it: she had been sent to bring Anastasia from Seeon to New York, and that was exactly what she meant to do. Passage was hastily booked for "Miss Gallagher and niece"[28] on the luxury Cunarder *Berengaria,* due to sail from Cherbourg on February 1. And so, on the twenty-ninth of January, 1928, Anastasia, with Miss Gallagher and the Duke, drove away from Castle Seeon, never to see it or any of the Leuchtenbergs again. To the Duke's astonishment she had paused to kiss the Duchess good-bye ("and she even thanked her!").[29] There was, as Faith Lavington observed, "a subdued but marked sigh of relief from the family." Miss Lavington went on:

Miss Gallagher and the Sick Lady went away by a very early train last Saturday morning . . . so it meant getting up at 6 o'c. Naturally I was up to see Miss G. off, and the Young Duchess [Catherine Leuchtenberg] was up in her bedroom and when she heard the first puffings of the motor car, as it began to get underway, she concentrated all of her mental powers on the Sick Lady and said to herself, "If you curse my husband, my children or this my household, then may this curse return upon you and yours forever," and this she continued to do until they were gone, then she appeared exhausted but victorious, having as she said "routed" the Sick Lady's last malediction. It was very curious that the Sick Lady looked earnestly up at our windows when going —was she mentally saying goodbye? — or was she surprised not to see the windows lined with attentive spectators, we shall never know, anyhow she is gone, and I sincerely hope that she will be a happier woman in America.[30]

After a day's shopping in Munich, where she bought a new wardrobe entirely in white, Anastasia and party moved on to Paris and booked into the Hôtel du Palais. Her stopover there had not been announced, of course, partly in order to spare her any further agitation and partly because one last confrontation had been planned that her friends hoped would not be compromised by the glare of publicity. Anastasia was now, at last, to meet Grand Duke Andrew.[31] The idea hadn't pleased her. "*Ten years* they have let me suffer like this," Anastasia cried; "now that I am quite broken, it is too late."[32] It was all Duke George could do to persuade her to see

"Uncle Andrew" even for a few minutes. "Anastasia looked at him and sobbed," said Agnes Gallagher, "but refused to talk to him. The Grand Duke himself was very much upset and looked as if he might be seeing a ghost."[33] When he emerged from Anastasia's room Andrew headed straight for a chair and sank into it with the words "I have seen Nicky's daughter, I have seen Nicky's daughter."[34]

It was, in Andrew's words, "an unshakable recognition."[35] He wrote Serge Botkin: "For two days I had occasion to observe the invalid, and I can tell you that no doubt remains in my mind: She is Grand Duchess Anastasia. It is impossible not to recognize her. Naturally, years and suffering have marked her, but not as much as I would have imagined. Her face is striking in its profound sadness, but when she smiles, it is she, it is Anastasia, without a doubt."

Andrew had made a promise to himself not to bother Anastasia with questions or advice and not to remain at her bedside any longer than she was willing to have him. When he left on the first evening he gave her a small potted plant to take with her on the trip to New York. She was pleased.[36] Later that evening she learned that Princess Lili Obolensky, a former lady-in-waiting to Empress Alexandra, was waiting downstairs and had very respectfully asked for an audience. She did not even bother to say no. "Anastasia said that [Princess Obolensky] was no good," Miss Gallagher reported, "that she was Russian and false to [the Empress]. When I repeated this to Grand Duke Andrew later, he said that was true and that Anastasia knew too much."[37]

She gave her friends and her enemies one last item to quarrel over before she left Europe. Probably she was not aware of what she was doing. At breakfast Miss Gallagher was confronted with a waiter who did not speak English, the only language Miss Gallagher knew. When Anastasia saw her companion waving her hands in despair, she stepped forward impatiently and ordered the meal herself — in French. ("I'm not sure she actually spoke French," said Miss Gallagher later, "but we got exactly what we wanted for breakfast.")[38] Then Anastasia and Miss Gallagher went down to the lobby, where a number of Russian monarchists, alerted to the news of Anastasia's presence in Paris, sat behind their newspapers and pretended not to stare. Grand Duke Andrew escorted the ladies and the Duke of Leuchtenberg to the Gare du Nord, where they sat for about an hour in Anastasia's compartment. Andrew's wife, Mathilde Kschessinska, had brought flowers, which broke the ice and moved Anastasia to remark that Mathilde was "really very nice." [39] Finally everyone said good-bye and the train moved off to Cherbourg.

During the trip Anastasia barely uttered a word, only looked out the window at the flat French countryside and occasionally whispered, "*Ich habe Angst, ich habe Angst* [I am afraid, I am afraid]." [40] At Cherbourg the Duke rode out with her on the cutter to the *Berengaria*. They said good-bye at the railing.

"Are you still angry with me because I brought so many people to see you?" the Duke asked. He was crying.

"She did not answer," the Duke reported to Harriet von Rathlef, "nor thank me, but only smiled roguishly and without malice. And the last thing she said was, 'All this is the fault of Frau von Rathlef.' So, dear madam, the last word was for you." [41]

Anastasia stood at the rail and watched until the cutter had steamed from sight. She had started crying, too, and as she walked down to her cabin with Agnes Gallagher she stammered her regrets at leaving Europe.

She spoke in English. [42] By the time she docked in New York a week later she was speaking nothing else.

With Anastasia gone, "the opposition" in Europe crumbled. Pierre Gilliard's *False Anastasia* fell with a thud when it was published exactly a year later and quickly went out of print. "Let us hope that this creature will stay in America," the Grand Duchess of Hesse wrote her son, "and that we'll be rid of her here." [43]

The news of Grand Duke Andrew's recognition of Anastasia, meantime, had spread rapidly, provoking, Andrew said, "a real storm in many circles and most unexpected protests." [44] Against his wishes, the Duke of Leuchtenberg had broken the news to the press. "Not only have I not permitted [him] to publish my opinion," Andrew complained, "but I also requested that he not even speak of the meeting until I had communicated my ideas to the members of our family. . . . My position, which was already delicate, has become more complicated, and this has cast an undesirable aura around the matter." [45] In fact the Grand Duke was under fire from all sides. "Everyone is persecuting me because of the identification I made," Andrew wrote, "saying that this is not the time, and even that it is dangerous, etc. But I cannot hide the truth to satisfy others; I stated what I saw and what I had no doubt of. . . ." [46] I cannot understand why she has not been recognized sooner. It is completely incomprehensible." [47] Only one task remained for Andrew.

The strength of his feeling and the sheer awfulness of Anastasia's situation now moved him to abandon the polite game he had been playing with his cousin in Copenhagen, Grand Duchess Olga:

Dear Olga,

Once again, and probably for the last time, I am writing to you about Anastasia Tschaikovsky, because I feel I must carry out my duty to the end.

You probably know that Guigui [George of] Leuchtenberg, due to lack of funds, could no longer house Anastasia Tschaikovsky and take care of her. Also for lack of funds we were unable to place her in a sanatorium. That is why it has been necessary, to our great regret, to accept the proposition to send her to America, where the necessary provisions for her housing and health have been assured.

On the 30th of January, while en route to America, Frau Tschaikovsky was brought to Paris, and I went there myself to see her at last and to form a personal opinion about this woman, to find out who she really is, about whom such bitter controversy has arisen, such legends have been born, and whose name inspires endless discussions of rights and family misunderstandings.

I spent two days with her. I observed her closely and attentively, and to the best of my conscience I must acknowledge that Anastasia Tschaikovsky is no one other than my niece, Grand Duchess Anastasia Nicolaievna. I recognized her at once, and further observation only confirmed my first impression. There is for me no doubt: she is Anastasia.

I only regret that you do not wish to see her again, now that she is settled. You would certainly have recognized her, just as surely as I have done.

You do not know, Olga, what I went through in those days, sitting beside her, looking at poor Anastasia — but so ill and careworn. If you had seen her lovely smile, still so childlike, her eyes filled with sadness and suffering, your heart, like mine, would have been broken.

Now she is already far away, in America. We shall not soon see her again, if we ever do see her again. What thoughts are going to haunt her in that distant country? God alone knows, but they will certainly be terrible, and a sorrowful question will obsess her, a question no one can answer for her. Will Anastasia survive these new ordeals? Who knows? But I am going to pray to God that she does survive, that she recovers her health and comes back to us from that distant land, not, this time, as a hunted and persecuted creature, but with her head high and with the strength of spirit to pardon those who have brought her so much misfortune.

Andrew[48]

There is no indication that Grand Duchess Olga, alone with the Dowager Empress in Copenhagen, ever answered her cousin Andrew's letter.

Gleb Botkin stood waiting with more than two dozen reporters on the East Thirteenth Street pier as the *Berengaria* moved into New York Harbor.[49] A dense fog over the bay had already held up the liner for several hours and now seemed likely to delay it overnight, so Botkin and the press corps boarded a Coast Guard cutter and went out themselves to welcome Anastasia to the United States. While Gleb prepared her for the ordeal ahead, the newsmen lounged outside the door of Cabin 419 and tried to piece together what they knew of Anastasia's story. The rumors were that she had come to New York to have the "bayonet scars" removed from her face. Someone had heard that she was hoping to break into films.[50] Everyone wondered in the meantime why her hostess, Princess Xenia, had not come down to meet the boat, but rather had left Gleb Botkin with authorization to act in her behalf. What was going on here?

All day and into the early evening the reporters kept their vigil. One go-getter planted himself outside the ladies' lavatory on D-Deck, taking pictures of every woman who went in and came out.[51] He explained that even a Grand Duchess had to go to the bathroom sooner or later and was crushed to learn that Anastasia had a private toilet in her cabin. Several times in the course of the long afternoon Gleb popped out to announce that "Her Imperial Highness" absolutely would not consent to an interview. Toward evening Agnes Gallagher appeared to make a statement: "I am sorry, but Madame cannot and will not see anyone. Neither now nor ever, tonight, tomorrow, will she speak with anyone of the press. . . . She will not talk, and there is no need of any of your remaining, for under no condition will any of you be allowed to speak with her." Gloomily the reporters sailed back to Manhattan, leaving the stewards to guard Anastasia's door through the night "as stoutly as could a company of palace guards."[52]

Nothing so equivocal as silence could stand in the way of the press and its story. The next morning every paper in New York carried a front-page feature on Anastasia's arrival: " 'Lost Daughter' of Tsar Hides on Ship in Bay";[53] "Legendary 'Duchess' Lands"[54] — the press had a holiday. "She comes surrounded," said the *Herald Tribune* in an editorial, " — like the exploits of Colonel T. E. Lawrence — with the full publicity of a complete reticence. . . . She granted no interviews, but locked herself in her cabin, preserving an impenetrable manner that divided between regal hauteur and utter indifference to openly expressed skepticism."[55] But her purchases in Paris had been disappointingly "meagre, and of uncostly nature," not at all the kind of thing one expected of a grand duchess. Only three times during the voyage, the reporters found out, had Anastasia appeared on deck. Twice she attended movie showings. No one on board had had any idea who she was.[56]

February 9, 1928, dawned clear and bright and the *Berengaria* at last managed to dock. The reporters had come back in force: more than fifty stood on board this morning with their cameras ready. Gleb Botkin had returned in the company of Charles Foley, an American friend who was also the personal manager of Serge Rachmaninoff.[57] The reporters went mad with excitement when they discovered that the great Rachmaninoff had "endorsed the woman's claim" and helped provide the funds required to bring her over from Germany. "Mr. Botkin and Mr. Foley were flying about," wrote the correspondent for the *Evening Post*, "seeing customs officials and darting into the stateroom. . . . And then it became apparent that this passenger was to be accorded special privileges."[58] Considerately, the doctor whose job it was to examine aliens on arrival had agreed to descend in person to Anastasia's cabin with a uniformed immigrations officer.[59] She took this concession as deference, only nodding silently to Agnes Gallagher when the questions began. Within two minutes the procedure had been completed, and the doctor was able to assure the reporters outside: "Ya, she's all right."

"Sure," said his companion, "she's jake."[60]

By now the *Berengaria* had been emptied of its passengers; only Anastasia and her retinue still remained on board. Preceded by the stern Miss Gallagher, who carried one of her bags, and flanked by Gleb and Foley, she now stepped briskly from her door.[61]

"Here she comes!" someone cried.

"Bang went the flashlights," wrote the *Evening Journal's* man, "and down the narrow corridor came the party. . . . In the very center, protected on all sides, was a small woman. Only her eyes

and nose were visible." [62] For a moment everybody paused to stare
at Anastasia in her black fur and her brown felt hat, which she had
pulled down tightly over her brow. Someone ventured later that she
cut "really a pathetic figure" [63] as she stood quivering in the middle
of the hall. Then the flashes went off again and the reporters began
shouting:

"What kind of trip did you have?"

"Tell us who you are!"

"Where are you going?"

"Are you the Grand Duchess or an impostor?"

"Show us your face! Show us your face!"

"For a brief moment Madame Tschaikovsky seemed to smile,
timidly," one of the reporters observed. "She lowered her fur piece,
just enough so that one could catch a glimpse of her mouth. Her
cheeks were very pale and she looked frightened. . . . Members of
the party patted the young woman's shoulders and whispered to
her." Now, as Anastasia rushed down the gangplank and along the
docks to the freight elevator, the reporters surged forward. "Keep
them off!" Foley cried.[64] He began to swing at them wildly, knocking to the ground two or three who came too close. "I'm a witness!
I'm a witness!" one of the injured yelled.[65] Next to the elevator was
a circular staircase. Down it Anastasia went, practically flying off
the docks to a waiting Buick sedan. "Show us your face!" somebody shouted for the last time, and then Anastasia and company
sped off into the city.

In the back seat of the Buick Gleb handed Anastasia a bunch of
wilted flowers. "Are you glad to be here?" he asked.

"I don't know. Tell me, do you really like this country?" [66]

At the wheel of the getaway car was Mrs. Auguste Richard, another friend of Gleb's. A careful word to one of the reporters now
sent the whole pack dashing out to Hetty Richard's house in Lawrence, Long Island, where they camped on the lawn for several days,
pestering the maids and throwing pebbles at the windows.[67] It was
a clever trick. In reality Anastasia had gone to the Park Avenue
townhouse of Annie Burr Jennings, the elderly, wealthy daughter of
a director of the original Standard Oil Trust, who had agreed to
take care of her until Princess Xenia's return from the West Indies.
Everyone at Miss Jennings's — and there was quite a crowd —
wanted to know how Anastasia's voyage had been, and Anastasia
could only reply through Miss Gallagher that it had been awful.
She had not been much impressed by the *Berengaria,* said Miss Gal-

lagher: "She said it was clean, all right, but otherwise poor in comparison with the Tsar's yacht, the *Standart*." The weather, too, had been "stormy and disagreeable," unlike anything in her experience.[68] Finally the reporters — Gleb had warned her about them, said Anastasia, but nothing had prepared her for the animals waiting to greet her on the pier. She still had not recovered from the shock: "It nearly killed me . . . the photographers made me crazy with the apparatus — there were so many."[69]

By late afternoon Anastasia had pulled herself together sufficiently to take a look at her surroundings. She liked what she saw. The enormous windows overlooking Park Avenue were just to her taste — there was so much light! — and the flowers that filled all the rooms made her feel as if she belonged there, "as if I were at home." Miss Jennings had had the happy idea of presenting her with a gigantic orchid and thus endeared herself immediately, Anastasia declaring that "she hadn't had one since she left Russia."[70] And that evening, while the news of her landing blared over the radio and the reporters drank bourbon on Hetty Richard's lawn, Anastasia and Gleb Botkin slipped off to the movies.[71]

"Anyway," read one of the morning headlines, "She Disappears like a Story-Book Duchess." The attempts to track down Anastasia lasted for several weeks and resulted in "odd similes: As difficult to find as a Grand Duchess in New York."[72] In the end, the newspapers were obliged to take the information they needed from secondary sources. "The slender threads of this romance yesterday shot forth from New York to various parts of the country," read a report in the *American*, " — wherever groups of Russian refugees are to be found. Controversy appeared less casual and more tense as the fact of the woman's actual landing was carried to these centres by wire." In Austin, Texas, of all places, a gentleman known as "Bob Lukan" stepped forward, claiming to be the nephew of Leon Trotsky and declaring that he had personally saved Grand Duchess Anastasia from the bloodbath at Ekaterinburg.[73] Then there was Alexander de Zaroubine, who professed to have been a music teacher at Tsarskoe Selo and dismissed Anastasia's claim with this logic: "If she was Grand Duchess Anastasia, I would be welcome in her home."[74] Neither had Anastasia's antagonists across the ocean allowed her to begin her new life quietly. In Darmstadt, Count Hardenberg drafted a lengthy report denouncing Anastasia and had copies sent to all potential "believers" at home and abroad (Princess Xenia found one waiting for her when she returned from her cruise).[75] With suspicious regularity, too, European correspondents were wiring news of myriad "Anastasias" and "Tatianas" suddenly clamoring for their rights again all over the world, a phenomenon that was meant to cast doubt on Anastasia's own claim, and succeeded.[76] But the strongest words came direct from Moscow, when the Kremlin startled everybody by unexpectedly taking a stand on the identity question. In a cruel piece entitled "The Toothless Girl," *Izvestia* portrayed the "Anastasia" scandal as nothing more than a symbol of decadence and demoralization in the monarchist emigration.[77] The analysis could not have been more accurate.

Moscow needn't have bothered, because her foes in the West were doing a fine job attacking Anastasia on their own. Quickly another witness, again a man who had never laid eyes on Anastasia, took up the banner of her opponents and went to work in earnest. This was Grand Duke Alexander Mikhailovitch, the estranged husband of the Tsar's sister Xenia, a gifted public speaker and notorious rake who spent a good deal of his time in the United States. The Grand Duke wrote in his memoirs:

I remember the endless visits paid to me in connection with this story by the zealous New York reporters. They wanted a "statement": Did I or did I not accept the claims of Miss Tschaikovsky? Was she or was she not Grand Duchess Anastasia? I felt hurt for my wife and sister-in-law. "Now, gentlemen," I said to the newsgatherers, "let us forget for a while about myself. But do you think that Grand Duchess Xenia and Grand Duchess Olga would sit quietly in Europe ignoring the appeals of a daughter of their brother? Do you think that the King of England would let his cousin fight her case in the American newspapers?"

The gentlemen of the press were seemingly convinced.[78]

In exile Grand Duke Alexander had learned how to exploit common notions of royal altruism, but in reality he watched the course of the "Anastasia" affair with nothing like the serenity his memoirs suggest. In October 1928 Alexander authored a formal denunciation of Anastasia for the world press,[79] but even before that he had developed what had to be the most original idea yet. The Grand Duke was a confirmed spiritualist and table-rapper. On one of his extended lecture tours of the United States he declared of Anastasia, "the excitable pretender":[80] "[Grand Duchess Anastasia's] spirit has returned to this world and incorporated itself into another body. She knows so much about the intimate life of the Tsar and his family that there is simply no other explanation for it; and of course it wouldn't be the first time that a spirit has returned to earth in new physical form."[81]

The New York papers lapped it up. All in all, however, the press stopped short of any outright endorsement or rejection of Anastasia's claim.[82] The major newspapers, including the staid and skeptical *New York Times,* tried only to cover her story as accurately as they could, and if the reporters had wished to see more of Anastasia in the city's fashionable salons and night spots, in the end they had to be content that she had come to New York at all: she was terrific copy. "The visitor is said to be entirely unconcerned whether the public accepts the claim," one reporter remarked in disbelief, before conceding that "the skeptics appeared to be gaining more recruits."[83] Such thoughtful and sympathetic pieces as appeared in *The Nation, The North American Review,* and other journals, in fact, were no match for the easy slander of Anastasia's Russian opponents. When the president of the Paris Russian Monarchist Council saw fit to inform his compatriots in New York of Grand Duke Andrew's recent recognition of Anastasia he added, incredibly, that "the Grand Duke must be mistaken . . . for there is not a particle of evidence on which such a recognition can be based."[84] This dumbfounding presumption typifies Anastasia's dilemma, but nothing surpasses the bizarre statement of another monarchist organization in New York. Its leader, striving to remain anonymous, only let it be known that he had once enjoyed "access to the palace." He told reporters, verbatim: "We do not deny she is Grand Duchess Anastasia. We simply say that it is impossible for this woman to be she. She was incontrovertibly massacred with the remainder of her family."[85]

Not long after her arrival in New York, Anastasia learned that there had been a threat on her life. Someone, somehow, had discovered her whereabouts and had telephoned Annie Jennings to warn her of a bomb concealed on the premises. This was only the first of many hoaxes, but it sufficed to convince Anastasia that she had probably made a terrible mistake in coming to America. New York City had already left her totally bewildered. She had never seen anything like it: the mass of concrete, the frantic activity, the grimy subways, and such typically American conveniences as the five-and-dime: "I had never been in such a store. It is a store in which everything can be bought for ten cents — and people *eat* there — you can get lunch for ten cents." [86] She couldn't believe it. Nor had she been prepared for Miss Jennings's society friends, who gripped her by the hand and nearly broke her fingers while introducing her to their wives as "Grand Duchess." But to Miss Jennings and her set, Anastasia was a social find of the first rank — this was the Metropolitan Opera crowd, horse-lovers all, philanthropists, prizewinning gardeners, and patrons of the arts — and Anastasia was obliged to meet more of these friendly Americans than she might have wished.[87]

She spent three weeks or so on Park Avenue with Miss Jennings, appearing at dinners, cocktail parties, and afternoon teas while she waited impatiently for Princess Xenia's return. It was an exhausting experience for Anastasia, made bearable only by its novelty, and when she was not greeting the curious she remained in bed, wondering what on earth she had gotten herself into. Gleb Botkin came to see her often with his friends — sometimes Russians, sometimes Americans, always inquisitive. She could not begin to keep the names and faces straight, but she did recall the day she was introduced to Serge Rachmaninoff, who sat at her bedside and patted her hand,[88] and to Margharita Derfelden, the Dowager Empress's friend, who had first encouraged Princess Xenia to bring Anastasia to New York. Yes, Anastasia agreed, Mme. Derfelden was very kind, but she was tired now and wanted to go to Oyster Bay: "I came to America in the belief that I would find rest."[89] When would Xenia be back from her cruise?

Mme. Derfelden answered the question as best she could: soon, soon. She had been shocked by her meeting with Anastasia — deeply shocked. She had not wanted to believe in the identity. "I tried to keep an open mind," she wrote some time later, "and should have been glad, under the painful circumstances, to discover any small but logical fact to prove she was *not* what she claimed to be." It couldn't be done. "I treated her as if I were convinced of her identity," Mme. Derfelden went on. "This was the easier because upon first glance I was impressed by her resemblance to her family; especially by her carriage, which was that of her paternal grandmother, and by a particular trick of voice — a dropping from time to time to a deeper note — which was also characteristic of the Dowager Empress."[90] For the remainder of Anastasia's stay on Park Avenue Mme. Derfelden acted as a kind of chaperone and gave Anastasia some relief from the steady stream of Auchinclosses, Franklins, Jameses, Goulds, and minor Roosevelts who paraded through Miss Jennings's apartment.[91]

"I do believe!" Margharita Derfelden finally confessed. "I can't get away from that." [92] It was no different when Princess Xenia returned from the West Indies at the end of February, expecting to encounter a deranged invalid and meeting instead a woman who, she had to conclude, was a cousin long presumed dead. Xenia, too, had not wanted to believe it. She had no reason to challenge the negative attitude of her family in Europe until her own experience convinced her that the family was wrong. Before she brought Anastasia to Oyster Bay — before the two women had even been introduced to each other — Xenia took the time to watch her guest in action. Quietly, unannounced, she entered Annie Jennings's crowded salon and stood at a distance while Anastasia held court. The moment Anastasia gave her hand to Gleb Botkin, Xenia knew she was looking at an equal. "It was so matter-of-course," she remembered, "so unforced — in no way a theatrical gesture. With it she radiated a natural grandeur and I was impressed on the spot." [93]

Princesss Xenia was a granddaughter of King George of Greece and a grandniece of Queen Alexandra of England. [94] Her instant recognition of a shared background with Anastasia marked the beginning of a special, delicate relationship that would last until Xenia's death in 1965. Anastasia had never been so glad to be anywhere as she was now at Kenwood, the Leedses' sprawling, multi-tiered Long Island estate, on the water near Cold Spring Harbor and not far away from the Roosevelt mansion at Sagamore Hill. She had her own room and was free to do exactly as she pleased. She could receive visitors if she wanted to and turn them away if she wanted to. She could play tennis, ride horses, walk along the beach, or go for outings on the boat. She seemed content. All the while Xenia was watching her in her new-found freedom, and listening. "One of the most convincing elements of her personality," Xenia recalled, "was a completely unconscious acceptance of her identity. She was herself at all times and never gave the slightest impression of acting a part. . . . I am firmly convinced that the claimant is, in fact, Grand Duchess Anastasia of Russia." [95]

In Europe, the reaction to Xenia's acceptance of Anastasia was just as expected. Pierre Gilliard learned of her opinion in time to label it "valueless" in *The False Anastasia*. He could only take a very narrow approach: "There is nothing here that should surprise us. Princess Xenia left Russia in the spring of 1914; she was thus ten-and-a-half when she last saw Grand Duchess Anastasia, when the latter was twelve-and-a-half. Biased as she was in favor of the unfortunate survivor, it is easy to see how she believed she had recognized a woman whom, in fact, she didn't even know." [96] Xenia had no intention of joining battle with Gilliard, but she did endeavor to answer the charge. "I shouldn't say that even after prolonged association I recognized the claimant *visually*," she explained. ". . . Fourteen years had passed since I had last seen Anastasia in the Crimea in the spring of 1914, but I felt I was competent to make up my mind on the difference between a member of my own family and an unfortunate Polish peasant woman who, so it was claimed, had been taught these things." There were specifics. There was "an all-around family resemblance, particularly on her mother's side." There was Anastasia's chronic moodiness, which reminded Xenia of the "frightfully temperamental" cousin she had known in Russia. There was the commanding bearing, the hot temper, and the tendency to melancholy that Xenia remembered in her godmother, Empress Alexandra. And there were, as always, Anastasia's stunning blue eyes: "Her father, the Tsar, and his sister, Grand Duchess Xenia, had similarly expressive eyes as I recall." But Princess Xenia had not invited Anastasia to Oyster Bay to prove or disprove her identity. She had invited her in order to give her a rest — to give the whole family a rest — and she knew that she had to tread carefully. She explained:

I was playing a kind of double role with the claimant, and I deliberately chose not to ask her any questions about the past. I wanted to give her every chance to reveal her true personality to me, without my influencing her with memories of her childhood or with questions. . . . I felt that if she were separated from doubtful people accused of suggesting memories and facts which she claimed to know, then her true identity and personality must reveal itself. This in my opinion is exactly how it turned out, what I found and have therefore firmly believed ever since: that she is Anastasia. . . . I confined myself to a constant observation. And it was above all through this observation that I was able to convince myself finally that her behavior did not consist of studied posturings or words she had learned, but rather that she was herself. [97]

"She was herself" — in three words Princess Xenia spoke for everyone who knew Anastasia; everyone, that is, who had the patience and the grace to accept her as she was. The simplicity of the statement speaks louder than any argument, and indeed the days at Oyster Bay passed by at first without a ripple of controversy. There were no more confrontations, no more spot tests or surprise meetings. Anastasia had extracted a promise from her hostess that no member of the Romanov family would be brought to see her without her permission, and Xenia was as good as her word.[98] Sometimes Anastasia joined the Leedses for lunch or dinner — she dined occasionally with Serge Rachmaninoff[99] and with Adele Astaire[100] — but more often she sat alone in her room, resting or playing with Xenia's daughter, Nancy, who was three at the time. Even Xenia's sister, Nina, got to see Anastasia only once for about five minutes,[101] not sufficient time to reach any conclusion about her identity, but long enough to know this: "Whoever she is, she is no Polish peasant. She is a lady of good society, and it is not true that she cannot speak Russian." [102]

For the duration of her residence at Oyster Bay Anastasia spoke almost entirely in English. Princess Xenia never heard a German word out of her. "We are madly talking English with A. N.," Xenia wrote Grand Duke Andrew in France.[103] Anastasia's English accent was "good," Xenia said, although grammatically she was "a bit rusty. That is, English phrases failed her now and then." [104] But there were never any gaps in communication. "The family was so polylingual," Xenia's daughter recalled, "that, when speaking among themselves, they chose a word simply for its precision, from one of several languages, including Russian. . . . My mother deliberately substituted Russian words in the crux of a sentence to see if Anastasia would follow what was said. She always did." [105] Sometimes, too, without thinking about it, Anastasia herself still "burst into Russian." Xenia had brought her two parakeets as a gift from the West Indies. Anastasia was thrilled with the birds and often let them play outside their cage. "Look," she cried in Russian one day, laughing in delight, "they are dancing on the windowsill." She walked through the garden with Margharita Derfelden, talking about the flowers and "calling them by their quaint Russian names." [106] And then once, while Xenia stood unnoticed in her doorway, she heard Anastasia speak to her birds for several minutes entirely in Russian — "and perfectly acceptable Russian from the point of view of St. Petersburg society." [107]

"*Why* will you not speak Russian?" Xenia asked Anastasia, knowing how important it was, and Anastasia answered with a remark that made Xenia's blood run cold: "Because it was the last language we heard in that house." [108]

"She spoke rarely of Siberia," said Margharita Derfelden. "It obviously made her unhappy to do so. She said that when she remembered it, it made her heart ache." [109] Princess Xenia was careful to point out that Anastasia "never described the scene of her family's murder," nor ever entered into geographical detail about her flight from Russia. She spoke only of "a long, long journey," during which time she was mostly unconscious. And even this, after ten years, proved too much for her, because in recalling the flight from Siberia and the trek to Berlin Anastasia broke down completely. Sobbing, her fists pounding against the wall of her room, she cried out: "I went through all that, and now they will not believe that I am Anastasia!" Said Xenia: "I was myself extremely upset to see her like this, but I never had the faintest feeling that her agitation was or could possibly have been caused by some delusion of hers." [110]

So the months went by, for the most part, tranquilly, while the evidence of Anastasia's identity was allowed to emerge if and how it chose. "She spoke of the rooms in the palace at Tsarskoe Selo," said Mme. Derfelden, "of the colors and cretonnes. . . . She remembered the lilac bushes with which her mother's rooms at Tsarskoe had been filled in late winter and early spring. I remembered them, too, having seen them when the Empress received me." [111] When spring came to Oyster Bay Anastasia spent more and more of her time walking on the beach or in the woods — she and Xenia frequently went hunting for mushrooms together — until one day a cold snap drove her back indoors. [112] "It reminded her of the cold wave that always accompanied the passing of the ice from the Neva," said Mme. Derfelden.

"What was the name of the festival when the Ladoga ice passed?" Anastasia asked. "Not the first ice, but the second?"

Mme. Derfelden had no idea what Anastasia was talking about, "and she grew quite indignant that [Mme. Derfelden], who had lived so long in Russia, could not remember such a simple thing." Later, however, Mme. Derfelden consulted a Russian friend in New York, who told her: "Why, she means the Opening of Navigation (*otkritie navigatie*). But only the Imperial Family could have considered that important." For centuries, in fact, each spring, the commandant of St. Petersburg had taken a glass of water from the Neva after the final thaw and had brought it to the Tsar as a sign that navigation could commence.

"That is right!" said Anastasia. ". . . It has always been done since Peter the Great."

"There are many more things in this order that I could tell," said Mme. Derfelden. "I give these to show the sequence of thought, the casualness of the statements."[113] Princess Xenia, too, had stories. Her daughter, Nancy, always seemed to take Anastasia's thoughts back in time. Once, as she sat watching Xenia and Nancy play together, Anastasia remarked quietly that "she was very ashamed that she had been unable to give her own child any love." This led to "a more or less complete description of her stay in Rumania." One morning, from her window, Anastasia caught sight of Nancy playing in the garden. Later Xenia found her crying on the bed. "Please," said Anastasia, "don't dress her like that." Nancy had been wearing a sailor suit and cap similar to the outfit often worn by the Tsarevitch Alexis.[114] Then there was the day when the past surged up and nearly destroyed the tentative friendship Xenia had established with her unhappy guest. Xenia had invited her cousin, Prince Dmitri of Russia, to Oyster Bay for a tennis game. Dmitri was the son of the Tsar's sister Xenia and of Grand Duke Alexander, the fun-loving spiritualist, and consequently was also a cousin of Grand Duchess Anastasia. "The [tennis] court," Xenia explained, "was immediately behind the house opposite the windows of the room occupied by the claimant, but completely hidden by a wire fence covered with vines, so that the players could be heard but not seen from the claimant's window." When Xenia went up to Anastasia's room to say good morning, Anastasia turned her back and refused to reply.

"How can I know what is the matter when you won't speak to me?" Xenia asked.

"You lied to me," Anastasia replied; "you promised not to bring them here."

Xenia pretended not to understand: "What are you talking about?"

"I know his voice. It's one of the cousins."[115]

The break between Anastasia and Princess Xenia, when it came, was not this time the result of Anastasia's famous fits of nerves. On the contrary, she seemed happy to remain at Oyster Bay. It is true that she and Xenia's husband, William Leeds, never got on well together. "He didn't like me," said Anastasia, "and I didn't like him."[116] The Leedses, moreover, were undergoing serious marital difficulties at this time, which the presence of a stranger — and above all this stranger — could only have aggravated. But Xenia's devotion to Anastasia was not a charade, and she deeply regretted the gulf that had been created between them. She remained exquisitely tight-lipped about it, only telling a journalist many years later that "there were so many things, so many lies . . . and then somebody mixed up the cards." [117]

For years people tried to sort out exactly what had gone wrong; who, in reality, was responsible for the breach, whether Gleb Botkin — this was Xenia's "somebody" — Anastasia herself, an indiscreet William Leeds, or, as many thought, the Romanov family at large. All that is known for sure is that a new character had now entered Anastasia's saga — not a witness this time, not even a person, but a pall, a specter of money and greed, which quickly became the most compelling and by far the most notorious figure in her story. When did the talk of the Romanov inheritance begin? Who first spread the rumor that the Tsar of Russia's only surviving daughter might be heiress to a fortune worth over ten million dollars? It was a moot point. "There exists a strong belief," Gleb Botkin wrote on June 5, 1928, "that there is money in one of the British banks, presumably the Bank of England," which was due to go to Anastasia should her identity be established. Anastasia herself, Gleb went on, "insists" on this point, "and gets very angry at the expression of any doubts on the subject." In a letter to Edward H. Fallows, the New York attorney who would shortly become Anastasia's first legal representative, Gleb explained the situation as he understood it:

I know for a fact that the late Emperor did have considerable sums of money in the Bank of England, but that much of it he had either withdrawn or presented to the Russian state by paying with it during the war for some of the military supplies that had been purchased abroad. During our Siberian exile the Emperor told my father . . . that he had no money of his own left in any of the foreign banks. This, however, would not necessarily mean that his *daughters* did not have any money at the time in a British bank, as the Emperor would not refer to his daughters' money as to his own. [118]

This, then, was the subject on Gleb Botkin's mind in the summer of 1928. The issue might not have come up when it did had it not been for a certain confusion about the niceties of Russian and international law. "I had been informed," said Anastasia later, "that the matter of the inheritance had to be settled in ten years after my supposed death." [119] And July 1928 marked the tenth anniversary of the disappearance of the imperial family from Ekaterinburg. Thus it was that Gleb went to Edward Fallows, a casual acquaintance and specialist in corporate law, and asked him to do what he could to prevent the Bank of England from disposing of the Romanov treasure. "Those of us who believe in Anastasia and her claims," said Gleb, "ask only that whatever moneys may be found to exist in England shall not be turned over to any of the other heirs of the Romanov family until Anastasia's case had been fully and legally presented." [120] Fallows, in the meantime, had agreed to take on Anastasia as his client.

Now, there was an added problem in this already delicate state of affairs. Anastasia had not been seeing Gleb Botkin during her residence at Oyster Bay. "I was angry with him," Princess Xenia admitted, "because he had broken his promise to me. We had both agreed that no one should give the claimant's arrival in America any so-called publicity. But shortly after she came the papers in New York and indeed throughout the country were filled with news about 'Anastasia.' " [121] According to Xenia, Anastasia herself had blamed Gleb for the dread publicity and had declared that she no longer cared to see him. That was fine with her hostess, and until the summer of 1928 Gleb was kept at a distance.

Gleb's side of the story was rather different. [122] He claimed total ignorance of Anastasia's displeasure and before long began to fear that Princess Xenia, on the orders of the Romanov family, was keeping Anastasia a virtual prisoner on Long Island. In July matters reached a head when William Leeds gave an offhand interview to several reporters who had followed him on one of his many sporting adventures — Leeds was a daredevil amateur pilot — and declared that he and his wife were "not interested" in proving Anastasia's identity and had no plans "to obtain any fortune for her." [123] Suspicious, Gleb called a press conference to announce that Leeds had no right to decide Anastasia's future, whereupon Leeds, annoyed, issued another statement, affirming that he had been speaking only for himself and for Xenia, that he had no personal interest whatever in Anastasia's "inheritance," and that he would, in Gleb's words, "do nothing to prevent [Gleb] from doing what [Gleb] thought right in [his] efforts to protect the interests of Grand Duchess Anastasia." [124]

The situation had become hopelessly muddled. After consultation with Edward Fallows, Gleb wrote Xenia to tell her that court action would be required in order to block payment of the Romanov fortune to the next of kin. Xenia was horrified. "I am extremely apprehensive as to the advisability of the course you propose to take," she wrote Gleb tactfully, "for many reasons too long to write." [125] She invited him to come out to Oyster Bay to talk about it. Afterward Gleb described his conversations with Xenia at Kenwood as marathon shouting matches, during which the Princess, in a state of near-hysteria, warned Gleb that he would very much regret his meddling in the affairs of the House of Romanov. Then, according to Gleb, Xenia had issued a startling ultimatum: the Tsar's sisters, she said, the Grand Duchesses Xenia and Olga, were prepared to support Anastasia for life "in some secluded spot in Europe," provided she renounce her claim to identity. If Anastasia did not accept this proposal she was to leave Oyster Bay within forty-eight hours. [126]

One might well ask how matters had reached this point. Xenia, needless to say, denied Botkin's allegations on every count. "I would never, *never* have said that," she protested. "My aunts' attitude was far too negative for them to have dreamed of proposing such a thing." [127] But that was the offer Gleb Botkin and Anastasia discussed when Gleb went upstairs and saw her for the first time in months. He had already written her about the necessity of taking steps in court to protect her inheritance and had been careful to assure her that "the whole thing could be done without the slightest publicity so that nobody would know anything about it." Edward Fallows, Gleb continued, had recently told him that there were "reliable indications" that the money would be paid out to the Tsar's sisters if something were not done. [128] And that was the alarming news that sent Anastasia careening back into paranoia.

There was one other, supremely important, factor behind Anastasia's distress. Princess Xenia — rashly, she admitted — had promised Anastasia that she would take her to Copenhagen to see her grandmother. "I was very young," the Princess reflected, "and convinced that I could obtain anything I wanted. But I ran up against the categorical opposition of her two aunts, who were also mine, the Grand Duchesses Xenia and Olga. What could I do? I didn't dare challenge them." [129] Xenia's failure to make good on the trip to Denmark had already roused Anastasia's suspicions when the thought of "imprisonment" did the trick. She asked to be taken away.

Xenia, in the meantime, was going through her own private agony at the prospect of Anastasia's future. What was going to happen to Anastasia if she followed Gleb Botkin's advice and took the case to court? It could only lead to disaster. (At Castle Seeon, when he heard about the plan, Duke George of Leuchtenberg had the same reaction: "It's a catastrophe! . . . She will destroy her chances for recognition and commence to play a 'dirty role.' *That* expression I think she will understand. Tell her, *in my name,* I beg her not to do it.") [130] In the last days of Anastasia's residence at Oyster Bay Xenia tried to reason with her, explaining that the matter could best be handled *by the family,* that the Tsar's sisters were "saints" who would surely recognize their error in time, that no one was going to abandon Anastasia and let her starve "in the street," that she would be well taken care of.[131] Nothing worked. Xenia's arguments convinced Anastasia only that her hostess had been in communication with her enemies in Europe and had turned against her. "She will never do anything for me," said Anastasia bitterly, "but make these promises she does not intend to keep!" [132] When Gleb Botkin arrived at Kenwood with Edward Fallows on the morning of August 8 he found Xenia in despair, still hoping that something could be done to change Anastasia's mind. Gleb hoped so, too. But when Gleb came down to the drawing room after a brief conversation with Anastasia he told Xenia that her cousin would be leaving within the hour, whereupon Xenia, as Fallows observed, "burst into tears and ran upstairs."

This scene was Fallows's first introduction to Anastasia's case. Completely bewildered, he wandered out into the garden for a breath of air and was shortly joined by William Leeds. Xenia had already told Fallows that "there was no doubt that her guest was her cousin," and now Leeds added his own assurances on that point. Yes, he said, he believed it, too: "He said that he deplored the split between Anastasia and her aunts, whom he knew; that in order to effect a reconciliation he was ready to buy her a home anywhere in the world she might wish — and he mentioned Switzerland as one place she said she liked — and that he would set aside enough money so that she could live comfortably for the rest of her life, *if only she would not bring the family quarrel into court* by insisting that she be acknowledged publicly. . . . He then asked me if I would urge her to accept his offer. I answered that as yet I had never even met her, much less been retained as her attorney." [133]

Was this, in truth, where the story of "the offer" originated — the proposal "to support Anastasia for life" if she would give up her claim? It's possible. Leeds never spoke publicly on the subject again, in the first place because he eventually came to regard Anastasia's case as a scurrilous hoax,[134] and in the second place because

he and Princess Xenia were divorced eighteen months later.[135] A
press release issued at the time of the decree was careful to state
that the demise of the marriage was not in any way related to Anastasia. No one in New York society believed it. The incomparably
blasé "Billy Benedick," the chronicler of many a Long Island scandal, remarked in the *Evening Journal* that Anastasia had single-
handedly destroyed the union of "The Tin Plate Croesus" and his
Russian-princess bride. The story went that Leeds had done everything in his power to discourage his wife from involving herself
with Anastasia, but that Xenia had not given in: "Therefore the
clash . . . which led to Mrs. Leeds taking preliminary steps to free
herself from the thralldom of matrimony." [136]

It was great gossip, but in reality the mood at Kenwood after
Anastasia's departure was one of plain regret mixed with a certain
understandable relief and more than a little sadness. "You know,"
Princess Xenia confided to her closest family and friends, "she isn't
normal." [137] But Xenia always stipulated that their abrupt falling-
out had done nothing to alter her conviction about Anastasia's
identity. In line with the courtesy and the prudence that elevated
her whole involvement in the case, Xenia never claimed proof and
never pressed the point too far within the imperial family. She did
not argue or plead with the disbelieving. She knew it was useless.
There can be no more profound sign of the Romanovs' intransigence than the fact that Xenia was never able fully to convince her
own sister, Nina, of Anastasia's authenticity.[138] In 1971 Xenia's
daughter finally broached the subject with Nina and her husband,
Paul Chavchavadze. "They were sure it never was the Polish girl,"
she reported, "but both felt quite unsure if it was or was not [the
Tsar's daughter]. I said, 'Then who?' and shoulders were hunched
and no one could say but Nina said it upset her so much she couldn't
talk about it. Again that nebulous claw that stabs at them all." [139]

So Princess Xenia's plan to spare her family "much unpleasantness" had come to nothing. The next few years were very hard for
Xenia, as Anastasia's lawyers prepared to bring her case to court
and repeatedly pestered Xenia for an affidavit. "She dreads doing
anything that will bring on publicity or involve her relatives," Xenia's own attorney reported. And yet Xenia still saw her faith in
Anastasia as a kind of trust: "She said she suffered from great mental distress, that she was between two fires — on the one side her
relatives and on the other side her sense of justice and the fact that
she knows Grand Duchess Anastasia is living. She told Mr. Albert

that notwithstanding the great distress it would undoubtedly cause her, and the opposition of her husband who does not wish her to be mixed up in the case in any way, she will do the right thing, come what may. . . . Princess Xenia deserves real praise for her action, as we know what tremendous pressure has been brought upon her not to testify." [140]

Anastasia had found a friend indeed. Princess Xenia was ready in court, as promised, when the time came.

10

CHANGING FORTUNES

*O*n Gleb Botkin's advice, Anastasia relinquished power of attorney to Edward Fallows immediately after her surprise return to New York City from Oyster Bay, on August 9, 1928.[1] In addition, she drew up a will. She thought it wise under the circumstances. After stipulating that Prince Waldemar of Denmark, the Dowager Empress's brother, be reimbursed for expenses incurred on her account, she divided the bulk of her potential estate among the Botkin children in memory of their father. Gleb was embarrassed, and, without Anastasia's knowledge, he directed that any money he might receive from her be given over to the Red Cross in *her* memory.

One hour after signing the will Anastasia summoned Fallows again. She asked that efforts be made without delay to locate her son in Rumania.[2] Then she informed Fallows that the idea of taking her case to court was "indecent" and that she would agree to it only if it was absolutely necessary and only because there seemed to be no other way to get justice.[3] But she expressly forbade Fallows to sue any member of the Romanov family in his efforts to establish her identity. With that, Fallows was dismissed from her presence.

Having lost the shelter of Oyster Bay, she was in need of a new protector. She had been staying at the cramped Lexington Avenue apartment of John Colter, a journalist friend of Gleb's and director of the North American Newspaper Alliance.[4] It was no place for a woman who demanded constant privacy. Gleb suggested that they might be able to rent a duplex together — he and his family could live in one half, said Gleb, while Anastasia occupied the other — but Anastasia had never heard such a foolish idea.[5] Help soon came from Auguste and Hetty Richard, who earlier had rescued Anastasia from the reporters on the *Berengaria*. The Richards offered to support her now "for a month to six weeks" at the Garden City Hotel.[6] Accordingly, Anastasia and her parakeets went back to Long Island.

If only for her greater peace of mind, it was essential that no one at the posh Garden City Hotel know the true identity of the lady in Room 205. On August 10 Anastasia booked in as "Mrs. Eugene Anderson."The "Eugene" was for Gleb Botkin's father, while the "Anderson," all speculation to the contrary, had simply been picked out of a hat by Auguste Richard. Anastasia's friends never guessed that the alias would stick and that one day, in melodic combination with "Anna," a shortened version of her Christian name, it would become her legal identity.[7]

"Mrs. Anderson" stayed on in Garden City for nearly six months, first at the hotel and later in a small cottage rented for her by Serge Rachmaninoff.[8] Gleb Botkin, who lived not far away in Hempstead, saw her almost every day now, introducing himself to the hotel staff as her brother in order to avoid any suspicion of impropriety.[9] Anastasia thought the charade vastly amusing, just as the full absurdity of her situation struck her, on good days, as more and more funny. She liked to confound Gleb with guessing games, history lessons, and spot "memory tests." Hanging in her room at the hotel, by coincidence, was a portrait of Queen Louise of Prussia, Grand Duchess Anastasia's great-great-great-grandmother. Anastasia took it as an omen and teased Gleb mercilessly when she discovered that he didn't know who the lady was. Another time she showed him a paper knife that had belonged to his father; Tatiana Botkin had given it to her in 1926 because it bore the crest of Empress Alexandra and had been presented to Dr. Botkin personally by the Empress.

"Have you ever seen this paper knife before?" Anastasia asked innocently.

Gleb answered that it meant nothing to him, and Anastasia squealed in delight: "Oh no! . . . If you are Gleb Botkin you must know where you have seen this paper knife. Otherwise I shall send you to Gilliard for identification." [10]

Life in Garden City, for all the jokes, could not have been called cheery. Anastasia had probably never felt more alone, and the weight of her insecurity further wore her down. In an enlightened moment she warned Gleb that she would quarrel with him sooner or later and with some tenderness asked him not to abandon her cause when the time came.[11] Once sure of his devotion, she gave free rein to her mounting frustration. On any one day Gleb could expect to be received cordially, dismissed angrily, and summoned again within the hour. There were times when Anastasia would speak to no one but her parakeets. "The nervous strain of looking after the Grand Duchess's affairs," Gleb remembered, "besides serving as a buffer between her and the outside world, was rapidly becoming too great to be long endured. At times Anastasia was as charming and delightful as she had been in the days of her childhood; but for the greater part of the time she acted in a way which reminded me of her mother. Like the late Empress, she suspected everybody of some malicious intention and suffered, alternatively, from attacks of uncontrollable rage and complete depression."[12] After their break several months later Gleb wrote about his "charming and delightful" friend in a letter to Edward Fallows: "And what does it lead to? . . . I feel plunged back into the days when the whole of Russia tried to bring the Empress back to her senses. . . . Nothing helped. She went to her grave praising Rasputin and denouncing everybody and everything. But she was always right. Same with Anastasia. She is always right. If something goes wrong it will always be the fault of everybody [else], but not hers. What can we do? What could anybody do in the situation?"[13]

Anastasia held on to Gleb Botkin longer than either of them had expected. She badly needed his support in the autumn of 1928. In October the Dowager Empress died at Villa Hvidøre, never having seen her supposed granddaughter and never having wanted to. The Empress's death dealt Anastasia a mighty blow. "She said nothing," Gleb wrote, "did not voice a single complaint. But for days thereafter she remained extremely depressed and I often surprised her sitting in a sort of stupor, her eyes wet, her thoughts apparently far away."[14]

Once again, anger gave Anastasia some relief from the shock of misfortune. Up till now the Romanov family, as a group, had not taken steps to disown her officially. Even Grand Duchess Olga, although she had lent her tacit support to the propaganda that had made Anastasia's life so miserable, would not take personal responsibility for the denial of her identity. Now, however, in October 1928, twelve members of the Russian imperial family affixed their signatures to a document that utterly and finally denounced Anastasia as a fraud.

It came to be called the Copenhagen Statement, but that was a misnomer. The royal declaration had been released to the Associated Press from the court of the Grand Duke of Hesse, not twenty-four hours after the death of the Dowager Empress. Two days later the Romanovs in Copenhagen, assembled for the Empress's funeral, issued a duplicate, billed as "the Declaration of the Russian Imperial Family Concerning the Tschaikovsky Affair." [15] Why the family had needed to wait for the Empress to die in order to issue the statement remains a mystery, but in any case the Romanovs now wanted to make known their "unanimous conviction that the person currently living in the United States is not the daughter of the Tsar." As evidence to back the family's stand there was advanced the "expert opinion" of Pierre Gilliard, Baroness Sophie Buxhoeveden, the criminologist Professor Bischoff, and the imperial dentist, Dr. Kastritsky. Grand Duke Alexander is thought to have drawn up the official disclaimer. He closed with an affirmation of familial love that, under the circumstances, was distinctly malicious:

For us, the nearest relatives of the Tsar's family, it is very difficult and painful to reconcile ourselves to the fact that not a single member of that family is still alive. How gladly we would like to believe that one of them, at least, had survived the murderous destruction of 1918. We would shower our love on the survivor. . . . But in the case of the lady in question our sense of duty compels us to state that the story is only a fairy tale. The memory of our dear departed would be tarnished if we allowed this fantastic story to spread and gain credence. [16]

It was with real surprise that Grand Duke Andrew and Princess Xenia of Russia read about the imperial family's "unanimous conviction" that Anastasia Tschaikovsky was not the daughter of the Tsar. Needless to say, they had not been consulted when the Copenhagen Statement was signed. Andrew, in particular, drew attention to its deceptive nature, pointing out that of the forty-four members of the Romanov family then living, only twelve had signed the statement — the Tsar's sisters, Xenia and Olga; Xenia's husband, Grand Duke Alexander; her six sons and her daughter, Irina Yussoupov; and two new opponents, Grand Duke Dmitri Pavlovitch and Grand Duchess Maria Pavlovna, the Tsar's cousins — and of those twelve, only one, Grand Duchess Olga, had ever seen Anastasia.

In New York, Gleb Botkin and Edward Fallows understood that this "utterly unprovoked" [17] attack required some kind of response. Gleb had been told that the United States immigration authorities were considering deporting Anastasia on the basis of what he called "Grand Duchess Xenia's declaration." Wrote Gleb: "The only thing that could be done was for me to issue a counter-statement strong enough to make it a grave libel if untrue. Should Grand Duchess Xenia bring a libel suit against me, Washington would allow Anastasia to remain in this country for all the duration of the litigation. And should Xenia fail to bring suit against me, Washington would accept it as an admission on her part that she knew my statement to be true."

Gleb's "counter-statement" was a violent personal attack on the Tsar's sister, into which, as he said, he "poured all the indignation and bitterness which had accumulated in [his] heart." [18] Edward Fallows dignified Gleb's assault with a simultaneous statement to the press: "I regard the claim of Grand Duchess Anastasia not as a case but as a cause. I appeal to all who love truth and justice and mercy not to prejudge this young woman, broken in body by the frightful suffering she has endured, but clear in mind, courageous in spirit and resolute in purpose to win her heroic fight for recognition." Fallows capped this gallantry with a formal notice that "from now on any person or corporation libeling or slandering Grand Duchess Anastasia will be held by her legally responsible." [19] This was nothing less than a dare, and it worked. There was not a word out of the Romanovs when Gleb published his letter to Grand Duchess Xenia:

> Your Imperial Highness!
> Twenty-four hours did not pass after the death of your mother . . . when you hastened to take another step in your conspiracy to defraud your niece. . . . It makes a gruesome impression that even at your mother's deathbed your foremost worry must have been the desire to defraud [Anastasia], and it is appalling that you did not have even the common decency of waiting if only a few days before resuming your ignoble fight. . . .
> That you personally are convinced of the real identity of Grand Duchess Anastasia Nicolaievna is evident enough from the fact that in the course of your whole fight against her you have never made a truthful statement nor mentioned a single

fact, but resort exclusively to the vilest slander and most pre-
posterous lies.

Before the wrong which Your Imperial Highness [is] committing pales even the gruesome murder of the Emperor, his family
and my father by the Bolsheviks. It is easier to understand a
crime committed by a gang of crazed and drunken savages than
the calm, systematic, endless persecution of one of your own
family . . . the Grand Duchess Anastasia Nicolaievna, whose
only fault is that being the only rightful heir to the late Emperor she stands in the way of her greedy and unscrupulous
relatives.[20]

Gleb Botkin accomplished more than he'd bargained for when he
published his open letter to the Tsar's sister. Without knowing it,
he had given the Romanov family a perfect excuse never to take
Anastasia seriously again. "All is lost," Grand Duke Andrew wrote
Gleb's sister, Tatiana. "Does he realize what he has done? *He has
completely ruined everything.*" [21] But Gleb, in the face of all criticism, continued to insist that his letter to the Tsar's sister had been
required in "Anastasia's interest." He had an excellent point: "It is
impossible, to my mind, to permit the Grand Duchess to be system-
atically slandered and vilified in the press without making the slightest protest. . . . Whatever I say about the enemies of the Grand
Duchess I say because I believe it to be true. . . . I am willing to
take full legal responsibility for my stand in the matter and bear the
consequences." [22]

Unfortunately, it wasn't Gleb, in the end, who had to bear the
consequences. Grand Duke Andrew explained to Edward Fallows
later that he had been trying to "appear to be impartial" on the
matter of Anastasia's identity in order better to effect a reconciliation with the Romanovs, but that there was no point in trying to
influence the Romanovs at all anymore, thanks to Gleb.[23] "Grand
Duke Andrew also remarked that the case was beginning to take on
the aspect of an intrigue for the Tsar's fortune," Tatiana Botkin
wrote. "This profoundly disgusted the Grand Duke, and he did not
further wish to involve his name in it." [24] Tatiana herself shared the
Grand Duke's point of view. When Fallows asked her two years
later to join a committee to raise funds for Anastasia's court battles
Tatiana had to turn him down — "and it is because of Gleb. . . .
Will he not influence the Committee to act in his own way, something like his letter to Grand Duchess Xenia . . . ? Gleb's methods
are so different from what I could endorse. Were I nearer I would

not fail to take part in the work and try to prevent such outbursts, but being so far away — how can I know what my name will be made to stand for? . . . I would very much rather not travel in his wake." 25

As the years went by Gleb Botkin found himself more and more isolated from the mainstream of Anastasia's supporters. Nor, when all was said and done, were Gleb's feelings of outrage and injustice directed only at the members of the imperial family. No one escaped the fires of his indignation — not the Romanovs, not the Duke of Leuchtenberg or Princess Xenia, not Harriet von Rathlef or Ambassador Zahle, not even his sister, whom he accused of faintheartedness. "Ultimately I found myself deserted by all relations and friends in Europe," Gleb wrote, "and do not expect to hear from them again until the day of Anastasia's final rehabilitation. They will be all back on that day, with flowers, candies and assurances of their 'profound respect and equal devotion.' That, however, is one consequence of Anastasia's recognition for which I feel no impatience." 26

And Anastasia? What did she think her chances now were ever to enjoy that "profound respect and equal devotion"? "Had it not been for her knowledge of the exact circumstances," Gleb explained, "and the realization that my public rebuke to her aunt was necessary for her own protection, Anastasia would, undoubtedly, have been quite as horrified as everybody else. As it was, she seemed hurt and in her attitude toward me ready to forgive rather than to approve." 27

She didn't forgive right away. Before long, inevitably, the "quarrel" had taken place. Anastasia received Gleb Botkin for the last time in January 1929 and did not see him again for nearly ten years.

She was now without a single Russian protector, her formal acknowledgment farther away than ever, her legal interests in the hands of strangers. In 1929 she began eighteen tragi-comic months of life as the Toast of Society. That was the role her hosts wanted her to play, at any rate. With great misgiving Anastasia accepted an invitation to live again on Park Avenue with Annie Jennings, the wealthy spinster who had first given her shelter when she came to the United States.28 Neither party understood what she was getting into. Miss Jennings merrily disregarded Princess Xenia's warning that Anastasia was prone to fits of despair and liable to accuse her friends of the blackest deeds. Anastasia, in turn, was due for some severe shocks at the hands of her American champions, whose main concerns went no farther than Wall Street.

She had her first taste of big business in February 1929, when she signed another of Edward Fallows's contracts and unwittingly turned herself into an international joke. Later Anastasia said that she had been misled — "I was alone, I did not understand these legal words" [29] — but in any event she had signed over control of the Romanov inheritance, whatever it might amount to and wherever it might be found. Fallows had found the perfect way to raise money for Anastasia's cause: by subscription. A corporation was formed under the name "Grandanor" — a witless acronym for "Grand Duchess Anastasia Nicolaievna of Russia" — and Miss Jennings's friends were invited to invest. If and when Anastasia obtained her fabulous millions all investors were to take a cut.[30]

The idea behind "Grandanor" was not so unsavory as it sounds. While protecting Anastasia's inheritance, the corporation also provided funds for Fallows to prepare her case and offered a real incentive for cooperation. Fallows himself, working for the moment without retainer, was eventually due to receive one quarter of all monies recovered under four hundred thousand dollars and then ten percent of all the rest, while the shareholders in "Grandanor" were scheduled to recoup five times their original investment. Anastasia had insisted on that, "because, as she said, her friends were taking a double risk, first that she was not Grand Duchess Anastasia, and second, that there was no money or property." [31]

It appears that Anastasia had understood more about the "Grandanor" corporation than she wanted to admit. "It is now eleven years that I have suffered and been maligned by those who would wish me out of the way," she said. "It is true that I am claiming monies and properties that my father left to my sisters, brother and me, and I am now sole heir to these monies and properties. . . . I intend to have them." [32] In August 1928 Edward Fallows had drawn up a statement for Anastasia's signature:

I, Grand Duchess Anastasia Nicolaievna, youngest daughter and only surviving child of the late Emperor Nicholas II and Empress Alexandra of Russia, do hereby declare that after our family had left St. Petersburg and were in exile at Ekaterinburg in Siberia, very shortly before the deaths of the other members of my family, my father told my three sisters and myself that before the World War in 1914, he had deposited in the Bank of England Five Million Roubles each for my three sisters and myself.

In 1925, when I was in Berlin, the Danish Ambassador Zahle, at Berlin, whom I had told of this deposit, of monies, made official enquiries, and very shortly afterward informed me that there were monies on deposit for my sisters and myself in the Bank of England, but the Bank was unwilling to state the amount.[33]

In the years ahead, Anastasia's attorneys dreamed of the day the Danish royal family would open up Ambassador Zahle's papers and, so they believed, confirm this statement. For if Zahle had made any inquiries at all at the Bank of England, some record of the bank's response ought to exist in his dossier; and if that response were positive, the bank's subsequent denials of any Romanov funds in its possession would, to say the least, be substantially shaken. In 1929, as it was, when investigations were first undertaken, the bank's solicitors preferred to fall back on the right of any bank, anywhere, to decline comment on a private deposit. Edward Fallows, preparing the case for Anastasia's legal identification, had asked a lawyer friend in London, Gilbert F. Kennedy, to put every bank in Great Britain on formal notice that the Tsar's daughter was still alive and that any property belonging to her must be held in reserve. This Kennedy achieved before holding a series of off-the-record discussions with J. Arthur Gallop, a senior partner of the Bank of England's solicitors, Freshfield, Leese, and Munns. Gallop did not deny to Kennedy that there were Romanov deposits at the Bank, but declared that he could not discuss the matter further in the absence of an *authenticated* claimant to the funds. "Judging from my conversation with Mr. Gallop," Kennedy wrote Fallows later, "I doubt very much if we shall be able to obtain any information from him, since his firm are the solicitors for the Bank of England, but from the guarded manner in which he discussed the matter, I imagine that the Bank of England now holds some or all of the Russian money you mention. . . ."[34] When Fallows met Gallop himself some time later nothing had changed in this regard: "He did not indicate in any manner that I was wrong in my assumptions [about the Romanov deposit] or that Anastasia was wrong in her allegations. . . . I, too, at that time got a very definite impression that the money was there, from what [Gallop] did *not* say."

What *did* Gallop say? Simply this: "Ordinarily, Mr. Fallows, I would go more than half way with you in any matter, but in this case we are representing a Government Institution, the Bank of England, and I cannot take even the first step. You must go all the way alone."

What was Fallows supposed to do, in that case?

"Go to the Court of Chancery and get an order that your client is Anastasia and then come to the Bank and we will open our books."

Was there any statute of limitations on the claim to the deposit?

"No. One could come a hundred years hence and draw it out on proper credentials."[35] Neither could any other member of the Romanov family, in theory, at least, withdraw the funds until Anastasia was either dead or her claim disproved. The mystery of her identity had effectively put the matter on ice.

Before the Revolution it was generally understood that the Tsar of Russia was one of the wealthiest men in the world. His assets at home were of course incalculable — they have been estimated in excess of twenty billion dollars — and it is futile to guess at the extent of his holdings abroad. These were certainly considerable; none of them, in any case, would ever have been registered under the name of "Romanov," but would have been shrouded by a variety of trustees, nominees, holding companies, and any number of dummy corporations. It was that immovable policy, undoubtedly, which enabled the Bank of England eventually to deny that it held any funds "in the name of" the Tsar or his children.[36] Sir Edward Peacock, who had been a director of the bank for more than twenty years, later prepared a statement for inclusion in the biography of his good friend and financial advisee, Grand Duchess Olga. "I am pretty sure there never was any money of the Imperial Family of Russia in the Bank of England," he wrote, "nor in any other bank in England. Of course it is difficult to say 'never,' but I am positive at least there never was any money after World War I and during my long years as director of the Bank."[37]

This disclaimer, coming as it did from an impeccable source, was a small masterpiece of dissemblance, because prior to the Russian Revolution Nicholas II had maintained substantial deposits both in England and around the world. In 1917 Alexander Kerensky's Russian Provisional Government estimated the Tsar's foreign holdings at at least fourteen million rubles,[38] while Count Benckendorff, the grand marshal of the Russian court, wrote that at the time of the Revolution Nicholas's children had possessed private fortunes amounting to "several million" rubles *each* "abroad and in the State

Bank."[39] The existence of Romanov deposits in Europe, in fact, and specifically in England, appears to have been another of those "open secrets" for which the "Anastasia" case became famous. In a 1959 series on the history of the great British banks, for example, *The Observer* of London remarked of Baring Brothers: "The Romanovs were among their distinguished clients. . . . It is affirmed that Barings' still holds a deposit of more than forty million pounds that was left with them by the Romanovs." Inquiries with Anthony Sampson, at that time editor-in-chief of *The Observer*, revealed that this affirmation had passed by without disclaimer either from Barings' or from Tsar Nicholas's peripheral heirs (ordinarily these things generate great rounds of protest). "If I am correctly informed," Sampson continued, "British banks are most reticent on this subject. . . . But this story is generally considered to be true."[40]

Anastasia maintained all of her life that the subject of the Tsar's money had first arisen during Grand Duchess Olga's visits to the Mommsen Clinic in 1925: "My aunt came and asked the doctors how long I would live. They said maybe a month, maybe less. It was at this time when I was expected to die that I told Mr. Zahle that my father had deposited money in England. . . . Mr. Zahle then told my aunt."[41]

But hadn't Anastasia told the Grand Duchess about the money herself?

No: "I told it to Mr. Zahle and *he* told it to my aunt." And Olga, many believed, had told her own sister, Grand Duchess Xenia, about the deposit, thereby destroying Anastasia's chances for recognition. Gleb Botkin, in fact, seeking a rational explanation for Anastasia's troubles, declared that she had been denied her identity for no more complicated a reason than the greed of her two aunts, who hoped to obtain the Tsar's fortune for themselves.[42]

Gleb's theory, amounting to an accusation of rampant, cold-blooded avarice, was a massive slur on the reputations of two women who, by all other accounts, were models of charity. The friends and relations of the Tsar's sisters indignantly rejected the notion that they had denied their brother's daughter for pecuniary reasons, particularly since the Grand Duchesses, in the words of one relative, "didn't know a ruble from a kopeck."[43] Here, however, there was a tendency to reflect only on the person and to overlook the personage, to forget *who* these ladies were and how many other people had an interest in their good fortune and, by extension, their patronage — former courtiers and servants, nieces and nephews, lawyers, bankers, and a variety of exiled Russian entrepreneurs. Anastasia herself, in fact, had provided the first telling clue to the fate of the Romanov inheritance by declaring that the deposit in the Bank of England had been registered in a secret account that she thought could be opened only through the revelation of a certain name, a name she recalled as "short" and "German-sounding."[44]

Working with this fuzzy description, it wasn't long before Anastasia's attorney remembered Sir Peter Bark, an Anglicized Russian who had been Nicholas II's last finance minister and who, after the Revolution, managed the generally chaotic financial affairs of the Tsar's sisters.[45] Bark had also been appointed trustee by King George V for the estate of the late Dowager Empress, and, in that capacity, presided over the sale of the Empress's fabulous jewel collection, which, for the duration of her exile, she had kept hidden in a box under her bed. More than two hundred and fifty thousand pounds realized from the sale of the jewels simply vanished in Bark's hands ("There were certain aspects of this affair which I could never understand," said Grand Duchess Olga.)[46] Although Bark, very likely, was the only man alive who knew the truth about the disposition of the Tsar's fortune, he persistently refused to discuss the matter with outsiders, including Edward Fallows. After Bark's death, his daughter stepped forward to affirm that her father had told her that none of the Tsar's money had remained abroad after the Revolution. She went further and said that "in 1916, the Emperor had refused to transfer even the smallest part of his capital outside of Russia."[47]

This conforms absolutely to the story the peripheral heirs of Nicholas II have presented to the world and, by and large, to each other. There was no money in England, they claim, because the Tsar, in 1914, had commanded that every member of the imperial family withdraw his foreign holdings in order to help the Russian war effort on the home front.[48] Nicholas himself, as "First Citizen of the Land," was naturally also the first to comply with his own order. "Would my mother have accepted a pension from King George V if we had any money in England?" Grand Duchess Olga asked ingenuously. "It does not make sense."[49] But Anastasia had a plausible explanation for the preservation of her inheritance. When Gleb Botkin asked her why her father had left his money in England, she replied, "Because it wasn't his money, it was our money."[50] Evidently the Tsar had felt he had no right to deprive his daughters of their future livelihood since, if any of them were to marry foreign princes, they would be stricken from the imperial Russian civil list: the money constituted latter-day dowries. Even in the emergency situation of World War I it could not have been regarded as a great crime to leave funds deposited in easy reach with England, the favored ally, and that, it seems, was exactly what the Tsar had done.[51] Lili Dehn, one of the two closest friends of Empress Alexandra, declared under oath in 1955: "In March 1917, when I was at Tsarskoe Selo with the imperial family, the situation being very grave on account of the Revolution, Her Majesty the Tsarina said this to me: 'At least we shan't have to beg, for we have a fortune in the Bank of England.' "[52] Mme. Dehn, when she issued this declaration, had not yet met Anastasia, and so could not be accused of any vested interest in Anastasia's identity with the daughter of the Tsar. "I don't remember exactly how much it was," she continued in reference to the British deposit, "but I know [the Empress] spoke of millions, and in gold."

It was with just such an eventuality as revolution in mind that the Tsar, after the insurrections of 1905, had been sure to make provisions for his children in the event of another. In coded accounts, "A. B. C. D. and E.," more than two million rubles were deposited in securities with the Mendelssohn Bank in Berlin.[53] "The bank purchased these securities and deposited them in their own name as trustees in the *Reichsbank*," Edward Fallows discovered, and took it for granted that Sir Peter Bark, the Russian finance minister, had "[followed] exactly the same course" at the Bank of England.[54] It was Fallows's belief that Bark, having assumed the deaths of Nicholas II and all his immediate heirs, could find no compelling reason to disclose the existence of the Tsar's money to anyone — and above all not to the other members of the Romanov family, who were most strenuously looking for it. In 1935, while researching the matter in London, Fallows consulted Sir Harold Brooks, one of the attorneys who had successfully prosecuted the famous libel suit brought by Grand Duchess Xenia's daughter, Irina Yussoupov, against Metro-Goldwyn-Mayer over the film *Rasputin and the Empress*. In conversation with Fallows, Brooks revealed that more than the family's good name had been on Xenia's mind: she had further authorized him and his colleague, the American Fanny Holtzmann, to conduct a search for her brother's money. "Brooks thinks there may be fire where there is so much smoke," Fallows observed,[55] and so, obviously, did Xenia. Fanny Holtzmann's biographer wrote:

By now, Fanny and Xenia were on intimate terms. The Grand Duchess indicated that the remaining Romanovs had other legal problems, including the whereabouts of enormous assets reportedly held overseas by the late Tsar. . . .

In [1920] Xenia had been named administratrix for the estate of her brother, the Tsar. For fifteen years a treasure hunt had been in progress all over the world, with lawyers and investigators angling for a percentage of assets variously described as gold bullion, real estate and stocks. . . .

Heavy investments in the United States were also attributed to the Tsar, mainly in railroads, steamship companies and timber; the New York *Sun* estimated the aggregate at $120,000,000. But as Fanny methodically checked out each lead, it slipped away into insubstantiality.

. . . A private letter to Fanny from a War Office official in close touch with the Bank of England provided a gallant footnote to history: "From a person well placed to know, I gather that *the very* high personage you mentioned, far from depositing funds abroad in 1914, actually sold and repatriated all their foreign deposits, investments, etc., as an act of patriotism. This I have confirmed elsewhere. . . ."[56]

And so the Tsar's fortune "slipped away into insubstantiality." It came as no surprise to Edward Fallows in 1939, when Anastasia's case was first scheduled to come before the bar in Berlin, that the lawyer representing the Grand Duchesses Xenia and Olga had been retained for them by Sir Edward Peacock, the Bank of England director who later denied so positively that the Tsar had ever held any money in Great Britain. "The intervention in the Berlin case of Sir Edward Peacock indicates the importance he attaches to any decision there," said Fallows,[57] noting that the Berlin proceedings had been delayed while English translations of the lawyers' memoranda were prepared for Sir Edward and for Grand Duchess Xenia's other British "advisor," Sir Peter Bark.[58] Fallows could not imagine that the opposition to Anastasia in England would have been so determined and so powerfully represented if there were not something at stake. "You know well how [Bark] kept both Xenia and Olga under his thumb," he wrote Harold Brooks in 1937, "and how bitter he was against Anastasia."[59] Fallows suspected that the Romanov deposit in London had gone "into the capitalization of the Anglo-International Bank, the Bank of England's largest subsidiary, of which Sir Peter became [at its founding] and to his death remained the President,"[60] and he did not doubt that the rest of the Romanov family had been duped by Bark just as surely as Anastasia had. "A private deposit draws no interest," Fallows observed. ". . . What a plum for the Bank of England!"

Edward Fallows never did succeed in solving the mystery of the Romanov fortune, nor, to date, has anyone else. What is certain is that the Tsar's family held out hopes of locating the treasure for many years, long after they had begun to say publicly that they knew the money didn't exist, and long after they had abandoned Anastasia.[61] The actual existence and whereabouts of the money, Fallows discovered, need never have been proven for it to play an important role in his client's life. The threat was there from the outset. For certainly even a *potential* sole heiress is a thorn in the side of anyone else who hopes to obtain — or retain — a princely sum. "I am pretty well convinced that powerful financial interests are at the back of it all," wrote one member of the Romanov family during the 1960s. "You may recall that whenever I was asked about the Anastasia case in the old days I used to answer what I had been told by my family, that the whole case is based on the nonexistent millions of the Tsar. I have since learnt better, and I don't think I'm exaggerating when I say that the legend of the *non*existence of the money has been carefully yet assiduously forced on my family so that they should never interfere in any way. What did the Dowager Empress and her two daughters know about the material side of life? Naturally they believed people like this Sir Peter Bark. . . . It is in the interests of those who play around with the capital that [Anastasia's] case should drag on as long as possible. Believe you me, as they say, it is more than unlikely that they would allow her to win."[62]

The matter of the Romanov inheritance remained uppermost in everyone's mind for the duration of Anastasia's sojourn in the United States. Backed now by Miss Jennings and the shareholders in the "Grandanor" corporation, Edward Fallows set off for Europe to unravel the secrets of Russian royalty. It was a quest that failed, in the end, for while Fallows did accomplish a great deal for Anastasia before he was finished, he was not equipped to break the back of her European opposition. "The Opposition here has been much more powerful, intense and bitter than any of us imagined," Fallows reported.[63] ". . . I did not dream how powerful and well organized this was when I accepted the case."[64] Nor did Fallows guess that his work for Anastasia would preoccupy him to the exclusion of all other concerns for the next (and final) twelve years of his life.

While Edward Fallows toiled in Europe, his client spent her days in borrowed rooms, dutifully following Miss Jennings from her Manhattan apartment to "Sunnie Holme," the Jennings country estate in Fairfield, Connecticut. Laden with gifts and stylish clothes, she moved with Miss Jennings from Park Avenue to the corner of Fifth and East Seventieth Street, where she endured an endless round of parties, teas, and dinner dances, receiving her guests with nervous courtesy and "imparting a highly spiced flavor to the fashionable chatter" of New York society.[65] The word was that "Miss Jennings . . . planned to adopt this 28-year-old enigma with the deep blue Slavic eyes and leave her the Jennings millions."[66] Rumors of Anastasia's engagement to one or another unnamed New York businessman or upper-crust party-goer were never long out of the columns. Anastasia had never read such nonsense — articles, as she remembered them, "saying that I would not dance with anyone but the Prince of Woho, everyone had to kneel and kiss my hand, for otherwise I would not speak or shake hands with anybody."[67] It was so silly. Already a silent movie had appeared based on Anastasia's story, inexplicably titled *Clothes Make the Woman* and, in a double twist of plot, dispatching its claimant heroine to Hollywood to play herself in a filmed recreation of the Ekaterinburg massacre.[68] Then there were Miss Jennings's friends, who might have expected Anastasia to wear a tiara and carry a scepter to the breakfast table, so little did they understand about her background. A woman who met her in Connecticut noted that "she had thick ankles and wrists and looked *anything* but patrician."[69] But even the people who judged her on these terms left her with the feeling that they had missed something. Guy Bolton, the grand old vaudevillian who later adapted the play based on her life, saw Anastasia at one of Miss Jennings' soirées:

I was a guest at a large party in the old Ritz-Carlton where, looking about me, I saw a woman, seemingly young but with eyes that were old, with a scarred face and a twisted mouth. She was seated in a corner and, as I looked at her, a woman approached her and, kneeling, kissed her hand. I turned to my hostess and said: "What's going on over there?"

"That," she said, "is the Grand Duchess Anastasia, youngest daughter of the Tsar."

"But surely," I protested, "she was killed together with the rest of her family. I remember reading about it in detail and have been haunted by the horror of it ever since."

"If you have been haunted by the horror of it," said my friend, "think of her. I doubt if she ever forgets it." [70]

All of 1929 was like this — parties, fashion shows, department stores, and more parties. Between these unaccustomed forays Anastasia found the quiet she wanted, alone in her room with her parakeets. She tried to help out at first, tried to be friendly and to cooperate with her lawyer so as to make things easier for everyone, but she tired so easily and had such a hard time keeping track of her legal and financial affairs. Her correspondence at this time was extensive.[71] When an American edition of Harriet von Rathlef's book appeared in New York, she fired off more than ten indignant letters on the subject and declared outrageously, "I feel very strongly now that I ought to have had the Rathlef woman arrested." [72] Her friends were agreeably surprised in the summer of 1929 when Anastasia, fed up with other people's talk, agreed to dictate her memoirs. Miss Jennings's brother, Oliver, had assured Anastasia that her book would "make millions," and that pleased her no end. "I was happy to think that I would have some money that I could feel was my own," she said, "and which I could feel I had helped to earn." [73] There was another consideration. It amounted to fairness: "Everyone the world over has had their say; they have said all sorts of terrible things about me, called me impostor. Now I have decided to lay before the public what I have to say. . . . *I* should have something to say." [74] But after two months of interviews given daily at the law offices of Curtis J. Mar, a colleague of Edward Fallows, nobody had the heart or the nerve to tell Anastasia that her rambling recollections were "utterly useless" for the kind of sentimental, "Dear Reader" melodrama her friends wanted her to publish.[75] The project was scrapped without her knowledge.

It may have been the fate of the book that first began to raise Anastasia's hackles. "What I am now going to write I ask you to report to Mr. Mar as coming from me," she commanded Miss Jennings's own attorney. "I have spent days, weeks, months working very hard over this book with Mr. Mar, giving him more than 120 pictures to use as illustrations. . . .[76] Now, no report has come to me in regard to this book. This was taken in shorthand and not a single word has come back to me for me to look over and read. I wanted this book to be finished and sold and the money coming from it used in these various expenses. . . . I am very tired of this treatment." [77]

She was beginning to get tired of New York altogether. The steady stream of Miss Jennings's awestruck friends, the parties at the Ritz and the Waldorf, the nights out at the Met and the glittering dinners on Fifth Avenue had left Anastasia cold. She was lonely. "I would have liked the freedom to find some friends of my own age and tastes," she said. Instead she felt shut up, confined, and not taken seriously. "The people whom I was brought in contact with at Miss Jennings' were not interested in any of the things I was interested in," said Anastasia, "nor I in their interests. To most of them I was some sort of exhibition animal. When a strange animal is brought into the zoo everybody rushes to see it. I was in the same position — they looked at me in the same way. I felt as if they might like to pet me in the same way. . . . I was not for them a woman, I was a spectacle. . . . I have had very trying experiences since 1918 — I had not much strength, I did what I could." [78]

Except in the newspapers, she had ceased to be known as "Frau Tschaikovsky." To the Jennings family and their friends she was "Mrs. Anderson," "the Lady," sometimes "Grandanor." "Grandanor" began to get difficult at the beginning of 1930. Her distress was brought on partly by the realization that she was irrevocably bound to her friends' business venture. Nor did she understand why Edward Fallows had to spend so much time in Europe when she wanted him with her in New York. "I am his client," she said; "Mr. Fallows is my lawyer, and employed by me to do all this work." [79] She got it into her head that Fallows was simply using Miss Jennings's money in order to have a high time abroad. Why else had she heard nothing from him? True, she had seen the reports Fallows sent to his colleague, Mar, and to Miss Jennings herself, but she felt she ought to be accorded the same courtesy. "I have not been treated in the proper way," she complained. "I don't wish Miss Jennings to send any more money to Mr. Fallows. . . . He has sent no reports in one year . . . not a word. . . . I feel it is not the proper way for a lawyer to treat his client." Miss Jennings asked Anastasia now if it would help to talk with Mar about her complaints, but Anastasia had no interest in that: "Mr. Mar can be left entirely out of the matter, I do not care to have anything more to do with him." In February, finally, Miss Jennings called in another attorney to help out. This was Wilton Lloyd-Smith of the firm of Cotton, Franklin, Wright & Gordon.

Anastasia had had reservations about Lloyd-Smith from the very start, when she went downstairs to meet him in the salon and found him sitting cross-legged on the floor. "I was surprised," she admitted later, "and terribly amused," but she tried not to show it: "I of course left the room, not because I am a Grand Duchess, but because in every country a man with the pretensions of Mr. Lloyd-Smith rises when a woman enters the room. If he does not, there may be several reasons for it, he may be drunk, he may wish to be rude. . . ."[80] In future Lloyd-Smith's breezy manner and studied insouciance were to leave Anastasia speechless — was he making fun of her? — and she had to conclude that he was "not the type of man whom [she] needed for this work involving contact with Europeans and with persons of culture." But in the meantime she appeared to be stuck with him, and she asked him to do what he could to sort out her agreements with Fallows. She couldn't make head nor tail of them.

Fallows himself returned to New York at the beginning of March 1930, after a full year's absence, to find Anastasia still out of sorts. With Lloyd-Smith's help he managed to smooth her feathers by telling her — not quite truthfully — that his investigation had netted tremendous results and that she could expect legal rehabilitation within the year. Having obtained more money from Miss Jennings, however, Fallows went straight back to Europe, driving his client to new heights of distraction.

This was the beginning of a series of tantrums, scenes, and cool machinations that ultimately led Anastasia to a nervous breakdown. Practically every day, according to Lloyd-Smith, now saw "another very serious altercation with our Lady."[81] Her behavior was as comical as it was exasperating. Lloyd-Smith (whom Fallows had now retained as associate counsel) was fired so many times he began to lose count. "I never knew why the trouble started," he wrote Fallows in Berlin, "but she took a violent exception to your return to Europe. She discharged me regularly every time I went to see her because I refused to cable for you. Each time, however, she would send for me again."[82] Then, when her visitor's visa came up for renewal, Anastasia angrily refused to be interviewed by the immigration authorities. When, after several weeks, she finally consented to receive an official from Ellis Island she was cooperative in spite of herself. "She behaved beautifully," Lloyd-Smith reported, "and scared him to death. When he came out he was so upset that he asked me to write his report."[83]

By this time Anastasia had begun to rue the day she ever left Castle Seeon. "What I went through at that time in Miss Jennings' house cannot be expressed in words," she said later.[84] Miss Jennings's own patience began to go when Anastasia started spending money too freely. She wrote Lloyd-Smith:

. . . You know, there is no doubt but that she is perfectly sure that she
is going to get her money and she said the other day that you had
told her that probably everything would be all right in a year. I told her
that she needed six dresses the other day, so she decided to go out —
she was in a very good humor — to these various stores, Altman's,
Kurzman's, and so on, with Josephine.
  Josephine reports that she ordered very expensively and that she
paid — or ordered — a wrap that will cost $450. Josephine protested at
intervals that the things she bought were very expensive, and she had
gone quite extensively into the purchase of lingerie. This is a new act on
her part, because in the past she has gotten only what she actually
needed and of course this is a great extravagance.
  We will accept what is being done now. There is nothing more for me
to say, but when Josephine would make these protests she would say,
"Yes, they are expensive, but I expect to pay back Miss Jennings when I
get my money."
  . . . Of course in my position I can't very well say anything, because I
told her she needed six dresses. I had in mind spring and summer
dresses, knowing that she really had nothing to put on, but I had no sort
of an idea that she would go to Altman's and buy so expensively in the
lingerie department.[85]

The Jenningses were beginning to wonder what they were going to do about the spoiled "Mrs. Anderson." All along Annie Jennings's two brothers, Walter and Oliver, had merely tolerated what they regarded as Anastasia's exploitation of their sister. When, in April 1930, Anastasia began to make silly accusations against Miss Jennings, Walter and Oliver complained directly to Princess Xenia, whom they felt to be somehow responsible for the unpleasant situation. "It was the combined opinion of the Jennings clan," one of their friends wrote, "that Mrs. Leeds grew so tired of her she foisted her upon Annie."[86] Mrs. Leeds, who had done nothing of the kind, failed to appreciate the complaint. The Jenningses had been precisely informed about Anastasia's difficult character. If she now resented acting the tragic princess at the Ritz, surely that was the Jenningses' fault.

Gradually the situation deteriorated. Nothing could please Anastasia anymore. She hated her room. She hated the servants. She hated the food and was wild with indignation when Miss Jennings sent the cook upstairs to discuss the menu with her: "*Nobody* sends the cook to her guest's room."[87] Wilton Lloyd-Smith did what he could to avert the inevitable clash. It was his opinion that Anastasia ought to be sent away somewhere for her own protection, and he made the mistake of urging her to see a doctor. A doctor! Anastasia knew what that meant. "I rose and told him to leave," she remembered, "and myself left the room. . . . I did at once send to Miss Jennings to ask if I could see her brother Oliver Jennings. Miss Jennings came at once herself to me — telling me that she had just met Mr. [Lloyd-] Smith and he wanted to know only if I was sane. When Miss Jennings entered my room, she laughed in my face — with such a mean expression I can never forget. She was horrible to look at." When Oliver Jennings arrived that evening Anastasia saw that he would be of no help to her. "If you do not do what we want you to do," she quoted Oliver, "we shall send you to an asylum from which you will never get out for the rest of your life."

Anastasia summoned her dignity. She looked Oliver straight in the eye, and she said, "Then I shall be a beggar indeed!"

Not at all, Oliver replied: the sale of her memoirs would take care of any financial difficulties if they could only get the damned thing written.

Anastasia was not amused: "I wonder how he supposed that they could put me in an insane asylum for life and at the same time expect me to be a popular author." But now she was obsessed with the threat. She began to see leers and horrid grins on every face around her. She thought the whole household was spying on her. She thought the telephone wires had been cut. She concluded that the Jenningses were out to steal her money and that the "Grandanor" contract had only been a means to cloak the theft. She went to her room now, and she did not come out. Miss Jennings knocked and called at her door for hours. She begged Anastasia to come with her to Fairfield for a rest. There was no response. "Utterly disgusted," Miss Jennings packed her bags and left.[88]

Now the Jenningses' home became a battleground. There entered into Anastasia's life at this time a bona fide adventuress, one Jill Lillie Cossley-Batt. "In private life she calls herself Miss Huntington," Oliver Jennings wrote in awe. "Actually she is the Dowager Countess of Huntington, her husband having been killed five weeks after their marriage. She apparently has had an extremely interesting past."[89] So she had. Jill was an authoress. She had recently published a book called *The Last of the California Rangers* and, she declared, was hard at work on another, *The Adolescent Life of Christ*. In the meantime Jill was on assignment for *The Times* of London and planned to write a sympathetic piece about the Anastasia dispute. "She said she had known Anastasia in Russia," Wilton Lloyd-Smith recalled, "was an intimate friend of the Queen of England and the Prince of Wales and felt sure she could have her recognized *instanter*." [90]

Jill Cossley-Batt and the man she called her manager, Irvin Baird, had burst into Anastasia's room without even knocking, taking her so completely by surprise that she could not speak a word. [91] "I know you!" cried Jill. "I have seen you! I am the Countess Huntington, Lady Huntington. I was born a Battenberg, and I am here to help you. . . . I have brought with me my boy friend. He is a lawyer, and he will help you."

"That was the first time I had heard the expressions 'boy friend' and 'gosh' and several such expressions," Anastasia pointed out. But she had no recollection of meeting any "Lady Huntington."

Oh, Jill replied, that was because she had been wearing glasses: they had met at the opera in St. Petersburg.

"I asked her to which Battenberg she belonged," Anastasia remembered, and Jill answered that she was the daughter of Prince Alexander — "Sandro." Now, Anastasia knew perfectly well that Alexander of Battenberg had died young and childless after a *disgraceful* marriage to an opera singer. Nor was she convinced when Jill's "boy friend" told her that he was the son of the King of England's physician, a Scottish duke: "I did not believe any of these stories. I had never heard of a physician of the King of England who was a Duke. Also, both showed at once that they could have had no contacts with *any* court. . . . But I was in such a dreadful position in that house, had had these alarming experiences and feared worse. It was worth taking the chance if by that means I could leave the house."

For the next two months Jill Cossley-Batt and Irvin Baird enjoyed the run of Miss Jennings's apartment while Anastasia sat in her room wondering what to do. Later it seemed to many that Jill and Baird had deliberately set out to drive a wedge between Anastasia and her American hostess. First of all, said Jill, the "Grandanor" contract was illegal, and Anastasia need not feel bound to honor its terms. By the time the Jenningses were through there would be nothing left of her inheritance at all. But Anastasia wasn't to worry about a thing: Jill and Baird would write her memoirs for her, make some money, and then obtain her a Canadian passport and bring her to England for recognition. "They were talking always about bringing me to England," said Anastasia, but how did they mean to do it?

Well, said Jill, they could cross the border into Canada secretly, without a visa, and then get a letter to the Prince of Wales. He would take care of everything.

Anastasia had reached the end of her rope. Whom was she going to trust? Miss Jennings kept calling and cabling and begging her to come up to Fairfield, but Jill and Baird were warning her that "for God's sake [she] should not go . . . for they would do something to [her] there. . . . The Jenningses had told them that they intended to lock [her] up." All the while Jill and Baird were getting bolder. "They drank without my permission," Anastasia observed sternly. They read her letters. One day she found them rummaging through her closet. And then Baird had a plan: Anastasia should marry him, thereby solving all of her legal problems. And if the notion of marriage didn't appeal to her, maybe they could arrange something else. Did she get the idea?

She did: "It was awful. It was unendurable." Anastasia had to get away now. But where to go? All her things were in Fairfield, priceless things, "things I had brought with me from Germany, many things that were valuable and many things that I cared for because they were mementos of great kindness." Anastasia was made frantic by indecision. How was she to know who and what "the Countess Huntington" really was? It was Wilton Lloyd-Smith who found it out. "Cossley-Batt is entirely unauthorised to represent us," the London *Times* cabled in June.[92] Jill, it now appeared, was known in other parts as "Lady Lillian Mountbatten" and had claimed still grander titles in the past. One morning she told Anastasia that she and Baird were leaving. There would be no memoirs, no "sympathetic" article, no trip to England.

"Well," said Anastasia with her last shred of dignity, "that is all, I have nothing more to say."[93] Before leaving her room Baird told her to "go to hell."[94]

The Jennings family could only be thankful that they had not allowed Anastasia to leave the country in the company of "this strange Dowager" and her sleazy boyfriend. But Jill's company had done its work. "The awful result," Lloyd-Smith wrote, "was a complete break between Mrs. Anderson and Miss Jennings. . . . Mrs. Anderson began writing Miss Jennings the most absurd abusive letters. Miss Jennings was of course very much upset and both of her brothers were perfectly furious."[95] Anastasia's accusations against her hostess far outstripped the usual litany of imaginary offenses. "I am not referring to simple little matters like stealing her money," Lloyd-Smith wrote Edward Fallows later. "I mean the kind of thing that usually would not be printed but which a Hearst paper under these circumstances would have been delighted to publish." And that was the worst of it: Anastasia was threatening to go public with her charges. She had lost her illusions about Miss Jennings: "I said I knew she was a gossip and that she drank but I had not known she was a crook. . . . I said I would not rest until I saw them all in jail."[96]

Perhaps if some outsider had managed to see her; if Anastasia had been able to talk with someone who really liked her, she might have come back to her senses. But no one liked her now, it seemed. "Don't people think I have any feelings?" she cried to Miss Jennings's niece, Marguerite, after one of the maids had sailed into Anastasia's room with unsolicited advice.[97] Lloyd-Smith had already written Gleb Botkin asking if Gleb thought Anastasia was "crazy." "I answered that in the colloquial use of the word one can say that the Grand Duchess is 'a crazy person,' " Gleb wrote, "and does crazy things, but that she certainly was in no way insane in the medical sense."[98] Wasn't she? Lloyd-Smith wondered, and he knew that since Anastasia would never enter a sanatorium voluntarily, some way would have to be found to commit her. Annie Jennings froze at the thought. She wrote Lloyd-Smith: "I feel very strongly that any act taken by you toward sending in a physician to see Mrs. Anderson, or any act leading to the commitment of Mrs. Anderson to a sanatorium should be upon the decision of her cousin, Princess Xenia."[99] Above all, Miss Jennings dreaded what "the Public" might think if Anastasia were committed against her will: "I feel absolutely sure that the Public will consider this act on our part as a very great reflection upon us and that we will be criticized by the Public for doing this, I in particular." On the other hand, Anastasia was threatening to create a scandal herself. Already Miss Jennings's friends were looking at her ruefully and whispering, "Poor Annie, the Grand Duchess is costing her *so* much money."[100] One woman recalled:

The rumors were that Anastasia spent most of her time playing with Miss Jennings' old parrot. . . . Miss Jennings' old chauffeur, who had

been with her for years, took her out occasionally when Miss Jennings
insisted on her "taking the air." He reported that she always pulled
all the curtains down in Miss J's big old Rolls-Royce. She had a terrific
persecution complex. The few times she was ill — a bad cold or flu —
they had a violent scene before she would see a doctor. . . . But the
showdown came when Anastasia became convinced the cook (who had
been with Miss Jennings for some thirty years) was trying to poison
her and would eat nothing but crackers out of a sealed box! Then — and
not until then — she was sent back to Mrs. Leeds. . . . I find it hard to
believe that even Miss Jennings believed in her at the end — but, I
don't know.[101]

What did it mean in the light of Anastasia's disputed identity to
know that her experiences had finally caught up with her? Was it
the Tsar's daughter or someone else who broke down in the summer of 1930? It didn't matter one way or the other to the Jennings
family. They had an embarrassment on their hands, and they did
not send it "back to Mrs. Leeds." When she heard about the plan
to have Anastasia committed — the Jenningses had settled on the
elegant "Four Winds" sanatorium at Katonah, in Westchester
County — Princess Xenia took it upon herself to write Anastasia
and urge her to go. "I do hope you did not misunderstand me,"
Xenia wrote in a second letter after hearing about "dearest Anastasia's" hysterical reaction to the first. "You see, my only idea was
to help you in any way I could. . . . Do think over my suggestion
and try to go [to Four Winds]. And please always remember that I
am your friend."[102] But Anastasia was ill equipped to listen to any
advice at all. On July 15 Lloyd-Smith wrote Miss Jennings in Connecticut:

Last night, about a quarter after six, Mrs. Anderson, in a fit of anger
over Miss [Cossley-Batt] and Mr. Baird, stepped on and killed one of her
birds. She began screaming and shouting and demanding another bird.
She was told that no bird could be got at that time of night. She did not
believe it. . . . She spent the entire night screaming and did not sleep.
This morning she went out and actually purchased another bird for,
I understand, about $25. . . .
    Later in the morning she went to Altman's and found that her credit
had been cut off.[103]

Annie Jennings was not a miserly woman by any means. Having
decided to send Anastasia away, she had also agreed to pay the four
hundred and seventy-five dollars a week it would cost to keep An-

astasia at the sanatorium in Katonah. Her brothers were annoyed. "We understood from you that the board would be $150.00 per week and $75.00 for the nurse," Walter Jennings complained to Lloyd-Smith.[104] His concerns soon turned back to Anastasia herself, however, who, yelling and crying, refused to leave the apartment on Fifth Avenue. "She went into terrific tempers," Lloyd-Smith wrote, "attacked people who were waiting on her with sticks, or whatever she could find. She screamed and shouted. She ran about on the roof without anything on, attracting an enormous amount of attention. Altogether the situation was a holy mess."[105] Matters came to a head when Anastasia, threatening "more and more convincingly to kill herself," began throwing heavy objects out her window in an unsuccessful effort to attract the police. One morning she went down to Altman's again, where she stood on the main floor and "made speeches" about Miss Jennings. The time had come, said Lloyd-Smith, to obtain a commitment order. "It was a question of doing it that way quietly," he explained to Edward Fallows later, "or of having her bring it on herself publicly, together with the publication from the police station, or wherever she went, of the most awful and unbelievable charges against Miss Jennings and *you*. . . . The action taken was the informal action permitted by our law to detain a person under circumstances where it might be of harm to others or to themselves."[106] Before lodging petition for Anastasia's commitment, however, Lloyd-Smith took Miss Jennings's advice and discussed the matter with Princess Xenia.

"I am going to commit her this afternoon," he told Xenia over the telephone, "unless you really think I shouldn't. . . . I am having the three best doctors I can find in New York to examine her. . . . I am doing everything carefully in her interest. I am very sorry."

"I am sorry, too," said Xenia. She paused: "I can't understand — but it is the best thing for her. I think it is the best thing for her. Otherwise she will hurt her cause."[107]

Walter Jennings filed the formal application for commitment with Judge Peter Schmuck of the Supreme Court of New York:

. . . Mrs. Anderson, without any near relatives in this country, has been the guest of, and supported by, my sister for 18 months. She believes attempts are being made to poison her, refuses medical assistance, spends most of her time confined to her bedroom talking to two birds. She believes my sister has stolen her property. . . . She is abusive to my sister and has refused all attempts to persuade her to leave my sister's house for a sanitarium. She threatened to shoot the last representative whom my sister sent. My information is from personal observation, conversations with my sister, and reports of a trained nurse and servants who recently have been the only persons she would see.[107]

Anastasia had not yet been examined by a psychiatrist, nor would she be until she was carted off to the sanatorium at Katonah. The doctors Wilton Lloyd-Smith had engaged to sign the commitment papers were ready, all the same, to attest to her "untidiness," her "extreme suspicion," and her "delusions of persecution."[108] It cost the Jenningses over one thousand dollars. "Dr. K . . . called me up," Lloyd-Smith wrote Walter Jennings afterward, "and asked me if I considered $500 for himself, $500 for Dr. Z . . . and $250 for Dr. W . . . as an excessive charge for their services. . . . I told him that I considered this perfectly reasonable. In view of the importance to you and to Miss Jennings in having their names on the commitment papers, and in view of the notoriety of the case when it is discovered, the charges are extremely modest."[109]

On July 24, 1930, Anastasia was adjudged insane — "dangerous to herself and others."[110] That night, while Lloyd-Smith stood by, a nurse and two orderlies broke down the door of her room. They found her cowering in the bathroom, dragged her to her feet, and took her away.[111]

11

HOME AGAIN

*F*rieda Riesenfeld was a nurse at the Kuranstalt Ilten, a psychiatric home situated a few miles from the German city of Hannover. One morning late in August 1931 she took the train up to Cuxhaven to meet a new patient, an American lady due in that afternoon on the steamer *Deutschland*. The patient, Miss Anderson, was evidently an important person. Her reception at Ilten had been seen to with the utmost care. First, an American doctor studying in Berlin had inspected the facilities to make sure they were the finest available. Then an attorney from Paris had arranged with the local authorities for Miss Anderson's entrance visa. On August 13 a cable had arrived from the German consul in New York City asking if the costs of a six months' stay at Ilten had been assured. A thousand dollars were shortly forwarded from the National City Bank in New York. Finally another cable arrived from the lawyer in Paris informing that Miss Anderson would arrive at Cuxhaven on the twenty-eighth.

When the *Deutschland* had docked, Frieda Riesenfeld went directly down to Cabin 90 to fetch her charge. She found Miss Anderson closely guarded by a private nurse, a Finnish woman. "The patient made a very shy impression," Nurse Riesenfeld reported, "and seemed afraid. She spoke not at all and kept her handkerchief permanently to her mouth. . . . I said to her in German, which she

253

understood well, that I had orders to take her to a sanatorium at Ilten. She then asked by whom the arrangements had been made. I showed her the telegram from the attorney to the sanatorium direc- tor. She replied that she did not know this attorney. She had to make up her mind at last to leave her stateroom, as the steamer had to be vacated."[1]

The staff at Ilten had already been warned, both by the American doctor and the Paris attorney, that Miss Anderson was insane and in need of constant surveillance. No one, however, had been able to provide any details of her illness or even to say who had ordered Miss Anderson committed. It was no different with Miss Ander- son's Finnish nurse, as Frieda Riesenfeld discovered on the return train to Hannover. All the nurse would say was that Miss Anderson was "a dangerous lunatic" and that she would probably make an attempt to escape. When Nurse Riesenfeld ventured to the contrary that "Miss A. was entirely quiet and orderly and had not made the slightest move to escape," the Finnish woman lost her temper. She could not answer for the consequences, she declared, if Miss Ander- son were left by herself.

Nurse Riesenfeld looked again at Miss Anderson, who had sat the whole time staring out the window. Whenever she spoke a few words to her, however, Miss Anderson only looked up, smiled, nod- ded, and said, "I like Germany."

There was something peculiar about this case. Didn't the Finnish nurse have *any* background information?

No. All the nurse knew was that Miss Anderson was mad.

Mad? asked Nurse Riesenfeld. How so?

Well, said the Finnish woman, she was obsessed with cleanliness "and washed about fifty times a day." There you were. Typical symptoms.

But why had she been committed to Ilten? Why hadn't she been kept in the United States?

The Finnish nurse rolled her eyes, sighed, and replied "that she did not know exactly, but very little was known about Miss A. anyway."

When the party arrived at Ilten late that evening Miss Anderson was taken to an isolation room and put under guard.[2] The doctors at the sanatorium noted with astonishment that Miss Anderson's nurse had not brought along any of her patient's medical records — no letters, no documents of transferral, nothing. The most she could produce was a passport granted to "Anna Anderson" on August

18, 1931, by the German consul in New York. In lieu of a signature the document was marked only with a large X.

At the crack of dawn the Finnish nurse, without notifying the doctors or any member of the staff, disappeared from Ilten for parts unknown. Soon Dr. Nieper, the nephew of the sanatorium director, went to Miss Anderson's cell for a chat.

"Good morning, Miss Anderson," said Dr. Nieper.

Miss Anderson glared at him. Finally she asked that her trunks be brought. Rummaging through papers, photographs, dresses, furs, and some very fine lingerie she found what she was looking for. It was a certificate of identity, granted in May of 1927 to Anastasia Tschaikovsky.

Dr. Nieper was quiet for a moment. Then he went to fetch his uncle, the director. "The faces of these gentlemen," said "Miss Anderson" later, "I will never forget." [3]

Bit by bit her story came out. [4] She told it passionately: how the Jennings family had "held her prisoner" in New York; how she had been dragged in mortal terror to the sanatorium at Katonah and detained there for more than a year; how there had been attempts to poison her, and blow her up, ever since her arrival in America; how all at once she had been ordered to pack her things and was brought to the *Deutschland* — dragged again, against her will. During the week-long voyage to Cuxhaven the Finnish nurse (who was thoroughly "*unsympathisch*" in the first place) had kept her locked in her cabin and taken away the key to her trunk, so that she was forced to sit out the trip in her dressing gown: "I had no toothbrush, no soap, no comb, no face-cloth — nothing whatever. I was left without any sort of toilet article. . . . We had, of course, no conversation coming over. What was there to say to such a person?" [5] Anastasia swore now that she had no idea where "Anna Anderson's" passport had come from, and she asked Dr. Nieper to find out how and why all this had been done to her — at once!

Dr. Nieper never did find out exactly. No one did. The American immigration authorities learned of Anastasia's return to Germany only a month after the event, and when the *Times* and other newspapers endeavored to get to the bottom of her mysterious voyage they turned up nothing. [6] The most anyone would say at the Four Winds sanatorium was that Anastasia had many times expressed a wish to leave the country: "While she was offered an opportunity to return to Germany, she quickly took advantage of it. . . . What port she intended to go to, we do not know." [7]

"The Public" in New York, in the meantime, whose opinion Miss Jennings had so dreaded, had never learned about the humiliating tactics that had been employed the year before to hospitalize Anastasia at Four Winds. Neither, at first, had Edward Fallows, her attorney, who was still hunting clues in Europe at the time. When he heard nothing from or about his client in over six weeks, Fallows started to worry.[8] "Have been silent because of very unexpected and strange complications," Wilton Lloyd-Smith cabled him in Berlin. "Having a devil of a time. . . ."[9] Eight more appeals for news from Fallows were left unanswered and unacknowledged. Only in August 1930, when her visa once again came up for renewal, was Anastasia's disappearance from the Jenningses' home made publicly known.[10] While the Jenningses kept quiet on the subject, Anastasia's photograph was printed in newspapers as far away as Rockford, Illinois, along with an announcement that the immigration authorities were searching for her. "Deport Anastasia as 'Royal' Fraud!" the New York *Mirror* screeched in its ignorance. The *Mirror* informed that "the most astonishing hoax of the century" had been seen through at last, that "prominent Americans [had] been victimized," that Anastasia had fled to England to avoid arrest, and so forth.[11] Since she had most obviously not returned to Europe, however, the headlines on that side of the ocean announced that she had been kidnapped and was probably dead. Those were the stories Fallows saw.

"Newspaper reports absurd . . . ," Lloyd-Smith finally cabled Fallows. "If Grandanor dead I'm a rhinoceros."[12]

Only months later did Edward Fallows find out what had been done to "Grandanor." He was furious: "I have never lived through five months of more intense anxiety and worry, because of this persistent silence in spite of repeated cables from myself begging for information. . . . The way Mr. Lloyd-Smith and his helpers took to capture the Grand Duchess by breaking down the door of her room . . . does not seem humane, to say the least. That alone would have been enough to derange temporarily any sensitive, high-strung, ill woman."[13]

When the news of Anastasia's move to the Four Winds sanatorium finally leaked out, there were few in New York society who could honestly blame Annie Jennings for forcing the treatment on her wayward protégée. "She is reported to have insulted the hundred percent. American servitors of her hostess," said the *Sunday News,* "causing them to depart in indignant droves."[14] Miss Jennings should have known better than to mix herself up with Europeans: "Meanwhile Anastasia remains at the Sanatorium. She isn't deranged, they say up there, just — well — just in need of attention for her disordered nerves." No one had known anything about the faked medical reports until Adelene Moffat,[15] an elderly painter from Boston, formed a committee "for the Recognition of the Grand Duchess Anastasia" and began pestering Wilton Lloyd-Smith for information. Miss Moffat's snooping might well have provided the incentive to transfer Anastasia to Ilten — that and the fact that her stay at Katonah had already cost Miss Jennings well over twenty-five thousand dollars, no small price in the middle of the Depression. Evidently her brothers had persuaded her to move Anastasia to more modest quarters: six months at Ilten cost only as much as two weeks at Katonah. By now, however, Anastasia had ample reason to resist other people's plans for her future, and she had refused — loudly — to leave Four Winds. (She may have had other reasons than the memory of "Mr. Lloyd-Smith and his helpers"; Four Winds was not the snake pit she later liked to make it out. Four hundred and fifty dollars a week gave her four private rooms, a personal attendant, use of the tennis courts, shopping trips to town, and an occasional night out at the opera or the theatre. It is true that for the first eight months of her hospitalization Anastasia had been kept under a twenty-four-hour guard and that she had never wanted to be at Katonah in the first place, but that appears to have been the extent of her degradation.) [16]

When the Jennings family learned that Anastasia was still not ready to cooperate with them, they resorted once more to force. Again Wilton Lloyd-Smith took care of the details. "I had a lot of trouble with Mrs. Anderson lately," he told Princess Xenia. "What would you think if I sent her to a sanitarium in Germany? She is very anxious to go, apparently."

"Yes? Well, I don't know, Wilton." Xenia explained that she had recently encountered Walter Jennings in New York, who told her that he had dispatched two former officers of the Tsar's yacht to Katonah to look at Anastasia, and that these two officers, Basil Woitinsky and George Taube, had both rejected Anastasia's identity out of hand. "He was quite disagreeable about it," Xenia remarked of Walter. ". . . He got quite pompous."

"I do think Woitinsky's opinion made a great difference with the Jenningses," Lloyd-Smith went on.

Xenia sighed: "Don't you see they *hoped* he would have that

opinion? They are bored with her, as I told them they would be.
. . . I hear the old lady [Miss Jennings] does not agree with her
brothers."

"I don't know," said Lloyd-Smith, before returning to the matter
at hand: "How to get her abroad, and just when, I don't know. But
I think I will give it a try." [17] In the end, Anastasia's return to Europe had to be arranged extralegally. Application for a German
passport was filed with the consulate. Some diminutive, dark-blond
woman was brought in to play the part of "Anna Anderson," and,
pleading illiteracy, signed the passport with a cross. Then one night
Anastasia was seized and driven off to New York Harbor.[18] She
was livid with rage when she discovered that she had been *imper-
sonated*. Arrived at Ilten, she bombarded Edward Fallows — who,
she said, was lucky to have his head on his shoulders — with angry
typewritten letters demanding that he have the Jennings family "arrested."[19] She was going to unleash "the police in New York" on
Lloyd-Smith, she added — "will you please tell him that!" But it
wouldn't have done any good to press charges. The Jennings clan,
Lloyd-Smith, and the German consulate all had no comment. "Miss
Jennings never converses on that subject," her butler informed the
New York papers. "She does not permit any of her people to converse on that subject." [20] And indeed Miss Jennings is said never to
have mentioned the name Anastasia again.

"What a mess!" Anastasia often said later when she referred to
her ill-starred years in America.[21] The Duke of Leuchtenberg, she
remembered, had cautioned her about leaving Germany to begin
with. Anyway, she was glad to be back. One of her first acts after
her ignominious return was to telegraph Princess Xenia, who, divorced now from Mr. Leeds, had moved into a small house in Syos-
set alone with little Nancy. Anastasia confessed to Edward Fallows
that she had been "a fool" ever to quarrel with Xenia and that she
regretted her behavior at Oyster Bay almost more than anything
else.[22] "Your mother was right," she told Nancy Leeds many years
later, "quite right. And I was not." [23]

As soon as the doctors at Ilten realized who the "dangerous lunatic" in their midst actually was — or said she was — they moved
her from her room to an apartment on the grounds of the sanatorium. "They did not seem to know what to do, at first," said Anastasia. "I think they felt as if they were seeing a ghost. They later
told me that I looked like one. . . . Then at once I began to get
letters from friends whom I had not heard from since I left Ger-

many. They all told me the same story, that they had written to me many times in America but that I had never answered any of their letters. Also from all over the world came . . . letters of all sorts. Some with offers of marriage, with offers of their homes, offers to take my case into court, to give me cheap rates in their pensions and hotels. . . . People, including princes, came asking me for money, which was humorous, considering my plight, that I had not so much money that I could buy a stamp for a letter!"[24] Anastasia made a point of ignoring these appeals, just as she had decided to ignore forevermore anyone's advice about her future. The day would come, she grew fond of saying, when she would "pave the way from Petersburg to Moscow with the skulls of her enemies."[25]

At Ilten, meantime, the doctors had been taking notes. "The lack of any symptoms of insanity," wrote Dr. Hans Willige, "was proved so conclusively during the very first examination that we were already able to tell Frau Tschaikovsky on the second day that she was not insane and not in need of treatment in an institution. . . . Hers is, however, a personality of unique character, consisting to a high degree of a strong willfulness, a highly egocentric outlook and an interior haughtiness." Anastasia's sanity was a condition attested to by "every doctor here," Willige went on, although he could not "entirely abandon the diagnosis of a psychopathic condition; after all, one might well designate so peculiar a personality as Frau Tschaikovsky obviously is . . . as psychopathic." But Willige wanted it understood once and for all that there was an essential difference between emotional disturbance and madness. His was the last formal examination of her much-debated psyche Anastasia would ever consent to, and it echoed without reservation the conclusions of every doctor who had treated her previously. "She had good reason to assume she was being persecuted," said Willige, refusing even to consider the possibility of fraud in this case: "To be able to [impersonate another] would require a surpassing intelligence, an extraordinary degree of self-control and an ever-alert discipline — all qualities Frau Tschaikovsky in no way possesses." Willige's verdict was unequivocal and unapologetic: "It will not be necessary for us to describe in detail the observations which led to our conclusion. . . . We are very well able to judge."[26]

It was 1931, and Anastasia, "the unknown woman," was back where she had started out, in a psychiatric institution. Eleven years of scrutiny and scandal had done nothing to alter her personality. The diagnosis at Ilten was exactly what it had been in 1920, when the gentle nurses of the Dalldorf Asylum sat with her in the night and promised not to reveal her secret. Dr. Willige told her that she was free to go.

Looking ahead, she must have seen a grim future. There were people in Europe she could turn to, she knew. She might impose on Tatiana Botkin in France, for instance, but with two passports, under two different names, how could she ever be sure she would not be stranded there? The Duke of Leuchtenberg had sent her a touching letter when her grandmother died, calling her, as always, "my dear child" and telling her that everyone at Seeon still thought about her often. But now the Duke was dead of a brain tumor — she suspected he had been poisoned — and she was not ready to face his formidable Duchess. It would never have occurred to her to seek out Grand Duke Andrew — not "that family" — or "the Rathlef woman," and while Ambassador Zahle and his wife would undoubtedly have helped, they had already endured enough on her account. She could not bring more trouble down on them.

Miss Jennings had paid her expenses for six months. Anastasia liked Ilten, and she stayed there. The world would not see her again until she had been immortalized on the stage and in the movies. Then, when she was old, still sick, part harridan and part fairy princess, her case went to court.

PART THREE

Mrs. Anderson

12

"HOHE FRAU":

THE HERMIT OF THE BLACK FOREST

*T*he village of Unterlengenhardt lies at the crest of a rocky cliff on the western edge of the Black Forest. Boasting a single paved road, an inn, a general store, and a small, cozy restaurant, it is little more than a well-tended clearing in the hills above the Nagold and practically indistinguishable in appearance from scores of other farming communities in the state of Baden-Württemberg. But Unterlengenhardt enjoys a distinction its neighbors cannot share. First of all, it is home to the Anthroposophists, those hardy disciples of Rudolf Steiner, the Christian visionary who once lived in Unterlengenhardt and in whose honor a community health center has been erected at the fringe of the woods. About five miles away, down the hill from Steiner's clinic, are the red roofs of Bad Liebenzell and, beyond them, Calw, where Hermann Hesse was born and where he laid the action for many a romantic fable. *Romantic* is the right word for Unterlengenhardt. It appears to be populated exclusively by children and old ladies, and while this part of the Black Forest has not entirely escaped the stucco blight of reconstructed Germany, most of the houses for miles around still look as though they might be made of gingerbread. "Unterlengenhardt was perfect," said one who came to know it well. "Time seemed to stop when you arrived. The Celts built there, you know."[1]

The reporters who streamed through Unterlengenhardt during the

1950s were not interested in the Celts, nor even in the still-flourishing science of Anthroposophy. They gathered one and all around a dilapidated wooden hut some few hundred yards off the main road, diagonally behind the village inn. During World War II this one-story cabin had served as army barracks, but now, in peacetime, it was virtually smothered in a variety of brambles, fences, creeping vines, weeds, and wild shrubbery. The overgrowth had gotten so bad that after a few years nothing could be seen of the barracks but the rusted chimney pipe puffing its smoke into the air. Even the dwarf fruit trees that surrounded the compound looked run-down, in need of repair.

This forlorn estate, so conspicuous among the tidy houses of the Black Forest, was the home of "Anna Anderson," [2] the legendary old lady who claimed to be the youngest daughter of the Russian Tsar. It was she, Anastasia, the reporters had come to see. Nobody in Unterlengenhardt would ever forget the onslaught of the journalists — hundreds of them every year, scrambling about in the woods; fighting over the use of the telephones; trying to bribe the farmers; calling for food, swilling beer, pounding, banging, yelling: "Anastasia! Hey, Anastasia! Grand Duchess! Open up!" The villagers had been almost as apprehensive as Anastasia herself. But they were loyal. They did not sell postcards or souvenirs. They did not give interviews without permission. True, there had been some talk at the inn. It was only natural: you couldn't live down the road from one of the most famous women in Europe and pretend that you didn't. But the gentlemen of the press had found out very quickly that Anastasia made no distinctions. If she didn't want to see anybody, she didn't want to see anybody, and that was all there was to it. Prince Sigismund of Prussia had knocked at her door for three days before she let him in — he a nephew of the Kaiser and Anastasia's own ("alleged") cousin! [3] Then there was Tatiana Botkin, one of her oldest friends, who had come all the way from Paris in the dead of winter to see her and who, after eight days in the snow, had gone home in defeat. [4] "I am old and sick," Anastasia had protested in tears. "Let them come again in the spring, when it will be nice. We will have tea in the garden — if I am not dead!" [5]

Any reporter who was not daunted by the prospect of a siege and who could prove to the wary citizens of Unterlengenhardt his seriousness and goodwill, might at length have been introduced to one of the several ladies who still enjoyed Anastasia's limited trust. There was Adele von Heydebrandt, first of all — Anastasia's live-in companion and chief confidante — but *she* never talked and lived under the constant threat of banishment. There were Frau von Heydebrandt's sprightly younger sister, Maria von Mutius; Gertrude Lamerdin and Louisa Mayhoff; the well-meaning but chronically imprudent Miss Thomasius; and Baroness Monica von Miltitz, an exiled Thuringian matriarch with a severe countenance, who was generally thought to be "the High Priestess of the Anastasia Cult."[6] All of them old, most of them spinsters, these women had built a well-nigh impenetrable wall around the lady in the barracks, and it was their job to see to it that she had whatever she might need at any moment: food, clothing, maid service, consolation, advice. They were her link with the world outside, in many ways her best friends, but they could not persuade her to meet a journalist, nor ever be sure that she wouldn't bolt her door against them, too, if they tried.

So the reporters had a choice: they could leave, or they could wait. Anastasia sometimes had other callers, and in Unterlengenhardt news traveled fast: "Somebody important is here to see 'Her.' " It might have been the former Crown Princess of Prussia, or a Romanov nephew come to meet "the family riddle."[7] It might have been one or the other of Anastasia's celebrated attorneys; Alexis Miliukoff, a Russian émigré whom she called "a scoundrel" but whose company she much enjoyed;[8] Baron Ulrich von Gienanth, her "Minister of Finance"; or Prince Frederick Ernest of Saxe-Altenburg, her most devoted champion, her friend, the man who had rescued her from the Soviet Zone in 1946 and brought her to the West. For that matter, because Anastasia attracted as many crackpots as she did journalists, her illustrious visitor might have been a Dutch housewife who claimed to be the *fifth* daughter of the Tsar, kidnapped from Tsarskoe Selo in babyhood;[9] or, again, a persistent, dangerous woman who swore she was Nicholas and Alexandra's illegitimate grandchild[10] — born in 1916, somehow being the offspring of Olga Nicolaievna and a Bolshevik soldier — and who threatened to shoot her way inside the barracks if her "Aunt Anastasia" wouldn't open the door.

While the reporters pondered these weird claimants — much truer to the type, they agreed, than "Mrs. Anderson" — Anastasia sometimes did open the door. No one could ever divine the reasons for her sudden cooperativeness. Perhaps she felt she had something to say. More likely she was tired of arguing and hoped that by seeing one reporter she might placate them all. (Of course she never could satisfy the curiosity of the press and she always regretted having

tried. "I have been speaking . . . ," she once wrote in her no-non-
sense style. "Myself an idiot.") [11] Thus in 1955 Adele von Heydebrandt escorted a reporter from *Life* magazine into the barracks,
where he found Anastasia lying on her camp-bed, ailing as always,
surrounded by portraits, photographs, medallions, and stacks of unopened mail, fretting about her peach trees and convinced that she
would never live out the year. The camera caught her smiling thinly,
and American readers were able to determine for themselves whether
she was, as stated, "still pretty." Pretty or not, she was unhappy,
unwell, and uninterested in the future. "People want me to die,"
she told *Life,* "certain people. I shall soon oblige them." [12]

Anastasia was at length forced to erect a high palisade of wire
and straw matting around her property in order to fend off the
curious. In the early 1960s, after her friends had built her a small
chalet to take the place of the rotting barracks, she put up iron
gates, let the shrubbery grow wilder than ever, and desperately
coated the tree trunks with lard so the reporters couldn't climb them
to take pictures. And it wasn't just the reporters. Bus tours of the
Black Forest included her house on the itinerary and sometimes
promised "a meeting with Anastasia." When they failed even to
catch a glimpse of Anastasia, disappointed Germans sent their young
children crawling through the bushes with cameras in the hope of
catching her unaware as she puttered about her yard. [13] "They
climbed trees," one of her friends recalled, "pressed against the fence,
tried to vault the gate, peered through the gaps in the hedge, threw
stones and whistled for her to come out." [14] How long could it go
on, Anastasia wondered — this prying and poking about, this incessant torment? "This moment were again two newspaper men here
. . . ," she wrote her attorneys. "I send them to you. . . . Please be
so kind and take care of these people." [15] Then she stopped count-
ing. To her friend Gleb Botkin she was not afraid to express her
abiding resentment. One letter, dictated in the third person, told
Gleb in something other than the King's English: "You are not able
to imagine what here goes on about the poor barrack. The reporters
are simply coming from all over the world. . . . Of course you will
imagine that her health is in a very poor condition. Without any
fresh air at all, because she cannot even look out, everywhere stands
somebody. She is a real prisoner in her own little home." [16]

Anastasia's complaints fell on deaf ears. One daring soul, crawling on hands and knees beneath her window, had a jug of cold
water poured over his head, [17] but afterward Anastasia was ashamed

of herself and henceforth relied for protection on her dogs: four great hybrids, half wolfhound, half St. Bernard. They had cute, innocent names — "Tillie," "Polly," "Baby," "Naughty" — but they were vicious, and they obeyed Anastasia alone.[18] The sight of her holding these beasts on a leash was enough to give anybody second thoughts. On those rare, dreaded occasions when she had to leave her forest redoubt, people heard Anastasia pacifying the huge creatures, softly, in English: "Darlings, wait for me here; I shan't be long." [19] Then she would emerge suddenly through the trees to conduct her business, swathed, summer and winter, in a full-length coat, a fur hat, gloves, and innumerable scarves, a handkerchief or paper napkin always pressed against her twisted jaw. A reporter from Paris saw her like that in the summer of 1960, just after her new house had been built and furnished, but before she had mustered the courage to move into it:

Suddenly, accompanied by an infernal uproar of barking, we saw the door open and there entered the strangest creature I have ever seen in my life. It was a little Madam Butterfly disguised as a Tyrolean. She was wearing a Japanese kimono, over which she had slipped a loden coat, and over the coat a black, hooded cape. The cowl was drawn up over the Tyrolean hat, which crowned a head of chestnut hair, streaked with white. The face had a great delicacy about it, but her mouth was sheltered behind a napkin, folded like a fan, which she held in one black-gloved hand. Her feet were buried in enormous fur boots, and the indecision of her step, the hesitation you could sense, conferred an unreal quality on her presence.[20]

This was "the Empress of Unterlengenhardt," "the Hermit of the Black Forest." [21] In those colorful, royalty-mad women's magazines that thrive especially in the Federal Republic of Germany, Anastasia took her place alongside Grace of Monaco, the Persian Empresses Soraya and Farah Diba, Princess Margaret Rose, and America's youthful queen, Jacqueline Kennedy. *Quick, 7-Tage, Frau im Spiegel, Frau in Welt* — the weeklies couldn't get enough of her. "I am the milch cow for the journalists," Anastasia complained.[22] She had no doubt that half of Germany had made a fortune on her story. And then her mail! The marriage proposals alone would have filled a trunk. One gentleman from New Zealand, pining for her hand, kept sending her money orders made out for twelve-and-a-half pence, evidently not thinking that New Zealand currency was of no earthly use to her in the Black Forest.[23] Piles of letters arrived at the barracks every day,[24] sometimes addressed to "Grand Duchess Anastasia, Black Forest, Germany," and sometimes — from the doubters — to the "Anderson Impostor." Altogether Anastasia's mail was fascinating. "Honoured Imperial Highness!" a letter might read, "Do you mind if I call you that?" Or: "My aunt has a great friend who was a cook at the royal palace [sic], and I feel sure that if you would only meet her . . ." Or this, from an especially demented correspondent: "Why do you say you are Anastasia, I know that you been murdered. . . ." There were death threats aplenty, along with pornographic notes and any number of outrageous propositions: to make movies, to invest in diamond mines, to go on safari — what did Anastasia care about it? She had her pictures, her ikons, her ladies, and her dogs. She needed nothing else. Some mysteries do not want solving:

> Anastasia, tell me who you are.
> Are you someone from another star?
> Anastasia, are you what you seem?
> Do your sad eyes remember a dream?
>
> Why do you tremble, and why do you sigh?
> Could you be lonely, as lonely as I?
> Do you remember, when summer has flown,
> Another world, a world that is yours alone?
>
> Anastasia, smile away the past!
> Anastasia, spring is here at last!
> Beautiful stranger, step down from your star.
> I only know I love you so,
> Whoever you are.[25]

Wholesome Pat Boone sang those words to the haunting main theme of Twentieth-Century Fox's *Anastasia,* the film that marked Ingrid Bergman's return to the American screen and won her an Oscar as Best Actress of 1956. The Fox film had been adapted loosely from Guy Bolton's popular New York stage version, which in turn had been adapted from the French original by Marcelle Maurette. Mme. Maurette might well have been annoyed to hear Pat Boone crooning his love for a heroine she had tried hard to make real, but no one would deny the romantic appeal of *Anastasia,* Marcelle Maurette least of all. Long before she wrote her play she had been captivated by the saga of the Tsar's lost daughter, seeing beyond the mystery to a fundamental, even existential problem of truth, identity, and, ultimately, choice. Mme. Maurette did not need to probe archives or go on interviews to know that Anastasia had become the powerless victim of "witnesses." As proof she had before her the radically opposite masterworks of Harriet von Rathlef and Pierre Gilliard, both of whom had presumed to judge a matter about which Anastasia, whoever she was, must have known far more than they. "Whether the witnesses accept her or reject her," wrote Mme. Maurette, "the surprising thing is that not one of them hesitates. Whoever she is, I am amazed."[26]

With that thought Marcelle Maurette went to work, crafting an "unquestionably old-fashioned, sentimental, rococo and somewhat neo-Sardou" melodrama[27] from the "Anastasia" story. Her plot revolved around "Anna," a beautiful, clever, and dignified amnesiac who is found contemplating suicide in Berlin and is finally persuaded by three money-hungry Russian émigrés to impersonate the daughter of the Tsar. The New York cast starred Viveca Lindfors as the mysterious claimant — "the Galatea I have fashioned out of the mud of the Landwehr Canal,"[28] as one of Anna's sponsors calls her in the play — and the great Eugénie Leontovich as her grandmother, the Dowager Empress, on whose meeting with the heroine the plot turns. In the Ingrid Bergman film version[29] the setting had shifted from Berlin to Paris and Copenhagen, where the Eiffel Tower and the Tivoli gardens better suited the wide screen, while Yul Brynner, fresh from his triumph in *The King and I,* had stepped in as Anna's lover. Starring along with Miss Bergman and Mr. Brynner was America's "First Lady of the Theatre," Helen Hayes. Her portrayal of the Dowager Empress satisfied everybody but the Romanovs, one of whom called it "a travesty."[30]

Hiding out in the Black Forest, Anastasia had never asked for this kind of publicity. She had certainly never expected her quarter century of obscurity to end the way it did, with her name emblazoned on posters and marquees all over the globe and her identity, already doubted in most quarters, further confused with a fictional beauty who ran off with Yul Brynner at the end of the story. But henceforth, like it or not, Anastasia could never escape the legend. The stage and film versions of her life made a greater impression on the public than all the books and newspaper articles put together. When Anastasia's photographs began to reappear in America, as a result, people were seriously put out to discover that "she didn't look a thing like Ingrid Bergman," and nobody likes to learn that in real life she never saw her grandmother again. World historians and Russian scholars, in the meantime, greeted the success of *Anastasia* with a shrug and a metaphorical smirk, suggesting that the fictional retelling of the story was as reliable as any other.

Among all those responsible for Anastasia's resurgent notoriety, only Marcelle Maurette, who had begun it all, felt a twinge of guilt. She had written her play without thinking that the von Rathlef/Gilliard heroine might still be alive. When she found out that the lady in the barracks was not only living but mortified, Mme. Maurette got in touch with Anastasia's attorneys and voluntarily offered to cede a share of her royalties. She was under no legal obligation to do so. Although the theatrical "Anastasia" had plainly been modeled on a real person, she bore such small resemblance to the character in the Black Forest that Mme. Maurette might reasonably have expected a finding in her favor if sued for libel. Pity, rather, lay behind Marcelle Maurette's offer of money to her beleaguered heroine — pity, fairness, and a certain "profound respect."

The decision to accept Marcelle Maurette's generosity had not been reached easily.[31] Anastasia's attorneys knew that by taking money, however nobly proffered, they would only appear to confirm the decades-old accusation that her claim was nothing but a grand swindle. On the other hand, if her lawyers took some compensation for the unauthorized use of her life story — the only identity Anastasia had — they could also ensure themselves a voice in the proceedings and protect her, they hoped, from any further exploitation. Added to which, they had not received a penny for their services in the eighteen years since they had first taken up the fight.

Thus it was that Anastasia, not without remark, was induced to sign a document pledging noninterference in the development of her myth. She never saw *Anastasia* and she never wanted to, but she agreed that Twentieth-Century Fox might "produce, distribute everywhere, exhibit and transmit [*Anastasia*] by all means now or hereafter known. . . . To the extent that the character of Anastasia depicts me and/or points to me you may depict such character. . . . It is understood that changes must under no circumstances be defamatory to my personal dignity and reputation or to the dignity and reputation of any member of my family."[32]

From the "deal" with Marcelle Maurette, Guy Bolton, and Twentieth-Century Fox, Anastasia and her attorneys extracted approximately thirty thousand dollars[33] (the Fox film alone grossed over five million in its theatrical release). Of this sum her lawyers took what they needed to cover minimal costs, while the rest was invested for Anastasia, giving her an income of about twenty dollars a week after the new chalet had been constructed in Unterlengenhardt.[34]

"I was with her when she signed the papers," Marcelle Maurette remembered. " *'Anastasia Tschaikovsky, alias Anna Anderson.'* That is to say: Nobody."[35]

For Anastasia, the road to the Black Forest and lasting fame was as hard as any she had previously traveled. She had survived World War II, for one thing. She had survived a leap of nearly forty feet during a bombing raid on Hannover (and later had the pleasure to read of her own demise in the newspapers: "Now She Really Is Dead!").[36] She used so many aliases and turned up in so many places as to give the impression that there were dozens of "Anastasias" around Germany. She endured a year and a half of occupation under the Red Army; two years of famine after the war; repeated surgery; and a tubercular swelling "as large as a lemon" on her throat, which had nearly choked her to death in 1939.[37] Everyone alike marveled at her stamina — what one of her friends called "Mrs. Anderson's unlikely powers of regeneration."[38] Once in 1936, while furious with one noble hostess or another, she shut herself in her room, refused food for three days, and then vanished.[39] She was found more than one month later on the edge of the Teutoburg Forest, her feet bleeding, her dress in tatters. She had subsisted on wild berries and mushrooms, she said. And that was all she said.

Anastasia's adventures had recommenced the moment she left the Ilten Sanatorium in 1932. She had been leading a quiet, pleasant life at Ilten, sewing, painting, playing tennis, and acquainting herself with the more genteel families in the environs of Hannover. Then suddenly, as one of her doctors recalled, "she began to pursue the matter of proving her identity."[40] Adelene Moffat, the president of "The Committee for the Recognition of the Grand Duchess Anastasia," had dashed over to Ilten from New York as soon as she learned that Anastasia was there and, like Curtis J. Mar and Jill Cossley-Batt before her, had agreed to help Anastasia with her memoirs. For weeks Miss Moffat slaved over the project, until Anastasia, having said what she wanted to say about all the "horrible persons" in her life, sent Miss Moffat home without a thank-you or a good-bye.[41] Then one afternoon in October 1931, while she pondered what to do next, she was introduced to Prince Frederick

Ernest of Saxe-Altenburg, the man who was going to protect her, defend her, represent her, and bear stoically with her for the next fifty years.

Prince Frederick was the younger son of the last Duke of Saxe-Altenburg, who, like all the German sovereigns, had abdicated in 1918. Although he had never met the children of the Tsar, the Prince still enjoyed an especially tight connection with the members of the Russian imperial family. His mother was a cousin of the Dowager Empress. His father's sister, Elisabeth, had married Grand Duke Constantine of Russia and raised her eight children at Pavlovsk, a country seat only a few miles away from Tsarskoe Selo. Three of Prince Frederick's first cousins were murdered by the Bolsheviks in the Revolution, and, latterly, his sister Charlotte-Agnes had married Sigismund of Prussia, the son of Grand Duchess Anastasia's "Aunt Irene." It was on Sigismund's behalf, in fact, that Prince Frederick first arrived at Ilten to interview Anastasia. Sigismund had devised a list of eighteen "test questions" concerning his last meeting with the Tsar's daughter before World War I. "Together my brother-in-law and I had determined that this final meeting at the Russian court . . . had not been mentioned anywhere in the memoirs or literature of the period," Prince Frederick wrote.[42] "I — we — stress this point, because it is known how suspicious those people are who believe themselves capable of passing judgment."[43] But Anastasia wanted to conduct a test of her own.[44] How was she to know that the man who had introduced himself as a prince of Saxe-Altenburg really was who he said he was? How was she to know that he was not, say, a Polish factory worker?

Prince Frederick was impressed. After a few strained conversations in the company of her doctors, Anastasia finally received the Prince alone and told him that she could answer Prince Sigismund's questions if Prince Frederick would give her time to think. On that condition, she took up the list and read it. She put it down. She picked it up and read it again. Then she thought about it for five days. The answers she finally gave, Prince Frederick said, were "perfectly accurate," and by themselves were sufficient to convince Prince Sigismund of her identity.[45] No one but the Tsar's daughter, Sigismund insisted, would possibly have known how to answer correctly. But for many years he refused to tell which questions he had asked Anastasia and exactly what her responses to them had been.[46] Why? Because he knew that if he published the details of this special test someone might come forward and make his own claims on the hitherto private information. Someone could say that Sigismund had given the answers in advance to Prince Frederick (as he had); from there it was only one step to alleging that Anastasia had been clued in — in other words, that Prince Frederick was a cheat. Someone — and Sigismund had Pierre Gilliard in mind — could point out that he, too, had been a witness to the last meeting with the Tsar's daughter before the war and could easily, at no risk to himself, declare that Anastasia's answers were false. What matter if she or Sigismund protested? Who could prove the point? Realizing that Anastasia could not win either way, Sigismund and Prince Frederick deprived her opponents of their lone weapon — specifics. They, at least, had convinced themselves of her authenticity. "This one incident," said Prince Frederick, " — apart from my whole impression of her — sufficed for me to support the invalid's case from that day forward."[47]

Frederick of Saxe-Altenburg was a professional historian, an archaeologist of some repute, a genealogist, an amateur philologist, a would-be linguist — his energies and his interests knew no limit. He was a royal whirlwind, nicknamed "Fritz the Sudden" by his naughtier friends, one of those intense, compact gentlemen who are bound to be described as "wiry." Like Anastasia, the Prince was given to sudden entrances and disappearances, and when his friends were asked his whereabouts they used to joke that "he may be upstairs or he may be in Istanbul."[48] But from 1931 onward all of Prince Frederick's other concerns were effectively subordinated to Anastasia's interests. There were many who suspected that Anastasia, only four years his senior, secretly hoped to marry the Prince. If so, she still maintained the outward signs of propriety. "Stop speaking Prussian!" Anastasia would command with a mock scowl when Prince Frederick addressed her in his native German.[49] She liked to say that the Prince was "a *charmeur*" — unless he had displeased her somehow, in which case he was apt to be ridiculed as "the greatest donkey in Europe."[50] Prince Frederick, in turn, was permitted certain liberties forbidden Anastasia's lesser acquaintances. He could talk back to her, for one thing, and he learned how to break through her frightened opposition to whatever plans had been made for her in his never-ending quest for her recognition. If, for instance, Anastasia was told that she had to meet a doctor or a potentially important witness, she customarily raised a tremendous fuss and flatly refused. "Wind velocity up!" Prince Frederick would cry before sitting back to wait out the storm. In the end, having been wheedled, cajoled, and lightly threatened into submission, Anastasia usually capitulated. Prince Frederick knew he had won when he heard her shout at him through her perennially closed door, her *r*'s rolling madly, "Prince Frederick! You are a devil!"[51] This was his friend speaking again, whom once, in devoted exasperation, he had christened "Madame Mutabor."[52] The nickname was their special secret. It was the Latin for "I will be changed."

Prince Frederick had not been gone long after their first meeting before Anastasia decided that she wanted a change of scenery. She left the Ilten Sanatorium at the beginning of 1932 on the unsound advice of Friedrich Völler, an ambitious lawyer who had convinced her, yet again, that her agreements with her American attorney, Edward Fallows, were illegal, and who swore that he could have her recognized in the courts within six months. With Völler Anastasia went off to a spa in Bad Liebenstein and shortly thereafter moved in with the Heyden-Rynsch family in Eisenach. There she continued the pattern already set in the 1920s. After weeks of gracious cooperation and manifest gratitude she suddenly and for no apparent reason broke with her friends, calling Völler "a swine" and "a mess" and declaring that she would see him in jail.[53] The Heyden-Rynsch family preferred not to discuss the unpleasantness between themselves and their irascible guest. Instead they told Anastasia that if she did not apologize to Völler she would have to leave. So she left. She walked to a phone booth, connected with Berlin, and engaged Harriet von Rathlef on the line, telling Frau von Rathlef to fetch her at once.

In the six years since their quarrel at Lugano, Frau von Rathlef had never lost hope that Anastasia would one day come to her senses. Now she brought her in triumph to Berlin, advised Ambassador Zahle that "the little one" was back, and soon had Anastasia installed in a respectable pension.[54] From there Anastasia set out to rekindle her old friendships and to cultivate some new ones: with Simon Douvan, who had once been mayor of Eupatoria, in the Crimea, and who had last seen the Tsar's daughter in 1916; with Catherine Lavrova, a former music teacher in St. Petersburg, who remembered Grand Duchess Anastasia from the semiannual concerts she and her pupils used to give for Empress Alexandra and her daughters at Tsarskoe Selo; and with Lieutenant Ivan Arapov, who had known the Tsar's daughter as a patient in her hospital during World War I.[55] Arapov had already met Edward Fallows in 1929, while Fallows was in Paris attempting to pry information from the

Russian monarchists. "Ask your client if she remembers me," Arapov had said, and Fallows had sent off a wire to his colleagues in New York City: "If Grand Duchess Anastasia remembers Lieutenant Ivan Arapov 1915 will she cable detailed description giving place he will become valuable witness with data."

The response was quick: "Does Arapov limp one leg short?"

Fallows had seen nothing the matter with Arapov's legs and presumed that Anastasia was confused. "Arapov limp unnoticed," he wired back.

"Grand Duchess Anastasia cannot identity Arapov unless he limps," the next cable informed. Baffled, Fallows asked Arapov about it and discovered that Arapov had in fact been wounded in the leg during the war; the infirmity had since healed. After this news reached New York the identification was complete: "Grand Duchess Anastasia distinctly remembers Arapov patient her hospital Russia." When Arapov and Anastasia finally met in Berlin there was no doubt in either's mind about the other's authenticity.[56] They went to dinner together and then spent several hours reminiscing and looking at Arapov's photographs from Tsarskoe Selo.

"Is that supposed to be Grand Duchess Maria?" asked Anastasia, pointing to one blurred picture.

"Yes," said Arapov, "that is Maria."

Anastasia looked at him sharply: "Yes, that is Grand Duchess Maria." Invitations to dinner did not warrant lapses of etiquette.

Anastasia stayed on in Berlin for more than a year, holding court at her pension, appearing at parties, concerts, and art galleries in her "flowing white tea gown,"[57] sometimes calling herself "Frau Lange,"[58] sometimes "Miss Brown,"[59] and sometimes "Mrs. Anderson," but never again, in view of its notoriety, "Frau Tschaikovsky." It was a good time for her, a relaxed and happy time. Not only were her new acquaintances in the city anxious to help her out, but — thanks to the indomitable spirit of Harriet von Rathlef — many of her first sponsors shed their creeping fears and once again rallied to her side. Anastasia was genuinely saddened and deeply suspicious when Frau von Rathlef suddenly died of a burst appendix in 1933, at the age of forty-four. Meanwhile Professor Serge Rudnev, Anastasia's one-time surgeon at the Mommsen Clinic, again stepped in to attend to her precarious health. Anastasia's trust in Rudnev was so great that she periodically triumphed over that greatest of all her fears: speaking Russian. Often Rudnev gave her Russian books to read — Anastasia's only condition was that they be "something interesting" — and remarked that her spoken Russian reminded him in its grammar, emphasis, and tone of that of Empress Alexandra's sister, Grand Duchess Elisabeth, whom Rudnev had known in Moscow.[60] Serge Botkin, whose benign work in her behalf might be said to have prevented Anastasia's ruin in the 1920s, also proved a worthy friend. He remained chief of the Russian Refugee Office in Berlin until the Nazis, unable to tolerate his fair-mindedness, drove him into exile. Botkin died in Paris in 1945.

Of all Anastasia's friends it was Herluf Zahle, her "Tall Man," who earlier had endured the most embarrassment on her account. Now the bad trouble of the twenties was forgotten, and the Zahles proved as kind as they had ever been before the scandal of Anastasia's claim forced them into silence. Often they let Anastasia stay with them at the Danish embassy when she found herself between hotels.[61] Whatever threat she may still have posed to his reputation as a diplomat now seemed to Zahle less compelling than her need for protection. Zahle, of course, could not know that the evidence he had collected for Anastasia would, in 1947, be confiscated by the Danish royal family, but he had seen already how her return to Europe had opened the gates to fresh attacks on her dignity. Almost immediately after her departure from Ilten in 1932, in fact, an article had appeared in London's popular scandal sheet, the *News of the World,* under the dramatic and by now tiresome headline "Impostor Unmasked! 'Princess' Confesses She Is a Fraud!"[62] According to the latest information, Anastasia had admitted to "attorneys for the Romanovs" that she was a Rumanian actress who had been hypnotized into playing the role of the Tsar's daughter by an unnamed "former manservant in the Romanov household." Luckily for her, she was now fully repentant and ready to take her punishment: "On the understanding that she signs a complete admission of the imposture and enters a convent within six weeks[!], the Romanov family will not take criminal proceedings against her."

This imaginative story was reprinted in newspapers and magazines all over Europe. But Anastasia was not nearly so friendless as her adversaries must have hoped: the publishers of the *News of the World* found themselves with a libel suit on their hands.[63] The case dragged on for years and finally lapsed during World War II, but not before the *News of the World* had identified the source of the latest "unmasking" operation. "The article in question was sent by our correspondent in Paris," a bewildered editor protested, "who informs us that the information was supplied to him by the Paris

lawyer of the Romanov family." [64] Suspicion fell immediately on
Grand Duke Kyril, the ever-hopeful pretender to the Russian throne.
It was no secret that Kyril had recently ordered his brother, Grand
Duke Andrew, to cease all activity in Anastasia's interest.[65] Soon,
in May of 1933, Anastasia was summoned to a meeting with a
number of international attorneys at the Hotel Bristol on Unter den
Linden.[66] She arrived in the protective company of Anna Samweber,
a German friend who had met the Tsar's daughter once in the Crimea and who had acknowledged Anastasia without reservation now.
"The meeting had been prearranged," Frau Samweber recalled. "One
of the attorneys read aloud from a photocopy of a letter in English
from Grand Duke Kyril to Prince [Felix] Yussoupov." The essential
passage in Kyril's letter, of course, touched on Anastasia: it was
openly suggested that she might be persuaded to renounce her claim
to identity in return for a substantial settlement and a periodic al-
lowance.

No sooner had Grand Duke Kyril's proposal been voiced than
Anastasia rose to her feet and declared, in words that sounded less
like a daughter of Nicholas II than one of her great ancestresses, "If
I had a horsewhip, I would strike him in the face with it!"

With that, the meeting at the Hotel Bristol came to an abrupt
end.

Her unpleasant business in Berlin concluded, Anastasia wanted
to move on. Never again would she willingly lay herself open to the
double-edged mercy of the Romanovs. "They are dead to me," [67]
she declared and then embarked in earnest on that scattered trip
through Old Germany that so distinguishes this part of her life.
She had no want of people to turn to. Each new friend felt bound
by honor to introduce her to another, until Anastasia, transporting
an ever-growing collection of photographs and imperial Russian
knickknacks, was "at home" in every province of the Reich. From
Berlin she went back to Hannover; from Hannover to Starnberg, in
Bavaria; thence to Pomerania; back down into Westphalia, Hesse,
and the Palatinate; over to Saxony and Thuringia, stopping, among
other fine places, at Weimar, Herleshausen, Meissen, Detmold,
Gotha, and Reutlingen. She lived in small cottages and on grand
estates, in borrowed apartments (seven in Hannover alone), at spas,
hotels, rest homes, and, not infrequently, in castles. When she arrived at these places she might stay for two days, or for six
months — no one ever knew ahead of time. She simply "popped
up" when she felt like it, sometimes telephoning ahead and some-

times not, but always confident that her rooms would be waiting.

If Anastasia's itinerary sounds like a frantic tourist's guide to Germany, the roster of her benefactors reads like a page from that *Who's Who* of royalty, the *Almanach de Gotha,* for in these vagabond years she found protection and support in the highest ranks of the German aristocracy. One of her regular hosts was Prince William of Hesse-Philippsthal, a cousin and nephew by marriage of her archenemy, the Grand Duke of Hesse. Another was Feodora, Princess Reuss, whose own grandmother, the German Empress Frederick, had been the eldest daughter of Queen Victoria. "She is my very good friend," said Anastasia of Feodora proudly.[68] "She had promised the German Kaiser that if she could see me she would know if I belonged to the family or not. Instantly when she saw me, she knew it, that I did." In 1932, from his exile in Holland, the Kaiser himself had sent his young wife, the Empress Hermine, to the Ilten Sanatorium for a meeting with Anastasia. Thereafter Anastasia enjoyed with the Kaiser's family a tacit understanding that culminated after the war in an intimate friendship with the German Crown Princess — her "loving Aunt Cecile."[69] And the hereditary Grand Duke of Saxe-Weimar-Eisenach, the bearer of one of the oldest titles in Europe, invited Anastasia to stand as godmother to his son, Prince Michael Benedict.[70] Anastasia was happy to oblige, and when Michael Benedict had grown up, his "Aunt Andy" thought that he would make a fine Tsar — "because he is good-looking and he has brains. You need not be good-looking to be Tsar, but you must have brains."[71]

Thus it went on for many years: those who got to know Anastasia spoke in her favor, and those who did not did not. One of her most faithful protectors at this time was Baroness Monica von Miltitz,[72] whom she had met through Prince Frederick and who often invited her to stay at Sieben Eichen, the Miltitz castle near Meissen. "I only did so," the Baroness remembered, "on the condition that I would not be drawn into the fight over her identity." It was a vain hope. To be sure, the Baroness's first impressions of Anastasia were "purely negative: she looked poor and shabby . . . and seemed constrained." But on first meeting the Baroness had considered only the physical creature, whose weird appearance startled even those with the best intentions. Bundled up in her fur coats, smothered with scarves, the lower part of her face covered with a handkerchief and the upper part shaded by a hat, Anastasia looked all too like the Madwoman of Chaillot. Then all at once, with a particular choice of phrase, a word to the servants, a sudden laugh, and "a flashing of the eyes," [73] her freakish exterior fell away to reveal a lovely woman still at home with the highest of the Baroness's guests. Time and again the people who knew Anastasia used the words *miracle* and even *transfiguration* to describe these moments, but Baroness von Miltitz, no romantic, avowed only that her attitude and demeanor were "decidedly aristocratic." That was all the Baroness needed or wanted to know, and after the war she — "the Good Fairy of Schloss Sieben Eichen" [74] — took refuge with Anastasia at Unterlengenhardt.

During all this time, as she flitted from one haven to another, Anastasia retained the city of Hannover as her base of operations. She loved Hannover, partly on account of the good friends she had made at the nearby Ilten Sanatorium. Chief among them were Paul Madsack, the owner and operator of the *Hannoverscher Anzeiger,* the largest German daily outside Berlin, and his wife, Gertrude, "full of fun and firm as a rock," [75] who together had published the first articles about Anastasia after her return to Germany in 1931. "Mrs. Madsack is a diplomat of the very highest order," wrote Edward Fallows, "and yet [she] *insists* on obedience from A. . . . *and she gets it.* To me this is most remarkable." [76] Throughout the thirties the Madsacks continued to care for Anastasia as for their own daughter, patiently supporting her childish temper, her illnesses, her depressions, and a variety of other miseries that came their way in connection with her claim to identity. If she had no castle or health spa to turn to, the Madsacks always found Anastasia a place to stay in town until, finally, they rented a small apartment for her on the Johannes-Trojanstrasse.

Now Anastasia was supposed to live alone, but the experiment failed, because she simply did not know how to take care of herself. She almost starved during the war, for instance, when her lifelong fear of "the brass buttons" prevented her from applying for a ration card.[77] Such, at least, was the explanation offered by Baroness von Miltitz, who regularly received thinly disguised cries for help. Once the Baroness had seen Anastasia standing alone outside the gates of Sieben Eichen. Anastasia had not been invited to stay, nor, as it turned out, did she want to. Dressed in white, a wide-brimmed hat hanging from her hand, she stared hard at the walls of the Miltitz castle, seemed at length to reach a decision, and then walked briskly away. Instantly the Baroness set off in pursuit, but Anastasia had reached the train depot in record time and gone home. "Two days later," the Baroness recalled, "I had a card from her in Hannover in which she told me that she was ill. I went to Hannover at once and found her positively famished. For eight days she had been living only on what little food there already was in the house." [78]

Gradually Anastasia's way of life began to extract its toll. In 1935, her nerves in a sorry state and her brain, as she put it, "burned out," she suffered another breakdown and then fell ill with some infection that was never properly diagnosed. In London, where he was preparing the libel case against the *News of the World*, Edward Fallows heard that "the end was near" and rushed across to Hannover with wills and codicils and plans to take a deathmask. [79] Anastasia, however, rebounded as always, and Fallows did not hear another word out of her for nearly two years, when the rumor spread over Europe that she had "died of shock" upon receiving an anonymous note: "We are finished with your case!" [80] Anastasia's reassuring letter to her attorney was a model of optimism. "The Black Angel does not get the permission to fetch me," she wrote Fallows; "he several times touched me with his wings, but of course he was not allowed to take me. I have such a good health now, as I have never had since I am away from home, and I hope it will be still better." [81] Indeed, when Fallows arrived in Hannover again at the beginning of 1938 he found his client fairly bubbling over with good spirits. "Oh, Mr. Fallows," she said as she walked into the room, as though they had only seen each other the weekend before, "how well you are looking."

"I returned the compliment quite sincerely," said Fallows, "for I have never seen her looking so well; a real transformation. Sparkling eyes, face glowing with health and natural color; very poised, bright and gay." Fallows had brought Anastasia a package of Yardley soap to break the ice: "She could not have made more of the little present if it had been a casket of priceless jewels. . . . It is hard for me to adequately express the unbelievable change in her appearance, [her] interest in everything, her outgoing responsiveness to each one, her wit, her rippling conversation, her laughter, when stars literally shone in her beautiful eyes." And as they stood together talking and watching the fish in Paul Madsack's aquarium Anastasia suddenly moved her attorney to tears when she wheeled around and exclaimed, "I do so love life! The birds and flowers and good things to eat, and jokes. I do get sad at times, but then I remember that God is good and that he will not give me more to bear than I can bear. He is going to let me live as long as I ought to."

She paused and then said, "I am going to help you in our case just as much as I can."

For the rest of his visit to Hannover, Fallows watched in amazement as Anastasia, "free from all inhibition," joined in parlor games with the Madsack family, chitchatted about her life in Russia, teased her hostess about the food, and giggled with delight as she rode the roller coaster at a nearby amusement park. "You have risen very high with me, young man, since last night," she said to Fallows, tapping him on the shoulder most flirtatiously and then breaking into peals of laughter. She was not even offended when Gertrude Madsack, ready to take her out for a drive, slammed on the brakes and said, "Go back to your apartment and get your teeth, or you shall not go with me." This was one of Frau Madsack's eternal complaints, for Anastasia could never find a denture that fit her properly and preferred to cover her mouth with a paper towel. Finally Frau Madsack tried to humiliate her into compliance by calling her "Miss Paper" in front of her friends.

"Miss Paper?" But Anastasia had never heard anything so funny! Now, she declared, everyone was going to call her "Miss Paper" or pay a fine of ten pfennigs. After she had collected a mark or two, Anastasia announced the formation of "the Paper Court Committee," saying that she would be its president, Fallows its treasurer, and Gleb Botkin, in absentia, its "Minister of Propaganda." The very thought sent her into new squeals of laughter. How Gleb would love it! she said, her committee and its stated goal: "The object of this Organisation is to raise funds for a journey to Utopia, where each day is happier than the one before it." She was still laughing when she saw Fallows off on the train to Berlin.[82]

It was Edward Fallows's belief that Anastasia's good humor might have prevailed throughout 1938 and beyond had it not been for the untimely interference of the Nazi government. "It seems that the Hannover police are instructed by some higher source to push this . . . 'famous Criminal Case' through *now*," Fallows wrote, "to decide whether Anastasia is genuine or an impostor; if the latter, she will be punished."[83] No one ever found out who had rekindled the authorities' interest in Anastasia's legal status, but it was understood in Hannover that Hitler himself had ordered the case to be settled. The threat coincided with the death of Grand Duke Kyril and the assumption of Kyril's claim to the throne by his son, Vladimir. In Berlin Vladimir's mentor, the fascist general Vassili Biskupsky, had taken over the leadership of the Russian Refugee Office and made it his task to collect on certain favors the anti-Semitic, right-wing monarchists of the Russian emigration had rendered to Hitler during his struggling days. Anastasia, when she heard about the Nazis' interest in her case, froze in terror, shutting herself in her apartment, refusing to see Fallows, refusing to see the Madsacks, and refusing, maddeningly, to speak Russian anymore, a language she had recently been using again fluently with Professor Rudnev and with Albert Coyle, an American colleague of Fallows's.[84] Fearing another breakdown, Fallows had an idea that he hoped might keep Anastasia in balance. She had said to him not long before, when he had given Gertrude Madsack a card for her birthday, "Mr. Fallows, I have known you now for ten years and you have never given *me* a birthday card." Then she took a slip of paper and wrote her name and date of birth on it in Russian, handing it over to Fallows with the words, "Please do not forget my next birthday."[85] Now, as Grand Duchess Anastasia's thirty-seventh birthday approached in June, Fallows organized a party at the Hotel Kastens in Hannover, writing as many of Anastasia's friends as he could locate and asking that they send their good wishes for the occasion.

The greetings poured in from all over the world — from friends, from doctors and nurses, from lawyers and secretaries she had never met, from everyone, in fact, who understood through Fallows that the moment was critical. Still Anastasia would not answer the knocks at her door, seeing no one but "Garba," the Madsacks' chauffeur, when he came to take her out for the long drives she liked so much. Finally Fallows decided that games were in order. He sent "Mrs. Anderson" a letter asking her, tongue-in-cheek, if she would use her influence to make sure Anastasia turned up at the birthday party. Then he sent Gertrude Madsack out to buy her a gift.

When the guests assembled on June 18 there had still been no word from Anastasia. Fallows was already wondering what to do with the cake when suddenly, nodding and smiling to everyone around her, Anastasia swept in wearing an elegant, magical-looking floor-length cape.

"Mr. Fallows," she said, sotto voce, "Mrs. Anderson had a very hard time of it persuading Anastasia to come to the party, but this lovely gift won her over."[86]

All this while Fallows had been looking for some way to avoid or postpone the latest decree from Nazi Berlin: Anastasia was supposed to be confronted again with the family of the missing Polish factory worker, Franziska Schanzkowska. It was supposed to be the final proof. The Schanzkowskis, not surprisingly, snatched from their fields and their coal mines by the Nazi police, were ready to do anything they were told, but Anastasia declined to commit herself, declaring that she would do nothing at all until Gleb Botkin came from America to advise her. She meant it, too: "Nothing without Botkin."[87] In New York Gleb got ready to sail — he had not seen Anastasia since 1929 — but only on one condition: Anastasia would have to agree to the Schanzkowski confrontation in advance. It was high time she met her friends halfway, said Gleb.

Anastasia was in no mood for negotiation. It was "Botkin or nothing." Gleb finally arrived in Hannover at the beginning of July without any assurance that Anastasia would cooperate. She seems to have realized that the Nazis meant business, however, and on July 9, sporting a smart wool suit bought for the occasion, she went down with Fallows, Gleb, and Frau Madsack to police headquarters. There, in a room normally reserved for convicts and their families, she saw the Schanzkowskis — the brothers Valerian and Felix, and the sisters Gertrude and Maria Juliana.[88] Gleb was surprised to see that Gertrude, the elder sister, did bear a physical resemblance to Anastasia: "It was, however, the kind of resemblance which a horse or a bird can have to a human being." Meantime Anastasia walked up and down along the wall while the Schanzkowskis chatted among themselves in their Low German, shaking their heads and looking "exceedingly doubtful." Finally Valerian Schanzkowski spoke: "No, this lady looks too different."

And did all the brothers and sisters agree?

They did. Not only did Anastasia not look a thing like Franziska, said Felix Schanzkowski, but she didn't even look like the same woman he had met near Seeon eleven years before. Could they go home now?

Anastasia made ready to leave. Then suddenly Gertrude Schanzkowska started shouting, banging her fists on the table and turning red in the face. "You are my sister!" she cried, grabbing Anastasia by the shoulders and shaking her. "You are my sister! I know it! You must recognize me!"

The police were looking at Anastasia now as though they had caught her picking pockets: "Well, what have you got to say?"

"What am I supposed to say?" said Anastasia.

"How many brothers and sisters did you have?"

"Four."

"But here we are," said Valerian Schanzkowski, "— four!"

"This is crazy," said Anastasia.

"Where were you born?"

"In Russia."

The answer took everyone by surprise. "In Russia?" Valerian asked, shaking his head. "In *Russia?*" Now Valerian, Felix, and Maria Juliana turned back to Gertrude. This was crazy indeed: you could tell at a glance that the lady was not Franziska. But the more her family protested the louder Gertrude got — "Admit it! Admit it!" — until Anastasia, pale with fury, walked from the room.

No one, including Gertrude Schanzkowska, agreed to sign anything that day.

Anastasia went straight from the police station to her apartment. She locked the door, locked the windows, pulled the blinds, and disconnected the telephone. "I will call the police!" she cried when Gleb came by to see her.

"I thought she was about to burst out laughing," said Gleb, "but she suppressed it."[89] For weeks, then, not a word emerged from Anastasia. Gleb went home. When the Madsacks' daughter Irmel finally saw Anastasia standing in the central square in Hannover one day, she tried to start a conversation, but Anastasia turned on her heel and fled. Then eventually she began sending vicious notes to Irmel's parents, whom she held responsible for her recent humiliation — as Fallows said, "the most horrid, untruthful and libelous letters" Anastasia had ever sent to anybody, "including Miss Jennings." Paul Madsack declared that he would never have Anastasia in the house again. Gertrude Madsack wept. And Edward Fallows, ten years wiser and many thousands of dollars short, informed his client by mail that if she did not send a *written* apology to the Madsacks he might sue her himself for libel: "YOU HAVE NOW BEEN WARNED!"[90]

There was no apology. There was nothing but silence. From New York Fallows's daughter, Annette, had already endeavored to give her father a piece of advice. "People don't understand that inner pride that is being humiliated all the time," Annette wrote. ". . . We may not like it, but it is there. And what I would so strongly urge [is] a most prayerful consideration of her fears, and her point of view, until a sincere sympathy takes the place of a desire to put through any specific course of action. . . . Any move or plan that seems to us important at the moment, even terribly important, drops to complete insignificance if it costs her confidence." [91] Now Fallows began to fear that he had been too harsh. What if Anastasia wasn't eating? he wondered. What if she had committed suicide? "Could you ever forgive yourself," he wrote Frau Madsack, "or would your friends or the world ever understand, if you now abandon her and leave her in a flat you have rented for her, mentally and physically sick and perhaps dying? Each day without food or care she surely is growing weaker, and the danger of death is becoming more imminent and horrible to contemplate." [92]

Actually, Anastasia had slipped away from her apartment several days before and joined a bus tour of the castles along the Rhine. She had a wonderful time.

At the outbreak of the world war Anastasia endeavored to settle down. Travel had become dangerous, first of all, and then, as she soon discovered, the Nazis did not look kindly on absentee tenants: in 1943 Anastasia was obliged to return overnight from a trip to Sieben Eichen, having been informed that she would lose her apartment in Hannover if she did not commence to live in it. And when the Allied bombs began to fall on Hannover she took it philosophically, facing the long nights in the bunkers with a stout heart and true serenity. "At the moment when there is danger," she said, "I do not get frightened. It makes me nervous but not afraid. If I should be afraid in danger I should now be dead." [93]

With Hannover reduced to rubble, Anastasia fled eastward to Schloss Winterstein, the castle of Louisa of Saxe-Meiningen. There she stayed put, more or less, until the autumn of 1946, when it became obvious that the Soviet occupation of the region was not likely to be temporary. Fears for Anastasia's safety were more than justified as the Red Army repatriated hundreds of thousands of Russian nationals to the Soviet Union; what they might do with a woman who claimed to be the Tsar's daughter was anyone's guess. Her hostess had already experienced some difficulty concealing Anastasia's identity from the Russian troops who periodically raided the castle — "and that my head is still on my shoulders," said Anastasia later, "I have only to thank the chief-leader of the SS in Eisenach — you know, the Wartburg." [94] She never explained what she meant. But for years thereafter she told hair-raising stories of her close brushes with death and worse — rape. (The latter atrocity she had every reason to fear, for few women escaped it as the Red

Army marched on Berlin.) "Frau! Come here!" a young Bolshevik had commanded Anastasia one day in the kitchen at Winterstein, where she was pretending, not very successfully, to be the maid. But Anastasia had grabbed a bread knife and would willingly have slit the fellow's throat before giving in.[95] Finally Prince Frederick, having walked five hundred kilometers out of Altenburg to safety, approached a friend in the Swedish Red Cross about bringing Anastasia across the sealed border of what was soon to become East Germany. The Red Cross refused to explain how it had been done, but on the night of December 18, 1946, Anastasia, with no papers or official travel documents, crossed the Weser River and next turned up at Aalen, where the Allies issued her pass number 018 774:

NAME: Anderson, Anna
NATIONALITY: Not cleared up
PROFESSION: No profession
REASON FOR TRAVELING: To return home

She had lied wholeheartedly in order to get the pass,[96] and she went straightaway to join Prince Frederick at Bad Liebenzell, in what was then the French Occupational Zone. Seven kilometers up the hill lay the hamlet of Unterlengenhardt. It was never Anastasia's intention to remain in the Black Forest, but it wasn't long before she had taken sick again with a breast infection, and, while she struggled with the thought that it might be cancer, she wrote Gleb Botkin from a clinic in Liebenzell:

At Hannover I am not, for Hannover does not exist anymore, and the beautiful house of Dr. Madsack does not exist anymore, and so many a dear friend is killed.

I am now in the Black Forest in a Sanatory, and am facing just now an operation. It is very difficult everything here, no place, no home, Prince Frederick and all friends have lost everything, we are all without a home.

Life here is altogether very very difficult, very cold, nothing to heat [with], no food, no clothing. Prince Frederick has only what he has on his body. I as well have nothing whatever. And it would be very kind of you if you could manage that we could get out of this frightful mess.[97]

In America, with no money to speak of, Gleb Botkin could see no way to rescue the royal refugees in the Black Forest "out of this frightful mess." Over the years, he had abandoned his writing career and turned full-time to religion and spirituality, his first true love and the object of his childhood aspiration. Gleb's was a curious faith, to be sure: at his home in Cassville, New Jersey, he now led a small sect in worship of the goddess Aphrodite. It was Gleb's opinion that patriarchal society had contributed nothing to the happiness and well-being of humankind — "Men!" he exclaimed. "Just look at the mess they've made" — and the Church of Aphrodite was not nearly so wanton as it sounds. It drew its precepts from the most ancient pagan rituals and owed a lot to the "Old Believers" in Russia. Anastasia never joined the Church of Aphrodite, nor did she care to discuss Aphrodite's powers with anyone, but she saw no real contradiction between one religion and another, and in future she accepted it without protest when Gleb closed each of his letters with a prayer: "May the Goddess bestow Her tender caress on Your Imperial Highness's head."

In 1949, as the Federal Republic of Germany struggled to its feet, Prince Frederick spent the last of his ready cash on the lopsided army barracks that became Anastasia's first permanent home. She moved in officially sometime later amid great celebration and much picture-taking. The children of the village, each with an enormous bouquet, had lined the road that led away from the inn and solemnly, bowing, handed her the flowers as she walked toward the house. There she remained as *"Hohe Frau"* [98] — "Great Lady" — until the world press rediscovered her in the early fifties — "a fuzzy-minded, aging woman," as *Time* magazine reported, "surrounded by a court of solicitous refugees." [99] In fact, this was one of the happiest and most peaceful times of Anastasia's life. When Lili Dehn,[100] the dear friend of Empress Alexandra who had been caught with the Empress and her daughters at Tsarskoe Selo during the Revolution, came to the Black Forest from Caracas for a six-day visit, Anastasia was touched beyond words. Lili had not thought to bother with Anastasia until Prince Frederick, on one of his South American archaeological expeditions, tracked her down and pleaded Anastasia's case.

"Do you know me?" Lili asked Anastasia gingerly.

"First I recognized the voice," said Anastasia, "and then you remind me of my mother."

"I never thought there was a likeness."

"In your ways."

"I had a shock," Lili confessed, "a real shock when first I saw her — a poor, pale and wrinkled little face!" She and Anastasia began to talk about Tsarskoe Selo, about rugs and curtains and the colors of the Empress's dresses. Then Anastasia asked if Lili remembered the night in March 1917 when Mamma and Maria had thrown on their cloaks and gone outdoors to plead for the loyalty of the troops.

"We were together," said Anastasia.

"Yes," said Lili.

And did Lili remember how they had played cards while they waited for Papa to come back? Did she remember Kerensky? Did she remember when Grand Duchess Anastasia had broken the vase in the drawing room, saying, "Don't worry about it. It isn't ours. It belongs to the government"?

"Do not bother to tell me that she had read these things in books," said Lili Dehn.[101] "I have recognized her, physically and intuitively, through signs which do not deceive. . . . As I was going away and turned round once more to look at her, she said, 'Good-bye, Good-bye,' and the way she said it went straight to my heart, for it was exactly the way my Empress used to do it. . . .[102]

"What can I say after having known her? I certainly cannot be mistaken about her identity."

13

THE TRIALS — FIRST INSTANCE

(1958–1961)

*A*nastasia's suit for legal recognition as the daughter of the Tsar of Russia was the longest-running court case of this century in Germany.[1] It may be said to have begun in 1933, when the Central District Court in Berlin, at the instance of the Countess Brassova, the widow of the Tsar's brother Michael, ruled for the first time that all of Nicholas II's children were dead and that his collateral heirs — Countess Brassova; the Grand Duchesses Xenia and Olga; the Grand Duke of Hesse; and the Empress's sisters Victoria and Irene — were thus entitled to anything that remained of his property in Germany.[2] Anastasia's attorneys had taken no formal action against this ruling until 1938, when the Berlin court issued a certificate of inheritance and the Tsar's deposits at the Mendelssohn Bank were actually paid out to the next of kin. Through revolution and inflation the money at Mendelssohn's had been reduced to a mere one hundred and fifty-seven thousand marks,[3] but money was never the real issue in the suits that followed. The bank itself had written Anastasia to tell her that the money was gone, addressing her politely as "Imperial Highness" and advising her to protect herself by demanding the withdrawal of the certificate of inheritance.[4] Thus commenced one of the strangest and most complicated proceedings in the history of law — an ordinary civil action studded with great names and royal titles, a gargantuan process of accusation and recrimination, which the German press, before it ended, had christened "Anastasia's Monster Trial." [5]

When Anastasia's "Petition for the Revocation of the Certificate of Inheritance" was first lodged in Berlin, on August 17, 1938, ten years had already been spent in search of the "right" means to prove her identity in court. "I could not do much for her in the early months," Edward Fallows recalled, "as she refused to have her claim submitted to the courts on the grounds that her father made the courts and she was superior to them." Only when she heard about a suit Grand Duchess Xenia had brought to recover some of the Tsar's lands in Finland did Anastasia agree to go ahead with the case, naively assuming, according to Fallows, "that all she had to do . . . was retain a lawyer and make a claim through him." [6]

She had summoned Fallows to the Ilten Sanatorium at the beginning of 1932, still shaking with indignation over the villainy of the Jennings family but ready to renew Fallows's power of attorney on the condition that he obey her wishes to the letter.[7] It had long been Fallows's intention to introduce some kind of claim in Berlin, where the money lay waiting at Mendelssohn's, but in order to do that he was obliged to retain associate counsel: Fallows was not licensed to practice law in Germany. The intervention of "the German group of attorneys"[8] appears to have been the spark that ignited Anastasia's next attack of wrath, for within a month she had "dismissed" Fallows and gone off with Friedrich Völler to Eisenach. After her quarrel with Völler she had retained another advocate in Berlin, and then another and another, until, as one of Fallows's partners said, there was "a whole club of people holding power of attorney."[9] It was not until 1935, at Munich, that Anastasia gave it back to Fallows permanently.

All this time Fallows had been exploring the various avenues open to him to introduce his client's suit. He had hoped to arrange matters in such a way that the burden of proof would fall on Anastasia's opponents — that "the opposition," in other words, would be required to prove that she was *not* the Tsar's daughter — and for a while Fallows considered employing the "Grandanor" corporation for that purpose. If "Grandanor" were to sue the Bank of England, for instance, for the release of the Tsar's fortune, the bank might then have to prove that "Grandanor" had no right to it. That way the identity could be established by default. A suit by the corporation, moreover, might free Anastasia from the burden of a personal appearance in court, and that was a constant worry for Fallows.

When suit for libel was eventually brought against the *News of the World* in London, in fact, over the "Rumanian actress" scandal of 1932, the only obstacle Fallows could see to its success was Anastasia herself, who was capable of contradicting anything her attorney said and who might, in all her strangeness, make the wrong impression on a judge not completely familiar with her background.

It had taken Edward Fallows more than six years to introduce the libel suit in London, the case having been postponed over and over again on account of the plaintiff's "precarious health." Altogether Fallows's work for Anastasia had been a tedious, painstaking, and nightmarish affair. It ruined his health and had cost him more than forty thousand dollars before he died in 1940. It is true that Fallows expected to be repaid when the Bank of England finally opened its coffers, but in the meantime his American colleagues looked on in horror as Fallows, at sixty-five, sold his insurance policies, his stocks, his bonds, his country house, and his New York apartment, sending his wife and daughter to live in rented rooms while he followed the quest in Europe. There is no doubt that Fallows was something of a mystic — he was a lay preacher and the proud son of a bishop of the Reformed Episcopal Church — who saw his work for Anastasia as a sacred trust. Nevertheless, Fallows entertained few illusions about his client. "I would like to give her a good spanking," he wrote after Anastasia had broken some agreement with him.[10] In 1932 he actually declared that he was ready to give up the case "honorably" and move on to something else, until the prospect of suing the *News of the World* flamed his passion once again.[11] Then for eight more years there were complaints in his letters home. "I am nearly broken in spirit as I am entirely in purse," Fallows wrote in 1933. ". . . It begins to look as if I had been a big fool to persist so long in an unappreciated effort to win the girl a name and fortune."[12] And then two years later: "Anyway, I return with the knowledge that I have done everything that any lawyer could do for 'A' — that is a little satisfaction, though it does not pay taxes, interest, rent and living expenses."[13]

"I hope you will get him home now and put a stop to this Anastasia business," a friend wrote Fallows's impoverished wife, Julia, at the outbreak of the war in Europe in 1939, "— certainly under present circumstances it's useless going on."[14] Before his decline, however, Fallows managed to perform one final and lasting service for his client. Through Count Albrecht Bernstorff, a former attaché at the Imperial German Legation in London, and Dr. Kurt Riezler, who had been acting German ambassador in Moscow in July 1918 —that is to say, at the very moment of the Russian imperial family's disappearance — Fallows met Paul Leverkuehn, one of the most successful and well-connected young lawyers in Berlin. It hadn't taken Leverkuehn long after reading the dossier and conferring with Dr. Riezler to convince himself that Anastasia's claims were just, and he had agreed to take on her case with his partner in Hamburg, Kurt Vermehren. Secure in the knowledge that his client was well represented, Fallows returned third-class to New York, where he died six weeks later. Bearing in mind "the temperament of the principal person," Fallows's daughter remarked with understandable regret, "I don't wonder that it killed him." [15]

Paul Leverkuehn and Kurt Vermehren were going to represent Anastasia now for the next quarter-century, sometimes with her cooperation and sometimes not, through all of the Berlin proceedings and beyond to the first trial at Hamburg. Equally talented, equally sophisticated, they were very different in style: Leverkuehn was quiet, sometimes aloof and somber; while Vermehren had an easygoing manner about him, an outward flair, and a taste for drama. Together they formed a brilliant team, arguing Anastasia's case with precision, imagination, and nothing less than respect. Discharged as frequently as any of their predecessors, Leverkuehn and Vermehren worked for twenty-four years without retainer and were always willing to wait while Anastasia threw her tantrums, slammed her doors, tore up contracts, and blamed everyone around her for "this mess." In that one respect, perhaps, her lawyers did not take her quite seriously.

Neither Leverkuehn nor Vermehren was overly surprised when, in September 1941, Anastasia's petition to have the certificate of inheritance revoked was first denied as "unwarranted" by the Central District Court in Berlin.[16] Before lodging appeal, Leverkuehn had begun to explore the possibility of a "compromise" with her royal opponents, an idea he felt would best serve the interests of everyone involved and which he continued to pursue on and off into the 1950s. His friend from the German embassy in Moscow, Dr. Riezler, had already suggested that "an umpire or referee" might be found to resolve the case for the family — the Kaiser, say, or the King of Denmark.[17] Leverkuehn, too, had his eye on Denmark, where Herluf Zahle, now retired, sat "with his hands tied," still hoping that he would receive permission from his government to testify for Anastasia.[18] "The Danish King has more than once expressed that the Danish royal family is entirely neutral," said Leverkuehn, "and only wants the truth to be found out. If the Zahle papers are not produced and the Danish court is used as an excuse, this would be entirely contrary to the intention of seeing the case cleared up and the truth found out." [19] But such was the event, and such the excuse. Meantime Leverkuehn and Vermehren forged ahead.

During the first appeal, in 1942, Anastasia's case was suspended for the duration of hostilities. Leverkuehn was dispatched to Turkey, where he served with Admiral Canaris as chief of intelligence; while Vermehren, following the surprise defection of his son to England, had the bad luck to be interned for more than a year in a room with his ex-wife at the concentration camp at Oranienbaum.[20] Then during the bombing of Berlin Leverkuehn's law offices were destroyed. All that remained of the "Anastasia" dossier in Germany was contained in the files of the Central District Court, a building which had escaped serious damage but which, by a miserable mischance, now lay in the Soviet sector of the city. The files were eventually reconstructed from court transcripts, but not before many of the original exhibits had disappeared — specifically, a great deal of the evidence in Anastasia's favor. The only hope seemed to be Annette Fallows, who, since her father's death, had taken possession of Fallows's papers.

Miss Fallows appears to have become more than a little resentful by this time about the whole "Anastasia" matter. It was not alone the strain her father had endured on Anastasia's account that irked Annette: Fallows had never been paid for his work either. As the new director of the "Grandanor" corporation, therefore, and in the belief that right was right, Annette intended to hold Anastasia to "Grandanor's" terms. Only after several years did she realize that all of the corporation's stock was supposed to have gone to Anastasia years before, and since no stock had ever been issued, Anastasia was in fact bound to nothing.[21] Still Annette held on to her father's papers as her only security, while Kurt Vermehren repeatedly begged her for their release — "because the pieces we got from your father and handed over to the Court, and all copies of those pieces, have been destroyed by war or lost in the Court." [22] Annette thought that was an excellent reason not to trust any more papers to the court and refused to comply.

"Under present conditions," Kurt Riezler had written Annette in 1947, "there is no hope at all for the case. How could it be otherwise? Nobody will take any interest in such a claim in the middle of the present misery of Europe."[23] And indeed, as Vermehren said, for ten years "as good as nothing happened."[24] Vermehren and Leverkuehn had finally brought their appeal to the High Court in West Berlin, where, in January 1957, the surprise testimony of a new witness resulted in another negative verdict.

The man was Hans-Johann Mayer, an Austrian, who in May of 1956 had published a series of articles in the sensationalist weekly *7-Tage*.[25] Mayer affirmed that he had been held as a prisoner of war in Ekaterinburg in 1918; that he had been recruited as a guard in the Ipatiev house and had been in the house on the night of the murder of the imperial family; that he had seen their bodies on the floor of the cellar and then had followed the corpses into the woods, where, before they were destroyed, he had counted them and made sure that all seven members of the family were dead. Mayer had also published a number of documents — including an official Bolshevik announcement of the imperial family's execution — which, he said, he had obtained from the Ural Regional Soviet in Ekaterinburg and smuggled out of Russia.

When Mayer was called as a witness before the High Court in West Berlin — the only witness, in fact, heard in person during the first appeal — the judges accepted his story without reservation, on faith.[26] "The Lady's No Duchess," *Newsweek* magazine proclaimed after the negative ruling had been handed down.[27] Perhaps the Berlin tribunal should not be judged too harshly for its credulity: Mayer's story, a lie from beginning to end, put a tidy stop to an otherwise maddeningly complicated procedure, and the perjury was not conceded by the opposition until 1964, when Mayer was dead. "The judges accepted that Mayer had spoken with such vividness, precision, and clarity," said a friend of Anastasia, "that his knowledge could not have been gleaned from the literature of the period nor founded in the experience of others."[28] It was ironic, to say the least. But the judges had refused to hear Anastasia's own witnesses on the subject: a friend of Mayer's who remembered the day Mayer had come to him with his "official Bolshevik documents" and announced that he had just had them printed in Berlin, and Robert von Lerche, a Russian émigré scholar who took the time to point out some of the more glaring errors and inconsistencies in those same documents. No, the judges had ruled: "The objections raised by the petitioner against the credibility of the witness Mayer are not valid."[29]

The next appeal was lodged in fury, but before it had gone very far a judge of the Berlin Court of Appeals advised Leverkuehn and Vermehren that Anastasia, even without the Fallows papers, probably had enough evidence of her identity not to bother any longer with the troublesome certificate of inheritance and to sue directly for her recognition. And so the petition was withdrawn, the case was moved for convenience from Berlin to Hamburg, and Anastasia prepared to accuse a relative of the Tsar's daughter of wrongfully denying her identity and spending her money.[30] The unlucky defendant was Barbara of Prussia, the current Duchess Christian Louis of Mecklenburg. As the granddaughter and adopted heir of "Aunt Irene," Duchess Barbara had inherited about six thousand marks from the fund at the Mendelssohn Bank, and Anastasia, technically, was asking for it back with interest. The Duchess had been only one of several possible defendants for the purposes of the suit, but in choosing her — for no other reason than that they wanted to confine the case to the boundaries of West Germany — Anastasia's attorneys had thrown the spotlight on all the tangles of the controversy. The Duchess's father was Prince Sigismund, who had acknowledged Anastasia sight unseen in the 1930s and had recently come away from a visit to the barracks at Unterlengenhardt;[31] while her mother's brother, Prince Frederick, hoping to avoid any further division within the family, had written Barbara twice warning her to return her share of the Tsar's money or face the consequences. "It is still not clear whether a certain inactivity was the cause," wrote a lighthearted friend of Prince Frederick, "or whether the postal services were to blame, but no reply was ever received."[32] At the last minute Duchess Barbara was joined as "voluntary codefendant" by Prince Louis of Hesse, the only surviving child of the late Grand Duke. Thus the battle against Anastasia continued to be waged from Darmstadt, and on January 9, 1958, the Duchess and Prince Louis sent their lawyers to meet Anastasia's lawyers in the Twenty-fourth Chamber for Civil Cases, Room 607, at the High Court of Hamburg.

Twelve days before Anastasia's case was due to open before the High Court, Dominique Auclères, a reporter for the *Figaro* in Paris, was called to the offices of her editor, Louis Gabriel-Robinet, the second-in-command to the *Figaro*'s redoubtable publisher, Pierre Brisson.

"What do you know about Anastasia?"

"I saw the movie, that's all."

"Well, you'd better find out what you can because we want you to cover her trial." [33]

Dominique Auclères was nineteen years old when, as a girl in Vienna, she ran to the apartment of Arthur Schnitzler and asked him if she could translate his works into French. Schnitzler was so taken aback that he agreed. From then on Mme. Auclères held his copyright in France. She was already married and a mother in 1934, when the King of Yugoslavia was assassinated at Marseilles and one of her friends, in great excitement, asked her to cover the story. Mme. Auclères had never "reported" anything in her life, but after accepting the challenge she did not look back. She wound up decorated by the government of France, famous throughout the country, and sensible, to boot. "I tried to write about the Anastasia affair for the *Figaro*," she remembered, "without making the affair or the *Figaro* look ridiculous." [34]

Within twenty-four hours Mme. Auclères had been to a library and in touch with Tatiana Botkin, who had divorced her husband some years before and had left the south of France for Paris. Then she paused to ask her readers for a favor: "I asked them to write me about it. I encouraged it. I wanted to know what *they* knew about Anastasia." [35] And so she did. Letters were already pouring in before the first session of the trial. The *Figaro,* in fact, became the serious, pan-European forum for everything concerning "The Grand Duchess and the Skeptic," [36] and it was not unusual to find a story about Anastasia on the front page next to an article about the French war in Algeria. "Anastasia became our rubric," Dominique Auclères explained with a laugh. "It didn't matter what else we were doing — the Test Ban, the Wall, the Kennedy assassination — we always found a little room for her." [37] With her own connections in Europe and through her gigantic correspondence, Mme. Auclères was going to prove an invaluable source for Anastasia's attorneys and, ultimately, a pivotal member herself of the small band fighting for Anastasia at Hamburg. "Anyhow," she said, "that's how I tumbled into the files, and that's how Anastasia took over my life." [38]

The first session of the trial was adjourned for a "completion of information." [39] Judge Werkmeister, the president of the Hamburg tribunal, sitting at the bench between Judge Backen and the lovely Judge Reisse — as Dominique Auclères described her, "a ravishing

pinup blond in judge's robes"[40] — wanted to know a good deal
more than the mountain of evidence was telling him. In Germany,
judges have a rather different role to play than they do under An-
glo-Saxon law.[41] They are not trained as jurists but rather as civil
servants. It is their job to dig for the truth while the lawyers, through
their oral argument and their memoranda, try to advise them of the
right questions to ask. During a civil proceeding like Anastasia's the
judges are free to hear or not hear, as they please, any witness cited
by the lawyers, and they may issue a ruling whenever they feel the
accumulation of evidence warrants it. The system adds a certain
understandable tension to every court session. No one but the judges,
furthermore, ordinarily questions the witnesses in court, and the
witnesses themselves are never sure in advance whether or not they
will be required to swear to their testimony. A witness *may* be asked
to take the oath when his testimony is finished, if the judges regard
the evidence as particularly important or if they hope to catch a
witness in perjury. And so the oath takes on a special significance
in German law.

"I think we're drowning in detail," said Judge Werkmeister after
two months on the "Anastasia" case.[42] But on the first morning he
had only issued some stout-hearted orders. He wanted more photographs of Anastasia and the young girl she claimed to have been.
He wanted handwriting specimens. He wanted "nearer proofs" of
the degree of relationship between the Tsar's daughter and certain
of Anastasia's witnesses. He ordered the defendants, who were nowhere in sight, to hand over to the tribunal any and all documents
they might have in Darmstadt or elsewhere with bearing on the
case. And he ordered Anastasia — also, of course, in absentia — to
decide as quickly as possible whether or not she was ready to appear in person before the court. "If she is not prepared to come to
Hamburg," said the judge, "she is to tell the tribunal why not and
let it know where she may be heard. . . . We will now move on to
the case of *Leiner and Sons* versus *Ziegelmeyer*."[43]

The press corps at Hamburg was profoundly disappointed. Nobody had known what to expect from the first audience, but it certainly wasn't this brief, lackadaisical pronouncement from the bench,
"squeezed in between two merchants in discord."[44] The German
press, on the assumption that the "Anastasia" affair might at last
be settled, had welcomed the new trial with great excitement. Now
the reporters realized that the process would be long and tedious,
when not totally unintelligible to outsiders. "Anyone not already

familiar with the details of the story of the true or the false Anastasia will have difficulty following the proceedings," Paul Noack
advised in the prestigious *Frankfurter Allgemeine Zeitung*.[45] The
scandalmongers and tabloid photographers, as a result, quickly
dropped out of the picture, turning up at Hamburg only when manifestly important witnesses were called to the bar and contenting
themselves with vague predictions about the outcome of this "Trial
of Doubt and Coincidence," this "Lawsuit of Ghosts."[46] Only six
weeks later, at the end of March 1958, did action commence, with
an examination of Anastasia's most ferocious enemy, Pierre Gilliard.

Having decided to hear in person the witnesses cited by the lawyers in their memoranda, the tribunal of Hamburg had repaired to
the tiny, rococo Hall of Justice in Wiesbaden for the deposition of
Felix Dassel, who was gravely ill with emphysema and could not
travel. It seemed appropriate and only fair to hear Gilliard at the
same time, along with Tatiana Botkin and several others, rather
than ask them to come all the way to Hamburg from their homes
in Paris and Lausanne. Prince Frederick had arrived — as Anastasia's legal proxy, he would attend the trial in her stead — along
with Gertrude Madsack and "*oh! miracle,* a genuine Hesse." It was
Marianne of Hesse-Philippsthal, the widow of Prince William, who
had "thumbed her nose at the spirit of the family"[47] and become
one of Anastasia's most indefatigable partisans. Pierre Gilliard,
white-haired now, seventy-eight years old and a widower (Shura
had died in 1955), took the stand on the morning of March 30,
1958, dressed in a plain dark suit and totally unbending in his denunciation of Anastasia.[48]

Briefly Gilliard outlined the essential points of his testimony —his
visits to Berlin in 1925; his immediate conviction that Anastasia
was a fraud; his late wife's like belief; and his abiding hatred of
Harriet von Rathlef. Then this: "The intimates of the Russian court
have been categorical on this subject. Not Grand Duchess Olga; not
Princess Irene of Prussia; not the Tsar's aide-de-camp, Colonel
Mordvinov; not Baroness Buxhoeveden, the Empress's maid-of-
honor; not Prince Yussoupov — none of them could find the slightest resemblance between the unknown woman and Anastasia."

Judge Werkmeister interrupted: "How do you know that?"

Gilliard had not expected the question. "Baroness Buxhoeveden
told me a hundred times," he began, his voice getting louder, when
Werkmeister cut him off again.

"A hundred times?" said the judge. "I remind the witness that he must be ready to swear to what he says."

"If I said a hundred times," said Gilliard, annoyed, "I meant many times. As for Grand Duchess Olga, she issued a peremptory declaration to the Danish newspapers."

"You do not represent the imperial family of Russia," said Judge Werkmeister. "You are a witness, and you are called to tell us only what you yourself have seen and experienced."

Now the interrogation began in earnest. The questions went on for hours — "When? What day? Where? What time? How long?" — until Gilliard, increasingly flustered and tired, was left to mumble over and over, "I don't know. I don't know anymore."[49]

The irony was lost on no one who knew the story; who knew about another "thorough interrogation" that had taken place in Berlin more than thirty years before. "Ordinarily," said Judge Werkmeister dryly, "a witness who knows that he is going to be heard finds a way to freshen his memory."

"M. Gilliard lowered his head," wrote Dominque Auclères, "like a bad schoolboy who's been reprimanded." She felt sorry for him: "In his hands he was nervously twisting a copy of his bible, *The False Anastasia*. He hadn't reread it very well; he had overestimated his powers. Probably he thought he could just swear to the whole thing in a block." And so, at last, he tried to do.

"*Monsieur le Président,*" said Gilliard, "I wrote this book thirty-five years ago, and I can swear that everything in it is true."

"One gets the impression," wrote the correspondent for *Die Zeit*, "that this rather pedantic man had been trapped by a decision he reached too hastily. How could such a fastidious teacher and amateur detective admit that he had made a mistake?"[50]

Judge Werkmeister refused to be sidetracked: "A book is not evidence, M. Gilliard." But now the judges did turn their attention to the contents of *The False Anastasia*. They wanted to examine some of the original documentation — above all, the excited letter Shura Gilliard had received in 1925 from Grand Duchess Olga, the letter that had first moved the Gilliards to meet Anastasia in Berlin.

"I don't have it anymore."

Then what about Gilliard's correspondence with the Duke of Leuchtenberg: "Is it true that you failed to reply to three of his letters?"

"Yes . . . no . . . I don't know anymore."

The correspondence with Harriet von Rathlef?

"No, I have nothing."

With Grand Duke Andrew?

"I have not spoken to him since the Revolution!"

"In his voice," said Dominique Auclères, "there was nothing but disdain for this one Romanov who had dared to recognize 'the actress.' " But there wasn't much point in going on.

"Refresh your memory over the weekend," Judge Werkmeister snapped. "I have more questions to ask you."

Evidently Gilliard took the judge's advice, because when he reappeared at the bar on Monday morning he was a changed man — bright, sardonic, and once again passionate in telling his version of the story. Paul Leverkuehn stepped up to the bench now to request that the court, in view of the enormous gaps in the evidence, make every possible effort to obtain the papers of the late Danish ambassador, Herluf Zahle, from the King of Denmark. Then, Leverkuehn whispered something to Judge Werkmeister, eliciting a nod.

"In *The False Anastasia*," said the judge to Gilliard, "you published certain photographs and handwriting specimens. We would like to see the originals. If you don't have them with you, the tribunal asks that they be sent."

Gilliard fairly cried the words: "I don't have them anymore! They're burned! I destroyed them. I have nothing anymore."

The silence in the chamber was deafening. Then "a suppressed murmur" moved through the court: "A historian who burns his archives . . ."[51] ("A corpse that stinks . . . ," said Prince Frederick later). Gilliard had no trouble sensing the thoughts that filled the room at that moment. Hastily he explained that he had burned his "Anastasia" dossier after the negative ruling of the High Court in West Berlin, thinking that the case was closed. He added, however, before he was dismissed for good that day, "Maybe there still is something in the safe-deposit box."

Maybe there was, said the judge. Gilliard would do well to look and inform the tribunal.

The court never heard another word from Pierre Gilliard. On his return to Lausanne he suffered an automobile accident. He never recovered from his injuries and died four years later, in 1962.

Felix Dassel was heard in the dining room of his house in Wiesbaden, gasping his testimony from a couch in the corner. His doctors had advised him not to make the effort to testify at all, but

Dassel had insisted: he hadn't waited this long to testify for "[his] Grand Duchess"[52] only to have a wretched case of emphysema stand in the way. And so, while his wife looked on anxiously and the judges posed their questions from a long table across the room, Dassel told his story from the beginning: about the military hospital at Tsarskoe Selo; the two merry Grand Duchesses who came to visit; the Revolution and the Civil War; then the meetings with Anastasia at Castle Seeon and the particular moments and events that had convinced him of her identity once and for all.

Dominique Auclères was the only journalist admitted to the hearing in Dassel's house, apart from the representatives of the wire services, thereby fueling the growing suspicion of the European press that there was more to her involvement with Anastasia than met the eye. Leverkuehn and Vermehren, as it turned out, already impressed by Mme. Auclères's thoroughness in reporting the case, had asked that she be present in order to fill in the gaps for the wire reporters. "He must have been handsome once," she observed of the dying Felix Dassel,[53] and was struck most of all by his sense of humor and his eloquence. Dassel, too, had been a writer and knew how to turn a phrase.

If Judge Werkmeister and his assistants had been firm during their interrogation of Pierre Gilliard, they were no less so with Felix Dassel — a little more indulgent of his health, certainly, but equally insistent that his answers be precise.[54] Thus when Werkmeister had led up to the inevitable questions about Anastasia's use of languages he did not want to hear that she spoke German "badly." He wanted to know *how* she spoke it badly, and Dassel replied by way of example, "She had a sovereign disdain for articles. Masculine, feminine, neuter — they were beyond her. The verb tenses were always wrong."

And Russian? The judges were already obsessed with the question: "Did you speak Russian with her?"

"She didn't speak Russian," Dassel replied, "although I was convinced that she understood it perfectly. One day when we were walking in the woods she tapped me on the shoulder and then pointed to a little mushroom. '*Ryzhik!*' she said."

A *ryzhik*, Dassel explained, is a certain type of red-capped mushroom common in Russia: "No foreigner can pronounce that word without betraying himself."

"But a Pole," said Judge Werkmeister meaningfully, "could perhaps pronounce it just as well?"

"A Pole?" said Dassel, who knew exactly what the judge was driving at. "No, I don't think so."

The audience was suspended quickly when Dassel's strength gave out; it was resumed the following morning. In a German civil proceeding, when a witness deposes, notes are taken from his testimony and then put together to form a continuous narrative. Only then is it decided whether the oath should be administered. "I don't want to let you sign your deposition," said Judge Werkmeister this morning, "until I've read to you the verdict of the Berlin tribunal that defeated the plaintiff in 1957. You can think about it, and perhaps you will want to tone down your deposition."

"I've been thinking about it for thirty years," said Dassel. "What for?"

Werkmeister went ahead with the reading, reminding Dassel also of the four anthropological experts who, on the basis of selected photographs, so far had all rejected Anastasia's claim to identity. Dominique Auclères had already been struck by something. When Pierre Gilliard declared that Anastasia was not the Tsar's daughter, she observed, nobody had asked him how he knew it, or bothered to remind him of the testimony of other people who said that she was. Dassel, on the other hand, was being treated as though his evidence went against an established truth. It was the first sign of a double standard that was going to run through the remainder of the trial — a tendency on the judges' part to credit automatically the testimony of Anastasia's opponents and thus, in effect, require that she prove everything twice: first, that her witnesses were telling the truth; and second, that her opponents were not. And when Felix Dassel — having declared that the Berlin verdict and the anthropological evidence were "all Chinese" — prepared to take the oath, he was not permitted to swear that Anastasia was the Tsar's daughter, only that he "had the certitude" that she was.

Werkmeister read the testimony aloud: "From all I have seen and experienced I believe I can say —"

"I did not say 'I believe,'" Dassel broke in sharply. "I affirm it! I *affirm* that she is Anastasia Nicolaievna."

"Do you want to use the religious formula for the oath?" asked Judge Werkmeister, apparently unmoved by the objection.

"Yes," said Dassel, wheezing and coughing and trying to get to his feet.

"Don't get up," said Werkmeister, concerned now. "You don't have to get up."

Dassel looked at him: "I am going to get up." He was standing with the aid of his wife when he declared, "I swear by God to 'have the certitude' that Mrs. Anderson is Anastasia Nicolaievna, Grand Duchess of Russia." [55]

The audience was adjourned.

There were no more dramatic oaths during the sessions in Wiesbaden, only a lengthy, tedious examination of Tatiana Botkin, much of which was devoted to an absurd confusion about her age ("Can we get it clear once and for all that the witness was quite old enough to have an opinion on this matter?"). "Anyone who has attended these four days of hearings will know that nothing has been decided," Paul Noack wrote in the *Frankfurter Allgemeine,* "and that nothing can be." [56] Before packing up, the judges cited the documents they wanted to see, the witnesses they wanted to hear, and then declared that under the circumstances, in view of the missing evidence and the amazingly contradictory testimony, there was simply no choice: Anastasia would have to depose in person.

Anastasia was already sick of the trial. When she found out that she was expected to make an appearance before her judges she snorted in contempt and declared that she would do no such thing. Dr. Vermehren was responsible for this, she had no doubt. For some reason, Anastasia had taken a severe dislike to Vermehren, announcing in her dictated letters that "Mrs. Anderson now thinks him not quite normal" and, mixing her images, charging, "That man only uses me for a golden calf!" [57] Finally she appeared to understand that it was a question of testifying or losing her case for sure, but she still would not agree in so many words. "At most," she said, "I may receive the president of the tribunal. I will invite him for tea if he is intelligent and a gentleman." [58]

Judge Werkmeister, wrote Dominique Auclères, "had not had the occasion to follow attentively the highs and lows of Mrs. Anderson's stormy humors . . . , but his doubts about her mental state were perfectly well founded." [59] In fact Werkmeister, when the judges met again in Hamburg, began by addressing himself to that very question: was Anastasia in full possession of her wits? What had she meant when she stated on a government form in 1949: "My name is Anna Anderson, I am a widow, my parents were called Tschaikovsky, I was born in Berlin and am a Protestant"? [60]

It turned out to have been nothing more than an attempt to avoid possible repatriation to the East, as Prince Frederick quickly explained to the judge; it was understandable, if slightly illegal.

But what about this? asked Werkmeister: in 1954 Anastasia had been brought to Paris for a meeting with Sydney Gibbes, the former English tutor at Tsarskoe Selo, and then had refused to speak English with him.[61] How to explain it? She had hardly used any other language since boarding the *Berengaria* in 1928.

Even Prince Frederick could not provide a satisfactory explanation for the fiasco with Gibbes. "She had decided to be sick," he suggested limply, not once leaving her bed during Gibbes's two-day visit and barely uttering a word at all.[62] Now the opposition had obtained an affidavit from Gibbes denouncing Anastasia as a fraud. Where would it end?

The journalists at Hamburg had begun to pay careful attention to "the opposition" — that is, the lawyers for the Duchess of Mecklenburg and Prince Louis of Hesse: the dour, more than slightly nasty Hans-Hermann Krampff[63] and the much younger, attractive, and flamboyant Günther von Berenberg-Gossler. Initially, Anastasia's attorneys had avoided suing Prince Louis precisely because they hoped not to have to deal with Krampff, but Louis's voluntary intervention had ruined their plans. Krampff and his young colleague, in the meantime, had announced that their sole motive in combatting Anastasia was "to discover the truth" and to restore the honor of the Russian imperial family and the House of Hesse. Anastasia's opponents, said Krampff, had always dealt with her case honestly, "out of responsibility and family feeling," and they would continue to do so in order to solve the mystery of her identity.[64] It was clear to everyone at Hamburg that the opposition's team was just as determined to succeed as Anastasia's, and that the battle would be hard. Now Judge Werkmeister pleaded with the reporters to take Anastasia's state of mind into account when they filed their dispatches by not making any predictions about her ultimate victory or defeat. Any excitement, the judge realized, made her appearance before the court less likely.

They were all back in Hamburg on May 21, 1958, in order to hear Doris Wingender and her younger sister, Louise, who had come from Berlin to testify about the missing Polish factory worker, Franziska Schanzkowska. The opposition had asked the judges to do more than deny Anastasia's claim to be the Tsar's daughter: they had brought a countersuit alleging that she *was* Franziska, and the moment was dangerous. The press had returned in force for the occasion. Without being entirely clear about the details of the Schanzkowska story, the reporters still knew that it was crucial to the trial, and they gave their full attention to Doris, who, in the years since the "unmasking," had married a car salesman and become Frau Rittmann. "She carries her fifty-four years well . . . ," said Dominique Auclères, "this ex-good-looker, ample-figured now but still spick-and-span." [65] The reporters watched in amusement as Doris "obligingly allowed herself to be photographed." [66] Then Doris took the stand. [67]

After a few hours everybody in the courtroom was stupefied, not excepting the judges, who already knew the details of the Schanz-kowska story and were better equipped than the German press to keep track of "the clothing and the teeth, the hair color and the tones of voice, an ominous mole and the strikingly good behavior of the Schanzkowksa woman." Said Paul Noack in the *Frankfurter Allgemeine:* "No mystery writer shooting for a best-seller would ever ask his readers to accept so many unlikely coincidences as the judge now finds in the evidence heaped before him." [68] Still Judge Werkmeister interrogated the witness with his usual thoroughness, in a patient if "rather Prussian" manner, [69] asking for more information; exact dates; further descriptions of the flowered hats and the mauve dresses of Franziska Schanzkowska; her shoes, her underwear, and the bunions on her feet, until the courtroom was nearly emptied of spectators.

"Do you mean there are no *photographic* exhibits that might permit us to identify the plaintiff with Franziska Schanzkowska?" Werkmeister asked finally, shaking his head. But there were. Doris Wingender brought two pictures out of her bag now. One depicted herself in 1920, wearing, she said, the famous blue suit she had given to Franziska in the summer of 1922, when Anastasia was missing from the home of Baron von Kleist. The second picture showed Anastasia later on in the Tiergarten. "You are going to see the same suit in this photograph," said Doris triumphantly, handing the photographs to the judge.

Werkmeister looked at the pictures in silence. Then he looked back at Doris and said with a frown, "But something has been erased on this picture of you." [70]

Yes, said Doris, that was true. In the original photograph a man had been standing at her shoulder: "I had his face removed because at the time certain wicked people were accusing me of having loose morals."

Werkmeister sniffed. Then he passed the pictures around the courtroom, while lawyers and journalists stared at them both and shrugged their shoulders.

"You can easily see that the two suits are identical," said Doris, umprompted, from the bar; "they've got the same buttons, the same belt . . ." But Werkmeister wasn't sure.

"Listen," said the judge, "we're going to get an expert opinion on these."

Doris Wingender was exceedingly displeased to hear it.

It was Louise's turn to be heard now, the younger sister, but she had nothing of importance to add to what Doris had already said. In fact she repeated Doris's testimony practically word for word. Even those journalists unfamiliar with the case could tell that the Wingender sisters had gotten their story down pat. Then on May 24 Gerda von Kleist, the Baron's daughter, was called to tell the court the truth about "Fräulein Unbekannt," about the goings-on at the Dalldorf Asylum in 1920 and the first days of the "Anastasia" scandal in Berlin.

Gerda von Kleist had become an extremely hostile witness. She remembered Anastasia as "a person without culture, with no real education, who liked to put on distinguished airs without succeeding in the least." [71] The court heard that Anastasia did not know a word of Russian or English; that she had cried out in Polish in her sleep; that she had once mistaken a German doctor for a relative of the imperial family, and so on. But when Gerda recalled the day that Anastasia — "Fräulein Anny" — had ducked beneath a table in order to wipe her nose, Prince Frederick leaped to his feet. This was too much! cried the Prince. He had known the plaintiff now for nearly thirty years and he could assure the court that her manners were better than *that*.

In reality the Kleist family, like the Leuchtenberg family and many others, was still deeply divided over the issue of Anastasia's identity. One of the sisters, Irina — who Gerda kept insisting was dead — now lived in East Berlin, where she was active in the theatre, and kept fond and "favorable" memories of Anastasia. The Baron, true enough, had died in 1929 "feeling he had been fooled," [72] but not so the Baroness, Gerda's mother, who had signed an affidavit the same year affirming that she had *never* wavered in her belief in Anastasia, "despite all attempts to the contrary." [73] But when a copy of the Baroness's affidavit was read aloud to her now, Gerda von

Kleist only remarked in a superior tone of voice, "My mother was crazy after my father died." [74]

"Where is the original of this document?" Judge Werkmeister asked.[75]

Leverkuehn replied that the Baroness's affidavit had been destroyed in the bombing of Berlin. Actually it had been kept by Annette Fallows, but that was a minor point at the moment: no one was able to contradict Gerda's testimony, not even when she declared that Felix Dassel, Anastasia's star witness, had already met her once at the Kleists' apartment in Berlin, several years *before* the supposedly revelatory meetings at Castle Seeon. That, said Gerda, was how Anastasia had learned what she knew about the military hospital at Tsarskoe Selo. Dassel had heard this charge before and had denied it, but he was not going to live out the summer and could not be called as a witness again.

Gerda von Kleist was asked to take the oath before she stepped down. She declined.

The May audiences closed with a number of peripheral witnesses and a little comic relief. Martha Borkowska, an old acquaintance of Franziska Schanzkowska from Poland, had been called to reminisce. When presented with a stack of photographs, she recognized each one of them as Franziska *except* the one of Franziska. Then when she, too, began to talk about Franziska's "pretentious airs," the increasingly grouchy Judge Werkmeister asked for examples, whereupon Martha, a bulky women, rose to her feet and pranced about the room in grotesque imitation of a movie queen.

One more session, when the arguments of the lawyers were heard and a number of documents were read into the record, left the judges obviously bored. A rogatory commission was going to be sent out now, Werkmeister announced, in order to hear various witnesses in Europe and America. Only then would the tribunal decide whether it had heard enough evidence to rule on the case.

Anastasia's lawyers, in the meantime, were impatiently awaiting the results of the forensic analysis that had been ordered on Doris Wingender's photographs. They had been conducting their own search for Franziska Schanzkowska and had tracked down a new witness, Bruno Grandsitzki, who claimed that he had met Franziska at Danzig in July 1920, at a time when Anastasia was already confined at the Dalldorf Asylum. Grandsitzki remembered that Franziska and "some other girls" had been making ready to sail for England, where they had found employment as domestic servants. The ship was called the *Premier,* Grandsitzki recalled, and Franziska had even given him her new address in London. It was "Bedford Road" — "unfortunately, I've forgotten the number." [76]

"Things had become exciting," wrote Dominique Auclères,[77] but alas, no information could be obtained from the British Home Office about Polish immigrants to England. In London, there were any number of "Bedford" thoroughfares, from streets to roads, with lanes, mews, gardens, terraces, places, and walks between. And of six steamers called *Premier* operating out of Danzig in 1920, three had never carried any Franziska Schanzkowska as a passenger; one was nowhere to be found; one was "too small to cross the oceans"; and one "made no reply." [78] But Anastasia's friends were heartened considerably when, in October 1958, the police experts at Hamburg-Altona delivered their report on Doris Wingender's pictures. The clothing in the two photographs, the police informed, was not only not identical, but on one of the suits "the buttons and the belt have been drawn in after the fact." [79]

The judges at Hamburg passed over this announcement in total silence.

A year went by. With Judge Backen at the helm, the tribunal's rogatory commission went to Paris, London, New York, and Montreal to hear some dozen witnesses, among them Felix Yussoupov, Faith Lavington, Gleb Botkin, Princess Xenia, Natalie Leuchtenberg and her brother Dmitri (she was "for," he "against"), and, in one of the most pathetic moments of the trial, the widowed Grand Duchess Olga, who was heard in Toronto much against her will. The years had not been easy for Olga. She and Colonel Kulikovsky had emigrated to Canada in 1949, where they operated a small farm until age and infirmity required that they give it up. Kulikovsky had been dead only a year when, as Olga's biographer, Ian Vorres, explained, "two German lawyers flew to Toronto to establish some details about the Grand Duchess's visit to Berlin in 1925." [80] In fact, Judge Backen and his assistant had wanted Olga to tell the story from the beginning, but Olga was in no mood. Her answers were curt and evasive — when Backen asked her if she had ever discussed Anastasia's case with her mother, the Dowager Empress, Olga replied with a frown, "It was not customary in our family to 'discuss' things overmuch" — and, after several hours of questioning, "the Grand Duchess began wondering if she were being trapped into answering questions which she did not properly understand."[81] Finally Olga rose and declared that the "interview" was over, left the room in the German consulate, and ran slap into a woman who cried, "Aunt Olga! Dear Aunt Olga! At last!"

"The Grand Duchess," wrote Ian Vorres, "too angry for speech, walked past her without a glance. . . . How proud and reserved was the Grand Duchess, and how bitterly all these impostors must have hurt her! I can still hear her voice:

" 'I know I am very near death and now at the end of a long life I think I have told you everything I remember about Anastasia. There is nothing to add to it. I think I have done my duty to the memory of my poor *Malenkaya.*' "

Grand Duchess Olga died in an apartment over a barbershop in Toronto on November 24, 1960.

On the morning of May 12, 1959, Anastasia, walking her dogs in the "garden" at Unterlengenhardt, stumbled across the body of her long-time companion, Adele von Heydebrandt, who had died there of a heart attack. The shock of the discovery left her with a physical reaction — a swelling of the arms and a terrible rash on her chest. The judges of Hamburg could not have chosen a worse moment, only eight days later, to come to meet her.[82]

There had been some changes at Hamburg in the long year since the court had last met. The elderly Dr. Krampff, one of the two lawyers for the Duchess of Mecklenburg, had bowed out of the case because of illness, and Judge Werkmeister had had to step down for the same reason, leaving Judge Backen to lead the trial through to its conclusion. Backen had taken matters in hand immediately by transporting the court to Bad Liebenzell, Anastasia's neighboring town in the Black Forest. There the judges proceeded to hear more of the witnesses: Theodor Eitel and Agnes Wasserschleben, Anastasia's doctor and nurse from the sanatorium at Oberstdorf; Fritz Schuricht, Harriet von Rathlef's one-time private detective in Berlin; and Gertrude Ellerik, born Schanzkowska, the only member of Franziska Schanzkowska's family to have "recognized" Anastasia as her sister ("Admit it! Admit it!"). There were no surprises in any of these testimonies, but the sessions were unusually tense as the judges waited for a word from the lady up the hill. They had brought with them a Russian expert, who was supposed to test Anastasia's knowledge of the language.

At eight o'clock on the morning of May 20 Kurt Vermehren advised the court that one of his client's "ladies," Louisa Mayhoff, had told him that Anastasia would not agree to see anyone. The reason: "her companion's recent death." It was decided, therefore, that Dr. Eitel, after giving his evidence that day, should go up to Unterlengenhardt and "use his influence on the plaintiff."

The whole court went up with him. Toward evening Baroness von Miltitz engaged Anastasia on the line of her newly installed telephone to say that Dr. Eitel wanted to speak with her.

Anastasia hung up. She hung up again when Miss Mayhoff called.

There was no use, said Miss Mayhoff. She would try again in the morning when she brought Anastasia her milk.

At eight-thirty the next day the court was back, only to be told the same thing. Anastasia would see no one, including Dr. Eitel: "She wished to remember him as he was years ago, at Oberstdorf." Suddenly Miss Mayhoff dashed out of the barracks and called for Gertrude Lamerdin, another of Anastasia's ladies: Miss Lamerdin was to come in with her at once!

The court stenographer, meanwhile, stood at a distance from the cabin taking her notes. Through the trees she caught sight of "a person — not Miss Lamerdin" and cautiously moved closer. She just had time to see this "person," wearing an enormous straw hat and holding two dogs on a leash, turn on her heel and reenter the barracks. There was no time to take a picture.

"No! No! I will not see them!" Miss Mayhoff quoted Anastasia when she next emerged.

In that case, said Judge Backen, the court would return at ten o'clock in the morning with the district doctor. If Anastasia was "too ill" to receive the judges and the Russian expert, the doctor would have to confirm the fact.

By the next day Anastasia had stopped making excuses. "Do not fight with me," she warned Miss Mayhoff; "leave me in peace!" Again the stenographer had crept up to the cabin door where, for the first time, she heard "a voice":

"I have nothing to do with the court!"

Later that morning Agnes Wasserschleben deposed in Liebenzell. The court had just finished with her when Gertrude Lamerdin came down and asked to speak with the judge. "The plaintiff," read the protocol, "is determined to see no one, and in particular not her attorney, Dr. Vermehren."

Vermehren grinned sheepishly: he was used to this.

"I tried to impress on Mrs. Anderson the importance of the occasion," Miss Lamerdin went on, but Anastasia would hear no argument. Somebody ought to write a new book about her case, she had said. And with the proceeds, perhaps, *somebody* could build her a house that was fit to live in! Then they could turn the old barracks into a museum, which the public could tour — *for a fee.* Anyway, said Miss Lamerdin, that was Anastasia's suggestion. Perhaps Dr. Leverkuehn could do something?

Leverkuehn had a better idea. He telephoned Baron Ulrich von Gienanth, the man who managed Anastasia's limited "finances," and asked him to come down to Unterlengenhardt. If Gienanth did not succeed, said Leverkuehn, no one could.

It was dusk on the evening of May 23 before Baron von Gienanth arrived. The judges waited near the cabin for more than half an hour while the stenographer lurked at the door. Finally, once again, she heard the voice:

"He can stare at me for ten minutes!"

By "he" Anastasia meant Judge Backen and Judge Backen alone: no assistants, no doctor, no Russian expert.

Backen found her sitting on the veranda between Miss Lamerdin and Baron von Gienanth. No, she would not shake his hand: she was afraid of germs.

They spoke in English "to break the ice." And then Judge Backen led up gradually to the matter at hand, asking Anastasia a variety of disconnected questions about the previous forty-one years of her life.

Did she remember when Irene of Prussia had come to see her?

Certainly: the Princess had recognized her "instantly" and invited her to Hemmelmark.

What about Grand Duchess Olga?

"No." But Anastasia did remember Shura and Pierre Gilliard: "Gilliard had been very kind to her at first and had sent her chocolates."

Now Anastasia tried to tell the judge "how difficult it was" — "because during all this long time she had been 'stormed' by curiosity-seekers." Could he not understand?

Did Anastasia know French?

She had been tutored in French, yes, but no, she did not know it anymore.

Backen tried to speak with her in French: "The plaintiff put an end to this conversation immediately."

Russian? Was Anastasia aware that there were people who claimed she could not speak Russian?

Of course Anastasia was aware of it, and she freely admitted that she had "partly" lost the ability to speak the language. And also she never had the opportunity.

Well, said Backen, here was her opportunity. But Anastasia turned her head away and made no reply when Backen, groping in his own memory, began asking her: "How do you say 'customs' in Russian? How do you say 'passport' in Russian?"

A moment later the judge heard Anastasia call to "Baby," the youngest and favorite of her dogs: "Babaka!"

Perhaps Anastasia ought to see the Russian language expert, said Backen.

That was enough: when Anastasia had said ten minutes she had meant ten minutes. Baron von Gienanth was to inform the judge that the meeting was over.

From the protocol:

[The plaintiff] gives the impression of a very self-confident and energetic lady. She seems . . . to be thoroughly clear and mentally competent. She speaks in a regal manner, with a deliberate distance. Sometimes she will look her conversation partner directly in the eye, while burying the lower part of her face in a high collar; sometimes the face turns all the way to the left side and is hidden entirely in the collar of her coat.

It is difficult to get the plaintiff to concentrate on certain questions and events. After thinking, she gives her answers with conviction in her voice. She pauses every now and then and gives her partner the impression that she wants a rest. She turns her gaze away mainly when she hears arguments which speak against her identity with the daughter of the Tsar. Repeatedly she says that she cannot understand the arguments of her enemies at all.

"I don't know who she is," said Judge Backen to the waiting crowd, "but she is a lady."[83] Before leaving Unterlengenhardt the court was able to procure from among the effects of the late Adele von Heydebrandt a Russian exercise workbook, with lessons written out in Frau von Heydebrandt's hand. Apparently Anastasia had been tutoring her companion in the language. Inside, in Russian, she had recently inscribed the words, "With God."[84]

"Dear Mrs. Anderson," read a letter from Paul Leverkuehn, "I am sending you a copy . . . [of] a most satisfying document . . . which I am sure you would not care to read. But perhaps you are interested in the conclusions on the last pages."[85]

The document was a report of the results of an anthropological study conducted at the University of Mainz by Baron von Eyckstedt, Professor and Honorary Doctor, and his partner, W. Klenke.[86] It had concluded on the basis of a comparison of more than three hundred photographs — some of Anastasia, some of the Tsar's daughter, and some of the various members of the Russian imperial family and the House of Hesse — that "with respect to none of the physical characteristics [of the face] were there any certain and constantly recurring deviations between Mrs. Anderson and Grand Duchess Anastasia" — in plain words, that the two women were identical. "It is not only possible that we are dealing with an identity," said Eyckstedt and Klenke; "it is the only acceptable solution."

Leverkuehn was right: Anastasia did not care to read about it. There had been several of these studies before, all of them negative in their conclusions, beginning with Professor Bischoff's analysis in 1927 and moving on through four other eminent specialists in Germany.[87] But Eyckstedt and Klenke had included those reports as part of their own research and had pointed out at considerable length the deficiencies of their predecessors' work. The earlier studies, they said, had each employed "a limited and therefore limiting" number of amateur and retouched photographs, and the negative judgments had all rested primarily on "alleged discrepancies of the ear region." By selecting photographs for comparison that had been taken at the same angles and under similar lighting conditions, however, Eyckstedt and Klenke had satisfied themselves that these "discrepancies" were only an illusion.

When the University of Mainz report was submitted in evidence to the judges at Hamburg, there was talk around Europe that the Duchess of Mecklenburg and Prince Louis of Hesse would be forced to reach a compromise with Anastasia. The new evidence was so compelling that no other solution seemed possible apart from Anastasia's total victory. But the Hesses were not about to compromise after so many years. Immediately Günther von Berenberg-Gossler, now the sole lawyer for the opposition, began to downplay the importance of expert opinion, while at the same time resubmitting the earlier photographic analyses for the court's consideration.

Finally the judges, with the agreement of both parties, ordered a new study, which — it was expressly stated — would be accepted as the last word on the subject. Selected for the task was Professor Otto Reche, "the Nestor of modern anthropology," as he was known in Germany,[88] the founder and former president of the German Anthropological Society, an expert in genetics and scientific criminology and an experienced witness for the courts. At the same time the court asked its own graphologist, Dr. Minna Becker (who had recently helped authenticate Anne Frank's diary), to conduct an analysis of Anastasia's handwriting. That, too, was going to be "the last word." Both Reche and Becker emphasized later that the opposition had cooperated with them fully in the matter by releasing numerous photographs and samples of Grand Duchess Anastasia's handwriting from the private archives at Darmstadt.

When Dr. Reche's sixty-page report was submitted to the court in 1960 he had already spent more than a year at his task, collecting every available photograph of the Tsar's daughter, the Romanovs, and the Hesses; traveling to Unterlengenhardt and gaining entrance — eventually — to Anastasia's barracks, where he photographed her under the *exact* angles and approximate lighting conditions of the earlier pictures; and studying the results, "millimeter by millimeter," under the magnifying glass. He had also busied himself with charts, grids, blood tests, and a comparison of Anastasia's features with those of Franziska Schanzkowska and her family.

Under German law, the only evidence accepted as "proof positive" of an identity is a set of fingerprints. Expert opinion like Dr. Reche's is regarded only as "probability tending on certitude."[89] The judges at Hamburg had to make up their minds now what to do, because Reche's conclusion was peremptory:

1. Mrs. Anderson is *not* the Polish factory-worker, Franziska Schanzkowska.

2. Mrs. Anderson *is* Grand Duchess Anastasia.

The results had far exceeded anyone's expectations. And there was more to come: when Minna Becker's graphological analysis arrived, it was no less categorical than Reche's had been. "I have never seen this many identical traits," said Dr. Becker, "in two scripts that did not come from the same hand. . . ."[90] Identity of traits, therefore: identity of person. . . . Mrs. Anderson is no one else than Grand Duchess Anastasia."[91]

There was universal rejoicing in Unterlengenhardt, as might have been expected. Anastasia herself decided that she wanted to give a party in the garden, to which she invited the entire village, along with a few select friends around Germany. She stood on the veranda one night under a row of Japanese lanterns, greeting each one of the villagers in person while a Russian singer and a string quartet rhapsodized in the background. There was hardly a newspaper in West Germany that had not already predicted her forthcoming victory. Her new house had just been completed, too — she called it "the dacha" — and her future, for the first time, looked positively rosy.

Paul Leverkuehn died in March 1960, just in time to have heard the happy news of Otto Reche's photographic report. At Kurt Vermehren's request, Dominique Auclères now secured permission from the *Figaro* in Paris to assist in the monumental task of keeping the evidence in order. So much material had accumulated by this time that it had to be wheeled into the courtroom on carts whenever the judges sat. Now Mme. Auclères spent each morning at Vermehren's house, sorting papers, taking and leaving notes and suggestions, until she had established a familiarity with the dossier as comprehensive as that of any of the lawyers.

There wasn't much left to do in the trial. Vermehren called a few more witnesses to give an accounting of Anastasia's incredibly difficult character, in the hope that the judges would regard her stubbornness and her chronic anxiety as a crucial aspect of the case and not as an obstruction of justice. The court also made a concerted effort through the West German Foreign Ministry to obtain Herluf Zahle's dossier from Denmark, but finally the Danish government, having refused the papers "on principle," warned of "serious diplomatic repercussions" if such requests did not cease: the Zahle dossier was going to remain where it was.[92]

The last sessions opened on May 9, 1961. Things were being "sped up,"[93] because, as Vermehren explained, the judicial recesses were at hand, and if the court were to wait until the fall a new president would have to be appointed to the tribunal, who would then have to familiarize himself with the case from the beginning — a terrifying prospect. The audience began with an oral "recapitulation of the facts" from the bench, a breathtakingly involved narrative of the "Anastasia" affair and the trial, point by point, detail by detail. When the evidence had been sifted, everyone waited for the judges to call the expert witnesses. Minna Becker, the graphologist, was "haunting the corridors," [94] while Professor Reche sat confidently at home, figuring he would be summoned the moment he was needed. Slowly it dawned on Anastasia's friends that the judges weren't going to hear them — that they were going to ignore the testimony of their own appointed experts.

Kurt Vermehren appeared to have gone into a trance. When the final pleas began on the third day his summation was somehow off-key, dry and uninspired, not at all the kind of impassioned defense of Anastasia's claim his friends knew he was capable of giving. Günther von Berenberg-Gossler, on the other hand, arguing for the opposition, gave a performance that was nothing short of brilliant, deriding Anastasia and her witnesses for more than three hours, "with talent, with striking force," marveling at Anastasia's "abnormally strong powers of suggestion" and wondering if the judges, too, like the court experts and so many others, were going to "fall under her spell." Did the judges know how many "Anastasias" Berenberg-Gossler had already met while working on this case? *Fourteen.* ("Dr. von Berenberg-Gossler deserves our sympathy," Paul Noack remarked in the *Frankfurter Allgemeine*. "He is beset by psychopaths.") With obvious pleasure Berenberg-Gossler attacked Anastasia's most vocal witness, Gleb Botkin, holding up Gleb's "Church of Aphrodite" as a telltale sign of the moral worth and mental stability of all of Anastasia's friends and inviting the judges to assess their testimony accordingly. What further evidence did the judges need to know that Anastasia and her "dream factory" were a matter for psychiatry and not the law? [95]

When Kurt Vermehren got up to speak again, Anastasia's friends were desperate for him to do something — to play some trump, to respond to the opposition in kind. Why had the judges made no mention of Ambassador Zahle's confiscated papers in their résumé of the facts? Why had they ignored Doris Wingender's retouched photographs and Pierre Gilliard's scandalous bonfires? How could they even think of ruling on the case without hearing the testimony of the expert witnesses? But Vermehren was content to let these matters rest. He left his client's fate, with patience and dignity, to the wisdom of the court.

The judgment came on May 15. "The claim is unfounded," read the verdict.[96] "The plaintiff, Mrs. Anderson, is defeated." [97] It was no consolation to hear that the counterclaim had also been defeated — the claim that Anastasia was actually the missing Franziska Schanzkowska. No consolation at all: the counterclaim was dismissed in the judgment merely on the grounds that it was "irrelevant," although the identity with Franziska, in the judges' opinion, was "eminently likely." [98]

Only a few hours had gone by before the judges understood that Anastasia would appeal.

14

THE TRIALS — SECOND INSTANCE

(1964–1967)

*T*he judgment of the first tribunal in Hamburg was so arbitrary, so hastily put together, and so superficial in its reasoning as to defy belief. Having spent three and a half years probing Anastasia's case to its depths, the judges of the High Court appear to have finally rebelled at the thought of making any decision that went against the status quo — for their verdict, in actuality, was no verdict at all. It had done nothing to alter Anastasia's position in the world. The point was lost on the international news services, which held that her claim to identity had been disproved, but the *Frankfurter Allgemeine* put it best in its headline of May 16, 1961: "Anna Anderson *May Not Be* the Tsar's Daughter." [1]

She had taken the news badly: "Her eyes became very sad, and she said, simply, 'Well, the only thing left to do is to die.' " [2] Then she shut her doors and for weeks refused to see anyone. When she emerged again she had made up her mind that there would be no more court trials. What for? she asked: "I know perfectly well who I am; I don't need to prove it in any court of law." [3] It was all Prince Frederick and Kurt Vermehren could do to persuade her, after months of arguing, to consent to the appeal "for the sake of the truth and the honor of the family she survived." [4]

Vermehren based his plea — and it was accepted immediately — on what he called "the one-sidedness, if not the prejudice" of the

318

Hamburg tribunal and the failure of the judges to consider "the many psychological difficulties of this singular case."[5] Some of the court's arguments Vermehren could understand: the fact that "the plaintiff's behavior did not allow the tribunal to gather all of the evidence it wanted," for example;[6] and the inability of the court to satisfy itself that she knew the Russian language. That was as far as Vermehren's appreciation went, however, because the remainder of the Hamburg verdict was a biased, presumptuous litany of Anastasia's failings in her role as a Russian grand duchess. The court had expressly apologized to the defendants, first of all, the Duchess of Mecklenburg and Louis of Hesse, for any embarrassment they may have endured on account of the trial. Pointing out that as many as "fifteen intimates of the Russian court" had denied Anastasia's claim to identity, the judges further alleged — falsely — that there had been "no spontaneous recognition" of Anastasia as the daughter of the Tsar. If Anastasia were genuine, the court reasoned, her relatives would have "dissolved into tears of joy and embraced her on the spot." Anything she knew about life at the Russian court — and the judges conceded that she knew a lot — she could theoretically have uncovered through "extensive research." The court argued that she had spoken English only since 1927, "after taking lessons" (evidently these were the nursery rhymes she had studied with Faith Lavington at Seeon), and that the Tsar's daughter would not, under any circumstances, have forgotten her Russian — "because the Russian is so devoted to his homeland and his mother tongue." The judges were "surprised," finally, by the "apodictic statements" of their scientific experts, ruling without explanation that Minna Becker, the graphologist, had been working with "insufficient material"; and that Otto Reche, the forensic anthropologist, had undermined his own expertise by addressing himself to only one question — grand duchess or Polish factory worker? — while ignoring the possibility that Anastasia might have been someone else altogether.

It was the failure of the tribunal, above all, to confront its experts with these limp, layman's objections that led the *Oberlandesgericht* in Hamburg — the High Court of Appeals — to declare Anastasia's case receivable in 1962. Kurt Vermehren had already submitted his first memorandum to the court's Second Civil Senate when, in October, he was killed in a car crash. "It's as though it were destiny," sighed Prince Frederick, to whom Anastasia's full power of attorney now reverted, "one miserable misfortune after another."[7] In January 1963 the Senate informed the Prince that Anastasia had six weeks to find a new attorney or drop the case. There was no want of lawyers in West Germany willing to represent her, of course. The problem was that they wanted to be paid ("Out of the question," said Prince Frederick: he had already had to obtain for Anastasia the so-called Rights of the Poor), and that most of them were not licensed to practice law in Hamburg. Only one, Carl-August Wollmann, had written the Prince to say that he would be happy to take on Anastasia's case without charge.

Wollmann had entered the ranks of what the German press called "the Anastasians" after a single reading of the published verdict of the first tribunal. A native of Tilsit, in East Prussia, Wollmann was "a tall man, with a handsome profile and wide shoulders,"[8] who had fled to the West in the migration of 1945. The bones of his right leg had been shattered in battle during World War II, but Wollmann had refused to have the leg amputated, preferring to limp along painfully with the aid of a rubber-tipped cane. Vehement, argumentative, pugnacious, and frequently abrasive, he was going to give a performance in court the likes of which the judges in Hamburg had never seen. Not for him the polite, "gentleman's agreement" tactics of Paul Leverkuehn and Kurt Vermehren. In Wollmann's opinion, altogether too much time had been wasted trying to be "nice." *Each one* of the testimonies against Anastasia, he pointed out, had been valued by the first tribunal as "true," "factual," and "comprehensive"; while *her* witnesses had been dismissed as "uncritical," "vague," and "predisposed in her favor." Wollmann saw nothing sinister in this double standard, only a want of imagination and a failure "to examine fully the very possibility that one of the Tsar's daughters might have escaped Ekaterinburg. . . . Since the judges were convinced from the outset that no one *could* have survived the general massacre, they proceeded to treat with inconceivable lightness the positive conclusions of their own experts." It was Wollmann's first task to remedy that mistake by examining the mystery of Ekaterinburg from beginning to end. For the rest of it, he intended to subject Anastasia's opponents to the same kind of criticism — if not the same kind of slander — to which she herself and all of her witnesses had at one time or another been exposed. While understanding that Anastasia bore the burden of proof in this marathon procedure, Wollmann also understood that each hostile witness "knocked out of the running, so to speak," could be taken as a point in her favor. He apologized to the judges in advance, but he meant to spare no one's feelings.

Wollmann's antagonism and that "outsider's" anger that invariably surfaced when he argued in court were to lead to serious conflicts among the "Anastasians" themselves. Prince Frederick, above all, found Wollmann grating and worried about the end result of his tactics. "You don't know Hamburg," the Prince explained to Dominique Auclères, who could not understand why he had hesitated before giving Wollmann the brief.[9] In fact Hamburg, the ancient city-state, fiercely proud of its independence and its glorious mercantile history, remained a bastion of modern bourgeois sensibility. What kind of impression might Wollmann, a dispossessed Prussian monarchist, a man of passion and quick temper, make on the stolid, republican judges of the Senate? And what kind of laughingstock might Günther von Berenberg-Gossler, the lawyer for the defense, make of Wollmann in court — Berenberg-Gossler, "the picture of health and prosperity," one of the leading lights of the clubbish Hamburg bar?

Prince Frederick need not have worried on the last score. "If Berenberg-Gossler imagined that he could just make mincemeat out of this younger man, this Prussian," Mme. Auclères observed, "he was sorely mistaken. He was no more aware than we were then of the conscientiousness, the meticulousness, the stubbornness of the man from Tilsit."[10] Wollmann and Berenberg-Gossler had met only once before the trial, in Berenberg-Gossler's office, and they detested each other immediately. But Anastasia liked Wollmann, or seemed to, and that was all that mattered. Her first act after she met him in Unterlengenhardt was to entertain her ladies with an uncannily exact imitation of his mannerisms — a sure sign that someone had impressed her favorably. "His leg is in a bad condition," she wrote Gleb Botkin sympathetically, "and he must take remedies against the terrible pains. I fear that he is not very long alive."[11] Anastasia wasn't far wrong. The next three years were to see a dramatic decline in Wollmann's health as he chain-smoked, drank endless cups of strong black tea, popped pain-killers and amphetamines, and stayed up night after night to prepare his memoranda, while his shattered leg began to twist and buckle and his stomach was eaten out by ulcers.

The opening of the new trial was delayed while Wollmann — "in the incredibly short time of one year"[12] — acquainted himself with the dossier. His first memorandum to the Senate was three hundred and thirty pages long, as opposed to Berenberg-Gossler's confident sixty. (It would always be that way: Wollmann would produce his hundreds of cheaply mimeographed pages, scarred by underlining and crawling with exclamation points, while the opposition contented itself sometimes with an elegant, three-page denial of everything he said.) Finally the first session was scheduled for April 1964 and the "Anastasians" gathered again in Hamburg. There had been some new additions to the group. Marianne of Hesse-Philippsthal, more devoted than ever to Anastasia, had offered to help Wollmann and his wife, Brigitte, keep the material in order. Prince Metfried of Wied [13] darted in and out of court, helping where he could and frequently lending his brother's shiny Mercedes for the innumerable excursions around Germany required in the search for witnesses. And from England came Ian Lilburn, a young friend of Prince Frederick, an assistant to Garter King of Arms at the College of Heralds in London, a devoted student of music and architecture and connoisseur of fine wines, with a photographic memory and an invaluable mania for detail. With the Prince, Ian Lilburn would become Wollmann's legs, traveling to Lausanne, Vienna, Stuttgart, Berlin — wherever he was needed — and often accompanying the Prince to the Black Forest to do battle with the increasingly testy, increasingly frustrated plaintiff.

"You must go to Munich," said Anastasia to Prince Frederick one day (after the Prince had just been to Munich), "to see Mr. Schacht. He is the witness of all."

"Madame Mutabor!" Prince Frederick replied. "Munich isn't just around the corner! It costs *money* to go to Munich" — whereupon Anastasia signaled that he should wait, went into her bedroom, and returned with a twenty-mark note: "Now go." Another time she told the Prince that he ought to get in touch with Alexander Kerensky, the leader of Russia's short-lived Provisional Government in 1917: "He will help."

"Is he still in New York?" asked Prince Frederick.

"Don't be ridiculous. Nobody in his right mind is in New York in July." [14]

"We were never long out of touch with one another," said Dominique Auclères of the "Anastasians." "Our solidarity expressed itself in a sort of communal existence." [15] Mme. Auclères herself, with the *Figaro*'s blessing, had leaped into the fray and now maintained only the professional appearance of neutrality. When the court was in session she stayed at the Hotel Vier Jahreszeiten, where she and the others would usually repair for lunch and where they frequently gathered at the close of each day's audience, sometimes not until long after midnight. Then the group would meet again in the morning to map out their plans and try to guess the moods and the wishes of the tribunal: Gustav Petersen, the "mild-mannered, courteous and heroically patient" president of the Senate, whose last case this was before retiring; the middle-aged, bespectacled Judge Bäthge, first assistant and clerk of the court, with an "astonishing knowledge" of the thirty-three volumes of evidence and "a comic way of talking without moving his upper lip"; and finally the youthful Judge Prusz, with his "sympathetic face" and "friendly smile," who rarely, if ever, spoke a word.[16]

Judge Petersen had hoped to have done with it by Christmas 1964. "The court is not here to consider gratuitous testimony," he announced on Thursday, April 9.[17] The European press corps, after a three-year respite, had taken up the story again with its usual vigor but also with unmistakable skepticism, directed not so much at Anastasia's claim to identity as at the ability of any court to resolve the issue. "Anastasia Trial," read the headlines,"— Again."[18] There were photographers everywhere in the somber, black-marbled chamber at the Palace of Justice, lounging near the great arched doorways and along the walls, where priceless manuscripts and books of law rose to the ceiling. Because of "the private, personal nature of the proceedings," however, Judge Petersen commanded that cameras never again be brought into court. The tribunal was not dealing with a case of "world-historical significance," said Petersen. It was solely a matter of establishing a woman's identity and, if necessary, sorting out a tangled inheritance. In the meantime the judge wished to hear nothing from anybody about "high stakes" or "fortunes in England" and emphasized that the tribunal would not conduct its own independent investigation of the case.[19] The court was going to rule only on the evidence presented by the lawyers, and above all by the lawyer for the plaintiff: "With her and with her alone lies the burden of proving this claim. . . . She *will* be heard, and the court will not see her in her house. . . . If the tribunal goes to Unterlengenhardt, the meeting will take place on neutral ground."[20]

"We were right back at the beginning," said Dominique Auclères. "Ground zero."[21] Her point was proved when the lawyers began the tedious process of reviewing the facts — the simple dates, places, and times of the "Anastasia" affair, which each of them had to accept as accurate before the trial could proceed. Already Klaus Wagner, the new correspondent for the *Frankfurter Allgemeine,* had been "irritated" by "the profusion of details and the endless possibilities" for argument.[22] Could it be that the judges and lawyers were only *now,* after forty-four years, finally determining the exact date of Anastasia's suicide attempt? But so they were. Efforts had been made after the destruction of the Berlin dossiers to move the date ahead from February 17 to February 27, 1920, a date that better coincided with the alleged disappearance of Franziska Schanzkowksa. As the months went by — and especially when the heavy fog rolled over Hamburg from the North Sea, shutting out the view from the windows in the Palace of Justice — Wagner sometimes felt that nothing else existed but Anastasia's trial. "Thick air outside, thick air in," he wrote as he gazed at the stack of evidence before the judges. "The representatives of the press may claim with the British Islanders — the rest of the world is cut off, only here does life go on . . . as though the identity of Mrs. Anna Anderson, sixty-three years of age, were the most important question on earth."[23]

So battle was joined. The anthropological and graphological experts were scheduled to be heard first. If the court could decide the issue solely on the basis of their evidence, then so much the better. If not, the round of witnesses would be heard again, along with any others the lawyers were holding in reserve. Then the spectators rose and left the court — "Old ladies with fine faces," mused the man from *Die Welt,* "who once were young, wearing fur coats that once were new"[24] — and it became clear to everyone present that the cast of characters in this "Trial Without End"[25] was, like the audience and the leading lady, rapidly aging. Time, it seemed, was running out.

Professor Otto Reche was eighty-four years old by the time he was allowed to take the stand at Hamburg, on April 16, 1964, and testify about the positive results of his "Anastasia" studies. A giant of a man with an enormous head, he was opposed in court by Professor Karl Clauberg, one of his own former pupils and paid assistants, who in 1955 had conducted a similar — but negative — study for the Berlin tribunal and who had now been called as a rebuttal witness for the opposition. Within a few hours the audience had degenerated into a shouting match. None of the reporters in the

chamber could keep track of the "wearisome and truly incomprehensible" debate,[26] but they all knew what it meant when Reche,
red in the face, stormed from the courtroom, having declared that
he would listen to no more nonsense and that if the judges wanted
to hear about his conclusions they could send away that pompous
little creature in the corner. *"Um Gottes Willen!"* Reche cried;
Clauberg was a *blood* specialist, ill equipped for the kind of work
involved here.

When Reche appeared again the next day, calmer but unbending
in his contempt for Professor Clauberg, he took a deep breath and
declared: "I am not going to participate in a session like yesterday's.
I am *not* going to be interrupted by my colleague, who wants to
sidetrack us with material of no bearing on this case." Clauberg
kept pointing out that Anastasia had the same blood type as one of
Franziska Schanzkowska's sisters — an utterly meaningless observation, since neither the Tsar's daughter's nor Franziska's blood
group was known. Said Reche: "If the Senate does not permit me
to explain myself, I'm going to leave."

Judge Petersen, "surprised," explained that the court had an obligation to hear all sides of the question. But he granted Reche's
request by asking Clauberg to withhold his comments and objections while the older man talked.

Reche began by citing what, in his opinion, was the matter with
all of the previous photographic comparisons: they had not employed a sufficient number of pictures; they had not taken into account the defects of amateur photography nor made allowances for
the cosmetic retouching of all formal portraits of the Russian imperial family; and they had all been executed at a time when this
kind of morphological science was more or less in its infancy. None
of the earlier reports, Reche insisted, could be endorsed by any
modern expert. Next, there was the famous portrait of Franziska
Schanzkowska, which Reche introduced as evidence of the bad faith
of Anastasia's opponents. "This photograph has been retouched
twice," he maintained, first for its publication in 1927 in the *Berliner Nachtausgabe;* and next, much more extensively, for its publication in Pierre Gilliard's *False Anastasia:* "The only purpose of
these retouchings was to heighten the resemblance between Fräulein
Schanzkowska and Mrs. Anderson."[27] Still the operation had not
succeeded. During his study of the photographs Reche had observed
that the height, the width, and the form of Franziska's face deviated
grossly not only from Anastasia's, but *identically* from the face of

the Tsar's daughter. That fact, Reche said, had to be taken as another indication that Anastasia and the Tsar's daughter were one
and the same.

The lights were dimmed in the courtroom now while pictures of
the faces were projected over a grid, showing just how and where
the features and the bones coincided. Reche had focused on four
"cardinal points":

1. the width of the cheekbones in relation to the height of the
   face, from the root of the nose to the chin,
2. the width of the cheekbones in relation to the lower jaw,
3. the height and width of the eyesockets,
4. the height and width of the forehead.[28]

Anastasia's face, Reche continued, had matched the face of the
Tsar's daughter "sometimes to the very millimeter." The only deviations were the normal ones brought about by age, but there had
been no fundamental differences in the structure of the bones. "Such
coincidence between two human faces," Reche summed up, "is not
possible unless they are the same person or identical twins." [29]

Reche did not wait to hear Professor Clauberg's response, nor the
evidence of Willy Beutler, the Senate's photography expert, who had
been called to testify to the authenticity of the pictures and who
agreed now with Clauberg that Anastasia's right ear presented "difficulties." Clauberg had criticized Reche on this point with particular severity, submitting that Anastasia's ear bore a certain curve and
indentation that he had been unable to locate on any photograph
of the Tsar's daughter. The reporters heard with relief, however,
that there would be no further debate. Rather, Beutler was going to
be sent to the Black Forest to lay siege and obtain new pictures of
the bothersome ear, while Professor Clauberg would leave his report for Reche's *written* consideration.

"We won't set the program for the hearing of the witnesses until
we've listened to the handwriting experts," said Judge Petersen after
the anthropologists had retired to their corners. But Carl-August
Wollmann had not finished with Clauberg, even if the court had.
When the tribunal met the following morning he asked for and obtained the floor.

"I cannot omit to repeat," said Wollmann, "that the competence
of Professor Clauberg is in grave doubt. I would like permission to

read here a letter Professor Reche has received from Dr. Ilse Schwidetzki, professor and Director of the Anthropological Institute at Mainz. These are the two essential passages: 'I know Professor Clauberg's work. It has not satisfied the German Anthropological Society. . . . One fact is indisputable, and that is the *unanimity* with which the Anthropological Society had refused to include Clauberg on its list of expert witnesses for the courts.' "

There was a moment of silence. "Why did you wait until now before bringing up such an important point?" asked Judge Petersen finally, annoyed by this first example of Wollmann's courtroom theatrics.

"It wasn't my intention to make Professor Clauberg look ridiculous," Wollmann replied innocently, "but in view of his peremptory attitude I felt I would be doing my client a disservice if I did not bring this letter to the attention of the court." [30]

When the Senate met again on April 23 it had received some unexpected news. The judges had ordered a physical examination of the plaintiff, Anastasia, in the hope that the medical experts might be able to determine the age and probable origin of the scars on her body, and to universal amazement Anastasia had agreed to it. With this heartening development the Senate turned to the evidence of Minna Becker, the court graphologist, who had been waiting now for four years to testify.

"I have never before seen two sets of handwriting," said the petite, white-haired Dr. Becker, triumphant to have finally won her moment in court, "bearing all of these concordant signs, which belonged to two different people. I have done thousands and thousands of these studies. I also know what difficulty people can have with writing after they have passed through some tragic or traumatic event. I've observed the phenomenon in adults, in children, and even in myself, having escaped from a near-fatal automobile accident this past summer.

"There remain in Mrs. Anderson's handwriting *all* of the traits that were already apparent in the handwriting of the young Anastasia. As for the Russian letters" — and here Dr. Becker glanced in the direction of Georg Dulckeit, another handwriting expert employed by the opposition to refute her testimony — "it isn't the mistakes in the language that matter. It is the *cursiveness* of the traits. . . . Mrs. Anderson's Russian script reveals a certain liveliness which is not to be found in her Latin characters. It's as though she had rediscovered her familiar climate." [31]

The questioning of Dr. Becker and her opponent, Dulckeit, went on for two days and seemed dull to the reporters in comparison with the violent "battle of the anthropologists." Dulckeit's main objection was that Anastasia, in two brief notes she had written in Russian during the 1950s, had made so many errors of grammar and structure as to preclude any Russian origins: "It was as if she had simply picked up a dictionary and copied out the words."[32] And so another of the court's language experts was called in, Dr. Bertha Weintraub, who explained that (a) Anastasia's errors were not nearly so gross as Dulckeit believed, and (b) that the Russian employed by the Tsar's daughter, in written form at least, had been little better. The court need only examine those Russian workbooks, said Dr. Weintraub.[33]

This, in fact, was the great drama of the graphological audience — when Wollmann entered the court bearing in his arms the school workbooks of the children of the Tsar, which Ian Lilburn had recovered at auction in London. Wollmann had not authorized their purchase (at five hundred pounds) merely in order to obtain new samples of Grand Duchess Anastasia's handwriting; there were plenty of those already in the court's files. Rather, he had hoped against hope that the young Grand Duchess, in haste or carelessness, might have left a smudge of ink with a fingerprint. The anonymous owner of the language workbooks, however, had refused to let anyone see them before their sale, and Wollmann had had to wait to discover that the Tsar's daughter, although she couldn't spell, was impeccably neat: there was not a mark out of place in her lessons. Still, the workbooks served a valuable and long-overdue purpose, demolishing in one blow the contention of the opposition that the Grand Duchess, as a child, had not known German. Anastasia had labored under that false claim ever since Pierre Gilliard first made it in the 1920s. Here, however, in black and white, were the lessons to prove that the Grand Duchess had studied German "in a serious manner," that her German lessons, in fact, bore fewer errors than her Russian lessons did.

It was Wollmann's idea now to submit the workbooks to another set of experts in order to find out if fingerprints might still be lifted from the pages. Berenberg-Gossler, having already lost one argument, objected on the spot, with the remark that "it is not out of the question that these books have been in the plaintiff's hands."[34] Meanwhile, the graphological experts were dismissed, not to be summoned again until July.

"There can be no mistake," Minna Becker repeated at her last audition.[35] In just one set of documents she had found "one hundred and thirty-seven identical characteristics" in the handwriting of Anastasia and the Tsar's daughter.[36] "After thirty-four years as a sworn expert for the German courts," Dr. Becker concluded, "I am ready to state on my oath and on my honor that Mrs. Anderson and Grand Duchess Anastasia are identical."[37] And when Willy Beutler, the Senate's photography expert, shortly returned victorious from Unterlengenhardt with new pictures of Anastasia's ears, he had only one remark: "What, are they crazy? Can't they see that it's the same ear? The same face? You'd have to be blind."[38]

The court had no choice but to move on to the next chapter, what Carl-August Wollmann called "The Rescue Complex."

It was unfortunate that neither Wollmann nor the judges of the Senate in Hamburg were privileged to consult the original dossier of Inspector Nicholas Sokolov concerning the murder at Ekaterinburg, which would not be tracked down in America for another eight years. If they had had it, they might have dispensed with weeks of argument on the unmistakable evidence that Grand Duchess Anastasia's escape from Russia was a moot point. As it was, however, Günther von Berenberg-Gossler continued to rely on Sokolov's edited report, published in 1924, as on an infallible oracle, using it to refute Wollmann's every argument and only occasionally, when it suited him, bringing in a witness to testify from personal experience. During the first trial, for example, Berenberg-Gossler had obtained the sworn deposition of Colonel Paul Rodzianko, who had been dispatched to Ekaterinburg in 1918 by the Empress's sister in order to search for the imperial family.[39] Rodzianko later testified that Inspector Sokolov, "one month" after the murder of the Romanovs, had shown him the very spot on the floor of the cellar where Grand Duchess Anastasia had died. Now, in May 1964, Wollmann had to undo the damage, pointing out among other things that one month after the murder of the imperial family, Sokolov had been nowhere near Ekaterinburg and thus could not have shown Rodzianko anything at all. There were dozens of these "errors" to be corrected. Wollmann proceeded to take apart the Sokolov report piece by piece — almost line by line — arguing that Sokolov's case was entirely circumstantial and that Anastasia's claim to identity could not and must not be dismissed on the grounds that the Tsar's daughter was dead. Wollmann could only wonder why the courts had not been able to grasp such a simple thing before.

The judges took their time before deciding whether or not to hear the new witnesses Wollmann had cited in his latest memorandum. They were still waiting for the results of Anastasia's medical examination, first of all, and in any case were obliged to hear the so-called intermediate pleas of the lawyers. These two, in the meantime, Wollmann and Berenberg-Gossler, were practically at each other's throats whenever they met in court. There was no longer even a pretense of civility or goodwill between them, and the judges were beginning to lose patience with the sarcastic outbursts of both.

The intermediate pleas had first been announced for September 1964 but were postponed when Wollmann came down with "a pernicious grippe" and rescheduled for February 4.[40] "Whether or not the present accumulation of evidence in the Anderson case will permit a judgment is completely open to question," said Judge Petersen when the court finally met.[41] It was Wollmann's job to convince the Senate that indeed the evidence would *not* permit a judgment, unless it were a favorable one. He spent more than seven straight hours arguing Anastasia's case, focusing on the mystery of Ekaterinburg and dismissing as presumptuous any and all witnesses who still insisted that the Tsar's daughter had been killed there.

"Killed!" Wollmann cried after an especially dramatic pause. *"How do we know that?"* [42]

The truth, said Wollmann, was that "we" did not know anything of the kind. Now, he announced, his client had left her compound in Unterlengenhardt for the first time in seven years in order to go to the hospital in Calw, where she had been examined from top to toe — literally — by the district doctors. Among the scars caused by her bouts with bone tuberculosis (which, said the doctors, might originally have been stab wounds where tuberculosis had developed) Anastasia bore, behind the right ear, a scar, "three and a half centimeters long and lengthened by a troughlike indentation into which the finger slides when touching it." On the middle finger of the left hand, after six decades, could still be seen the scar left by some "total crushing" — just what you would expect to find on a finger that had been slammed violently in a carriage door, as Anastasia claimed. Finally, through the right foot, was Wollmann's pièce de résistance: a "star-shaped" scar, which the medical experts confirmed corresponded in shape and appearance to the mark that would be left by "the triangular-pointed bayonets manufactured for the Russian army during World War I and used by the Bolsheviks during the Revolution and the Civil War." [43] If the exact origin of the other scars could no longer be determined, there was no doubt about this one: Anastasia had been stabbed in Russia.

"Why have the X-rays revealed no trace of head wounds?" Berenberg-Gossler demanded to know in his rebuttal. Why, if Anastasia was the Tsar's daughter, was her body not "larded with bayonet scars"? [44] The court should examine the report of another doctor in Calw, who gave it as "his opinion, even his belief," [45] that some of the scars on Anastasia's body could have been self-inflicted (there was an audible gasp in the courtroom).

The medical testimony went on for hours and led precisely nowhere. For every document Wollmann could produce in support of his thesis, Berenberg-Gossler could produce another in support of his. Even the dentists who examined Anastasia's few remaining teeth drew a blank, declaring that after so many years there was simply no way of telling what her teeth might once have looked like — whether they had been loosened, as Wollmann suggested, "by a blow from a rifle-butt," or simply removed in 1920 by some amazingly irresponsible dentist at the Dalldorf Asylum. And so Berenberg-Gossler moved on generally to what he called the "Romanov ballyhoo." There was more to this case, he argued, than the delusion of one aging madwoman: it had become a genuine, international "mass psychosis." [46] A little over a year ago, Berenberg-Gossler reminded the judges, echoing the summation he had delivered during the first trial, a Mrs. Eugenia Smith, from Chicago, Illinois, had made a great splash in the United States on the cover of *Life* magazine, introducing herself as Grand Duchess Anastasia and passing a lie-detector test in order to prove it. [47]

Dominique Auclères groaned aloud when she heard Mrs. Smith's name mentioned. She had been brought by *Life* to New York to meet Mrs. Smith (they had wanted Tatiana Botkin to come, but Tatiana had refused: "I already know where Anastasia is, and it isn't in New York") [48] and had returned to Paris to write an article for the *Figaro* that was a model of understated amusement. [49] It hadn't escaped Mme. Auclères's attention that this "new Anastasia" — who actually had been wandering about Europe and America for years with her claim — had achieved international prominence only at the very moment when Anastasia's case was first due to open in Hamburg, in October 1963. Then, when the trial had been postponed and rescheduled for the following April, there was suddenly a "Tsarevitch" in play — a blustering, seemingly unbalanced former KGB agent who had defected to the West and, in the words of one CIA deprogrammer, "flipped his lid." [50] Coincidence? None of the "Anastasians" thought so, and they listened in outraged silence as Berenberg-Gossler read the report of one of Hamburg's most prominent psychiatrists, who, without having met Anastasia, still affirmed that her case bore all the signs of *"pseudologia phantastica."* [51] Undoubtedly, said Berenberg-Gossler, when Anastasia finally entered "history's gallery of pathological frauds" she would find herself in excellent company.

The lawyers finished their pleas on February 7, 1965, and waited for the judges' decision. In the weeks that preceded the next session the "Anastasians" kept hard at work, getting in touch with the more than twenty new witnesses Wollmann had asked to testify at Hamburg: soldiers, diplomats, and White Army officers who had heard about Grand Duchess Anastasia's escape in 1918; several people who remembered the carriage accident at Tsarskoe Selo when the Grand Duchess's finger had been crushed; a few who had known the Grand Duchess before the Revolution and who had since recognized Anastasia; and others who were scheduled to testify about the "third complex" of the trial — the *Hessenreise,* the Grand Duke of Hesse's secret trip to Russia in 1916.[52] The Hesse trip, in fact, as the quintessential dispute of Anastasia's life, had assumed a role in the trial second only to the Ekaterinburg tragedy in importance.

In Austria, meanwhile, near Innsbrück, Wollmann and Prince Frederick had been conducting a series of clandestine "interviews" with another potential witness. It was Rudolf Lacher, an Austrian former prisoner of war in Ekaterinburg who had served in the Ipatiev house as the personal orderly to Commandant Yurovsky and who, so far as anyone could tell, was the only person left alive who had actually been in the house when the imperial family disappeared. No one in Lacher's village of Steinach knew that "the respected little burgher" among them had once participated, however peripherally, "in one of the cruelest and most moving dramas in history." [53] Said Lacher later: "I served the Bolsheviks well. I kept quiet." [54] And in fact Lacher, refusing to testify at Hamburg, had consented to see Wollmann and the Prince only on the condition that he not be named, cited, or otherwise identified *even by nationality,* so deeply he feared for his reputation and for his life should the Soviets get wind of his whereabouts. It hardly seemed to matter, in the end, for Lacher insisted that "he had seen nothing, heard nothing, and knew nothing" [55] about the last hours of the imperial family. Yurovsky had locked him into his basement room that night and had only released him the next day. He had no information whatever about the fate of the youngest Grand Duchess.

"Ask your client if she remembers Rudolf," said Lacher as Wollmann left. "And good luck." [56] Then Lacher had a thought: "If these can be of any use to you . . ." [57] He opened a box containing various articles that had belonged to the imperial family — a gold case, a handkerchief or two, and a small cigarette holder, shaped like a tobacco pipe. It had belonged to the Tsar.

Wollmann's thoughts went back to the notes Harriet von Rathlef had taken so long ago at the Mommsen Clinic, when Anastasia first met Baron "Willy" Osten-Sacken and had become so agitated because he was smoking "Papa's pipe." Now the chain was linked: the Tsar's pipe and Baron Osten-Sacken's were identical. In great excitement Wollmann rushed to Unterlengenhardt to show his find to Anastasia, but she, far from being impressed, merely took the thing in her hands, turned it over several times, handed it back, and said, "My father's pipe was darker than that." [58]

It wasn't long before Dominique Auclères had gotten to the bottom of this particular mystery. In Paris she located J. Sommer, one of the jewelers' firms that had fashioned Nicholas II's cigarette holders before World War I. It turned out that the Tsar had commissioned seven identical pipes from various precious materials.

"Were there any in black?" asked Mme. Auclères.

"Certainly, some were in onyx." The last to be manufactured at Sommer, in fact, had been crafted out of dark amber. That was the pipe the Tsar had last used, and that was the pipe, evidently, that Anastasia remembered. [59]

She did not remember "Rudolf." The closest anyone came to rousing her memories of the Ipatiev house was when Wollmann mentioned the name of Paul Medvedev, Commandant Yurovsky's chief henchman, and Anastasia let loose what appeared to be a small shriek of terror. [60] That name was never to be spoken in her presence again.

On June 10, 1965, the Senate in Hamburg announced that the "Anastasia" debates would continue and that all the new witnesses would be heard. "How long we will have to wait for a decision on the actual question concerned in this trial," said Klaus Wagner in the *Frankfurter Allgemeine,* "remains to be seen." [61]

The citizens of Unterlengenhardt began to notice an ominous change in Anastasia during the summer of 1965.[62] Two of her dogs had died, and instead of replacing them she had turned to cats — dozens of them. They ran about everywhere, fouling the premises, chewing the crops, and generally beginning to cause a public nuisance. Only rarely now did Anastasia admit even one of her devoted ladies to the "dacha," preferring to keep herself entirely to herself and allowing the new house to deteriorate as badly as the barracks had done. She had taken to sleeping on her sofa, giving the master bed to the cats. She spread newspapers on the floor, and after the cats had messed them up sufficiently she tossed the dirty paper onto an extraordinary "compost heap" that steamed in her backyard. When Wollmann or Prince Frederick came to call, she usually left them standing on the front porch while she spoke to them, if at all, from the window or the door. All the while she kept talking about going back to America. Gleb Botkin had written her from his new home in Charlottesville, Virginia, that "everything was arranged," and that a Southern gentleman of his acquaintance, a Dr. Manahan, had agreed to pay for her trip.

For years Anastasia had been conducting an extensive, friendly, often funny, but — for the purposes of the trial — devastating correspondence with Gleb Botkin. Anastasia, of course, was willing to believe the worst about anyone, and in her letters to Gleb she did not hesitate to express her opinions.[63] "The Baroness Miltitz, Miss Mayhoff, Miss Lamerdin, and Prince Frederick have lost their reason," she might say. ". . . The judge they have sent to a sanatorium. He is really insane . . . . Every letter from you goes to Madame Auclair [sic] and what she does with your letters — I don't care to think about. . . . It is no human life here anymore. . . . One wants to force me that I shall see again television people — French, Italian and German. Not very agreeable. Since many weeks I am fighting against this. The Baroness Miltitz has already arranged, it shall be done as soon as the weather is warmer and more friendly. . . . I was hoping that they would leave me in rest now. And now it shall go on again. You can imagine how troubled I am about this."

Ordinarily Anastasia closed her letters to Gleb with a quick, "Now good-bye! For today, enough of this terrible dirt." The extent of Gleb Botkin's influence was made plain in July 1964, when Anastasia, in one of the last of the "confrontations," met Alexander Nikititch Romanov, a grandson of the Tsar's sister Xenia and of

Grand Duke Alexander — in other words, a man born to "the opposition."

Prince Alexander was a good friend of Ian Lilburn in London. Lilburn, having entered the "Anastasia" dispute "with a strictly hostile attitude," had since switched sides completely and was now "absolutely convinced" of Anastasia's authenticity.[64] Naturally Alexander was slower to come around, and indeed he never lost his attitude of extreme caution toward the affair. "I asked him if he would like to pay her a visit," Lilburn remembered later, "and he replied very modestly that he could well understand it if she refused to see him."[65] On July 6, nevertheless, Alexander, with Lilburn and Prince Frederick, arrived in Unterlengenhardt to meet Anastasia. The trio had hoped to take her by surprise, and they succeeded. Sitting in the garden when Alexander came through the gate, Anastasia took one look at him, leaped from her chair and rushed into the dacha, bolting the door and crying to Prince Frederick, "That can only be a descendant of Grand Duke Alexander. I recognize him by his oceanlike walk."

Eventually Anastasia was coaxed outside for tea and chatted with Prince Alexander for about two hours. Later Alexander explained that she had reminded him in her appearance of his grandmother, Grand Duchess Xenia, and in her manner of his "Aunt Irina," Princess Yussoupov.[66] But since Alexander had not been born until long after the Revolution, he had no way and no intention of taking a public stand on the matter. He caught a plane from Stuttgart after tea with Anastasia and that night went to dinner with Earl Mountbatten of Burma in London.

Lord Mountbatten, in the opinion of many, had taken over from the late Grand Duke of Hesse as the villain in Anastasia's story and had put up the money for the battle against her in court. Few people, indeed, were unaware that Lord Mountbatten, Empress Alexandra's nephew and the de facto leader of the House of Hesse, had become the guiding force behind Anastasia's opposition. As one of the original defendants in Anastasia's first suit before the Berlin courts, he had made a point of soliciting testimony against her from witnesses in England[67] and when the BBC planned a documentary on the case, Mountbatten quickly had it squelched.[68] Later he admitted publicly that the "Anastasia" controversy had cost him "thousands of pounds." Now Gleb Botkin could not dismiss the notion that all of Anastasia's royal opponents were taking their orders from Mountbatten, and that Prince Alexander, in particular, had been forbidden to testify in Anastasia's behalf and had been sent to Unterlengenhardt as a spy. In reality, Alexander had done what little he could to influence his family gently in Anastasia's favor — or at least into neutrality — "but was merely asked how he could be so 'stupid' as to imagine that people such as Baroness Buxhoeveden and Pierre Gilliard could possibly have lied. He spoke to his uncles [the Princes] Andrew and Dmitri, but he might just as well have been talking at a stone wall." [69]

After this particular comedy of errors had played itself out, Gleb Botkin stepped up his campaign against the Hamburg Senate, advising Anastasia not to cooperate with "a kangaroo court, . . . determined to rule against you," [70] and warning her to be careful about whom she admitted to the dacha in the future. Ian Lilburn was selected to right the balance, telling Gleb that "the position has never looked better in the whole long and tragic history of the case"; that "the tribunal is entirely objective and fair"; and that Anastasia's friends would "have to pull together." [71] But the advice, not for the first time, was rejected.

The Senate met again in Hamburg on July 27 in order to hear the testimony of two capital witnesses. One was a high-ranking German Communist who claimed to have learned from the Bolshevik hierarchy that Grand Duchess Anastasia was dead. The other was a master tailor from Vienna who claimed to have seen the Grand Duchess alive after the massacre at Ekaterinburg.

Erich Wollenberg, seventy-two years of age, had been born in Königsberg and, for a time, was the editor of the *Rote Fahne* in Berlin.[72] An early and "old-style" leader of the German Communist Party, he had gone to the Soviet Union for military training and had stayed there as a member of the Comintern until Stalin's purges began to annihilate the ranks of the main-line Bolsheviks. In 1929, however, before returning to Germany, Wollenberg had been posted to Siberia. There he had encountered "the murderer of the Tsar" [73] (he meant Alexander Beloborodov, the leader of the Ural Regional Soviet), who had assured him that all of the Russian imperial family was dead and that the then "Frau Tschaikovsky," as everyone knew, was really the Polish factory worker, Franziska Schanzkowska.

Even the judges shook their heads on hearing the last remark,[74] but Wollenberg's testimony had just begun. The Soviet regime, he declared, had employed the "Anastasia" affair during the 1920s as a means to divide the Russian monarchists and, through Europe's nobility, to infiltrate "the Western High Command." [75] A Russian grand duke, said Wollenberg, known in Moscow as "Uncle Paul," had worked to that end as an agent *for* the Soviets. It quickly became apparent that the grand duke in question, the "Romanov spy," was meant to be Grand Duke Andrew, the only one of the grand dukes to have acknowledged Anastasia as his niece.

The testimony, as Ian Lilburn said, was "quite appalling in its implications." [76] Lilburn had been listening to Wollenberg with a mixture of fascination and pure revulsion. "He was a repugnant person," Lilburn wrote, "and extremely conceited, whose very presence made everyone's hair stand on end." But the testimony was one of the most sensational to date. "She Was a Red Agent!" the tabloid headlines proclaimed, [77] greatly exciting the German housewives who followed the course of Anastasia's trial as religiously as they checked prices. Wollenberg went on to say that he had met the Russian Grand Duke, this "Uncle Paul," in Moscow in 1925; that the Grand Duke had been "somewhat smaller than himself, with a pointed beard and a very elastic walk"; that he was a cousin of the Tsar and a friend of the King of England, with a mistress in the south of France; that his family had believed him to be in Egypt at the time of his mission to Moscow; and that he had been instructed by the Soviets to "recognize" Anastasia. [78]

"Are you sure it wasn't the other way around?" asked Wollmann when he had secured permission to interrogate the witness. [79]

"What do you mean?"

"Are you sure this grand duke was not instructed to *deny* that my client was Anastasia?" The effect would have been no different if the goal were to divide the monarchists.

Wollenberg confessed that he couldn't be sure.

Which one of the grand dukes was it? Wollmann asked.

Again Wollenberg couldn't be sure — "but . . . Dr. von Berenberg-Gossler had said that it was probably Grand Duke Andrew."

The judges looked at Berenberg-Gossler.

"I would recognize a photograph," said Wollenberg.

Anastasia's lawyer had already foreseen the possibility. With Ian Lilburn's help he had prepared a chart bearing photographs of all eight of the Russian grand dukes who had been alive in 1925 (some of them depicted twice), along with those of four others who were dead. Wollenberg was "taken by surprise," Lilburn remembered, "and before he had time to think, his finger went straight to the bottom lefthand corner of the chart." [80]

"Obviously he got the wrong one," Klaus Wagner wrote, "because the Anderson party [were] all laughing."[81] In fact Wollenberg's finger had landed next to a photograph of Grand Duke Alexander, the author of the Copenhagen Statement of 1928 and one of Anastasia's most determined opponents. Was it possible, Ian Lilburn wondered in a letter to the Grand Duke's namesake, Prince Alexander, that this was the elusive "Uncle Paul," with the "elastic walk" and the mistress in France? "I need only add, perhaps," Lilburn wrote, "that in the German translation of the second volume of his memoirs . . . Grand Duke Alexander mentions . . . that he was in Cairo in 1925. Please note also the present plaintiff's recognition of *your* 'oceanlike' walk, which she said reminded her of Grand Duke Alexander."[82]

"Maybe Grand Duke Andrew was wearing a false beard," Berenberg-Gossler suggested lamely · before Wollenberg was dismissed.[83] Erich Wollenberg's testimony, in any case, had boomeranged.

Next came the deposition of Heinrich Kleibenzetl, "the little Viennese tailor" who, as another prisoner of war in Ekaterinburg, claimed to have seen Grand Duchess Anastasia, wounded but alive, after the murder of her family.[84] Dominique Auclères had already interviewed Kleibenzetl for the *Figaro* and had thereby been able to answer the question everybody was asking: why had Kleibenzetl waited so long before coming forward with his story?

In fact Kleibenzetl hadn't: he had already told a friend in Vienna about it in 1923.[85] But as Kleibenzetl added in his Viennese dialect, "When you've seen the Revolution, you'd rather keep your mouth shut." Kleibenzetl hadn't even mentioned the matter to his first wife.

"Is she dead?"

"No, but she drank too much, I got rid of her. . . . It wasn't till 1958, when I read all the nonsense they were saying about Anastasia, that I went to my second wife and said, 'Hey, they're crazy! I *saw* Anastasia, me, on the night of the murder.' After I'd told her about it, she said, 'Heini,' that's what she said, 'Heini, you can't keep quiet anymore.' "

At Hamburg Heinrich Kleibenzetl produced his identity and work papers, which demonstrated that he had indeed lived in Ekaterinburg in July 1918; in fact, that he had been an apprentice to the tailor Baoudin in a building directly opposite the Ipatiev house. Kleibenzetl had been the one who repaired the uniforms of the soldiers guarding the imperial family. In that capacity he had often had to go into the house to fetch and deliver clothing, and had frequently seen the members of the family walking in the enclosed courtyard. He had never spoken a word to any one of them. One evening, however, a friend of Kleibenzetl's in the guard had come over to the Baoudins' to say that "something [was] happening." Kleibenzetl was curious. He had entered the courtyard carrying some uniforms: "The guards knew me, they didn't ask any questions, they were drinking." Kleibenzetl had hidden behind some boxes and suddenly heard gunshots, screams, and a single female cry: "Mamma!"

" 'Heini,' I says, 'they're shooting people; if they find you they'll shoot you too.' " Quickly he had slipped out of the yard and spent about an hour and a half walking around the town. When he got back home his landlady, Anna Baoudin, was boiling water and told him not to go up to his room. He would have to spend the night on the ironing board.

"Great," said Kleibenzetl, noticing that "Frau Annouchka" kept running up and down the stairs.

"What's going on here?" he finally asked, and she told him: "I'm making tea."

There was a silence. Then: "Oh, never mind, we can trust you. It's Anastasia, the Grand Duchess, she's in your room. She's wounded, I'm trying to get her to drink some tea."

"I'll help you," said Kleibenzetl. He had gone upstairs with Anna Baoudin where, in his bed, he recognized "one of the women" he had seen walking in the courtyard of the Ipatiev house: "The lower part of her body was covered with blood, her eyes were shut and she was pale as a sheet. We washed her chin, Frau Annouchka and me, then she groaned. The bones must have been broken. . . . Then she opened her eyes for a minute."

The "Grand Duchess," Kleibenzetl went on, had remained at the Baoudin house for three days: "The first day the Red guards came, but they knew us too well to search the house. They went like this: 'Anastasia's disappeared, but she's not here, that's for sure.' We were scared, but they didn't come back. . . . The third day a Red guard came to get her, one of the same men who had brought her, Frau Annouchka said. And that was it. The Whites came, then the Reds came back. . . . That was it."

Heinrich Kleibenzetl was questioned at Hamburg for more than six hours, and, said Ian Lilburn, "gave such a good account of himself that even Dr. von Berenberg-Gossler treated him with sincere courtesy." [86] Try as they would, the judges could not find a hole in Kleibenzetl's story. When they asked him to describe the Ipatiev house and its environs, Kleibenzetl complied without hesitation, even drawing a map of the grounds. Klaus Wagner observed that his memory for detail was "flabbergasting." [87] Only when the lawyers began their arguments, after Kleibenzetl's departure, did things begin to fall apart. It was hot, and tempers were fraying. Before hearing Kleibenzetl's oral testimony Berenberg-Gossler had been content to dismiss him as an opportunist and "a little Austro-Marxist." Now, however, after Kleibenzetl's manifestly successful audition, the master tailor had become "a psychopath . . . not normal mentally."

Wollmann snorted: "He's only the latest on a long and distinguished list, where he joins the German Kaiser and the Crown Princess of Prussia!" [88]

The sessions closed with an announcement that the police experts could not lift fingerprints from Grand Duchess Anastasia's recovered school workbooks without destroying the documents, and that in any case there could be no guarantee that such fingerprints would still exist. The court would have to plunge ahead on its own. "And so," said Klaus Wagner, "after the surprise testimony . . . of the master tailor . . . one is, if not wiser, at least more certain that in this monster trial anything is possible." [89]

The trial was suspended till the autumn.

On September 16, 1965, Judge Bäthge and Irene Neander, the Senate's Russian-language expert, arrived at the town hall in Unterlengenhardt for the meeting Wollmann had promised them would take place with Anastasia that day.[90] Actually, she hadn't agreed to it yet. "It was an absolute nightmare trying to persuade her that the whole performance was necessary . . . ," wrote Ian Lilburn, who had come with Wollmann, Prince Frederick, and Princess Marianne for the occasion. "Princess Marianne drove down from Herleshausen (near Kassel) three times in two weeks, and was a tower of strength. As she is by birth a princess of Prussia, and Herr Wollmann is a very monarchist and patriotic East Prussian, he was furious with his client for making a member of 'his' Royal Family wait around ('antechambrieren') sometimes for hours." [91] Nobody had dared to tell Anastasia that a test of her knowledge of Russian was supposed to take place. She thought she was simply going to meet the judge, as she had done in 1959, and on that understanding, at the eleventh hour, she agreed.

Just before the hearing was due to begin Prince Frederick asked to speak with Judge Bäthge. Anastasia, he explained, would never cooperate if she had to deal with Berenberg-Gossler, the lawyer for the opposition. "If he is there," she had warned the Prince, "I will call him a *durak* (an 'ass')!" [92] Bäthge was willing to waive the regulations so far as to forbid both of the lawyers to participate in the hearing, but he insisted that they remain in the room.

At 12:10, "very much agitated," Anastasia arrived.[93] Immediately she spotted Berenberg-Gossler. "In spite that Mr. Wollmann had sworn to me that this man shall not be there," she wrote Gleb Botkin when it was all over, "he *was* there, sitting in a corner. I pointed with the finger and told loud: 'Is that not Berenberg-Gossler?' Mr. Wollmann ran at once to him and took him out."

With Berenberg-Gossler gone, Wollmann was obliged to leave, too. Anastasia was still furious: "I mean, Mr. Berenberg-Gossler is a playboy . . . and a copy of Yussoupov when he was young. . . . You can believe me, everybody fell in love with him." [94]

The test began before Anastasia had time to object. "She was questioned in Russian for 1½ hours," wrote Ian Lilburn, "and although she insisted on answering the questions in English, she occasionally used a few Russian words. . . . Herr Bäthge and Frau Neander could not have been more patient." [95] At last Bäthge brought out a book of Russian poetry and asked Anastasia to read from it aloud.

Anastasia had forgotten her glasses. Prince Frederick gave her his to wear, which she balanced on her nose with her one good arm while endeavoring at the same time to hold the book. It was useless. She put the thing down and asked Judge Bäthge, "Are you married to this nice lady?" [96]

Bäthge laughed. He had never participated in anything like this before, and now, on the chance that it would help Anastasia relax, he began to sing Russian songs to her ("which must surely," said Ian Lilburn, "be the first time that a High Court judge has been heard to sing during a hearing").[97] Dr. Neander kept prodding her with questions in Russian — "Have you ever heard of a poet called Lermontov?" [98] — while Prince Frederick encouraged her in English and Princess Marianne spoke to her quietly in English and German at once. Dazed, Anastasia finally fell silent altogether.

When the session had concluded at one-forty, Anastasia wanted to know when the questions were going to begin — about the case, she meant. But there weren't going to be any. The Russian expert had evidently found out, or not found out, whatever it was she needed to know. Judge Bäthge, Lilburn explained, "only happened to be present when [Anastasia] was examined by the Russian expert. In other words, her official meeting with her judges is apparently still to come. . . . That is perhaps an encouraging sign: It seems to show at least that Herr Bäthge was not immediately convinced that she was a Polish factory-worker. Poor Prince Frederick, however, is showing signs of collapse, and would give his eye-teeth not to have to go through the whole ordeal again." [99]

In Unterlengenhardt, meanwhile, Anastasia had entered a slow burn. "Just this moment Miss Thomasius brought me journals," she wrote Gleb Botkin several weeks later.[100] "Where I was photographed, when I was here to the Town Hall. A monkey — I am looking so foolish. . . . Mr. Wollmann and Prince Frederick had promised me that under no condition I would be photographed and made to look ridiculous. I have been made officially ridiculous." [101]

Since Wollmann was obviously so ill, Anastasia continued, "the Baroness Miltitz and Prince Frederick are therefore looking for other lawyers. And this of course I don't want anymore to permit. . . . I never liked that this was done in Hamburg. . . . I want the lawyer for myself and not for Prince Frederick and the Baroness Miltitz. And I have taken the necessary steps in this direction. I have chosen a *woman* lawyer."

She never explained what she was talking about, and soon returned to the greater concerns of her forest kingdom. "Here has been a very hard and sudden winter again," she wrote Gleb at the end of the year. "Many trees are hurt." [102]

At Bremen, in camera, the Senate heard Princess Kyra Kyrilovna of Russia, the eldest child of the late Grand Duke Kyril and Grand Duchess Victoria.[103] Kyra had met Anastasia only briefly in 1952 at the behest of her mother-in-law, Cecilie of Prussia (Kyra had married Prince Louis-Ferdinand, the pretender to the German throne). Although her testimony was strictly negative, Wollmann, too, had wanted Kyra to be heard. He wanted her to explain to the court why she had kept up such a friendly correspondence with Anastasia's attorneys for so many years; why she had discussed with them the possibility of acknowledging Anastasia in order to present "a united front" to the Bank of England. He wanted Kyra to tell the judges what her uncle, Grand Duke Andrew, had tried to do the last time they met before the Grand Duke's death in 1956.

"He tried to convince me," said Kyra reluctantly.[104] But she had never taken the case seriously herself. No, it had been obvious that the woman was an impostor.

And how would Kyra know that? Wollmann asked. She had been seven years old at the time of the Revolution. Before that, her parents had been banished from Russia after marrying against the Tsar's orders. "Isn't it true," said Wollmann, "that your mother-in-law, the [former] Crown Princess, introduced you to my client?"

"Yes."

"Isn't it true that she did it with the words, 'That is your cousin'?"

"That's correct."

"And what did you think of her after the little tête-à-tête you had?"

"That she was repellent. That she was not a lady. That she spoke a Slavic-tainted English, Polish, maybe, or Czech, but not the English used in the family."

"And your mother-in-law, the Crown Princess — did she speak this 'family English'?"

"Yes, that goes without saying."

"Well then, don't you think she might have noticed before you did that the plaintiff had neither the language ability nor the manner of a Russian Grand Duchess?"

"Well, there can be differences of opinion. Besides, my mother-in-law wasn't well at the time." [105]

Prince Frederick — "friendly, patient Prince Frederick" [106] — was beginning to be angry. He had heard all about the Crown Princess's "failing health" and "drifting wits" at the time of her recognition of Anastasia. He'd heard about her "loose morals," too, just as he'd heard for years that all of Anastasia's supporters had some kind of blot on their record.[107] Prince Frederick himself had obtained the Crown Princess's handwritten affidavit, at the bottom of which her son, Louis-Ferdinand, had had the cheek to scrawl the words: "Kyra and I find *no* resemblance." [108] For once the Prince was glad when Wollmann, in embarrassing detail, began to describe the terrible relations that had existed between Nicholas and Alexandra and Kyra's parents, and when he reminded the judges of Grand Duke Kyril's desertion of the Tsar at the outbreak of the Revolution.

"What good is all this doing?" asked Kyra's husband.[109]

Wollmann had warned the court, had he not? The opposition must be ready to take as good as it gave.

Two days later the press had flocked again to Hamburg to hear

the deposition of Prince Dmitri Galitzin, an elderly Russian émigré
who had come from Paris to testify. The reporters invariably returned to the Palace of Justice when royalty and nobility took the
stand. "All those moth-eaten princes," as Gleb Botkin called them,[110]
lent an air of glamour and romance to the trial and more than compensated for the crashing dullness of the judges' ordinary routine.
The testimony of Prince Galitzin served as a vivid reminder of the
world which hung as a backdrop to the trial but which was frequently obscured by the mound of yellowing protocols and the bar-
rage of expert opinion — the vanished world of imperial Russia.

The court had begun to examine the evidence for and against
Anastasia's claim that the Empress's brother, the Grand Duke of
Hesse, had come to see her parents in Russia during World War I.
"If you can bring me somebody who actually saw the Grand Duke
at the train station in Tsarskoe Selo . . . ," Berenberg-Gossler had
said to Wollmann, "and gave him a light, then I'll acknowledge that
he really did make the trip, with all the consequences that would
have for your client."[111] Now, through Dominique Auclères, Wollmann had found his witness. In 1963 Mme. Auclères had been giving a lecture about Anastasia in Paris when Prince Galitzin, con-
gratulating her on a fascinating evening, remarked offhandedly that
he himself had seen the Grand Duke at the palace in Tsarskoe Selo.

"I couldn't believe my ears," said Mme. Auclères.[112] She had
wanted to grab Galitzin by the collar and whistle for the police, but
instead she smiled and asked if he would care to testify at Hamburg.

"Why not?" the Prince replied.

Mme. Auclères explained that she had already met a number of
Russian exiles — seven, to be exact — who knew about the Grand
Duke's "secret" trip but who did not want to do anything that might
be interpreted as support for "that woman."

"I will testify because it is the truth," said Galitzin.[113] At Hamburg, the first surprise came when the Prince asked for permission
to depose in French.

"Why do you want to do that?" asked Wollmann with a knowing smile.

"Because I am more at ease in that language."

"Have you forgotten your Russian?" asked Judge Petersen.

"No, but when I speak Russian I always translate from English
and French; the words don't come to me automatically. I might
make a mistake."[114]

The point was not lost in a trial that had turned the Russian language into a sacred cow. In French, then, Prince Galitzin told his story.[115]

The Prince had been mobilized in 1914 and shortly afterward had suffered shell shock in the field. After that, he had been put to work for Vladimir Vladimirovitch von Mekk, former private secretary to the Empress's sister, Grand Duchess Elisabeth, and now the director of the Empress's relief services. "We were at Tsarskoe Selo twice in 1916," said Galitzin, "once in the spring and once in the autumn. During one of these trips I was waiting for Mekk in a large corridor at the Alexander Palace, while he gave his report to the Empress, when suddenly I saw a gentleman in civilian dress come in rather furtively and then disappear through another door."

"You were struck by his dress?" asked the judge.

"Yes, at a time when everybody was in uniform."

A little later, Galitzin went on, Mekk had returned and asked "with a faintly worried air" if he had seen anybody go by.

Yes, Galitzin had replied: "Who is it?"

"That's none of your affair," said Mekk. But "that same evening — or maybe the next day, I can't be sure after forty-nine years — when I came back to the subject, he put his finger to his lips and told me that it was the Empress's brother, the Grand Duke of Hesse, whom I had seen in the corridor. He told me again to keep quiet about it. That was an order."

"When did this take place?" asked Judge Petersen.

"In 1916, maybe in the autumn."

Wollmann rose: "In a letter I have here the witness says that it was at the beginning of the year."

"We've got to know if it was spring or if it was autumn," said Berenberg-Gossler. "The witness doesn't seem to be sure."

Prince Galitzin was not interested in arguing with the lawyer for the Duchess of Mecklenburg. "If I wrote that letter," he replied loftily, "and signed it, and said it was at the beginning of the year, then it was at the beginning of the year. There's nothing to discuss."

Berenberg-Gossler did what he could now to take the wind out of Prince Galitzin's sails.[116] Perhaps the gentleman he had seen at Tsarskoe Selo was the American YMCA representative who had come over to Russia around that time to discuss the treatment of prisoners with the Empress.

Galitzin stared at him.

Perhaps Vladimir von Mekk had made a mistake.

Galitzin laughed: Mekk had been Grand Duchess Elisabeth's secretary and had accompanied the Grand Duchess on any number of
visits to her brother in Darmstadt.

Perhaps Mekk had been joking.

Galitzin stared again. Finally he turned to Judge Petersen: "If I
am not going to be believed, I should not have been called." [117]

"Why have you waited so long before coming forward with this
story?" asked Berenberg-Gossler, not ready to give up. [118]

Prince Galitzin replied that in the 1920s, at the time of Anastasia's greatest notoriety, he had been living in Turkey. Later, when
he returned to Europe, he hadn't realized how important the matter
was.

And how had Galitzin come to realize that the matter *was* so
important?

He had read about it in the newspapers.

"Yes, but how did you come in contact with the Hamburg tribunal? Somebody must have alerted you."

All eyes turned to Dominique Auclères, who sat behind Prince
Frederick calmly taking notes. "This was not the first time Berenberg-
Gossler had tried to involve me in the trial," she wrote. ". . . But
Prince Galitzin was no dupe."

Yes, Prince Galitzin answered, somebody had "alerted" him.

Who had?

"A *lady*," said Galitzin, looking at Berenberg-Gossler as though
he were some noxious insect.

That was as far as this line of questioning went. When Prince
Galitzin returned to Paris his Russian émigré landlady threw him
out of his apartment. "So much fuss over a testimony!" he exclaimed. [119] ". . . Perhaps if they'd all told the truth we might have
settled this affair a long time ago." [120]

Two months later it was the opposition's turn to address the subject of "the Hesse trip." Berenberg-Gossler had employed an expert
historian from the University of Hamburg, Professor Egmont Zechlin, who took the stand now and produced in evidence letters, diaries, notebooks, and timetables from the private archives at Darmstadt. These, Zechlin maintained, could prove that the Grand Duke
of Hesse had never left his troops on the Western Front during the
first months of 1916 and thus could never had taken the disputed
trip to Russia. Not that the Grand Duke would have dreamed of
doing such a thing in the first place, Zechlin continued: he had already been "badly compromised" by his tentative efforts to estab-

lish negotiations for a separate peace with Russia and would never have risked further embarrassment. Argument was superfluous, in any case, because the documents could account for the Grand Duke's whereabouts at all times.

The ensuing debates about the Grand Duke's Russian trip were fully as lengthy and involved as any that had gone before. Wollmann was not impressed even by the Grand Duke's letters to his wife in the spring of 1916, which Zechlin had recovered at Darmstadt and which still bore postmarks from France. The very fact that they *did* bear postmarks was grounds for suspicion, said Wollmann, because the Grand Duke ordinarily sent his letters home by personal courier. It stood to reason that he would have established some kind of cover before embarking on the trip to Russia: letters and diary entries were as good as any. "In all I reckon on nine days," the Grand Duke had written his wife mysteriously on February 20, 1916, "three for the first thing, three for the new, and then three to the end." [121] If the Grand Duke had been with his troops at the end of February, Wollmann asked, how could anyone explain what he had written about the final stages of the siege of Douaumont, when, in the space of three days, he lost six hundred men of his own bodyguard regiment, many of them his personal friends? "All is going well," the Grand Duke remarked on February 24, after three hundred had been killed. And on the same day, in his diary: ". . . if only the losses are not too heavy." Then on the twenty-fifth, the Grand Duke was still "satisfied, because everything is going so well." [122]

Consider the letters of Empress Alexandra, Wollmann went on. In February 1916 the Tsar had been with his family for the opening of the Duma. He had just returned to GHQ at Moghilev when suddenly, for no apparent reason and to'the Empress's obvious surprise, he came back to Tsarskoe Selo: "What joy! On Thursday you will be home, it is truly heavenly news." [123] But when the Tsar once again returned to the front the Empress's joy had faded. In her next letter she spoke of "worry without end" and closed with a remark which, in context, made no sense: "The good will come and you are patient and will be blessed, I feel so sure, only much to be gone through still. When I think what the 'losses' of lives mean to yr. heart — I can imagine Ernie's suffering now. Oh this hideously bloody war!" [124]

Why "Ernie"? asked Wollmann quietly. And why "now"? "Because, I submit, the Empress and the Tsar had just seen the Grand

Duke at Tsarskoe Selo." Look in the Grand Duke's field diaries, said Wollmann, his voice rising: "You will find that for the whole period between January 27 and April 1, 1916, the Grand Duke is recorded as being 'In the field, near Verdun,' nothing more precise than that." [125]

"That's false," said Professor Zechlin. [126]

"That's true," said Prince Frederick, handing copies to the judge.

"*I* am the historian," Zechlin grumbled. The debate, as was happening more and more frequently, had become heated and ugly, until the lawyers for both parties were yelling in open court.

"You tell me," Wollmann shouted at Professor Zechlin, "if the Grand Duke himself were to rise from the grave, walk into this room and say, 'You're wrong, this trip *did* take place' — would you tell him that he was *mistaken?*"

"Yes!" cried Berenberg-Gossler, out of turn, and after the court had recovered from its surprise Professor Zechlin turned back to Wollmann and answered, "Yes. I would say, 'Yes, Your Highness, because the documents say it did not.'" [127]

The Wingender sisters were back. Having agreed to reopen the debates on "the Schanzkowska complex," the judges of the Senate proceeded to listen to the witnesses with a boredom they made no effort to conceal. "The tribunal didn't really take the Schanzkowska business very much to heart," Ian Lilburn remembered. [128] After an initial hearing in Hamburg, Judge Petersen had moved the court to West Berlin for Doris Wingender's final deposition. "This time," Wollmann said, "'Frau Doris Rittmann-Wingender is *not* going to escape. When she has finished testifying I'm going to demand that she take the oath. She's either going to perjure herself, and I'm going to prove it, or she's going to have to retract." [129]

There were no unexpected revelations in the audience that followed; for once, the Schanzkowska story had not changed by so much as a comma. Louise Wingender, whom Lilburn called "the gentler one," did confide to several reporters in the hallway that she was tired of it all: "We had no idea it would go this far." As for Doris, she wasn't up to form. She broke down under Wollmann's attack, sobbing out loud and crying, "I can't anymore! I have the flu!" [130]

Wollmann would not let up. He had located a copy of *Die Woche,* the Berlin magazine in which, said Doris, she had first recognized Franziska Schanzkowksa in a photograph of Anastasia.

"In *this* photograph?" Wollmann asked.[131]

"Yes."

"And it was on seeing *this* picture that you went off to the *Nachtausgabe?*"

"Yes. I don't feel well."

"And it was *this* picture which allowed you to conclude that the invalid at Castle Seeon . . . was your Polish girl?"

"*Yes.*"

"I suppose the fifteen hundred marks weren't going to be paid unless you made an identification."

"Correct. As soon as the identification was made."

Wollmann handed the magazine to the judges. The photograph of Anastasia's face, they saw, was little more than a smudge of ink — a white blob with two black circles for eyes and another where the mouth was supposed to be.

"Why," said Judge Bäthge, "from that you could recognize anybody or nobody."[132]

Doris got the point. Dominique Auclères observed that she had gone "as white as the wall."

"I'm sick!" she cried. "I've got the flu!"

"A chair for my witness!" cried Berenberg-Gossler.

"You're going to take the oath," said Judge Petersen to Doris.

"I can't. I can't tonight! Take my pulse."

"Well," said Mme. Auclères, "a judge isn't a hangman, after all." Wollmann was furious: "I want that oath given and given now!"

Bäthge tried to calm him: "She'll be given the oath later by one of the Berlin magistrates."

"*Now!*"

While they were arguing Doris Wingender slipped from the room. She never came back. And that, for all intents and purposes, was the end of the legend of Franziska Schanzkowska.

The trial was almost suspended permanently in January 1966, when Wollmann, in an unprecedented move, accused Judge Bäthge of bias and asked that he be removed from the tribunal. The occasion was a closed hearing,[133] meant to be a secret, held in Göttingen for the sworn deposition of Rudolf Lacher, the Austrian orderly from the Ipatiev house. Berenberg-Gossler, too, had tracked Lacher down, and had advised him that West Germany enjoyed a reciprocal agreement with the Republic of Austria that enabled him to insist on Lacher's testimony. To the horror of the "Anastasians,"

Lacher was now swearing that on the night of the murder of the imperial family, from the window of his room, he had counted "eleven bloody bundles" which he took to be the bodies of the Romanovs and their servants. "Eleven, mind you," said Dominique Auclères. It was Hans-Johann Mayer all over again, only this time the testimony came from a witness whose credentials were rather better.

Mme. Auclères wasn't supposed to be in Göttingen when Lacher was heard. She wasn't even supposed to know about it. The only people authorized to attend the hearing were Lacher, the two lawyers, Prince Frederick, and Judge Bäthge, who had come from Hamburg as a one-man rogatory commission. While Lacher gave his evidence, however, Mme. Auclères and Ian Lilburn lurked guiltily in the hall outside, pressing their ears against the doors "and pretending to be potted plants" [134] whenever anyone went by.

Lacher's testimony was a grisly experience. He was a cold man, Wollmann reported later, "cold as ice," who talked with a total lack of expression in his voice of the sight of the Tsar's four daughters being hurried down the staircase on the night of the murder, sobbing as they went and clutching each other. What did he care what had happened to them? asked Lacher: "They weren't my relatives." [135] Lacher had no information to give about the circumstances of the assassination, because, as he had said, he had been locked in his room by Commandant Yurovsky; he had been able to see the family at all only by peering through the keyhole. Later, however, after he heard the sound of gunfire, Lacher had stepped onto the bed in his basement room and looked out the window into the courtyard, where he saw the "bloody bundles" [136] — bodies wrapped in sheets — being piled onto a truck. And counted them.

"It isn't possible," Wollmann exclaimed after the session had ended. "It just isn't possible." [137] He stayed up all night that night, going over his photographs and his maps of the Ipatiev house, reading and rereading the Sokolov report and the testimony of the Red guards in Ekaterinburg. "He could *not* have seen out that window," Wollmann insisted the following morning. Lacher's room had been built at the same level as the cellar into which the imperial family had been taken. The window sat at the top of the wall, near the ceiling. Even if Lacher had set a stool on the bed his eyes would not have reached high enough to see out. And what could he have seen if they had? The walls of the house were more than two feet thick; the glass was on the *inside* of the aperture; the view out was blocked on one side by the stairs to the main entrance of the house and on the other by the palisade the Bolsheviks had erected around the building: *"Lacher could not have seen out that window."*

The day's session, Ian Lilburn remembered, was so ugly and so loud that he and Mme. Auclères could hear the shouting at the far end of the hall outside.

"Where *were* you that night?" Wollmann bellowed.

"I told you, I was locked in my room."

"Either you're lying when you say you were locked in your room or you're lying when you say you saw the bodies." Wollmann hoped he did not need to tell the court what that might mean. Was it necessary to state that they might now be looking at one of the murderers of the family of the Tsar? Anyway, they were looking at a liar and a thief. How had Lacher come into possession of the Tsar's cigarette holder if he did not steal it? *"Where were you?"* Wollmann cried again.

"I already told you."

All Wollmann could do now was try to discredit the witness. To that end, he called to the stand Rudolf Bouzek, another Austrian, a man who had long ago written Anastasia's attorneys about Lacher's theft of relics from Ekaterinburg. But now it was Judge Bäthge's turn to get angry. It was his turn to start yelling.

"We are not in criminal court!" the judge barked. "This man" — meaning Lacher — "is not on trial here." [138] It was plain to everyone in the room that Bäthge's patience had worn out; in fact, that he had been hoping to provide the long-awaited "last word" on the "Anastasia" affair. Lacher was the means, and Bouzek was an obstacle. "Answer the question!" Bäthge hollered whenever Bouzek paused to think. "Answer the questions put to you! Get on with it! Get to the point!" [139] When the time came for Bouzek to take the oath, he hesitated over the form.

"Do you want the religious form?" asked Bäthge impatiently.

Bouzek didn't know. He was an apostate, he explained, and didn't know what to do. Might he not be charged with perjury if he swore by God?

"Yes or no!"

"Yes!" cried Bouzek. He was practically in tears by the time he was dismissed that evening. Prince Frederick brought him over to the Gasthof Sonne and tried to cheer him up: "He didn't mean it badly. You must understand how hard it is for the judges, how tired they must be." [140]

Was that it? That the judges were tired? Or had the full meaning dawned on them of the decision they had been asked to make —the responsibility of deciding the identity of·a human being, of telling her, "Yes, you are who you say you are," or telling her, "No, you are not"? By the next morning, in any case, Wollmann had made up his mind: Judge Bäthge intended to rule against his client on the testimony of a lying witness. His treatment of Bouzek had made that plain enough. "Judge Bäthge called for silence and declared that the deposition of the witness was finished," wrote Dominique Auclères, "and since the lawyers had completed their questions the audience was closed." Wollmann was beside himself: he would not allow it! The judge would be removed. They would go right back to the beginning if they had to. Then Wollmann and Bäthge started screaming at each other.

"No one in living memory had challenged a judge of the Hamburg Senate," said Dominique Auclères after the court had left Göttingen.[141] In the end, Wollmann's request was denied, but the challenge, coupled with judicial vacations and the increasingly poor state of Wollmann's health, prevented the debates from opening again until November. The "Anastasians" had lost another year.

When Gertrude Lamerdin moved into a house across the road from Anastasia's dacha, Anastasia took it into her head that Miss Lamerdin was spying on her. "It would be high time that I got here out," she wrote Gleb Botkin in comic confusion.[142] "This dirty business" in Hamburg was making her ill: "Princess Marianne from Herleshausen is playing a very strange part in all this. She don't separate anymore from Mr. Wollmann nor Prince Frederick. She is constantly travelling with them together." And then, said Anastasia — as though this were strange — "She has her own car and drives it herself."[143] Even Ian Lilburn, whom Anastasia manifestly liked and "who is in England so important," had come under her suspicion: "I fear that he is playing a bleak part at the Bank of England."[144] Now, she told Gleb, she let no one into the dacha — not even "the girls."

The third of her dogs had died. Anastasia had arisen in the middle of the night, dragged the beast outside, and, with her good arm, dug it a shallow grave. Now the carcass had begun to rot, spreading its noisome odor across the whole village. Meantime the cats had multiplied. There were more than forty of them, inbred, undernourished, some of them blind and crippled. The exceptionally patient

Herr Berger, mayor of Unterlengenhardt, realized that something would have to be done about the situation, but what? Anastasia took nobody's advice.

On July 16 she sat in her house and heard outside her gate the Russian Orthodox priest who came every year on that day to pray for the souls of her family. People wondered what it was she *did* in there all day long. She kept sending Gleb copies of her correspondence, begging him to "take great care" and scolding him for not following up clues. "Why did one not go to him in time?" Anastasia chided Gleb after a certain witness had died. "You are almost fifty years in America?" [145] But Gleb was her only true friend, she thought. So many others had died: Gertrude Madsack, Princess Xenia, Faith Lavington — "They are all dead." [146] Anastasia's letters became shorter and ever more desultory. She simply began to list things that had happened to her, without explanation or apparent connection. "The Baroness Miltitz" was "dangerous," she said. All of "the girls" were dangerous. [147] If Gleb could not bring her to Charlottesville, maybe she would go to Switzerland. Or Herleshausen. She loved Herleshausen, no matter what her current opinion of Princess Marianne. "Count Pourtalès," she wrote one day, "the nephew of the Ambassador in Petersburg before the First War, . . . has sent to me through Prince Frederick a Christmas *stollen*. It is a long cake, like a bread. Very sweet, and many raisins in." [148]

The "foto-reporters" were back, Anastasia went on: "They were behaving like crazy devils. It was very difficult to get rid of them. . . . Then were television people here from Hamburg, and I have been for many hours troubled." [149]

She closed: "I am tired of all this. . . . I am sick to death of all." [150]

The next set of pleas had been scheduled for the end of November 1966. The complications in Wollmann's leg had already raised the specter of an amputation when his wife was ill for several months, forcing another round of sleepless marathons for the preparation of the final memoranda. The year before, Wollmann had dismissed his secretary and given up his office for want of funds. Now Princess Marianne stepped into the breach and helped him over the last hurdle. In the space of fifteen days Wollmann bombarded the judges of the Senate with no fewer than five separate briefs, each of them designed to encourage the judges either to rule in Anastasia's favor immediately or call more witnesses.

None of the "Anastasians" thought that the November pleas would be the last. New evidence was cropping up all the time, and then there were witnesses who had been waiting for years to be called. One of the last the court heard, in fact, was Prince Ferdinand of Schönaich-Carolath, the stepson of the Kaiser, who testified that "His Majesty himself" had told his family about the Grand Duke of Hesse's Russian peace mission in 1916.[151] When the inevitable questions arose about why Prince Ferdinand had waited so long before telling his story, the Prince did not bother to explain that he had only just been called to the stand. Rather, he threw Judge Petersen a disdainful look and replied, "The unwritten law at Doorn was that no one who heard His Majesty speak would repeat His words outside the walls of the castle. . . . We never commented on what His Majesty said."

The pervasively monarchist flavor of the trial had begun to irk the judges. Wollmann, referring to the Kaiser, kept calling him "She," since the German word *Majestät* is a feminine noun; thus, in a strictly formal sense, when the Kaiser confirmed the Hesse trip to Russia *"She* was speaking the truth."

"Who *are* you talking about?" snapped Judge Petersen.

"Of His Majesty."

"Oh, no, not you too." [152]

On November 25 Wollmann argued Anastasia's case for eleven hours, beginning at eight in the morning and not finishing until after seven that night.[153] His plea ran along the lines of what he called "the obvious" — that only the Tsar's daughter could know what Anastasia knew; only the Tsar's daughter could think and behave the way Anastasia did; and only the Tsar's daughter, above all, would ever have been treated so shabbily as Anastasia had. What point was there in persecuting a demented Polish factory worker? Wollmann wondered: "I am only asking for justice for a woman whose destiny has been, from beginning to end, one cruel tragedy. What further proof are you looking for? What must she do in order that she may be herself again? What on God's earth must this lonely woman do in order to prove that she has a legitimate claim in law to the name and the identity of Grand Duchess Anastasia?" Wollmann's closing lines, while provocative, were far calmer than usual: "The Senate's task is a difficult one. . . . But I ask the court to remember this: behind all the evidence — the papers, the documents, the photographs — a human being . . . stands waiting for justice. *Her* task is the hardest of all. . . .

"May the court's regard for the truth be commensurate with its responsibility. . . .

"May the verdict be just."

The next day, November 26, was a Saturday. It gave the reporters some time to think about Berenberg-Gossler's rebuttal before calling in their stories. "Herr Wollmann appears to have stolen my thunder," said Berenberg-Gossler ironically, not bothering to reply to a single one of Wollmann's arguments.[154] In fact Berenberg-Gossler's summation had fallen flat. All he could deliver was another *"éloge à la folie,"* [155] renewing his assault on Anastasia's troubled mind and wondering when, if ever, the judges at Hamburg would recognize her case for the pathetic delusion that it was. Dominique Auclères, for one, was tired of Berenberg-Gossler's armchair psychoanalysis — "all wrapped up in neat little Freudian packages, which, it seemed to me, were designed to knock the judges unconscious and impress the spectators with Berenberg-Gossler's own intelligence." Besides, said Mme. Auclères, "we were not there to prove Mrs. Anderson's sanity. We were there to prove her identity with the daughter of the Tsar, something which, by itself, would by no means preclude derangement."

At the bench, Judge Petersen, Judge Bäthge, and Judge Prusz were sitting in silence. They gave no indication, in Mme. Auclères's phrase, "that D-Day might have arrived." [156] The judges did not so much as lift an eyebrow when Wollmann, exercising his right to rejoinder, told them about the three nurses who had recently run across the published photograph of Franziska Schanzkowska and had written him to say that Franziska had been a patient under their care in the asylum at Herrenprotsch, near Breslau, from 1929 to 1934. But here was the strangest thing, said Wollmann: the woman at Herrenprotsch, because no one knew her true identity, had been known at the asylum as "Anastasia."

It may have been on hearing about this latest evidence that the judges in Hamburg decided they had heard enough.

"All the German papers are saying that there's going to be a verdict tomorrow," said Ian Lilburn to Prince Frederick and Dominique Auclères as they sat together at the Vier Jahreszeiten in Hamburg, on February 27, 1967.

"It can't be," said Prince Frederick. "Not unless it's a favorable one."

The next morning Mme. Auclères just had time to warn the *Fi-*

garo to reserve some space on the front page before she and the rest of the press corps were more or less hustled into a small auxiliary chamber of the court — not the room ordinarily employed for "Anastasia's Monster Trial." The gallery was packed, and there was an air of expectancy that had the audience jumping at every sound from the door at the far wall.

The moment the judges walked into the room Anastasia's friends knew they had lost. There couldn't have been any other reason for those long faces. "The only thing missing was a funeral march and the official mourners," said Mme. Auclères bitterly. "Petersen was ghastly pale and seemed almost to have swallowed his cheeks, they were so hollow." [157]

"Not good," Ian Lilburn whispered.

The judge's hands were shaking when he read the verdict: "The plaintiff is defeated in appeal . . ."

Nobody moved. Nobody jumped up and clapped anybody else on the back. There was total silence in the chamber.

"It isn't possible for me to give the motivation for the judgment this morning," Judge Petersen continued. "The considerations in this monumental trial are so many that they would fill a book. Briefly, I will say that the plaintiff, who has asked for recognition as Anastasia Nicolaievna, Grand Duchess of Russia, has not been able to provide sufficient proof for that recognition, any more than she was able to do so in the first instance." [158]

The judges shuffled out of the room as gloomily as they had entered it. Suddenly a soft cry rose from the audience: "There is no more justice in Germany." [159] Then the reporters dashed to the telephones.

The news had hit the wires within minutes: "The Court of Appeals Refuses to Recognize Anna Anderson"; [160] "Anderson, Alias Anastasia — She Isn't It"; [161] "Was There a Rescue of Russia's Little Mother? Hamburg Says No." [162] An old photograph of Anastasia, showing her in a ratty fur, with a slight smile and an expectant look on her face, was flashed around the world and turned up in newspapers from California to Australia. In New York, the *Today* show gave its attention to the story before moving on to an interview with Alexander Kerensky in commemoration of the fiftieth anniversary of the Russian Revolution. And within a day the Bank of England, for its own reasons, had formally denied that it held any funds in wait for the heir of the Tsar.[163] This time, or so it seemed, the "Anastasia" case was good and finished.

At the Palace of Justice Anastasia's friends found themselves in an empty chamber. "All we wanted to do was get out of there," said Dominique Auclères.[164] No one had the courage to walk out the main entrance, where the reporters had surrounded the victorious Günther von Berenberg-Gossler. Wollmann led his friends to a side door, which turned out to be a mistake, because out in the hallway they came upon an elderly, dumpy German *Hausfrau,* dressed in a brown wool coat, who stood with a smile of triumph and cried at the top of her voice: "The verdict is just! *I* am Anastasia!"[165]

"No coup de theatre could have been more ridiculous," wrote Klaus Wagner in the *Frankfurter Allgemeine,* "and nothing more informative about the whole identity question: the way Anna Anderson maintains her dignity."[166] The photographers who came tearing down the hall now caught Prince Frederick and Wollmann gaping at the woman with grotesque, baffled grins on their faces. Then quickly the "Anastasians" ran from the building into a taxi.

Nobody said a word back at the Vier Jahreszeiten.[167] Dominique Auclères went into her bedroom and telephoned Baroness von Miltitz in Unterlengenhardt: would the Baroness please break the news to Anastasia? Then she sat down to write her article and found herself getting angrier by the minute. "I could not believe it," she recalled. "I just could not believe it." Her article revealed as much. It was uncharacteristically confused, one minute defensive, the next weepy and sentimental, finally building up steam to attack "this judgment, such as it is, which cannot disguise its sordid nature . . . . Those who still believe in Anastasia, and I count myself among them, had better hope that they are mistaken, because this verdict — if it strikes down the martyred girl who managed to escape the slaughter of Ekaterinburg — this verdict is an atrocity."[168]

Mme. Auclères put down her pen and joined the others in the living room. She ordered lunch.

"My regrets, Highness," said the waiter to Prince Frederick as he came up with the food. "We're all devastated for you."

They ate their lunch in silence. "We sat there like poor sinners," said Mme. Auclères. "We were really knocked down." Then another thought came to her: she wasn't going to be seeing these people anymore. The "Anastasians" had lost their reason for being. "You're going back to Unterlengenhardt," said Mme. Auclères to Prince Frederick, ". . . Marianne's going home, Ian's going back to that house of his in London — and I?. . . I've got to go back to the *Figaro* with a broken Grand Duchess."

"Why don't you come with me to Unterlengenhardt for a few days?" said Prince Frederick.

Mme. Auclères was touched. After lunch she went back to her room, called in her story, packed her things, and with the Prince left Hamburg — a town she hoped she would never see again, nor the massive Palace of Justice, nor the words emblazoned over the judges' bench: *"Recht ist Wahrheit, und Wahrheit Recht* [Law is Truth, and Truth is Law]."

PART FOUR

Anastasia

15

CHARLOTTESVILLE

*T*he judgment of the Senate in Hamburg left Anastasia's friends with time on their hands. Ian Lilburn returned to London to start work on a book about the case, while Prince Frederick attended to his long-neglected archaeological concerns and Dominique Auclères answered her mail. The vast outpouring of loyalty and regret had astonished even the intrepid secretaries of the *Figaro,* who had been screening letters about Anastasia for nine years. "The way in which the judgment had been handed down," Mme. Auclères observed, " 'taking it on the lam,' so to speak, had cut short all possibility of comment and allowed for only a futile protestation. . . . Among the many correspondents who wanted to tell me how disappointed they were by the verdict of 28 February, certain ones asked me what arguments Herr Wollmann might be able to bring before the Supreme Court."[1]

There was never any doubt that the case would go to the Federal Supreme Court at Karlsruhe. Wollmann had said as much immediately after the judgment. Two things needed to be accomplished beforehand, however. First of all, an advocate had to be found for Anastasia who was eligible to plead before the judges there, and then the appeal had to await the publication of the verdict of the Hamburg Senate. At the Palace of Justice, in the meantime, a special room had been set aside just to contain the forty-nine volumes of evidence while the judges wrote their opinion. When the first section, a résumé of the facts totaling three hundred and six pages, was released in May of 1967, Wollmann exercised his right to petition for the correction of mistakes in the text. There were scores of them: "factual inaccuracies, incompleteness, vagueness . . . and finally clerical errors, which garbled everything." [2] Because Wollmann had had to introduce his new brief before the judicial recesses, however, the judges of the Senate found themselves in the unique position of hearing his objections to the verdict *before* they had delivered the second half in July: the four hundred and four pages that gave the reasons for the negative ruling. "That in itself is believed here to be adequate justification for an appeal to the Federal Supreme Court in Karlsruhe," wrote Ian Lilburn, "but it is not the only point." [3]

Anastasia had found her attorney in Karlsruhe before the year was out. He was Curt, Freiherr von Stackelberg, himself the scion of the Baltic-Russian nobility, "one of the most respected legal brains in Germany" [4] and later the president of the association of lawyers licensed to practice before the Supreme Court. Baron von Stackelberg, like Wollmann in 1963, had had no difficulty identifying the weaknesses of the Hamburg verdict, which he narrowed down for the sake of argument to three:

1. an excessive and unreasonable demand for proof

2. a questioning of the credibility of the witnesses for the plaintiff solely on account of other testimonies coming from the opposition, which were not intrinsically any more valid than the first [in other words, Anastasia had labored under a double standard]

3. a failure to conduct a recapitulation of the evidence that militates in favor of the plaintiff. [5]

A friend of Anastasia's once remarked that each judgment in the long course of her trial was slightly more reasonable than the one before it. To a certain extent, that was true. There had been some significant victories at Hamburg. The judges had gone out of their way, first of all, to emphasize that their verdict did not deny Anastasia's identity: it held only that she had failed to prove it to the satisfaction of the court. "The verdict in Hamburg" said Ian Lilburn, "was as near to a finding of 'not proven' as is permissible in German law." [6] Then on page 401 of the written explanation, for the first time, it was acknowledged that "the death of Grand Duchess Anastasia at Ekaterinburg cannot be accepted as a conclusively proven historical fact." [7] That was Carl-August Wollmann's personal triumph — he had managed after all to discredit the testimony of Rudolf Lacher, the Austrian orderly from the Ipatiev house — and it led to speculation that the Tsar's collateral heirs, including the Duchess of Mecklenburg, might be required to refund the money they had taken so long ago from the Mendelssohn Bank. But these concessions, as Baron von Stackelberg argued in his brief to the Supreme Court, could not disguise the fact that the Hamburg Senate, no less than the High Court in the first instance, had been guilty of a "capricious and arbitrary" interpretation of the evidence,[8] thereby denying Anastasia a fair trial.

Baron von Stackelberg centered his appeal in the "fundamental rights of man" as spelled out in the West German constitution. "The right to identity," he maintained, "as well as the right to a name, is included in the basic rights of human dignity and the free development of the personality. Thus it follows that, in cases of this sort, the usual official procedures are not in order; on the contrary, the procedural rules of civil law, in such cases of fundamental rights and human identity, must be modified in consideration of those rights. At the least, this leads to an alleviation of the burden of proof. . . . In cases where a fundamental right is at stake, the burden of proof must be reversed: it must be borne by the person *contesting* the claim. . . ." Stackelberg likened the problem to cases involving the sincerity of conscientious objectors, where proof can never be furnished and "a reasonable certainty" must suffice. The Hamburg Senate, said Stackelberg, had not only elected not to believe Anastasia's witnesses, but in effect had been asking her to provide evidence which it was impossible to furnish, inasmuch as it didn't exist: there could be no positive proof of her identity in the absence of fingerprints. Under the unique circumstances, the court had an obligation to place the same demands of proof on the opposition, because *only* the unproven allegations of Anastasia's opponents stood in the way of her recognition.

As for the judges' interpretation of the evidence, Stackelberg submitted a list of more than eighty examples of what appeared to him to be crass prejudice. First and foremost was the failure of the court, once again, to believe its own scientific experts; then, its failure to submit to expert evaluation the new photographs it had commissioned of Anastasia's ears in 1964; then, its failure to hear more than thirty witnesses cited by Wollmann during his last plea;[9] and, finally, its decision to value the witnesses it did hear *only insofar as their testimony agreed with the arguments of the opposition*. Some of the people who had deposed about the escape of the Tsar's daughter, for example, were dismissed in the Hamburg verdict merely on the grounds that their testimony contradicted the findings of the Sokolov investigation, leading Anastasia's friends to wonder why the judges had bothered to hear the case at all. The extent of the tribunal's bias was plain enough, said Baron von Stackelberg, in view of its unsubstantiated — and completely unnecessary — ruling that the much-disputed trip of the Grand Duke of Hesse to Russia was not really in dispute at all. Said the tribunal: "This trip did not take place." [10] Stackelberg went on: "When Colonel Mordvinov, the former aide-de-camp to the Tsar, declares that 'the Unknown Woman of Berlin' is not Anastasia, no one asks him when he last saw Anastasia or what reasons he might have had for refusing to acknowledge her. (It is known that Mordvinov abandoned the Tsar on the very day of his abdication.) On the other hand, if a witness appears who swears to have recognized the fourth daughter of the Tsar, suddenly Hamburg wants to know if his memory is reliable, if the degree of his intimacy with the Grand Duchess would permit him to have an opinion, if age or infirmity might not be causing him to hallucinate, if self-interest is not, perhaps, at the back of his testimony." [11]

Finally there was the matter of "the recapitulation of the evidence in favor of the plaintiff." Stackelberg compared Anastasia's case to an enormous canvas, to a mosaic, actually, which cannot be appreciated in isolated fragments, but only as a whole. Striking though any one piece of the mosaic may be, it is finally telling only in relation to all of the others. And that, said Stackelberg, was the greatest failing of the Hamburg Senate — "the failure to take an *overall* view of the case. . . . The plaintiff is constructing a case based on circumstantial evidence. . . . Just because some of the stones in the mosaic may be imperfect or slightly chipped, they are not to be isolated or cast aside, because when placed in conjunction to form a picture, and when viewed from the proper perspective, they create a very definite and conclusive impression."

The Supreme Court at Karlsruhe was not being asked to issue a ruling about Anastasia's identity. It was being asked only to examine the procedure of the lower court for judicial errors. If Karlsruhe were to rule in Anastasia's favor the whole process would begin again before another tribunal. If not, Anastasia would likely remain forever where the judges of the Hamburg Senate had left her: in legal limbo.

Baron von Stackelberg completed his brief in July 1968. It would be eighteen months before the Supreme Court had time to review the case.

The second negative judgment in Hamburg had had a far more debilitating effect on Anastasia than the first. There were no outbursts this time, and no snide remarks about the tribunal. Instead, Anastasia sank into a morbid and ultimately frightening depression. She told her friends that the actual winning of the case hadn't mattered to her: she had only been hoping "to die under the name with which she was born." [12] In Unterlengenhardt, meanwhile, her living conditions had deteriorated even further. The dacha was filthy now, the floors encrusted with cat dirt and littered with papers, empty cans of pet food, and milk bottles.[13] Anastasia's friends were heartened at the end of August 1967, when she snapped out of her torpor momentarily and agreed to take a trip with them to Paris. "I love Paris," she remarked later. "It is the most beautiful city in the world." [14]

A film was being prepared in Paris that summer by the French director Gilbert Prouteau, a documentary about the "Anastasia" affair [15] that began with a fictional premise: two attorneys (to be played by Vittorio de Sica and Paul Meurisse) arguing Anastasia's case before the World Court at the Hague. The idea was to dramatize the story while at the same time recording for posterity the actual testimony of the witnesses. Although Anastasia had no intention of making an appearance on the screen, she did seem to like the idea of the new movie. It allowed her to believe that she had not been forgotten in the wake of the Hamburg verdict. But there was a more important reason for the Paris trip: the widow of Grand Duke Andrew — formerly the prima ballerina Mathilde Kschessinska, the instructress of Dame Margot Fonteyn and one-time mistress of the Tsar — had asked Prince Frederick if she might see Anastasia again. Mathilde was ninety-five now and "did not want to die without telling Anastasia that she and her husband had never ceased to believe in her." [16] At first Anastasia had resisted. "No!" she cried to Louisa Mayhoff every morning when Miss Mayhoff brought her breakfast to the door. "I will never go to Paris. Prince Frederick would do better to look after my affairs with the King of Denmark, now that he has lost my case in the court!" [17] Finally, however, Anastasia, too, seemed eager for a journey into the past, and with the Prince, Ian Lilburn, and Countess Elisabeth Oppersdorf,[18] in a flurry of packing and forgotten toilet articles, she climbed into the car for the twelve-hour drive to Paris.

Anastasia proved to be an avid tourist, tireless, inquisitive, and game for adventure as she walked through the cathedral of Notre Dame and up the Eiffel Tower, pausing for a moment of silence on the bridge named for Tsar Alexander III. She cut a striking, even jolly, figure in her furs, her veils, and the comical sunglasses she had insisted on wearing, but the journey was not without pathos. On the first morning of her trip Anastasia had gone out to Gilbert Prouteau's studio, where Prouteau had arranged a screening of old newsreel clips of the Russian imperial family.

"I saw how her hand went up to her heart," wrote Dominique Auclères, "as though struck by some invisible weapon, when she saw the Emperor Nicholas II walking past with the Empress, the Tsarevitch between them, and then three adolescent Grand Duchesses, wearing their bright bonnets, each of them escorted by a dashing cavalier."

"There's one missing," said Anastasia, perplexed, when finally "a little girl came running up behind them, a bit frantic because she was late, her hair falling down to her shoulders, her wide-brimmed hat balanced on the back of her head — in a word, it was Anastasia, the fourth daughter of the Tsar."

"There," said Anastasia. "It was the tercentenary of the Romanovs in Moscow." Then the pictures changed, suddenly, to a shot of the storming of the Winter Palace.[19]

Anastasia gasped. "You are killing me!" she whispered. And then: "*Must* we have this?"[20]

She rose and walked over to the wall, where she buried her face in her arms and stood for several minutes. She was crying. "How could you do this to me?" she asked Countess Oppersdorf, who had followed her to see if she was all right.

"Do you want to go home?"

"I am here," said Anastasia, wiping her eyes. "And I will stay to the end." But for the rest of the day she remained in a pensive, touchy mood, and when she joined Tatiana Botkin for lunch later that day she astonished everyone by leading the conversation around to the imperial family's imprisonment at Tobolsk. It was obvious that she was trying to remember something.

"Where was Maria?" she asked finally. "Why didn't I go with her?"

Nobody doubted that Anastasia was thinking of the night the Tsar, the Empress, Grand Duchess Maria, and Tatiana Botkin's father had been taken by the Bolsheviks to Ekaterinburg. "Where was she?" Anastasia asked again. "We were everywhere together. I was looking for her. . . . I am looking. . . ." She turned to Dominique Auclères: "Do you have a tape-recorder running somewhere?"

Mme. Auclères was shocked: "Oh, no, madame, I would never do that to you."

"That's too bad," said Anastasia. "Sometimes I say things and then I forget them. I forget that I have said them." She paused and smiled almost in apology. "I have lost touch with myself." [21]

When Anastasia got ready the next morning to meet Grand Duke Andrew's widow she decided that she wanted to wear one of those enormous hats she had seen in the newsreels the day before. Yes, she said, it was appropriate. It took her friends some time to convince her that a hat from 1914, provided they could find one, might attract unwelcome stares on the streets of Paris. Finally Anastasia settled for a simple black lace veil and moved off with her entourage to "the home of friends," where she expected to greet Mathilde Kschessinska but instead encountered Mathilde's son, Prince Vladimir Romanov, known in the family as "Vova." [22]

Prince Frederick groaned: he had been dodging Vova for weeks. After Mathilde Kschessinska had made known her desire to meet Anastasia again, her son had done everything in his power to prevent it. It wasn't that Vova doubted Anastasia's identity so much as he feared the wrath of his cousin and namesake, "Grand Duke" Vladimir Kyrilovitch, [23] the current pretender to the Russian throne and the man who, by dubious fiat, had raised Vova from his morganatic status as a mere "Prince Romanovsky-Krassinsky" to a full-fledged "Prince Romanov." It was Vova's "fiancée," Liliane Ahlefeld — "a little masterpiece of God's creation" — who during the trials had approached Dominique Auclères with the letter Grand Duke Andrew had written to Grand Duchess Olga after his encounter with Anastasia in 1928, the letter in which Andrew gave his opinion that she was "no one other than my niece, Grand Duchess Anastasia Nicolaievna." Liliane had offered it to the *Figaro* for a million francs. "True," said Mme. Auclères, "this was in old currency. Even so . . . " The *Figaro* had declined to pay, and Liliane had been obliged to take her letter to the editors of *L'Aurore*.[24] Its publication had had such an impact that Vova, acutely embarrassed, had released the copy of a second letter from his father's papers, written to Grand Duchess Olga nearly thirty years later, in which Andrew appeared to have modified his views: "I have never formally stated my opinion on the matter, because I have never been entirely convinced. . . . The mystery remains unsolved. . . ."[25] Although the letter had not been signed and may never even have been sent, the opposition at Hamburg had seized on it as proof that Andrew, before his death, had changed his mind about Anastasia's identity.

"Ha!" said Liliane Ahlefeld to Dominique Auclères. She had spoken with the Grand Duke about it just before he died: "The truth is that he was in terror of the anger of the family." But that was how matters stood when Anastasia met Andrew's son in Paris. Vova bowed and kissed her hand when she walked into the room — endearing himself forever and earning the sobriquet "the sweetest little sweetheart"[26] — then sat down at her side to apologize for his mother's absence, saying that her doctors had forbidden her to go anywhere or participate in any meeting that might upset her. Surely Anastasia would understand, said Vova:"She's terribly sorry."

"But I must see her!" Anastasia replied. "I must! Absolutely!" Had she come to Paris for this?

By now Prince Frederick was fed up with Vova's timidity. "Vova," he said, with a sternness unusual for him, "you know that your father fully recognized our friend here — your cousin here — as Anastasia Nicolaievna."

"Such was his belief, yes," said Vova.

"You *know* that he identified her as such. . . ."

"Yes," Vova whispered.

"And your mother, too . . ."

"Any more of this and I'm leaving!"[27] Shortly afterward Vova escorted Anastasia to the car and kissed her good-bye. Then Anastasia decided it was time to go home — back to Unterlengenhardt, the dacha, and the cats.

"A retraction!" Vova cried several days later, when he read Dominique Auclères's deliberately accusatory article about his meeting with Anastasia. "I demand a retraction!" Mme. Auclères took him out for a drink and they discussed the case from the beginning.[28]

"It's a horrifying story," said Vova when he had calmed down somewhat. "It's just a horrifying story. . . ."

"Horrifying for her," Mme. Auclères answered coldly, after Vova "had repeated this phrase for the fifth time" — "but for you? All you're upset about is that you haven't been able to say what you know to be the truth."

"Yes," said Vova desperately, bowing his head and "positively weighed down with grief."

"I didn't bother to publish this," said Mme. Auclères. "What good would it have done? Vova would only have denied it." In fact Vova was more anxious than ever not to make waves within the imperial family. Two weeks later Gilbert Prouteau's film crew had gained entrance to the Villa Molitor in order to record the testimony of Vova's mother, Mathilde Kschessinska. The old princess's health seemed to have improved dramatically since Vova had forbidden her meeting with Anastasia. She was bright, cheerful and, at ninety-five, extraordinarily lucid.

"Princess," said Gilbert Prouteau, "in 1928, in Paris, you met the woman who at that time was called 'the Unknown Woman of Berlin.' Is that right?"

"I saw her once."

"And what did you think?"

"That it was she. . . ."

"*Nyet!*" cried Vova from across the room. "*Nyet!* Cut! You've got to cut!" He went over to scold his mother in Russian: "You must answer only what is written!"

What had been written was a cautious, tepid endorsement of Anastasia's claim, based on Mathilde's "feeling" that Anastasia was the daughter of the Tsar. Resigned to it, Mathilde read the prepared statement into the camera: "I was never formally presented to Grand Duchess Anastasia Nicolaievna and only saw her from a distance. The comparison I was able to make between her and the unknown woman could only be relative. . . . My impressions must not be taken as a affirmation. . . ."

"Did we tire you out, madame?" asked Gilbert Prouteau when the crew had finished. He had left the sound recorder running.

"Not at all, not at all, everyone has been so kind. . . ."

"You were great, madame," said Prouteau. ". . . I know that you take this problem very much to heart, that it's upsetting for you. . . ." Prouteau stammered: "Anastasia . . . Mrs. Anderson . . ."

"Now," said Mathilde, "I am still certain it is she. When she looked at me, you understand, with those eyes . . . that was it, it was the Emperor. It isn't that I have to say anything, you know. No, it's just what I think. . . . It was the exact same look. It was the Emperor's look. And anyone who saw the Emperor's eyes will never forget them."

"And you knew those eyes well?" Prouteau asked carefully.

"Very well," said the Tsar's former mistress, "very well, very well. . . . It is she, you know, I am certain it is she."[29]

Mathilde Kschessinska died in 1971; her son Vova three years later. On Vova's death Vladimir Kyrilovitch, the pretender, came immediately to Paris and took charge of Grand Duke Andrew's papers, sealing them off from all scrutiny.[30]

The decline was swift, alarming, and looked at first to be fatal. Returned to Unterlengenhardt, Anastasia resumed her solitary existence in the dacha, not allowing anyone inside and bellowing with rage when it was suggested to her that she put the more debilitated of her animals out of their misery. The farmers had begun to kill any of the cats they found rooting in their fields. How was Anastasia going to know the difference? She had ceased to pay attention to anything beyond the walls of her house, and when Prince Frederick told her that he had orders from the mayor of Unterlengenhardt and the district board of health to clean up the premises she responded with a threat: "Then I shall go to America at once."

Nobody thought she really meant it. She had been talking about leaving Germany for years now, pointing out that Dr. Manahan, Gleb Botkin's friend in Charlottesville, had sent her the money for the trip and had agreed to take care of her once she got there. It had become her refrain, her answer to every challenge: "America." Her friends had stopped listening.

She made her last appearance in Unterlengenhardt on the hundredth anniversary of the birth of Nicholas II, in May 1968, sitting at her window while her friends held a small party outside. Later, opinion was divided about the cause of her subsequent collapse — whether it had been brought on by the painful associations of the Tsar's birthday, or by the fact that Prince Frederick, before leaving the village on some business, had carted away her "compost heap." At the end of the month, in any case, Anastasia bolted herself inside the dacha and for four days refused to see anyone. Her ladies knew that there was no food in the house, and finally Miss Mayhoff, made bold by anxiety, ordered that the door be broken down. She found Anastasia lying half-conscious on the sofa, twisting in pain and moaning repeatedly, "Mamma, Mamma, where is Mamma? Mamma, I'm dying. . . ."[31]

A doctor was called, who gave Anastasia an injection and ordered that she be taken immediately to the district hospital at Neuenbürg. Anastasia was sufficiently alert to protest before she fainted, "I will not go to the hospital! You cannot take me there! I forbid it!" Then the ambulance arrived. When she recovered consciousness several days later Anastasia was gripped by "an insane rage" and demanded that she be taken home at once.

It wasn't possible, her nurses replied: she needed rest and care, and, besides, the compound at Unterlengenhardt was being cleaned.

The shouting that emerged from Anastasia's room on receipt of this news sent the nursing sisters shrinking in terror. The doctors at Neuenbürg had been worried about the weak state of her heart, but no longer. *Who* had done this to her? Anastasia cried. Who had given her "the deadly injection" at the dacha? She had been poisoned! It was Prince Frederick's fault. He was "a criminal."

"*Me!*" Prince Frederick exclaimed when he heard Anastasia's latest charge. "I wasn't anywhere around!"

Word of Anastasia's displeasure was brought to Unterlengenhardt on the lips of Alexis Miliukoff, a Russian friend who worked for the American military administration in Frankfurt. Miliukoff had been known to fling himself on his knees in front of Anastasia, begging her forgiveness if he had offended her, but doing it always with a twinkle in his eye which indulged her undying sense of the absurd. She liked Miliukoff tremendously and called him "Tartar."

"She has forbidden the nurses to give out any information on her condition to anyone from Unterlengenhardt," Miliukoff informed Prince Frederick.

"But her heart," asked Dominique Auclères, who had rushed to the Black Forest on hearing about Anastasia's collapse. "How is her heart?"

"Her heart?" Miliukoff replied. "Her heart is just fine."[32]

Mme. Auclères was, for the moment, still in Anastasia's good graces. She went to see her several times at Neuenbürg and was thereby able to keep the others informed of her progress. The nurses, she reported, "disciplined and terrorized," had taken Anastasia at her word and refused to discuss the case. Worse, Anastasia had found out the one thing Prince Frederick had wanted to tell her in person: that her cats — more than sixty of them — had been gassed on the orders of the board of health. The neighbors had tried to save "Baby," the last of the hounds, but with his mistress gone the dog had lain down to die, refusing to eat "and howling through the night," and he, too, had been destroyed. Now the rupture was complete. *Criminal* was not a strong enough word to describe Prince Frederick, in Anastasia's opinion. He was "a murderer," working in conspiracy with Baroness von Miltitz. It was the old Baroness, Anastasia fantasized, "who had allowed her to be given a shot of morphine in order to put her in the hospital, in order to murder her animals and steal from her her priceless documents and other valuables."[33] Later Anastasia insisted that papers worth "more than ten thousand dollars" had disappeared from the dacha during her absence.[34] In reality, a great many of them had simply been left behind in boxes when Miliukoff, on Anastasia's command, entered the house and hastily packed her things.

She said good-bye to no one. Miliukoff, having arranged her American visa, came to fetch her on the thirteenth of July, 1968, and the next day the two of them flew from Frankfurt to Dulles Airport outside Washington. She had arrived in Charlottesville before any of her friends in Europe knew she had left.

In Unterlengenhardt, Prince Frederick and Ian Lilburn finished cleaning up the house. It took them days to scrape the cats' mess off the floors and tidy up the grounds, and while resting Lilburn enjoyed the opportunity to look at Anastasia's "priceless documents." To his surprise (and to Prince Frederick's consternation), he found that for years people had been sending Anastasia money in the form of checks and postal orders — hundreds of dollars' worth, which she had never cashed and which would have been of great help to them all, inasmuch as Anastasia had managed every month to spend about four times her income.[35] There was nothing remaining of the *Anastasia* royalties now. The dacha had been mortgaged twice, while Lilburn himself had "ceased to count [his] own personal contributions to the cause when they passed the $5,000 mark."[36] He brought Anastasia's papers back to London for safekeeping, and in the meantime began to wonder what all of her friends were wondering: "What on earth are we going to do with her when her visa runs out?"[37]

One of Anastasia's first acts upon her arrival in Virginia was to give an interview in which she roundly denounced her friends in Europe, declaring that "her trial had profited no one but her lawyers,"[38] that she had been lied to and abused "in every way," poisoned, spied upon, and held up to public ridicule in the French press. Her remarks were so vitriolic that even Gleb Botkin, who had met her at the airport, began to refer to her "perfectly absurd accusations" and her "nonsensical statements," finally admitting in a letter to Prince Frederick that "the Grand Duchess's mental faculties appear to be seriously impaired."[39]

"I am ill, deranged and tired . . . ," said Anastasia with a sigh. "One becomes ill when one must again and again repeat."[40]

She was speaking from Fairview Farm in Scottsville, the country home of her new host, Dr. John E. Manahan, a former professor of history and political science and the only child of a dean of the University of Virginia. To the surprise of everyone who knew her, Anastasia had been granting interviews on a more or less regular basis. The headlines said it all: " 'Anastasia' Finds Haven in Virginia — Mystery Woman to Stay";[41] "Fight to Prove Identity Wearisome — She Doesn't Care Anymore";[42] " 'Daughter' of Last Tsar Steals Show at City D.A.R. Luncheon."[43] Generally Anastasia appeared in the company of Gleb Botkin, the bearded, chain-smoking "Most Reverend Archbishop of the Church of Aphrodite," who seemed to fascinate the reporters almost as much as the tiny woman in the "sleeveless flowered blouse, two silk scarves around her neck, maroon slacks and fluffy white slippers."[44] The two of them together, chatting about the past and utterly oblivious to the world's opinion of their respective creeds, were a sight the American reporters did not easily forget. After Anastasia's arrival at Dulles Airport, a waggish speechwriter in Lyndon Johnson's White House thought it might be fun if Marjorie Merriweather Post gave a reception for her in Washington (it never came off),[45] and later in the year she received an invitation to Richard Nixon's inaugural.[46] She declined to attend.

For the moment the jovial, rotund Dr. Manahan, "Jack" to his friends, remained largely in the background. "She is my guest for as long as she wants to stay," he said.

And why had Jack Manahan brought Anastasia to Charlottesville in the first place?

"To get the history written straight," he replied, "to see that she has a happy and a safe life and to help her win her case in court."[47]

The alias "Anna Anderson" had been discarded the moment she touched down at Dulles. Gleb continued to call her "Your Imperial Highness" in public (although, as Anastasia said, "I was done with that long ago"),[48] while Jack, when enough time had gone by that he could feel himself an intimate, addressed her only as "Anastasia," drawing out the long *a*'s in his piercing, Southern-aristocrat accent.

"Anastasia!" Jack called when reporters or visitors came around. "Come on out now." [49]

Anastasia may have temporarily modified her opinion of journalists, but she had not altered her habits. She kept them waiting as usual. "She is taking a bath," Jack might explain. Or: "She hates having her picture taken." Or: "The clock in her room is always wrong. . . ." [50] Ordinarily, however, she would make a brief appearance, "frail and birdlike, with a short plume of white hair. . . .

"Yes, yes, please do come in," said Anastasia to a reporter for the *Washington Star* from behind the screen door at Scottsville. She even sat down in an armchair to talk with him — something she was rarely seen to do in the company of strangers. She spoke about her first visit to America in 1928. "I was a bit younger then," she remarked with a giggle, pressing her Kleenex against her mouth, "and not with the white hair. . . . Maybe I would one day be an American citizen. That was always my wish, but until now it has not been possible." When the questions turned to her childhood in Russia she was more bored than offended: "That is so far back and so dead, all so past, Russia doesn't exist." The word *dead* had begun to crop up in her conversation almost as frequently as the word *mess*. She pointed to Gleb: "That's the only one alive of my friends. My old friends all are dead." [51]

In August 1968 a picture appeared on the "People" page of *Time* magazine under the caption "Anna and Maria." [52] The "Maria" was Maria Grigorievna Rasputin, the daughter of the "Holy Father," who had come to Charlottesville "uninvited" in the company of her companion and ghostwriter, Patte Barham. Gleb Botkin, loyal as he was, was disgusted: "A Rasputin gives the case a bad name. Where has she been all these years?" [53] In fact Maria had written Anastasia several times in the Black Forest — "I hope, dear, you do remember Maria Rasputin" — saying that she had many things to tell her that could be spoken only "in private." [54] Now the two ladies had their chance to talk, and Maria's subsequent acknowledgment of her "childhood friend" made headlines around the world.

"Yes, she has something," said Maria Rasputin, "— she has the nobility in her, in her gestures, in her voice. I think she is Anastasia. . . . It's been so many years. We all change — she can't recognize me, I can't recognize her. But I think she is genuine." It was Patte

Barham who informed a fascinated press that Maria "was more certain of the identity than she was willing to say to a reporter." The night after her first meeting with Anastasia, Maria had "paced the floor instead of sleeping," saying, "Bless God, it is [she], but it is such a decision, I am afraid almost to think about it. . . . It gives me chills."[55]

"I would say that Maria is completely sold," said Patte Barham,[56] but there is no lasting record of Anastasia's own ideas about Maria. Jack Manahan later ventured that "a Rasputin in the house is an albatross around the neck." Indeed, the ladies shortly had a falling-out. Jack explained that Maria "wanted Anastasia to come to Hollywood to make movies" and that Anastasia had ordered her evicted.[57] Maria protested to the contrary that it was Anastasia's stunningly unexpected marriage to Jack at the end of the year that changed her mind about Anastasia's identity. "This is a shocking thing," said Maria Rasputin,[58] and indeed it was: it left Anastasia's old friends reeling.

The wedding had been performed on December 23 in the office of City Sergeant Raymond Pace, with Gleb Botkin as best man. After they had recovered from the shock, Anastasia's friends in Europe were content — eager, as a matter of fact — to regard the match as a mere marriage of convenience, brought about by the imminent expiration of Anastasia's visa and her adamant refusal to approach the German embassy in Washington for a renewal. The pictures taken after the ceremony showed the new Mrs. Manahan sitting in her furs, with Gleb at her side and Jack — at forty-nine nearly twenty years his bride's junior — standing behind them both, beaming. Gleb had seriously considered marrying Anastasia himself, but, with a heart condition, he wondered who would be obliged to take care of whom, and finally he rejected the notion on the grounds that it would be "like marrying [his] sovereign."[59] So Jack was the obvious choice, and if the union began with expedience in mind it quickly developed into something else. Some said it was comradeship, others that it was folie à deux, but in fact Anastasia doted on Jack and believed, with some justification, that she owed him "everything." She need never again worry about where she would go or, for that matter, who she would be. She was a proud, defiant, and *legal* Anastasia Manahan.

"Well," Jack asked Gleb Botkin after the wedding, "what would Tsar Nicholas think if he could see his new son-in-law?"

"I think he would be grateful," said Gleb.[60]

Gleb died of a heart attack at the end of December 1969, just before Anastasia's case was due to be argued before the Supreme Court in Karlsruhe. The death of her friend left her in a state of shock. Of course Gleb had been poisoned; he was only one of many to meet "a strange end." [61] The timing, however, as so often in Anastasia's life, could not have been worse. For weeks her attorney in Karlsruhe, Baron von Stackelberg, had been writing Jack Manahan to urge that Anastasia be present in court when the judges met to hear the pleas. Prince Frederick, too, had written Charlottesville begging Anastasia to come, so that the judges could see her as she "really" was, "natural and straightforward." It would be a fine opportunity, too, the Prince added pointedly, to "thank all [her] many friends for their everlasting activities in [her] interest." [62] But Anastasia refused even to consider the possibility, with the argument that her "so-called friends" would try to imprison her if she returned to Germany: "They would never let me leave again." [63] In lieu of a personal appearance, therefore, she sent a portrait of herself to Kurt Pagendarm, the President of the Court, signed with the best wishes of "Anastasia and John E. Manahan."

"These things happen," said Judge Pagendarm on the morning of January 19, 1970. "I don't think anyone will imagine I'm being unfairly influenced by this." [64] Pagendarm was smiling. He sat at the bench with his four colleagues in the former palace of the Grand Dukes of Baden and observed the turnout. Prince Frederick had arrived with his elder brother and with Ian Lilburn, who, in the past two years, had "performed miracles" by organizing the evidence for Baron von Stackelberg and preparing a seventy-page index just to contain the names of the witnesses. Princess Marianne was there, along with Dominique Auclères and Carl-August Wollmann, who had kept his distance from the others since 1967 and who, according to Mme. Auclères, was looking "more transparent and emaciated than ever."

"This Anastasia trial has ruined his career, you know," whispered Ferdinand of Schönaich-Carolath, the Kaiser's stepson, who had also appeared. "Just imagine — an East Prussian immigrant daring to treat the Hamburg judges the way he did!"

On the other side of the chamber, in the area reserved for the defense, sat Günther von Berenberg-Gossler with Edward Kersten, the Duchess of Mecklenburg's new attorney at Karlsruhe, and between them, for the first time, the Duchess herself. What had possessed her to come? the reporters wondered as they watched Barbara staring calmly ahead at the judges. Dominique Auclères took note ironically of the "extraordinary resemblance" the Duchess bore to her mother's brother, Prince Frederick: "the same straight brow, the same profile, the same jaw and high cheekbones, and the same stony faces when their eyes met." [65] But the final session of "Anastasia's Monster Trial" held no surprises in store. The lawyers' briefs had long ago been read and the hearing was only a formality.

"The court is going to go over certain points in the dossier," said Judge Pagendarm. "And then it will decide. It will decide in all fairness." [66]

The night before the judgment Ian Lilburn dreamed that Anastasia had won. Next morning, on February 17, 1970, he found himself sitting in a high box in the courtroom as "the plaintiff's historical advisor." [67] It was fifty years to the day since "Fräulein Unbekannt's" attempt at suicide in the Landwehr Canal. Lilburn observed that Judge Pagendarm, when he read the negative ruling, kept calling the plaintiff "Anastasia" without correcting himself.

The appeal was rejected, but the case, technically, was not closed. The judgment held that Anastasia's claim must be regarded as "non liquet" — "neither established nor refuted," "unsatisfactory to both parties." [68] The court could not accept Baron von Stackelberg's argument that the burden of proof had been exaggerated at Hamburg, could not agree to bend the rules of German civil law by shifting that burden to the opposition ("It would be incompatible with a well-ordered state to require that one party surrender property to another merely because he cannot prove that the other has no right to it"),[69] and could not urge the German courts to compare the cases before them to mosaics. True, Grand Duchess Anastasia's death had never been proven, but neither had her escape. True, the judges at Hamburg had refused to credit their scientific experts, but that was a matter for their own decision: "It rests solely in the discretion of the presiding judge." [70] The plaintiff had been free at any time to change her name legally to "Anastasia Nicolaievna Romanov," just as she was now free to bring a new suit against any other member of the imperial family in the lowest court. In closing, Judge Pagendarm wanted it understood that his ruling constituted no reflection on Anastasia's true identity: "We have not decided that the plaintiff is not Grand Duchess Anastasia, but only that the Hamburg court made its decision without legal mistakes and without procedural errors." [71]

The Karlsruhe verdict — the "draw" at the Supreme Court — left

Anastasia's friends emotionally flattened; not "knocked down," as they had been at Hamburg, but feeling drained and empty. It could be looked on as a kind of victory, they agreed, for how many claimants in the long and colorful history of royal pretenders had ever battled her case so far, or won a judgment of such passing respect? Later Judge Pagendarm advised Baron von Stackelberg privately that the Supreme Court could just as easily have ruled in Anastasia's favor — "but what good would it do?" [72] Should she be dragged back to the beginning as she neared the age of seventy, to go through the whole ordeal of the trials *again?* Should her new life in Charlottesville be disrupted? Was there any guarantee that another tribunal would prove more imaginative and fair-minded than those in Hamburg? Pagendarm felt the weight of the decision he had made, and when he later attended a lecture Prince Frederick gave about Anastasia, he listened with approval to the arguments in her favor. "I am glad you told that story, Your Highness," the judge remarked when Prince Frederick had finished a particular anecdote, "because if you had not, I would have." [73]

In Charlottesville, Jack Manahan declared that he was "surprised" by his wife's defeat before the Supreme Court — "because people there said she would win" — but in reality he was not much bothered by the verdict. [74] Neither was Anastasia. "We go on," she said. [75] ". . . It was wrong to have it in the newspapers. It cannot be risked again, and it won't be." [76] For the next several years she nodded silently whenever her husband said that he was going to bring the case before the World Court. Finally Jack, too, stopped talking about courtrooms. "For myself," said Jack, "I feel this is a case to go before the bar of history." [77]

Thus the "Anastasians" were disbanded for good. Baron von Stackelberg realized that another trip through the courts would probably be a waste of time unless he had some dramatic and conclusive new evidence to offer. He waited for it patiently in Karlsruhe, but it was not until 1977 that someone came forward with the proof he was looking for — what Dominique Auclères called *"la chose nouvelle."* [78]

The next years were spent very much on the go, in a kind of bizarre, uninterrupted royal progress. The Manahans were never idle. *"If one stops,"* said Anastasia, *"then it is over."* [79] When they were not receiving guests at their elegant one-story colonial house on Charlottesville's exclusive University Circle, they were dining at the

Farmington Country Club, touring Monticello or the Blue Ridge Mountains, tending to the animals down at the farm, hopping into the station wagon or the pickup truck for an impromptu drive to Washington or New York City, calling on Romanov and Manahan relations or genealogical conventions in North Carolina, Florida, Georgia, Texas. "At the recent National Assembly of the Huguenot Society of Manakin held in Dallas, Texas, at the Sheraton-Dallas," wrote Jack in his *Coppage Family Bulletin,* "your editor was unanimously elected Honorary National President. Accompanied by his wife Anastasia, last Grand Duchess of Russia still surviving, who took an emu Easter egg with her and made Dallas headlines, he made in the month of May a 3,027-mile trip by car, visiting twice Emily Virginia Mills in Pine Bluff, Arkansas, who introduced them to Mrs. H. L. Knorr, National Honorary President General of the Order of the Crown, who has in her house the largest card index file of Virginia marriages in existence, which was carefully checked for Coppage and Coppedge . . . "[80] And so on. This was the kind of printed announcement that streamed out of University Circle all the time, and which Jack sent to genealogy enthusiasts and "Anastasia" buffs alike, without clear regard for his correspondents' sphere of interest. Reporters frequently came away from Charlottesville in a daze, and not because Anastasia had confounded them. Jack Manahan was a nonstop talker, unflaggingly gracious and hospitable, ebullient, opinionated, with a southern gentleman's inscrutable courtesy and a story to tell about any subject.

Anastasia was more than happy with her husband's gregariousness. It kept people at a distance from her. All inquiries she referred to Jack ("You must speak with my husband"), just as she refused to accept in person the gifts people brought her ("It is much too valuable; you must give it to my husband").[81] If she was present during one of Jack's marathon speeches — and frequently she was not — she ordinarily sat with her head bowed, listening very intently but making no remark until he had said something she regarded as inaccurate, or foolish, or embarrassing. "Don't believe a word he says," Anastasia advised.[82] Then she would begin to berate him in German, the language they most often used together, calling him by the simple nickname she had chosen: Hans.

"Hans!" she would cry. "Hans! *Mach ein Ende! Mach ein Ende!*"[83]

"Yes, dear," Jack would reply, *"I'll make an end."* Then he would go right on talking until his guest had either excused himself or become so plainly inattentive that Jack had to change the subject. Many people were frustrated by the situation. They had come to meet the legendary Anastasia, to hear Anastasia's story from her own lips, they supposed, and instead they encountered this walking encyclopedia, in his plaid jacket and his patriotic tie, with his white leather shoes and, later on, his official Bicentennial hat, connecting his wife's case with the "International Communist Conspiracy" and declaring that "the world is due to be overturned sometime soon. . . . A second George Washington will emerge to preside over a true American independence."[84] Dave Smith of the *Los Angeles Times* left Charlottesville with the disagreeable impression that Anastasia had been reduced to the status of a *"holy object"* in Jack Manahan's collection — *"a relic. A totem. A thing."*[85] But the "totem" still had a terrific sense of humor. For weeks she carried in her handbag a table-card from a local restaurant advertising a variety of red wine and promising, "If you drink a glass of this, you'll think you're Anastasia, too."[86]

The journalists who saw Anastasia were, as ever, divided on the subject of her identity. Some, like Dave Smith, took the time to research her story in advance, but most arrived in Charlottesville on the spur of the moment and had trouble agreeing even on her physical appearance. One reporter talked about her *"cold"* eyes, *"not at all merry,"*[87] while another went into raptures over their brightness and charm, their color "as blue as the windows of heaven." One mentioned her *"haughty, inscrutable, arrogant"* manner,[88] while the next noted that "she seems about to flee in terror." Her hair, "iron-grey with a trace of rust, is cut short and wispy over the forehead, in a kind of Prince Valiant, medieval style. . . . She wanders about the room a lot, and sometimes just vanishes into another part of the house. She seems royal, if at all, in her reticence. Mostly, she gives the impression of being a delicate, well-raised, somewhat addled spinster who has lived most of her life sheltered from the world." Anastasia had taken to answering questions with a shrug: "Many believe me, many do not. . . .[89] *I think maybe I live too long."*[90] Then Jack would break in to argue her case in his particular fashion while she ran off to tend to an ever-growing menage of dogs (there were seven Irish setters) and stray cats (no one knew how many). "They are very ill behaved," said Anastasia of "the kittens." "It looks as if seven devils have been at work here."[91]

She had instantly set about turning the grounds of the house on University Circle into a replica of the yard at Unterlengenhardt.

Within a year the weeds had grown, a wire fence had gone up, and the exquisite front windows were covered over with cardboard. She was seen scattering huge branches, rotted tree-stumps, and sacks of coal and dried leaves around the lawn, remarking that these were regrettable but necessary "traps." [92] Jack protested that there was nothing he could do about the mess, because "that's the way Anastasia likes to live." [93] Inside, she and Jack occupied separate bedrooms at the end of the hall on the main floor. The living room, meantime, had been transformed into an "Anastasia" museum, where sat the accumulated memorabilia of a lifetime, some of it valuable, some of it pure junk — she made no distinction. Books lined the walls from floor to ceiling, piled on top of each other when shelf space ran out and sometimes running seven rows deep. Until his death in 1976 the Manahans were waited on daily by Jack's black butler, James, who imagined that he had been through a lot in his life but who never accustomed himself to his employer's new wife or to the steady deterioration of the Manahan estate.

"I know you must feel like you've taken your life into your hands to come here," said Jack to a guest. "But we do all this to discourage visitors. We had to, they bothered us so." [94] Actually, Jack did not seem in the least inclined to discourage visitors. Anastasia's old friends were amazed to find out how public her life had become. She still fussed about meeting people, of course, but it seemed to be more out of habit than anything else. "Anastasia!" Jack would shout through her door after an hour or two of arguing. "We're going out to the car now, and I'm going to honk four times when we're ready to leave. Then *you* are going to come out of that room and join us." [95]

Loudly regretting his wife's "Russian" temperament, Jack would herd his guests into the station wagon, picking up a dog or two along the way. Then he would lean on the horn until he heard the front door slam and saw Anastasia, her face set in a scowl, march toward the car, her red patent-leather handbag slung over her paralyzed arm, waving aside the stammered greetings of her visitors and saying brusquely, "Do not shake my hand." But she wasn't angry at them. She was angry at "this husband of mine. . . . Do other men treat their wives like this? . . . I am married to a most unreasonable man."

Jack grinned, victorious, and went right on talking. "I am married to the White Queen," he liked to say, "and the White Queen usually wins."

"What nonsense you are talking. *Ruhe!* [Be quiet!]"

"Uh-oh. I think I've said the wrong thing. Have I said the wrong thing, Anastasia?"

"Entirely."

Her voice and her vocabulary still carried the traces of a girl who had learned English in the first years of the century. Her world was peopled with "scoundrels," "rascals," and "scalawags." She was the victim of "so much nonsense" and a husband who would not "fetch" her a clean "cushion-sheet" — a pillow case — when she wanted one. Of course her husband was "quite mad" — "tipsy-tipsy-tra-la-la," as Anastasia said. But by and large her English had been overtaken by her German, which she now employed in the same way she had used the other in the Black Forest: in order that she might speak freely among strangers. Verbs were banished to the end of her sentences, modifiers dangled every which way, while each affirmation or objection to her husband's stories was qualified by a brisk, German "*Absolut!*" or, as circumstance demanded, "*Absolut not!*" Ignorant of the long and incredible journey of Anastasia Tschaikovsky-Anderson-Manahan, and not much enlightened by the occasional stories about her in the newspapers, people in Charlottesville judged her on sight, as she sat in restaurants or at the country club picking at her cottage cheese, her mashed potatoes, and her ice-cream sundaes — she had become a strict vegetarian and believed firmly in reincarnation — and scooping the remains of everyone's lunch into wads of tinfoil to take home for the cats.

"May I just ask you a personal question about your life now?" asked a correspondent for ABC television's "Good Morning America." He was sitting with Anastasia in a room at the country club, Jack having decided that the house on University Circle was no longer fit for public viewing.

"What is your life like now?"

"Now," said Anastasia, "it is a happy life."

"It is?"

"Yes, so."

There was a long silence.

The ABC people wanted Anastasia to make a public affirmation, to say aloud the three words which, since 1920, she had always been loath to say: "I am Anastasia." When her interlocutor led up to it she was completely baffled, and the simple question of who she was had to be repeated several times. "I am the daughter of the Tsar of Russia," said Anastasia finally. "That's all. And nothing else. What should I be otherwise?"[96] By the time she had consented to a second television appearance a year later the "shouting" had resumed in the world press and she was in no mood for pleasantries.

"How shall I tell you who I am?" she asked, taunting the camera and the public behind it. "In which way? Can you tell me that? Can you really prove to me who you are?"[97]

"I can prove who *I* am," said Jack unhelpfully.

Anastasia was quiet a moment. Then she said, "You believe it or you don't believe it. It doesn't matter. In no anyway whatsoever."

The television interviews were merely the highlights of a new burst of publicity that had attended the publication of Anthony Summers's and Tom Mangold's *The File on the Tsar* in the autumn of 1976. The book had become a best-seller in England on the strength of its theory that the Empress of Russia and her four daughters had not been murdered at Ekaterinburg and that Grand Duchess Anastasia had probably escaped to the West. Now the house on University Circle was under siege. It was as bad as anything Unterlengenhardt had seen.

"I know what you want," said Anastasia to the ABC reporter. "For the mystery. I know exactly."[98] But she would not talk with anyone about the murder of the Russian imperial family. When pestered about it, she turned to Jack and said, "*Zu diesen Sachen kann ich doch nicht antworten* [I cannot answer to these things]." "I cannot tell it. I cannot. I will be killed at once."[99]

People suspected that she enjoyed being mysterious, that she was taking some small revenge after all these years, now that the scholars were turning to *her* to know what had happened. "Events in Ekaterinburg were quite different from what they say," she had told Prince Frederick years before, "but if *I* say that, they think I'm mad." Then she had been quoted in *The File on the Tsar:* "There was no massacre there, but I cannot tell the rest."[100]

She would not budge on this subject. "She has her reasons," said Jack. "And I respect her reasons." Maybe she would tell it one day, and maybe not. Then again, said Jack, "perhaps Anastasia is fooling us all on this point. . . ."[101] It certainly began to look like it as the months went by and stories emerged from University Circle about "doubles" being murdered in the imperial family's place, about royal trains hurtling across Siberia to the Russian frontier, about the Tsar ending his days in Denmark and his daughters finding refuge with the Grand Duke of Hesse in Darmstadt. Only a few of

Anastasia's inquisitors had the courtesy to let the subject rest, and the deathly silence was edited out of the *Good Morning America* tape when the correspondent asked her to tell him directly what had happened to her sisters. Still the pilgrimage to Charlottesville kept up unabated. There had never been such an incongruous living legend — this frail old lady in her grimy leather coat, wearing a hat that might have done a Cossack proud and looking more and more like a granny apple doll; dragging her brambles and her sacks of coal across her front yard; one day finding an oppossum and a dead rabbit among her kittens and saying, in a most dramatic tone of voice, "Look what I have come to! I must live like a gypsy!"[102] People read mystery into her every word and tragedy in the still dignified way she held out her hand, *"as if across an abyss."*[103] But Anastasia had played out her role. "Write no more," she entreated her guests. "Enough has been said. It is all a nonsense. Throw it in the fire."[104]

She did not forgive Prince Frederick until the autumn of 1977. Jack had been trying to effect a reconciliation for a number of years, but Anastasia had not forgotten the mass extermination of her pets in Unterlengenhardt. When her young friend Brien Horan went to Europe in 1973 he asked her if he ought to see the Prince, and she replied, "Better not, better not. He is very dangerous, very strange; no, no, better not."[105]

In the end, somehow, with Brien's help, Jack managed to overrule his wife's objections and sent Prince Frederick the money for a plane ticket to Charlottesville. Why not have Ian Lilburn come too? Jack figured, making out another check and inviting them both. Lilburn had only one day to get ready, and he flew out of his town house in London trailing shirts and ties and carrying a present he had been saving for Anastasia for several years.

The year 1977 was Anastasia's last "good year" and the year, many believed, of her vindication. Since 1970 her attorney in Karlsruhe, Baron von Stackelberg, had been looking for some irrefutable evidence with which to reintroduce her case. In February word came from Munich that Dr. Moritz Furtmayr, one of West Germany's most prominent forensic experts, had concluded on the basis of selected photographs that "the current Mrs. Manahan" and the daughter of the Tsar were one and the same person.[106] This was no mere repetition of the earlier studies at Hamburg. Furtmayr had already satisfied himself of Anastasia's authenticity several years before, when he submitted her pictures to a system of identification he had devised himself and which, at least in criminal cases, had been accepted as positive proof by the courts. His method — known as "P.I.K." — employed a comparison of "the cardinal points of the skull, [which,] once formed, retain the same relation with each other until death."[107] Working with graphs and grids, Furtmayr demonstrated that every human face produces a clear and distinct "headprint" when lines are drawn to connect the bones, and he added that in his hundreds of studies he had never seen two of these "headprints" match unless the subjects were identical. With "P.I.K." Furtmayr had been able to identify the victims of fires, gunshot blasts to the face, and other calamities, and now he took his study of Anastasia one step farther. From the very beginning the anthropological experts had been confounded by Anastasia's controversial right ear, which appeared in several twists and curves not to correspond with photographs of the Tsar's daughter. Fifty years after the first negative comparison ordered by the court of Darmstadt Furtmayr found out why: the Darmstadt experts, and all of the others after them, had been working with a photograph taken of Anastasia at the Dalldorf Asylum, the negative of which had been reversed when the picture was printed. Thus her *left* ear had been compared to the Grand Duchess's *right* ear. In reality, said Furtmayr when he had set things right, the ears were "identical in 17 anatomical points and tissue formations, five more than the dozen points normally accepted by West German courts to establish a person's identity."[108]

Anastasia's friends felt a tremendous rush of righteous triumph when they heard about Dr. Furtmayr's studies. At the Supreme Court Baron von Stackelberg announced that Anastasia's case could reopen as soon as she or her proxy, Prince Frederick, gave the signal. It was Prince Frederick who decided not to go ahead with it.[109] He had taken to heart the reasoning of Judge Pagendarm at Karlsruhe: "What good would it do?" What would Anastasia gain now through legal identification? The royal families of Europe, undoubtedly, would not admit to a mistake and embrace Anastasia as one of their own. She would still be required to submit to an interrogation by her judges, and, as Prince Frederick knew, in her current mood she would just as soon "spit at them" all.

"Of course," Anastasia had said[110] when she heard that her ear matched "the ear of the Grand Duchess" — "How could it be anything else? . . . I am ill of this dirt. I will not read this dirt. Is my ear so important? I am ill of the constant, constant questions. Even little children ask me, 'Anastasia, when will you get your jewelry back?' I will never get it back. I have no desire for wealth. I would never wear it." [111]

"We had won a Pyrrhic victory," said Dominique Auclères as she closed her memoirs of the "Anastasia" affair. "A victory without a happy end." [112]

Prince Frederick arrived in Charlottesville with Ian Lilburn in December 1977, there to enjoy a week of parties, dinners, and country drives *à la Manahan*. Her neighbors had never seen Anastasia so "open and free" as she was with the Prince. "They were like brother and sister," said one — Prince Frederick, the "charmeur," and Anastasia, the irrepressible "Madame Mutabor." [113] It was no reflection on Jack, the neighbors pointed out: it was just a different kind of relationship. It was a relationship that did not need to explain itself. And when Ian Lilburn gave Anastasia the present he had been saving for her she threw him that radiant smile that still had the power to take his breath away. She had said to him in the Black Forest, many years before, that she remembered a song her mother had sung to her — "a song about swallows." [114] Lilburn had found it for her in a book of student drinking songs: "Wenn die Schwalben heimwärts ziehn [When the Swallows Homeward Fly]" by Franz Abt:

> *Wenn die Schwalben heimwärts ziehn,*
> *wenn die Rosen nicht mehr blühn,*
> *wenn der Nachtigall Gesang*
> *mit der Nachtigall verklang,*
> *fragt das Herz in bangem Schmerz,*
> *fragt das Herz in bangem Schmerz*
> *ob ich dich auch wiederseh'?*
> *Scheiden, ach Scheiden, Scheiden thut weh!*
> *Scheiden, ach Scheiden, Scheiden thut weh!*
>
> When the swallows homeward fly,
> When the rose begins to die,
> When the nightingale's sweet song
> With the nightingale is gone,
> Then the heart cries out in pain,
> Then the heart cries out in pain,
> Will I see you once again?
> Parting, ah, parting — parting is sad!
> Parting, ah, parting — parting is sad!

She was delighted with the gift, thrilled, but she had to tell Lilburn the truth: "My mother sang it in English." ("I'll bet she did, too," Lilburn remarked. "It was just the kind of sentimental London music-hall turn the Empress would have loved.") [115]

They said good-bye just before Christmas, Ian Lilburn moving on to New Haven and New York and Prince Frederick heading south to see his sister and brother-in-law at Finca San Miguel in Costa Rica. From now on the Prince was a welcome guest at University Circle and thus, to his regret, was witness to the sad and degrading last years of "Madame Mutabor." By September 1978 the house had deteriorated so drastically and been so thoroughly befouled by cats and dogs as to pose a health hazard to the entire neighborhood, and Jack and Anastasia were haled into court [116] on charges of "failing to maintain clean and sanitary premises, allowing refuse to collect on their premises and allowing weeds and brush to grow in excess of 18 inches." It wasn't the first time Jack had been warned. The neighbors had been complaining for some time now. "There's a great smell emanating from the property," said Dr. Richard A. Meade, a professor of education at the university and one-time patient friend of the Manahans. "I think it could be described as a stench."

Anastasia's day in court was not without comedy. "We haven't used a vacuum in at least six years," Jack told Judge D. B. Marshall, "and now it's too late." Jack's old friends had been worrying about him a lot lately. They could see how tired he was, how thin he had become, how the strain of looking after Anastasia had turned him into an old man before his time. Now, in court, Jack produced in evidence samples of the kudzu vine, which, he said, had overrun his yard. "Manahan," wrote Ray McGrath in the *Daily Progress,* "whose striped tie bore the Virginia colors of orange and blue, said the vines were invading his property. . . . He held up a small vine and a four-foot vine more than an inch in diameter. 'The little vine becomes this,' he said, holding up the larger vine and noting that the kudzu can grow as much as 27 inches on a hot, wet July night.

Be that as it may, said the judge, it did not explain the trash on the lawn. Jack replied that his wife's dogs ate more than ninety cans of food every week. "I am hard put to it," he said, "to keep the family going, to feed all the livestock [at the farm] and pick up all the cans."

It was Anastasia's turn now to answer the charges against her. She had been sitting in the last row of the courtroom, evidently paying no attention whatever to the proceedings, and when Judge Marshall called her before the bench she didn't move. Jack beckoned to her, and she still didn't move.

"I think she feels she's not subject to American law," said Jack.

"She's going to have to answer these charges like any other person," said the judge. Did she prefer to be cited for contempt? But Marshall agreed to continue her case for the moment, and in the end nobody heard another word about it.

Judge Marshall found Jack guilty and gave him three weeks to clean up the property on University Circle. Cats and dogs would henceforth stay out in Scottsville, he ruled, before declaring, "Charlottesville has been known for its diverse people, and I don't want to punish you for your diversity. But I want spectacular improvements on those conditions."

The house was soon restored to a semblance of neatness, but it was only a matter of months before it had degenerated again. The pattern held. Each time Jack was ordered to clean up his property, he did so, and each time he did so, the premises quickly filled again with papers, branches, and other trash. People began to wonder where Anastasia's "eccentricity" ended and Jack's began, or if there was a difference any longer. At least the animals were gone (although Anastasia still insisted on bringing some of the dogs with her when she came back from her daily excursion to Scottsville). Then one day Jack came running to the house of their good friends, Dr. Nathaniel Ewell and his wife, Mildred, to tell them that Anastasia was dying. He was very upset.

Dr. Ewell found her on her camp bed. Something was seriously wrong: this was not another collapse brought on by starvation or fatigue. At the hospital it was discovered that she had an intestinal blockage, common enough in the elderly but life-threatening all the same, and Dr. Ewell later remarked that Anastasia had been saved by only a matter of hours.

"Do you *want* to live?" he had asked her when she rallied momentarily, and she had answered, "Yes, I do." [117]

She never walked again. She had developed arthritis in her feet, but it wasn't bad enough to cripple her. Rather, it seemed to everyone when she came home that she had just given up, that she was too tired to do anything more than sit in her blue wheelchair or in the front seat of the station wagon, which itself had come to resemble a junk heap. A woman who came from Manassas to meet her saw boxes of cornflakes, a bottle of port wine, empty Styrofoam cups, a package of unopened cherry tarts, and more brown bags than she could count lying on the floor beneath Anastasia's feet. She was so tiny, so thin, and so bent now that people wondered in black amusement if she wouldn't one day disappear among the refuse. Nevertheless, she took the time to admire her visitor's young son, saying that the baby was "a darling, such a darling." She liked his name: Andrew.[118]

She and Jack had more or less been driven by their possessions out of the main house and now stayed mostly in a small apartment in the building they owned across the driveway. There Jack gave Anastasia the bath she still insisted on having every day, fed her her meals when she would eat them, and set her gently down on her bed at night, jumping up at all hours when she called to him. Her cry — "Hans!" — was not the brisk command it had once been. It was plaintive, dragged out, and repeated ceaselessly until he either woke up or dropped whatever he was doing to attend her.

Lame, increasingly disoriented, sometimes unsure of her surroundings but still perfectly lucid when she wanted to be heard, Anastasia somehow kept up her frantic pace. Jack would carry her out to the car first thing in the morning for the trip to Scottsville, and she would sit all day in the front seat while he drove around the city to call on neighbors, go to the bank, eat lunch and dinner at Ken Jonson's cafeteria, or take her to attend some funeral, lawn sale, or genealogical gathering. They were known by sight all over Virginia. Once, when their car broke down near Culpeper, a nervous companion tried to explain to the state police that Anastasia would never consent to leave the vehicle and that the car would have to be towed with her in it, never mind the law.

"Don't worry about it," the officer replied. "We all know these two."

She had begun to pine for Unterlengenhardt. "It breaks my heart," she said. "It breaks my heart." America was no longer the haven she had thought it. Malicious teenagers had taken to harassing her, breaking windows, shooting at the dogs on the farm for sport, poking holes in the tires of the car, and making unkind remarks about "bag ladies."

"This was once a beautiful car," Anastasia told a friend in May of 1981. "Look at it now." She and Jack were on their way to a garden party in Richmond.

"I am tired of garden parties," said Anastasia suddenly.

Jack began to sing to her. He did it frequently, because his songs always seemed to cheer her up. Her favorite was "Dominique."

"Hans!" she said. "Hans, I want to go back to Europe. I want to go to Paris and have tea with Tatiana Botkin." She ordered that he stop the car. She wanted a cup of coffee — "boiling hot, boiling hot." She had become addicted to coffee, she admitted, while saying it was strange: "Never until I was here in America did I drink coffee." Jack disapproved, but there was "nothing I can do about it, nothing I can do." He watched as Anastasia poured five or six packets of sugar into the cup.

"Russian," she said with a grin. "It is very Russian."

"I'm just trying to keep Anastasia alive until her eightieth birthday," said Jack. "Just to keep her alive until then."

"I will go back to Germany," Anastasia continued. "I will go back to Unterlengenhardt. I will go in a sanatorium." Then she nodded off. She was often asleep now. She would be talking and then her head would fall to her chest.

"Next time we meet in Germany," she said, awake again, when Jack dropped off their guest at the bus station in Fredericksburg. Then the battered station wagon, crammed to bursting with trash, Anastasia's wheelchair poking out the back window, roared off in the direction of Richmond.[119]

More than seventy-five people had gathered on the front lawn of Anastasia's house on University Circle on June 18, 1981. She had made it — eighty years. She sat in her chair in a white wool shawl, a blanket over her legs, a pink straw hat with a jaunty feather stuck on her head, and snapped at Jack only half-heartedly when he announced to their guests that she was a descendant of Genghis Khan. She smiled at her friends and told them how she had been poisoned in 1979 and taken to the hospital: "I came twelve days to the end." Prince Frederick had sent her his greetings from the train station in Karlsruhe on his way to see the Grand Duchess of Saxe-Weimar. She ate a little bit and had a glass of punch. She was very tired.[120]

A few days later Jack and Anastasia met the reporters again on the lawn.

"They think I'm insane," said Anastasia of the world at large.

"If Anastasia had the power," said Jack, "she says she would change her birthright."

Anastasia nodded.

"It has been a curse," said Jack.

Anastasia nodded again. Then she asked Jack to take her back to the car. She wanted to be alone.[121]

She sat by herself for an hour or two, watching the students run to their rehearsals at the university theatre behind her house, probably talking to "Perevel," the dog in the back seat, telling him what "a bad boy" he had been and worrying about his hind leg, which had been hit by a bullet in Scottsville. She was going to live long enough to know about Dominique Auclères's death in September, to know that a new play based on her life had opened in New York, York, and to receive a copy of the commemorative ikon issued by the Russian Orthodox Church Outside of Russia, which, in October 1981, had canonized the Russian imperial family — the Tsar, the Empress, Alexis, and the four Grand Duchesses. She looked at the image of Anastasia — "The Holy Martyr Anastasia Nicolaievna" —a light mantle cast over her shoulders, a taper in her hand, and a halo shining at the back of her hair. She wept over it for a while, then she put it among her most cherished possessions: a massive portrait of Nicholas II, an oil painting of Duke George of Leuchtenberg, a book of stories by Harriet von Rathlef, and a tinted photograph of herself, taken at Miss Jennings's in 1929.[122]

She had never let anybody copy that picture. "I cannot give it out of my hands," she said. "I could never replace it." [123] It shows her laughing, facing the light that streams in from the tall windows on Park Avenue, dressed in a powder-blue gown and a heavy white fur, her right hand stretched out to balance her parakeets on her fingers.

ACKNOWLEDGMENTS

It seems to be customary for writers to conclude their acknowledgments by thanking their families. I would like to begin by thanking mine: my parents, Frederick Kurth and Constance Schindler Kurth; sisters, Barbara Kurth and Gillian Randall; brothers, Richard and Robert, and their wives, Virginia and Elizabeth, for their unfailing support, material and otherwise, and the faith they have always demonstrated in this project and in me. It is my honor also to acknowledge publicly the contribution of H. H. Prince Frederick Ernest of Saxe-Altenburg, of Ian R. Lilburn, Brien Purcell Horan, Mme. Tatiana Botkin, Mrs. Edward J. Wynkoop, and the late Mme. Suzanne D'Adler, known in her profession as Dominique Auclères — six generous people, who, from the start, did not hesitate to share with me their knowledge, ideas, and private papers concerning the "Anastasia" affair. This book could never have been written without their cooperation and kind assistance.

Many, many others need to be thanked for the help they gave me during my research, beginning with Rodney G. Dennis, Curator of Manuscripts, and his staff at the Houghton Library at Harvard University; Ron Bulatoff at the Hoover Institution on War, Revolution and Peace in Palo Alto; and the staff at the Bibliothek fur Zeitgeschichte in Stuttgart. For interviews given, time spent, permissions granted, and letters promptly answered I must thank Frau Hedwig

Breitfeld, David and Eugenia Chavchavadze, Prince Paul and Princess Nina Chavchavadze, Hubert Clauser, Professor Robert V. Daniels, Dr. and Mrs. Nathaniel Ewell, the Reverend Andrew Hartsook, Paul Ilyinsky, Willa Iverson, Rosemary Jampolsky-Clauser, Count Vladimir Kleinmichel, Tikhon Kulikovsky, Dr. Charles I. Lambert, Duke Dmitri and Duchess Catherine of Leuchtenberg, Isaac Don Levine, Tom Mangold, Freya von Moltke, Maria Rasputin, Gregg Rittenhouse, Alexander Romanoff, Princess Vera Constantinovna of Russia, Sophie Satin, Marina Schweitzer, Bella Spewack, Curt, Freiherr von Stackelberg, Anthony Summers, Alexandra Tolstoy, Konrad Wahl, and Dr. and Mrs. John J. Weber.

The following people have all helped with criticism, advice, encouragement, footwork, photography, translation, sleeping arrangements, and patience where it counted: Alan Altshuld, Suzon and Georges Balaes, Fran Bradfield, Lane Brown, Mina Caminis, Francine Casanova, Ed Chemaly, Gladys Colburn, William C. Collier, Terrance L. Demas, Sally MacNichol Gavin, Brooke Gladstone, Nancy Haynes, Jane Horner, Jean-Bernard Houriet, Fred Kaplan, Deborah S. Leete, Liz MacFarlane, Susan Mack, Terry McClymonds, Cate McKegney, John Meyer, Kenneth Nalibow, Edith O'Brien, Mary Pappas and the late John Pappas, Olga Pomar, W. Thompson Randall, Nancy Reitano, Nancy Rosenberg, Barbara Sauer Sandage, Verna Siegrest, Mari Siegrest-Jones, Simone Suchet, Craig A. Toth, Charles Towers, Steve VandeGriek, James Wimsatt, Margaret Wimsatt, Bradford Wright, and Ethel Goldstein Wright.

Special thanks to David Sokol.

Separate acknowledgments must go to my agent, Raphael Sagalyn, whose enthusiasm and devotion to *Anastasia* were boundless from the first; to Mary Tondorf-Dick, my editor at Little, Brown, whose pencil is as swift as her hunches are sure; Glea Humez, a woman who gives new meaning to the process of copyediting; Professor Veronica Richel, who struggled with me through the densest and most convoluted of German sentences; Lisa Devlin, who spent many a well-earned vacation poking into archives that for her were unintelligible; Kaye Danforth, whose overseeing of the final manuscript preparation has been invaluable and who may now be surprised to find herself an honorary "Anastasian"; above all to Betty Berman, "the Divine Miss B.," whose warmheartedness, sharp eye, and loving understanding have far exceeded the call of ordinary friendship.

These acknowledgments would not be complete without a word

of thanks to Dr. John Manahan and his wife, the heroine of this book. The subject of publication was never explicitly discussed between Anastasia and me until after I had signed the contract with Little, Brown, and then, to my astonishment and trepidation, she had already heard the news before I had had a chance to tell her. When I went to Charlottesville, however, to inform Anastasia that several of our conversations were going to be published, she smiled and, for the first time, offered me her hand unbidden. It was a reward I had never expected.

NOTES

ABBREVIATIONS USED IN NOTES

A	The unknown woman/Frau Tschaikovsky/Anna Anderson/Anastasia
A "Interviews"	Interviews of Anastasia at the offices of Curtis J. Mar, summer 1929, in EHF
A "Memoirs"	Edward Fallows's proposed version of Anastasia's "autobiography," with separate designation for "My American Experiences," in EHF
Auclères I	*Anastasia, qui êtes-vous?*
Auclères II	"L'Inconnue de Berlin"
BA	Serge Botkin Archive
Botkin I	*The Real Romanovs*
Botkin II	*The Woman Who Rose Again*
Botkin MS.	"Grand Duchess Anastasia"
EHF	Fallows papers
FA	Gilliard and Savitch, *La Fausse Anastasie* (The False Anastasia)
FAZ	*Frankfurter Allgemeine Zeitung*
FOT	Summers and Mangold, *The File on the Tsar*
Hamburg	Records of the *Oberlandesgericht*
Horan MS.	"Anastasia?"
IA	Krug von Nidda, trans. Coburn, *I Am Anastasia* (translation of *Ich, Anastasia, erzähle*), the 1957 "autobiography" commissioned and approved for publication by Anastasia's attorneys
Lavington Diary	Diary of Faith Lavington, kept at Castle Seeon in 1927, transcript (unpaginated) at Hamburg.

PK   Peter Kurth
Rathlef   *Anastasia, Ein Frauenschicksal* . . .
Rathlef MS.   English translation, prepared as affidavit, of above, in
                            EHF
Rathlef/Noeggerath   "Summary" of the Schanzkowska affair
Rathlef notes   Notes of Frau von Rathlef, June 19–July 4, 1925, taken
                            at St. Mary's Hospital, in EHF. All others designated
                            as "loose" and by date where available.

Preface

1. See FA, *passim.*
2. Grand Duke Andrew Vladimirovitch to Grand Duchess Olga Alexandrovna, February 4, 1928, Hamburg (see my Chapter 9).
3. Testimony of Princess Xenia Georgievna of Russia, given at New York City, March 16–17, 1959, transcript at Hamburg.
4. Interview with Ian Lilburn.
5. Lilburn MS.
6. Dehn, *The Real Tsaritsa,* 78.
7. Viroubova, *Memories of the Russian Court,* 343.
8. See Rathlef MS.
9. Buxhoeveden, *The Life and Tragedy of Alexandra Feodorovna,* 342.
10. FOT, 70.
11. Ibid., 52.
12. Vorres, *The Last Grand Duchess,* 254.
13. Transcribed from endpapers in Trewin, *The House of Special Purpose.*
14. Ibid., 75.
15. Bulygin in *The Murder of the Romanovs,* 238–239.
16. John Terraine, *The Life and Times of Lord Mountbatten* (New York: Holt, Rhinehart, and Winston, 1980), 27.
17. Vorres, 256.
18. Francis McCullagh, *Prisoner of the Reds* (London: John Murray, 1921), 133.
19. FOT, 196.

1. Dalldorf

1. Rathlef notes.
2. Interview with Prince Frederick Ernest of Saxe-Altenburg. The Netherlands Palace in Berlin was used as a city residence by various members of the Prussian royal family, among them Empress Alexandra's elder sister, Irene of Prussia. It was A's assumption that if Irene were in the city at all she would be here.
3. Rathlef notes.
4. A "Memoirs," EHF. In 1932, when interrogated by the police in Hannover, A could not recall falling into the water at all. See Hamburg verdict, 28.
5. Police bulletin, quoted in IA, 89.
6. Auclères I, 33.
7. Redern notes. According to the Bonhoeffer report A spoke "an affected Southern German, apparently Franconian in origin, possibly Alemannic," but the note is added that "she was at pains to conceal her dialect." No other report mentions a German accent of any kind.
8. The records of the Berlin police, of the Elisabeth Hospital, and of the Dalldorf Asylum disappeared along with other documents relating to A's case at the end of World War II. The account of A's hospitalization is drawn from four sources: Affidavit of Dr. Friedrich Reich, July 19, 1929, EHF; notes of Erika von Redern, secretary to Edward Fallows, from the records and the bulletin of tne Dalldorf Asylum, May 16, 1929, EHF; report of Captain Nicholas von Schwabe, June 10, 1922, including his observations from the Elisabeth Hospital

records and conversations with the doctors at Dalldorf, EHF; and report of Dr. Karl Bonhoeffer, March 18, 1926, who studied the Dalldorf files and interviewed the nurses before examining A, in EHF and BA.

9. Schwabe report, EHF.

10. Frau Chemnitz (Thea Malinovsky) to Kurt Pastenaci, September 27, 1927, in Rathlef (German 189). Frau Chemnitz was a nurse at the Dalldorf Asylum, where the questioning of A continued.

11. Reich affidavit, EHF.

12. Bonhoeffer report.

13. Protocol of Dr. Wilhelm Völler's visit to Clara Peuthert ("Fräulein P."), April 29, 1927, EHF and Hamburg.

14. Memorandum of Paul Leverkuehn and Kurt Vermehren, October 31, 1938, EHF.

15. Bonhoeffer report, EHF.

16. Reich affidavit, EHF.

17. Redern report, EHF.

18. Police bulletin, IA, 89.

19. Bonhoeffer report, EHF.

20. Hamburg verdict, 31.

21. Fritz Schuricht's protocol of conversations with "Kommissar X," April 29, 1927, EHF.

22. Nogly, 12.

23. Bonhoeffer report, EHF.

24. Redern notes, EHF.

25. Affidavit of Erna Bucholz (nurse), June 29, 1929, EHF. The nurses at the Dalldorf Asylum were interviewed by Dr. Bonhoeffer in March 1926; most had already left statements with Baron Arthur von Kleist in the summer of 1922, as cited. Others given to Edward Fallows.

26. Letter of Frau Chemnitz (Thea Malinovsky) to the *Berliner Nachtausgabe,* March 5, 1927.

27. Bonhoeffer report, EHF.

28. Affidavit of Emilie Barfknecht (nurse), June 12, 1922, EHF.

29. Schwabe report, EHF.

30. Bonhoeffer report, EHF.

31. Chemnitz letter to *Nachtausgabe.*

32. Bucholz affidavit, EHF.

33. Bonhoeffer report.

34. Bonhoeffer report; Schwabe report, EHF.

35. Bonhoeffer report, EHF. The word employed was *Nordlandreise.*

36. Bucholz affidavit, EHF.

37. Barfknecht affidavit, EHF.

38. Hamburg verdict, 30.

39. Bonhoeffer report, EHF.

40. Bucholz affidavit, EHF.

41. Bonhoeffer report, EHF.

42. This was, understandably, one of the most controversial moments of the Anastasia affair — exactly when and to whom A first claimed to be the Tsar's daughter, and which of the daughters, at that. The testimony of Nurse Chemnitz (Malinovsky) on pages 11–12 speaks for itself; for the rest, the nurses only insisted that they had begun to suspect A's identity "before she had received a single visit" from anyone outside the asylum (Bucholz affidavit). It was alleged repeatedly in later years that the nurses themselves first "suggested" to A that she make the claim. There is no evidence to support that contention.

43. Barfknecht affidavit, EHF.

44. Deposition of Dr. Theodor Eitel, May 20, 1959, Hamburg. Eitel treated A during eight months in 1926.

45. Bonhoeffer report, EHF.

46. Bucholz affidavit, EHF.

47. Bonhoeffer report, EHF.

48. Chemnitz letter to *Nachtausgabe.*

49. It has never been established if the magazine in question here was the same one later seen by Clara Peuthert. Nurse Chemnitz (Malinovsky) insisted that the magazine A showed

her during the night shift was a "very old" edition of the *Berliner Illustrierte Zeitung* dating from before World War I. Evidently A herself kept the magazine(s) at her bedside.

50. Affidavit of Bertha Walz (nurse), June 17, 1922, EHF.

51. Bucholz affidavit, EHF.

52. Walz affidavit, EHF.

53. Testimony of December 17, 1958, Hamburg; quoted in memorandum of Kurt Vermehren, March 31, 1962.

54. Chemnitz (Malinovsky) to Fallows, April 15, 1929, EHF.

55. Chemnitz letter to *Nachtausgabe.*

56. The scurrilous notion that the Russian Revolution was the work of some "International Jewish Conspiracy" was so widespread in Germany and elsewhere during the 1920s as to require no actual reference in the minds of its adherents. For particulars about the presumed role of the Jews in the murder of the Russian imperial family, see FOT.

57. Correspondence with Fallows, EHF.

58. Rathlef/Noeggerath.

59. Völler protocol of conversation with Clara Peuthert.

60. Rathlef/Noeggerath.

61. Völler protocol, EHF.

62. Schwabe report, EHF.

63. The *Berliner Illustrierte* was dated October 23, 1921 (photocopy in EHF), and recounted the bare outlines of the slaughter of the imperial family at Ekaterinburg, adding that the Tsar's youngest daughter, Grand Duchess Anastasia, was supposed to have escaped. Those who did not accuse the nurses of "suggesting" to A that she claim the identity accused Clara instead. Since Clara left the asylum declaring to have discovered Grand Duchess *Tatiana,* however, it would seem that she acted independently of anything she had read in the magazine.

64. A to Harriet von Rathlef: Report (undated, 1925–1926) of Harriet von Rathlef, BA.

65. Schwabe report.

66. For further information about the Russian emigration to Europe and the monarchist battles, see Robert C. Williams, *Culture in Exile,* the finest and only complete study of the subject in English.

67. Schwabe report, EHF. Captain von Schwabe claimed descent from the Estonian nobility.

68. This phenomenon continued well into the 1930s, providing the basis for the common assumption that A was just one of many "Anastasias." The only claimants who generated any kind of serious attention besides A, however, were Mrs. Marga Boodts, who claimed to be Olga Nicolaievna; Mrs. Eugenia Smith, who claimed to be Anastasia Nicolaievna (see *Life* magazine, October 18, 1963); and the Polish defector Michal Goleniewsky, who claimed to be the Tsarevitch and still enjoys a certain following. For further reading, see FOT, chapter 17.

69. Schwabe report, EHF; statement of Franz Jaenicke, dated "June 1922," EHF; and statement of Jaenicke, February 27, 1956, Hamburg.

70. Statement of Clara Peuthert, June 10, 1922, EHF.

71. The whole account above is taken from Schwabe report, EHF.

72. Schwabe to A, reported by A to Harriet von Rathlef, in Rathlef notes; also in A "Memoirs," EHF.

73. Statement (*Gutachten*) of Sophie Buxhoeveden, Hamburg; also in FA, 34–36.

74. Auclères I, 36.

75. Schwabe report, EHF.

76. Ibid.

77. Auclères I, 36.

78. Protocol (undated) of Baron Arthur von Kleist, attached to the affidavit of Baroness Maria von Kleist, EHF; the Baron's protocols, whose authenticity has been much disputed, are reproduced in FA, 46–51. For the rest of her life A labored under the charge that she had "switched her story around" after Baroness Buxhoeveden's denial of her identity as "Tatiana." Such evidence as there is, however, plainly indicates that at this stage A had no story to switch.

79. Schwabe report, EHF.

80. Arthur von Kleist to director of Dalldorf, March 22, 1922, EHF. Permission for A's release was granted on May 22 by the *Polizeiamts-Reinickendorf*.

81. Affidavit of Maria von Kleist, June 5, 1929, EHF.

82. IA, 96.

83. Maria von Kleist affidavit, EHF.

84. Bonhoeffer report, EHF.

85. Barfknecht affidavit, EHF.

2. "The Story"

1. Auclères I, 45. Although one continually hears and reads about the Russian monarchist "hordes" who saw A at the Kleists', neither the Baron, his wife, nor, later, his daughter Gerda ever provided names and exact details. When A later lived with Franz Jaenicke the same phenomenon occurred, i.e., a monarchist "invasion" of Jaenicke's apartment: Jaenicke statement 1956, Hamburg.

2. IA, 92.

3. Jaenicke statement 1956, Hamburg.

4. Protocol of Baron von Kleist, EHF.

5. Letter (statement?) of Baron Vassili Lvovitch von der Osten-Sacken Tettenborn, "Berlin, February 1926," Hamburg.

6. Baroness von Kleist affidavit, EHF.

7. Affidavit of Zinaida Tolstoy, May 3, 1929, EHF; Fallows "Entry," April 29, 1929.

8. Baroness von Kleist affidavit, EHF.

9. Testimony of Olly Reim, quoted in the memorandum of Kurt Vermehren, January 31, 1961, Hamburg.

10. Testimony of Gerda von Kleist, November 19, 1965, Hamburg. Transcript prepared by Prince Frederick of Saxe-Altenburg.

11. Baroness von Kleist affidavit, EHF.

12. This was only loosely employed. See Jaenicke statement 1956 and Gerda von Kleist testimony, Hamburg.

13. Jaenicke statement 1956, Hamburg.

14. Gerda von Kleist testimony, Hamburg.

15. Baroness von Kleist affidavit, EHF.

16. The word crops up frequently in conversation with A's friends.

17. English translation in EHF; original (missing) dated May 18, 1923.

18. A used the Russian diminutive, "Verunitchka." A note in pencil (possibly but not necessarily appended by Dr. Schiler) followed the reference to A's speaking Russian: "Supposed to have done so."

19. The special difficulty of reconstructing "The Story" I hope to have made clear in the text. Repeatedly, those who spoke with A about Ekaterinburg and her flight from Russia remarked that she did so only "in a disjointed manner, talking first of one thing and then of another" (Rathlef MS.). Inspector Franz Grünberg, the Berlin police commissioner who managed, after three years, to piece together a fairly intelligible account of A's adventures, still insisted: "I did not get this narrative from her in the above coherent form, but only in rather disconnected fragments over a period of weeks and months. And even then I had to proceed in a most careful way, since in recalling these dreadful experiences she would become indescribably upset and then would break down completely" (Letter of Inspector Franz Grünberg, June 19, 1925, in EHF, hereafter referred to as "Grünberg letter"). In view of this situation and the ceaseless pressure on A's friends to provide a whole and convincing account of her experiences, it is more than likely that some of them attempted to fill in the gaps and thus bound her to a narrative not entirely hers. Her eventual disavowal of every published description of the murder of the Romanovs, her sojourn in Bucharest, and her journey to Berlin may have sprung from confusion, defiance, and resentment as much as anything else, but there is no doubt that during the 1920s she stood by the bare outlines of "The Story" in all its improbability, and as late as May 1982 she remarked to me that she still recalled seeing the body of Alexander Tschaikovsky "in the coffin" in Bucharest. See also Dr. Eitel's report of December 1926: "Regarding the murder and the first stage of the rescue the patient says as good as nothing. To my question, what the flight was like, she gives me a Berlin daily

newspaper containing an article about her, saying that some of it is true, but much of it is false. She herself cannot yet speak of it" (Eitel report: December 22, 1926, EHF).

20. Rathlef notes.

21. A "Memoirs," EHF.

22. Loose notes of Harriet von Rathlef (December 1925), BA.

23. Protocols of Arthur von Kleist, EHF.

24. Rathlef notes.

25. Quoted in Leverkuehn/Vermehren memorandum, October 31, 1938, EHF. Much is made in FA about the boy's ostensible birthdate at the beginning of December 1918, the implication being that if A were the Tsar's daughter she would have had to have conceived the child while still a prisoner with her family at Tobolsk. On balance, there is nothing to preclude the possibility.

26. Auclères I, 235.

27. This was no more than a rumor, but it found wide currency among the monarchists.

28. Report of Harriet von Rathlef, undated, BA.

29. Rathlef notes.

30. A "Interviews."

31. The "Interviews" with Curtis J. Mar were conducted over a period of two months.

32. Loose notes of Harriet von Rathlef, BA.

33. Many, many attempts, none of them successful or convincing, have been made over the years to identify the Tschaikovsky brothers. These have focused generally on the published lists of the Red guards at the Ipatiev house, on the assumption merely that only one of the Bolshevik soldiers would have been in a position to rescue the Tsar's daughter. A described Alexander to Harriet von Rathlef as being "of medium height," with dark blond hair, a small moustache, and a face "as if carved from stone . . . as if he did not know how to laugh." Serge Tschaikovsky was equally nondescript, while their mother, Maria, was "not yet old," and their sister had a rosy, "peasant" face. According to Frau von Rathlef, A did not recall seeing Tschaikovsky among the guards at Ekaterinburg, while, according to Edward Fallows, she did: See Fallows memoranda, EHF; and Leverkuehn/Vermehren memorandum, October 1938, EHF. In view of the mysteries, large and small, which attend the true circumstances of the murder of the imperial family, A's various remarks may only be accepted or rejected at face value.

34. Rathlef notes.

35. A "Interviews."

36. Interview with Ian Lilburn.

37. Interview with Tatiana Botkin; also in Figaro, January 17, 1958.

38. Tolstoy affidavit, EHF. When, in the 1930s, word spread that Grand Duchess Tatiana had surfaced in Poland, A shook her head, saying, "I stood behind her." See testimony of Baroness Nina von Osten-Sacken, née von Hoyningen-Huené, quoted in memoranda of counsel, Hamburg.

39. A "Interviews."

40. Loose notes of Harriet von Rathlef (December 1925), BA.

41. Rathlef notes.

42. Rathlef MS.

43. Grünberg letter, EHF.

44. Report of Harriet von Rathlef, undated, BA.

45. Rathlef (German 107).

46. Affidavit of Agnes Gallagher, December 22, 1930, EHF. Many fragments of smashed and burned jewelry were uncovered by the White army at the "Four Brothers" mineshaft near Ekaterinburg, where the bodies of the Romanovs were ostensibly destroyed. It was impossible, under the circumstances, to provide a matching inventory of the remains and the jewelry known to be in the possession of the imperial family.

47. A "Interviews."

48. Grünberg letter, EHF.

49. A "Interviews." A told Harriet von Rathlef that she had always traveled in a first-class compartment, while Serge Tschaikovsky sat elsewhere: Rathlef (German 32).

50. Rathlef (German 32).

51. A "Interviews."

52. Rathlef makes no mention of this, but see IA, 86.

53. Eitel report, EHF.

54. A remarked that the Tschaikovsky family always spoke to her in Russian, while conversing among themselves in Polish. See report of Harriet von Rathlef, undated, BA.

55. A "Memoirs."

56. Clara Peuthert to Irene of Prussia, August 23, 1922, Hamburg; also in FA, 52.

57. Schwabe report, EHF.

58. Verdict of the *Landgericht-Hamburg* (the High Court), printed privately, "nicht rechtskräftig."

59. Loose notes of Arthur von Kleist, undated (presumably August 1922), attached to affidavit of Maria von Kleist, EHF.

60. Schiler report, EHF.

61. To list all the published information on the fate of the imperial family and the Sokolov investigation would be next to impossible and is beyond the scope of these notes. For further reading on the subject, see O'Conor, *The Sokolov Investigation*, and, above all, FOT. The lone "eyewitness" to the murder of the imperial family was Paul Medvedev, chief assistant to Yakov Yurovsky, the commandant of the Ipatiev house. All of the other guards who testified for Inspector Sokolov about the circumstances of the assassination based their narratives on hearsay evidence.

62. FOT, 135–136.

63. FOT, 149. The bones recovered at the "Four Brothers" mine were never certified as human.

64. Memorandum of General Michael Constantinovitch Diterichs, April 10, 1919, quoted in memorandum of Carl-August Wollmann, December 30, 1963, Hamburg; also Ian Lilburn to David Clegg, September 5, 1966, in Lilburn's collection.

65. FOT, 103.

66. See Wilton, *The Last Days of the Romanovs*, and Diterichs, *Ubiistvo tsarskoi semi'i.*

67. Gilliard, *Le Tragique Destin*, 242.

68. FOT, 103.

69. Quoted in FOT, 111.

70. Letter of Alexis Golovin, quoted in *Figaro*, June 8, 1965. According to Golovin, Sokolov himself privately conceded the possibility of the escape of one of the Tsar's daughters, but seemed to have no interest in pursuing the matter further. That the Whites knew about the rumors is evident enough from the suppression of much of the material in the original Sokolov file and the various efforts — which continue to this day — to prove Anastasia's death *specifically*. The common story of her being stabbed to death with bayonets is based on the thirdhand report of Anatoly Yakimov, one of the Red guards at Ekaterinburg, who claimed to have learned about the murder of the imperial family from two other soldiers, who claimed to have watched the crime through a window in the Ipatiev house courtyard: "Of the members of the Tsar's family, only Anastasia was mentioned as having been pierced with bayonets" (see FOT, Wilton, and O'Conor). But why Anastasia? The first reports to filter out of Siberia after the White occupation cited *Tatiana* as the girl who was stabbed during the murder. Colonel Paul Rodzianko, a monarchist officer sent to Ekaterinburg at the request of the Empress's sister Victoria, reported back to London that fourteen bayonet thrusts, "corresponding roughly to the shape of a human body [!]," had been found at "the exact spot" on the floor of the cellar where Grand Duchess Tatiana had died. But when the rumors of Anastasia's escape reached Europe, something else was needed. Thus the identity of the Grand Duchess was switched and the number of stabs increased for good measure to "eighteen." In his excellent and otherwise scrupulous *Romanovs* (New York: The Dial Press, 1981), W. Bruce Lincoln perpetuates this story: "Only slightly wounded, [Anastasia] cried out, more in fear than in pain [?]. Unwilling to bother with reloading their weapons, the guards seized several rifles that stood nearby and calmly bayoneted her to death" (746).

One final example of the Whites' determination to "kill off" the youngest Grand Duchess will suffice. At the "Four Brothers" mineshaft, in June 1919, the Whites uncovered the perfectly preserved corpse of the spaniel "Jemmy," which had been given to Grand Duchess Tatiana by Anna Viroubova before the outbreak of World War I. The official explanation was that the dog had been "frozen in ice" at the bottom of the shaft for nearly a year (an absurdity, inasmuch as there *was* no ice in the shaft for six months out of the year [see FOT 173]). More important, however, is the fact that "Jemmy," overnight, ceased to be described as Tatiana's pet and suddenly became Anastasia's. The story was swiftly concocted that Anastasia had carried the animal down to the cellar on the night of the murder, and the implication is obvious: if the dog was dead, so was the Grand Duchess. No amount of evidence seems able to shake this smart fiction from the heads of otherwise reputable historians.

71. This was Summers's and Mangold's coup, and the chief emphasis of their work. See FOT, *passim.*

72. FA, 24, and in Wollmann memorandum, December 31, 1963, Hamburg.

73. Testimony of November 19, 1925, Hamburg.

74. Rathlef; IA and FOT all contain representative samples. The largest collection is at Hamburg, with others in EHF. See also the correspondence of Alois Hochleitner with Harriet von Rathlef, BA; and in Rathlef (German 205–212).

75. See as example the statement of Dr. Vladimir Poletyka, May 23, 1929, EHF; and of Baron von Schenk, who saw one of the posters in Russia nearly twenty years later: Testimony of July 27, 1965, Hamburg.

76. Testimony of Arthur Rohsé, November 1956, in IA, 69–70.

77. Testimony of General Himitch, March 19, 1958, Hamburg.

78. Julius Holmberg to Harriet von Rathlef, April 20, 1929, EHF.

79. Letter to Prince Frederick of Saxe-Altenburg, October 13, 1952, Hamburg; in FOT 375. Bonde had already told this story in 1926. See letter of Herluf Zahle to Serge Botkin, January 24, 1927, BA.

80. Vorres, 177.

81. More than "shame" kept A from approaching the King and Queen. The former Princess Victoria Melita of Edinburgh and Coburg, a sister of Queen Marie, had divorced Empress Alexandra's brother and married Grand Duke Kyril of Russia, who in exile claimed the title of Emperor. The entire branch became "those Coburgs" in A's mind. See the "questionnaire" prepared in lieu of personal testimony by Herluf Zahle, Danish Minister Plenipotentiary to Berlin, EHF.

82. Loose notes of Harriet von Rathlef (December 1925), BA.

83. See report of Fritz Schuricht, undated (1927), EHF.

84. Paul Ionescu-Voiculescu to Ian Lilburn, July 24, 1968, in Lilburn's collection.

85. Sworn statement of Sarjo Gregorian, May 4, 1927, in Rathlef (German 233–234).

86. Deposition of Constantine C. Anastasiu, April 8, 1926, BA.

87. Testimony of Lieutenant-Colonel Werner Hassenstein, May 12, 1955, Hamburg.

88. See FOT, *passim.* It is remarkable that throughout her long life and in spite of many attempts to have her expelled from Germany or arrested for fraud, the German government, sooner or later, never failed to come to A's rescue. A letter to Harriet von Rathlef from a Wilhelm Abegg at the Prussian Ministry of the Interior, dated August 29, 1931 (EHF), informs that according to the information the ministry had received, the youngest daughter of the Tsar had indeed escaped Ekaterinburg. A remarked further that the house occupied by the Tschaikovsky family in Bucharest had been situated on a tiny street which (in the protocols of Baron von Kleist) was rendered as "Sventa Voyevoda." An entrance to the imperial German embassy, held by caretakers after 1916, was at Number 56, Sfintii Voyevozi in Bucharest.

89. Letter to Paul Leverkuehn, August 27, 1958, Hamburg.

90. Serge Dmitrievtch Botkin to Grand Duke Andrew of Russia, March 7, 1927, Hamburg; see also Rathlef (German 266–268).

91. Affidavit of Ilse-Irene Hoffmann, June 24, 1929, EHF.

92. Rathlef (German 268); also in IA, 216.

3. To and Fro with the Émigrés

1. Baroness von Kleist affidavit.

2. Quoted in Nogly, 41.

3. Jaenicke statement 1956, Hamburg.

4. Loose notes of Arthur von Kleist, EHF.

5. Baroness von Kleist affidavit, EHF.

6. See IA, 102.

7. Grünberg letter, EHF.

8. See statement of Princess Henry (Irene) of Prussia, in FA, 43; and Grünberg letter, EHF.

9. Grünberg letter, EHF.

10. Irene statement, FA.

11. Jaenicke statement, 1956, Hamburg.

12. Rathlef notes.

13. Rathlef (German 41).

14. Grünberg letter, EHF.

15. Irene statement. To say that there is some question about the extent of Irene's "firm conviction" that A was not her niece is an understatement. Lori von Oertzen, the lady-in-waiting who accompanied Irene to Funkenmühle, later testified that Irene had practically begged A to return with her to Hemmelmark, where, presumably, she hoped to resolve her doubts (see testimony of Eleonore von Oertzen, September 16, 1958, Hamburg). Later on in the decade Irene was deeply anxious to know what other family members thought about A, and before her death in 1953, according to Grand Duke Andrew of Russia, she admitted that she "might have made a mistake and that it probably [was] Anastasia" (see letter of Grand Duke Andrew to Grand Duchess Olga Alexandrovna, February 10, 1955, Hamburg).

16. Prince Frederick of Saxe-Altenburg to Brien Purcell Horan, quoted in Horan MS.

17. Interview with Prince Frederick of Saxe-Altenburg; in FOT, 235.

18. Lillan Zahle to Maria Debagory, January 1, 1927, BA. Mlle. Debagory was the aunt of Tatiana and Gleb Botkin.

19. She was back with Baron von Kleist on October 11 (see Schiler report and protocols of Arthur von Kleist, EHF); A to Jaenicke: Jaenicke statement 1956, Hamburg; Jaenicke to Munich: Notes of Baron von Kleist, EHF.

20. Baroness von Kleist affidavit, EHF.

21. See IA, 111–112.

22. Konrad Wahl to PK, January 30, 1977.

23. Wahl to A, January 20, 1967, left in A's papers.

24. Marie-Louise Hiller, "*Mit Frau von Tschaikowsky unter einem Dach,*" article in the *Berliner Nachtausgabe,* March 21, 1927.

25. Lavington Diary, Hamburg.

26. Rathlef (German 39).

27. IA, 112.

28. A "Memoirs"; Rathlef/Noeggerath.

29. Rathlef notes. A never lost her faith in Rasputin.

30. A "Interviews."

31. A "Memoirs."

32. Rathlef/Noeggerath. "Too dreadful" was A's catchall phrase for anything that upset or displeased her.

33. Jaenicke statement 1956, Hamburg.

34. A "Interviews."

35. Jacoby, *Le Tsar Nicolas II et la révolution,* 381.

36. Protocol of Dr. Wilhelm Völler's conversation with Clara Peuthert, EHF.

37. Notes of Baron von Kleist; Leverkuehn/Vermehren memorandum, October 1938, EHF.

38. This story, which is frequently told, was related to me by Prince Frederick of Saxe-Altenburg.

39. Notes of Baron von Kleist, EHF.

40. Notes of Baron von Kleist, EHF; also in Leverkuehn/Vermehren memorandum, October 1938, EHF. Zinaida Tolstoy made no mention of the incident in her own affidavit.

41. IA, 99.

42. Statement (in English) of Grand Duchess Olga Alexandrovna, attached to her 1959 deposition, Hamburg; undated, but introduced in evidence during the Berlin trials, and thus written before 1956.

43. Grünberg letter, EHF.

44. Notes of Harriet von Rathlef (December 1925), BA. With this accusation A raised an issue which, many believed, did as much to destroy her chances for recognition as the specter of her missing child. Many are convinced that the lost dossier of Ambassador Zahle (see my chapter 5) contains vital information on the matter: See Zahle "questionnaire," EHF. Interestingly, Baroness Buxhoeveden was the only member of the imperial suite who refused to testify for Inspector Sokolov in Siberia or, later, in Europe. There were awkward attempts to cover for her, the most common being that the Bolsheviks had spared her life at Ekaterinburg

because they thought she was a foreigner. Says Ian Lilburn: "The even more obviously foreign name of Fräulein Schneider [the Empress's lectrice] did not save the poor woman from being shot."

45. Quoted in a letter of Harriet von Rathlef to Fallows, December 29, 1929, EHF.

46. Letter (statement?) of Baron Osten-Sacken, "February 1926," Hamburg.

47. FA, 38–41. Princess Elisabeth Naryshkin-Kurakin described Sablin as "the fine wretch of an aide-de-camp": Naryshkin-Kurakin, *Under Three Tsars*, 218.

48. Baroness von Kleist affidavit, EHF; also in *Figaro*, May 24, 1958.

49. Countess Lareinty-Tholozan in *Figaro*, June 30, 1959.

50. Gerda von Kleist testimony, Hamburg.

51. See police *Vermerk*, December 23, 1926, Hamburg.

52. Clara Peuthert to Irene of Prussia, September 24, 1924, Hamburg. A herself had sent an appeal to the Princess on August 30 (letter at Hamburg): "Must implore your forgiveness that I did not speak that time at Funkenmühle. Everything came so unexpectedly and you were introduced to me as a strange lady, so that I lost all courage. I entreat you to bring me someplace else, they intend to put me in an asylum or a hospital. Love and kisses, your Anastasie." The members of the Russian imperial family always employed the French spelling of their names when not writing in Russian.

53. Letter to Baron von Kleist, September 21, 1924, Hamburg and EHF.

54. Lori von Oertzen to Baron von Kleist, July 22, 1925, Hamburg and EHF.

55. Rathlef/Noeggerath.

56. Rathlef (German 39).

57. Grünberg letter, EHF.

58. Rathlef notes; Police *Vermerk*, December 23, 1926, Hamburg.

59. Grünberg letter, EHF.

60. The story is discussed briefly in Rathlef; in Botkin I and II; in the *Berliner Nachtausgabe* (April 1927); and in the protocol of Wilhelm Völler of his conversation with Clara Peuthert. The original photograph of A, bearing the penciled inscription, which Clara Peuthert sold to Harriet von Rathlef for thirty marks (Rathlef/Noeggerath), is now in EHF.

61. *New York Times*, February 14, 1928.

62. A "Interviews."

63. Rathlef notes.

64. Affidavit of Cecilie, Crown Princess of Prussia, October 2, 1953, Hamburg.

65. Rathlef notes.

66. Cecilie to Frederick Franz IV, Grand Duke of Mecklenburg, July 1, 1925; quoted in Hamburg verdict.

67. Grünberg letter, EHF.

68. Cecilie affidavit, Hamburg.

69. Grünberg letter, EHF.

70. Grünberg to Fallows, April 28, 1929, EHF.

71. Grünberg letter, EHF.

72. Rathlef and Rathlef notes.

73. Rathlef (English 19).

74. Rathlef meeting with A: Rathlef notes.

4. The Shadows of the Past

1. Unless specifically noted, all of the material relating to A's first days with Harriet von Rathlef at St. Mary's Hospital is taken from the Rathlef notes.

2. Botkin MS.

3. Testimony of Marie Adèle Amy Smith, December 18, 1965, Hamburg.

4. Smith testimony, Hamburg.

5. Loose notes of Harriet von Rathlef (December 1925), BA.

6. Botkin MS.

7. Curtis J. Mar to Edward Fallows, December 27, 1929, EHF.

8. Lavington Diary, Hamburg.

9. Gitta Müller-Mittler to Fallows, September 5, 1935, EHF.

10. A "Memoirs" ("My American Experiences").

11. Statement of Harriet von Rathlef, undated, BA.

12. Affidavit in lieu of oath (*"Eidesstattliche Versicherung"*) of Harriet von Rathlef, EHF. There are a number of these loose affidavits in the Fallows archive, prepared for possible submission in court.

13. Rathlef to Duke George of Leuchtenberg, April 2, 1927, EHF.

14. Rathlef (German 62).

15. A "Interviews."

16. Rathlef (German 117).

17. Notes of Harriet von Rathlef (December 1925), BA.

18. Rathlef (German 88).

19. Rathlef (German 101, German 30).

20. Notes of Harriet von Rathlef (December 1925), BA.

21. Rathlef (German 137).

22. Notes of Harriet von Rathlef (December 1925), BA.

23. Copies of the reports of Drs. Rudnev ("End of March, 1926"), Nobel ("End of March, 1926"), and Bonhoeffer (March 16, 1926) are held in BA; EHF; Hamburg, and edited in IA. I have cited the IA translations where employed.

24. IA, 162.

25. Rathlef notes.

26. Letter of Dr. Reinhardt to Harriet von Rathlef and Asta Noeggerath (who helped Edward Fallows with his investigation in 1929), April 5, 1929, EHF.

27. This is a total mystery. Fallows obtained copies of the X rays from the Leuchtenberg family in 1929, and had more copies made in Paris that same year. They are no longer in his files. It might be that they vanished with the other documents from the *Amtsgericht Berlin-Mitte* after World War II, but there is no mention of their being submitted in evidence in the Leverkuehn/Vermehren memorandum of October 1938. Another set, also missing, had been taken on June 6, 1922, just after A's release from Dalldorf. These were the photographs that allowed Dr. Schiler to conclude: "Earlier, a severe injury of the head took place." See Hamburg verdict and memoranda of counsel.

28. Nobel report, BA and EHF.

29. Bonhoeffer report, BA and EHF. An attempt was made to hypnotize A at Castle Seeon on June 28, 1927. It failed miserably. See statement of Dr. E. Osty in Rathlef (German 254–255).

30. Rathlef (German 91).

31. Vorres, 176. Gilliard appears to have been the one to propagate this "error," which did immeasurable damage. There was, however, a German tutor at the Russian court, a Herr Kleinenberg, right up to the moment of the Revolution. Gilliard's own timetables, now on deposit at the University of Lausanne, demonstrate that Grand Duchess Anastasia had a German lesson every Monday, Wednesday, and Friday from 8 to 9 o'clock in the morning while still at Tobolsk.

32. Statement of Dr. Ludwig Berg, May 10, 1929, EHF.

33. Rathlef (German 176).

34. Lavington Diary, Hamburg.

35. Bonhoeffer report, BA and EHF.

36. Rudnev report, BA and EHF.

37. Nobel report, in IA, 118.

38. A said this to Princess Xenia Georgievna of Russia in 1928; quoted in Horan MS. See also my chapter 9.

39. Nobel report, BA and EHF.

40. Rathlef notes.

41. Affidavit in lieu of oath of Harriet von Rathlef, EHF.

42. A to PK.

43. Bonhoeffer report, BA and EHF.

44. Nobel report, BA and EHF.

45. Rathlef (German 44).

46. Report of Amy Smith, in Rathlef (German 45, English 42).

47. Smith testimony, Hamburg.

48. In her testimony at Hamburg, Miss Smith gave as an example of Count Hardenberg's intransigence the quarrel over the name "Nini." A had said that her mother's sister, Irene of Prussia, had been known as "Nini" in the family. Hardenberg replied that Irene had never

been called "Nini" *by the Tsar's children*. A's use of the diminutive "Ania" when describing her mother's confidante, Anna Viroubova, led Hardenberg to reply not only that "the Christian name is wrong: it should be Anna," but also that Mme. Viroubova "was never an intimate friend of the Empress." Later Miss Smith located a copy of Empress Alexandra's correspondence, where, on practically every page, she found some reference to "Ania." Said Miss Smith: "This was the nature of the arguments used against me" (Smith report, Rathlef [German 49]).

49. Smith report, Rathlef (German 49–50).

50. Smith testimony, Hamburg.

51. The remainder of the chapter is based on Rathlef notes, except for "*Im Kriege bei uns zu Hause*": Smith testimony, Hamburg. These were the words A employed to Miss Smith's "exact recollection." See also her letter to Baroness Monica von Miltitz, March 10, 1967, left in A's papers.

5. The Family Reacts

1. A "Interviews."

2. Ibid.

3. Smith testimony, Hamburg.

4. For information on the Grand Duke of Hesse's various efforts to secure a separate peace with Russia, see *Die Zeit*, March 27, 1958 ("Weltpolitische Schatten um eine unbekannte Frau"); the memoirs of Sir George Buchanan, *My Mission to Russia* (2 vols., London: Cassel, 1923); Alexandra, *The Letters of the Tsaritsa to the Tsar*, in particular the Empress's letter to her husband of April 17, 1915; IA; and FOT, 236–239.

5. Viktoria Luise, Duchess of Brunswick, *The Kaiser's Daughter* (New York: Prentice-Hall, 1977), 101.

6. Cecilie affidavit, Hamburg. A's lawyer, Kurt Vermehren, asked the Crown Princess what she had thought when she heard about the Grand Duke of Hesse's Russian journey, and she replied, "We were very elated" — suggesting to Vermehren that she had indeed heard about the trip at the time when it took place, and not later on, when the mission had failed. Interview with Ian Lilburn.

7. See Auclères I, 217–218; FOT, 238.

8. Interview with Dominique Auclères. Affidavits on this subject are still being collected, as, for instance, the recent statement of Frau Ingrid Ellen von Pistolkors (currently in the possession of Prince Frederick of Saxe-Altenburg). Many people who knew about the Grand Duke's trip, however, including members of Europe's royalty, still prefer not to be named, on the correct assumption that their testimony will be marshaled in support of a woman whom most of them consider to be an impostor.

9. *Die Zeit*, March 27, 1958.

10. *Figaro*, November 26–27, 1966 (from testimony of Princess Marianne of Hesse-Philippsthal).

11. Rathlef (German 50).

12. Statement (undated) of Harriet von Rathlef, BA.

13. The Crown Princess wrote her brother (letter of July 1, 1925, Hamburg), "The case must be followed up."

14. Statement of Harriet von Rathlef, BA; also Rathlef (German 50–51).

15. Vorres, 173.

16. For the best-informed account of Maria Feodorovna's adventures and her life in exile, see Vorres.

17. Interview with Prince Paul Chavchavadze.

18. Philip Whitwell Wilson, "Anastasia?" *North American Review* (January 1929).

19. *New York Times*, December 13, 1924. Grand Duke Nicholas Nicolaievitch carefully avoided any proclamation like his cousin's, and was the far more popular choice for the position of Emperor. His candidacy remained passive, however, up through his death in 1929. A herself thought his selection for the job would be a good joke on Kyril (Rathlef notes).

20. See Williams, *passim*.

21. Alexander, *Always a Grand Duke*, 212.

22. This point was stressed over and over again. See Rathlef (German 17–18). (The Dan-

ish legation in Berlin was not, strictly speaking, an embassy, but a ministry, and Zahle bore the title of Minister to Berlin. I have used the terms *ambassador* and *embassy*, however, for simplicity.)

23. See *Souvenirs d'Alexis Volkov* (Paris: Payot, 1928). No one has ever been able to explain satisfactorily why the Bolsheviks in Siberia would have murdered the imperial family at Ekaterinburg while keeping their servants alive for two more months, actually bothering to transfer them to Perm.

24. The most important evidence on the visits — the notes and other documentation collected by Ambassador Zahle — has been confiscated by the Danish royal family (see page 118). All that remains are the various reports, letters, affidavits, and manuscripts of Harriet von Rathlef. According to Frau von Rathlef, Grand Duchess Olga read the one chapter concerning herself in the first Rathlef manuscript ("Lebt Anastasia?") and reported to Ambassador Zahle that it was "correct in its depiction [of the meetings in Berlin]; but she hadn't read the rest because she had no great command of German" (Rathlef [German 200]). I have followed Frau von Rathlef's account of the meetings because there is no other choice. For Gilliard's version (which agrees with Frau von Rathlef's on points of time and place but does not enter into conversational detail), see his "very confidential" letter to Count Vladimir Kokovtzov, July 18, 1926, BA; his various letters to Frau von Rathlef and Zahle, all in BA; and FA, 64–68 and 69–78. By the time Gilliard had published his narrative, it had solidified into a kind of gospel, and it is, in my opinion, grossly distorted if not directly false in its claims. (One example: in his letter to Count Kokovtzov, Gilliard had rendered A's response to his ceaseless questioning as "I cannot, I cannot"; while in FA it became "I don't know, I don't know.") In 1964 Grand Duchess Olga's biographer, Ian Vorres, pieced together her rather scattered recollections to form a narrative: Vorres, 173–180. It contributes nothing new to the story and, in its tone and lucidity, bears small resemblance to Olga's formal testimony at Toronto (March 23–24, 1959, Hamburg). Olga died in 1960 and never saw Vorres's finished book. Meantime, Dr. Ludwig Berg, the chaplain at St. Mary's, took the trouble to confirm explicitly Frau von Rathlef's account of the meetings with Alexis Volkov, while Professor Rudnev backed her up when and as he could. As for Ambassador Zahle, he wrote after reading Frau von Rathlef's report: "By and large it agrees with my memories and my notes, and in any case contains nothing which speaks more for the identity . . . than the material I either possess or which has come to my attention" (Zahle to Serge Botkin, November 26, 1926, BA).

Before his death the ambassador prepared a ten-page "questionnaire" (EHF) in lieu of personal testimony, consisting of the questions he said he *would* answer should his government ever give him permission to do so (it did not). It is a fascinating document, because the questions are phrased in such a way that they answer themselves and serve as de facto corroboration of Frau von Rathlef's reports. Finally, Grand Duke Andrew of Russia, after he had studied the case in depth, reported that in his opinion Frau von Rathlef's narrative was not only accurate, but in fact "a minimization of what really took place. . . ." He continued, "Sadly, I must report that everything Gilliard writes to me about the meetings in Berlin deviates very much from the truth." See Andrew correspondence with Serge Botkin, 1926–1929, BA (also in English and German translation in Ian Lilburn's collection), in particular the letters of November 30, 1926, and of February 19 and March 8, 1927.

25. Volkov visit taken from Rathlef (German 51–55) and protocol of Harriet von Rathlef (undated, July 1925), BA.

26. Zahle "questionnaire," EHF.

27. General Tatischev was shot by the Bolsheviks in 1918, as was also Klementy Nagorny, the Tsarevitch's attendant. The sailor Derevenko deserted at the outbreak of the Revolution, while the doctor of the same name disappeared during the Civil War. He had been the only member of the imperial suite allowed access to the Ipatiev house in Ekaterinburg.

28. See Christopher, Prince of Greece and Denmark, in the *Saturday Evening Post,* May 26, 1928: "She has always dressed in black since the death of her husband."

29. All direct quotes, pages 101–105, are from Rathlef, *passim*.

30. See affidavit of Tatiana Botkin-Melnik, May 11, 1929, EHF.

31. See statement of Margharita Derfelden, undated (1929–1930), original left in A's papers, copies in EHF.

32. Affidavit in lieu of oath of Harriet von Rathlef, EHF.

33. Viroubova, 76.

34. From IA, 141; in FA, 64. This was one of the documents Gilliard destroyed in 1957 (see my chapter 13).

35. Rathlef (German 59).

36. Rathlef (German 59–61); and memorandum of Harriet von Rathlef, November 20, 1926, BA.

37. A critical point. The malformation *hallux valgus* is not uncommon among people who spend a great deal of time on their feet (waitresses are prone to it, for example), but the odds against any particular claimant to the identity of the Tsar's daughter suffering the complaint must be regarded as strong. The similarity of the feet was confirmed again by Grand Duchess Olga in her testimony at Toronto in 1959: Olga testimony, Hamburg.

38. From Rathlef articles in the *Tägliche Rundschau* ("Wie eine Frau vernichtet werden sollte"), October 1927.

39. Rudnev report.

40. Quotes on pages 106–112 are from Rathlef (German 102–103) unless otherwise noted.

41. Statement, undated, of Harriet von Rathlef, BA.

42. Affidavit in lieu of oath of Harriet von Rathlef, EHF.

43. Olga's children were both born after the Revolution and never knew the Tsar's daughter.

44. See letter of Harriet von Rathlef to Serge Botkin, July 29, 1926, BA; and Rathlef (German 109).

45. Affidavit in lieu of oath of Harriet von Rathlef, EHF. The telegram from Grand Duchess Xenia is presumed, perhaps erroneously, to be in the Zahle papers. Duke George of Leuchtenberg wrote Frau von Rathlef in 1927 that "a near relative of the Tsar's family" had told him what the telegram said: "Do not go to Berlin. Recognition in any case out of the question." The Duke, himself a member of the Romanov family, requested that Frau von Rathlef *not* mention the matter, because he and Grand Duke Andrew, who at that time was investigating the affair, "did not want this compromising fact to be made public."

46. Statement of Harriet von Rathlef, November 20, 1926, BA.

47. Affidavit of Serge Rudnev, December 29, 1929, EHF.

48. Rathlef to Leuchtenberg, March 27, 1927, EHF.

49. Affidavit in lieu of oath of Harriet von Rathlef, EHF.

50. "How are things in Berlin?" etc: The originals of Gilliard's letters to Frau von Rathlef are in EHF, and additional correspondence with Zahle in BA.

51. The original letters written in Russian and employing the formal mode of address, were still in A's possession during the 1960s. Olga also gave to A one of her personal photograph albums. Photostats on file in EHF. The translations here are from Botkin, II, 97–98.

52. In IA, 167.

53. Rathlef (German 114).

54. Rathlef (German 51).

55. Testimony of Pierre Gilliard at Wiesbaden, March 29 and March 31, 1958, Hamburg. The truth about the strange collaboration between the Swiss tutor and the former Grand Duke was lost forever when Gilliard destroyed his files on the case after the ruling of the High Court of West Berlin in 1957 (see my chapter 13). Many took the simplest view and assumed that Gilliard had been paid by the Grand Duke of Hesse to fight against A. Certainly the salary of a language professor at the University of Lausanne could not have compensated for the time and travel required over the next three years in the attempt to destroy her. What is not in dispute is that Gilliard, after the Berlin meetings, worked in exclusive cooperation with the Grand Duke.

56. Zahle "questionnaire."

57. Olga wrote Gilliard: "I will never forget the horrible dinner that evening Mme. von Schwabe came to call. How he [Zahle] brooded!" Quoted in Gilliard to Kokovtzov, BA. "A Polish vagabond": Rathlef to Leuchtenberg, June 16, 1927, EHF.

58. One of the most famous exchanges of the "Anastasia" affair. See Olga testimony, Hamburg.

59. Gilliard's four points: Gilliard to Kokovtzov, BA.

A's inability to answer questions, yet "put in touch with everything concerning the imperial family": the point cannot be emphasized strongly enough that A was caught in an impossible double-bind here. If any one of her statements about her childhood could be traced to some source, it instantly lost its value as evidence, and if it could not, it could never be verified.

In FA Gilliard devoted two full chapters to what he called "Frau Tschaikovsky's mistakes." These consisted of about thirty of her "memories," as recorded by Harriet von Rathlef, which Gilliard declared were false. The attempts to contradict him continue successfully to this day, but I gave up the quest myself some time ago, in the belief that no person's childhood recollections may be regarded as objective truths and that they are not to be treated as exhibits. See FOT, 234, on "the malachite room"; and Auclères I, chapter 11, on the "blue regiment" and the samovar at Moghilev. These will serve to demonstrate with what caution Gilliard's affirmations must be received.

60. I have heard the story from many people, among them Prince Frederick of Saxe-Altenburg and Mrs. Edward J. Wynkoop (the former Nancy Leeds).

61. Vorres, 179.

62. Viroubova, 316. Frau von Rathlef wrote: "The Grand Duchess [Olga] said several times that the patient resembled her niece Tatiana more. Herr Gilliard and his wife were of the same opinion. The Grand Duchess even said that she would believe it immediately if anyone told her the patient was her niece Tatiana" (Rathlef [German 112]).

63. Olga testimony, Hamburg.

64. Rathlef to S. Botkin, July 29, 1926, BA.

65. FA, 76; Rathlef (German 116–117).

66. Gilliard testimony, Hamburg, quoted in memorandum of Kurt Vermehren, January 31, 1961. Serge Botkin wrote Grand Duke Andrew on January 19, 1927 (BA): "Nobody took the psychological aspect into account. During their visit they immediately proceeded with an interrogation. In line with her character, the invalid answers an interrogation with silence and withdraws into herself entirely. . . . She simply cannot deal with an 'exam,' which paralyzes and depresses her. . . . I am convinced that if the people who visited her had really understood all this, things would be different."

67. Gilliard to Kokovtzov, BA.

68. Fallows "Entry," March 27, 1929 (EHF); and Fallows's notes on Gleb Botkin's *Woman Who Rose Again* (EHF).

69. Letter of March 16, 1935, taken from Horan MS. Zahle's dossier consisted of fifteen volumes of evidence.

70. *Sunday Times* (London), October 23, 1977. On May 12, 1981, the private secretary to Queen Margrethe wrote me: "In reply to your letter Her Majesty has asked me to tell you that the said reports, made by Mr. Zahle for King Christian X, form part of the Royal Archives which are inaccessible even to writers and scientists; it is, therefore, not possible to grant your request."

71. Quoted in Auclères I, 74.

72. Zahle to Danish Foreign Ministry, December 12, 1928, Hamburg. The letter was released to the Hamburg courts by the Ministry.

73. The original is, of course, in Zahle's papers, with a certified copy in BA. When asked about this document during her testimony at Toronto, Olga claimed ignorance: "If I wrote that letter, I can no longer say what I had in mind with those words, because so far as I was concerned it was established that the claimant was not Anastasia."

74. Testimony of Princess Xenia Georgievna of Russia, given at New York City, March 16–17, 1959, Hamburg.

75. Andrew to Serge Botkin, March 8, 1927, BA (Ian Lilburn's translation).

76. Olga to Princess Olga of Hannover, May 13, 1958, Hamburg.

77. December 4, 1925, Hamburg.

78. Statement of Grand Duchess Olga, attached to her testimony of March 1959, Hamburg.

79. General Spiridovitch informed Tatiana Botkin, the daughter of the imperial family's private physician, about the letter from Olga to Prince Dolgorouky. See letter of Tatiana Botkin (Melnik) to Serge Botkin, October 14, 1926, BA.

80. Interview with Ian Lilburn.

81. Mrs. Edward J. Wynkoop to PK, March 30, 1972.

82. Testimony of Princess Xenia Georgievna of Russia, March 16–17, 1959, Hamburg.

83. Vorres 173, and *passim*, for Olga's marital woes and life in exile.

84. Gilliard to Kokovtzov, BA.

85. Olga to Irene, December 22, 1926 (original English), Hamburg.

86. Vorres, 180.

87. Olga to Mordvinov, March 30, 1927, Hamburg.

88. Interview with Mrs. Edward J. Wynkoop.

89. Andrew to Serge Botkin, March 29, 1928, BA (Ian Lilburn's translation). As Zahle explained it to Prince Frederick of Saxe-Altenburg, Grand Duchess Olga, during the second consultation with the Dowager Empress, was so nervous that she never took her eyes off her embroidery. When Zahle asked the Empress to consider how it would look to the world and to history if everything were not done that could be done to clear up this case, the Empress replied only: "My daughter Olga tells me this woman is not my granddaughter" (Interview with Prince Frederick of Saxe-Altenburg). And from the Zahle questionnaire: "Did Grand Duchess Olga's behavior [at this meeting] give Excellency Zahle the impression that she was deeply shamed by the contradiction between her behavior after her visit to the claimant in Berlin, when the Grand Duchess took the identity of the claimant with her niece to be *as good as certain,* and her subsequent denial of that identity in the press?" (Emphasis added.)

90. Rathlef to Leuchtenberg, March 27, 1927, EHF.

91. In *Poslednyi Novosti* (Reval), January 15, 1926; also in FA, 61–62. The denial had obviously been timed to coincide with the other issued from Copenhagen.

92. Affidavit of Serge Ostrogorsky, May 21, 1929, EHF.

93. Rathlef (English 107, German 114).

94. Gilliard to Kokovtzov, BA.

95. Rathlef (German 129).

96. Fallows "Entry," March 6, 1938, recording report of Albert F. Coyle, who had just spoken with Grand Duke Andrew in Paris.

97. Notes of Harriet von Rathlef (December 1925), BA.

98. Alexandra Gilliard to Lillan Zahle, December 14, 1925, BA.

99. Fallows "Entry," March 6, 1938 (Coyle report).

100. Notes of Harriet von Rathlef (December 1925), BA.

6. Tanya

1. Rathlef (German 120–121).

2. Information from police reports, quoted in Hamburg verdict and in Nogly; see also the protocol of conversation with "Kommissar X," EHF.

3. See Hamburg verdict, 59–60.

4. Notes of Harriet von Rathlef (December 1925), BA.

5. Notes of Harriet von Rathlef (December 1925), BA. The rumor that A had crossed herself like a Roman Catholic was too convenient for her opponents; it could not be easily dispelled. The controversy continued the following year when A was living at Castle Seeon with the Leuchtenberg family. Duke Dmitri of Leuchtenberg heard from the Orthodox priest at Seeon that A had made her confession in German at Easter; the same priest informed Duchess Olga of Leuchtenberg that she had confessed in Russian (see testimony of Dmitri, Duke of Leuchtenberg, given at Montreal, March 20–21, 1959; transcript at Hamburg; and Hamburg verdict). Duke Dmitri and his wife, Duchess Catherine, swore that A continued to use the Catholic genuflection, while Dmitri's sister, Duchess Natalie, remembered that it seemed to be "a mixture" of the Catholic and Orthodox forms. According to Natalie, A remarked that after her marriage to Alexander Tschaikovsky she no longer knew to which faith she belonged. The priest at Seeon then informed her that in his opinion she could still consider herself a member of the Orthodox Church. "After that," said Natalie, "she showed no signs of hesitation. . . . She was very well acquainted with the Orthodox rites" (see testimony of Natalie, Baroness Meller-Zakomelsky, Hamburg; quoted in memorandum of Kurt Vermehren, January 31, 1961, Hamburg).

6. Letter of Gertrude Spindler, July 27, 1926; in Rathlef (German 124).

7. Laqueur, 82ff., 118.

8. Nothing at all is known about Schwabe's death or the fate of his wife and daughter.

9. Many believe that Savitch had all along been an agent for the Bolsheviks and that he simply returned to Moscow.

10. A used this term in later life to describe a number of her adversaries.

11. A "Interviews."

12. A "Memoirs."

13. Letter (statement) of Baron Osten-Sacken, dated "February 1926," Hamburg.

14. See Williams, *passim.*

15. Botkin MS.

16. Serge Botkin's "commentary" to the BA archives.

17. Gilliard to Rathlef, February 28, 1926, EHF.

18. FOT, 220.

19. Affidavit of Vera Urvantzov, April 6, 1929, EHF.

20. Rathlef (German 133–134).

21. Frau von Rathlef's Lugano letters (some only in extract) are in BA; also IA, 184–185. See also Rathlef (German 233) and IA, 120, about A and the "English guest" at the Hotel Tivoli.

22. Rathlef (German 138).

23. Affidavit in lieu of oath of Harriet von Rathlef, EHF.

24. IA, 184.

25. The Prince retained his faith in A despite the negative attitude of his niece, Grand Duchess Olga. See Gilliard to Kokovtzov, BA.

26. IA, 184.

27. Osten-Sacken letter, Hamburg.

28. Report of Baron Osten-Sacken to Herluf Zahle, June 29, 1926, BA.

29. Combined from Rathlef letters to Serge Botkin (June 9, 1926) and to Zahle (June 10, 1926), BA.

30. Rathlef to Osten-Sacken, June 9, 1926, BA.

31. Osten-Sacken report to Zahle, BA.

32. Telegram of June 21, 1926, BA.

33. Osten-Sacken report to Zahle, BA.

34. Report of Dr. Theodor Eitel (December 22, 1926), BA and EHF.

35. Letter of Dr. Saathof to Duke George of Leuchtenberg (December 7, 1927), in BA and EHF.

36. Testimony of Dr. Eitel, given at Bad Liebenzell on May 20, 1959, transcript at Hamburg.

37. Saathof letter, BA and EHF.

38. Eitel report, BA and EHF.

39. Affidavit of Nurse Agnes Wasserschleben, July 28, 1929, EHF.

40. IA, 188.

41. Wasserschleben affidavit, EHF.

42. Quoted in letter of Nina von Hoyningen-Huené (later Osten-Sacken) to Paul Pavlovitch von Kügelgen (who edited Frau von Rathlef's book), in Rathlef (German 153).

43. Eitel testimony, Hamburg.

44. Eitel report, BA and EHF.

45. The section on Tatiana Botkin is taken from a number of sources: Botkin (Melnik), *Vospominanya* (authorized English translation, "Memories of the Tsar's Family" in EHF), and *Au temps des tsars.* Concerning her meeting with A, see her affidavit of May 11, 1929, EHF and Hamburg; her letters to her uncle, Serge Botkin, in BA; her articles in *Figaro,* January 16–22, 1958; Auclères I and II; and Horan MS. I have also drawn on my own conversations with Tatiana since 1971.

46. In Horan MS.; also conversations with Tatiana Botkin and emendations by her to my original manuscript.

47. *Au temps des tsars,* 84.

48. Horan MS.

49. *Au temps des tsars,* 81, and emendations by Tatiana Botkin to my manuscript.

50. *Vospominanya,* EHF.

51. Interview with Tatiana Botkin.

52. Interview with Tatiana Botkin.

53. Report of Baron Osten-Sacken to Herluf Zahle, September 9, 1926, BA.

54. Osten-Sacken report to Zahle, BA; and Tatiana Botkin affidavit, EHF.

55. *Figaro,* January 16–17, 1958.

56. Auclères I and II; and interview with Tatiana Botkin.

57. Osten-Sacken report to Zahle, BA.

58. Tatiana Botkin affidavit, EHF.

59. Lillan Zahle to Maria Debagory, September 11, 1926, BA.

60. Serge Botkin to Herluf Zahle, September 14, 1926, BA.

61. Osten-Sacken report to Zahle, BA.

62. Tatiana Botkin affidavit, EHF.

63. Osten-Sacken report to Zahle, BA.

64. Tatiana Botkin to Serge Botkin, September 4/17, 1926, BA.

65. Gilliard to Tatiana Botkin, October 30, 1926, BA.

66. Letter of August 30, 1926, BA; quoted in IA, 197–198.

67. Tatiana to Serge Botkin, September 18, 1926, BA.

68. Interview with Tatiana Botkin; in *Figaro,* January 18, 1958; Tatiana to Serge Botkin, October 14/27, 1926, BA.

69. Tatiana Botkin to Fallows, January 3, 1930; *Figaro,* January 18, 1958; Tatiana to Serge Botkin, October 14/27, 1926, BA. Tatiana wrote me in 1982 that Countess Alexandra Shuvalov, a great friend of the Botkin family, had "immediately" arranged for her to see "some members of the best Russian families. They all seemed disturbed. Ladies had tears in their eyes. But only one gentleman declared later: 'If there is even the slightest possibility that this invalid is our Tsar's daughter, we must help her.' " The gentleman was Serge Rachmaninoff, who, two years later, did provide A with financial and moral support (see my chapter 9).

70. *Figaro,* January 18, 1958.

71. Sokolov, *Enquête judiciaire,* 28.

72. *Figaro,* January 18, 1958.

73. Botkin MS. Peter Botkin pointed out that Tatiana was expecting a child at the time of her meeting with A, and thus "suffering from the hallucinations common to a pregnant woman" (Botkin I, 273).

74. Notes (*Bemerkungen*) of Tatiana Botkin, April 1961, Hamburg.

75. Horan MS.

76. Andrew to Serge Botkin, March 2, 1927, BA (Ian Lilburn's translation).

77. Serge Botkin to Andrew, October 19, 1926, BA (Lilburn's translation).

78. Mathilde had been the mistress not only of Nicholas II, but later of his cousin Grand Duke Serge Mikhailovitch, who was murdered by the Bolsheviks at Alapayevsk along with the Empress's sister Grand Duchess Elisabeth and other members of the Romanov family. The date of the assassination is given as July 17, 1918. Mathilde waited for three years, until she was certain that Serge was dead, before marrying Andrew. Her son, Vladimir (see Part IV), was thought to be Serge's child.

79. An important point, inasmuch as A's adversaries sought to minimize Andrew's qualifications for recognizing or not recognizing the Tsar's daughter. Faith Lavington, the governess at Castle Seeon, was informed erroneously that Andrew had not seen the Tsar's children "in donkey's years" — that is, since before World War I — when, in fact, he was one of the last in the family to see them at all. See Lavington Diary, Hamburg.

80. Andrew to Serge Botkin, November 30, 1926, BA.

81. Quoted in Andrew's letter to Serge Botkin, above.

82. Andrew to Serge Botkin, November 30, 1926, BA.

83. See Part IV. Andrew's letters are, for the most part, in BA. Translations submitted at Hamburg. Some of the letters are published in FOT and in Auclères I, with others (mostly Serge Botkin's replies) at Hamburg alone. I have worked from the certified copies submitted at Hamburg and followed Ian Lilburn's English translations where noted.

84. Andrew to Serge Botkin, February 8, 1927.

85. Andrew's provisions for release of his dossier: FOT, 387. Andrew wrote Serge Botkin on February 2, 1927: "Zahle is mistaken somewhat if he thinks I am taking this case lightly. The difficulty has been completely clear to me from the very first, and I am convinced that Zahle himself does not suspect how complicated and confused this case is. . . . The affair does not concern the invalid alone, but a whole network of other circumstances. . . . Unfortunately I cannot reveal even schematically the details of the investigation in a letter; that would be imprudent on my part. But I can assure you that this case is extremely serious and, I repeat, much more complicated than Zahle imagines"; BA.

86. Andrew to Serge Botkin, February 26, 1927 (Lilburn translation), BA.

87. Andrew to Serge Botkin, March 2, 1927, BA.

88. Andrew to Tatiana Botkin, May 18, 1927, in Auclères I, 171.

7. "What Have I Done?"

1. Osten-Sacken to Rathlef, November 6, 1926, BA.
2. Rathlef to Osten-Sacken, October 12, 1926, BA. Baron Osten-Sacken had in fact seen A once while she was still at Dalldorf: Schwabe report, BA.
3. Zahle to Rathlef, November 12, 1926, BA.
4. Alfred Hugenberg wielded tremendous power in Weimar Germany and probably did more than any other private citizen to influence public opinion in favor of the Nazis.
5. See Rathlef/Noeggerath.
6. Zahle to Rathlef, November 12, 1926, BA.
7. Andrew to Tatiana Botkin, May 18, 1927, Hamburg.
8. Andrew to Serge Botkin, March 14, 1927, BA. See also Andrew's letters of January 23 and March 8, 1927, concerning his conversations with King Christian X and Queen Alexandrine and the children of Prince Waldemar.
9. Serge Botkin to Andrew, February 15, 1927, Hamburg.
10. Dr. Eitel's correspondence with Zahle, Serge Botkin, and others is in BA.
11. Eitel testimony, Hamburg.
12. Osten-Sacken to Zahle, September 1, 1926, BA.
13. Lillan Zahle to Maria Debagory, January 1, 1927, BA.
14. Lillan Zahle to Maria Debagory, January 1, 1927; and to Tatiana Botkin, March 9, 1927, BA.
15. Rathlef to Leuchtenberg, July 4, 1927, EHF.
16. Andrew to Serge Botkin, February 8, 1927, BA.
17. Andrew to Serge Botkin, March 15, 1927, BA.
18. Zahle to Serge Botkin, January 24, 1927, BA.
19. The Dukes of Leuchtenberg were descended from Napoleon Bonaparte's stepson, Eugène de Beauharnais, whose son Maximilian married a daughter of Tsar Nicholas I. As members of the imperial house, the Leuchtenbergs were considered "Romanovs in everything but name," but remained outside the line of succession. See Horan MS. Duke George had also been influenced in A's favor by Zahle.
20. Serge Botkin to Andrew, March 7, 1927, Hamburg.
21. Andrew to Serge Botkin, February 8, 1927 (Lilburn translation), BA.
22. Zahle to Serge Botkin, January 24, 1927, BA.
23. The Grand Duke of Hesse's "investigation" was nothing of the kind, inasmuch as he had no intention other than to find the means to prove A false. The very simple solution of a meeting between the Grand Duke and A seems not to have been even considered in Darmstadt.
24. Serge Botkin to Andrew, January 19, 1927, Hamburg.
25. Frau von Rathlef had no desire to indulge the Grand Duke of Hesse, but Zahle advised her to cooperate — "otherwise Darmstadt will naturally claim that the casts are proof *against* the invalid" (letter of March 21, 1927, EHF).
26. She had actually signed her statement in 1925, but this was the first time it had been mentioned publicly. Wrote Duke George of Leuchtenberg: "Nothing would surprise me coming from that person. . . . I wonder if her current employer knows that she has written an abusive book in French about her former mistress [Empress Alexandra]": Leuchtenberg to Rathlef, July 16, 1927, EHF.
27. See article in the *Königsberger Allgemeine,* March 7, 1927, reproduced in Rathlef (German 125–127).
28. Andrew to Serge Botkin, March 28, 1927 (Lilburn translation), BA.
29. Zahle to Serge Botkin, January 24, 1927, BA; and Botkin to Andrew, February 15, 1927, Hamburg.
30. It is not clear when and how the meetings between Zahle and the Grand Duke of Hesse were arranged, but Zahle certainly did not hesitate to go when asked.
31. IA, 203–204. The phrase about "the status quo" is in the original German, reproduced in *Ich, Anastasia, erzähle.*
32. Zahle to Andrew, February 15, 1927, BA.
33. See Eitel correspondence, BA.
34. Telegram to Serge Botkin, February 5, 1927, BA.
35. Zahle to Serge Botkin, February 5, 1927, BA.

36. Andrew to Zahle, February 10, 1927, BA.

37. Interview with Prince Frederick of Saxe-Altenburg.

38. Harriet von Rathlef's articles were published in the *Berliner Nachtausgabe* as "Lebt Anastasia?" Clippings in BA and EHF.

39. In 1928 Frau von Rathlef was charged with bribing a police official in Berlin and was acquitted (see *New York Times,* May 15, 1928); the *Nachtausgabe* also later sued the rival *Tägliche Rundschau* over charges about the origin and nature of the "unmasking" (see pages 164–175). That case was dropped.

40. Quoted in Gilbert Guilleminault, ed., *Grandes Enigmes de l'histoire* (Paris: Gautier-Languereau, 1964), 154.

41. Editorial in the *Nachtausgabe,* March 10, 1927.

42. Article in the *Königsberger Allgemeine,* March 7, 1927.

43. Zahle to Tatiana Botkin, March 10, 1927, BA.

44. Andrew wrote Serge Botkin on February 26, 1927 (BA): "Gilliard writes me that he very much regrets it, but he has had to challenge Frau von Rathlef's assertions and conclusions in the newspapers, that is, insofar as they relate to him and to his wife."

45. Letters of March 8 and March 20, 1927, EHF.

46. See FA, 152–163; *L'Illustration,* June 25, 1927; and in the *Berliner Nachtausgabe,* April 1927.

47. See FA, 163–164.

48. Quoted in Nogly, 182.

49. Letter to Kurt Vermehren, undated (June 1958), Hamburg; in Auclères I, 163; see also pp. 158–162 for the analysis of Maurice Delamain, the former president of the French Graphological Society, which also concluded in A's favor.

50. FA, 173.

51. Botkin MS.

52. Interview with Tatiana Botkin.

53. Letter in BA.

54. Andrew to Serge Botkin, March 5, 1927.

55. Tatiana was outraged at the thought that she was to be *paid* to assist A. "Please understand me," Zahle wrote her in his letter of March 10, 1927 (BA), "it is only natural that you, who are obliged to leave your family, should not also suffer financially."

56. Zahle to Tatiana Botkin, March 10, 1927, BA.

57. Zahle to Tatiana Botkin, March 10, 1927, BA.

58. Serge Botkin to Andrew, March 7, 1927, BA.

59. See A "Memoirs."

60. Zahle to Serge Botkin, February 15, 1927, BA.

61. Wasserschleben affidavit.

62. Tatiana Botkin affidavit, EHF.

63. Report of Tatiana Botkin, in Rathlef (English 149, German 155).

64. Interviews with Tatiana Botkin; in Auclères I, 99–100 and II; *Figaro,* January 21, 1958; and emendations of Tatiana Botkin to my manuscript.

65. Dominique Auclères, for delicacy's sake, changed the word to *gamin* (urchin), but informed me privately of A's actual remark.

66. See testimony of Natalie, Baroness von Meller-Zakomelsky, Hamburg.

67. Notes of Duke George of Leuchtenberg, EHF.

68. Andrew to Tatiana Botkin, March 12, 1927, Hamburg.

69. Andrew to Serge Botkin, August 4, 1927, BA.

70. Leuchtenberg notes, EHF.

71. Her statement against A is published in FA, 141–142. She refers to A's "vulgar manner" and adds that she had "not a trait, not a gesture to remind one of Grand Duchess Anastasia Nicolaievna." In reality Mme. Hessé, by her own admission, had seen the Tsar's daughter only fleetingly in the years after 1905. The Duke of Leuchtenberg reported: "The widow of General Hessé, the Tsar's former palace commandant, frequently came to visit us. One day she sought out the invalid, whom in general she rejected, and asked her a series of questions which she [A] was unable to answer. Finally she asked: 'Who is Conrad (or Konrad)?' whereupon the invalid, instead of answering, smiled and imitated the movement of hands over a piano.

"[Mme. Hessé told the Duke]: 'Now today your invalid has really staggered me! Because the piano teacher Conrad was known by only a very few people even at Court, his name was scarcely mentioned' " (from the Duke of Leuchtenberg's notes, EHF and Rathlef).

72. See testimony of Darya Gordeyev, given at New York City, March 17, 1959; transcript at Hamburg.

73. Lavington Diary, Hamburg.

74. Gordeyev testimony, Hamburg.

75. Wasserschleben affidavit, EHF.

76. Natalie, Baroness Meller-Zakomelsky to Brien Horan, in Horan MS.

77. Serge Botkin to Andrew, April 1, 1927, Hamburg.

78. Headline in the *Berliner Nachtausgabe* ("Fall Anastasia geklärt!"), March 31, 1927.

79. Andrew to Serge Botkin, April 4, 1927, BA.

80. For considerations of length and clarity, I have discussed only the major points of the so-called Schanzkowska Legend. So confused is the evidence on this subject as to make A's other affairs look simple by comparison. There is not a single detail of the "unmasking" that is not in dispute, beginning with the date of Franziska's disappearance from Berlin in 1920 and ending with the allegation nearly fifty years later that Franziska was actually a patient at the lunatic asylum at Herrenprotsch in the late twenties (see my chapter 14). In the course of my research I have met only one royal witness against A — Duke Dmitri of Leuchtenberg — who actually believed the Schanzkowska story.

81. *Berliner Nachtausgabe,* March 31, 1927.

82. Serge Botkin to Andrew, April 1, 1927, Hamburg.

83. Andrew to Serge Botkin, April 4, 1927, BA.

84. Leuchtenberg's emendations to Rathlef's account, EHF.

85. Andrew to Serge Botkin, April 4, 1927, BA.

86. Reported in the *Nachtausgabe,* April 6, 1927.

87. Andrew to Serge Botkin, April 4, 1927, BA.

88. Fallows "Entry," March 6, 1938 (containing report of Albert F. Coyle), EHF.

89. This is the story of the "unmasking" as first reported in the *Nachtausgabe;* over the years, it changed considerably.

90. According to Frau von Rathlef's attorney, A had been staying with Clara Peuthert during the time in question (see protocol of Dr. Wilhelm Völler of his conversation with Clara, April 29, 1927, EHF).

91. All of the clothing disappeared after the *Nachtausgabe* ostensibly handed it over to Detective Knopf. That being the case, it will not be necessary to take a detailed inventory of what Dominique Auclères called "Doris Wingender's wardrobe."

92. Testimony of Doris Rittmann and Louise Fiedler (the Wingender sisters), November 17–18, 1965, Hamburg.

93. She was declared mad on September 19, 1916, and spent time in and out of the lunatic asylums at Berlin-Schöneberg and Neu-Ruppin.

94. Rathlef (German 184).

95. Agatha Grabisch's report of her conversations with Lucke is dated "May 1927," EHF.

96. Lucke testimony, Hamburg.

97. Protocol of conversations with "Kommissar X," EHF.

98. Letter of Darmstadt police to Berlin police, May 20, 1927, Hamburg.

99. "Kommissar X" protocol, EHF.

100. Andrew to Serge Botkin, May 13, 1927 (Lilburn translation), BA.

101. Lucke testimony, Hamburg. The contract with Doris Wingender is reproduced in Rathlef (German, facing page 193).

102. In the *Nachtausgabe,* April 6, 1927.

103. Rathlef/Noeggerath.

104. Rathlef/Noeggerath; also protocols of Gleb Botkin and Wilhelm Völler, May 19 and 21, 1927, EHF.

105. Leuchtenberg report, in Rathlef (German 179–180).

106. Letter of Fritz Spengrüber to the *Tägliche Rundschau,* October 4, 1927; in Rathlef (German 187–188).

107. Leuchtenberg to Rathlef, July 28 and October 2, 1927, EHF.

108. See Grand Duke Andrew correspondence, BA, in particular his letters to Serge Botkin of August 18, 1927; and to Tatiana Botkin of May 18, 1927, Hamburg.

109. The confrontation with Felix Schanzkowski is described in Rathlef (German 183),

and in greater detail in "Wie eine Frau," etc. See also Andrew's correspondence with Serge Botkin, BA; the testimony of Duke Dmitri and Duchess Catherine of Leuchtenberg and of Natalie, Baroness Meller-Zakomelsky, Hamburg; and, finally, the affidavit of Felix Schanzkowski, May 9, 1927, EHF; with further information in the protocol of Dr. Wilhelm Völler of May 10, 1927.

110. Botkin MS.
111. Völler protocol, EHF.
112. Unsigned affidavit, copy in EHF.
113. "Wie eine Frau," etc.
114. IA, 217.
115. Affidavit of Felix Schanzkowski, EHF.
116. Rathlef/Noeggerath.
117. Serge Botkin to Andrew, March 7, 1927, Hamburg.
118. See Rathlef-Leuchtenberg correspondence, EHF.
119. Leuchtenberg to Rathlef, June 27, 1927, EHF.
120. Rathlef to Leuchtenberg, June 29, 1927, EHF.
121. "Wie eine Frau," etc.; Völler protocol, EHF.
122. Leuchtenberg to Rathlef, October 12, 1927, EHF.
123. Serge Botkin to Andrew, April 2, 1927, Hamburg.

8. At Castle Seeon

1. Quoted in the *Frankfurter Allgemeine,* April 2, 1958 (from testimony of Felix Dassel).
2. Lavington Diary, Hamburg.
3. See Botkin MS; and Botkin I and II.
4. A "Memoirs."
5. Botkin MS.
6. See Princess Xenia testimony, Hamburg; and Botkin I, 281.
7. Botkin MS.
8. See Leuchtenberg-Rathlef correspondence, EHF.
9. The word *mess* was a favorite of A's all of her life. People, places, and things were all "messes" when they stood in her way.
10. Leuchtenberg to Rathlef, June 8, 1927, EHF.
11. "L'Histoire d'une imposture," *L'Illustration* of June 25, 1927.
12. Felix Dassel to Rathlef, January 6, 1928, EHF. A's literal phrase was *machte schlechte Sachen in die Zeitungen.*
13. A's phrase quoted in Dassel, *Grossfürstin Anastasia lebt!*
14. Rathlef to Leuchtenberg, April 8, 1927, EHF.
15. Leuchtenberg to Rathlef, April 22, 1927, EHF.
16. Botkin MS.
17. See their testimonies at Hamburg. Of the two youngest Leuchtenberg children, Constantine came out against A, while Tamara stood "for" with reservations.
18. Wasserschleben affidavit, EHF.
19. Lavington Diary, Hamburg.
20. Automobiles of the Russian court — that is, those bearing the imperial arms — were free of all restriction.
21. Darya had not seen the Tsar's daughter since 1916, and no more "lived" with the Grand Duchesses than the Botkin children had. Like the Botkins, Darya, in Gilliard's words, "never came to the palace." In her Hamburg testimony, moreover, Darya confessed that the similarity between A's eyes and the eyes of the Tsar's daughter had disturbed her.
22. Diary of Vera von Klemenz, authorized English translation signed and amended by Vera von Klemenz in 1929 for submission as affidavit in court, in EHF.
23. Leuchtenberg to Rathlef, June 19, 1927, EHF.
24. Affidavit in lieu of oath in Harriet von Rathlef, EHF; see also Leuchtenberg to Rathlef, December 23, 1927, EHF.
25. Leuchtenberg to Rathlef, July 7, 1927, EHF.
26. Serge Botkin to Andrew, August 9, 1927, Hamburg.
27. Andrew to Serge Botkin, August 4, 1927, BA.
28. Colonel Mordvinov's account of his meeting with A is in FA, 92–97.

29. Quoted in testimony of Duke Dmitri of Leuchtenberg, Hamburg.
30. Grand Duchess Olga to Colonel Mordvinov, March 30, 1927, Hamburg.
31. See testimony of Prince Felix Yussoupov, July 15, 1959, Hamburg; and Yussoupov, Felix, *En exil* (Paris: Plon, 1954), pp. 113–116.
32. Marie, *A Princess in Exile,* 103–104.
33. Yussoupov to Gilliard, December 10, 1928, in FA, 143–145.
34. FA, 144.
35. Quoted in Auclères I, 116.
36. See Yussoupov testimony, Hamburg; and *En exil.*
37. Yussoupov to Andrew, September 19, 1927, Hamburg.
38. See the statement prepared by Major-General Alexander Spiridovitch (offered grandly as an "expert evaluation") of June 30, 1928, in FA, 164–165.
39. Auclères I, 130 (from an interview with Kastritsky's daughter, Dr. Kastritsky-Procé).
40. Auclères I, 130. At Hamburg Dr. Kastritsky's testimony was ruled "too vague" for serious consideration: FOT, 249.
41. Fallows "Entry," September 19, 1938, EHF.
42. The account of Felix Dassel's meetings with A is taken from his *Grossfürstin Anastasia lebt!* except where noted.
43. Testimony of Felix Dassel, given at Wiesbaden, April 1 and 2, 1958, transcript at Hamburg.
44. *Figaro,* April 2, 1958.
45. Bornemann's statement concerning the meetings at Castle Seeon is dated September 18, 1927, in EHF.
46. Dassel testimony, Hamburg.
47. Bornemann statement, EHF.
48. A had already remembered the medallion during Tatiana Botkin's visit to Oberstdorf. See Tatiana Botkin affidavit, EHF.
49. On page 29 of the English translation of Tatiana's *Vospominanya* (in EHF) the line reads: "They daily visited the hospital dedicated to their names."
50. Bornemann statement, EHF.
51. Lavington Diary, Hamburg.
52. There were further examples of this kind of thing. Dassel recalled the day when the Tsar's daughters had brought their commonplace books to the hospital at Tsarskoe Selo for the wounded officers to sign. In Maria's, on the first page, were inscribed the words: "To the famous Mandrifolie, from Dmitri." When Dassel had the Duke of Leuchtenberg ask A if she knew the significance of "the famous Mandrifolie," she answered simply: "Maria had many nicknames."
53. The next few pages are based on the Lavington Diary, Hamburg.
54. See *Grossfürstin Anastasia lebt!* A declared that the Kodak camera was exactly like the one she had owned in Russia, and when she first used it at Seeon she did not need to read the instructions.
55. The remainder of the chapter is drawn from Lavington Diary, Hamburg.

9. "She Was Herself"

1. These were not Gleb's words, but rather the tag attached by the majority of American reporters.
2. *New York Times,* January 2, 1926.
3. New York *Herald Tribune,* February 9, 1928.
4. *Herald Tribune,* February 10, 1928.
5. The feature article in the *New York Times,* dated March 28, 1926, had been written by Bella Cohen (later Spewack) and was based on her conversations at the Mommsen Clinic wih Frau von Rathlef and at the Danish embassy with Zahle and Shura Gilliard.
6. Botkin I, 260.
7. The North American Newspaper Alliance was managed by Gleb's friend John Colter, who later became friendly with A.
8. Botkin I, 265; 274.
9. Botkin II, 52.
10. Botkin MS. See also Gleb Botkin's affidavit of July 20, 1938, EHF.

11. Botkin MS., I and II, *passim.*

12. Botkin MS.

13. His accusations against the Romanovs and the Russian monarchists stopped just short of libel, and would undoubtedly have led to civil action had A's opposition dared to bring her case into court. After an especially vitriolic article of Gleb's had appeared in the New York press, Grand Duke Andrew wrote Serge Botkin: "The tone of the last part of the article is absolutely unwarranted. . . . Gleb is no longer relying here on facts, but on notoriously untrue gossip. Has Gleb really not got enough feeling and tact to understand how inappropriate, even harmful, it is for a Russian to sling mud at his own people in the columns of the foreign press? His insinuations against the Grand Duke of Hesse I find equally distasteful. . . . It must not be forgotten that ultimately the recognition of the invalid will depend primarily on Grand Duchess Olga Alexandrovna, but when she hears into whose hands the invalid has fallen she will no longer believe anything — and she will be right, because after this article of Gleb's everyone will lose faith. Can he really not understand such a simple thing, that he is completely ruining the invalid?" (Andrew to Serge Botkin, December 25, 1927) (Lilburn translation), BA.

14. Botkin MS.

15. Botkin II, 129–130. Margharita was the widow of Christopher Derfelden, and an American by birth. Her daughter Maria (Maya) was the first wife of Hugh D. Auchincloss, who later married Janet Bouvier. It was through the Auchinclosses that A came in contact with Hugh's aunt, Annie B. Jennings (see page 210).

16. See Botkin II, 130–141; and testimony of Princess Xenia of Russia, March 16–17, 1959, Hamburg. Xenia, a goddaughter of Empress Alexandra, was born in 1903; her sister, Nina, in 1901, just two days after Grand Duchess Anastasia.

17. Xenia testimony, Hamburg.

18. Interview with Princess Paul Chavchavadze (Princess Nina).

19. Leeds's mother, the former Nancy Stewart, had married Xenia's uncle, Prince Christopher of Greece and Denmark, and became Princess Anastasia after her reception into the Orthodox Church.

20. See New York *Evening Journal,* February 3, 1930.

21. Princess Xenia testimony, Hamburg.

22. Lavington Diary, Hamburg.

23. Ibid.

24. See Andrew's correspondence with Serge Botkin, May–December, 1927, BA. On December 8 the Grand Duke finally acknowledged that the trip to New York was not only advisable but essential: "I should tell you of my deep conviction that certain people [in Europe] are bent on destroying her [A]."

25. Lavington Diary, Hamburg.

26. She used the Scots spelling "Gallacher." Her affidavit is dated December 22, 1930, in EHF. See also her letters to Fallows, EHF.

27. Gallagher affidavit, EHF. Since A's first identity certificate had been granted in Berlin, that was where Darmstadt focused its attempts to have it revoked.

28. Gallagher affidavit, EHF.

29. Leuchtenberg to Rathlef, January 29, 1928, EHF.

30. Lavington Diary, Hamburg.

31. There was a great hue and cry among the Russian monarchists after A's passage through Paris became known. After her departure for the United States a number of monarchists claimed that they had tried to see A at the Hôtel du Palais, but, according to Miss Gallagher, no one but Princess Obolensky (page 205) actually endeavored to do so.

32. Leuchtenberg to Rathlef, July 16, 1928, EHF; see also Gallagher affidavit, EHF.

33. Gallagher affidavit, EHF.

34. Prince Vladimir Romanov to Dominique Auclères, quoted without citation in Auclères I, 178.

35. Andrew to Serge Botkin, February 17, 1928, BA; in Auclères I, 178.

36. Andrew to Serge Botkin, February 6, 1928.

37. Gallagher affidavit, EHF.

38. Gallagher affidavit, EHF; and interview with Mrs. Edward J. Wynkoop (Nancy Leeds).

39. Gallagher affidavit, EHF.

40. Quoted in Lavington Diary, Hamburg.

41. Leuchtenberg to Rathlef, February 11, 1928, EHF.

42. Gallagher affidavit, EHF.

43. Eleonore, Grand Duchess of Hesse, to Prince Louis of Hesse, February 15, 1928, Hamburg.

44. Andrew to Gleb Botkin, April 3, 1928; in Botkin II, 217.

45. Andrew to Serge Botkin, February 17, 1928.

46. Andrew to Maria Debagory, February 16, 1928, in Auclères I, 179.

47. Andrew to Serge Botkin, February 17, 1928, BA.

48. Andrew's letter to Olga (Lilburn translation) is dated February 4, 1928, and was first published on February 10, 1960, in *L'Aurore* (Paris). See Part IV.

49. See Botkin II, 157–166. In 1935 Agnes Gallagher sent Fallows a number of newspaper clippings concerning A's arrival. They are now in EHF, but are not clearly identified by date and publication. All of the clippings in question are from the period between February 7 and February 12, 1928.

50. Undated, unattributed article, EHF.

51. Botkin II, 163.

52. *Herald Tribune*, February 9, 1928.

53. *Herald Tribune*, February 8, 1928.

54. Undated, unattributed article, EHF.

55. *Herald Tribune*, February 13, 1928.

56. *Herald Tribune*, February 9, 1928.

57. Gleb quoted Rachmaninoff: "I shall be very frank with you and tell you right now, that I am by no means convinced that she is actually Grand Duchess Anastasia. Hers seems to be one of those stories which are too fantastic to be believed, yet require even more fantastic explanations to be disbelieved. But I am convinced that she is no deliberate imposter. . . . I want to be of help" (Botkin II, 153). Rachmaninoff's sister-in-law, Sophie Satin, wrote me on April 23, 1971, that he "was one of the Russians who supplied some money for her coming to America, [saying] that this claim must be settled, that her presence here might help to learn the truth."

58. Undated, unattributed article, EHF.

59. Botkin II, 161–162.

60. Undated, unattributed article, EHF.

61. Botkin II, 165–166.

62. Undated, unattributed article, EHF.

63. Undated, unattributed article, EHF.

64. Undated, unattributed article, EHF.

65. Botkin II, 165.

66. Gleb Botkin in *Evening World*, July 19, 1928.

67. See articles in the *Herald Tribune*, February 10–11, 1928; and Botkin II, 174.

68. Gallagher affidavit. Miss Jennings was seventy-four at this time and lived at 48 Park Avenue.

69. A "Interviews."

70. Gallagher affidavit, EHF.

71. A "Memoirs" ("My American Experiences").

72. Undated, unattributed article, EHF.

73. *New York American*, February 10, 1928.

74. *New York Mirror*, March 29, 1930.

75. Princess Xenia testimony, Hamburg.

76. BA contains a number of clippings.

77. *Izvestia*, February 25, 1928.

78. Alexander, *Once a Grand Duke*, 335–336.

79. See page 229.

80. Alexander, *Once a Grand Duke*, 335.

81. *Literary Digest*, July 7, 1928.

82. For fun, see Donald Ogden Stewart's satire "Introducing Anastasia," in *The New Yorker*, February 25, 1928.

83. Undated, unattributed article, EHF.

84. *New York Times*, February 28, 1928.

85. *Herald Tribune*, February 11, 1928.

86. A "Memoirs" ("My American Experiences"), EHF.

87. See A "Memoirs" ("My American Experiences"). Miss Jennings's gardens at Fairfield, Connecticut, were open to the public.

88. Botkin II, 184.

89. A "Interviews."

90. Derfelden affidavit, EHF.

91. See A "Memoirs." Nicholas Roosevelt took an abiding interest in A's case. See Fallows's "Entries" and letters on this subject in EHF.

92. Derfelden to Annie B. Jennings, May 15, 1930 (? — no year in letter), Hamburg.

93. Princess Xenia testimony, Hamburg.

94. King George I of Greece was the brother of Queen Alexandra and of the Dowager Empress.

95. Affidavit of Princess Xenia Georgievna, February 10, 1958, attached to her Hamburg testimony.

96. FA, 106.

97. Princess Xenia testimony, Hamburg.

98. Princess Xenia testimony, Hamburg.

99. Sophie Satin reported that "she did not take any part in the conversation and was very reserved" (to PK, April 23, 1971).

100. Adele Astaire was a great friend of William Leeds, and was with Leeds during an accidental explosion at the boathouse at Kenwood; A was sure the blast had been meant for her: Interview with Mrs. Edward J. Wynkoop.

101. Letter of Prince Paul Chavchavadze to PK, February 1971 (undated).

102. Interview with Princess Nina.

103. Quoted in Andrew to Serge Botkin, May 6, 1928, BA.

104. Princess Xenia testimony, Hamburg.

105. Mrs. Edward J. Wynkoop to Brien Horan, in Horan MS.

106. Derfelden affidavit, EHF.

107. David Chavchavadze to Brien Horan, in Horan MS.

108. Notes and emendations of Mrs. Edward J. Wynkoop to my manuscript. David Chavchavadze reported A's reply differently as "Because it was the last language we heard before we were all shot." See Horan MS.

109. Derfelden affidavit, EHF.

110. Princess Xenia testimony, Hamburg.

111. Derfelden affidavit, EHF.

112. See Princess Xenia testimony, Hamburg.

113. Derfelden affidavit, EHF.

114. Princess Xenia testimony, Hamburg; also in Auclères I, 185.

115. Princess Xenia affidavit, attached to Hamburg testimony.

116. A to Mrs. Edward J. Wynkoop (in my presence).

117. Xenia to Dominique Auclères, in Auclères I, 183–184.

118. Gleb Botkin to Fallows, June 5, 1928, EHF.

119. A "Memoirs."

120. Gleb Botkin in Evening World, July 19, 1928.

121. Princess Xenia testimony, Hamburg.

122. For Gleb Botkin's account of the goings-on at Oyster Bay in August 1928 see Botkin II, 221–280, an account disputed not only by Xenia, but on many points of detail by Edward Fallows (see Fallows notes on The Woman Who Rose Again, EHF).

123. Quoted in Evening World, July 19, 1928. See also Botkin II, 231.

124. Gleb Botkin in Evening World, July 19, 1928.

125. Xenia to Gleb Botkin, July 18, 1928, EHF.

126. Botkin II, 259, and Gleb's correspondence with Fallows in EHF.

127. Xenia to Dominique Auclères, in Auclères I, 184.

128. Gleb Botkin to A, July 12, 1928, EHF. This was the famous "sealed letter" that Gleb alleged Xenia had withheld from A to nefarious purpose (Botkin II, 226). Xenia explained to the contrary that she had only been hoping to spare A further distress. The envelope and Gleb's copy are both in EHF.

129. Xenia to Auclères, in Auclères I, 184.

130. Leuchtenberg to Rathlef, November 8, 1928, EHF.

131. See Princess Xenia testimony, Hamburg; and A "Memoirs" ("My American Experiences").

132. A to James R. Sheffield, January 4, 1930, EHF and Hamburg.

133. Affidavit of Edward H. Fallows, March 1, 1938, EHF.

134. Interview with Mrs. Edward J. Wynkoop.

135. Clippings in EHF.

136. *Evening Journal*, July 26 (?), 1930. "Billy Benedick" was just one of the noms de plume (among them "Dolly Madison" and "Cholly Knickerbocker") of the society columnist Maury Paul.

137. Interview with Mrs. Edward J. Wynkoop.

138. This is hazy, as Nina herself was on the subject. When I met the Princess in 1971 she declared that she did not believe in A's identity, while arguing consistently in her favor. At the end of the twenties, however, she was widely quoted as being on A's side. See Curtis J. Mar to Fallows, November 21, 1929, EHF.

139. Mrs. Edward J. Wynkoop to PK, July 7, 1971.

140. Mar to Fallows, December 10 and 27, 1930, EHF.

10. Changing Fortunes

1. All of A's signed agreements with Fallows between 1928 and 1940 are in EHF.

2. See Fallows "Entries," August 1928, EHF.

3. Gleb Botkin to Andrew, October 24, 1928, EHF.

4. Botkin II, 265–266.

5. A "Memoirs" ("My American Experiences").

6. Botkin II, 275.

7. A never knew when and how the name "Anna" was chosen, but it seems to have been picked when she was sent back to Germany in 1931.

8. A "Memoirs" ("My American Experiences").

9. Botkin II, 276; see also 290–327.

10. Botkin II, 308.

11. Botkin II, 204.

12. Botkin I, 310–311.

13. Gleb Botkin to Fallows, October 17, 1929, EHF.

14. Botkin II, 282.

15. The Copenhagen Statement is reproduced in FA, 9–11. The version issued from Darmstadt also bore the signatures of the Grand Duke of Hesse and his sisters Victoria and Irene.

16. Nogly, 84; in *Evening Post,* January 14, 1929.

17. Gleb Botkin to Fallows, October 26, 1928, EHF.

18. Botkin II, 284–285.

19. Statement of Edward H. Fallows, October 28, 1928, EHF; also in *New York Times,* October 30, 1928.

20. Letter of October 18, 1928, in EHF and BA.

21. Interview with Tatiana Botkin.

22. Gleb Botkin to Fallows, October 26, 1928, EHF.

23. See Fallows "Entries," March 1929, EHF.

24. Tatiana Botkin quoted in Horan MS.

25. Tatiana Botkin to Fallows, December 8, 1930, EHF.

26. Botkin II, 286–287.

27. Botkin II, 287.

28. See A "Memoirs" ("My American Experiences").

29. A "Memoirs" ("My American Experiences").

30. The Grandanor Corporation had actually been formed in August 1928, but was not incorporated until February 9, 1929. All material relating to the corporation is in EHF.

31. Statement of Edward Fallows, December 5, 1928, EHF.

32. A "Interviews" ("Tentative for Introduction").

33. Affidavit of A, December 15, 1928, EHF; in Botkin II, 203.

34. Kennedy to Fallows, July 3, 1928, EHF.

35. Fallows and Kennedy conversations with Gallop: from Fallows's "Entries" of February 25 and April 11, 1929, EHF.

36. Bank of England to Earl Mountbatten of Burma, April 18, 1958, Hamburg.

37. Vorres, 245.

38. See the testimony of Alexander Kerensky and Prince Lvov in the Russian edition of the Sokolov report; also quoted in the memorandum of Kurt Vermehren, January 31, 1961, Hamburg.

39. Benckendorff, *Last Days at Tsarskoe Selo,* 125.

40. *Observer* and Sampson: in Auclères I, 132–133.

41. A "Interviews."

42. See Botkin II, *passim;* and in particular pp. 201–204; and 99.

43. Interview with Princess Nina.

44. Affidavit of A, August 10, 1938, EHF.

45. See Fallows's "Entries" and letters, EHF; also Ponsonby, Sir Frederick, *Recollections of Three Reigns* (London: Eyre and Spottiswoode, 1951).

46. Vorres, 185. For an account of the sale of the Dowager Empress's jewelry collection, see Vorres, 180–185; and Ponsonby, 339. Grand Duchess Olga received forty thousand pounds from the sale, while her elder sister, Xenia, took sixty thousand — something Olga still resented thirty years later: "Xenia took it upon herself to arrange things. I was given to understand that the matter could not concern me very closely because I had a commoner for a husband."

47. Letter of Mme. Nina Semenov-Tian-Chansky to Dominique Auclères, in Auclères I, 131.

48. Interview with Princess Nina; see also memorandum of counsel, Hamburg.

49. Vorres, 180. The Dowager Empress, after several years of chaos, had been granted an annuity of ten thousand pounds by the British royal family.

50. See Botkin II, 201; I have heard A use these words.

51. In *Nicholas and Alexandra,* Robert K. Massie cites a letter from the Empress to the Tsar in 1915 in which she writes that Sir George Buchanan, the British ambassador to Russia, is coming to the palace — "as he brings me again over 100,000 p [pounds] from England." Massie concludes on the basis of this note, "By the end of the war there was nothing left." So it might seem, but this line from the Empress's letters demonstrates by itself that the Tsar's fortune was not brought back to Russia from England in a burst of patriotism at the outbreak of hostilities, as most of the family claimed. It also completely discredits Sir Edward Peacock's contention that there was "never" any money in England. If we knew how much the Tsar had kept there to begin with, it might be possible to determine how much was left at the time of the Revolution, but we don't, and Massie is only guessing that the funds had all been spent. See Massie, 530.

52. Sworn statement of Lili Dehn, September 23, 1955, Hamburg; and in IA, 261–262.

53. See IA, 260; Williams, 348–349; and Fallows's "Entries," letters, and statements, EHF. The money in Berlin later became the nominal object of A's court battles.

54. Statement of Edward Fallows, dated 1936, EHF.

55. Fallows "Entry," October 15, 1935, EHF.

56. Berkman, Edward O., *The Lady and the Law* (Boston: Little, Brown, 1976), 141, 149.

57. Fallows to Paul Leverkuehn, May 12, 1939, EHF.

58. See Fallows "Entries," 1935–1938, EHF.

59. Fallows to Harold Brooks, November 9, 1937, EHF. Brooks's widow later told Fallows that in her opinion Bark had "engineered" the negative attitude of the Grand Duchesses Xenia and Olga toward A. See Fallows "Entry" January 22, 1938, EHF.

60. Fallows "Entry," May 12, 1939, EHF.

61. See the articles in the *New York Times* of July 29 and 30, 1929, concerning the application of Prince Serge Romanovsky (Leuchtenberg), as representative of the Romanov family, to order a search for the Tsar's wealth in the United States.

62. Private correspondence seen by PK.

63. Fallows to A, January 13, 1930, EHF.

64. Fallows to Curtis J. Mar, October 27, 1929, EHF.

65. *Evening Journal,* February 3, 1930.

66. *New York Sunday News,* August 2, 1931.

67. A "Memoirs" ("My American Experiences").

68. A review is in the *New York Times,* June 5, 1928.

69. Unattributed transcript of letter received by Duncan Edwards, "Southport, Connecticut, January, 1960," in the possession of Mrs. Edward J. Wynkoop.

70. Guy Bolton in *Theatre Arts,* May 1956 ("Riddle of Anastasia").

71. Some of her letters, dictated frequently to Miss Jennings and, when not, to Miss Jennings's secretary, are in EHF.

72. A to James R. Sheffield, January 4, 1930, EHF; Hamburg.

73. "My American Experiences," EHF.

74. A "Interviews" ("Tentative for Introduction").

75. See Mar's correspondence with Fallows, EHF.

76. All of her life A kept a collection of photographs of the Russian imperial family, some of which she clipped from newspapers and magazines and others that had been sent to her at random by her friends and, frequently, by "the public." Sydney Gibbes, the English tutor at Tsarskoe Selo, who met A in 1954, remarked: "I did not show her any pictures or photographs of the imperial family as she would probably have recognised them. I understand she had a collection of 2,000 postcards and photographs" (Trewin, *The House of Special Purpose,* 147).

77. A to Sheffield, January 28, 1930, EHF.

78. "My American Experiences."

79. A to Sheffield, January 28, 1930.

80. "My American Experiences."

81. Wilton Lloyd-Smith to Foster M. Kennedy, March 27, 1930. A document was prepared for submission at Hamburg under the heading "*Auszüge der Briefe aus der Amerikazeit*" ("Extracts from the letters from the American period"). Most, but not all, of the letters cited to the end of the chapter are now in EHF, others in the *Auszüge.*

82. Lloyd-Smith to Fallows, August 22, 1930, EHF.

83. Lloyd-Smith to Sheffield, March 28, 1930, *Auszüge.*

84. "My American Experiences."

85. Annie B. Jennings to Lloyd-Smith, March 25, 1930, *Auszüge.*

86. Duncan Edwards's extract, sent to Mrs. Wynkoop.

87. "My American Experiences."

88. Lloyd-Smith to Fallows, August 22, 1930, EHF.

89. Oliver Jennings to Wilton Lloyd-Smith, April 28, 1930, *Auszüge.*

90. Lloyd-Smith to Fallows, August 22, 1930, EHF.

91. The Baird–Cossley-Batt material is taken from "My American Experiences."

92. *Times* to Lloyd-Smith, June 17, 1930, *Auszüge.*

93. "My American Experiences."

94. Jill and Baird went promptly to Miss Jennings's brothers to demand payment of one thousand dollars for services rendered to "Mrs. Anderson." They were shown the door. "You realize I spent hours talking to that awful woman," said Baird during a meeting with Lloyd-Smith. "That is worth something" — to which Lloyd-Smith replied that it probably wasn't worth arrest for extortion. A transcript of the conversation with Lloyd-Smith is in EHF, dated June 6, 1930.

95. Lloyd-Smith to Fallows, August 22, 1930, EHF.

96. "My American Experiences."

97. Dictated notes of Marguerite Jennings, June 26, 1930, from the files of Wilton Lloyd-Smith, currently in the collection of Mrs. John J. Weber.

98. Gleb Botkin to Fallows, November 20, 1930, EHF.

99. Miss Jennings to Lloyd-Smith, June 11, 1930, *Auszüge.*

100. Report of Adelene Moffat of her conversation with Lloyd-Smith, undated (1931, notes and transcript in EHF). Miss Moffat was a painter from Boston who had formed the "Committee for the Recognition of the Grand Duchess Anastasia" and who became a lifelong friend of A's. It was she who took down A's dictation for "My American Experiences" in 1932.

101. Report to Duncan Edwards, sent to Mrs. Wynkoop.

102. Xenia to A, undated, EHF.

103. Lloyd-Smith to Miss Jennings, July 15, 1930, *Auszüge.*

104. Walter Jennings to Lloyd-Smith, August 2, 1930, *Auszüge.*

105. Lloyd-Smith to Fallows, August 22, 1930, EHF.

106. Lloyd-Smith to Fallows, March 19, 1932, EHF.

107. Transcript of telephone conversation, July 24, 1930, in the collection of Mrs. John J. Weber.

108. "Petition for the Commitment of the Insane," filed with the Supreme Court of New York, July 24, 1930.

109. Lloyd-Smith to Walter Jennings, August 1, 1930, *Auszüge*.

110. See IA, 250.

111. See Fallows to James R. Sheffield, October 23, 1930 (EHF): "I had to wait until my return to New York . . . to learn from yourself the details of this untoward action. . . ."

11. Home Again

1. Frieda Riesenfeld's affidavit is dated January 24, 1932, Hamburg.

2. For A's reception at Ilten, see report of Dr. Hans Willige, November 5, 1938; also letters of Dr. Wahrendorff and Dr. Nieper, EHF and BA.

3. "My American Experiences."

4. See the articles of Dr. Paul Madsack in the *Hannoverscher Anzeiger* (in particular his "Anastasia Tschaikowsky in der Kuranstalt Ilten").

5. "My American Experiences."

6. See articles of September 26 and 27, 1931.

7. *New York Times*, September 27, 1931.

8. See his letters and "Entries" for 1930, EHF.

9. Lloyd-Smith to Fallows, May 19, 1930, EHF.

10. See the clippings Fallows kept, in EHF.

11. *New York Mirror*, March 29, 1930.

12. Lloyd-Smith to Fallows, August 9, 1930, EHF.

13. Fallows to Sheffield, November 24, 1930, EHF.

14. *Sunday News*, August 2, 1930.

15. See notes to my chapter 10.

16. The records of A's hospitalization were routinely discarded by the staff at Four Winds. There are, however, several letters to Lloyd-Smith in EHF from the sanatorium's director, Dr. Lambert, along with his report of A's being visited by the Russian émigré George Taube, who had served as an officer on the imperial yacht and who denounced her as a fraud. To right the balance, see the letter to Fallows from the Russian Olga Smirnoff, who worked at Four Winds and who "discovered the falseness of the statements made against [A]. . . . Unfortunately, our Russians discarded the question of her identity, fearing responsibility and other complications" (letter in EHF).

17. Transcript of telephone conversation, August 15, 1931, in the collection of Mrs. John J. Weber.

18. The German general consulate in New York informed Dr. Wahrendorff at Ilten on October 29, 1931: "The application for the passport came through Mr. C. J. Foley [Rachmaninoff's manager, who evidently had taken to working with Lloyd-Smith], whose secretary personally accompanied Miss Anderson to the General Consulate" (letter in EHF). The staff at Four Winds would say only that A had not left the grounds of the sanatorium on August 18, 1931, when the document was signed. See letter to Wahrendorff, February 24, 1932, EHF.

19. A's letters to Fallows, typewritten by her, are in EHF.

20. *New York World Telegram*, January 7, 1933.

21. A's remark repeated frequently in my presence.

22. See Fallows "Entries" for 1938, EHF.

23. Notes of Mrs. Edward J. Wynkoop to PK.

24. "My American Experiences." A did not explain whom she meant by "princes" asking for money.

25. A favorite remark of A's.

26. Willige report, EHF.

12. "Hohe Frau":
The Hermit of the Black Forest

1. Interview with Ian Lilburn.
2. The name was made official on October 26, 1957, when the Interior Ministry of Baden-Württemberg granted it to A for the purposes of her lawsuit against the Duchess of Mecklenburg (see my chapter 13).
3. See his affidavit of September 13, 1957, Hamburg.
4. Her abortive trip to Unterlengenhardt (in company of Dominique Auclères) is described in Auclères I, chapter 4 ("A l'assaut du petit Kremlin").
5. Auclères II.
6. Interview with Dominique Auclères.
7. Interview with Mrs. Edward J. Wynkoop.
8. Interview with Ian Lilburn.
9. See *Figaro,* October 3, 1968.
10. Interview with Ian Lilburn.
11. A to Gleb Botkin, January 14, 1966, copy left in A's papers.
12. *Life,* February 14, 1955.
13. Interview with Ian Lilburn.
14. Unpublished manuscript of Baroness Monica von Miltitz, quoted in Horan MS.
15. A to Paul Leverkuehn and Kurt Vermehren, February 14, 1955, left in A's papers.
16. A to Gleb Botkin, February 9, 1957.
17. *Figaro,* August 20, 1960.
18. See *Paris-Match,* November 26, 1960.
19. Interview with Dominique Auclères.
20. Auclères I, 248.
21. Titles in general use. See Auclères I; and *Paris-Match,* January 25, 1958.
22. *Der Spiegel,* March 5, 1967. See also *Spiegel* of May 9, 1956.
23. Interview with Ian Lilburn.
24. A great many of the letters were left in boxes in Unterlengenhardt when A moved to Virginia in 1968. It is not possible to identify all of her correspondents. The letters are now with Ian Lilburn in London.
25. Lyrics copyright by Paul Francis Webster. (1956)
26. Marcelle Maurette in *La Revue de Deux Mondes,* February 15, 1958, pp. 703–715.
27. *New York Evening Post,* December 30, 1954.
28. Maurette, Marcelle, *Anastasia.* English adaptation by Guy Bolton. (New York: Random House, 1955).
29. The Ingrid Bergman film was by no means the end of the "Anastasia" dramatizations. In 1967 Lynn Fontanne came out of retirement to play the Dowager Empress opposite Julie Harris in a Hallmark Hall of Fame television adaptation. At the time of her death in 1981, Natalie Wood was preparing a new film version of the story, while in June 1982 a musical adaptation of the Maurette/Bolton script premiered in Miami as *I, Anastasia.* A new play by Royce Ryton, *I Am Who I Am,* opened in New York in September 1982. Finally, in 1956 Lilli Palmer won the German Federal Film Prize for her portrayal of A in a loosely fictionalized version of the story, called in German *Anastasia, Die letzte Zarentochter* and in English *Is Anna Anderson Anastasia?* The film never opened in the United States.
30. Interview with Mrs. Edward J. Wynkoop.
31. Interviews with Ian Lilburn and with Prince Frederick of Saxe-Altenburg.
32. Agreement of June 4, 1954, left in A's papers.
33. Letter of Ulrich von Gienanth to A, undated, left in A's papers.
34. Interview with Ian Lilburn. The chalet, prefabricated, was erected in 1960.
35. Maurette in *La Revue.*
36. Interview with A.
37. Fallows's "Entry," July 4, 1939.
38. Prince Frederick of Saxe-Altenburg to Spes Stahlberg, April 13, 1938, EHF.
39. See Auclères I, 15.
40. Willige affidavit, EHF.
41. See "My American Experiences."
42. Affidavit of Prince Frederick of Saxe-Altenburg, August 1, 1938, EHF and Hamburg.

43. Frederick to Spes Stahlberg, April 13, 1938, EHF.

44. Interview with Prince Frederick.

45. Frederick to Spes Stahlberg, April 13, 1938, EHF.

46. Affidavit of Prince Sigismund of Prussia, July 5, 1938, EHF and Hamburg.

47. Frederick to Spes Stahlberg, April 13, 1938, EHF. Prince Sigismund's questions remained a secret to all but a few insiders until 1976, when details were first published in FOT. Among other things, the Prince had asked A to tell him when they had last met, where that meeting had taken place, and exactly where he, Sigismund, had been lodged at the time. A replied correctly that they had last seen each other at Spala, the Tsar's hunting estate in Poland, in the autumn of 1912, and that Sigismund had been given the room normally reserved for Baron Fredericks, the court chamberlain.

48. Interview with Dominique Auclères.

49. Interview with Ian Lilburn.

50. Interview with Prince Frederick of Saxe-Altenburg.

51. Interview with Ian Lilburn. A ordinarily used the German "Friedrich."

52. Interview with Prince Frederick.

53. See Fallows's notes, December 1932, EHF.

54. See Fallows's "Entries" and letters to Julia and Annette Fallows, EHF; also correspondence in BA.

55. Fallows's correspondence with him is in EHF, along with copies of the cables exchanged at the end of May 1929.

56. See affidavit of Ivan Arapov, October 11, 1938, EHF.

57. Gitta Müller-Mittler to Fallows, September 5, 1935, EHF.

58. See Fallows's notes, EHF.

59. See testimony of Anna Samweber, August 10, 1965, Hamburg.

60. See Fallows's "Entries," 1938, EHF, in particular February 8 and August 7, 1938.

61. Samweber testimony, Hamburg.

62. The article in the News of the World was dated September 4, 1932, copies in EHF.

63. The claim was lodged on April 7, 1938. As a German resident, A could not sue in England in the years between 1939 and 1949.

64. Letter to Friedrich Völler, September 22, 1932, EHF.

65. Interviews with Tatiana Botkin and Prince Frederick of Saxe-Altenburg.

66. Samweber testimony, Hamburg.

67. The phrase now became a permanent part of A's repertory.

68. A to Gleb Botkin, February 12–14, 1937; EHF.

69. FOT, 244. These were Cecilie's words. The Crown Princess's recognition of A had been unconditional after their reunions at Schloss Lichtenstein in the early 1950s.

70. Another of Prince Michael Benedict's godmothers was Queen Juliana of the Netherlands.

71. A to PK.

72. See her affidavit of March 10, 1961, Hamburg.

73. Müller-Mittler to Fallows, EHF.

74. IA, 265.

75. Fallows to Julia Fallows, February 9, 1938, EHF.

76. Fallows's "Entry," February 8, 1938, EHF.

77. Annette Fallows to Fallows, April 1938, EHF.

78. Miltitz affidavit, Hamburg.

79. See Fallows's "Entries" for October–December, 1935, EHF.

80. Prince Frederick to Spes Stahlberg, April 13, 1938, EHF.

81. A to Fallows, October 25, 1937, EHF.

82. Fallows's visit to Hannover: quotes from Fallows's "Entries" for January 28 and 29 and February 8 and 9, 1938, EHF.

83. Fallows's "Entry," July 1, 1938.

84. When Fallows arrived in Hannover at the end of January 1938, in the company of Albert F. Coyle, his Russian-speaking colleague from New York, A remarked: "Please come with me into the other room. I have something to tell you." She explained that Coyle's presence had embarrassed her deeply, that it was "a disgrace" for her not to speak her mother tongue, and then confided: "I took up a Russian book I had and looked at the words. Suddenly I recognized them and began to read. I was terribly excited. It seemed as if a curtain

had rolled up from before my brain. Soon I am sure I shall be speaking it again." And so she was within several weeks. See Fallows's "Entries" for January and February 1938. Fallows continued: "She asked me to keep quiet about it. . . . I asked if there was not someone in Hannover who might talk with her to refresh her memory; she was very emphatic that there was no one whom she could trust; they would say afterward that she had been *taught* to speak Russian, whereas she only wanted to *practice* and bring back her vocabulary" (See Fallows's "Entry" of February 8, 1938). A's progress was cut short by the attentions of the Nazi government.

85. The notes are in EHF, with Fallows's statement attached.

86. See Fallows's "Entries" for the end of June 1938, EHF.

87. See Fallows's correspondence and "Entries," April–July 1938, EHF.

88. The account of the meeting in Hannover is taken from the statement and notes of Paul Leverkuehn (who was also present at police headquarters), in EHF; and the report of Gleb Botkin, written just two days after the meeting, in EHF.

89. Fallows's "Entry," July 16, 1938, EHF.

90. Fallows to A, October 6, 1938; copy in EHF.

91. Annette Fallows to Fallows, April 29, 1938, EHF.

92. Fallows to Gertrude Madsack, July 18, 1938, EHF.

93. In "My American Experiences."

94. A to Gleb Botkin, August 2, 1965.

95. Quoted in *Piedmont* magazine (supplement to the Charlottesville, Virginia, *Daily Progress*), September 7, 1974.

96. See my chapter 13, page 303.

97. A to Gleb Botkin, March 11, 1947, EHF and Hamburg.

98. In general use; see also *Der Spiegel*, March 5, 1967.

99. *Time*, February 11, 1957.

100. Her affidavit, the first to be submitted at Hamburg, is dated November 5, 1957. See also FOT, 246–247.

101. *Figaro*, February 24, 1958.

102. From Dehn affidavit, Hamburg.

13. The Trials — First Instance

1. A general note on use of sources for the two chapters on the Hamburg trials: the depositions of the witnesses at Hamburg are not drawn up in question-and-answer form, but are rather pieced together as a narrative; frequently the questions asked by the tribunal are not recorded on the final transcripts. For accounts of the actual words used in the courtroom I have relied heavily on the articles in the *Figaro* and in the *Frankfurter Allgemeine Zeitung* (henceforth abbreviated as FAZ) as the best-informed coverage of the proceedings; and on my extensive interviews with Prince Frederick, Dominique Auclères, and Ian Lilburn (who was the only person to attend every session of the second trial). Where I have cited the court transcripts I have simply referred to the witnesses' "testimony, Hamburg" by date. A complete listing of Dominique Auclères's articles is available at the offices of the *Figaro* in Paris and in the Horan MS. Her unpublished manuscript (Auclères II) is in the possession of her family. It is unpaginated.

2. The declaration of the Tsar's heirs was issued on September 8, 1933. Countess Brassova had sued as the heir of her son George, who had been killed in a car crash in 1931. The certificate of inheritance was issued on November 24, 1937: see Hamburg verdict.

3. See Hamburg verdict.

4. Letter of February 8, 1938, EHF. The use of the address "Imperial Highness" appears to have been no more than a courtesy.

5. In general use; see FAZ articles, 1964–1967.

6. Fallows to Vermehren, July 15, 1938, EHF.

7. For information on Fallows's activities see his letters and "Entries" from 1929 to 1940, EHF.

8. Fallows's notes, December 1932, EHF.

9. Alfred Fuchs to Fallows, January 13, 1933, EHF.

10. Fallows to Julia Fallows, September 25, 1932, EHF.

11. Fallows to Julia Fallows, August 30, 1932, EHF.

12. Fallows to Gleb Botkin January 16, 1933, EHF.
13. Fallows to Julia Fallows, November 26, 1935, EHF.
14. Grace Leeds to Julia Fallows, October 22, 1939, EHF.
15. Annette Fallows to Gleb Botkin, February 27, 1948, EHF.
16. See Hamburg verdict.
17. See Fallows's "Entry," April 20, 1938, EHF.
18. See letter of Fallows to Thomas J. Watson, July 10, 1939, EHF.
19. Leverkuehn to Fallows, May 24, 1939, EHF.
20. Interview with Ian Lilburn.
21. Alan McHenry to Annette Fallows, June 24, 1952, EHF.
22. Kurt Vermehren to Annette Fallows, August 20, 1954, EHF.
23. Kurt Riezler to Annette Fallows, February 8, 1947, EHF.
24. Memorandum of Kurt Vermehren, January 31, 1961, Hamburg.
25. See FOT, 228–230, and Lilburn MS.
26. Mayer was heard in Berlin on November 8, 1956.
27. Headline in *Newsweek,* February 11, 1957.
28. Lilburn MS.
29. Quoted in Lilburn MS. from verdict of the Berlin High Court.
30. A's petition for the revocation of the certificate of inheritance was withdrawn on October 29, 1957, two weeks exactly after battle was formally lodged at Hamburg. According to Ian Lilburn, Hamburg was chosen "only out of consideration for the Duchess of Mecklenburg, who would not have liked the case to be conducted in her own town." Hans-Hermann Krampff, who represented the Duchess and her codefendant, Louis of Hesse, practiced in Düsseldorf; the younger attorney, Berenberg-Gossler, was, like Vermehren, based in Hamburg.
31. See Sigismund's affidavit of September 13, 1957, Hamburg. Sigismund, "disinherited" by the Nazis in the 1930s, had left Germany to live in Costa Rica; after the war, he never bothered to obtain formal reinstatement. He had married Prince Frederick's sister, Charlotte Agnes. Their daughter Barbara, born in 1920, was adopted by her grandmother, Princess Irene, who did not, however, sever ties with her son.
32. Lilburn MS.
33. Auclères I, 11.
34. Interview with Dominique Auclères.
35. Auclères II.
36. Headline in the *Figaro,* April 12, 1958.
37. Auclères II; also interview with Dominique Auclères.
38. Interview with Dominique Auclères.
39. Auclères I, 14.
40. Auclères II.
41. Interview with Ian Lilburn.
42. FAZ, May 22, 1958.
43. *Figaro,* January 10, 1958.
44. Auclères I, 14.
45. FAZ, March 31, 1958.
46. See FAZ, May 21 and 23, 1958.
47. Auclères I, 194–195. Gertrude Madsack and A had long been reconciled.
48. Pierre Gilliard's interrogation is reported in Auclères I, 196–200, and in the *Figaro,* March 31 and April 1, 1958. Other references as cited.
49. Auclères II.
50. *Die Zeit,* April 10, 1958.
51. FAZ, April 1, 1958.
52. Auclères II.
53. Auclères I, 200; and II.
54. Dassel's testimony reported in Auclères I, 200–206; and from the court transcript as reported in *Figaro,* April 2 and 3, 1958.
55. Auclères II.
56. FAZ, April 5, 1958.
57. A to Gleb Botkin, February 9, 1957.
58. Auclères II; and I, 230.
59. Auclères II.

60. Quoted in *Figaro*, May 21, 1958.

61. Gibbes had already provided a statement denouncing A for publication in FA (138–140). No mention of that fact was made in his subsequent deposition, nor in the book prepared from his private papers (Trewin, *The House of Special Purpose*), where both statements are reproduced as if there were *two* claimants in play. Gibbes was heard in London on January 17, 1959 (testimony at Hamburg); see also Trewin, 146–147.

62. Interview with Prince Frederick.

63. Interview with Ian Lilburn. After Krampff's withdrawal from the case in 1959 his colleague, Berenberg-Gossler, was assisted by Krampff's wife.

64. FAZ, April 5, 1958.

65. Auclères II.

66. Auclères I, 227.

67. Doris Wingender's testimony is reported in Auclères I, 226–233; in *Figaro* and FAZ, May 22 and 23, 1958.

68. FAZ, May 22, 1958.

69. FAZ, March 31, 1958.

70. Auclères II; and I, 228.

71. *Figaro*, May 24, 1958.

72. See memorandum of Kurt Vermehren, January 31, 1961, Hamburg.

73. Baroness von Kleist affidavit, EHF.

74. Auclères II.

75. Auclères I, 234.

76. See the letter of Bruno Grandsitzki to Paul Leverkuehn of June 1958; and his Hamburg testimony of November 24, 1958.

77. Auclères II.

78. Mme. Auclères took on as a personal responsibility the tracking down of the *Premier*. See Auclères I, 150.

79. Police report of October 1, 1958, Hamburg.

80. Vorres, 203, 206.

81. Olga testimony, Hamburg.

82. A's hearing in Unterlengenhardt reported in the court's protocol of May 20–24, 1959, Hamburg.

83. Auclères I, 240.

84. Auclères I, 239.

85. Paul Leverkuehn to A, August 23, 1958, Hamburg.

86. The Eyckstedt/Klenke report is dated July 26, 1958, Hamburg.

87. The four other specialists were the Professors Fischer, Curtius, Müller-Hess, and Clauberg. Only Clauberg remained to defend his study after the new evidence was submitted (see my chapter 14).

88. FAZ, April 17, 1964.

89. See Horan MS.

90. Quoted in *Figaro*, April 20, 1964.

91. Auclères I, 243.

92. Lilburn MS. It should be noted that the opposition was as eager to see Zahle's papers released as Vermehren was.

93. Auclères II.

94. Auclères I, 253.

95. Berenberg-Gossler's summation appears in FAZ, May 12, 1961.

96. Verdict of the Landgericht-Hamburg, printed privately (*nicht rechtskräftig*).

97. Auclères I, 259.

98. Verdict of the Landgericht-Hamburg.

14. The Trials — Second Instance

1. FAZ, May 16, 1961.

2. Unpublished manuscript of Monica von Miltitz, quoted in Horan MS.

3. FOT, 256.

4. Quoted in Horan MS.

5. Memorandum of Kurt Vermehren (*Berufungsbegründung*), March 31, 1962, Hamburg.

6. Auclères I, 259.
7. Interview with Prince Frederick.
8. Auclères II.
9. Ibid.
10. Ibid.
11. A to Gleb Botkin, November 9, 1965.
12. *Sunday Times* (London), March 15, 1964 ("Sorting Out the Tangled House of Romanoff").
13. He was a close friend of Ian Lilburn.
14. Interview with Ian Lilburn.
15. Auclères II.
16. Ian Lilburn to Gleb Botkin, May 1, 1965, copy in Lilburn's collection.
17. Lilburn MS.
18. FAZ, April 9, 1964.
19. FAZ, April 10, 1964.
20. FAZ, April 11, 1964.
21. Auclères II.
22. FAZ, April 10, 1964.
23. FAZ, February 5, 1965.
24. *Die Welt*, April 10, 1964.
25. FAZ, November 19, 1965.
26. FAZ, April 17, 1964.
27. *Figaro*, April 17, 1964.
28. From report of Dr. Reche of December 5, 1959, as reported in *Figaro*, April 17, 1964.
29. *Figaro*, April 17, 1964.
30. *Figaro*, April 20, 1964. Dr. Schwidetzki's letter, dated February 29, 1964, submitted at Hamburg.
31. *Figaro*, April 24, 1964.
32. FAZ, April 24, 1964.
33. Among the school workbooks were two belonging to Grand Duchess Anastasia, each thirty-two pages long, containing her German and Russian lessons, the latter revealing "copious and extensive errors and corrections."
34. Quoted in Wollmann memorandum of March 15, 1965.
35. Becker testimony, Hamburg.
36. *Figaro*, July 22, 1964.
37. Becker testimony, Hamburg.
38. *Figaro*, July 22, 1965; and interview with Dominique Auclères.
39. Rodzianko had testified during the first trial, on January 15, 1959. Deposition at Hamburg.
40. Auclères II.
41. FAZ, February 5, 1965.
42. *Figaro*, February 5, 1965.
43. Ibid., quoted in Horan MS.
44. *Figaro*, February 8, 1965.
45. FAZ, February 5, 1965.
46. FAZ, February 6, 1965. See also Berenberg-Gossler's memoranda of October 13, 14, and 22, 1964, Hamburg.
47. See *Life*, October 18, 1963.
48. Auclères II.
49. Auclères's article on Smith was coauthored with Nicolas Châtelain, in *Figaro*, October 18 and 19, 1963.
50. FOT, 209.
51. The Hamburg psychiatrist was Professor Bürger-Prinz, whose report — still unsupported by a meeting with A — was submitted on June 14, 1966.
52. See Auclères's articles of June 4 and 8, 1965.
53. Auclères II.
54. Testimony of Rudolf Lacher, January 17–18, 1966, Hamburg (see my pages 349–351).
55. *Figaro*, June 4, 1965.

56. Wollmann memorandum, February 19, 1967, Hamburg.
57. *Figaro,* June 4, 1967.
58. Interview with Ian Lilburn.
59. Auclères II.
60. Interview with Ian Lilburn.
61. FAZ, November 23, 1965.
62. Interviews with Ian Lilburn and Prince Frederick.
63. Quotations are combined from A's letters of March 16, 1966, August 2, 1965, and February 9, 1957.
64. Interview with Ian Lilburn.
65. Lilburn to Gleb Botkin, May 1, 1965.
66. Interviews with Ian Lilburn and Alexander Romanov.
67. This was another of the family's "open secrets." The noted Russian journalist Isaac Don Levine informed by way of example that Mountbatten had arranged for the deposition of the former British vice-consul at Ekaterinburg, Sir Thomas Preston, who testified against the possibility of A's escape. See Vorres, 247–253.
68. FOT, 230.
69. Lilburn to Gleb Botkin, May 1, 1965.
70. Gleb Botkin to A, January 19, 1965.
71. Lilburn to Gleb Botkin, May 1, 1965.
72. See Wollenberg testimony, July 27–28, 1965, Hamburg; *Figaro* and FAZ, July 28, 1965.
73. Wollenberg testimony, Hamburg.
74. FAZ, July 28, 1965.
75. Wollenberg testimony, Hamburg.
76. Lilburn to Alexander Romanov, August 28, 1965.
77. Quoted in *Figaro,* February 9, 1965, from headline in *Bild-Zeitung.*
78. Lilburn to Alexander Romanov, August 28, 1965.
79. Interviews with Ian Lilburn and Dominique Auclères.
80. Lilburn to Alexander Romanov, August 28, 1965.
81. FAZ, July 28, 1965.
82. Lilburn to Alexander Romanov, August 28, 1965.
83. Interview with Ian Lilburn.
84. See Auclères's interview with Heinrich Kleibenzetl in *Figaro,* May 12, 1964; and Kleibenzetl testimony, July 28, 1965, Hamburg; reported in *Figaro* and FAZ of July 29, 1965.
85. Affidavit of Anton Hornik, May 30, 1963, Hamburg.
86. Lilburn to Alexander Romanov, August 28, 1965.
87. FAZ, July 29, 1965.
88. Quoted in Wollmann memorandum of December 30, 1966.
89. FAZ, July 29, 1965.
90. The court's protocol is dated September 30, 1965. See also *Figaro,* September 22, 1965.
91. Lilburn to Alexander Romanov, October 10, 1965, copy in Lilburn's collection.
92. *Figaro,* September 22, 1965.
93. Lilburn to Alexander Romanov, October 10, 1965.
94. A to Gleb Botkin, September 20, 1965.
95. Lilburn to Alexander Romanov, October 10, 1965.
96. Interview with Ian Lilburn.
97. Lilburn to Alexander Romanov, October 10, 1965.
98. *Figaro,* September 22, 1965.
99. Lilburn to Alexander Romanov, October 10, 1965. The tribunal never did arrange another hearing of A.
100. A to Gleb Botkin, October 18, 1965.
101. A to Gleb Botkin, November 19, 1965.
102. A to Gleb Botkin, undated.
103. Testimony of September 20, 1965, Hamburg.
104. Kyra testimony, Hamburg.
105. *Figaro,* September 23, 1965.
106. Interview with Dominique Auclères.

107. Interview with Prince Frederick.
108. Interview with Ian Lilburn.
109. *Figaro,* September 23, 1965.
110. Gleb Botkin to A, June 17, 1965.
111. Quoted in Wollmann memorandum, February 19, 1967.
112. *Figaro,* June 8, 1965.
113. Auclères's conversation with Galitzin: Auclères II.
114. *Figaro,* September 25, 1965.
115. Galitzin's testimony dated September 24, 1965, Hamburg. Quotes through page 346 from *Figaro,* September 25, 1965.
116. Interview with Ian Lilburn.
117. *Figaro,* September 25, 1965.
118. Auclères II.
119. Prince Galitzin in *Figaro,* October 7, 1965.
120. Interview with Dominique Auclères.
121. Ernest Louis of Hesse to Eleonore, Grand Duchess of Hesse, February 20, 1916, Hamburg.
122. Copies of the Grand Duke's diary submitted at Hamburg and quoted frequently in memoranda of counsel.
123. Alexandra to Nicholas, February 16, 1916; in Alexandra, *Letters of the Tsaritsa to the Tsar.*
124. Alexandra to Nicholas, March 2, 1916 (Russian Old Style); in *Letters of the Tsaritsa to the Tsar.*
125. Interviews with Ian Lilburn and Prince Frederick.
126. *Figaro,* November 23, 1965.
127. Interview with Ian Lilburn. See also *Der Spiegel,* No. 11, March 5, 1967.
128. Interview with Ian Lilburn.
129. Auclères II.
130. Interview with Ian Lilburn.
131. For Doris's deposition, see *Figaro,* December 29, 1965, and Auclères II.
132. Interview with Ian Lilburn.
133. Hearing of Lacher and Bouzek: see their testimonies of January 17 and 18, 1966, Hamburg; *Figaro,* February 5 and 9, 1966; and Auclères II. I have also relied on interviews with Prince Frederick (who was present during the hearings) and with Ian Lilburn and Mme. Auclères (who listened through the doors at Göttingen).
134. Interview with Dominique Auclères.
135. Interview with Ian Lilburn.
136. Lacher testimony, Hamburg.
137. Auclères II.
138. Auclères II.
139. Interview with Ian Lilburn.
140. Auclères II.
141. Auclères II.
142. A to Gleb Botkin, undated (March 1966?).
143. A to Gleb Botkin, September 20, 1965.
144. A to Gleb Botkin, January 14, 1966.
145. A to Gleb Botkin, January 14, 1966.
146. This was a habitual remark of A's.
147. A to Gleb Botkin, August 2, 1965.
148. A to Gleb Botkin, March 16, 1966.
149. A to Gleb Botkin, September 20, 1965.
150. A to Gleb Botkin, January 14, 1966.
151. Testimony of November 18, 1966, Hamburg; see also *Figaro,* November 19, 1966.
152. Auclères II.
153. For Wollmann's summation, see his memoranda of February 15 and 19, 1967, Hamburg. I have relied also on interviews with Ian Lilburn and Dominique Auclères; Auclères II; and *Figaro,* November 26, 1966.
154. Auclères II.
155. *Figaro,* November 28, 1966.

156. Auclères II.
157. Interviews with Ian Lilburn and Dominique Auclères; Auclères II.
158. *Figaro*, March 1, 1967.
159. *Die Welt*, March 1, 1967.
160. *Figaro*, March 1, 1967.
161. *Die Zeit*, March 3, 1967.
162. *Der Spiegel*, March 5, 1967.
163. *Die Welt*, March 2, 1967.
164. Interview with Dominique Auclères.
165. *Die Welt*, March 1, 1967.
166. FAZ, March 1, 1967.
167. Auclères II and interview with Dominique Auclères.
168. *Figaro*, March 1, 1967.

15. Charlottesville

1. *Figaro*, March 10, 1967.
2. Wollmann memorandum, May 29, 1967, Hamburg.
3. Ian Lilburn to Michael Sissons, November 25, 1967, copy in Lilburn's collection.
4. Lilburn to Sissons.
5. From memorandum of Curt von Stackelberg of July 5, 1968, as reported in *Figaro*, July 30, 1968.
6. Ian Lilburn to Andrew Hartsook, February 10, 1970, copy in Lilburn's collection.
7. Hamburg verdict.
8. See memorandum of Curt, Freiherr von Stackelberg, July 5, 1968, in Lilburn's collection.
9. The majority of the witnesses were set to depose about the peace mission of the Grand Duke of Hesse to Russia and about the escape of the Tsar's daughter from Siberia; one of the witnesses to the latter had been the mistress of Peter Ermakov, a leading member of the Ural Regional Soviet in Ekaterinburg. See Stackelberg memorandum.
10. Quoted from Hamburg verdict in the *Neue juristische Wochenschrift*.
11. From memorandum of Stackelberg of July 5, 1968, as reported in *Figaro*, July 30, 1968.
12. Interview with Stackelberg.
13. Interview with Ian Lilburn.
14. A to PK.
15. Prouteau's documentary was tentatively titled *Le Dossier Anastasia* and was scrapped in 1969 when investors' funds dried up.
16. Interview with Prince Frederick.
17. Auclères II.
18. Countess Oppersdorf, born Princess Radziwill, passed through Unterlengenhardt periodically to be of service to A.
19. *Figaro*, September 7, 1967.
20. Interview with Ian Lilburn.
21. Interview with Dominique Auclères.
22. Auclères II.
23. By edict of Tsar Alexander III, only the children and grandchildren of the sovereign bore the title of Grand Duke or Grand Duchess; Vladimir's title is recognized only by those who also recognize his claim to the Russian throne; to others he remains "Prince" Romanov.
24. Auclères II; and interview with Dominique Auclères.
25. Andrew to Olga, February 10, 1955, Hamburg.
26. A to PK.
27. Quoted from Auclères II; also reported in *Figaro*, September 12, 1967.
28. Auclères II.
29. *Figaro*, September 21, 1967.
30. See Horan MS.
31. Gertrude Lamerdin to John E. Manahan, July 13, 1968, copy in Lilburn's collection.
32. Auclères II.
33. Gertrude Lamerdin to John Manahan.

34. A to PK.
35. Interview with Ian Lilburn.
36. Ian Lilburn to Andrew Hartsook, in Lilburn's collection.
37. Interview with Ian Lilburn.
38. *Figaro,* January 23, 1970.
39. Gleb Botkin letter to Prince Frederick, quoted in Lilburn to Andrew Hartsook, in Lilburn's collection.
40. *Washington Post,* August 24, 1968.
41. *Washington Evening Star,* exact date unknown. The article appeared after A's arrival in America on July 13, 1968, and before her meeting with Maria Rasputin on August 12.
42. *Piedmont,* September 7, 1974.
43. *Halifax* (Virginia) *Gazette,* March 25, 1974.
44. *Evening Star,* 1968.
45. Interview with Russell Roberts (with special thanks to Ellen Donlan).
46. Interview with John E. Manahan. Dr. Manahan has saved the invitation.
47. *Evening Star,* 1968.
48. Horan MS.
49. Conversation in PK's presence.
50. *Argosy,* April 1977.
51. *Evening Star,* 1968.
52. *Time,* August 23, 1968.
53. *Washington Post,* August 24, 1968.
54. Maria Rasputin to A, January 6, 1960, left in A's papers.
55. *Evening Star,* August 12, 1968.
56. *Evening Star,* August 13, 1968.
57. John E. Manahan to PK.
58. Charlottesville *Daily Progress,* January 20, 1970.
59. Interview with Mildred Ewell.
60. Ibid.
61. A to PK.
62. Prince Frederick to A, October 13, 1969, copy in Lilburn's collection.
63. *Daily Progress,* January 19, 1970.
64. FAZ, January 20, 1970; and interview with Ian Lilburn. In future, Dr. Manahan did not hesitate to sign pictures, cards, and letters for A, employing the Cyrillic letters.
65. Auclères II.
66. *Figaro,* January 20, 1970.
67. Interview with Ian Lilburn.
68. FOT, 217.
69. *Neue juristische Wochenschrift,* 21 (1970): 946–951.
70. Press release of the Bundesgerichtshof (Supreme Court), February–March, 1970.
71. Quoted in *Richmond* (Virginia) *Times-Dispatch,* February 18, 1970.
72. Interviews with Ian Lilburn and with Prince Frederick.
73. Interview with Ian Lilburn.
74. *Daily Progress,* February 18, 1970.
75. *Time,* March 2, 1970.
76. *Times-Dispatch,* February 18, 1970.
77. *Daily Progress,* January 19, 1970.
78. Auclères II.
79. *Los Angeles Times,* November 30, 1976 ("Claimant to a Bloody Legend").
80. *Coppage Family Bulletin,* in private circulation.
81. A to PK.
82. A to PK; see also *Daily Progress,* October 28, 1976.
83. *Los Angeles Times,* November 30, 1976.
84. *Argosy,* April 1977.
85. *Los Angeles Times,* November 30, 1976.
86. *South Boston* (Virginia) *News,* March 26, 1974.
87. *Los Angeles Times,* November 30, 1976; *Transgas,* July–August 1969.
88. *Los Angeles Times,* November 30, 1976.
89. *Argosy,* April 1977.

90. *Los Angeles Times,* November 30, 1976.
91. A to PK.
92. *Daily Progress,* October 28, 1976.
93. John Manahan to PK.
94. *Times-Dispatch,* October 31, 1976.
95. Conversations in PK's presence.
96. ABC interview for *Good Morning America;* edited version broadcast on October 26, 1976.
97. Interview for "In Search of . . . Anastasia," broadcast 1977–1978 in national syndication (Alan Landsburg Productions).
98. ABC interview.
99. Ibid.
100. FOT, 259.
101. *Times-Dispatch,* October 31, 1976.
102. A to PK.
103. *Los Angeles Times,* November 30, 1976.
104. *Daily Progress,* August 7, 1979.
105. Conversation in presence of PK.
106. The results of his study were first published in *Quick,* February 24, 1977.
107. FOT, 255. Furtmayr's first report was dated May 17, 1970. See *Figaro* of June 15, 1970.
108. Associated Press dispatch, February 25, 1977.
109. Interviews with Prince Frederick and with Baron von Stackelberg.
110. Auclères II.
111. *Daily Progress,* February 28, 1977. See also *New York Times,* March 2, 1977.
112. Auclères II.
113. Interview with Mildred Ewell.
114. Interview with Ian Lilburn.
115. Ibid.
116. *Daily Progress,* September 2, 1978.
117. Interview with Mildred Ewell.
118. Meeting and conversation in PK's presence.
119. Conversations in PK's presence.
120. See *Daily Progress,* June 20, 1981.
121. *Daily Progress,* June 28, 1981.
122. Dominique Auclères died on September 11, 1981; Royce Ryton's *I Am Who I Am* premiered on September 25, 1982; the imperial family was canonized along with some thirty thousand other "martyrs" to Soviet Communism on October 31–November 1, 1981, in New York City. PK gave A a copy of the ikon.
123. A to PK.

For permission to quote from previously copyrighted material, the author gratefully acknowledges the following companies, archives, and individuals:

ABC Television for quotations from an interview with Anastasia Anderson from the "Good Morning America" program broadcast on the ABC Television Network on October 26, 1976. Used by permission.

CBS Songs for the song "Anastasia," Lyric by Paul Francis Webster, Music by Alfred Newman. © 1956 Twentieth Century Music Corporation. All rights assigned to CBS Songs, a division of CBS, Inc. International Copyright Secured. All rights reserved. Used by permission.

Hubert Clauser and Rosemary Jampolsky for quotations from *L'Inconnue de Berlin: Le Vraie Historie de nos treize années de lutte pour la reconnaissance d'Anastasia,* an unpublished work by Dominique Auclères. Used by permission.

Éditions Payot for quotations from *La Fausse Anastasis* by Pierre Gilliard. By permission of the publisher.

Figaro Littéraire for quotations from several articles by Dominque Auclères, which appeared in *Figaro* during the years 1964–1967.

Hachette, Éditeur, for quotations from *Anastasia, qui êtes-vous?* by Dominque Auclères. By permission of the publisher.

Harper & Row, Publishers, Inc., for quotations from *The File on the Tsar* by Anthony Summers and Tom Mangold. Copyright © 1976 by Anthony Summers and Tom Mangold. By permission of the publisher.

The Hoover Institution on War, Revolution, and Peace for access to the papers of Serge Dmitrievitch Botkin.

Brian Horan for quotation from his unpublished work *Anastasia: The Anna Anderson–Anastasia Case.* Used by permission.

The Houghton Library at Harvard University, Tatiana Botkin, and Clara Lloyd-Smith Weber for access to the papers of Edward H. Fallows and for quotations from these documents. Used by permission.

The New York Times for quotations from two articles: "Anastasia's Issue up in Berlin Suit," February 14, 1928; and "Anastasia to Fight for Czar's Fortune," October 30, 1928. © 1928 by The New York Times Company. Reprinted by permission.

Marina B. Schweitzer for quotations from *The Real Romanovs,* from *The Woman Who Rose Again* by Gleb Botkin, and from his unpublished manuscripts and letters. Used by permission.

Societäts-Verlag, Frankfurt-am-Main, for quotations from *Ich, Anastasia, erzähle* by Roland Krug von Nidda. By permission of the Publisher.

The Washington Post Company for quotations from two articles: "Claimant to Russian Crown: 'Anastasia' Finds Haven in Virginia," July, 1968; and "Maria Sold on Anastasia," August, 1968. Reprinted from the *Washington STar.* Copyright reserved. Used by permission.

Nancy Leeds Wynkoop for quotations from her unpublished letters. Used by permission.

SELECTED BIBLIOGRAPHY

This list does not attempt to be an exhaustive survey of the literature concerning the last imperial family of Russia, the Revolution, or the mystery of Ekaterinburg. I have included here only those books I have cited frequently in the text and which I think will be most informative and accessible to the reader.

MANUSCRIPT COLLECTIONS

There are three major archival sources for a study of the "Anastasia" affair:

(1) The archives of Serge Dmitrievitch Botkin "relating to the case of Mrs. Chaikovski" at the Hoover Institution on War, Revolution and Peace at Stanford University. The papers were donated by Serge Botkin in 1937 with provision for a fifteen-year seal. The archive consists overwhelmingly of the correspondence of Botkin and his private secretary, Baron Osten-Sacken, with various principals in the "Anastasia" controversy. Of chief value are the letters of Grand Duke Andrew and Tatiana Botkin (Melnik). (The Andrew letters were submitted at Hamburg in translation from the original Russian, and it is from those translations that I have worked.) Also among the Botkin papers there are loose notes of Harriet von Rathlef, letters of Ambassador Zahle and Pierre Gilliard, newspaper clippings, the reports of doctors and nurses attending Anastasia, and, as the catalogue to the archives reports, "various informations and memorandums."

(2) The archives of Edward H. Fallows, Anastasia's attorney from 1928 until his death in 1940. The papers were donated to the Houghton Library at Harvard University by Fallows's daughter, Annette. There is a great deal of duplication between the Fallows and the Botkin archives (copies of the same letters, statements, news clippings, and so on). The Fallows papers consist of thirteen cartons of evidence, among them seven that, at the time when they were donated, betrayed no discernible attempt at organization, and six that contain folders filed alphabetically under the names of one hundred and twenty witnesses and correspondents. The papers contain the original signed affidavits of the witnesses from the period 1925–1940 (documents that had been believed to have been lost during the bombing of Berlin in World War II), Harriet von Rathlef's notes of her conversations with Anastasia at St. Mary's Hospital, Fallows's correspondence, his letters to his wife and daughter, and his daily diary "Entries." Finally, there are the transcripts of the interviews given (in English) by Anastasia at the law offices of Curtis J. Mar in New York City during the summer of 1929, and the various drafts of her proposed "memoirs," based on her dictations and bearing such

437

working titles as "The Truth about Anastasia" and "Anastasia: Her Own Story." Of these, I have relied most heavily on the interviews and the section of the memoirs entitled "My American Experiences," which bear the unmistakable ring of her own English and are not distorted by Fallows's editorial efforts.

Certain documents in the Fallows archive consist only in Helene Noeggerath's English translation, prepared for Fallows between 1929 and 1939. In such cases, I have taken the liberty of correcting Frau Noeggerath's English grammar and substituting standard usage for her often awkward words and phrases.

(3) The records of the Oberlandesgericht-Hamburg relating to Anastasia's suit for recognition against Barbara, Duchess of Mecklenburg (No. III ZPO 139/67). Copies of all the material submitted in evidence at Hamburg, along with the transcripts of the witnesses' depositions and memoranda of counsel, are currently in the possession of Prince Frederick of Saxe-Altenburg and of Ian Lilburn. Lilburn also holds in safekeeping the papers left behind in Anastasia's house at Unterlengenhardt in the Black Forest.

INDIVIDUAL MANUSCRIPTS

Auclères, Dominique. "L'Inconnue de Berlin: La Vraie Histoire de nos treize années de lutte pour la reconnaissance d'Anastasia." Loaned to me by the author.
Botkin, Gleb. "Grand Duchess Anastasia." Unpaginated, dated "June-July-August, 1927." In the Fallows papers.
Horan, Brien. "Anastasia? The Anna Anderson–Anastasia Case." Loaned to me by the author.
Lilburn, Ian R. Untitled manuscript, three chapters. In Lilburn's collection.
Rathlef-Keilmann, Harriet von, with Helene Noeggerath. "Summary" of Frau von Rathlef's answer to the Schanzkowska affair. In the Fallows papers.

BOOKS AND ARTICLES

Alexander, Grand Duke of Russia. *Once a Grand Duke* (New York: Garden City, 1932).
———. *Always a Grand Duke* (New York: Garden City, 1932).
Alexandra, Empress of Russia. *Letters of the Tsaritsa to the Tsar* (London: Duckworth, 1923).
Alexandrov, Victor. *The End of the Romanovs* (Boston: Little, Brown, 1967).
Auclères, Dominique. *Anastasia, qui êtes-vous?* (Paris: Hachette, 1962).
Benckendorff, Count Paul. *Last Days at Tsarskoe Selo* (London: Heinemann, 1927).
Botkin, Gleb. *The Real Romanovs* (New York: Fleming H. Revell, 1931).
———. *The Woman Who Rose Again* (New York: Fleming H. Revell, 1937).
Botkin, Pierre (Peter). *Les Morts sans tombes* (Paris, 1922).
Botkin, Tatiana (Melnik). *Vospominanya o Tsarskoi Sem'i* (Belgrade: Stefanovitch, 1921). (Authorized English translation in EHF as *Memories of the Tsar's Family*.)
———. *Au temps des tsars* (Paris: Bernard Grasset, 1980).
Bulygin, Paul. "The Sorrowful Quest," in *The Murder of the Romanovs* (New York: Robert M. McBride, 1935).
Buxhoeveden, Baroness Sophie. *The Life and Tragedy of Alexandra Feodorovna, Empress of Russia* (New York and London: Longmans, Green, 1928).
———. *Left Behind: Fourteen Months in Siberia during the Revolution* (New York and London: Longmans, Green, 1928).
Bykov, P. M. *The Last Days of Tsardom* (London: Martin Lawrence, 1934).
Castelot, André. "Le Mystère de la grande-duchesse Anastasia," in *Drames et tragédies de l'histoire* (Paris: Librairie Académique Perrin, 1966).
Christopher, Prince of Greece and Denmark. *Memoirs* (London: Hurst and Blackett, 1938).
Cowles, Virginia. *The Last Tsar* (New York: G. P. Putnam's Sons, 1977).
Crankshaw, Edward. *The Shadow of the Winter Palace* (New York: The Viking Press, 1976).
Dassel, Felix. *Grossfürstin Anastasia Lebt!* (Berlin: Verlagshaus für Volksliteratur und Kunst, 1928). First published (October 1927) in the *Tägliche Rundschau* as "Zarskoje Sjelo — Schloss Seeon: Grossfürstin Anastasia wie ich sie kannte, wie ich sie wiederer kannte."
Decaux, Alain. *L'Enigme Anastasia* (Paris: La Palatine, 1961).

Dehn, Lili. *The Real Tsaritsa* (London: Thornton Butterworth, 1922).

Diterikhs, General Mikhail Konstantinovich. *Ubiistvo tsarskoi sem'i i chelnov Doma Romanovykh na Urale.* 2 vols. (Vladivostok: Military Academy, 1922).

Escaich, Réné. *Anastasie de Russie: La Morte vivante.* (Paris: Plantin, 1955).

Gilliard, Pierre. *Le Tragique Destin de Nicolas II et de sa famille: Treize années à la cour de Russie* (Paris: Payot, 1921).

———. *Thirteen Years at the Russian Court* (London: Hutchinson, 1921).

Gilliard, Pierre, and Savitch, Constantine. *La Fausse Anastasie: Histoire d'une prétendue grande-duchesse de Russie* (Paris: Payot, 1929).

Jacoby, Jean. "La Légende," in *Le Tsar Nicolas II et la Révolution* (Paris: A. Fayard, 1931).

Kerensky, Alexander. *The Crucifixion of Liberty* (New York: Day, 1934).

———. "The Road to the Tragedy," in *The Murder of the Romanovs* (New York: Robert M. McBride, 1935).

———. *La Vérité sur le massacre des Romanov* (Paris: Payot, 1936).

Kochan, Miriam. *The Last Days of Imperial Russia* (London: Weidenfeld and Nicolson, 1976).

Krug von Nidda, Roland ("editor"). *Ich, Anastasia, erzähle* (Frankfurt: Scheffler, 1957). In English as *I Am Anastasia,* trans. by Oliver Coburn (New York: Harcourt, Brace and Co., 1958).

Kschessinska, Mathilde (Maria Felixovna). *Dancing in Petersburg,* trans. by Arnold Haskell (Garden City: Doubleday, 1961).

Kyril Vladimirovitch, Grand Duke of Russia. *My Life in Russia's Service — Then and Now* (London: Selwyn and Blount, 1939).

Laqueur, Walter. *Russia and Germany* (London: Weidenfeld and Nicolson, 1965).

Lasies, Joseph. *La Tragédie sibérienne* (Paris: Editions Françaises Illustrées, 1920).

Maria Pavlovna, Grand Duchess of Russia. *A Princess in Exile* (New York: The Viking Press, 1931).

Massie, Robert K. *Nicholas and Alexandra* (New York: Atheneum, 1967).

Massie, Robert K., and Swezey, Marilyn Pfeifer. *The Romanov Family Album* (New York: The Vendome Press, 1982).

Moorehead, Alan. *The Russian Revolution* (New York: Harper and Brothers, 1958).

Mossolov, A. A. *At the Court of the Last Tsar* (London: Methuen, 1935).

Naryshkin-Kurakin, Princess Elisabeth. *Under Three Tsars* (New York: Dutton, 1931).

Nogly, Hans. *Anastasia: Ein Frauenschicksal wie kein Anderes* (Hamburg: Verlag der Sternbücher, 1957). In English as *Anastasia* (London: Methuen, 1959).

O'Conor, John F. *The Sokolov Investigation* (New York: Robert Speller and Sons, 1971).

Pares, Sir Bernard. *The Fall of the Russian Monarchy* (New York: Vintage Press, 1961).

Preston, Sir Thomas. *Before the Curtain* (London: John Murray, 1950).

Pridham, Vice-Admiral Sir Francis. *Close of a Dynasty.* Foreword by H.I.H. the Grand Duchess Xenia Alexandrovna (London: Allen Wingate, 1956).

Rathlef-Keilmann, Harriet von. *Anastasia, Ein Frauenschicksal als Spiegel der Weltkatastrophe* (Leipzig and Zürich: Grethlein and Co., 1928). In English as *Anastasia: The Survivor of Ekaterinburg* (New York: Payson and Clarke, 1929). First published (Part I) as "Lebt Anastasia?" in the *Berliner Nachtausgabe,* February–March, 1927. Original manuscript in authorized English translation in the Fallows papers, signed and amended by Harriet von Rathlef.

———. "Wie eine Frau vernichtet werden sollte: Die Wahrheit über Anastasia Tschaikowsky," first published in the *Tägliche Rundschau* (Berlin), September 1927; portions adapted for inclusion in the above *Anastasia* (Privately printed).

Rodzianko, Colonel Paul. *Tattered Banners* (London: Seeley Service, 1939).

St.-Pierre, Michel, Marquis de. "Epilogue: Anastasia," in *Le Drame des Romanov,* vol. 2 (Paris: Robert Laffont, 1969).

Smirnoff, Serge. *Autour de l'assassinat des grands ducs* (Paris: Payot, 1928).

Sokolov, Nicolas. *Enquête judiciaire sur l'assassinat de la famille impériale russe* (Paris: Payot, 1924).

———. *Ubiistvo tsarskoi sem'i* (Berlin: Slovo, 1925).

Spéranski, Valentin. *La Maison à destination spéciale* (Paris: Ferenczi et Fils, 1929).

Spiridovitch, Major-General Alexander. *Les Dernières Années de la cour de Tsarskoié-Selo.* 2 vols. (Paris: Payot, 1928).

Summers, Anthony, and Mangold, Tom. *The File on the Tsar* (New York: Jove/Harcourt Brace Jovanovich edition, 1978).

Thierry, Jean-Jacques. *Anastasia, La Grande-Duchesse retrouvée* (Paris: Belfond, 1982).

Tisdall, E. E. P. *Maria Feodorovna: Empress of Russia* (New York: Day, 1958).

Trewin, J. C. *The House of Special Purpose: An Intimate Portrait of the Last Days of the Russian Imperial Family, Compiled from the Papers of Charles Sydney Gibbes* (New York: Stein and Day, 1975).

Viroubova, Anna. *Memories of the Russian Court* (New York: Macmillan, 1923).

Vorres, Ian. *The Last Grand Duchess: Her Imperial Highness Grand Duchess Olga Alexandrovna* (New York: Scribners, 1965).

Williams, Robert C. *Culture in Exile: Russian Emigrés in Germany 1888–1941* (Ithaca: Cornell University Press, 1972).

Wilson, Colin. *Rasputin and the Fall of the Romanovs* (New York: Farrar, Strauss, 1964).

Wilton, Robert. *The Last Days of the Romanovs* (New York: Doran, 1920).

INDEX

441

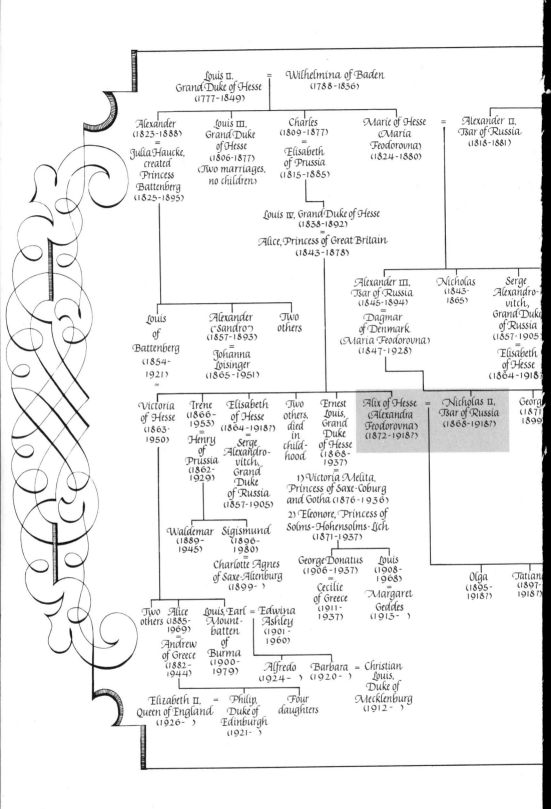

Louis II,
Grand Duke of Hesse
(1777-1849)
=
Wilhelmina of Baden
(1788-1836)

Alexander
(1823-1888)
=
Julia Haucke,
created
Princess
Battenberg
(1825-1895)

Louis III,
Grand Duke
of Hesse
(1806-1877)
(Two marriages,
no children)

Charles
(1809-1877)
=
Elisabeth
of Prussia
(1815-1885)

Marie of Hesse
(Maria
Feodorovna)
(1824-1880)
=
Alexander II,
Tsar of Russia
(1818-1881)

Louis IV, Grand Duke of Hesse
(1838-1892)
=
Alice, Princess of Great Britain
(1843-1878)

Alexander III,
Tsar of Russia
(1845-1894)
=
Dagmar
of Denmark
(Maria Feodorovna)
(1847-1928)

Nicholas
(1843-
1865)

Serge
Alexandro-
vitch,
Grand Duke
of Russia
(1857-1905)
=
Elisabeth
of Hesse
(1864-1918?)

Louis
of
Battenberg
(1854-
1921)
=

Alexander
("Sandro")
(1857-1893)
=
Johanna
Loisinger
(1865-1951)

Two
others

Victoria
of Hesse
(1863-
1950)

Irene
(1866-
1953)
=
Henry
of
Prussia
(1862-
1929)

Elisabeth
of Hesse
(1864-1918?)
=
Serge
Alexandro-
vitch,
Grand
Duke
of Russia
(1857-1905)

Two
others,
died
in
child-
hood

Ernest
Louis,
Grand
Duke
of Hesse
(1868-
1937)
=
1) Victoria Melita,
Princess of Saxe-Coburg
and Gotha (1876-1936)
2) Eleonore, Princess of
Solms-Hohensolms-Lich
(1871-1937)

Alix of Hesse
(Alexandra
Feodorovna)
(1872-1918?)
=
Nicholas II,
Tsar of Russia
(1868-1918?)

Georg
(187
1899

Waldemar
(1889-
1945)

Sigismund
(1896-
1980)
=
Charlotte Agnes
of Saxe-Altenburg
(1899-)

George Donatus
(1906-1937)
=
Cecilie
of Greece
(1911-
1937)

Louis
(1908-
1968)
=
Margaret
Geddes
(1913-)

Olga
(1895-
1918?)

Tatian
(1897-
1918?)

Two
others

Alice
(1885-
1969)
=
Andrew
of Greece
(1882-
1944)

Louis, Earl
Mount-
batten
of
Burma
(1900-
1979)
=
Edwina
Ashley
(1901-
1960)

Alfredo
(1924-)

Barbara
(1920-)
=
Christian
Louis,
Duke of
Mecklenburg
(1912-)

Elizabeth II,
Queen of England
(1926-)
=
Philip,
Duke of
Edinburgh
(1921-)

Four
daughters